Northern Ireland Yearbook

agendaNi
Digital | Events | Print

2022

Welcome to the 21st edition of the Northern Ireland Yearbook.

The Northern Ireland Yearbook is an invaluable guide to the public sector in Northern Ireland, both central and local government are fully detailed, with focused chapters on key sectors.

2021 saw the Covid-19 pandemic put further pressure on a health service which has reached breaking point, however the vaccination programme is now offering some hope of a 'new normal' in 2022. The education sector has also faced much disruption over the past two years and is making progress towards normality.

Chapter one provides readers with a comprehensive look at the political landscape both at Stormont and Westminster. The May 2022 election will see a shake-up at Stormont, bringing with it new challenges and opportunities. Readers will receive an update with the full election results when available.

This edition of the Yearbook includes a focused economy chapter which provides a detailed overview of the Northern Ireland and wider economy and how it has responded to challenges such as the impact of Covid-19 and Brexit.

The local government chapter gives an overview of the 11 councils, their responsibilities, and key people. The Yearbook also features a directory of representative groups and organisations.

I hope the Northern Ireland Yearbook is a useful addition to your organisation throughout the course of 2022. A special thanks to the agendaNi team, advertisers and readers for their contribution to this edition.

Fiona McCarthy, Editor

ISBN: 978-1-8384314-0-2

No part of this publication may be reproduced, stored in a retrieval system or transmitted in any form or by any means electronic, electrostatic, magnetic tape, mechanical, photocopying or otherwise without the express permission in writing from the copyright holder.

The Publishers regret that while every effort has been made during the compilation of this Yearbook to ensure the accuracy of information obtained and published, they cannot be held responsible in any way for inaccuracies in the information supplied to them for publication, nor for any errors or omissions. Users of the Yearbook should satisfy themselves that all the services offered by those listed are acceptable, before commissioning.

Inclusion of a company or individual in this Yearbook should not be interpreted as a recommendation of that company or individual listed to undertake particular instructions. Similarly, no criticism is implied of any company or individual who may for any reason have been omitted from the Yearbook.

Editorial
Fiona McCarthy, Editor
fiona.mccarthy@agendani.com

David Whelan

Ciarán Galway

Odrán Waldron

Sharon Morrison

Advertising
Leanne Brannigan
advertising@agendani.com

Circulation and Marketing
Lynda Millar
lynda.millar@agendani.com

Design
Gareth Duffy, Head of Design
gareth.duffy@agendani.com

Paul Rooney, Design
paul.rooney@agendani.com

agendaNi
bmf Business Services
19a Maghaberry Road
Maghaberry
Co Antrim
BT67 0JE
Tel: +44 (0) 28 9261 9933
Web: www.agendani.com
Twitter: @agendani
Printed by: GPS Colour Graphics, Belfast

Acknowledgements
The authors and publishers owe a debt of gratitude to the many people who have contributed their advice and efforts to this publication, especially those who have supplied copyright material. We have made every effort to ensure that permission has been obtained and the source attributed for all such material. Any lapse in this respect is entirely accidental.

Thanks also to our advertisers and our 'hands on' team who provided the research, production design and proofing required for the publication. Mapping is reproduced with the permission of Land and Property Services Permit ID 40399.

www.northernirelandyearbook.com

Contents

The Northern Ireland Assembly — 05

Directory of MLAs	13
Other institutions of government	24
Assembly election 2017	35

Northern Ireland at Westminster — 71

Directory of Northern Ireland MPs	72
UK Government	73
2019 election results	75

Government departments and agencies — 81

| Departments | 83 |
| Agencies and other public bodies | 143 |

Local government — 151

| Councils | 158 |

Health — 185

| Health and social care trusts | 188 |
| Other organisations | 191 |

Housing — 193

| Northern Ireland Housing Executive | 195 |
| Housing associations | 207 |

Contents

Education and skills — 209

Agencies and organisations in education — 218

Skills — 221

Justice — 223

Courts, judiciary and prosecutions — 228

National policing, security and justice — 229

Tourism and Conferencing — 231

Tourism organisations — 234

Conference venues — 244

Economy — 247

Economic overview and sectoral analysis — 248

Local enterprise agencies — 270

Representative groups and organisations — 273

Chambers of commerce — 276

Trade unions — 277

Charities — 279

193 Housing

209 Education and skills

223 Justice

231 Tourism and Conferencing

Advertise in the 2023 edition

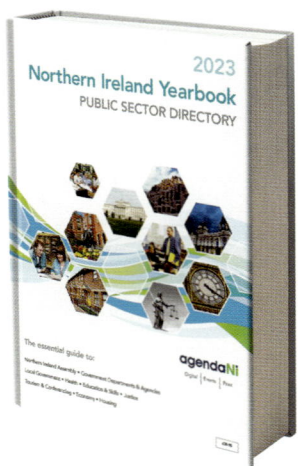

Advertise in the Northern Ireland Yearbook

With a shelf-life of at least a year, the Northern Ireland Yearbook presents an ideal platform for organisations to showcase their brand and services to a unique senior executive readership. Choice of marketing activity is key when communicating important messages to an already influential audience – our advertising team can help you to establish the most cost-effective return for your investment.

Creative marketing opportunities include advertisements, advertorials, sponsorship, gatefolds and many more. We work closely with all of our clients to guarantee maximum exposure and customer satisfaction and we are also happy to take care of any design requirements on behalf of the client (at no extra cost).

Benefits of sponsorship and advertising:

- An excellent platform for organisations to raise their profile
- Create awareness of the organisation's services
- Communicate key messages to important stakeholders
- Yearlong profiling opportunity
- Feature in a unique publication used as an essential reference guide across all sectors
- Prime positions available within particular chapters of key sectors
- Package options available across a series of bmf business services publications
- Be a thought leader in your area

Advertising opportunities:

- **Display advertising**
- **Advertorials (branded-style articles)**
- **Front cover profile**
- **Sponsorship of the directory**
- **Sponsorship of individual chapters**
- **Roundtable discussion features**

To discuss advertising opportunities in the Northern Ireland Yearbook contact us on 028 9261 9933 or email info@agendani.com.

Northern Ireland Yearbook

The Northern Ireland Assembly

Northern Ireland Assembly | Northern Ireland Yearbook

The Northern Ireland Assembly

Devolution in Northern Ireland

Political power was first devolved to Northern Ireland with the establishment of the Northern Ireland Parliament in 1921. The introduction of direct rule from Westminster in 1972 was intended as a temporary measure and attempts to restore devolution continued throughout the Troubles. A Northern Ireland Assembly met from 1973 to 1974 and formed a brief power-sharing government. This was followed by a second Assembly between 1982 and 1986 which had no legislative powers.

The Belfast Agreement in April 1998, also known as the Good Friday Agreement, established the present Assembly. A devolved government was formed in 1999 but was suspended in 2002 after a breakdown of trust between the parties. Two shadow assemblies met during suspension to provide a forum for political discussion and the St Andrews Agreement in October 2006 led to the restoration of devolution in May 2007.

Assembly restored: January 2020

January 2020 saw the return of devolved government in Northern Ireland after three years of deadlock under the New Decade, New Approach (NDNA) agreement. The NDNA agreement was announced by the Irish and British governments on 9 January 2020 and subsequently endorsed by the main political parties on 10 January. Draft Assembly legislation related to the language and cultural aspects of the deal was also published. This included three separate (draft) bills to establish: the Office of Identity and Cultural Expression (OICE); an Irish language Commissioner; and a Commissioner focusing on Ulster Scots and Ulster British language, arts and literature.

The Northern Ireland Assembly collapsed in January 2017. Sinn Féin withdrew from government over the botched non-domestic Renewable Heat Incentive Scheme which came at a large cost to the tax payer. During the next three years of talks, Sinn Féin and the DUP clashed over the creation of stand-alone Irish language act and wider cultural issues. The devolved government departments were ran in the interim by civil servants with no overall political direction. In October 2019 it was announced that the 90 MLAs had been paid a total of £15 million since the Assembly collapsed.

The resignation of deputy First Minister Martin McGuinness in protest over the Renewable Heat Incentive scandal in January 2017 triggered an election. It was the sixth election since the Assembly's formation and took place on 2 March 2017, just 10 months after a previous election in May 2016. The next election will take place in May 2022.

The Northern Ireland Assembly has 90 members – five for each of the 18 Westminster constituencies – who are termed Members of the Legislative Assembly (MLAs). This had been reduced from 108 members in the previous 2016 Assembly. The Assembly has full authority for all transferred matters i.e. those for which Parliament is not responsible. The Assembly has a five-year term.

As part of a comprehensive review of the way the Stormont Executive operates, 2016 saw the number of Northern Ireland government departments reduced from 12 to nine. The functions and services delivered by the former departments were restructured and transferred to the relevant new departments. The new departments were named: Agriculture, Environment and Rural Affairs, Infrastructure, Economy, Education, Finance, Health, Justice, Executive Office and Communities.

Plenary meetings of the Assembly take place on Monday and Tuesday of each week. Members are required to designate themselves as nationalist, unionist or other.

MLAs elect a Presiding Officer, or Speaker, and three deputy speakers, of which one is appointed as Principal Deputy Speaker. The Speaker keeps order in the Chamber and scrutinises legislation to check that it lies within the Assembly's competence. They select amendments to motions for debate and questions for oral answer during Question Time.

The Assembly Commission is the body corporate of the Assembly and provides the property, staff and services required for the Assembly to carry out its work.

Executive

The First Minister is nominated by the largest party in the largest designation and a deputy

First Minister by the largest party in the second largest designation; the two posts form a joint office.

Seven ministerial positions are then allocated between the parties through the d'Hondt system. The Justice Minister is elected through a cross-community vote.

The First Minister, the deputy First Minister and the eight other departmental ministers form the Executive Committee, also known as the Northern Ireland Executive.

Two junior ministers are also appointed to assist the First and deputy First Ministers.

The Executive meets every two weeks and is a forum for discussing cross-cutting issues, prioritising executive and legislative proposals, recommending common positions where necessary, and reviewing progress on the Programme for Government and Budget. Significant or controversial ministerial decisions may also be discussed at Executive level. Major ministerial decisions may be referred back to the Executive for further discussion by a petition of 30 MLAs.

Ministers are required to participate fully in the Executive, North/South Ministerial Council and British-Irish Council, observe the joint office of the First and deputy First Ministers, uphold the rule of law and serve all the people of Northern Ireland equally.

Another change to the operation of the Executive in 2016 seen an opposition for the first time in the history of devolved government in Northern Ireland. The Ulster Unionist Party and the SDLP both declined ministerial seats that were allocated to them and entered into a cross-community opposition. When the Executive returned in 2020 all the main parties entered the Executive.

Committees

There are three types of committee: statutory, standing and ad hoc.

Statutory committees scrutinise the work of the Executive departments. There are therefore nine statutory committees and each has nine members. Chairpersons and deputy chairpersons are allocated under the d'Hondt system, in the same manner as ministers in the Executive are appointed, and committee membership reflects party strengths in the Assembly.

These committees are tasked with advising and assisting their respective ministers on the formulation of policy, and have the power to:

- initiate legislation;
- take the committee stage of primary legislation;
- consider secondary legislation;
- initiate inquiries and make reports;
- consider and advise on departmental budgets and annual plans;
- consider matters brought to their attention by ministers; and
- call for persons and papers.

The seven standing committees assist the Assembly in its work. These are the Business Committee, the Procedures Committee, the Standards and Privileges Committee, the Assembly and Executive Review Committee, which considers changes to how the institutions work, the Public Accounts Committee, which scrutinises how departments and agencies use public money, the Audit Committee, which oversees the finances of the Northern Ireland Audit Office and the Chairpersons' Liaison Group.

Ad hoc committees are also established to consider specific issues and report back to the Assembly within a set period of time, usually two months. Chairpersons and deputy chairpersons for statutory and standing committees are appointed using the d'Hondt system; ad hoc committee positions are elected within the committee.

Climate.
Waste.
Biodiversity.

Working together to help people and nature to thrive.

Inspiring action by individuals, communities and organisations through our world class programmes.

Environmental Engagement Index

What does our environment mean to you?

Have your say

KEEP NORTHERN IRELAND BEAUTIFUL

Carbon Literacy Programmes

Northern Ireland Assembly | Northern Ireland Yearbook

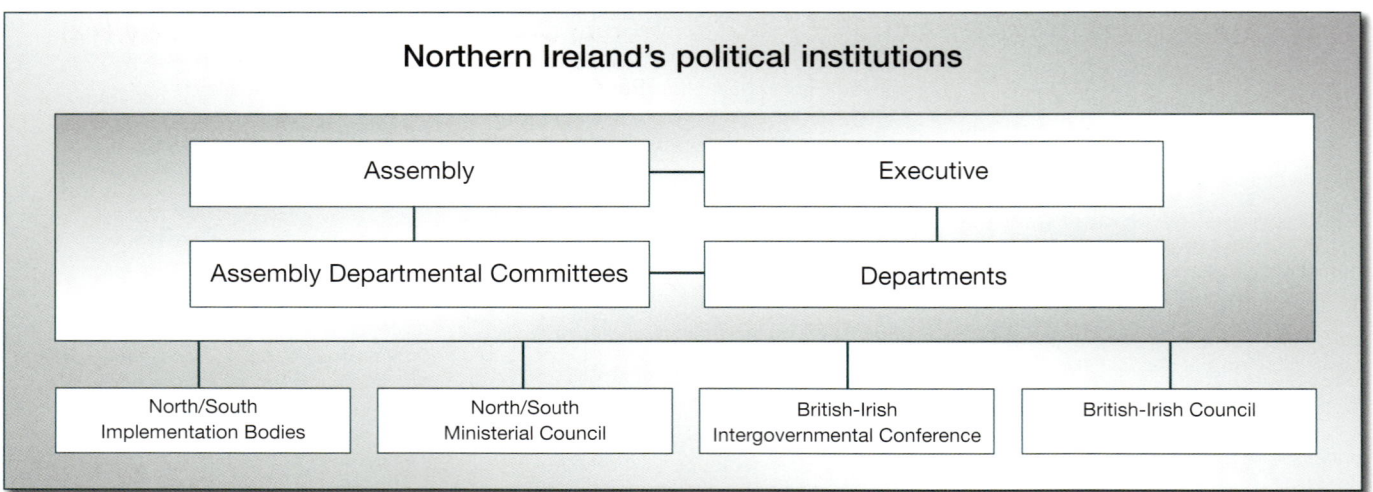

Northern Ireland's political institutions

Legislation

Bills may be brought forward by ministers, committees or private members and generally pass through the following legislative procedure:

1. First reading (formal reading of title);
2. Second reading (debate and vote on general principles);
3. Committee stage (scrutiny by relevant statutory committee);
4. Consideration stage (considers committee report, allows amendments);
5. Further consideration stage (allows debate on final amendments);
6. Final stage (passing or rejecting of Bill).

A reconsideration stage can take place if the Bill is found to be defective – e.g. if it lies outside the Assembly's competence – after the final stage. This allows additional amendments to be debated.

Accelerated passage bypasses the committee stage and requires cross-community support. If the Bill is approved, the Speaker asks the Secretary of State to seek royal assent to enact it. The Assembly also approves secondary legislation, known as statutory rules, either in statutory committees or in plenary session, which add more detail to its acts.

During the 2011 to 2016 mandate the Assembly passed a total of 67 Bills.

State of the parties 2017

Party Votes*	Seats*	%
DUP	28	28.1
Sinn Féin	27	27.9
SDLP	12	11.9
UUP	10	12.9
Alliance	8	9.1
Green	2	2.3
TUV	1	2.6
PBPA	1	1.8
Independent	1	1.8
Others	0	1.8
Total	90	100

(Source - Northern Ireland Assembly, Research and Information Service)
* first preferences, 2017 Assembly election
**as of March 2017

Northern Ireland Assembly

Parliament Buildings
Belfast, BT4 3XX
Tel: 028 9052 1137
Web: www.niassembly.gov.uk
Email: info@niassembly.gov.uk
Twitter: @niassembly

Clerk to the Assembly / Chief Executive: Lesley Hogg

Director of Parliamentary Services: Gareth McGrath

Director of Corporate Services: Richard Stewart

Director of Legal, Governance and Research Services: Tara Caul

Examiner of Statutory Rules: Angela Kelly

Editor of Debates: Simon Burrowes

Adviser to the Speaker / Head of Corporate Support: Robin Ramsey

Comptroller and Auditor General: Kieran Donnelly

Northern Ireland Public Services Ombudsman: Margaret Kelly

Clerk Assistant: Paul Gill

Northern Ireland Yearbook | Northern Ireland Assembly

MLAs by party (as of November 2021)

Democratic Unionist Party (27)

Maurice Bradley	East Londonderry
Paula Bradley	North Belfast
Keith Buchanan	Mid Ulster
Thomas Buchanan	West Tyrone
Jonathan Buckley	Upper Bann
Joanne Bunting	East Belfast
Pam Cameron	South Antrim
Trevor Clarke	South Antrim
Diane Dodds	Upper Bann
Stephen Dunne	North Down
Deborah Erskine	Fermanagh and South Tyrone
Paul Frew	North Antrim
Paul Givan	Lagan Valley
Harry Harvey	Strangford
David Hilditch	East Antrim
William Humphrey	North Belfast
William Irwin	Newry and Armagh
Gordon Lyons	East Antrim
Michelle McIlveen	Strangford
Gary Middleton	Foyle
Robin Newton	East Belfast
Edwin Poots	Lagan Valley
George Robinson	East Londonderry
Christopher Stalford	South Belfast
Mervyn Storey	North Antrim
Peter Weir	Strangford
Jim Wells	South Down

Sinn Féin (27)

Caoimhe Archibald	East Londonderry
Cathal Boylan	Newry and Armagh
Nicola Brogan	West Tyrone
Pádraig Delargy	Foyle
Linda Dillon	Mid Ulster
Jemma Dolan	Fermanagh and South Tyrone
Sinéad Ennis	South Down
Ciara Ferguson	Foyle
Órlaithí Flynn	West Belfast
Colm Gildernew	Fermanagh and South Tyrone
Deirdre Hargey	South Belfast
Declan Kearney	South Antrim
Gerry Kelly	North Belfast
Liz Kimmins	Newry and Armagh
Alex Maskey	West Belfast
Declan McAleer	West Tyrone
Philip McGuigan	North Antrim
Maolíosa McHugh	West Tyrone
Áine Murphy	Fermanagh and South Tyrone
Conor Murphy	Newry & Armagh
Carál Ní Chuilín	North Belfast
John O'Dowd	Upper Bann
Michelle O'Neill	Mid Ulster
Aisling Reilly	West Belfast
Emma Rogan	South Down
Pat Sheehan	West Belfast
Emma Sheerin	Mid Ulster

Social Democratic and Labour Party (12)

Sinéad Bradley	South Down
Pat Catney	Lagan Valley
Mark Durkan	Foyle
Cara Hunter	East Londonderry
Dolores Kelly	Upper Bann
Nichola Mallon	North Belfast
Daniel McCrossan	West Tyrone
Patsy McGlone	Mid Ulster
Colin McGrath	South Down
Sinead McLaughlin	Foyle
Justin McNulty	Newry and Armagh
Matthew O'Toole	South Belfast

Ulster Unionist Party (10)

Steve Aiken	South Antrim
Andy Allen	East Belfast
Rosemary Barton	Fermanagh and South Tyrone
Doug Beattie	Upper Bann
Roy Beggs	East Antrim
Robbie Butler	Lagan Valley
Alan Chambers	North Down
Mike Nesbitt	Strangford
John Stewart	East Antrim
Robin Swann	North Antrim

Alliance Party (7)

Kellie Armstrong	Strangford
John Blair	South Antrim
Paula Bradshaw	South Belfast
Stewart Dickson	East Antrim
Naomi Long	East Belfast
Chris Lyttle	East Belfast
Andrew Muir	North Down

Independent (3)

Alex Easton	North Down
Trevor Lunn	Lagan Valley
Claire Sugden	East Londonderry

Green Party (2)

Clare Bailey	South Belfast
Rachel Woods	North Down

People Before Profit Alliance (1)

Gerry Carroll	West Belfast

Traditional Unionist Voice (1)

Jim Allister	North Antrim

Consumer protection in Northern Ireland

Noyona Chundur, Chief Executive of the Consumer Council

The Consumer Council is Northern Ireland's consumer body and is responsible for protecting and safeguarding the rights and interests of its 1.9 million citizens. Noyona Chundur, Chief Executive of the Consumer Council outlines the vision of the organisation and the work they are doing to ensure that consumer confidence and resilience continues to build.

The Consumer Council has multiple statutory functions in the areas of consumer affairs, energy, post, transport, water and sewerage, and food accessibility. Alongside this, we have the designation to raise a super-complaint to the relevant regulator here or in the UK, if we believe a market in the UK is, or appears to be, significantly harming the interests of consumers.

This wide-ranging remit affords us the opportunity to look across the consumer landscape and see what challenges exist, where pressures are felt, and importantly what prevention and solutions can be implemented. This privilege is one that we use to bring positive change to the citizens of Northern Ireland through our consultation, education, outreach, research, and campaigns on the issues affecting them, so that their needs and wants are at the centre of public policy and decision making. Complementing this is our complaints and investigations service which offers consumers free redress when things go wrong.

How the Consumer Council helps people in Northern Ireland

Empowering consumers

Our focus is always on the consumer. We provide free, expert advice and confidential guidance on a variety of issues. We work on behalf of everyone in Northern Ireland, particularly those who are disabled, have long term health conditions, are of pensionable age, on low incomes or living in rural areas. For this reason, we make every effort to be available for consumers in a way that suits them, be it over the phone, online, or in person. Our freephone number is a key source of support for consumers, with our team returning over £1 million to the people of Northern Ireland in 2020-21. Despite the challenges of the Covid-19 pandemic, we maintained a 99.8 per cent customer satisfaction score, delivered outstanding levels of workplace engagement, and improved our customer service excellence standards.

Our website also offers consumers free advice and online interactive tools designed to help them save money. They can find out if they are on the best electricity or gas tariff available to them, where the most affordable petrol or diesel can be found, or learn ways to make their household budgets go further.

Our extensive communication, outreach, and empowerment work culminates in our annual Northern Ireland Consumer week, which began in March 2021 and returns for a second time in March 2022.

Driving change through policy

It is our job to campaign for consumers to be placed at the heart of public policy, ensuring it meets their needs, safeguards their rights, is citizen-focused and supports inclusive economic recovery. We do this through consultation responses, tariff reviews, customer service and complaints handling audits, and representation at consumer, industry and sector forums here, in the UK and in Europe. We represent their interests to stakeholders and industry and give their concerns and aspirations a voice, in order to improve service delivery to consumers, help them to access better products and services, and support them to meet emerging priorities.

This is underpinned by our extensive research catalogue, where we carry out quantitative and qualitative projects to better understand the Northern Ireland consumer position, including how they are impacted by emerging issues, their perceptions, and potential solutions. The cornerstone in our research calendar is our annual Insight Survey, published every April, which provides detailed findings into current consumer experiences and the impact on their lives and livelihoods. This year, we will also undertake a range of studies into consumer vulnerability and affordability, and deliver the UK's first regional Consumer Price Index in partnership with the Office of National Statistics.

The future for the Consumer Council

As we emerge from the pandemic, life remains challenging for many citizens. There is significant disparity in consumer experiences brought about by the rising cost of living, the risks and opportunities resulting from digitalisation, the growing response to climate change alongside the need for a just and fair energy transition, reducing financial inclusion and increasing consumer detriment. The need to protect and empower consumers has never been more important. Everyone at the Consumer Council works extremely hard at being Northern Ireland's trusted consumer partner. Every aspect of our work is delivered through the lens of consumer protection principles that set out minimum standards for access, choice, safety, information, fairness, representation, redress and education.

There is no single consumer perspective. Partnerships are important, as is connection, shared ideas and pulling together to deliver the best outcomes for the citizens of Northern Ireland. We must work collectively to ensure the diverse consumer interests necessary for developing effective public policy are represented, that regulatory frameworks prioritising education, empowerment and accountability are in place, and that standards for protection, compliance and enforcement are met.

We remain in unchartered territory and as civic society, policy makers, regulators and industry, we won't have all the answers and won't know all the challenges. To deliver for consumers, we need to come together to ask the right questions and find the right solutions, so that markets and services work for consumers and all of society.

Consumers can contact the Consumer Council:
T: 028 9025 1600
E: info@consumercouncil.org.uk
W: www.consumercouncil.org.uk

Northern Ireland Assembly | Northern Ireland Yearbook

Political parties in the Assembly

Contact details for parties at Stormont are as follows:

Democratic Unionist Party (DUP)
Room 207
Parliament Buildings
Stormont Estate, Belfast, BT4 3XX
Tel: 028 9052 1322
Email: info@mydup.com
Party Leader: Jeffrey Donaldson

Sinn Féin (SF)
Room 264
Parliament Buildings
Stormont Estate, Belfast, BT4 3XX
Tel: 028 9052 1471
Email: admin@sinnfein.ie
Party Leader: Michelle O'Neill

Social Democratic & Labour Party (SDLP)
Room 272
Parliament Buildings, Stormont Estate
Belfast, BT4 3XX
Tel: 028 9052 1319
Email: info@sdlp.ie
Party Leader: Colum Eastwood

Ulster Unionist Party (UUP)
Room 214
Parliament Buildings, Stormont Estate
Belfast, BT4 3XX
Tel: 028 9052 1935
Email: uup@uup.org
Party Leader: Doug Beattie

Alliance Party of Northern Ireland (APNI)
Room 220
Parliament Buildings, Stormont Estate
Belfast, BT4 3XX
Tel: 028 9052 1315
Email: alliance@allianceparty.org
Party Leader: Naomi Long

Traditional Unionist Voice (TUV)
Room 252
Parliament Buildings, Stormont Estate
Belfast, BT4 3XX
Tel: 028 9052 1175
Email: info@jimallister.org
Party Leader: Jim Allister

Green Party
Room 259
Parliament Buildings
Stormont Estate, Belfast, BT4 3XX
Tel: 028 9052 1790
Email: info@greenpartyni.org
Party Leader: Clare Bailey

People Before Profit Alliance
Parliament Buildings, Stormont
Belfast, BT4 3XX
Email: info@peoplebeforeprofit.ie
Party Leader: Gerry Carroll

MLAs by constituency (as at November 2021)

East Antrim
Roy Beggs	UUP
Stewart Dickson	APNI
David Hilditch	DUP
Gordon Lyons	DUP
John Stewart	UUP

East Belfast
Andy Allen	UUP
Joanne Bunting	DUP
Naomi Long	APNI
Chris Lyttle	APNI
Robin Newton	DUP

East Londonderry
Caoimhe Archibald	SF
Maurice Bradley	DUP
Cara Hunter	SDLP
George Robinson	DUP
Claire Sugden	IND

Fermanagh and South Tyrone
Rosemary Barton	UUP
Jemma Dolan	SF
Deborah Erskine	DUP
Colm Gildernew	SF
Áine Murphy	SF

Foyle
Pádraig Delargy	SF
Mark Durkan	SDLP
Ciara Ferguson	SF
Sinead McLaughlin	SDLP
Gary Middleton	DUP

Lagan Valley
Robbie Butler	UUP
Pat Catney	SDLP
Paul Givan	DUP
Trevor Lunn	IND
Edwin Poots	DUP

Mid Ulster
Keith Buchanan	DUP
Linda Dillon	SF
Patsy McGlone	SDLP
Michelle O'Neill	SF
Emma Sheerin	SF

Newry and Armagh
Cathal Boylan	SF
William Irwin	DUP
Liz Kimmins	SF
Justin McNulty	SDLP
Conor Murphy	SF

North Antrim
Jim Allister	TUV
Paul Frew	DUP
Philip McGuigan	SF
Mervyn Storey	DUP
Robin Swann	UUP

North Belfast
Paula Bradley	DUP
William Humphrey	DUP
Gerry Kelly	SF
Nichola Mallon	SDLP
Carál Ní Chuilín	SF

North Down
Alan Chambers	UUP
Stephen Dunne	DUP
Alex Easton	IND
Andrew Muir	APNI
Rachel Woods	Green

South Antrim
Steve Aiken	UUP
John Blair	APNI
Pam Cameron	DUP
Trevor Clarke	DUP
Declan Kearney	SF

South Belfast
Clare Bailey	Green
Paula Bradshaw	APNI
Deirdre Hargey	SF
Matthew O'Toole	SDLP
Christopher Stalford	DUP

South Down
Sinéad Bradley	SDLP
Sinéad Ennis	SF
Colin McGrath	SDLP
Emma Rogan	SF
Jim Wells	DUP

Strangford
Kellie Armstrong	APNI
Harry Harvey	DUP
Michelle McIlveen	DUP
Mike Nesbitt	UUP
Peter Weir	DUP

Upper Bann
Doug Beattie	UUP
Jonathan Buckley	DUP
Diane Dodds	DUP
Dolores Kelly	SDLP
John O'Dowd	SF

West Belfast
Gerry Carroll	PBPA
Órlaithí Flynn	SF
Alex Maskey	SF
Aisling Reilly	SF
Pat Sheehan	SF

West Tyrone
Nicola Brogan	SF
Thomas Buchanan	DUP
Declan McAleer	SF
Daniel McCrossan	SDLP
Maolísa McHugh	SF

Northern Ireland Yearbook | Northern Ireland Assembly

MLA individual profiles
As at November 2021

Steve Aiken
Party: Ulster Unionist Party
Constituency: South Antrim
Address: 3 The Square
Ballyclare, BT39 9BB
Tel: 028 9334 4966
@SteveAikenUUP

Email: steve.aiken@mla.niassembly.gov.uk
Year elected as an MLA: 2016
Committee membership: Chairpersons' Liaison Group; Chair, Finance; Standards and Privileges

Andy Allen
Party: UUP
Constituency: East Belfast
Address: 174 Albertbridge Road
Belfast, BT5 4GS
Tel: 028 9046 3900
@AndyAllen8

Email: andy.allen@mla.niassembly.gov.uk
Year elected as an MLA: 2016 (co-option in 2015)
Committee membership: Communities

Jim Allister
Party: TUV
Constituency: North Antrim
Address: 38 Henry Street
Ballymena, BT42 3AH
Tel: 028 2564 0250
@JimAllister

Email: info@jimallister.org
Year elected as an MLA: 2011
Committee membership: Assembly and Executive Review; Audit; Finance

Caoimhe Archibald
Party: Sinn Féin
Constituency: East Londonderry
Address: 81 Main Street
Dungiven, BT47 4LE
Tel: 028 7774 2488
@CArchibald_SF

Email: caoimhe.archibald@mla.niassembly.gov.uk
Year elected as an MLA: 2016
Committee membership: Chairpersons' Liaison Group; Chair, Economy

Kellie Armstrong
Party: Alliance
Constituency: Strangford
Address: 14 South Street
Newtownards, BT23 4JT
Tel: 028 9181 1414
@Kelmba

Email: kellie.armstrong@mla.niassembly.gov.uk
Year elected as an MLA: 2016
Committee membership: Assembly and Executive Review; Deputy Chair, Communities

Clare Bailey
Party: Green Party
Constituency: South Belfast
Address: 132 University Street
Belfast, BT7 1HH
Tel: 028 9031 4455
@ClareBaileyGPNI

Email: clare.bailey@mla.niassembly.gov.uk
Year elected as an MLA: 2016
Committee membership: Agriculture, Environment and Rural Affairs; Business

Rosemary Barton
Party: UUP
Constituency: Fermanagh and South Tyrone
Address: 1 Regal Pass
Enniskillen, BT74 7NT
Tel: 028 6632 2028
@RosemaryBarton1

Email: rosemary.barton@mla.niassembly.gov.uk
Year elected as an MLA: 2016
Committee membership: Agriculture, Environment and Rural Affairs; Business; Procedures

Doug Beattie
Party: UUP
Constituency: Upper Bann
Address: 103 Bridge Street
Portadown, BT38 8AF
Tel: 028 3835 0004
@BeattieDoug

Email: doug.beattie@mla.niassembly.gov.uk
Year elected as an MLA: 2016
Committee membership: Justice

Northern Ireland Assembly

MLA individual profiles

Roy Beggs
(Deputy Speaker)
Party: UUP
Constituency: East Antrim
Address: 3 St Bride's Street
Carrickfergus, BT38 8AF
Tel: 028 9336 2995
@roybeggs

Email: roy.beggs@mla.niassembly.gov.uk
Year elected as an MLA: 1998
Committee membership: Infrastructure; Deputy Chair, Public Accounts

John Blair
Party: Alliance
Constituency: South Antrim
Address: Unit 2, 21 Carnmoney Road
Newtownabbey, BT36 6HL
Tel: 028 9084 0930
@JohnBlairMLA

Email: john.blair@allianceparty.org
Year elected as an MLA: Co-opted 2018
Committee membership: Agriculture, Environment and Rural Affairs; Northern Ireland Assembly Commission

Cathal Boylan
Party: Sinn Féin
Constituency: Newry and Armagh
Address: 59 Thomas Street
Armagh, BT61 7QB
Tel: 028 3751 1797
@cathalboylansf

Email: cathal.boylan@mla.niassembly.gov.uk
Year elected as an MLA: 2007
Committee membership: Infrastructure; Public Accounts

Maurice Bradley
Party: DUP
Constituency: East Londonderry
Address: 2 Park Street
Coleraine, BT52 1BD
Tel: 028 7035 6990
@bradley_mla

Email: maurice.bradley@mla.niassembly.gov.uk
Year elected as an MLA: 2016
Committee membership: No main committee membership

Paula Bradley
Party: DUP
Constituency: North Belfast
Address: 23A Ballyclare Road
Glengormley, BT36 5EU
Tel: 028 9083 0066
@PBradleyMLA

Email: paula.bradley@mla.niassembly.gov.uk
Year elected as an MLA: 2011
Committee membership: Chairpersons' Liaison Group; Chair, Communities

Sinéad Bradley
Party: SDLP
Constituency: South Down
Address: 11-14 Newry Street
Warrenpoint, BT34 3JZ
Tel: 028 4175 4000
@SineadBradleySD

Email: sinead.bradley@mla.niassembly.gov.uk
Year elected as an MLA: 2016
Committee membership: Justice; Procedures; Standards and Privileges

Paula Bradshaw
Party: Alliance
Constituency: South Belfast
Address: 100 University Street
Belfast, BT7 1HE
Tel: 028 9032 4274
@PaulaJaneB

Email: paula.bradshaw@mla.niassembly.gov.uk
Year elected as an MLA: 2016
Committee membership: Business; Health

Nicola Brogan
Party: Sinn Féin
Constituency: West Tyrone
Address: 4 James Street, Omagh
BT78 1DQ
Tel: 028 8225 3040
@nbrogan087

Email: nicola.brogan@mla.niassembly.gov.uk
Year elected as an MLA: 2020 co-opted
Committee membership: Education; Procedures

Northern Ireland Yearbook | Northern Ireland Assembly

MLA individual profiles

Keith Buchanan
Party: DUP
Constituency: Mid Ulster
Address: 2 Queens Avenue
Magherafelt, BT45 6BU
Tel: 028 7930 0295
@Buchanan_dup

Email: keith.buchanan@mla.niassembly.gov.uk
Year elected as an MLA: 2016
Committee membership: Economy; Deputy Chair, Finance

Thomas Buchanan
Party: DUP
Constituency: West Tyrone
Address: 52 Market Street
Omagh, BT78 1ES
Tel: 028 8224 7702

Email: thomas.buchanan@mla.niassembly.gov.uk
Year elected as an MLA: 2003
Committee membership: Agriculture, Environment and Rural Affairs; Deputy Chair, Procedures

Jonathan Buckley
Party: DUP
Constituency: Upper Bann
Address: 6 West Street
Portadown, BT62 3PD
Tel: 028 3889 4477
@JBuckleyMLA

Email: jonathan.buckley@mla.niassembly.gov.uk
Year elected as an MLA: 2017
Committee membership: Chairpersons' Liaison Group; Chair, Infrastructure

Joanne Bunting
Party: DUP
Constituency: East Belfast
Address: 220 Knock Road
Belfast, BT5 6QD
Tel: 028 9079 7100
@Joanne_Bunting

Email: joanne.bunting@mla.niassembly.gov.uk
Year elected as an MLA: 2016
Committee membership: Business; Procedures

Robbie Butler
Party: UUP
Constituency: Lagan Valley
Address: 59 Bridge Street
Lisburn, BT28 1XZ
Tel: 079 1502 0777
@RobbieButlerMLA

Email: robbie.butler@mla.niassembly.gov.uk
Year elected as an MLA: 2016
Committee membership: Assembly and Executive Review; Business; Education; Northern Ireland Assembly Commission

Pam Cameron
Party: DUP
Constituency: South Antrim
Address: 12A Beverley Road
Newtownabbey, BT36 6QD
Tel: 028 9034 2234
@PCameronMLA

Email: pam.cameron@mla.niassembly.gov.uk
Year elected as an MLA: 2011
Committee membership: Deputy Chair, Health; Standards and Privileges

Gerry Carroll
Party: People Before Profit Alliance
Constituency: West Belfast
Address: 208 Falls Road
Belfast, BT12 6AH
Tel: 028 9023 1628
@GerryCarrollPBP

Email: gerry.carroll@mla.niassembly.gov.uk
Year elected as an MLA: 2016
Committee membership: Health; Procedures

Pat Catney
Party: SDLP
Constituency: Lagan Valley
Address: 12-14 Smithfield Square
Lisburn, BT28 1TH
Tel: 028 9252 8203
@PatCatney

Email: pat.catney@mla.niassembly.gov.uk
Year elected as an MLA: 2017
Committee membership: Finance

MLA individual profiles

Alan Chambers
Party: UUP
Constituency: North Down
Address: 1A Donaghadee Road
Groomsport, BT19 6LG
Tel: 028 9147 7555
@alcham49

Email: alan.chambers@mla.niassembly.gov.uk
Year elected as an MLA: 2016
Committee membership: Audit; Health

Trevor Clarke
Party: DUP
Constituency: South Antrim
Address: 1 Railway Street
Antrim, BT41 4AE
Tel: 028 9446 3273
@trevorclarkeMLA

Email: trevor.clarke@mla.niassembly.gov.uk
Year elected as an MLA: 2007
Committee membership: Business; Northern Ireland Assembly Commission

Pádraig Delargy
Party: Sinn Féin
Constituency: Foyle
Address: 53 Falls Road
Belfast, BT12 4PD
Tel: 028 9034 7350
@padraig_delargy

Email: padraig.delargy@mla.niassembly.gov.uk
Year elected as an MLA: Co-opted 2021
Committee membership: Infrastructure; The Executive Office

Stewart Dickson
Party: Alliance
Constituency: East Antrim
Address: 8 West Street
Carrickfergus, BT38 7AR
Tel: 028 9335 0286
@stewartcdickson

Email: stewart.dickson@mla.niassembly.gov.uk
Year elected as an MLA: 2011
Committee membership: Economy; Standards and Privileges

Linda Dillon
Party: Sinn Féin
Constituency: Mid Ulster
Address: 7 The Square
Coalisland, BT71 4LN
Tel: 028 8774 8689
@LindaDillon81

Email: linda.dillon@mla.niassembly.gov.uk
Year elected as an MLA: 2016
Committee membership: Chairpersons' Liaison Group; Chair, Standards and Privileges

Diane Dodds
Party: DUP
Constituency: Upper Bann
Address: 7 Bridge Street
Banbridge, BT32 3JL
Tel: 028 6052 0048
@DianeDoddsMLA

Email: diane.dodds@mla.niassembly.gov.uk
Year elected as an MLA: 2003-2007, 2020 co-opted
Committee membership: Education; The Executive Office

Jemma Dolan
Party: Sinn Féin
Constituency: Fermanagh and South Tyrone
Address: 5-7 Market Street
Enniskillen, BT74 7DS
Tel: 028 6632 8214
@jemma_dolan

Email: jemma.dolan@mla.niassembly.gov.uk
Year elected as an MLA: 2017
Committee membership: Finance; Justice

Stephen Dunne
Party: DUP
Constituency: North Down
Address: 8 Church Road
Holywood, BT18 9BU
Tel: 028 9042 3322
@StephenDunneMLA

Email: stephen.dunne@mla.niassembly.gov.uk
Year elected as an MLA: Co-opted 2021
Committee membership: Communities; Economy

Northern Ireland Yearbook | Northern Ireland Assembly

MLA individual profiles

Mark Durkan
Party: SDLP
Constituency: Foyle
Address: Frank Long's Complex
141H Strand Road, Derry
BT48 7PB
Tel: 028 7136 5516
@MarkHDurkan

Email: markh.durkan@mla.niassembly.gov.uk
Year elected as an MLA: 2011
Committee membership: Communities

Alex Easton
Party: Independent
Constituency: North Down
Address: 7 High Street
Donaghadee, BT21 0AA
Tel: 028 9188 9620

Email: alex.easton@mla.niassembly.gov.uk
Year elected as an MLA: 2003
Committee membership: The Executive Office

Sinéad Ennis
Party: Sinn Féin
Constituency: South Down
Address: 14A Charlotte Street
Warrenpoint, BT34 3HZ
Tel: 028 4175 4448
@EnnisSinead

Email: sinead.ennis@mla.niassembly.gov.uk
Year elected as an MLA: 2017
Committee membership: Business; Deputy Chair, Justice

Deborah Erskine
Party: DUP
Constituency: Fermanagh and South Tyrone
Address: 1 Quay Lane
Enniskillen, BT74 6AG
Tel: 028 6632 0722
@deborah_cheryl

Email: deborah.erskine@mla.niassembly.gov.uk
Year elected as an MLA: Co-opted 2021
Committee membership: Health

Ciara Ferguson
Party: Sinn Féin
Constituency: Foyle
Address: 53 Falls Road
Belfast, BT12 4PD
Tel: 028 9034 7350
@ciaraf44

Email: ciara.ferguson@mla.niassembly.gov.uk
Year elected as an MLA: Co-opted in 2021
Committee membership: Communities; Procedures

Órlaithí Flynn
Party: Sinn Féin
Constituency: West Belfast
Address: Unit 23
The New Dairy Farm Centre
Stewartstown Road
Poleglass, Dunmurry, BT17 0AW
Tel: 028 9061 1176
@OrlaithiFlynnSF

Email: orlaithi.flynn@mla.niassembly.gov.uk
Year elected as an MLA: Co-opted in 2016
Committee membership: Health; Public Accounts

Paul Frew
Party: DUP
Constituency: North Antrim
Address: 45 Mill Street
Ballymena, BT43 5AA
Tel: 028 2565 9800
@paulfrewDUP

Email: paul.frew@mla.niassembly.gov.uk
Year elected as an MLA: 2010
Committee membership: Assembly and Executive Review; Communities

Colm Gildernew
Party: Sinn Féin
Constituency: Fermanagh and South Tyrone
Address: 46 Market Square
Dungannon, BT70 1DQ
Tel: 028 8772 2776
@GildernewColm

Email: colm.gildernew@mla.niassembly.gov.uk
Year elected as an MLA: 2017
Committee membership: Chairpersons' Liaison Group; Chair, Health

MLA individual profiles

Paul Givan
Party: DUP
Constituency: Lagan Valley
Address: The Old Town Hall
29 Castle Street, Lisburn, BT27 4DH
Tel: 028 9266 1100
@paulgivan

Email: paul.givan@mla.niassembly.gov.uk
Year elected as an MLA: 2011 (co-option in 2010)
Committee membership: None (attends Executive)

Deirdre Hargey
Party: Sinn Féin
Constituency: South Belfast
Address: 178 Ormeau Road
Belfast, BT7 2ED
Tel: 028 9024 3194
@DeirdreHargey

Email: deirdre.hargey@mla.niassembly.gov.uk
Year elected as an MLA: 2020 co-opted
Committee membership: None (attends Executive)

Harry Harvey
Party: DUP
Constituency: Strangford
Address: 10a The Square
Ballynahinch, BT24 8AE
Tel: 075 9074 2280
@harveyscrossgar

Email: harry.harvey@mla.niassembly.gov.uk
Year elected as an MLA: Co-opted 2019
Committee membership: Agriculture, Environment and Rural Affairs; Education

David Hilditch
Party: DUP
Constituency: East Antrim
Address: 2 Joymount
Carrickfergus
BT38 7DN
Tel: 028 9332 9980
@dwh_crfc

Email: david.hilditch@mla.niassembly.gov.uk
Year elected as an MLA: 1998
Committee membership: Deputy Chair, Infrastructure; Public Accounts

William Humphrey
Party: DUP
Constituency: North Belfast
Address: Parkgate House
35 Woodvale Road
Belfast, BT13 3BN
Tel: 028 9074 4008
@WmHumphreyDUP

Email: william.humphrey@mla.niassembly.gov.uk
Year elected as an MLA: 2011 (co-option in 2010)
Committee membership: Chairpersons' Liaison Group; Chair, Public Accounts; Procedures

Cara Hunter
Party: SDLP
Constituency: East Londonderry
Address: 1 Bellhouse Lane
Coleraine, BT52 1ED
Tel: 028 7034 8933
@CaraHunterMLA

Email: cara.hunter@mla.niassembly.gov.uk
Year elected as an MLA: 2020 co-opted
Committee membership: Infrastructure; Public Accounts

William Irwin
Party: DUP
Constituency: Newry and Armagh
Address: 18 Main Street
Richhill, BT61 9PW
Tel: 028 3887 0500

Email: william.irwin@mla.niassembly.gov.uk
Year elected as an MLA: 2007
Committee membership: Agriculture, Environment and Rural Affairs; Deputy Chair, Audit; Public Accounts

Declan Kearney
Party: Sinn Féin
Constituency: South Antrim
Address: Unit 1, 2 Main Street
Randalstown, BT41 3AB
Tel: 028 9454 8166
@DeclanKearneySF

Email: declan.kearney@mla.niassembly.gov.uk
Year elected as an MLA: 2016
Committee membership: None (attends Executive)

Northern Ireland Yearbook | Northern Ireland Assembly

MLA individual profiles

Dolores Kelly
Party: SDLP
Constituency: Upper Bann
Address: 74 William Street
Lurgan, BT66 6JB
Tel: 028 3832 2140
@upperbannsdlp

Email: dolores.kelly@mla.niassembly.gov.uk
Year elected as an MLA: 2003-2016, 2017
Committee membership: Business; Northern Ireland Assembly Commission

Gerry Kelly
Party: Sinn Féin
Constituency: North Belfast
Address: 202 Antrim Road
Belfast, BT15 3BU
Tel: 028 9521 5649
@GerryKellyMLA

Email: gerry.kelly@mla.niassembly.gov.uk
Year elected as an MLA: 1998
Committee membership: Assembly and Executive Review

Liz Kimmins
Party: Sinn Féin
Constituency: Newry and Armagh
Address: 1 Kilmorey Terrace
Patrick Street
Newry, BT35 8DW
Tel: 028 3026 1693
@LizK1988

Email: liz.kimmins@mla.niassembly.gov.uk
Year elected as an MLA: 2020 co-opted
Committee membership: Infrastructure

Naomi Long
Party: Alliance
Constituency: East Belfast
Address: 56 Upper Newtownards Road
Belfast, BT4 3EL
Tel: 028 9047 2004
@naomi_long

Email: naomi.long@mla.niassembly.gov.uk
Year elected as an MLA: 2003-2007, 2016-2019, 2020 co-opted
Committee membership: None (attends Executive)

Trevor Lunn
Party: Independent
Constituency: Lagan Valley
Address: 17 Graham Gardens
Lisburn, BT28 1XE
Tel: 028 9267 1177
@TrevorLunnLV

Email: trevor.lunn@mla.niassembly.gov.uk
Year elected as an MLA: 2007
Committee membership: The Executive Office

Gordon Lyons
Party: DUP
Constituency: East Antrim
Address: 116 Main Street
Larne, BT40 1RG
Tel: 028 2826 7722
@gordonlyons1

Email: gordon.lyons@mla.niassembly.gov.uk
Year elected as an MLA: 2016 (co-option in 2015)
Committee membership: None (attends Executive)

Chris Lyttle
Party: Alliance
Constituency: East Belfast
Address: 56 Upper Newtownards Road
Belfast, BT4 3EL
Tel: 028 9047 2004
@Chris_Lyttle

Email: chris.lyttle@mla.niassembly.gov.uk
Year elected as an MLA: 2011 (co-option in 2010)
Committee membership: Chairpersons' Liaison Group; Chair, Education

Nichola Mallon
Party: SDLP
Constituency: North Belfast
Address: 168 Antrim Road
Belfast, BT15 2AH
Tel: 028 9515 0100
@NicholaMallon

Email: nichola.mallon@mla.niassembly.gov.uk
Year elected as an MLA: 2016
Committee membership: None (attends Executive)

MLA individual profiles

Alex Maskey
(Speaker)
Party: Sinn Féin
Constituency: West Belfast
Address: 147 Andersontown Road
Belfast, BT11 9BW
Tel: 028 9080 8404
@AlexMaskeyMLA

Email: alex.maskey@mla.niassembly.gov.uk
Year elected as an MLA: 1998 (West Belfast);
2003 (South Belfast); Co-opted (West Belfast) in 2014
Committee membership: Chair, Business; Chair, Northern Ireland Assembly Commission

Declan McAleer
Party: Sinn Féin
Constituency: West Tyrone
Address: 4-5 James Street
Omagh, BT78 1DH
Tel: 028 8225 3040
@mc_mla

Email: declan.mcaleer@mla.niassembly.gov.uk
Year elected as an MLA: 2016 (co-option in 2012)
Committee membership: Chair, Agriculture, Environment and Rural Affairs; Chairpersons' Liaison Group; Standards and Privileges

Daniel McCrossan
Party: SDLP
Constituency: West Tyrone
Address: Wray House, 1 Church Brae
Strabane, BT82 8BS
Tel: 028 7188 2828
@McCrossanMLA

Email: daniel.mccrossan@mla.niassembly.gov.uk
Year elected as an MLA: 2016 (co-option in 2016)
Committee membership: Chair, Audit; Chairpersons' Liaison Group; Education

Patsy McGlone
(Deputy Speaker)
Party: SDLP
Constituency: Mid Ulster
Address: 54A William Street
Cookstown, BT80 8NB
Tel: 028 8675 8175
@patsymcglone

Email: patsymcglonemla@yahoo.ie
Year elected as an MLA: 2003
Committee membership: Agriculture, Environment and Rural Affairs; Standards and Privileges

Colin McGrath
Party: SDLP
Constituency: South Down
Address: 97A Main Street
Newcastle, BT33 0AE
Tel: 028 4379 8350
@ColinSDLP

Email: colin.mcgrath@mla.niassembly.gov.uk
Year elected as an MLA: 2016
Committee membership: Assembly and Executive Review; Business; Health

Philip McGuigan
Party: Sinn Féin
Constituency: North Antrim
Address: 12 Main Street
Dunloy, BT44 9AA
Tel: 028 2765 7198
@mcguigan_philip

Email: philip.mcguigan@mla.niassembly.gov.uk
Year elected as an MLA: 2003 (co-option in 2016)
Committee membership: Deputy Chair, Agriculture, Environment and Rural Affairs; Finance

Maolíosa McHugh
Party: Sinn Féin
Constituency: West Tyrone
Address: 1A Melvin Road
Ballycolman
Strabane, BT82 9PP
Tel: 028 7188 6464

Email: maoliosa.mchugh@mla.niassembly.gov.uk
Year elected as an MLA: Co-opted 2019
Committee membership: Deputy Chair, Assembly and Executive Review; Finance; Public Accounts

Northern Ireland Yearbook | Northern Ireland Assembly

MLA individual profiles

Michelle McIlveen
Party: DUP
Constituency: Strangford
Address: 24 Castle Street
Comber, BT23 5DZ
Tel: 028 9187 1441
@MMcIlveenMLA

Email: michelle.mcilveen@mla.niassembly.gov.uk
Year elected as an MLA: 2007
Committee membership: None (attends Executive)

Sinead McLaughlin
Party: SDLP
Constituency: Strangford
Address: Unit 4, Spencer House
12-22 Spencer Road
Derry, BT47 6QA
Tel: 028 7116 2900
@SMcLaughlinMLA

Email: sinead.mclaughlin@mla.niassembly.gov.uk
Year elected as an MLA: 2020 co-opted
Committee membership: Deputy Chair, Chairpersons' Liaison Group; Chair, The Executive Office

Justin McNulty
Party: SDLP
Constituency: Newry and Armagh
Address: 15 Trevor Hill
Newry, BT34 1DN
Tel: 028 3026 7933
@JustinMcNu1ty

Email: justin.mcnulty@mla.niassembly.gov.uk
Year elected as an MLA: 2016
Committee membership: Education

Gary Middleton
Party: DUP
Constituency: Foyle
Address: 1st Floor, Waterside Centre
23 Glendermott Road
Waterside, Derry
BT47 6BG
Tel: 028 7134 6271
@Gary_Middleton

Email: gary.middleton@mla.niassembly.gov.uk
Year elected as an MLA: 2016 (co-opted in 2015)
Committee membership: None (attends Executive)

Andrew Muir
Party: Alliance
Constituency: North Down
Address: 33 Church Road
Holywood, BT18 9BU
Tel: 028 9544 2944
@AndrewMuirNI

Email: andrew.muir@mla.niassembly.gov.uk
Year elected as an MLA: 2019 co-opted
Committee membership: Business; Infrastructure; Public Accounts

Áine Murphy
Party: Sinn Féin
Constituency: Fermanagh and South Tyrone
Address: 53 Falls Road
Belfast, BT12 4PD
Tel: 028 9034 7350
@ainemurphy116

Email: aine.murphy@mla.niassembly.gov.uk
Year elected as an MLA: Co-opted 2021
Committee membership: Communities; Standards and Privileges

Conor Murphy
Party: Sinn Féin
Constituency: Newry and Armagh
Address: 38 Cardinal O'Fiaich Square
Crossmaglen, BT35 9JH
Tel: 028 3086 1948
@conormurphysf

Email: conor.murphy@mla.niassembly.gov.uk
Year elected as an MLA: Co-opted 2015 (first elected 1998)
Committee membership: None (attends Executive)

Mike Nesbitt
Party: UUP
Constituency: Strangford
Address: 16 South Street
Newtownards, BT23 4JT
Tel: 028 9182 1587
@mikenesbittni

Email: mike.nesbitt@mla.niassembly.gov.uk
Year elected as an MLA: 2011
Committee membership: Economy

MLA individual profiles

Robin Newton
Party: DUP
Constituency: East Belfast
Address: 59 Castlereagh Road
Belfast, BT5 5FB
Tel: 028 9045 9500
🐦 @RobinNewtonMLA

Email: robin.newton@mla.niassembly.gov.uk
Year elected as an MLA: 2003
Committee membership: Education; Justice

Carál Ní Chuilín
Party: Sinn Féin
Constituency: North Belfast
Address: 545 Antrim Road
Belfast, BT15 2GZ
Tel: 028 9074 0817
🐦 @CaralNiChuilin

Email: caral.nichuilin@mla.niassembly.gov.uk
Year elected as an MLA: 2007
Committee membership: Chairpersons' Liaison Group; Health; Chair, Procedures

John O'Dowd
Party: Sinn Féin
Constituency: Upper Bann
Address: 57 Church Place
Lurgan, BT66 6HD
Tel: 028 3834 9675
🐦 @JohnODowdSF

Email: john.odowd@mla.niassembly.gov.uk
Year elected as an MLA: 2003
Committee membership: Business; Economy; Northern Ireland Assembly Commission

Michelle O'Neill
Party: Sinn Féin
Constituency: Mid Ulster
Address: 30F Fairhill Road
Cookstown, BT80 8AG
Tel: 028 8627 7680
🐦 @moneillsf

Email: michelle.oneill@mla.niassembly.gov.uk
Year elected as an MLA: 2007
Committee membership: None (attends Executive)

Matthew O'Toole
Party: SDLP
Constituency: South Belfast
Address: 30 University Street
Belfast, BT7 1FZ
Tel: 028 9023 3344
🐦 @matthewotoole2

Email: matthew.otoole@mla.niassembly.gov.uk
Year elected as an MLA: 2020 co-opted
Committee membership: Deputy Chair, Economy; Finance

Edwin Poots
Party: DUP
Constituency: Lagan Valley
Address: The Old Town Hall
29 Castle Street, Lisburn, BT27 4DH
Tel: 028 9260 3003
🐦 @poots_edwin

Email: edwin.poots@mla.niassembly.gov.uk
Year elected as an MLA: 1998
Committee membership: None (attends Executive)

Aisling Reilly
Party: Sinn Féin
Constituency: West Belfast
Address: 53 Falls Road
Belfast, BT12 4PD
Tel: 028 9034 7350
🐦 @aislingreilly11

Email: aisling.reilly@mla.niassembly.gov.uk
Year elected as an MLA: Co-opted 2021
Committee membership: Communities

George Robinson
Party: DUP
Constituency: East Londonderry
Address: 6-8 Catherine Street
Limavady, BT49 9DB
Tel: 028 7776 9191
🐦 @G_Rob44

Email: george.robinson@mla.niassembly.gov.uk
Year elected as an MLA: 2003
Committee membership: Assembly and Executive Review; Infrastructure

Northern Ireland Yearbook | Northern Ireland Assembly

MLA individual profiles

Emma Rogan
Party: Sinn Féin
Constituency: South Down
Address: 64 St Patrick's Avenue
Downpatrick, BT30 6ND
Tel: 028 4461 4405
@emmarogan12

Email: emma.rogan@mla.niassembly.gov.uk
Year elected as an MLA: 2017
Committee membership: Audit; Justice

Pat Sheehan
Party: Sinn Féin
Constituency: West Belfast
Address: 2a 689 Springfield Road
Belfast, BT11 8EB
Tel: 028 9061 3894
@PatSheehanMLA

Email: pat.sheehan@mla.niassembly.gov.uk
Year elected as an MLA: 2011 (co-option in 2010)
Committee membership: Deputy Chair, Education; The Executive Office

Emma Sheerin
Party: Sinn Féin
Constituency: Mid Ulster
Address: 79 Quarry Road
Knockcloghrim, BT45 8NS
Tel: 028 7964 4550
@SheerinOfficial

Email: emma.sheerin@mla.niassembly.gov.uk
Year elected as an MLA: Co-opted 2018
Committee membership: Chairpersons' Liaison Group; The Executive Office

Christopher Stalford
(Principal Deputy Speaker)
Party: DUP
Constituency: South Belfast
Address: 127-145 Sandy Row
Belfast, BT12 5ET
Tel: 028 9052 1322
@CStalfordMLA

Email: christopher.stalford@mla.niassembly.gov.uk
Year elected as an MLA: 2016
Committee membership: Deputy Chair, Standards and Privileges; The Executive Office

John Stewart
Party: UUP
Constituency: East Antrim
Address: 95 Main Street
Larne, BT40 1HJ
Tel: 028 2827 2644
@JohnStewart1983

Email: john.stewart@mla.niassembly.gov.uk
Year elected as an MLA: 2017
Committee membership: Deputy Chair, The Executive Office

Mervyn Storey
Party: DUP
Constituency: North Antrim
Address: 3 Market Street
Ballymoney, BT53 6EA
Tel: 028 2766 9753

Email: mervyn.storey@mla.niassembly.gov.uk
Year elected as an MLA: 2003
Committee membership: Chairpersons' Liaison Group; Chair, Justice

Claire Sugden
Party: Independent
Constituency: East Londonderry
Address: 1 Upper Abbey Street
Coleraine, BT52 1BF
Tel: 028 7032 7294
@ClaireSugden

Email: claire.sugden@mla.niassembly.gov.uk
Year elected as an MLA: 2016, (co-opted in 2014)
Committee membership: Economy

Robin Swann
Party: UUP
Constituency: North Antrim
Address: 13-15 Queen Street
Ballymena, BT42 2BB
Tel: 028 2565 9595
@RobinSwannUUP

Email: robin.swann@mla.niassembly.gov.uk
Year elected as an MLA: 2011
Committee membership: None (attends Executive)

MLA individual profiles

Peter Weir
Party: DUP
Constituency: North Down
Address: 6A North Street Newtownards, BT23 4DE
Tel: 028 9181 0858
 @peterweirmla

Email: peter.weir@mla.niassembly.gov.uk
Year elected as an MLA: 1998
Committee membership: Assembly and Executive Review; Chairpersons' Liaison Group; Economy; Justice

Jim Wells
Party: DUP
Constituency: South Down
Address: 12 Bridge Street Kilkeel, BT34 4AD
Tel: 028 4176 9900
 @Jim_Wells_MLA

Email: jim.wells@mla.niassembly.gov.uk
Year elected as an MLA: 1998
Committee membership: Finance

Rachel Woods
Party: Green Party
Constituency: North Down
Address: 12 Hamilton Road Bangor, BT20 4LE
Tel: 028 9127 3327
 @rachelwoods52

Email: rachel.woods@mla.niassembly.gov.uk
Year elected as an MLA: Co-opted 2019
Committee membership: Justice

Other institutions of government

As well as creating the Northern Ireland Assembly, the Belfast/Good Friday Agreement allowed for new structures for consulting with wider society in Northern Ireland, co-operation between Northern Ireland and the Republic of Ireland, and co-operation between all governments in Britain and Ireland.

The Agreement's structures covered the three 'strands' of relations affecting Northern Ireland:

Strand One (within Northern Ireland): Northern Ireland Assembly; Civic Forum
Strand Two (north-south): North/South Ministerial Council; North/South implementation bodies
Strand Three (east-west): British-Irish Council; British-Irish Intergovernmental Conference

Institutions in Strands Two and Three were formed by the British-Irish Agreement between the UK and Irish Governments in March 1999, which came into force with the introduction of devolution to Northern Ireland in December 1999.

North/South Ministerial Council
Joint Secretariat
58 Upper English Street
Armagh, BT61 7LG
Tel: 028 3751 8068
Web: www.northsouthministerialcouncil.org

Northern Ireland Joint Secretary: Tim Losty
Irish Joint Secretary: Mark Hanniffy

The Council brings together ministers from the Northern Ireland Executive and Irish Government to work together and take action on matters of mutual interest. Six areas of co-operation have been outlined to date: agriculture, education, environment, health, tourism and transport.

North/South implementation bodies

The implementation bodies develop cross-border co-operation in specific areas of mutual interest. They operate under the supervision of the North/South Ministerial Council and are funded by relevant departments in the Northern Ireland Executive and Irish Government.

Food Safety Promotion Board (safefood)
7 Eastgate Avenue, Eastgate
Little Island, Cork, T45 RX01
Tel: + 353 21 230 4100
Web: www.safefood.net
Email: info@safefood.net
Chief Executive: Ray Dolan

Foras na Gaeilge
63-66 Amiens Street, Dublin 1
Tel: 00 353 (1) 639 8400
Web: www.gaeilge.ie
Email: eolas@forasnagaeilge.ie
Chief Executive: Seán Ó Coinn

InterTradeIreland
Old Gasworks Business Park
Kilmorey Street, Newry, BT34 2DE
Tel: 028 3083 4100
Web: www.intertradeireland.com
Email: info@intertradeireland.com
Chief Executive: Margaret Hearty

Loughs Agency
22 Victoria Road, Waterside
Derry, BT47 2AB
Tel: 028 7134 2100
Web: www.loughs-agency.org
Email: general@loughs-agency.org
Designated Officer:
Sharon McMahon

Carlingford Regional Office
Dundalk Street
Carlingford, Co Louth
Tel: + 353 (42) 938 3888
Email: carlingford@loughs-agency.org

Enquiries about Irish lighthouses and marine navigation should be directed to:

Commissioners of Irish Lights
Harbour Road, Dún Laoghaire
Co Dublin
Tel: + 353 (1) 271 5400
Web: www.irishlights.ie
Email: info@cil.ie
Chief Executive:
Yvonne Shields O'Connor

The Commissioners of Irish Lights was established as a public body in 1867. The body is jointly accountable to the UK and Irish Governments as its services protect shipping on the approaches to Britain and Ireland.

Special EU Programmes Body (SEUPB)
The Clarence West Building
2 Clarence Street West
Belfast, BT2 7GP
Tel: 028 9026 6660
Web: www.seupb.eu
Email: info@seupb.eu
Chief Executive: Gina McIntyre

Tourism Ireland
4th Floor, Bishop's Square
Redmond's Hill, Dublin 2
D02 TD99
Tel: 00 353 (1) 476 3400
Web: www.tourismireland.com
Email: corporate.dublin@tourismireland.com
Chief Executive: Niall Gibbons

Ulster Scots Agency (Tha Boord o Ulstèr-Scotch)
The Corn Exchange, 31 Gordon Street
Belfast, BT1 2LG
Tel: 028 9023 1113
Web: www.ulsterscotsagency.com
Email: info@ulsterscotsagency.org.uk
Chief Executive: Ian Crozier

Waterways Ireland
2 Sligo Road, Enniskillen, BT74 7JY
Tel: 028 6632 3004
Web: www.waterwaysireland.org
Email: info@waterwaysireland.org
Chief Executive: John McDonagh

North/South Inter-Parliamentary Association
The North/South Inter-Parliamentary Association was established in July 2012. It meets on a rotational basis between the Oireachtas and the Northern Ireland Assembly.

Assembly Joint Clerk: Tony Logue
Northern Ireland Assembly
Parliament Buildings
Belfast, BT4 3XX
Tel: 028 9052 1930
Email: tony.logue@niassembly.gov.uk

Oireachtas Joint Clerk: Noel Murphy
Houses of the Oireachtas
Kildare House
Kildare Street, Dublin 2
Tel: + 353 (1) 618 3167
Email: noel.murphy@oireachtas.ie

Northern Ireland Assembly | Northern Ireland Yearbook

East-West co-operation

British-Irish Council
1st Floor, Thistle House
91 Haymarket Terrance
Edinburgh, EH12 5HE
Tel: 0131 479 5331
Web: www.britishirishcouncil.org
Email: secretariat@britishirishcouncil.org
Irish Government Joint Head:
Ciara Gilvarry
UK Government Joint Head:
William Wickman

The Council promotes good relations among its member administrations: the British and Irish Governments, the Northern Ireland Executive, the Scottish Government, the Welsh Assembly Government, and the Governments of Jersey, Guernsey and the Isle of Man.

British-Irish Intergovernmental Conference
Windsor House, 9-15 Bedford Street
Belfast, BT2 7EL
Tel: 028 9038 3700

The Joint Secretariat brings the British and Irish Governments together to promote bilateral co-operation on matters of mutual interest.

British-Irish Parliamentary Assembly (BIPA)
British Joint Clerk: Edward Beale
Table Office, House of Commons
London, SW1A 0AA
Tel: 020 7219 3927

Irish Joint Clerk: Paul Stephens
House of The Oireachtas
Kildare Street, Dublin 2
Tel: 00 353 (1) 618 3218
Web: www.britishirish.org

The Assembly was set up in 1990 and brings together parliamentarians from the legislatures of the British Isles i.e. the UK Parliament, Oireachtas, Scottish Parliament, National Assembly for Wales, Northern Ireland Assembly, Tynwald (Isle of Man Parliament), States of Jersey and States of Guernsey.

Assembly business: Communications

Head of Communications for the Northern Ireland Assembly, Susie Brown, discusses the Assembly's new communications strategy, including the role of social media in informing and engaging audiences.

Setting the context of a high-profile organisation under constant political and media scrutiny, Brown emphasises the critical nature of transparency and accountability in the Assembly's communications. Brown's team has recently embarked on a strategy to embed a more planned approach to what it publishes, how content is published and the creation of content.

"We can be very specific about what it is we want to achieve, with governance in place so that we know who is responsible for what and we have a workflow that helps us get from concept to publication, with structure."

The Head of Communications says that efficiencies are achieved not only through enhanced role identification in the content production process, backed up with data and intelligence to support quick and efficient decisions, but also through the building of team empowerment.

"The benefits to our users are that they only receive high quality content, it is trustworthy, it is user-centred and it will help them to become champions to amplify our content," she explains.

Brown outlines the core objectives of the strategy in supporting and demonstrating effective scrutiny and debate; helping to explain Assembly business and proceedings; and inspiring meaningful engagement and participation. To this end, social media has been a valuable tool. The Assembly uses YouTube, Facebook, Twitter and Instagram as its core channels.

The Assembly seeks to amplify its own accurate, timely and accessible content in the form of what is happening in the chamber and in committees, supported by experts across the Assembly. Explanation of business and proceedings evolves around the sharing of text, video and audio content, showcasing activity and engaging in discussion with audiences. This engagement is part of the wider participation objective, and signpost areas of possible participation such as visiting, campaign support and the influence of the Assembly's work on peoples' lives.

Brown explains that central to any ambitions is user need, with the Assembly utilising research and data to inform everything that it publishes. In particular, she points to moves to address misinformation, which requires educational and informative content.

Brown points to a range of content pillars which underpin the Assembly's objectives. "Each of our six pillars has content which supports the delivery of each objective. In creating topics, we then look to see if the content exists and if it does, if we can use it or if it needs tailored. If it doesn't exist, we look to see if we or a colleague can create it, what links we have to existing content and what we can re-use."

Governance

Explaining that as a public body, governance is at the heart of all that the Assembly does and very important in relation to communications, Brown points to challenges in delivering at speed. Providing agility, the Assembly's communications team has autonomy to create and publish content.

"We work in an environment of trust, professionalism and integrity," she states. "Our model is that the author will go through a period of discovery, they will work with a subject matter expert and create that content with appropriate research. We then get expert review prior to publication and post-publication, we review that content based on user experience, adding iterations where necessary."

On the topic of measuring success, Brown points to a range of overarching key performance indicators (KPIs) used across all content but stresses the use of additional targets and metrics where necessary, on different objectives.

Things like audience growth rate, amplification rate and social share of voice are all tools used by the Assembly to gauge success of content. Brown is pleased to highlight results that showcase progression including 1.62 million Facebook impressions in the last year and 13.6 per cent increase in Twitter followers since September 2020.

However, she is aware of the stark difference between followers and an engaged audience and places greater weight on the impressive 9.6 per cent engagement rate for Facebook and 7.3 per cent rate for Twitter held by the Assembly over the past 12 months.

Brown admits that not all engagement with the Assembly is positive and so, her team has a strategy in place to deal with negativity which involves firstly, understanding the complaint or problem and its motivation, secondly, offering a quick, accurate and impartial response and thirdly, if necessary, passing the complaint on to the relevant body.

Brown adds the stipulation: "We never respond to threats, abusive communications or communication that includes swearing. Our tone is helpful and calm. Always."

Concluding, Brown paid tribute to her team who continue to stay right up to date with the digital landscape and are never afraid to try new things to increase awareness of and participation with the Assembly.

Northern Ireland Assembly | Northern Ireland Yearbook

Assembly Committees

Committee for the Economy.

Assembly committees play an important role in holding ministers and departments to account and practically supporting the Assembly in its work. When the Executive was restored in January 2020, no official opposition was formed. There are three types of committee: statutory, standing and ad hoc.

Statutory committees

Statutory committees scrutinise the work of the Executive departments. There are nine statutory committees and each has nine members. Chairpersons and deputy chairpersons are allocated under the d'Hondt system, in the same manner as ministers in the Executive are appointed, and committee membership reflects party strengths in the Assembly.

These committees are tasked with advising and assisting their respective ministers on the formulation of policy, and have the power to:

- initiate legislation;
- take the committee stage of primary legislation;
- consider secondary legislation;
- initiate inquiries and make reports;
- consider and advise on departmental budgets and annual plans;
- consider matters brought to their attention by ministers; and
- call for persons and papers.

A summary of the activities of each committee for the 2021-2022 session (as at November 2021), named by their area of responsibility, is outlined below:

The **Agriculture, Environment and Rural Affairs Committee** met in November 2021 to continue its consideration of the Climate Change Bills, No.1 and No.2. The Committee also produced a Report on the Horse Racing (Amendment) Bill in October 2020. The Bill will enable the current operators of Down Royal and Downpatrick racecourses to apply to the Horse Racing Fund. They have also received a briefing on the upcoming Northern Ireland Peatland Strategy 2021-2040.

The **Committee for Communities** is currently calling for evidence on the Betting, Gaming, Lotteries and Amusements (Amendment) Bill. The objectives of this Bill are to address a number of specific anomalies with regard to the current regulation of land based betting, gaming, lottery and amusement activities. The Committee is also calling for evidence on the Private Tenancies Bill, which aims to assist in making the private rented sector a safer and more secure housing option for a wider range of households.

The **Committee for the Economy** is seeking views on the Small-Scale Green Energy Bill. This Bill will, if passed, require the Minister for the Economy to establish a small-scale green energy scheme for

Northern Ireland Assembly

Northern Ireland. It is also calling for evidence on the Parental Bereavement (Leave and Pay) Bill, which aims to create a legal requirement for all employers to grant a period of a minimum of two weeks of Parental Bereavement Leave, with pay (if eligible) at the statutory flat rate.

The **Committee for Education** recently received an oral briefing from the Minister of Education on Covid-19 safety in schools and staff shortages. The Committee is calling for evidence on the Integrated Education Bill. The purpose of the Integrated Education Bill is to make provision about the promotion and provision of integrated education. It will also provide for the reform and expansion of integrated education. The Committee for Education has also been considering Covid-19 Lockdown and Restart and the Impact on the Provision of Special Educational Needs. The Committee for Education has been considering Post-Primary Transfer Testing.

The **Committee for Finance** is currently scrutinising the Defamation Bill. The aim of the Bill is to reform the law of defamation to ensure that a fair balance is struck between the right to freedom of expression and the protection of reputation. The Committee for Finance is currently scrutinising the draft Financial Reporting (Departments and Public Bodies) Bill. The Committee has recently produced its report on the proposed Legislative Consent Memorandum for the Public Service Pensions and Judicial Offices Bill and has also agreed its report on an independent Fiscal Council for Northern Ireland.

The **Committee for Health** is currently calling for evidence on the Abortion Services (Safe Access Zones) Bill. The purpose of the Bill is to make provision for the establishment of 'safe access zones' around abortion clinics. The Committee Stage of the Health and Social Care Bill finished on 1 October 2021. The Autism (Amendment) Bill is currently at Committee stage and aims to strengthen and enhance the Autism Strategy through amendments to the Autism (Northern Ireland) Act 2011. The Committee also held an inquiry into Covid-19 and its impact on care homes.

The **Committee for Infrastructure** have launched an inquiry into decarbonising Northern Ireland's road transport. As part of this inquiry, the Committee has prepared a survey to find out how people feel about ultra-low emission vehicles, both pure electric and plug-in hybrids, as well as what they see as barriers to their use.

The **Committee for Justice** has begun to take oral evidence on the Justice (Sexual Offences and Trafficking Victims) Bill. This aims to enhance public safety and to improve services for victims of trafficking and exploitation. The Committee also issued a call for evidence on the Protection from Stalking Bill.

The **Committee for the Executive Office** met in November 2021 and received briefings from stakeholders in relation to the Travel Agents Coronavirus Financial Assistance Scheme.

Standing committees

Standing committees fulfil a number of separate functions which assist the work of the Assembly. Chairpersons and deputy chairpersons are allocated under the d'Hondt system. There are six standing committees with varying sizes.

The **Business Committee** (12 members) sets the agenda for Assembly meetings and is chaired by the Speaker and filled by the whips of the parties.

The **Procedures Committee** (9 members) considers and reviews standing orders and procedures on an ongoing basis.

The **Standards and Privileges Committee** (9 members) considers privilege, members' interests, the Assembly code of conduct, and any complaints on these issues. Complaints are referred to the Assembly Commissioner for Standards for investigation.

The **Assembly and Executive Review Committee** (9 members) considers changes to how the Assembly and Executive work. The Committee is required to review and report on the operation of Parts III and IV of the Northern Ireland Act 1998 that deal with Executive Authorities and Assembly Elections.

The **Public Accounts Committee** (9 members) scrutinises how departments and agencies use public money. It can follow up Northern Ireland Audit Office reports and also start its own investigations.

The **Audit Committee** (5 members) approves the budget and annual plan of the Northern Ireland Audit Office, which is otherwise independent.

All chairpersons of statutory and standing committees are members of the **Chairpersons' Liaison Group**, which represents the collective voice of committees and seeks to improve their effectiveness and to facilitate linkages between committees and the Executive.

Ad hoc committees

Ad hoc committees are established to consider specific issues and report back to the Assembly, normally within a two-month period. Information on the membership of the Assembly's statutory and standing committees follows.

Northern Ireland Assembly | Northern Ireland Yearbook

Statutory Committees

Committee for Agriculture, Environment and Rural Affairs

Chairperson: Declan McAleer (SF)

Deputy Chairperson: Philip McGuigan (SF)

Membership: Clare Bailey (Green); Rosemary Barton (UUP); John Blair (APNI); Thomas Buchanan (DUP); Harry Harvey (DUP); William Irwin (DUP); Patsy McGlone (SDLP)

Committee Clerk: Nick Henry
Tel: 028 9052 1742
Email: committee.agrienvrural@niassembly.gov.uk

Committee for Communities

Chairperson: Paula Bradley (DUP)

Deputy Chairperson: Kellie Armstrong (APNI)

Membership: Andy Allen (UUP); Mark Durkan (SDLP); Stephen Dunne (DUP); Paul Frew (DUP); Ciara Ferguson (SF); Áine Murphy (SF); Aisling Reilly (SF)

Committee Clerk: Janice Thompson
Tel: 028 9052 1369
Email: committee.communities@niassembly.gov.uk

Committee for the Economy

Chairperson: Caoimhe Archibald (SF)

Deputy Chairperson: Matthew O'Toole (SDLP)

Membership: Keith Buchanan (DUP); Stewart Dickson (APNI); Stephen Dunne (DUP); John O'Dowd (SF); Matthew O'Toole (SDLP); Mike Nesbitt (UUP); Claire Sugden (Ind); Peter Weir (DUP)

Committee Clerk: Peter Hall
Tel: 028 9052 1799
Email: committee.economy@niassembly.gov.uk

Committee for Education

Chairperson: Chris Lyttle (APNI)

Deputy Chairperson: Pat Sheehan (SF)

Membership: Nicola Brogan (SF); Robbie Butler (UUP); Diane Dodds (DUP); Harry Harvey (DUP); Daniel McCrossan (SDLP); Justin McNulty (SDLP); Robin Newton (DUP)

Committee Clerk: Aoibhinn Treanor
Tel: 028 9052 1628
Email: committee.education@niassembly.gov.uk

Statutory Committees

Committee for the Executive Office

Chairperson:
Sinead McLaughlin (SDLP)

Deputy Chairperson: John Stewart (UUP)

Membership: Pádraig Delargy (SF); Diane Dodds (DUP); Alex Easton (Ind); Trevor Lunn (Ind); Emma Sheerin (SF); Christopher Stalford (DUP); Pat Sheehan (SF)

Committee Clerk: Michael Potter
Tel: 028 9052 1830
Email: committee.executive@niassembly.gov.uk

Committee for Finance

Chairperson:
Steve Aiken (UUP)

Deputy Chairperson: Keith Buchanan (DUP)

Membership: Jim Allister (TUV); Pat Catney (SDLP); Jemma Dolan (SF); Matthew O'Toole (SDLP); Maolíosa McHugh (SF); Philip McGuigan (SF); Jim Wells (DUP)

Committee Clerk: Peter McCallion
Tel: 028 9052 1821
Email: committee.finance@niassembly.gov.uk

Committee for Health

Chairperson:
Colm Gildernew (SF)

Deputy Chairperson: Pam Cameron (DUP)

Membership: Paula Bradshaw (APNI); Gerry Carroll (PBPA); Alan Chambers (UUP); Deborah Erskine (DUP); Órlaithí Flynn (SF); Colin McGrath (SDLP); Carál Ní Chuilín (SF); Pat Sheehan (SF)

Committee Clerk: Keith McBride
Tel: 028 9052 0348
Email: committee.health@niassembly.gov.uk

Committee for Infrastructure

Chairperson:
Jonathan Buckley (DUP)

Deputy Chairperson: David Hilditch (DUP)

Membership: Cathal Boylan (SF); Roy Beggs (UUP); Padraig Delargy (SF); Cara Hunter (SDLP); Liz Kimmins (SF); Andrew Muir (APNI); George Robinson (DUP)

Committee Clerks: Cathie White and Alison Ross
Tel: 028 9052 1448 and 028 9052 1436
Email: committee.infrastructure@niassembly.gov.uk

Northern Ireland Assembly | Northern Ireland Yearbook

Statutory Committees

Committee for Justice

Chairperson:
Mervyn Storey (DUP)

Deputy Chairperson: Sinéad Ennis (SF)

Membership: Doug Beattie (UUP); Sinead Bradley (SDLP); Jemma Dolan (SF); Robin Newton (DUP); Emma Rogan (SF); Rachel Woods (Green); Peter Weir (DUP)

Committee Clerk: Christine Darrah
Tel: 028 9052 1629
Email: committee.justice@niassembly.gov.uk

Standing Committees

Assembly and Executive Review Committee

Chairperson:
Peter Weir (DUP)

Deputy Chairperson: Maolíosa McHugh (SF)

Membership: Jim Allister (TUV); Kellie Armstrong (APNI); Robbie Butler (UUP); George Robinson (DUP); Paul Frew (DUP); Gerry Kelly (SF); Colin McGrath (SDLP)

Committee Clerk: Shane McAteer
Tel: 028 9052 1843
Email: committee.assemblyexecutivereview@niassembly.gov.uk

Standing Committees (continued)

Audit Committee

Chairperson:
Daniel McCrossan (SDLP)

Deputy Chairperson: William Irwin (DUP)

Membership: Jim Allister (TUV); Alan Chambers (UUP); Emma Rogan (SF)

Committee Clerk: Marie Austin
Tel: 028 9052 0302
Email: committee.audit@niassembly.gov.uk

Business Committee

Chairperson:
Alex Maskey (SF)

Membership: Clare Bailey (Green); Rosemary Barton (UUP); Paula Bradshaw (APNI); Joanne Bunting (DUP); Robbie Butler (UUP); Trevor Clarke (DUP); Sinéad Ennis (SF); Dolores Kelly (SDLP); John O'Dowd (SF); Colin McGrath (SDLP); Andrew Muir (APNI)

Committee Clerk: Alex McGarel
Tel: 028 9052 1534
Email: business.office@niassembly.gov.uk

Northern Ireland Yearbook | Northern Ireland Assembly

Standing Committees

Procedures Committee

Chairperson: Carál Ní Chuilín (SF)

Deputy Chairperson: Tom Buchanan (DUP)

Membership: Rosemary Barton (UUP); Joanne Bunting (DUP); Sinead Bradley (SDLP); Nicola Brogan (SF); Gerry Carroll (PBPA); Ciara Ferguson (SF); William Humphrey (DUP)

Committee Clerk: Emer Boyle
Tel: 028 9052 1678
Email: committee.procedures@niassembly.gov.uk

Public Accounts Committee

Chairperson: William Humphrey (DUP)

Deputy Chairperson: Roy Beggs (UUP)

Membership: Cathal Boylan (SF); Órlaithí Flynn (SF); David Hilditch (DUP); Cara Hunter (SDLP); William Irwin (DUP); Maolíosa McHugh (SF); Andrew Muir (APNI)

Committee Clerk: Lucia Wilson
Tel: 028 9052 1208
Email: committee.publicaccounts@niassembly.gov.uk

Standards and Privileges Committee

Chairperson: Linda Dillon (SF)

Deputy Chairperson: Christopher Stalford (DUP)

Membership: Steve Aiken (UUP); Sinead Bradley (SDLP); Pam Cameron (DUP); Stewart Dickson (APNI); Declan McAleer (SF); Patsy McGlone (SDLP); Áine Murphy (SF)

Committee Clerk: Shane McAteer
Tel: 028 9052 1843
Email: committee.standardsprivileges@niassembly.gov.uk

Chairpersons' Liaison Group

Chairperson: Carál Ní Chuilín (SF)

Deputy Chairperson: Sinead McLaughlin (SDLP)

Membership: Steve Aiken (UUP); Caoimhe Archibald (SF); Paula Bradley (DUP); Jonathan Buckley (DUP); Linda Dillon (SF); Colm Gildernew (SF); William Humphrey (DUP); Chris Lyttle (APNI); Declan McAleer (SF); Daniel McCrossan (SDLP); Emma Sheerin (SF); Mervyn Storey (DUP); Peter Weir (DUP)

Clerk: Stella McArdle
Tel: 028 9052 1475
Email: committee.office@niassembly.gov.uk

Changes to Assembly Opposition standing orders

In October 2020, a New Decade, New Approach commitment was fulfilled when the Standing Order which regulates the Official Opposition was amended to enable a party to join the Opposition up to two years following the formation of an Executive.

Following the May 2016 Assembly election, the Assembly and Executive Reform (Assembly Opposition) Act (Northern Ireland) 2016 provided for the formation of an Assembly Opposition. Agreement on the legislation had been reached during the Stormont House talks in November 2015.

Section 2 of the 2016 Act provides that parties entitled to nominate an individual to ministerial office (or whose members comprise 8 per cent or more of the total cohort of MLAs) may choose to opt out and instead form an 'official' Opposition. This Opposition may be formed with one or more qualifying parties.

The Assembly Opposition is tasked with scrutinising the work and performance of the Northern Ireland Executive. Standing Orders provide enhanced speaking rights for the Opposition, or more speaking rights than a member of the Opposition would otherwise be entitled to on the basis of numerical size in the Assembly. This includes the allocation of at least 10 days per annum to Opposition business.

Formation

As per the 2016 Act, an official Opposition may be formed at the time when a ministerial office is to be filled following: the first meeting of the Assembly; all ministers ceasing to hold office; or the application of section 18 (10) of the Northern Ireland Act 1998 where a ministerial office is vacant for any reason (other than if a nominating officer of the party on whose behalf the previous incumbent was nominated does not nominate a person to hold that office).

The New Deal, New Approach agreement committed to amending the 2016 Act to provide for a party to join the Opposition up to two years following the formation of an Executive.

Standing Order 45A makes provision for the timing of the formation of an Assembly Opposition.

Originally, Standing Order 45A paragraph 1 outlined that where a party is entitled to nominate a person to hold Ministerial office and declines to do so, that party may choose to be recognised as part of the official opposition.

This was subject to paragraph 2: "A party is not to be recognised as part of the official opposition if any member of that party holds a Ministerial office, or held a Ministerial office and ceased to hold that office otherwise than at a time when all Northern Ireland Ministers ceased to hold office."

Paragraph 3 outlined that where only one party choose to be recognised as such, that party will be regarded as the official opposition.

Amendments

However, in October 2020, Standing Order 45A was amended.

Paragraph 1 now reads: "Where, at a time when all Northern Ireland ministers ceased to hold office", a party is entitled to nominate a person to hold Ministerial office and declines to do so, that party may choose to be recognised as part of the official opposition.

An alternative paragraph 2 was inserted and provides: "Subject to paragraph (3), where, during the relevant period, a party is entitled to nominate a person to hold a Ministerial office under section 18(10) of the Northern Ireland Act 1998, and declines to do so, that party may choose to be recognised as part of the official opposition".

Paragraph 3 removes the following line from the original paragraph 2 "or held a Ministerial office and ceased to hold that office otherwise than at a time when all Northern Ireland Ministers ceased to hold office".

Paragraph 4 co-opts the language of the original paragraph 3 and paragraph 5 defines the phrase "relevant period" in paragraph 2 as being a period of two years beginning with the date on which the Ministerial offices are filled under.

Following the Assembly's restoration in January 2020, the UUP and the SDLP chose to nominate ministers. Currently, therefore, there is no official Opposition. Instead, smaller non-Executive parties undertake an unofficial opposition role.

Northern Ireland Assembly elections

As well as the reduction of the Stormont Assembly by 18 seats, the March 2017 snap election also brought further significant change to the political landscape of Northern Ireland, most significantly the loss of a unionist majority at Stormont for the first time in the history of the State.

While the DUP remained the largest party at Stormont returning 28 MLAs, the result represented a loss of 10 seats on their previous total. In contrast Sinn Féin's loss of just one seat from its previous total is viewed as a significant gain with the context of an almost 4 per cent rise in their first preference vote share.

A strong surge in the nationalist vote was also represented in the SDLP's ability to hold on to their 12 seats, even though their share of first preference votes fell slightly. Despite entering into what is now viewed as an unsuccessful period of opposition, the SDLP's retention of seats in a shrinking Assembly has been credited not just to greater mobility among the nationalist electorate, but also from transfers received from voters of the UUP, their partners in opposition. The partnership was not as fruitful for the UUP however, despite marginally increasing their voter share, the party lost six seats, sparking the party leader Mike Nesbitt's decision to announce he was leaving the role, even as the counting was still ongoing.

The Alliance Party recorded their highest ever number of votes and achieved eight seats. The Green Party (2), the TUV (1) and Independent Claire Sugden (1) and People Before Profit (1) made up the remainder of allocation.

Added together, those designated as unionists (DUP, UUP, TUV and Claire Sugden) make up just 40 of the 90 possible seats. This, is in contrast to the DUP's failure to secure 30 seats, also means that it has lost the ability to wield the Petition of Concern unaided.

Overall voter turnout was up by 10 per cent to 64.8 per cent, an initial sign that recent controversy at Stormont appeared to strike a chord with the electorate, interest levels which were last present in 1998.

While the number of females represented in the Northern Ireland Assembly has fallen by three, the reduction of assembly members means that females now make up a more significant proportion of MLAs. The proportion of female membership of the Assembly (30 per cent) is consistent with the proportion of the 70 females who made up the overall candidate number (30.7 per cent).

In terms of party make up, Sinn Féin returned the most female MLAs (11), meaning females make up over 40 per cent of their elected members. The six DUP female MLAs are 21.4 per cent of its MLAS, while a third (33 per cent) of the SDLP's 12 members are female. Three (37.5 per cent) of the Alliance's MLAs are female.

As well as a number of high profile MLAs who chose not to contest the 2017 general election, including former Junior Minister Alastair Ross and the UUP's Ross Hussey, there was also a number of significant figures who contested but lost out on a seat in the new Assembly. Below is a list of defeated incumbents.

DUP
Nelson McCausland; Emma Little Pengelly; Adrian McQuillan; Maurice Morrow; Brenda Hale; Phillip Logan

People Before Profit
Eamonn McCann

Sinn Féin
Oliver McMullan

SDLP
Alex Attwood; Richie McPhillips

Independent
Jonathan Bell; Gerry Mullan

The following pages contain a detailed breakdown of the 2017 Assembly election, including the number of votes cast for each candidate, the first preference votes cast for major parties and the stage at which each candidate was elected or eliminated. Percentage vote shares from the 2016 election are also included. Results are accurate as of the time of declaration although elected representatives may subsequently be replaced by co-option.

Northern Ireland Assembly election 2017: Overall result by party share and seats

	Votes 2017	Votes 2016	% Share of vote 2017	Number of seats 2017	+/- since 2016
DUP	225,413	202,567	28.1	28	-10
Sinn Fein	224,245	166,785	27.9	27	-1
UUP	103,314	87,302	12.9	10	-6
SDLP	95,958	83,364	11.9	12	
APNI	72,717	48,447	9.1	8	
TUV	20,523	23,776	2.6	1	
Green	18,527	18,718	2.3	2	
PBPA	14,100	13,761	1.8	1	-1
Independents	14,407	22,650	1.8	1	
UKIP		10,109			
PUP	5,590	5,955	0.7		
Conservative	2,399	2,554	0.3		
NI Labour		1,577			
Others	6,122	6,745		28	
Total	803,315	694,314	100	90	

Belfast North

Total Valid Poll 41,486   Quota 6,915   Turnout 61.8%

Party performance

Party	Seats	1st Pref Vote	2016%	2017%
DUP	2	13,309	35	32.1
SF	2	12,204	26.5	29.4
UUP	-	2,418	5.4	5.8
SDLP	1	5,431	10.6	13.1
APNI	-	3,487	7	8.4
Others	-	4,637	15.5	11.2

At a glance...

The make-up of results from the Belfast North constituency remained largely the same as in 2016, aside from the exclusion of former DUP minister Nelson McCausland who lost his seat in the sixth count. Turnout increased by almost 12 per cent, but returned five familiar faces from the 2016 election. The two main parties Sinn Féin and the DUP each won two seats, with the final seat belonging to the SDLP. Paula Bradley and William Humphrey of the DUP were both elected on the sixth count. Gerry Kelly Sinn Féin, Carál Ní Chuilín Sinn Féin and Nichola Mallon SDLP were elected on the seventh count.

		Stage 1	Stage 2
		1st preference	Exclusion of Millar, O'Hara, We
Paula Bradley	DUP	4,835.00	(+8.00) 4,843.00
Julie-Anne Corr-Johnston	PUP	2,053.00	(+50.00) 2,103.00
Fiona Ferguson	PBPA	1,559.00	(+290.00) 1,849.00
Robert Foster	UUP	2,418.00	(+39.00) 2,457.00
William Humphrey	DUP	4,418.00	(+5.00) 4,423.00
Gerry Kelly	Sinn Féin	6,275.00	(+54.00) 6,329.00
Nichola Mallon	SDLP	5,431.00	(+142.00) 5,573.00
Nuala McAllister	APNI	3,487.00	(+312.00) 3,799.00
Nelson McCausland	DUP	4,056.00	(+13.00) 4,069.00
Adam Millar	Independent	66.00	(-66.00) 0.00
Carál Ní Chuilín	Sinn Féin	5,929.00	(+54.00) 5,983.00
Malachai O'Hara	Green	711.00	(-711.00) 0.00
Gemma Weir	The Workers Party	248.00	(-248.00) 0.00
Non transferable			(+58.00) 58.00

Northern Ireland Assembly election results 2017

Candidates elected

Candidates elected	Count
Paula Bradley (DUP)	6
William Humphrey (DUP)	6
Gerry Kelly (SF)	7
Carál Ní Chuilín (SF)	7
Nichola Mallon (SDLP)	7

Paula Bradley · William Humphrey · Gerry Kelly · Carál Ní Chuilín · Nichola Mallon

	Stage 3	Stage 4	Stage 5	Stage 6	Stage 7
	Exclusion of Ferguson	Exclusion of Corr-Johnston	Exclusion of Foster	Exclusion of McCausland	Transfer of Bradley's surplus
	(+22.00) 4,865.00	(+371.00) 5,236.00	(+766.00) 6,002.00	(+2,456.00) 8,458.00	(-1,543.00) 6,915.00
	(+71.00) 2,174.00	(-2,174.00) 0.00	-	-	-
	(-1,849.00) 0.00	-	-	-	-
	(+60.00) 2,517.00	(+624.00) 3,141.00	(-3,141.00) 0.00	-	-
	(+6.00) 4,429.00	(+508.00) 4,937.00	(+323.00) 5,260.00	(+2,016.00) 7,276.00	(+0.00) 7,276.00
	(+243.00) 6,572.00	(+10.00) 6,582.00	(+9.00) 6,591.00	(+2.00) 6,593.00	(+2.00) 6,595.00
	(+503.00) 6,076.00	(+49.00) 6,125.00	(+537.00) 6,662.00	(+30.00) 6,692.00	(+114.00) 6,806.00
	(+555.00) 4,354.00	(+161.00) 4,515.00	(+742.00) 5,257.00	(+39.00) 5,296.00	(+312.00) 5,608.00
	(+10.00) 4,079.00	(+293.00) 4,372.00	(+337.00) 4,709.00	(-4,709.00) 0.00	-
	-	-	-	-	-
	(+168.00) 6,151.00	(+4.00) 6,155.00	(+3.00) 6,158.00	(+1.00) 6,159.00	(+5.00) 6,164.00
	-	-	-	-	-
	-	-	-	-	-
	(+211.00) 269.00	(+154.00) 423.00	(+424.00) 847.00	(+165) 1,012.00	(+1,110.00) 2,122.00

Northern Ireland Assembly election results 2017

Belfast South

Total Valid Poll 43,053   Quota 7,176   Turnout 64.0%

Party performance

Party	Seats	1st Pref Vote	2016%	2017%
DUP	1	8,975	22	20.8
SF	1	7,610	14.2	17.7
UUP	-	3,863	6.7	9
SDLP	1	8,353	20	19.4
APNI	1	7,648	16.4	17.8
Others	1	6,604	20.7	15.3

At a glance...

Máirtín Ó Muilleoir continued to be the popular vote in South Belfast with 7,610 first preferences, well over the required quota and was therefore elected in the first count. All the MLAs elected in this area won their seats in the 2016 elections with little change in vote share. One casualty was the DUP's Emma Little Pengelly who did not return her seat. This is one of the few constituencies where each candidate is from a different party. Claire Hanna from the SDLP, Paula Bradshaw of APNI and Christopher Stalford, DUP were all re-elected. Clare Bailey also reached the quota on the ninth count and is the Green Party's second MLA.

		Stage 1	Stage 2	Stage 3
		1st preference	Transfer of Ó Muilleoir's surplus	Exclusion of Kerr and Jabbour
Clare Bailey	Green Party	4,247.00	(+45.78) 4,292.78	(+48.96) 4,341.74
Paula Bradshaw	APNI	5,595.00	(+37.26) 5,632.26	(+40.24) 5672.50
Sean Burns	Cross-Community Labour Alternative	531.00	(+8.76) 539.76	(+26.66) 566.42
Naomh Gallagher	SDLP	1,794.00	(+61.68) 1,855.68	(+10.24) 1,865.92
Claire Hanna	SDLP	6,559.00	(+197.28) 6,756.28	(+31.84) 6,788.12
Michael Henderson	UUP	3,863.00	(+3.00) 3,866.00	(+66.12) 3,932.12
John Andrew Hiddleston	TUV	703.00	(+0.36) 703.36	(+14.00) 717.36
George Jabbour	Conservatives	200.00	(+0.48) 200.48	(-200.48) 0.00
Lily Kerr	The Workers Party	163.00	(+5.22) 168.22	(-168.22) 0.00
Emma Little Pengelly	DUP	4,446.00	(+0.78) 4,446.78	(+22.06) 4,468.84
Emmet McDonough-Brown	APNI	2,053.00	(+27.96) 2,080.96	(+14.42) 2,095.38
Pádraigín Mervyn	PBPA	760.00	(+29.58) 789.58	(+39.14) 828.72
Máirtín Ó Muilleoir	Sinn Féin	7,610.00	(-434) 7,176.00	(+0.00) 7,176.00
Christopher Stalford	DUP	4,529.00	(+1.08) 4,530.08	(+21.00) 4,551.08
	Non transferable		(+14.78) 14.78	(+34.02) 48.80

Northern Ireland Assembly election results 2017

Candidates elected

Candidates elected	Count
Máirtín Ó Muilleoir (SF)	1
Paula Bradshaw (APNI)	6
Claire Hanna (SDLP)	6
Clare Bailey (Green)	9
Christopher Stalford (DUP)	9

	Stage 4	Stage 5	Stage 6	Stage 7	Stage 8	Stage 9
	Exclusion of Burns	Exclusion of Hiddleston, Mervyn	Exclusion of Gallagher, MacDonough-Brown	Transfer of Hanna's surplus	Transfer of Bradshaw's surplus	Exclusion of Pengelly
	(+181.34) 4,523.08	(+550.88) 5,073.96	(+376.04) 5,450.00	(+894.00) 6,344.00	(+375.36) 6,719.36	(+77.86) 6,797.22
	(+67.90) 5,740.40	(+125.98) 5,866.38	(+1,824.00) 7,690.38	(+0.00) 7,690.38	(-514.38) 7,176.00	(+0.00) 7,176.00
	(-566.42) 0.00	-	-	-	-	-
	(+27.50) 1,893.42	(+68.80) 1,962.22	(-1,962.22) 0.00	-	-	-
	(+51.44) 6,839.56	(+141.98) 6,981.54	(+1,671) 8,652.54	(-1,476.54) 7,176.00	(+0.00) 7,176.00	(+0.00) 7,176.00
	(+23.00) 3,955.12	(+285.30) 4,240.42	(+97.38) 4,337.80	(+310.00) 4647.80	(+113.60) 4,761.40	(+494.54) 5,255.94
	(+7.12) 724.48	(-724.48) 0.00	-	-	-	-
	-	-	-	-	-	-
	-	-	-	-	-	-
	(+8.00) 4,476.84	(+179.06) 4,655.90	(+20.36) 4,676.26	(+19.00) 4695.26	(+8.00) 4,703.26	(-4,703.26) 0.00
	(+23.54) 2,118.92	(+66.42) 2,185.34	(-2,185.34) 0.00	-	-	-
	(+142.14) 970.86	(-970.86) 0.00	-	-	-	-
	(+0.00) 7,176.00	(+0.00) 7,176.00	(+0.00) 7,176.00	(+0.00) 7,176.00	(+0.00) 7,176.00	(+0.00) 7,176.00
	(+3.00) 4,554.08	(+150.00) 4,704.08	(+11.18) 4,715.26	(+11.00) 4,726.26	(+2.24) 4,728.50	(+3,939.00) 8,667.50
	(+31.44) 80.24	(+126.92) 207.16	(+147.60) 354.76	(+242.54) 597.29	(+15.18) 612.47	(+191.86) 804.33

Northern Ireland Assembly election results 2017

Belfast West

Total Valid Poll 40,344   Quota 6,725   Turnout 66.8%

Party performance

Party	Seats	1st Pref Vote	2016%	2017%
DUP	-	4,063	10.4	10.1
SF	4	24,931	54.5	61.8
UUP	-	486	1.8	1.2
SDLP	-	3,452	7.3	8.6
APNI	-	747	0.8	1.9
Others	1	6,665	25.2	16.4

At a glance...

The nationalist stronghold of West Belfast remains largely green with Sinn Féin holding four seats. In 2016, Sinn Féin lost a seat to Gerry Carroll of People Before Profit who secured 3,000 more votes than the next candidate, however in the 2017 election he only reached the quota in the third count. New Sinn Féin candidate Órlaithí Flynn was elected on the first count. One notable exclusion was the SDLP former minister Alex Attwood who lost his seat on the third count. The unionist vote for the area slightly decreased overall in 2017. Sinn Féin's overall vote share inceased by 7.3 per cent.

Candidate	Party	Stage 1 – 1st preference
Alex Attwood	SDLP	3,452.00
Conor Campbell	The Workers Party	415.00
Gerry Carroll	PBPA	4,903.00
Michael Collins	PBPA	1,096.00
Sorcha Eastwood	APNI	747.00
Órlaithí Flynn	Sinn Féin	6,918.00
Alex Maskey	Sinn Féin	6,346.00
Fra McCann	Sinn Féin	6,201.00
Frank McCoubrey	DUP	4,063.00
Ellen Murray	Green	251.00
Fred Rodgers	UUP	486.00
Pat Sheehan	Sinn Féin	5,466.00
Non transferable		

Northern Ireland Assembly election results 2017

Candidates elected	Count
Órlaithí Flynn (SF)	1
Alex Maskey (SF)	3
Gerry Carroll (PBPA)	3
Fra McCann (SF)	4
Pat Sheehan (SF)	4

Órlaithí Flynn — Alex Maskey — Gerry Carroll — Fra McCann — Pat Sheehan

Stage 2	Stage 3	Stage 4
Exclusion of Murray, Campbell, Rodgers, Eastwood, Collins	Exclusion of Attwood	Transfer of Carroll's surplus
(+567.00) 4,019.00	(-4,019.00) 0.00	-
(-415.00) 0.00	-	-
(+1,611.00) 6,514.00	(-1,738.00) 8,252.00	(-1,527.00) 6,725.00
(-1,096.00) 0.00		-
(-747.00) 0.00	-	-
(+0.00) 6,918.00	(+0.00) 6,918.00	(+0.00) 6,918.00
(+105.00) 6,451.00	(+585.00) 7,036.00	(+0.00) 7,036.00
(-113.00) 6,314.00	(+322.00) 6,636.00	(+431.00) 7,067.00
(+309.00) 4,372.00	(+118.00) 4,490.00	(+31.00) 4,521.00
(-251.00) 0.00	-	-
(-486.00) 0.00	-	-
(+49.00) 5,515.00	(+224.00) 5,739.00	(+164.00) 5,903.00
(+241.00) 241.00	(+1,032.00) 1,273.00	(+901.00) 2,174.00

Northern Ireland Assembly election results 2017

East Antrim

Total Valid Poll 37,424 Quota 6,238 Turnout 60.1%

Party performance

Party	Seats	1st Pref Vote	2016%	2017%
DUP	2	13,164	36.1	35.2
SF	-	3,701	8.1	9.9
UUP	2	8,498	20.2	22.7
SDLP	-	1,524	3.8	4.1
APNI	1	5,996	14.6	16
Others	-	4,541	17.1	12.2

At a glance...
DUP David Hilditch, UUP Roy Beggs and DUP Gordon Lyons all retained their East Antrim seats. The DUP's Alastair Ross did not stand again in this election and his seat went to the UUP's John Stewart. The DUP's share of first preference votes dropped by -0.9% and the UUP increased the most by 2.5%. The Alliance's Stewart Dickson also was returned.

		Stage 1	Stage 2	Stage 3
		1st preference	Exclusion of Best, Dunlop, Sheridan, Patterson	Exclusion of Wilson
Roy Beggs	UUP	5,121.00	(+151.00) 5,272.00	(+317.00) 5,589.00
Ricky Best	Independent	106.00	(-106.00) 0.00	-
Stewart Dickson	APNI	4,179.00	(+437.00) 4,616.00	(+42.00) 4,658.00
Danny Donnelly	APNI	1,817.00	(+270.00) 2,087.00	(+18.00) 2,105.00
Alan Dunlop	Conservatives	152.00	(-152.00) 0.00	-
David Hilditch	DUP	6,000.00	(+37.00) 6,037.00	(+211.00) 6,248.00
Noel Jordan	UKIP	1,579.00	(+74.00) 1,653.00	(+280.00) 1,933.00
Gordon Lyons	DUP	3,851.00	(+18.00) 3,869.00	(+199.00) 4,068.00
Margaret Anne McKillop	SDLP	1,524.00	(+109.00) 1,633.00	(+20.00) 1,653.00
Oliver McMullan	Sinn Féin	3,701.00	(+49.00) 3,750.00	(+2.00) 3,752.00
Dawn Patterson	Green	777.00	(-777.00) 0.00	-
Stephen Ross	DUP	3,313.00	(+21.00) 3,334.00	(+193.00) 3,527.00
Conor Sheridan	Cross-Community Labour Alternative	393.00	(-393.00) 0.00	-
John Stewart	UUP	3,377.00	(+102.00) 3,479.00	(+230.00) 3,709.00
Ruth Wilson	TUV	1,534.00	(+53.00) 1,587.00	(+1,587.00) 0.00
Non transferable			(+107.00) 107.00	(+75.00) 182.00

Northern Ireland Assembly election results 2017

Candidates elected

Candidates elected	Count
David Hilditch (DUP)	3
Roy Beggs (UUP)	6
Stewart Dickson (APNI)	6
Gordon Lyons (DUP)	8
John Stewart (UUP)	9

	Stage 4	Stage 5	Stage 6	Stage 7	Stage 8	Stage 9
	Exclusion of McKillop	Exclusion of Jordan	Exclusion of Donnelly	Transfer of Dickson's surplus	Exclusion of Ross	Transfer of Lyons' surplus
	(+125.00) 5,714.00	(+442.00) 6,156.00	(+168.00) 6,324.00	(+0.00) 6,324.00	(+0.00) 6,324.00	(+0.00) 6,324.00
	-	-	-	-	-	-
	(+407.00) 5,065.00	(+106.00) 5,171.00	(+1,612.00) 6,783.00	(-545.00) 6,238.00	(+0.00) 6,238.00	(+0.00) 6,238.00
	(+365.00) 2,470.00	(+45.00) 2,515.00	(-2,515.00) 0.00	-	-	-
	-	-	-	-	-	-
	(+0.00) 6,248.00	(+0.00) 6,248.00	(+0.00) 6,248.00	(+0.00) 6,248.00	(+0.00) 6,248.00	(+0.00) 6,248.00
	(+22.00) 1,955.00	(-1,955.00) 0.00	-	-	-	-
	(+10.00) 4,078.00	(+395.00) 4,473.00	(+17.00) 4,490.00	(+23.94) 4,513.94	(+3,040) 7,553.94	(-1315.94) 6,238.00
	(-1,653.00) 0.00	-	-	-	-	-
	(+526.00) 4,278.00	(+14.00) 4,292.00	(+231.00) 4,523.00	(+167.58) 4,690.58	(+8.00) 4,698.58	(+2.19) 4,700.77
	-	-	-	-	-	-
	(+12.00) 3,539.00	(+277.00) 3,816.00	(+9.00) 3,825.00	(+9.12) 3,834.12	(-3,834.12) 0.00	-
	-	-	-	-	-	-
	(+79.00) 3,788.00	(+343.00) 4,131.00	(+129.00) 4,260.00	(+339.72) 4,599.72	(+435.27) 5,034.99	(+1,308.89) 6,343.88
	-	-	-	-	-	-
	(+107.00) 289.00	(+333.00) 622.00	(+349.00) 971.00	(+4.64) 975.64	(+350.85) 1,326.49	(+4.86) 1,331.35

Northern Ireland Assembly election results 2017 ⇢ 43

East Londonderry

Total Valid Poll 41,873   Quota 6,979   Turnout 62.7%

Party performance

Party	Seats	1st Pref Vote	2016%	2017%
DUP	2	14,040	36.8	33.5
SF	1	10,804	21.8	25.8
UUP	-	2,814	8.3	6.7
SDLP	1	3,319	9.5	7.9
APNI	-	1,841	3.7	4.4
Others	1	9,055	19.9	21.7

At a glance...

All five MLAs elected in East Londonderry had previously won their seats in the 2016 election. The exception was DUP MLA Adrian McQuillan who did not reach the quota. Independent former minister Claire Sugden reached the quota on the eighth count. The DUP retained two seats in the form of Maurice Bradley and George Robinson whilst Sinn Féin's Caoimhe Archibald also held on to her seat. Sinn Féin's vote share however increased by 4 per cent in contrast to the DUP's share which fell by 3.3 per cent. The SDLP share of votes also fell from 9.5 per cent to 7.9 per cent.

		Stage 1	Stage 2	Stage 3	Stage 4
		1st preference	Exclusion of Harding	Exclusion of Campbell, Flynn	Exclusion of Watton
Caoimhe Archibald	Sinn Féin	5,851.00	(+3.00) 5,854.00	(+80.00) 5,934.00	(+3.00) 5,937.00
Jordan Armstrong	TUV	1,038.00	(+10.00) 1,048.00	(+6.00) 1,054.00	(+93.00) 1,147.00
Maurice Bradley	DUP	5,444.00	(+18.00) 5,462.00	(+11.00) 5,473.00	(+359.00) 5,832.00
Gavin Campbell	PBPA	492.00	(+2.00) 494.00	(-494.00) 0.00	-
John Dallat	SDLP	3,319.00	(+6.00) 3,325.00	(+115.00) 3,440.00	(+3.00) 3,443.00
Anthony Flynn	Green	305.00	(+5.00) 310.00	(-310.00) 0.00	-
David Harding	Conservatives	219.00	(-219.00) 0.00	-	-
William McCandless	UUP	2,814.00	(+52.00) 2,866.00	(+33.00) 2,899.00	(+61.00) 2,960.00
Chris McCaw	APNI	1,841.00	(+31.00) 1,872.00	(+278.00) 2,150.00	(+13.00) 2,163.00
Adrian McQuillan	DUP	3,881.00	(+6.00) 3,887.00	(+3.00) 3,890.00	(+104.00) 3,994.00
Gerry Mullan	Independent	1,204.00	(+2.00) 1,206.00	(+87.00) 1,293.00	(+4.00) 1,297.00
Cathal Ó hOisín	Sinn Féin	4,953.00	(+1.00) 4,954.00	(+25.00) 4,979.00	(+0.00) 4,979.00
George Robinson	DUP	4,715.00	(+6.00) 4,721.00	(+9.00) 4,730.00	(+51.00) 4,781.00
Claire Sugden	Independent	4,918.00	(+72.00) 4,990.00	(+112.00) 5,102.00	(+176.00) 5,278.00
Russell Watton	PUP	879.00	(+3.00) 882.00	(+7.00) 889.00	(-889.00) 0.00
Non transferable			(+2.00) 2.00	(+38.00) 40.00	(+22.00) 62.00

Candidates elected

Candidates elected	Count
Claire Sugden (Ind)	8
Maurice Bradley (DUP)	9
George Robinson (DUP)	9
Caoimhe Archibald (SF)	12
John Dallat (SDLP)	12

Claire Sugden, Maurice Bradley, George Robinson, Caoimhe Archibald, John Dallat

	Stage 5	Stage 6	Stage 7	Stage 8	Stage 9	Stage 10	Stage 11	Stage 12
	Exclusion of Armstrong	Exclusion of Mullan	Exclusion of McCaw	Exclusion of McCandless	Exclusion of McQuillan	Transfer of Bradley's surplus	Transfer of Robinson's surplus	Transfer of Sugden's surplus
	(+3.00) 5,940.00	(+226.00) 6,166.00	(+133.00) 6,299.00	(+12.00) 6,311.00	(+9.00) 6,320.00	(+0.00) 6,320.00	(+8.00) 6,328.00	(+2.00) 6,330.00
	(-1,147.00) 0.00	-	-	-	-	-	-	-
	(+295.00) 6,127.00	(+5.00) 6,132.00	(+39.00) 6,171.00	(+568.00) 6,739.00	(+1,317.00) 8,056.00	(-1,077.00) 6,979.00	(+0.00) 6,979.00	(+0.00) 6,979.00
	-	-	-	-	-	-	-	-
	(+16.00) 3,459.00	(+266.00) 3,725.00	(+641.00) 4,366.00	(+777.00) 5,143.00	(+155.00) 5,298.00	(+145.00) 5,443.00	(+266.00) 5,709.00	(+382.00) 6,091.00
	-	-	-	-	-	-	-	-
	-	-	-	-	-	-	-	-
	(+308.00) 3,268.00	(+20.00) 3,288.00	(+293.00) 3,581.00	(-3,581.00) 0.00	-	-	-	-
	(+27.00) 2,190.00	(+137.00) 2,327.00	(-2,327.00) 0.00	-	-	-	-	-
	(+141.00) 4,135.00	(+7.00) 4,142.00	(+28.00) 4,170.00	(+396.00) 4,566.00	(-4,566.00) 0.00	-	-	-
	(+17.00) 1,314.00	(-1,314.00) 0.00	-	-	-	-	-	-
	(+1.00) 4,980.00	(+175.00) 5,155.00	(+41.00) 5,196.00	(+6.00) 5,202.00	(+9.00) 5,211.00	(+10.00) 5,221.00	(+15.00) 5,236.00	(+2.00) 5,238.00
	(+125.00) 4,906.00	(+56.00) 4,962.00	(+31.00) 4,993.00	(+342.00) 5,335.00	(+2,466.00) 7,801.00	(+0.00) 7,801.00	(-822.00) 6,979.00	(+0.00) 6,979.00
	(+159.00) 5,437.00	(+270.00) 5,707.00	(+854.00) 6,561.00	(+994.00) 7,555.00	(+0.00) 7,555.00	(+0.00) 7,555.00	(+0.00) 7,555.00	(-576.00) 6,979.00
	-	-	-	-	-	-	-	-
	(+55.00) 117.00	(+152.00) 269.00	(+267.00) 536.00	(+486.00) 1,022.00	(+610.00) 1,632.00	(+922.00) 2,554.00	(+533.00) 3,087.00	(+190.00) 3,277.00

Northern Ireland Assembly election results 2017

Fermanagh and South Tyrone

Total Valid Poll 52,263   Quota 8,711   Turnout 72.6%

Party performance

Party	Seats	1st Pref Vote	2016%	2017%
DUP	1	15,581	32.7	29.8
SF	3	22,008	40	42.1
UUP	1	6,060	12.8	11.6
SDLP	-	5,134	8.5	9.8
APNI	-	1,437	1.1	2.7
Others	-	2,043	4.9	4.0

At a glance...

Fermanagh and South Tyrone had the highest turnout of all the constituencies at 72.6 per cent. Michelle Gildernew, who topped the constituency back in 2011, came second with almost 8,000 votes to DUP leader Arlene Foster who topped the polls with 8,495 votes. DUP stalwart Maurice Morrow lost his seat, reducing the total number of DUP seats to one. Rosemary Barton held the seat for the Ulster Unionists although they have experienced a loss of almost 7 per cent vote share since 2011. The SDLP's Richie McPhillips lost his seat to Sinn Féin.

Candidate	Party	Stage 1 — 1st preference
Rosemary Barton	UUP	6,060.00
Noreen Campbell	APNI	1,437.00
Jemma Dolan	Sinn Féin	7,767.00
Richard Dunn	Conservatives	70.00
Alex Elliott	TUV	780.00
Arlene Foster	DUP	8,479.00
Michelle Gildernew	Sinn Féin	7,987.00
Tanya Jones	Green	550.00
Seán Lynch	Sinn Féin	6,254.00
Richie McPhillips	SDLP	5,134.00
Maurice Morrow	DUP	7,102.00
Donal O'Cofaigh	Cross-Community Labour Alternative	643.00
Non transferable		

Northern Ireland Assembly election results 2017

Candidates elected	Count
Arlene Foster (DUP)	2
Michelle Gildernew (SF)	3
Jemma Dolan (SF)	3
Seán Lynch (SF)	4
Rosemary Barton (UUP)	4

	Stage 2	Stage 3	Stage 4
	Exclusion of Dunn, Jones, O'Cofaigh, Elliott and Campbell	Exclusion of McPhillips	Transfer of Gildernew's surplus
	(+803.00) 6,863.00	(+1,471.00) 8,334.00	(+108.00) 8,442.00
	(-1,437.00) 0.00	-	-
	(+256.00) 8,023.00	(+905.00) 8,928.00	(+0.00) 8,928.00
	(-70.00) 0.00	-	-
	(-780.00) 0.00	-	-
	(+266.00) 8,745.00	(+0.00) 8,745.00	(+0.00) 8,745.00
	(+241.00) 8,228.00	(+1,157.00) 9,385.00	(-674.00) 8,711.00
	(-550.00) 0.00	-	-
	(+84.00) 6,338.00	(+836.00) 7,174.00	(+543.00) 7,717.00
	(+1,142.00) 6,276.00	(-6,276.00) 0.00	-
	(+230.00) 7,332.00	(+73.00) 7,405.00	(+6.00) 7,411.00
	(-643.00)	-	-
	(+458.00) 458.00	(+1,834.00) 2,292.00	(+17.00) 2,309.00

Northern Ireland Assembly election results 2017 47

Foyle

Total Valid Poll 44,616   Quota 7,437   Turnout 65%

Party performance

Party	Seats	1st Pref Vote	2016%	2017%
DUP	1	5,975	11.9	13.4
SF	2	16,350	28.5	36.6
UUP	-	1,660	3.6	3.7
SDLP	2	14,188	30.0	31.8
APNI	-	1,124	0.6	2.5
Others	-	5,319	25.4	12.0

At a glance...

The 2016 poll topper was the late deputy First Minister Martin McGuinness who moved to Foyle from Mid Ulster. His seat in the 2017 election was won by newcomer Elisha McCallion who had the highest number of first preference votes. She was closely followed by party colleague Raymond McCartney. Mark H Durkan and SDLP leader Colum Eastwood were comfortably returned. The DUP saw their only candidate Gary Middleton regain his seat. People Before Profit's 2016 MLA Eamonn McCann did not reach the quota.

		Stage 1	Stage 2
		1st preference	Transfer of McCallion's surplus
Stuart Canning	Conservatives	77.00	(+0.19) 77.19
Colm Cavanagh	APNI	1,124.00	(+8.93) 1,132.93
Shannon Downey	Green	242.00	(+2.09) 244.09
Mark H Durkan	SDLP	6,948.00	(+75.05) 7,023.05
Colum Eastwood	SDLP	7,240.00	(+92.53) 7,332.53
Julia Kee	UUP	1,660.00	(+1.52) 1,661.52
John Lindsay	Citizens Independent Social Thought Alliance	196.00	(+3.61) 199.61
Elisha McCallion	Sinn Féin	9,205.00	(+1,768.00) 7,437.00
Eamonn McCann	PBPA	4,760.00	(+90.63) 4,850.63
Raymond McCartney	Sinn Féin	7,145.00	(+1,463.76) 8,608.76
Arthur McGuinness	Independent	44.00	(+0.57) 44.57
Gary Middleton	DUP	5,975.00	(+0.00) 5,975.00
	Non transferable		(+29.11) 29.11

Northern Ireland Assembly election results 2017

Candidates elected	Count
Elisha McCallion (SF)	1
Raymond McCartney (SF)	2
Colum Eastwood (SDLP)	3
Mark H Durkan (SDLP)	5
Gary Middleton (DUP)	6

	Stage 3	Stage 4	Stage 5	Stage 6
	Transfer of McCartney's surplus	Exclusion of Canning, Downey, Lindsay, McGuinness	Exclusion of Cavanagh, Kee	Transfer of Durkan's surplus
	(+1.71) 78.90	(-78.90) 0.00	-	-
	(+46.74) 1,179.67	(+115.55) 1,295.22	(-1,295.22) 0.00	-
	(+20.33) 264.42	(-264.42) 0.00	-	-
	(+252.51) 7,275.56	(+105.12) 7,380.68	(+1,033.00) 8,413.68	(-976.68) 7,437.00
	(+262.77) 7,595.30	(+0.00) 7,595.30	(+0.00) 7,595.30	(+0.00) 7,595.30
	(+7.41) 1,668.93	(+35.57) 1,704.50	(-1,704.50) 0.00	-
	(+25.84) 225.45	(-225.45) 0.00	-	-
	(+0.00) 7,437.00	(+0.00) 7,437.00	(+0.00) 7,437.00	(+0.00) 7,437.00
	(+236.17) 5,086.80	(+204.83) 5,291.63	(+630.53) 5,922.16	(+451.00) 6,373.16
	(-1,171.76) 7,437.00	(+0.00) 7,437.00	(+0.00) 7,437.00	(+0.00) 7,437.00
	(+11.78) 56.35	(-56.35) 0.00	-	-
	(+1.71) 5,976.71	(+31.38) 6,008.09	(+894.28) 6,902.37	(+134.00) 7,036.37
	(+304.79) 333.91	(+132.67) 466.58	(+441.91) 908.49	(+391.68) 1,300.17

Northern Ireland Assembly election results 2017

Lagan Valley

Total Valid Poll 45,069 Quota 7,512 Turnout 62.60%

Party performance

Party	Seats	1st Pref Vote	2016%	2017%
DUP	2	18,614	47.2	41.3
SF	-	1,801	2.7	4.0
UUP	1	11,338	21.2	25.2
SDLP	1	3,795	7.5	8.4
APNI	1	6,105	9.5	13.5
Others	-	3,416	11.9	7.6

At a glance...

Despite a strong vote performance, the DUP failed to return their third seat in Lagan Valley. In one of the few surprises of Election 2017, SDLP candidate Pat Catney was elected on the eighth count, defeating the DUP's Brenda Hale, in this traditionally unionist stronghold. After serving as Minister for Communities since the last election, Paul Givan topped the poll significantly increasing his first preference vote tally from 5,364 in 2016 to 8,035. Former minister Edwin Poots was also returned for his fifth term. The UUP lost one seat in the form of Jenny Palmer, leaving Robbie Butler as their only MLA for the area. Trevor Lunn from the APNI was also returned to his seat.

		Stage 1	Stage 2
		1st preference	Exclusion of Gray and Robinson
Dan Barrios-O'Neill	Green	912.00	(+21.00) 933.00
Robbie Butler	UUP	6,846.00	(+34.00) 6,880.00
Pat Catney	SDLP	3,795.00	(+5.00) 3,800.00
Peter Doran	Sinn Féin	1,801.00	(+2.00) 1,803.00
Paul Givan	DUP	8,035.00	(+0.00) 8,035.00
Keith John Gray	Independent	76.00	(-76.00) 0.00
Brenda Hale	DUP	4,566.00	(+18.00) 4,584.00
Trevor Lunn	APNI	6,105.00	(+26.00) 6,131.00
Samuel Morrison	TUV	1,389.00	(+17.00) 1,406.00
Jonny Orr	Independent	856.00	(+53.00) 909.00
Jenny Palmer	UUP	4,492.00	(+50.00) 4,542.00
Edwin Poots	DUP	6,013.00	(+15.00) 6,028.00
Matthew Robinson	Conservatives	183.00	(-183.00) 0.00
Non transferable			(+18.00) 18.00

Candidates elected — Count

Candidates elected	Count
Paul Givan (DUP)	1
Robbie Butler (UUP)	7
Trevor Lunn (APNI)	7
Edwin Poots (DUP)	8
Pat Catney (SDLP)	8

Paul Givan  · Robbie Butler  · Trevor Lunn  · Edwin Poots  · Pat Catney

	Stage 3	Stage 4	Stage 5	Stage 6	Stage 7	Stage 8
	Transfer of Givan's surplus	Exclusion of Orr	Exclusion of Barrios-O'Neill	Exclusion of Doran and Morrison	Exclusion of Palmer	Transfer of Butler's surplus
	(+0.36) 933.36	(+284.00) 1,217.36	(-1,217.36) 0.00	-	-	-
	(+29.58) 6,909.58	(+121.06) 7,030.64	(+100.06) 7,130.70	(+331.72) 7,462.42	(+3,575.00) 11,037.42	(-3,525.42) 7,512.00
	(+1.32) 3,801.32	(+58.06) 3,859.38	(+162.00) 4,021.38	(+1,362.12) 5,383.50	(+309.42) 5,692.92	(+1,156.00) 6,848.92
	(+0.06) 1,803.06	(+26.06) 1,829.12	(+48.00) 1,877.12	(-1,877.12) 0.00	-	-
	(-523.00) 7,512.00	(+0.00) 7,512.00	(+0.00) 7,512.00	(+0.00) 7,512.00	(+0.00) 7,512.00	(+0.00) 7,512.00
	-	-	-	-	-	-
	(+306.90) 4,890.90	(+17.12) 4,908.02	(+19.12) 4,927.14	(+333.70) 5,260.84	(+300.86) 5,561.70	(+854.00) 6,415.70
	(+4.74) 6,135.74	(+205.06) 6,340.80	(+678.06) 7,018.86	(+374.00) 7,392.86	(+264.00) 7,656.86	(+0.00) 7,656.86
	(+5.88) 1,411.88	(+22.12) 1,434.00	(+14.00) 1,448.00	(-1,448.00) 0.00	-	-
	(+0.72) 909.72	(-909.72) 0.00	-	-	-	-
	(+11.46) 4,553.46	(+119.12) 4,672.58	(+64.12) 4,736.70	(+358.02) 5,094.72	(-5,094.72) 0.00	-
	(+118.92) 6,146.92	(+20.12) 6,167.04	(+18.00) 6,185.04	(+287.44) 6,472.48	(+348.34) 6,820.82	(+581.00) 7,401.82
	-	-	-	-	-	-
	(+43.06) 61.06	(+37.00) 98.06	(+114.00) 212.06	(+278.12) 490.18	(+297.10) 787.28	(+934.42) 1,721.70

Northern Ireland Assembly election results 2017

Mid Ulster

Total Valid Poll 49,678   Quota 8,280   Turnout 72.4%

Party performance

Party	Seats	1st Pref Vote	2016%	2017%
DUP	1	9,568	18.1	19.3
SF	3	26,207	46.7	52.8
UUP	-	4,516	11.9	9.1
SDLP	1	6,419	15.2	12.9
APNI	-	1,017	1.2	2.0
Others	-	1,951	6.9	3.9

At a glance...

Sinn Féin retained three seats in Mid Ulster with its new Northern Ireland Assembly leader Michelle O'Neill, who succeeded the late Martin McGuinness in 2016, topping the poll with 10,258 votes. The DUP's Keith Buchanan was also elected in the first stage with 9,568 first preferences. The SDLP's only name on the ballot Patsy McGlone retained his seat. UUP candidate Sandra Overend failed to reach the quota. The poll topper in the 2016 election Sinn Féin's Ian Milne was elected in the second stage along with his party colleague Linda Dillon.

Candidate	Party	Stage 1 1st preference
Keith Buchanan	DUP	9,568.00
Linda Dillon	Sinn Féin	7,806.00
Hannah Loughrin	TUV	1,244.00
Hugh McCloy	Independent	247.00
Patsy McGlone	SDLP	6,419.00
Ian Milne	Sinn Féin	8,143.00
Michelle O'Neill	Sinn Féin	10,258.00
Sandra Overend	UUP	4,516.00
Hugh Scullion	The Workers Party	217.00
Stefan Taylor	Green	243.00
Fay Watson	APNI	1,017.00
Non transferable		

Northern Ireland Assembly election results 2017

Candidates elected	Count
Michelle O'Neill (SF)	1
Keith Buchanan (DUP)	1
Ian Milne (SF)	2
Linda Dillon (SF)	2
Patsy McGlone (SDLP)	5

	Stage 2	Stage 3	Stage 4
	Transfer of O'Neill's surplus	Transfer of Buchanan's surplus	Exclusion of Loughrin, McCloy, Scullion, Taylor and Watson
	(+0.00) 9,568.00	(-1,288.00) 8,280.00	(+0.00) 8,280.00
	(+1,226.64) 9,032.64	(+0.00) 9,032.64	(+0.00) 9,032.64
	(+1.90) 1,245.90	(+446.94) 1,692.84	(-1,692.84) 0.00
	(+6.84) 253.84	(+3.12) 256.96	(-256.96) 0.00
	(+264.67) 6,683.67	(+15.34) 6,699.01	(+1,033.96) 7,732.97
	(+410.21) 8,553.21	(+0.00) 8,553.21	(+0.00) 8,553.21
	(-1,978.00) 8,280.00	(+0.00) 8,280.00	(+0.00) 8,280.00
	(+3.42) 4,519.42	(+740.61) 5,260.03	(+1,792.38) 7,052.41
	(+4.37) 221.37	(+0.78) 222.15	(-222.15) 0.00
	(+3.04) 246.04	(+1.69) 247.73	(-247.73) 0.00
	(+13.11) 1,030.11	(+6.50) 1,036.61	(-1,036.61) 0.00
	(+43.80) 43.80	(+73.02) 116.82	(+629.95) 746.77

Northern Ireland Assembly election results 2017

Newry and Armagh

Total Valid Poll 54,918   Quota 9,154   Turnout 69.4%

Party performance

Party	Seats	1st Pref Vote	2016%	2017%
DUP	1	9,760	16.7	17.8
SF	3	26,532	40.9	48.3
UUP	-	7,256	14.1	13.2
SDLP	1	8,983	18.2	16.4
APNI	-	1,418	1.0	2.6
Others	-	969	9.1	1.7

At a glance...

All five candidates were re-elected in Newry and Armagh where turnout had risen by 20 per cent, having dropped by 10 per cent at the last election. East Unionist candidate and former minister Danny Kennedy failed to be re-elected this time round. The DUP's only candidate William Irwin topped the poll closely followed by Sinn Féin's Cathal Boylan. Sinn Féin returned a further two MLAs; Megan Fearon and Conor Murphy. Former Armagh Gaelic footballer Justin McNulty was also returned for the SDLP. Two female candidates again stood for election after Newry and Armagh was the only ballot in 2011 without a female nominee.

Candidate	Party	Stage 1 1st preference
Cathal Boylan	Sinn Féin	9,197.00
Jackie Coade	APNI	1,418.00
Emmet Crossan	Citizens Independent Social Thought Alliance	704.00
Megan Fearon	Sinn Féin	8,881.00
William Irwin	DUP	9,760.00
Danny Kennedy	UUP	7,256.00
Justin McNulty	SDLP	8,983.00
Conor Murphy	Sinn Féin	8,454.00
Rowan Tunnicliffe	Green	265.00
Non transferable		

Northern Ireland Assembly election results 2017

Candidates Elected	Count
William Irwin (DUP)	1
Cathal Boylan (SF)	1
Megan Fearon (SF)	2
Justin McNulty (SDLP)	2
Conor Murphy (SF)	3

	Stage 2	Stage 3	Stage 4
	Exclusion of Tunnicliffe, Crossan and Coade	Transfer of McNulty's surplus	Transfer of Murphys' surplus
	(+0.00) 9,197.00	(+0.00) 9,197.00	(+0.00) 9,197.00
	(-1,418.00) 0.00	-	-
	(-704.00) 0.00	-	-
	(+294.00) 9,175.00	(+0.00) 9,175.00	(+0.00) 9,175.00
	(+0.00) 9,760.00	(+0.00) 9,760.00	(+0.00) 9,760.00
	(+419.00) 7,675.00	(+264.00) 7,939.00	(-7,939.00) 0.00
	(+1,102.00) 10,085.00	(-931.00) 9,154.00	(+0.00) 9,154.00
	(+227.00) 8,681.00	(+337.00) 9,018.00	(+0.00) 9,018.00
	(-265.00) 0.00	-	-
	(+345.00) 345.00	(+330.00) 675.00	(+0.00) 675.00

Northern Ireland Assembly election results 2017

North Antrim

Total Valid Poll 48,094   Quota 8,016   Turnout 63.2%

Party performance

Party	Seats	1st Pref Vote	2016%	2017%
DUP	2	19,540	43.1	40.6
SF	1	7,600	12.9	15.8
UUP	1	6,022	10.7	12.5
SDLP	-	3,519	7.5	7.3
APNI	-	2,616	3.2	5.4
Others	1	8,797	22.6	18.4

At a glance...

Sinn Féin's Philip McGuigan was first past the post in North Antrim, a position previously held in the 2016 election by the TUV's Jim Allister. McGuigan took the place of party colleague Daithí McKay who held the only North Antrim nationalist seat in the previous Assembly. The DUP lost their third seat from 2016, with two MLAs Paul Frew and Mervyn Storey being re-elected for the area. UUP MLA Robin Swann became party leader in April 2017, which may account for his increase in first preference votes which almost doubled.

		Stage 1	Stage 2
		1st preference	Exclusion of McBride
Jim Allister	TUV	6,214.00	(+1.00) 6,215.00
Mark Bailey	Green	530.00	(+17.00) 547.00
Monica Digney	Independent	435.00	(+19.00) 454.00
Connor Duncan	SDLP	3,519.00	(+8.00) 3,527.00
Paul Frew	DUP	6,975.00	(+2.00) 6,977.00
Timothy Gaston	TUV	1,505.00	(+1.00) 1,506.00
Phillip Logan	DUP	5,708.00	(+1.00) 5,709.00
Adam McBride	Independent	113.00	(-113.00) 0.00
Philip McGuigan	Sinn Féin	7,600.00	(+1.00) 7,601.00
Patricia O'Lynn	APNI	2,616.00	(+39.00) 2,655.00
Mervyn Storey	DUP	6,857.00	(+6.00) 6,863.00
Robin Swann	UUP	6,022.00	(+10.00) 6,032.00
Non transferable			(+8.00) 8.00

Northern Ireland Assembly election results 2017

Candidates Elected	Count
Philip McGuigan (SF)	6
Robin Swann (UUP)	6
Jim Allister (TUV)	7
Paul Frew (DUP)	7
Mervyn Storey (DUP)	7

Stage 3	Stage 4	Stage 5	Stage 6	Stage 7	Stage 8
Exclusion of Digney	Exclusion of Bailey and Gaston	Exclusion of O'Lynn	Exclusion of Duncan	Transfer of McGuigan's surplus	Exclusion of Logan
(+14.00) 6,229.00	(+1,335.00) 7,564.00	(+115.00) 7,679.00	(+155.00) 7,834.00	(+155.00) 7,989.00	(+0.00) 7,989.00
(+33.00) 580.00	(-580.00) 0.00	-	-	-	-
(-454.00) 0.00	-	-	-	-	-
(+138.00) 3,665.00	(+94.00) 3,759.00	(+1,233.00) 4,992.00	(-4,992.00) 0.00	-	-
(+7.00) 6,984.00	(+71.00) 7,055.00	(+80.00) 7,135.00	(+64.00) 7,199.00	(+32.00) 7,231.00	(+0.00) 7,231.00
(+3.00) 1,509.00	(-1,509.00) 0.00	-	-	-	-
(+2.00) 5,711.00	(+65.00) 5,776.00	(+34.00) 5,810.00	(+30.00) 5,840.00	(+20.00) 5,860.00	(-5,860.00) 0.00
-	-	-	-	-	-
(+128.00) 7,729.00	(+40.00) 7,769.00	(+191.00) 7,960.00	(+1,820.00) 9,780.00	(-1,764.00) 8,016.00	(+0.00) 8,016.00
(+66.00) 2,721.00	(+309.00) 3,030.00	(-3,030.00) 0.00	-	-	-
(+5.00) 6,868.00	(+28.00) 6,896.00	(+69.00) 6,965.00	(+48.00) 7,013.00	(+53.00) 7,066.00	(+0.00) 7,066.00
(+17.00) 6,049.00	(+78.00) 6,127.00	(+839.00) 6,966.00	(+1,465.00) 8,431.00	(+0.00) 8,431.00	(+0.00) 8,431.00
(+41.00) 49.00	(+69.00) 118.00	(+469.00) 587.00	(+1,410.00) 1,997.00	(+1,504.00) 3,501.00	(+0.00) 3,501.00

Northern Ireland Assembly election results 2017

North Down

Total Valid Poll 37,739   Quota 6,290   Turnout 59.20%

Party performance

Party	Seats	1st Pref Vote	2016%	2017%
DUP	2	14,152	41.7	37.5
SF	-	591	1.0	1.6
UUP	1	8,115	15.5	21.5
SDLP	-	679	1.3	1.8
APNI	1	7,014	16.8	18.6
Others	1	7,188	23.7	19.0

At a glance...

The DUP's Alex Easton topped the poll for the third election running. The breakdown of seats remained identical apart from the loss of one DUP seat, with Peter Weir moving into the Strangford constituency. Alan Chambers was returned for the Ulster Unionists in the first count, with the UUP increasing their vote share significantly by 6 per cent. The Green Party's Steven Agnew was re-elected in the seventh count, increasing his first preference share by around 1,000 votes. Alliance's Stephen Farry was also returned in the first stage of counting.

		Stage 1	Stage 2
		1st preference	Transfer of Easton's surplus
Steven Agnew	Green Party	5,178.00	(+42.24) 5,220.24
Chris Carter	Independent	92.00	(+2.20) 94.20
Alan Chambers	UUP	7,151.00	(+0.00) 7,151.00
William Cudworth	UUP	964.00	(+65.12) 1,029.12
Gordon Dunne	DUP	6,118.00	(+1,560.68) 7,678.68
Alex Easton	DUP	8,034.00	(-1,744.00) 6,290.00
Stephen Farry	APNI	7,014.00	(+0.00) 7,014.00
Melanie Kennedy	Independent	1,246.00	(+39.82) 1,285.82
Kieran Maxwell	Sinn Féin	591.00	(+0.22) 591.22
Caoímhe McNeill	SDLP	679.00	(+2.86) 681.86
Gavan Reynolds	Independent	31.00	(+1.54) 32.54
Frank Shivers	Conservatives	641.00	(+13.20) 654.20
	Non transferable		(+16.12) 16.12

Candidates Elected	Count
Alex Easton (DUP)	1
Alan Chambers (UUP)	1
Stephen Farry (APNI)	1
Gordon Dunne (DUP)	2
Steven Agnew (Green)	7

	Stage 3	Stage 4	Stage 5	Stage 6	Stage 7	Stage 8
	Transfer of Dunne's surplus	Transfer of Chamber's surplus	Transfer of Farry's surplus	Exclusion of Carter, Maxwell and Reynolds	Exclusion of Shivers	Exclusion of McNeill, Kennedy and Cudworth
	(+100.54) 5,320.78	(+67.44) 5,388.22	(+394.10) 5,782.32	(+197.64) 5,979.96	(+180.54) 6,160.50	(+0.00) 6,160.50
	(+21.78) 115.98	(+3.12) 119.10	(+7.60) 126.70	(-126.70) 0.00	-	-
	(+0.00) 7,151.00	(-861.00) 6,290.00	(+0.00) 6,290.00	(+0.00) 6,290.00	(+0.00) 6,290.00	(+0.00) 6,290.00
	(+852.50) 1,881.62	(+703.68) 2,585.30	(+105.20) 2,690.50	(+35.72) 2,726.22	(+331.84) 3,058.06	(-3,058.06) 0.00
	(-1,388.68) 6,290.00	(+0.00) 6,290.00	(+0.00) 6,290.00	(+0.00) 6,290.00	(+0.00) 6,290.00	(+0.00) 6,290.00
	(+0.00) 6,290.00	(+0.00) 6,290.00	(+0.00) 6,290.00	(+0.00) 6,290.00	(+0.00) 6,290.00	(+0.00) 6,290.00
	(+0.00) 7,014.00	(+0.00) 7,014.00	(-724.00) 6,290.00	(+0.00) 6,290.00	(+0.00) 6,290.00	(+0.00) 6,290.00
	(+85.80) 1,371.62	(+18.24) 1,389.86	(+40.00) 1,429.86	(+74.10) 1,503.96	(+92.92) 1,596.88	(-1,596.88) 0.00
	(+0.66) 591.88	(+0.72) 592.6	(+11.90) 604.50	(-604.50) 0.00	-	-
	(+4.40) 686.26	(+20.88) 707.14	(+93.40) 800.54	(+377.46) 1,178.00	(+24.88) 1,202.88	(-1,202.88) 0.00
	(+4.84) 37.38	(+0.96) 38.34	(+2.10) 40.44	(-40.44) 0.00	-	-
	(+86.46) 740.66	(+15.48) 756.14	(+21.10) 777.24	(+24.64) 801.88	(-801.88) 0.00	-
	(+231.70) 247.82	(+30.48) 278.30	(+48.60) 326.90	(+62.08) 388.98	(+171.70) 560.68	(+0.00) 560.68

Northern Ireland Assembly election results 2017

South Antrim

Total Valid Poll 42,344   Quota 7,058   Turnout 62.4%

Party performance

Party	Seats	1st Pref Vote	2016%	2017%
DUP	2	14,278	37.5	33.7
SF	1	6,891	13.2	16.3
UUP	1	8,792	22.2	20.8
SDLP	-	4,024	9.6	9.5
APNI	1	5,278	8.9	12.5
Others	-	3,081	8.6	7.2

At a glance...

Again, there is not much change to the political make-up of South Antrim aside from the loss of one DUP seat. There are no new faces with each of the MLAs having served in the previous Assembly. David Ford's vote share increased having previously lost 1,000 votes in 2016. Sinn Féin's only candidate, Declan Kearney was first to be elected in the fourth count. UUP MLA Steve Aiken was returned to his seat, having previous taken over the seat from MP Danny Kinahan. The DUP won two seats in the eighth count, Pam Cameron and Paul Girvan. After the June 2017 elections, Trevor Clarke has replaced Paul Girvan who was elected as MP for South Antrim.

		Stage 1	Stage 2	Stage 3
		1st preference	Exclusion of Logan	Exclusion of Bailey
Steve Aiken	UUP	6,287.00	(+3.00) 6,326.00	(+42.00) 6,368.00
Ivanka Antova	PBPA	530.00	(+5.00) 535.00	(+123.00) 658.00
Eleanor Bailey	Green	501.00	(+3.00) 504.00	(-504.00) 0.00
Richard Cairns	TUV	1,353.00	(+16.00) 1,369.00	(+9.00) 1,378.00
Pam Cameron	DUP	4,604.00	(+9.00) 4,613.00	(+11.00) 4,624.00
Trevor Clarke	DUP	4,522.00	(+18.00) 4,540.00	(+5.00) 4,545.00
Adrian Cochrane-Watson	UUP	2,505.00	(+20.00) 2,525.00	(+6.00) 2,531.00
David Ford	APNI	5,278.00	(+35.00) 5,313.00	(+181.00) 5,494.00
Paul Girvan	DUP	5,152.00	(+12.00) 5,164.00	(+1.00) 5,165.00
Declan Kearney	Sinn Féin	6,891.00	(+4.00) 6,895.00	(+30.00) 6,925.00
Mark Logan	Conservatives	194.00	(-194.00) 0.00	-
Roisin Lynch	SDLP	4,024.00	(+11.00) 4,035.00	(+34.00) 4,069.00
David McMaster	Independent	503.00	(+14.00) 517.00	(+46.00) 563.00
Non transferable			(+8.00) 8.00	(+16.00) 24.00

Northern Ireland Assembly election results 2017

Candidates Elected	Count
Declan Kearney (SF)	4
Steve Aiken (UUP)	5
David Ford (APNI)	7
Paul Girvan (DUP)	8
Pam Cameron (DUP)	8

Declan Kearney — Steve Aiken — David Ford — Paul Girvan — Pam Cameron

	Stage 4	Stage 5	Stage 6	Stage 7	Stage 8
	Exclusion of McMaster and Antova	Exclusion of Cairns and Cochrane-Watson	Transfer of Aiken's surplus	Exclusion of Lynch	Transfer of Ford's surplus
	(+126.00) 6,494.00	(+2,314.00) 8,808.00	(-1,750.00) 7,058.00	(+0.00) 7,058.00	(+0.00) 7,058.00
	(-658.00) 0.00	-	-	-	-
	-	-	-	-	-
	(+31.00) 1,409.00	(-1,409.00) 0.00	-	-	-
	(+20.00) 4,644.00	(+335.00) 4,979.00	(+378.12) 5,357.12	(+101.80) 5,458.92	(+220.00) 5,678.92
	(+14.00) 4,559.00	(+436.00) 4,995.00	(+363.40) 5,358.40	(+87.00) 5,445.40	(+82.00) 5,527.40
	(+52.00) 2,583.00	(-2,583.00) 0.00	-	-	-
	(+496.00) 5,990.00	(+232.00) 6,222.00	(+545.56) 6,767.56	(+3,094.00) 9,861.56	(-2,803.56) 7,058.00
	(+58.00) 5,223.00	(+353.00) 5,576.00	(+223.56) 5,799.56	(+73.08) 5,872.64	(+97.00) 5,969.64
	(+140.00) 7,065.00	(+0.00) 7,065.00	(+0.00) 7,065.00	(+0.00) 7,065.00	(+0.00) 7,065.00
	-	-	-	-	-
	(+160.00) 4,229.00	(+131.00) 4,360.00	(+235.52) 4,595.52	(-4,595.52) 0.00	-
	(-563.00) 0.00	-	-	-	-
	(+124.00) 148.00	(+191.00) 339.00	(+3.84) 342.84	(+1,239.64) 1,582.48	(+2,404.56) 3,987.04

Northern Ireland Assembly election results 2017

South Down

Total Valid Poll 49,399   Quota 8,234   Turnout 66.2%

Party performance

Party	Seats	1st Pref Vote	2016%	2017%
DUP	1	7,786	12.3	15.8
SF	2	19,083	31.1	38.6
UUP	-	4,172	8.5	8.4
SDLP	2	12,433	31.4	25.2
APNI	-	4,535	5.4	9.2
Others	-	1,390	11.3	2.8

At a glance...

Sinn Féin's Sinéad Ennis and Chris Hazzard topped the poll in South Down and were both elected in the first stage. The breakdown of seats remains largely the same, apart from the loss of the UUP's Harold McKee who did not reach the quota. Former health minister Jim Wells was the only DUP candidate and was re-elected on the fifth count. Sinéad Bradley and Colin McGrath were both comfortably returned for the SDLP.

		Stage 1	Stage 2
		1st preference	Exclusion of Hynds, Clarke, George and Rea
Sinéad Bradley	SDLP	7,323.00	(+164.00) 7,487.00
Patrick Brown	APNI	4,535.00	(+348.00) 4,883.00
Patrick Clarke	Independent	192.00	(-192.00) 0.00
Sinéad Ennis	Sinn Féin	10,256.00	(+0.00) 10,256.00
Hannah George	Green	483.00	(-483.00) 0.00
Chris Hazzard	Sinn Féin	8,827.00	(+0.00) 8,827.00
Gary Hynds	Conservatives	85.00	(-85.00) 0.00
Colin McGrath	SDLP	5,110.00	(+92.00) 5,202.00
Harold McKee	UUP	4,172.00	(+337.00) 4,509.00
Lyle Rea	TUV	630.00	(-630.00) 0.00
Jim Wells	DUP	7,786.00	(+302.00) 8,088.00
	Non transferable		(+147.00) 147.00

Northern Ireland Assembly election results 2017

Candidates Elected	Count
Sinéad Ennis (SF)	1
Chris Hazzard (SF)	1
Sinéad Bradley (SDLP)	3
Jim Wells (DUP)	5
Colin McGrath (SDLP)	7

	Stage 3	Stage 4	Stage 5	Stage 6	Stage 7
	Transfer of Ennis' surplus	Transfer of Bradley's surplus	Exclusion of McKee	Transfer of Wells' surplus	Transfer of Hazzard's surplus
	(+1,419.12) 8,906.12	(-672.12) 8,234.00	(+0.00) 8,234.00	(+0.00) 8,234.00	(+0.00) 8,234.00
	(+218.64) 5,101.64	(+93.24) 5,194.88	(+812.94) 6,007.82	(+723.00) 6,730.82	(+143.84) 6,874.66
	-	-	-	-	-
	(-2,022.00) 8,234.00	(+0.00) 8,234.00	(+0.00) 8,234.00	(+0.00) 8,234.00	(+0.00) 8,234.00
	-	-	-	-	-
	(+0.00) 8,827.00	(+0.00) 8,827.00	(+0.00) 8,827.00	(+0.00) 8,827.00	(-593.00) 8,234.00
	-	-	-	-	-
	(+310.80) 5,512.80	(+530.88) 6,043.68	(+588.74) 6,632.42	(+596.00) 7,228.42	(+385.20) 7,613.62
	(+13.44) 4,522.44	(+5.32) 4,527.76	(-4,527.76) 0.00	-	-
	-	-	-	-	-
	(+3.36) 8,091.36	(+0.28) 8,091.64	(+2,730.00) 10,821.64	(-2,587.64) 8,234.00	(+0.00) 8,234.00
	(+56.64) 203.64	(+42.40) 246.04	(+396.08) 642.12	(+1,268.64) 1,910.76	(+63.96) 1,974.72

Northern Ireland Assembly election results 2017

Strangford

Total Valid Poll 38,785   Quota 6,465   Turnout 60.9%

Party performance

Party	Seats	1st Pref Vote	2016%	2017%
DUP	3	15,492	43.0	39.9
SF	-	1,110	2.0	2.9
UUP	1	7,776	19.5	20.0
SDLP	-	3,045	8.3	7.9
APNI	1	5,813	10.7	15.0
Others	-	5,549	16.5	14.3

At a glance...

The DUP won three seats in Strangford; Simon Hamilton who topped the poll; Michelle McIlveen and Peter Weir. Former party member Jonathan Bell ran as an independent after a fall out with the party and was not re-elected. Former UUP leader Mike Nesbitt topped the poll in 2016, however he was in the seventh count this time round. Kellie Armstrong was also returned for APNI and first to be elected on the fourth count.

		Stage 1	Stage 2	Stage 3	Stage 4
		1st preference	Exclusion of Benton	Exclusion of Bamford	Exclusion of Kennedy
Kellie Armstrong	APNI	5,813.00	(+32.00) 5,845.00	(+527.00) 6,372.00	(+238.00) 6,610.00
Ricky Bamford	Green	918.00	(+12.00) 930.00	(-930.00) 0.00	-
Jonathan Bell	Independent	1,479.00	(+10.00) 1,489.00	(+60.00) 1,549.00	(+29.00) 1,578.00
Scott Benton	Conservatives	195.00	(-195.00) 0.00	-	-
Joe Boyle	SDLP	3,045.00	(+4.00) 3,049.00	(+71.00) 3,120.00	(+758.00) 3,878.00
Stephen Cooper	TUV	1,330.00	(+20.00) 1,350.00	(+20.00) 1,370.00	(+3.00) 1,373.00
Simon Hamilton	DUP	6,221.00	(+13.00) 6,234.00	(+25.00) 6,259.00	(+3.00) 6,262.00
Dermot Kennedy	Sinn Féin	1,110.00	(+0.00) 1,110.00	(+19.00) 1,129.00	(-1,129.00) 0.00
Michelle McIlveen	DUP	5,728.00	(+9.00) 5,737.00	(+9.00) 5,746.00	(+1.00) 5,747.00
Jimmy Menagh	Independent	1,627.00	(+7.00) 1,634.00	(+49.00) 1,683.00	(+6.00) 1,689.00
Mike Nesbitt	UUP	5,323.00	(+39.00) 5,362.00	(+57.00) 5,419.00	(+13.00) 5,432.00
Philip Smith	UUP	2,453.00	(+27.00) 2,480.00	(+27.00) 2,507.00	(+0.00) 2,507.00
Peter Weir	DUP	3,543.00	(+9.00) 3,552.00	(+4.00) 3,556.00	(+0.00) 3,556.00
Non transferable			(+13.00) 13.00	(+62.00) 75.00	(+78.00) 153.00

Northern Ireland Assembly election results 2017

Candidates Elected

Candidates Elected	Count
Kellie Armstrong (APNI)	4
Simon Hamilton (DUP)	5
Michelle McIlveen (DUP)	9
Mike Nesbitt (UUP)	9
Peter Weir (DUP)	11

Stage 5	Stage 6	Stage 7	Stage 8	Stage 9	Stage 10	Stage 11	Stage 12
Exclusion of Cooper	Transfer of Armstrong's surplus	Transfer of Hamilton's surplus	Exclusion of Bell	Exclusion of Menagh	Exclusion of Smith	Transfer of McIlveen's surplus	Exclusion of Boyle
(+0.00) 6,610.00	(-145.00) 6,465.00	(+0.00) 6,465.00	(+0.00) 6,465.00	(+0.00) 6,465.00	(+0.00) 6,465.00	(+0.00) 6,465.00	(+0.00) 6,465.00
-	-	-	-	-	-	-	-
(+204.00) 1,782.00	(+9.75) 1,791.75	(+2.25) 1,794.00	(-1,794.00) 0.00	-	-	-	-
-	-	-	-	-	-	-	-
(+22.00) 3,900.00	(+120.75) 4,020.75	(+0.25) 4,021.00	(+94.00) 4,115.00	(+114.25) 4,229.25	(+934.00) 5,163.25	(+3.84) 5,167.09	(-5,167.09) 0.00
(-1,373.00) 0.00	-	-	-	-	-	-	-
(+269.00) 6,531.00	(+0.00) 6,531.00	(-66.00) 6,465.00	(+0.00) 6,465.00	(+0.00) 6,465.00	(+0.00) 6,465.00	(+0.00) 6,465.00	(+0.00) 6,465.00
-	-	-	-	-	-	-	-
(+216.00) 5,963.00	(+0.75) 5,963.75	(+49.50) 6,013.25	(+316.75) 6,330.00	(+432.00) 6,762.00	(+0.00) 6,762.00	(-297.00) 6,465.00	(+0.00) 6,465.00
(+153.00) 1,842.00	(+3.00) 1,845.00	(+1.50) 1,846.50	(+343.25) 2,189.75	(-2,189.75) 0.00	-	-	-
(+212.00) 5,644.00	(+9.00) 5,653.00	(+4.00) 5,657.00	(+455.00) 6,112.00	(+428.00) 6,540.00	(+0.00) 6,540.00	(+0.00) 6,540.00	(+0.00) 6,540.00
(+141.00) 2,648.00	(+0.00) 2,648.00	(+3.00) 2,651.00	(+149.00) 2,800.00	(+279.25) 3,079.25	(-3,079.25) 0.00	-	-
(+80.00) 3,636.00	(+0.00) 3,636.00	(+3.50) 3,639.50	(+238.25) 3,877.75	(+313.75) 4,191.50	(+910.00) 5,101.50	(+290.88) 5,392.38	(+0.00) 5,392.38
(+76.00) 229.00	(+1.75) 230.75	(+2.00) 232.75	(+197.75) 430.50	(+622.50) 1,053.00	(+1,235.25) 2,288.25	(+2.28) 2,290.53	(+0.00) 2,290.53

Northern Ireland Assembly election results 2017

Upper Bann

Total Valid Poll 51,548   Quota 8,592   Turnout 62.5%

Party performance

Party	Seats	1st Pref Vote	2016%	2017%
DUP	2	16,885	31.1	32.8
SF	1	14,328	24.9	27.8
UUP	1	10,599	21.6	20.6
SDLP	1	5,127	9.5	9.9
APNI	-	2,720	3.1	5.3
Others	-	1,889	9.8	3.6

At a glance...

As per 2016, it was Carla Lockhart DUP who was first past the post being elected on the first count with 9,140 votes. The DUP also saw candidate Jonathan Buckley elected, taking the place of Sydney Anderson. Having lost her seat in the 2016 election, Dolores Kelly regained a seat for the SDLP. Doug Beattie was also returned for the UUP. Sinn Féin lost a seat, however former minister John O'Dowd was elected in the fifth count.

		Stage 1	Stage 2
		1st preference	Exclusion of Craig, Ferguson, Lee & Nickels
Doug Beattie	UUP	5,467.00	(+288.00) 5,755.00
Jonathan Buckley	DUP	7,745.00	(+493.00) 8,238.00
Colin Craig	The Workers Party	218.00	(-218.00) 0.00
Jo-Anne Dobson	UUP	5,132.00	(+272.00) 5,404.00
Tara Doyle	APNI	2,720.00	(+377.00) 3,097.00
Roy Ferguson	TUV	1,035.00	(-1,035.00) 0.00
Dolores Kelly	SDLP	5,127.00	(+121.00) 5,248.00
Simon Lee	Green	555.00	(-555.00) 0.00
Carla Lockhart	DUP	9,140.00	(+0.00) 9,140.00
Ian Nickels	Conservatives	81.00	(-81.00) 0.00
John O'Dowd	Sinn Féin	8,220.00	(+78.00) 8,298.00
Nuala Toman	Sinn Féin	6,108.00	(+61.00) 6,169.00
	Non transferable		(+199.00) 199.00

Northern Ireland Assembly election results 2017

Candidates Elected	Count
Carla Lockhart (DUP)	1
Jonathan Buckley (DUP)	4
Doug Beattie (UUP)	5
John O'Dowd (SF)	5
Dolores Kelly (SDLP)	6

	Stage 3	Stage 4	Stage 5	Stage 6
	Exclusion of Doyle	Transfer of Lockhart's surplus	Exclusion of Dobson	Transfer of Beattie's surplus
	(+419.00) 6,174.00	(+28.86) 6,202.86	(+4,526.00) 10,728.86	(-2,136.86) 8,592.00
	(+76.00) 8,314.00	(+450.84) 8,764.84	(+0.00) 8,764.84	(+0.00) 8,764.84
	-	-	-	-
	(+506.00) 5,910.00	(+59.58) 5,969.58	(-5,969.58) 0.00	-
	(-3,097.00) 0.00	-	-	-
	-	-	-	-
	(+1,261.00) 6,509.00	(+2.76) 6,511.76	(+678.16) 7,189.92	(+1,864.00) 9,053.92
	-	-	-	-
	(+0.00) 9,140.00	(-548.00) 8,592.00	(+0.00) 8,592.00	(+0.00) 8,592.00
	-	-	-	-
	(+262.00) 8,560.00	(+0.60) 8,560.60	(+33.00) 8,593.60	(+0.00) 8,593.60
	(+125.00) 6,294.00	(+0.30) 6,294.30	(+22.30) 6,316.60	(+25.00) 6,341.60
	(+448.00) 647.00	(+5.06) 652.06	(+710.12) 1,362.18	(+247.86) 1,610.04

Northern Ireland Assembly election results 2017

West Tyrone

Total Valid Poll 44,325   Quota 7,388   Turnout 69.9%

Party performance

Party	Seats	1st Pref Vote	2016%	2017%
DUP	1	9,064	22.0	20.4
SF	3	21,321	42.0	48.1
UUP	-	3,654	11.4	8.2
SDLP	1	6,283	11.0	14.2
APNI	-	1,252	1.3	2.8
Others	-	2,751	12.3	6.3

At a glance...

Turnout in West Tyrone increased significantly by 20 per cent. All those elected had served the area in the 2016 Assembly, with exception of the UUP's Ross Hussey who was not returned. The DUP's Thomas Buchanan topped with poll with just over 9,000 votes. Michaela Boyle and Barry McElduff were also returned for Sinn Féin in the first count, followed by Declan McAleer in the fifth count. The SDLP also held onto their seat with Daniel McCrossan being re-elected in the last stage.

Candidate	Party	Stage 1 – 1st preference
Michaela Boyle	Sinn Féin	7,714.00
Barry Brown	Citizens Independent Social Thought Alliance	373.00
Thomas Buchanan	DUP	9,064.00
Charlie Chittick	TUV	851.00
Alicia Clarke	UUP	3,654.00
Stephen Donnelly	APNI	1,252.00
Corey French	Independent	98.00
Roger Lomas	Conservatives	27.00
Declan McAleer	Sinn Féin	6,034.00
Sorcha McAnespy	Independent	864.00
Ciaran McClean	Green Party	412.00
Daniel McCrossan	SDLP	6,283.00
Barry McElduff	Sinn Féin	7,573.00
Roisin McMackin	Independent	85.00
Susan-Anne White	Independent	41.00
Non transferable		

Northern Ireland Assembly election results 2017

Candidates Elected

Candidates Elected	Count
Thomas Buchanan (DUP)	1
Michaela Boyle (SF)	1
Barry McElduff (SF)	1
Declan McAleer (SF)	5
Daniel McCrossan (SDLP)	5

	Stage 2	Stage 3	Stage 4	Stage 5
	Transfer of Buchanan's surplus	Transfer of Boyle's surplus	Transfer of McElduff's surplus	Exclusion of Brown, Chittick, Donnelly, French, Lomas, McAnespy, McClean, McMackin and White
	(+0.00) 7,714.00	(-326.00) 7,388.00	(+0.00) 7,388.00	(+0.00) 7,388.00
	(+7.60) 380.60	(+3.68) 384.28	(+1.14) 385.42	(-385.42) 0.00
	(-1,676.00) 7,388.00	(+0.00) 7,388.00	(+0.00) 7,388.00	(+0.00) 7,388.00
	(+577.79) 1,428.79	(+0.16) 1,428.95	(+0.02) 1,428.97	(-1,428.97) 0.00
	(+1,034.93) 4,688.93	(+0.56) 4,689.49	(+0.24) 4,689.73	(+1,584.81) 6,274.54
	(+7.98) 1,259.98	(+3.76) 1,263.74	(+1.86) 1,265.6	(-1,265.60) 0.00
	(+0.57) 98.57	(+2.92) 101.49	(+0.06) 101.55	(-101.55) 0.00
	(+4.75) 31.75	(+0.40) 32.15	(+0.04) 32.19	(-32.19) 0.00
	(+0.57) 6,034.57	(+254.76) 6,289.33	(+131.98) 6,421.31	(+613.68) 7,034.99
	(+2.47) 866.47	(+4.08) 870.55	(+4.38) 874.93	(-874.93) 0.00
	(+3.99) 415.99	(+1.32) 417.31	(+0.88) 418.19	(-418.19) 0.00
	(+17.10) 6,300.10	(+33.24) 6,333.34	(+9.26) 6,342.60	(+1,339.00) 7,681.60
	(+0.00) 7,573.00	(+0.00) 7,573.00	(-185.00) 7,388.00	(+0.00) 7,388.00
	(+0.76) 85.76	(+0.28) 86.04	(+0.44) 86.48	(-86.48) 0.00
	(+4.18) 45.18	(+0.04) 45.22	(+0.06) 45.28	(-45.28) 0.00
	(+13.31) 13.31	(+20.80) 34.11	(+34.64) 68.75	(1,101.12) 1,169.87

Northern Ireland Assembly election results 2017

Subscribe to agendaNi

Want to join 7,000 Northern Irish decision-makers and receive the latest in-depth articles and analysis for your sector?

agendaNi magazine offers diverse content covering Northern Ireland's key sectors. The magazine goes behind the headlines to produce focused analysis through specialised sectoral reports. Subscription is the easiest way to keep up to date with the latest editions of agendaNi delivered directly to you throughout the year.

Regular agendaNi reports include:

- Public affairs
- Round table discussions
- Latest political developments
- Business
- Digital government
- Housing
- Economy
- ICT
- Health
- Energy
- Infrastructure
- Education
- Banking and finance
- Transport
- Reform
- Environment
- …. and much more!

Taking out a subscription has never been easier, visit www.agendani.com to order
Annual Subscription: £17.70 + £4.95 Postage and Packaging = £22.65
E: subscriptions@agendani.com T: 028 9261 9933

Don't forget to follow @agendani on Twitter and find us on Facebook for the latest articles and exclusive content.

Northern Ireland at Westminster

The Act of Union 1800 brought Ireland and Great Britain together within the United Kingdom (UK), under a single national Parliament at Westminster. Northern Ireland was formed by the Government of Ireland Act 1920, which partitioned Ireland along the present border, and has remained within the UK while the rest of the island has attained full independence as the Republic of Ireland.

Parliament consists of the Crown, the House of Lords and the House of Commons. Northern Ireland is represented by 18 elected Members of Parliament: eight DUP, seven Sinn Féin, two SDLP and one Alliance. Sinn Féin MPs abstain from Westminster but are entitled to use its facilities on behalf of their constituents. APNI Northern Ireland MPs sit on the opposition benches. There are 650 MPs at Westminster in total. The latest Westminster election took place in December 2019.

The House of Lords consists of around 790 peers; its membership fluctuates with deaths and new appointments. Peers do not represent geographical areas and estimates of those with links to the province vary. There are currently five sitting DUP peers (Lord Browne, Lord Dodds, Lord Morrow, Lord Hay and Lord McCrea) and two UUP peers (Lord Empey and Lord Rogan), one SDLP peer (Baroness Ritchie) as well as a number of Northern Ireland residents or former residents who are either members of UK national parties or independents.

As the UK is a constitutional monarchy, the Queen plays a largely ceremonial role. Her Government is normally formed from the largest party in the House of Commons and is headed by the Prime Minister and his Cabinet. If no party has an overall majority after a general election, a coalition may be formed to secure a majority in the House.

The Secretary of State for Northern Ireland represents Northern Ireland's interests in the Cabinet and leads the Northern Ireland Office (NIO). Northern Ireland Question Time takes place in the Commons every fourth Wednesday and any MP may take part.

Westminster legislates for Northern Ireland through Acts of Parliament, Orders-in-Council or Statutory Instruments. Acts undergo full parliamentary scrutiny and may be amended while Orders-in-Council cannot. Statutory Instruments are pieces of secondary legislation which can be used to amend, update or enforce Acts and Orders.

While Parliament is sovereign and can make laws in any area, in practice it does not legislate on transferred matters without the Assembly's consent. The Assembly cannot overturn laws previously passed in Parliament.

UK Parliament
Parliamentary Switchboard:
020 7219 3000
Web: www.parliament.uk

House of Commons
London
SW1A 0AA
Information Office: 020 7219 4272
Email: hcenquiries@parliament.uk

House of Lords
London
SW1A 0PW
Information Office: 020 7219 3107
Email: hlinfo@parliament.uk

Contact details for Northern Ireland MPs

Órfhlaith Begley
Constituency: West Tyrone
Party: Sinn Féin
4-5 James Street, Omagh, BT78 1DQ
Tel: 028 8225 3040
Email: orfhlaith.begley@sinnfein.ie

Mickey Brady
Constituency: Newry and Armagh
Party: Sinn Féin
1 Kilmorey Terrace, Newry, BT35 8DW
Tel: 028 3026 1693
Email: mickey.brady28@gmail.com

Gregory Campbell
Constituency: East Londonderry
Party: DUP
25 Bushmills Road, Coleraine, BT62 2BP
Tel: 028 7032 7327
Email: dupcoleraine@parliament.uk

Jeffrey Donaldson
Constituency: Lagan Valley
Party: DUP
The Old Town Hall, 29 Castle Street
Lisburn, BT27 4DH
Tel: 028 9266 8001
Email: jeffrey.donaldson.mp@parliament.uk

Colum Eastwood
Constituency: Foyle
Party: SDLP
Northside Village Centre
111 Glengalliagh Road
Derry, BT48 8NN
Tel: 028 7135 0045
Email: colum.eastwood.mp@parliament.uk

Stephen Farry
Constituency: North Down
Party: APNI
58 Abbey Street
Bangor, BT20 4JB
Tel: 07775 687 152
Email: stephen.farry.mp@parliament.uk

John Finucane
Constituency: Belfast North
Party: Sinn Féin
7 Altantic Avenue, Belfast, BT7 2HN
Tel: 028 9050 0890
Email: john.finucane.mp@parliament.uk

Michelle Gildernew
Constituency: Fermanagh and South Tyrone
Party: Sinn Féin
89 Main Street
Clogher, BT76 0AA
Tel: 028 8556 9250
Email: michelle.gildernew.mp@parliament.uk

Paul Girvan
Constituency: South Antrim
Party: DUP
29A The Square
Ballyclare, BT39 9BB
Tel: 028 9334 0111
Email: paul.girvan.mp@parliament.uk

Claire Hanna
Constituency: Belfast South
Party: SDLP
1 Rushfield Avenue, Belfast, BT7 3FP
Tel: 028 9099 6066
Email: claire.hanna.mp@parliament.uk

Chris Hazzard
Constituency: South Down
Party: Sinn Féin
Circular Road, Castlewellan, BT31 9ED
Tel: 028 4377 0185
Email: southdownmp@gmail.com

Carla Lockhart
Constituency: Upper Bann
Party: DUP
31 High Street
Lurgan, BT66 8AH
Tel: 028 3831 0088
Email: carla.lockhart.mp@parliament.uk

Paul Maskey
Constituency: Belfast West
Party: Sinn Féin
51-55 Falls Road
Belfast, BT12 4PD
Tel: 028 9034 7350
Email: westbelfastmp@sinnfein.ie

Francie Molloy
Constituency: Mid Ulster
Party: Sinn Féin
30F Fairhill Road, Cookstown, BT80 8AG
Tel: 028 8676 5850
Email: francie.molloy.mp@parliament.uk

Ian Paisley
Constituency: North Antrim
Party: DUP
9-11 Church Street, Ballymena, BT43 6DD
Tel: 028 2564 1421
Email: ian.paisley.mp@parliament.uk

Gavin Robinson
Constituency: East Belfast
Party: DUP
Strandtown Hall, 96 Belmont Avenue
Belfast, BT4 3DE
Tel: 028 9047 3111
Email: gavin.robinson.mp@parliament.uk

Jim Shannon
Constituency: Strangford
Party: DUP
34A Frances Street, Newtownards, BT23 7DN
Tel: 028 9182 7990
Email: jim.shannon.mp@parliament.uk

Sammy Wilson
Constituency: East Antrim
Party: DUP
116 Main Street, Larne, BT40 1RG
Tel: 028 2826 7722
Email: barronj@parliament.uk

Northern Ireland Affairs Committee

The Northern Ireland Affairs Committee examines the administration, policy and expenditure of the Northern Ireland Office and conducts inquiries into related matters. Its contact details and membership are as follows:

7 Millbank, House of Commons, London, SW1P 3JA
Tel: 020 7219 2173
Email: northircom@parliament.uk

Committee Clerk: Margaret McKinnon
Tel: 020 7219 2172

Members

Member	Party	Constituency
Simon Hoare MP (Chair)	Con	North Dorset
Scott Benton MP	Con	Blackpool South
Gregory Campbell MP	DUP	East Londonderry
Stephen Farry MP	APNI	North Down
Mary Kelly Foy MP	Lab	City of Durham
Rt Hon Robert Goodwill MP	Con	Scarborough and Whitby
Claire Hanna MP	SDLP	Belfast South
Fay Jones MP	Con	Brecon and Radnorshire
Ian Paisley MP	DUP	North Antrim
Stephanie Peacock MP	Lab	Barnsley East
Bob Stewart MP	Con	Beckenham

Northern Ireland Grand Committee

A separate Northern Ireland Grand Committee meets occasionally to debate policy relating to Northern Ireland. Its membership includes sitting Northern Ireland MPs and up to 25 MPs from elsewhere. The committee does not have a full-time staff.

UK Government responsibilities in Northern Ireland

Central government departments and details of senior ministers are outlined below along with their main responsibilities in Northern Ireland (or across the United Kingdom as a whole).

All UK departmental websites are hosted at www.gov.uk/government

Prime Minister's Office
10 Downing Street
London, SW1A 2AA
Tel: 020 7930 4433

Prime Minister, First Lord of the Treasury and Minister for the Civil Service: The Rt Hon Boris Johnson MP

The Prime Minister is head of the UK Government and is ultimately responsible for its policy and decisions. He appoints members of the Government and is the principal Government figure in the House of Commons. Johnson took up leadership in July 2019.

Cabinet Office
70 Whitehall
London, SW1A 2AS
Tel: 020 7276 1234

Minister for the Cabinet Office:
The Rt Hon Michael Gove MP

Home Civil Service; honours and peerages; national security co-ordination; political and constitutional reform.

Office of the Advocate-General for Scotland
Victoria Quay
Edinburgh, EH6 6QQ
Tel: 0131 244 0359

Advocate-General for Scotland:
Keith Stewart QC

Attorney-General's Office
20 Victoria Street
London, SW1H 0NF
Tel: 020 7271 2492

Attorney-General for England and Wales:
The Rt Hon Michael Ellis QC MP

UK Government's chief advisor on Northern Ireland law (as Advocate-General for Northern Ireland).

Department for Business, Energy and Industrial Strategy
1 Victoria Street
London, SW1H 0ET
Tel: 020 7215 5000

Secretary of State for Business, Energy and Industrial Strategy: The Rt Hon Kwasi Kwarteng MP

Business; industrial strategy; science; innovation; energy and climate change.

COP26 President:
The Rt Hon Alok Sharma MP

Glasgow was chosen by the UK to host COP26 in November 2021.

Ministry for Housing, Communities and Local Government
2 Marsham Street
London, SW1P 4DF
Tel: 0303 444 0000

Secretary of State for Housing, Communities and Local Government: The Rt Hon Robert Jenrick MP

Regulation of architects.

Northern Ireland at Westminster | Northern Ireland Yearbook

Department for Digital, Culture, Media and Sport (DCMS)
100 Parliament Street
London, SW1A 2BQ
Tel: 020 7211 6000

Secretary of State for Digital, Culture, Media and Sport:
The Rt Hon Oliver Dowden MP

Broadcasting; National Lottery; telecommunications.

Ministry of Defence (MoD)
Whitehall
London, SW1A 2HB
Tel: 020 7218 9000

Secretary of State for Defence:
The Rt Hon Ben Wallace MP

Department for Education
Piccadilly Gate, Store Street
Manchester, M1 2WD
Tel: 0370 000 2288

Secretary of State for Education:
The Rt Hon Gavin Williamson MP

Department for Environment, Food and Rural Affairs (Defra)
Nobel House
17 Smith Square
London, SW1P 3JR
Tel: 03459 33 55 77

Secretary of State for Environment, Food and Rural Affairs:
The Rt Hon George Eustice MP

Foreign and Commonwealth Office (FCO)
King Charles Street
London, SW1A 2AH
Tel: 020 7008 1500

Secretary of State for Foreign and Commonwealth Affairs:
The Rt Hon Dominic Raab MP

Department of Health and Social Care
3-9 Victoria Street
London, SW1H 0EU
Tel: 020 7210 4850

Secretary of State for Health:
The Rt Hon Matt Hancock MP

Home Office
2 Marsham Street
London, SW1P 4DF
Tel: 020 7035 4848

Secretary of State for the Home Department:
The Rt Hon Priti Patel MP

Asylum, immigration and nationality; borders; counter-terrorism (international); drug classification; passports.

Department for International Trade
22 Whitehall
London, SW1A 2EG
Tel: 020 7023 0000

Secretary of State for International Trade:
The Rt Hon Elizabeth Truss MP

Ministry of Justice (MoJ)
102 Petty France
London, SW1H 9AJ
Tel: 020 3334 3555

Secretary of State for Justice & Lord Chancellor:
The Rt Hon Robert Buckland MP

Access to information; judicial appointments; National Archives; Supreme Court.

Office of the Leader of the House of Commons
70 Whitehall
London, SW1A 2AS
Tel: 020 7276 1005

Leader of the House of Commons & Lord President of the Council:
The Rt Hon Jacob Rees-Mogg MP

Office of the Leader of the House of Lords
Room 20, Principal Floor
West Front, House of Lords
London, SW1A 2AS
Tel: 020 7219 3200

Leader of the House of Lords & Lord Privy Seal: The Rt Hon The Baroness Evans of Bowes Park

Northern Ireland Office (NIO)
1 Horse Guards Road
London, SW1A 2HQ

Stormont House, Belfast, BT4 3SH
Switchboard: 028 9052 0700
Email: comms@nio.gov.uk

Secretary of State for Northern Ireland:
The Rt Hon Brandon Lewis MP

Electoral policy; oversight of political process and devolution; parading; regulation of political parties.

Scotland Office
1 Melville Crescent
Edinburgh, EH3 7HW
Tel: 0131 244 9010

Secretary of State for Scotland:
The Rt Hon Alister Jack MP

Department for Transport
Great Minster House
33 Horseferry Road
London, SW1P 4DR
Tel: 0300 330 3000

Secretary of State for Transport:
The Rt Hon Grant Shapps MP

Civil aviation; marine navigation and rescue; shipping; vehicle registration and licensing.

HM Treasury
1 Horse Guards Road
London, SW1A 2HQ
Tel: 020 7270 5000

Chancellor of the Exchequer:
The Rt Hon Rishi Sunak MP

Currency; customs; financial markets and services; taxation; UK Budget.

Wales Office
1 Caspian Point, Caspian Way
Cardiff, CF10 4DQ
Tel: 029 2092 4216

Secretary of State for Wales:
The Rt Hon Simon Hart MP

Department for Work and Pensions (DWP)
Caxton House, Tothill Street
London, SW1H 9NA
Tel: 020 7340 4000

Secretary of State for Work and Pensions:
The Rt Hon Thérèse Coffey MP

Child benefit; national insurance; national minimum wage.

Northern Ireland Yearbook | Northern Ireland at Westminster

Belfast East

Candidate elected:	Gavin Robinson
Eligible electorate:	66,245
Votes polled:	42,619
Valid votes:	42,450
Invalid votes:	169
Turnout:	**64.34%**

Candidate	Description	Votes Polled	% vote
Naomi Long	APNI	19,055	44.9
Carl Christian McClean	UUP	2,516	5.9
Gavin Robinson*	**DUP**	**20,874**	**49.2**

*Sitting MP

Belfast South

Candidate elected:	Claire Hanna
Eligible electorate:	69,984
Votes polled	47,527
Valid votes:	47,352
Invalid votes:	172
Turnout:	**67.91%**

Candidate	Description	Votes Polled	% vote
Paula Jane Bradshaw	APNI	6,786	14.3
Claire Hanna	**SDLP**	**27,079**	**57.2**
Michael Henderson	UUP	1,259	2.7
Emma Little Pengelly*	DUP	11,678	24.7
Chris McHugh	Aontú	550	1.2

*Sitting MP

Belfast North

Candidate elected:	John Finucane
Eligible electorate:	72,225
Votes polled:	49,425
Valid votes:	49,037
Invalid votes:	388
Turnout:	**68.43%**

Candidate	Description	Votes Polled	% vote
Nigel Dodds*	DUP	21,135	43.1
John Finucane	**Sinn Féin**	**23,078**	**47.1**
Gemma Weir	The Workers Party	4,824	9.8

*Sitting MP

Belfast West

Candidate elected:	Paul Maskey
Eligible electorate:	65,644
Votes polled:	38,988
Valid votes:	38,782
Invalid votes:	206
Turnout:	**59.39%**

Candidate	Description	Votes Polled	% vote
Gerry Carroll	PBPA	6,194	16
Monica Digney	Aontú	1,635	4.2
Paul Doherty	SDLP	2,985	7.7
Donnamarie Higgins	APNI	1,882	4.9
Paul Maskey*	**Sinn Féin**	**20,866**	**53.8**
Frank McCoubrey	DUP	5,220	13.5

*Sitting MP

Northern Ireland at Westminster

East Antrim

Candidate elected:	Sammy Wilson
Eligible electorate:	64,830
Votes polled:	37,431
Valid votes:	37,261
Invalid votes:	170
Turnout:	57.74%

Candidate	Description	Votes Polled	% vote
Steve Aiken	UUP	5,475	14.7
Danny Donnelly	APNI	10,165	27.3
Oliver McMullan	Sinn Féin	2,120	5.7
Angela Mulholland	SDLP	902	2.4
Philip George Randle	Green Party	685	1.8
Aaron Rankin	Conservative and Unionist	1,043	2.8
Sammy Wilson*	DUP	16,871	45.3

*Sitting MP

East Londonderry

Candidate elected:	Gregory Campbell
Eligible electorate:	69,246
Votes polled:	39,495
Valid votes:	39,302
Invalid votes:	193
Turnout:	57.04%

Candidate	Description	Votes Polled	% vote
Gregory Campbell*	DUP	15,765	40.1
Richard John Holmes	UUP	3,599	9.2
Cara Hunter	SDLP	6,158	15.7
Chris McCaw	APNI	5,921	15.1
Seán McNicholl	Aontú	1,731	4.4
Dermot Nicholl	Sinn Féin	6,128	15.6

*Sitting MP

Fermanagh and South Tyrone

Candidate elected:	Michelle Gildernew
Eligible electorate:	72,848
Votes polled:	51,087
Valid votes:	50,762
Invalid votes:	324
Turnout:	70.13%

Candidate	Description	Votes Polled	% vote
Matthew Beaumont	APNI	2,650	5.2
Tom Elliott	UUP	21,929	43.2
Adam Gannon	SDLP	3,446	6.8
Michelle Gildernew*	Sinn Féin	21,986	43.3
Caroline Wheeler	Independent	751	1.5

*Sitting MP

Foyle

Candidate elected:	Colum Eastwood
Eligible electorate:	74,346
Votes polled:	47,370
Valid votes:	47,144
Invalid votes:	226
Turnout:	63.72%

Candidate	Description	Votes Polled	% vote
Colum Eastwood	SDLP	26,881	57
Rachel Ferguson	APNI	1,267	2.7
Darren Guy	UUP	1,088	2.3
Shaun Harkin	PBPA	1,332	2.8
Elisha McCallion*	Sinn Féin	9,771	20.7
Anne McCloskey	Aontú	2,032	4.3
Gary Middleton	DUP	4,773	10.1

*Sitting MP

Lagan Valley

Candidate elected:	Jeffrey Donaldson
Eligible electorate:	75,735
Votes polled:	45,589
Valid votes:	45,405
Invalid votes:	184
Turnout:	60.20%

Candidate	Description	Votes Polled	% vote
Robbie Butler	UUP	8,606	19
Jeffrey Donaldson*	DUP	19,586	43.1
Sorcha Eastwood	APNI	13,087	28.8
Ally Haydock	SDLP	1,758	3.9
Gary Hynds	Conservative and Unionist	955	2.1
Alan Love	UKIP	315	0.7
Gary McCleave	Sinn Féin	1,098	2.4

*Sitting MP

Mid Ulster

Candidate elected:	Francie Molloy
Eligible electorate:	70,449
Votes polled:	44,968
Valid votes:	44,620
Invalid votes:	348
Turnout:	63.83%

Candidate	Description	Votes Polled	% vote
Mel Boyle	APNI	3,526	7.9
Keith Buchanan	DUP	10,936	24.5
Denise Johnston	SDLP	6,384	14.3
Francie Molloy*	Sinn Féin	20,473	45.9
Conor Rafferty	Independent	690	1.5
Neil Richardson	UUP	2,611	5.9

*Sitting MP

Newry and Armagh

Candidate elected:	Mickey Brady
Eligible electorate:	81,226
Votes polled:	51,120
Valid votes:	50,779
Invalid votes:	341
Turnout:	62.94%

Candidate	Description	Votes Polled	% vote
Mickey Brady*	Sinn Féin	20,287	40
Pete Byrne	SDLP	9,449	18.6
Jackie Coade	APNI	4,211	8.3
William Irwin	DUP	11,000	21.7
Martin Kelly	Aontú	1,628	3.2
Sam Nicholson	UUP	4,204	8.3

*Sitting MP

North Antrim

Candidate elected:	Ian Paisley
Eligible electorate:	77,134
Votes polled:	44,355
Valid votes:	44,051
Invalid votes:	304
Turnout:	57.50%

Candidate	Description	Votes Polled	% vote
Margaret McKillop	SDLP	2,943	6.7
Cara McShane	Sinn Féin	5,632	12.8
Patricia O'Lynn	APNI	6,231	14.1
Ian Paisley*	DUP	20,860	47.4
Stephen Palmer	Independent	246	0.6
Robin Swann	UUP	8,139	18.5

*Sitting MP

North Down

Candidate elected:	Stephen Farry
Eligible electorate:	67,099
Votes polled:	40,842
Valid votes:	40,643
Invalid votes:	172
Turnout:	**60.87%**

Candidate	Description	Votes Polled	% vote
Alan Chambers	UUP	4,936	12.1
Alex Easton	DUP	15,390	37.9
Stephen Farry	**APNI**	**18,358**	**45.2**
Matthew Robinson	Conservative and Unionist	1,959	4.8

*Sitting Ind MP not among candidates

South Down

Candidate elected:	Chris Hazzard
Eligible electorate:	79,175
Votes polled:	49,971
Valid votes:	49,762
Invalid votes:	209
Turnout:	**63.11%**

Candidate	Description	Votes Polled	% vote
Paul Brady	Aontú	1,266	2.5
Patrick Brown	APNI	6,916	13.9
Glyn Hanna	DUP	7,619	15.3
Chris Hazzard*	**Sinn Féin**	**16,137**	**32.4**
Jill Macauley	UUP	3,307	6.6
Michael Gerard Savage	SDLP	14,517	29.2

*Sitting MP

South Antrim

Candidate elected:	Paul Girvan
Eligible electorate:	71,711
Votes polled:	43,188
Valid votes:	42,974
Invalid votes:	214
Turnout:	**60.23%**

Candidate	Description	Votes Polled	% vote
John Blair	APNI	8,190	19.1
Paul Girvan*	**DUP**	**15,149**	**35.3**
Declan Kearney	Sinn Féin	4,887	11.4
Danny Kinahan	UUP	12,460	29
Roisin Lynch	SDLP	2,288	5.3

*Sitting MP

Strangford

Candidate elected:	Jim Shannon
Eligible electorate:	66,928
Votes polled:	37,669
Valid votes:	37,485
Invalid votes:	175
Turnout:	**56.28%**

Candidate	Description	Votes Polled	% vote
Grant Abraham	Conservative and Unionist	1,476	3.9
Kellie Armstrong	APNI	10,634	28.4
Joe Boyle	SDLP	1,994	5.3
Ryan Carlin	Sinn Féin	555	1.5
Maurice Macartney	Green Party	790	2.1
Jim Shannon*	**DUP**	**24,036**	**62**
Philip Smith	UUP	4,023	10.7
Robert Stephenson	UKIP	308	0.8

*Sitting MP

Upper Bann

Candidate elected:	Carla Lockhart
Eligible electorate:	82,887
Votes polled:	50,348
Valid votes:	50,045
Invalid votes:	303
Turnout:	60.74%

Candidate	Description	Votes Polled	% vote
Doug Beattie	UUP	6,197	12.4
Dolores Kelly	SDLP	4,623	9.2
Carla Lockhart	DUP	20,501	41
John O'Dowd	Sinn Féin	12,291	24.6
Eóin Tennyson	APNI	6,433	12.9

*Sitting DUP MP not among candidates

West Tyrone

Candidate elected:	Órfhlaith Begley
Eligible electorate:	66,259
Votes polled:	41,375
Valid votes:	41,186
Invalid votes:	189
Turnout:	62.44%

Candidate	Description	Votes Polled	% vote
Órfhlaith Begley*	Sinn Féin	16,544	40.2
Thomas Buchanan	DUP	9,066	22
Stephen Donnelly	APNI	3,979	9.7
Susan Glass	Green Party	521	1.3
James Hope	Aontú	972	2.4
Daniel McCrossan	SDLP	7,330	17.8
Andy McKane	UUP	2,774	6.7

*Sitting MP

Social Media Belfast Conference

Speakers: Paul McGarrity, Octave Digital; Michelle Baird, Ulster Orchestra; Mark Quinn, Guide Dogs NI; Aoife McGuigan, Suntory Beverage & Food Ireland and Chris Barnes, Public Health Agency.

The seventh annual Social Media Belfast Conference recently took place as a hybrid event in September 2021. The event is Northern Ireland's leading social media event and brought together an excellent line up of social media experts both local and visiting to share their knowledge and examples of successful campaigns.

A massive thank you to all speakers and delegates who joined us, both in the Europa Hotel, Belfast and virtually, who helped bring #SMBelfast to life across all social media channels and made the conference a huge success!

We have already started brainstorming for 2022! If you are interested in sponsoring, exhibiting or sharing your experiences as a speaker please do get in touch with the event director Fiona McCarthy, **Fiona.McCarthy@agendani.com**. Follow us on Twitter **@agendani** for all the latest information.

Speakers: Susie Brown, Northern Ireland Assembly; Paul McGarrity, Octave Digital and Steven O'Riordan, Department of Housing, Local Government and Heritage.

Dylan Burke, Honeycomb Jobs with Emma Sharkey, Mash Direct Ltd.

Speaker: John Hart, Sport Northern Ireland.

Andrew McFarline and Kristian Ross, Northern Ireland Housing Executive.

Francesca Woodman and Colleen Rainey, Power NI.

The 2021 Social Media Belfast crowd.

Northern Ireland Yearbook

Government Departments

The Executive Office
www.executiveoffice-ni.gov.uk

Department of Agriculture, Environment and Rural Affairs
www.daera-ni.gov.uk

Department for Communities
www.communities-ni.gov.uk

Department of Education
www.education-ni.gov.uk

Department for the Economy
www.economy-ni.gov.uk

Department of Finance
An Roinn Airgeadais
www.finance-ni.gov.uk

Department of Health
An Roinn Sláinte
Männystrie O Poustie
www.health-ni.gov.uk

Department for Infrastructure
An Roinn Bonneagair
www.infrastructure-ni.gov.uk

Department of Justice
www.justice-ni.gov.uk

Government Departments

The governance of Northern Ireland

Responsibility for the governance of Northern Ireland is divided between the devolved Northern Ireland Assembly at Stormont and the United Kingdom Parliament at Westminster. Most social and economic policy is set by the Northern Ireland Executive, a power-sharing coalition government drawn from the Assembly.

The Executive has the power to make decisions on transferred matters – i.e. those which have not been retained by Parliament – and delivers policy through the nine Northern Ireland Civil Service departments.

Departments and a brief summary of key responsibilities are as follows:

The Executive Office (TEO)
Policy co-ordination, external relations, equality, victims.

Department of Agriculture, Environment & Rural Affairs (DAERA)
Includes environmental protection, water, land, angling, animal health and welfare, waste, countryside management, EU exit, marine and pollution.

Department for Communities (DfC)
Includes housing, benefits and pensions, support for children, regeneration, local government, PRONI, arts and culture, sport, museums and libraries.

Department of Education (DE)
Education up to age 19, children and young people issues, schools and infrastructure.

Department for the Economy (DfE)
Economic policy, energy, employment and skills programmes, tourism, higher and further education, consumer affairs, employment rights and telecoms.

Department of Finance (DoF)
Includes finance, procurement, NICS, property rating and valuation, land registration, Ordnance Survey of NI, programme and project management and assurance.

Department of Health (DoH)
Includes policy, dentistry, mental health, governance, workforce, pharmacy, public health policy and advice, safety, and social services.

Department of Justice (DoJ)
Justice and the law, policing, courts, prisons, legal aid, forensic science and youth justice.

Department for Infrastructure (DfI)
Includes roads, transport, public transport, waterways, ports, planning, rivers and flooding.

The United Kingdom Government is accountable to Parliament and sets policy on non-devolved matters, which can be further sorted into excepted and reserved matters.

Excepted matters are areas of major constitutional and financial policy, and are the exclusive responsibility of Westminster.

Key excepted matters are:
- international relations;
- defence;
- taxation;
- the constitution.

Reserved matters are dealt with at Westminster but can be devolved with the consent of Parliament. Decisions on some social and economic policy areas are taken centrally as a common national policy is considered the best approach.

These include:
- shipping;
- civil aviation;
- postal services;
- telecommunications;
- broadcasting.

Policing and criminal justice powers were reserved to Westminster in March 1972, when direct rule was introduced, and most were devolved to the Assembly on 12 April 2010. Some justice-related matters — i.e. national security, counterterrorism, extradition and drug classification — remain reserved or excepted.

Northern Ireland Office

The Secretary of State for Northern Ireland represents the region's interests at Cabinet level and the UK Government's interests in Northern Ireland. He leads the Northern Ireland Office (NIO), which oversees the devolution settlement.

Secretary of State:
Rt Hon Brandon Lewis MP
Appointed: February 2020

Responsibilities: Overall direction and control of NIO, constitutional issues, relations with the Executive and Assembly, national security in Northern Ireland, UK Government's approach to the legacy of the Troubles.

Minister of State for Northern Ireland:
Conor Burns MP
Appointed: September 2021

Parliamentary Under Secretary of State:
Lord Caine is the Government's chief spokesman on Northern Ireland affairs in the House of Lords.

Law officers
Attorney-General:
Brenda King

The Attorney-General for Northern Ireland is the chief legal advisor to the Executive. She is independent of government and may participate but not vote in the Assembly's proceedings. Brenda King was appointed to the post on August 2020.

Advocate-General:
The Rt Hon Suella Braverman QC MP

The Advocate-General for Northern Ireland advises the UK Government on Northern Ireland law. The post is held by the Attorney-General for England and Wales, who is a government minister. The Rt Hon Suella Braverman QC MP was a QC MP was appointed in 2020.

The Executive Office (TEO)

The Executive Office
Stormont Castle
Stormont, Belfast, BT4 3TT
Tel: 028 9037 8055
Web: www.executiveoffice-ni.gov.uk

First Minister:
Paul Givan MLA

deputy First Minister:
Michelle O'Neill MLA

Principal Private Secretary (First Minister):
Deirdre Griffith
Tel: 028 9037 8221
Email: deirdre.griffith@executiveoffice-ni.gov.uk

Private Secretary (First Minister):
Karen Wilson
Tel: 028 9037 8222
Email: karen.wilson@executiveoffice-ni.gov.uk

Principal Private Secretary (deputy First Minister):
Donal Moran
Tel: 028 9037 8234
Email: donal.moran@executiveoffice-ni.gov.uk

Private Secretary (deputy First Minister):
Paula Magill
Tel: 028 9037 8235
Email: paula.magill@executiveoffice-ni.gov.uk

Junior Ministers:
Gary Middleton MLA
Declan Kearney MLA

Head of the NI Civil Service:
Jayne Brady
Tel: 028 9037 8133
Email: HOCS@executiveoffice-ni.gov.uk

Permanent Secretary:
Denis McMahon
Tel: 028 9037 8116
Email: perm.sec@executiveoffice-ni.gov.uk

Office of the Head of the Civil Service
Private Secretary and Head of Office: Roisin Coleman
Tel: 028 9037 8143

The Executive Office

The vision of TEO is to build a peaceful and prosperous society with respect for the rule of law where everyone can enjoy a better quality of life now and in years to come.

Underpinning this vision, the overall aim of TEO is to contribute to and oversee the co-ordination of Executive policies and programmes to deliver a peaceful, fair, equal and prosperous society.

TEO's vision and aim are supported through the following key functions and objectives:

- the effective operation of the institutions of government in the delivery of an agreed PfG;
- delivering the Executive's Good Relations strategy: Together: Building a United Community (T:BUC);
- tackling disadvantage and promoting equality of opportunity; and
- driving investment and sustainable development, including promotion of the Executive's policy interests internationally.

The work of the department includes the following functions:

Support to the Executive and the institutions of government

Head of the Civil Service Office

Office of the Legislative Counsel

Programme for Government (PfG) and Executive Support

Executive and Central Advisory Division

- Assembly and Legislation Section;
- Executive Secretariat;
- Machinery of Government;
- Intergovernmental Relations Team; and
- Information Management and Central Advisory Branch.

Government Departments | Northern Ireland Yearbook

The Executive Office

www.executiveoffice-ni.gov.uk

The Executive Office organisation chart

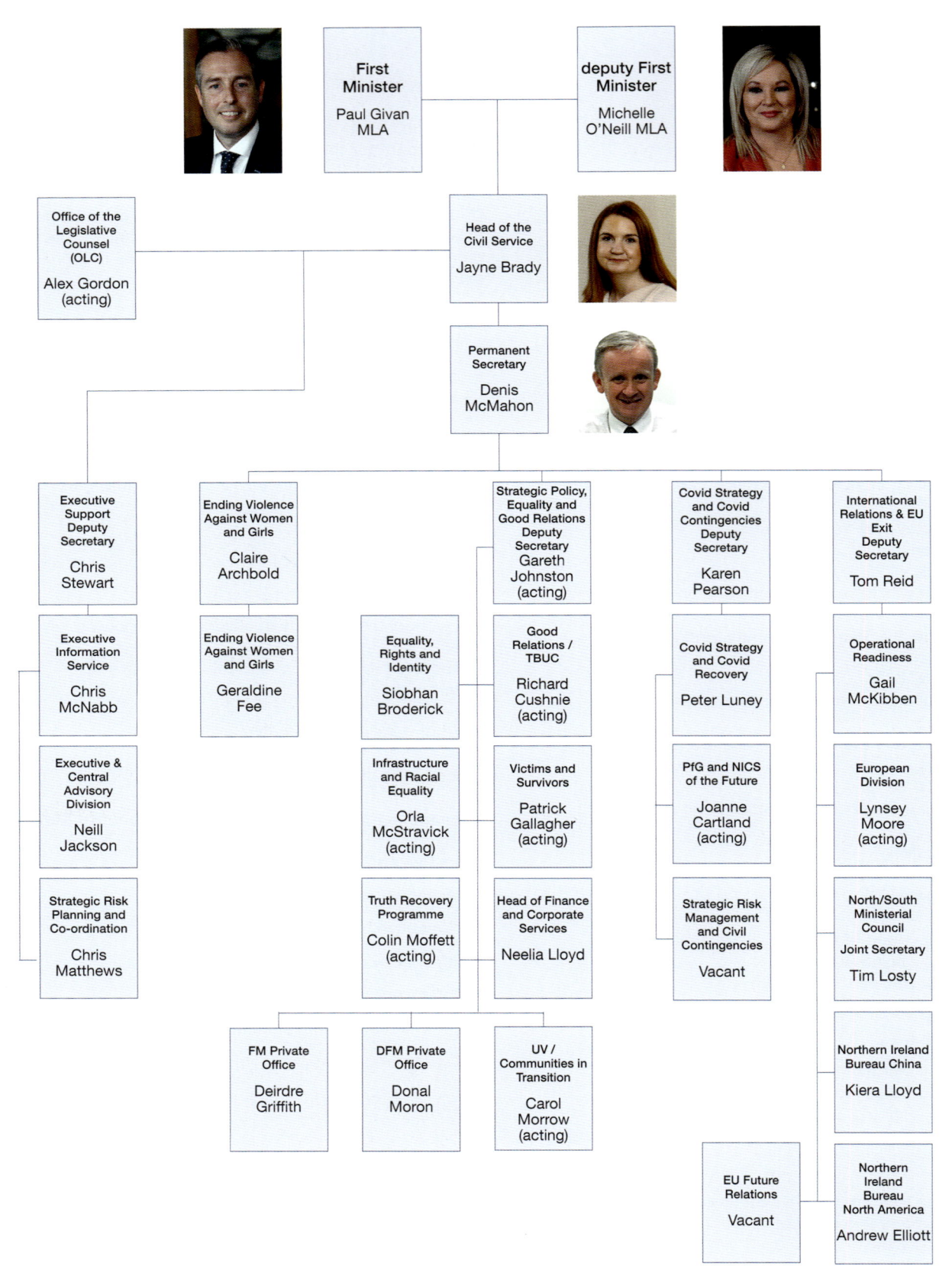

- **First Minister**: Paul Givan MLA
- **deputy First Minister**: Michelle O'Neill MLA
- **Head of the Civil Service**: Jayne Brady
- **Permanent Secretary**: Denis McMahon
- **Office of the Legislative Counsel (OLC)**: Alex Gordon (acting)

Executive Support Deputy Secretary: Chris Stewart
- Executive Information Service: Chris McNabb
- Executive & Central Advisory Division: Neill Jackson
- Strategic Risk Planning and Co-ordination: Chris Matthews

Ending Violence Against Women and Girls: Claire Archbold
- Ending Violence Against Women and Girls: Geraldine Fee

Strategic Policy, Equality and Good Relations Deputy Secretary: Gareth Johnston (acting)
- Equality, Rights and Identity: Siobhan Broderick
- Infrastructure and Racial Equality: Orla McStravick (acting)
- Truth Recovery Programme: Colin Moffett (acting)
- Good Relations / TBUC: Richard Cushnie (acting)
- Victims and Survivors: Patrick Gallagher (acting)
- Head of Finance and Corporate Services: Neelia Lloyd
- FM Private Office: Deirdre Griffith
- DFM Private Office: Donal Moron
- UV / Communities in Transition: Carol Morrow (acting)

Covid Strategy and Covid Contingencies Deputy Secretary: Karen Pearson
- Covid Strategy and Covid Recovery: Peter Luney
- PfG and NICS of the Future: Joanne Cartland (acting)
- Strategic Risk Management and Civil Contingencies: Vacant
- EU Future Relations: Vacant

International Relations & EU Exit Deputy Secretary: Tom Reid
- Operational Readiness: Gail McKibben
- European Division: Lynsey Moore (acting)
- North/South Ministerial Council Joint Secretary: Tim Losty
- Northern Ireland Bureau China: Kiera Lloyd
- Northern Ireland Bureau North America: Andrew Elliott

84 — Government Departments

The Executive Office
www.executiveoffice-ni.gov.uk

Executive Information Service
Strategic Planning and Co-ordination

Strategic Policy, Equality and Good Relations
- Victims and Survivors;
- Good Relations and T:BUC;
- Urban Villages and Communities in Transition;
- Equality Rights and Identity;
- FM Private Office;
- dFM Private Office;
- Infrastructure and Racial Equality; and
- Finance and Corporate Services.

International Relations and EU Exit
- EU Future Relations;
- Operational Readiness;
- North South Ministerial Council;
- Northern Ireland Bureau in North America;
- European Division and Office of the Northern Ireland Executive in Brussels; and
- Northern Ireland Bureau in China.

Covid Strategy and Covid Contingencies
- Covid Strategy and Covid Recovery;
- Strategic Risk Management and Civil Contingencies; and
- Programme for Government and NICS of the Future.

Office of the Legislative Counsel
First Legislative Counsel: Alex Gordon (acting)
Tel: 028 9037 8176
Email: alexander.gordon@executiveoffice-ni.gov.uk

Executive Support Directorate
Director: Chris Stewart
Tel: 028 9037 8651
Email: chris.stewart@executiveoffice-ni.gov.uk

Executive and Central Advisory Division
Head of Division: Neill Jackson
Tel: 028 9037 8149
Email: neill.jackson@executiveoffice-ni.gov.uk

Executive Information Service
Head of Communications: Chris McNabb
Tel: 028 9037 8003
Email: chris.mcnabb@executiveoffice-ni.gov.uk

Strategic Policy, Equality and Good Relations Directorate
Director: Gareth Johnston (acting)
Tel: 028 9052 8204
Email: gareth.johnston@executiveoffice-ni.gov.uk

Victims and Survivors Division
Head of Division: Patrick Gallagher (acting)
Tel: 028 9052 6807
Email: patrick.gallagher@executiveoffice-ni.gov.uk

Good Relations and T:BUC Division
Head of Division: Richard Cushnie (acting)
Tel: 028 9052 8531
Email: richard.cushnie@executiveoffice-ni.gov.uk

Equality Rights and Identity Division
Head of Division: Siobhan Broderick
Tel: 028 5052 8351
Email: siobhan.broderick@executiveoffice-ni.gov.uk

Urban Villages and Communities in Transition Division
Head of Division: Carol Morrow (acting)
Tel: 028 9052 8351
Email: carol.morrow@executiveoffice-ni.gov.uk

Infrastructure and Racial Equality Division
Head of Division: Orla McStravick (acting)
Tel: 028 9052 8153
Email: orla.mcstravick@executiveoffice-ni.gov.uk

Finance and Corporate Services Division
Head of Division: Neelia Lloyd
Tel: 028 9052 0553
Email: neelia.lloyd@executiveoffice-ni.gov.uk

Strategy on Violence Against Women and Girls
Director: Claire Archbold
Email: claire.archbold@executiveoffice-ni.gov.uk

Head of Division: Geraldine Fee
Email: geraldine.fee@executiveoffice-ni.gov.uk

International Relations and EU Exit
Director: Tom Reid
Tel: 028 9037 8155
Email: tom.reid@executiveoffice-ni.gov.uk

The International Relations Group aims to promote Northern Ireland overseas and develop mutually beneficial relationships with targeted countries, regions and organisations to secure investment, trade, tourism and to exchange knowledge and expertise.

The Executive Office
www.executiveoffice-ni.gov.uk

The Group is also responsible for coordinating the Executive's response to the UK's exit from the EU including supporting and advising Ministers and senior officials in North/South, East/West and European engagements, in the implementation of both the Withdrawal Agreement and the Future Relationship agreement; ensuring effective communication across Departments on issues relating to EU Exit; consideration of the implications for Northern Ireland legislation and post EU exit arrangements.

Operational Readiness:
Gail McKibbin
Tel: 028 9037 8075
Email: gail.mckibbin@executiveoffice-ni.gov.uk

European Division and Office of the Northern Ireland Executive in Brussels
Director: Lynsey Moore (acting)
Tel: 00 322 290 1342
Email: lynsey.moore@executiveoffice-ni.gov.uk

North South Ministerial Council
Joint Secretariat
58 Upper English Street
Armagh, BT61 7LG

Joint Secretary: Tim Losty
Deputy Joint Secretary: Richard Hill
Tel: 028 3751 5008
Email: tim.losty@executiveoffice-ni.gov.uk

Northern Ireland Bureau North America
Director: Andrew Elliott
Tel: 001 202 340 3363
Email: aelliott@nibureau.com

NI Bureau in China
Director: Kiera Lloyd
Tel: +86 105 192 4119
Email: nibchina@nics.gov.uk
kiera.lloyd@fco.gov.uk

Covid Strategy and Covid Contingencies Directorate
Director: Karen Pearson
Tel: 028 9037 8155
Email: karen.pearson@executiveoffice-ni.gov.uk

Covid Strategy and Covid Recovery Division
Head of Division: Peter Luney
Tel: 028 9041 2282
Email: peter.luney@executiveoffice-ni.gov.uk

PfG and NICS of the Future Division:
Head of Division: Joanne Cartland (acting)
Tel: 028 9052 3415
Email: joanne.cartland@executiveoffice-ni.gov.uk

Strategic Risk Management and Civil Contingencies
Head of Division: Vacant

TEO Agencies, Non-Departmental Public Bodies and other organisations

Commission for Victims and Survivors for Northern Ireland
4th Floor, Equality House
7-9 Shaftesbury Square
BT2 7DP
Tel: 028 9031 1000
Web: www.cvsni.org
Email: commission@cvsni.org
Commissioner: Vacant
Chief Executive: Andrew Sloan

Commissioner for Public Appointments for Northern Ireland
Dundonald House, Annexe B
Stormont Estate
Upper Newtownards Road
Belfast, BT4 3SB
Tel: 028 9052 4820
Web: www.publicappointmentsni.org
Email: info@publicappointmentsni.org
Commissioner: Vacant

Commissioner for Survivors of Institutional Childhood Abuse
5th Floor South
Queen's Court
56-66 Upper Queen Street
Belfast, BT1 6FD
Tel: 028 9054 4985
Email: info@cosica-ni.org
Commissioner: Fiona Ryan

NI Community Relations Council
2nd Floor, Equality House
7-9 Shaftesbury Square
Belfast, BT2 7DB
Tel: 028 9022 7500
Web: www.community-relations.org.uk
Chair: Martin McDonald
Chief Executive: Jacqueline Irwin

Equality Commission for Northern Ireland
Equality House
7-9 Shaftesbury Square
Belfast, BT2 7DP
Tel: 028 9050 0600
Web: www.equalityni.org
Email: information@equalityni.org
Chief Commissioner: Geraldine McGahey
Chief Executive: Evelyn Collins

Government Departments

Maze / Long Kesh Development Corporation
Halftown Road
Lisburn, BT27 5RN
Tel: 028 9250 1806
Email: contact@mazelongkesh.com
Interim Chief Executive: Bryan Gregory

Northern Ireland Judicial Appointments Commission
Headline Building
10-14 Victoria Street
Belfast, BT1 3GG
Tel: 028 9056 9100
Text phone: 028 9056 9124
Web: www.nijac.co.uk
Email: judicialappointments@nijac.gov.uk
Chair:
Lady Chief Justice The Right Honourable Dame Siobhan Keegan
Chief Executive: Tonya McCormac

Office of the Attorney General for Northern Ireland
PO Box 1272
Belfast, BT1 9LU
Tel: 028 9072 5333
Web: www.attorneygeneralni.gov.uk
Email: contact@attorneygeneralni.gov.uk
Attorney General: Brenda King

Strategic Investment Board Limited
5th Floor
9 Lanyon Place
Belfast, BT1 3LP
Tel: 028 9025 0900
Web: www.sibni.org
Email: contact@sibni.org
Chair: Gerry McGinn
Chief Executive: Brett Hannam

Victims and Survivors Service
1st Floor, Seatem House
28-32 Alfred Street
Belfast, BT2 8EN
Tel: 028 9027 9100
Email: enquiries@vssni.org
Chair: Oliver Wilkinson
Chief Executive: Margaret Bateson

Press office contacts

Heads of Press Office can be contacted as follows:

The Executive Office
Contact: Erin Craig and Libby Kinney
Tel: 028 9037 8207
Email: libby.kinney@executiveoffice-ni.gov.uk/
erin.craig@executiveoffice-ni.gov.uk

The Executive Office
www.executiveoffice-ni.gov.uk

Department of Agriculture, Environment and Rural Affairs
Contact: Joanne McCauley
Tel: 028 9052 4243
Email: joanne.mccauley@daera-ni.gov.uk

Department of Education
Contact: Clare Baxter
Tel: 028 9127 9772
Email: clare.baxter@education-ni.gov.uk

Department for the Economy
Contact: Ronan Henry
Tel: 028 9052 9611
Email: ronan.henry@economy-ni.gov.uk

Department of Finance
Contact: Ciarrai Conlon
Tel: 028 9081 6724
Email: ciarrai.conlon@finance-ni.gov.uk

Department of Health
Contact: Karina Meredith
Tel: 028 9052 0636
Email: karina.meredith@health-ni.gov.uk

Department of Justice
Contact: Karen Fullerton
Tel: 028 9052 6250
Email: karen.fullerton@justice-ni.x.gsi.gov.uk

Department for Infrastructure
Contact: Aine Gaughran
Tel: 028 9054 0817
Email: aine.gaughran@infrastructure-ni.gov.uk

Department for Communities
Contact: Gareth Bannon
Tel: 028 9082 3500
Email: gareth.bannon@communities-ni.gov.uk

Government Advertising Unit
Contact: Kathryn Napier/Catherine Heron
Tel: 028 9037 8208
Email: kathryn.napier@finance-ni.gov.uk /
catherine.heron@finance-ni.gov.uk

NI Direct
Contact: Philip Maguire
Tel: 028 9089 4604
Email: philip.maguire@finance-ni.gov.uk

Better together: Joined up working is key to a better future

The Commission's Chief Executive Andrew Sloan with Belfast US Consul General, Paul Narain.

The Commission was established as a non-departmental Public Body in May 2008 under legislation known as The Victims and Survivors (Northern Ireland) Order 2006.

Working under the sponsorship of The Executive Office, the Commission's role is to address the needs of victims and survivors of the Troubles, promote their interests and advise government on issues that help to reconcile Northern Ireland's divisions and build towards a better future.

Since August 2020, the Commission has operated without an appointed Commissioner.

There is no denying this presented its challenges in some regard; the very legal powers the office is founded on lie with that appointee. However, not a team to be deterred, the Commission, led by its Chief Executive, Andrew Sloan, seized the opportunity to reflect on how the office can work better at an operational level in the interests of those touched by Northern Ireland's violence.

From committee appearances and engagements around legacy issues with local, national and international policy influencers, to creatively exploring engaging ways to promote European Union PEACE IV-funded research, 2021 has laid some strong foundations for Northern Ireland's future.

Getting creative

During the summer, the Commission partnered with the Northern Ireland Housing Executive and Big Telly Theatre Company to produce part-installation, part-theatre piece, 'The House'.

Hosted at both Féile an Phobail and East Side Arts festivals, the event held a mirror up to the human experience in an ethical and trauma-informed way and encouraged reflection of personal contributions towards healing and a reconciled future.

Speaking at the time, Jennifer Hawthorne, Head of the Housing Executive's Belfast Region had said: "Innovative artistic projects like this can help us form a much better understanding of who we are and what our communities have experienced historically."

Sloan added: "'The House' demonstrated that feelings of hurt, loss, addiction and resilience are universal. Irrespective of backgrounds, political views or countless other things that may divide us, there is always common ground in human emotion."

This move towards artistic and creative expression is something the Commission are incredibly keen to take further in the years ahead.

A quarter of us

Very little in our society doesn't relate in some way to past and ongoing divisions. Yet conversations around victims and survivors are often viewed as being separate to the broader work of reconciliation. There can be a notion that those who witnessed or experienced harm are ringfenced in a particular sector.

"This isn't the case," says Sloan. "As recently as this year, we carried out a population survey which found around a quarter of our population meet that legal definition of a victim. Yet only a fraction of those access support through community based organisations.

"This survey left no doubt as to the far-reaching impact the Troubles have had; they span communities, jurisdictions and generations."

So, what have the Commission done to bring as many voices and experiences as possible into shaping government policy and decision-making on ways forward?

Departmental champions

In October 2021, the Commission gave evidence to The Executive Office Committee.

Focusing on key themes of education, health, community planning and economic development, they asked Committee members to support a more

Actors Niall Cusack and Jonny Cameron play a grandfather and grandson debating conflict legacy in production, 'The House'.

collaborative approach in working practice and the formal inclusion of victims and survivors' voices by establishing departmental champions on victims' issues.

Models for such a way of working already exist with race equality, disability and gender champions. The Commission are of the strong view that 'victim-proofing' by combining efforts and sharing expertise across government and the community and voluntary sectors, can help our society break the cycles of trauma, negative coping strategies and divisions we currently experience.

Speaking of the economic impact of Covid, Sloan states: "I have little doubt that we will see departmental budgets and funding streams tighten in the years ahead. It is imperative we find a way to share learning and expedite initiatives that seek to deliver real change."

The Commission are currently working with local councils and authorities to determine how similar cohesiveness can be considered at every level of government.

A new government strategy

Also drawing to a close in 2021, were key pieces of research funded by the EU's PEACE IV Programme, as managed by the Special EU Programmes Body (SEUPB).

The findings and recommendations of these will be a cornerstone in the development and delivery of a new 10-year Victims' Strategy.

Twenty-three years after the signing of the Belfast Good Friday Agreement, the Commission, The Executive Office and others are currently in a co-design process, developing a Strategy that meets the contemporary needs of victims and survivors.

EU funding provided the opportunity to expand the scope of research to Great Britain and the Republic of Ireland and capture voices and experiences that, in the past, have been underrepresented and needs left unmet.

Sloan continued: "The reality for those who lived through the worst of the violence is that we need to get this new Strategy right if those affected by the past are to feel empowered and supported in their journey moving forwards. We all want to see a future where the violence doesn't define us. It is not about forgetting the past, but about growing from it and healing.

"Promoting Northern Ireland, strategic investment and regeneration are heavily reliant on prolonged and sustainable peace. So too is incentivising our young people to see a worthwhile future with the best standard of living available to them.

"We have to put our hands up and say, 'I have something to bring to that.' It's the only way we gain enough momentum to keep going forward," concludes Sloan.

T: 028 9031 1000
E: commission@cvsni.org
W: www.cvsni.org

Department of Agriculture, Environment and Rural Affairs (DAERA)

Department of Agriculture, Environment and Rural Affairs
www.daera-ni.gov.uk

Dundonald House
Upper Newtownards Road
Ballymiscaw
Belfast, BT4 3SB
Tel: 028 9052 4999
Web: www.daera-ni.gov.uk

Minister: Edwin Poots MLA

Permanent Secretary:
Anthony Harbinson
Tel: 028 9052 4608
Email: anthony.harbinson@daera-ni.gov.uk

Private Office
Head of Private Office and Private Secretary:
Jonathan McFerran
Tel: 028 9052 0808
Email: jonathan.mcferran@daera-ni.gov.uk

The Department of Agriculture, Environment and Rural Affairs (DAERA) has responsibility for food, farming, environmental, fisheries, forestry and sustainability policy and the development of the rural sector in Northern Ireland. The Department assists the sustainable development of the agri-food, environmental, fishing and forestry sectors of the Northern Ireland economy, having regard for the needs of the consumers, the protection of human, animal and plant health, the welfare of animals and the conservation and enhancement of the environment, which helps deliver the Department's vision of a living, working active landscape valued by everyone.

DAERA provides a business development service for farmers and growers and a veterinary service for administration of animal health and welfare. The Department's College of Agriculture, Food and Rural Enterprise (CAFRE) delivers training and further and higher education courses in the agri-food sector. DAERA is responsible to the Department of the Environment, Food and Rural Affairs (Defra) in Great Britain for the administration of schemes affecting the whole of the United Kingdom. The Department also oversees the application of European Union agricultural, environmental, fisheries and rural development policy to Northern Ireland.

Press Office
Principal Information Officer: Joanne McCauley
Tel: 028 9052 4243
Email: joanne.mccauley@daera-ni.gov.uk

Central Services and Contingency Planning Group
Deputy Secretary: Brian Doherty
Tel: 028 7744 2252
Email: brian.doherty@daera-ni.gov.uk

Digital Services Division
Head of Division: Paul McGurnaghan
Tel: 028 9052 4999
Email: paul.mcgurnaghan@daera-ni.gov.uk

Data Protection and Information Management Branch
Head of Branch: Philip Gilmore
Tel: 028 7744 2350
Email: philip.gilmore@daera-ni.gov.uk

DAERA Data Protection Officer:
Philip Gilmore
Tel: 028 7744 2350
Email: dataprotectionofficer@daera-ni.gov.uk

Digital Transformation Unit
Head of Unit: Philip Spence
Tel: 028 9052 5015
Email: philip.spence@daera-ni.gov.uk

Digital Portfolio Management Branch
Head of Branch: Deirdre Mussen
Tel: 028 9052 0818
Email: deirdre.mussen@daera-ni.gov.uk

Digital Programme Support Office
Head of Branch: Noel McDonnell
Tel: 028 7131 9828
Email: noel.mcdonnell@daera-ni.gov.uk

Digital Programme Governance Branch
Head of Branch: Oliver McWilliams
Tel: 028 7744 2237
Email: oliver.mcwilliams@daera-ni.gov.uk

Information Management Unit
Head of Unit: Geraldine Devine
Tel: 028 7744 2227
Email: geraldine.devine@daera-ni.gov.uk

Science Digital Support Unit
Head of Unit: Gerry Hackett
Tel: 028 9052 0843
Email: gerry.hackett@daera-ni.gov.uk

Food, Farming and Forestry Digital Systems Branch
Head of Branch: Padraig McAuley
Tel: 028 9052 4036
Email: padraig.mcauley@daera-ni.gov.uk

Department of Agriculture, Environment and Rural Affairs (DAERA) organisation chart

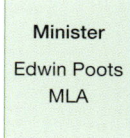

Minister: Edwin Poots MLA

Permanent Secretary: Anthony Harbinson

Northern Ireland Environment Agency Group
Tracey Teague (acting) — Chief Executive

- **Resource Efficiency** — Keith Bradley (acting)
- **Natural Environment NIEA** — Helen Anderson

Rural Affairs, Forest Service and Estate Transformation Group
Fiona McCandless — Deputy Secretary

- **Forest Service** — John Joe O'Boyle
- **Rural Affairs** — David Reid
- **Estate Transformation** — Alison Caldwell

Central Services and Contingency Planning Group
Brian Doherty — Deputy Secretary

- **Digital Services** — Paul McGurnaghan
- **Corporate Services** — Sharon McFlynn
- **NIFAIS** — Nigel Trimble
- **Staff Engagement, Equality and Diversity** — Pauline Keegan
- **Brexit Operational Readiness** — Mark Livingstone
- **Finance** — Roger Downey

Food and Farming Group
Norman Fulton — Deputy Secretary

- **College of Agriculture, Food & Rural Enterprise** — Martin McKendry
- **Policy, Economics and Statistics** — Seamus McErlean
- **Area Based Schemes** — Jason Foy
- **Brexit** — Rosemary Agnew
- **Sustainable Agri-food Development** — Colette McMaster
- **Science, Evidence and Innovation Policy** — Alistair Carson

Veterinary Service Animal Health Group
Robert Huey — Deputy Secretary

- **Enzootic Disease & Animal Welfare** — Michael Hatch
- **International Trade Facilitation** — Perpetua McNamee
- **Animal Health and Welfare Policy** — Neal Gartland
- **Veterinary Public Health, Portal Controls and Imports** — Brian Dooher

Environment, Marine and Fisheries Group
Tracey Teague — Deputy Secretary

- **Regulatory and Natural Resources Division** — Dave Foster
- **EU Transition** — John Mills
- **Environmental Policy** — Colin Breen
- **Marine and Fisheries** — Owen Lyttle
- **Green Growth and Climate Action** — Arron Wright (acting)

Department of Agriculture, Environment and Rural Affairs

www.daera-ni.gov.uk

Environment, Marine and Fisheries Digital Systems Branch
Head of Branch: Joanna McDonald
Tel: 028 9054 2166
Email: joanna.mcdonald@daera-ni.gov.uk

Digital Enterprise Services Branch
Head of Branch: Esther McMaster
Tel: 028 9076 5867
Email: esther.mcmaster@daera-ni.gov.uk

Veterinary Service Digital Systems Branch
Head of Branch: Leanne Mills
Tel: 028 9056 9625
Email: leanne.mills@daera-ni.gov.uk

NIFAIS Division
Head of Division: Nigel Trimble
Tel: 028 9052 4621
Email: nigel.trimble@daera-ni.gov.uk

NIFAIS Related Business Change
Head of Branch: Shane Collins
Tel: 028 3752 9091
Email: shane.collins@daera-ni.gov.uk

Staff Engagement, Equality and Diversity Division
Director of Staff Engagement, Equality and Diversity:
Pauline Keegan
Tel: 028 9052 4586
Email: pauline.keegan@daera-ni.gov.uk

Staff Engagement, Equality and Diversity Branch
Head of Branch: Colin Campbell (Wellbeing, Equality, Diversity and Inclusion) /
Chris Conway (Engagement and Leadership)
Tel: 028 7744 2046/028 9037 8596
Email: colin.campbell@daera-ni.gov.uk/
chris.conway@daera-ni.gov.uk

Corporate Services Division
Director of Corporate Services: Sharon McFlynn
Email: sharon.mcflynn@daera-ni.gov.uk

Central Management Branch
Head of Branch: Kathryn Clarke
Tel: 028 9052 4189
Email: kathryn.clarke@daera-ni.gov.uk

Media Services Branch
Head of Branch: Joanne McCauley
Tel: 028 9052 4243
Email: joanne.mccauley@daera-ni.gov.uk

Business Management Branch
Head of Branch: Marc Little
Tel: 028 7744 2385
Email: marc.little@daera-ni.gov.uk

Health and Safety Coordination Branch
Head of Branch: Lorrayne Simmons
Tel: 028 9052 0811
Email: lorrayne.simmons@daera-ni.gov.uk

ALB Corporate Sponsor and Public Appointments Branch
Head of Branch: Paddy Griffin
Tel: 028 9076 5396
Email: patrick.griffin@daera-ni.gov.uk

AFBI Sponsor Branch
Head of Branch: Ashley McGinnis
Tel: 028 7744 2316
Email: ashley.mcginnis@daera-ni.gov.uk

Brexit Operational Readiness Division
Director of Brexit Operational Readiness/Food Supply Security:
Mark Livingstone
Tel: 028 9056 9363
Email: mark.livingstone@daera-ni.gov.uk

Operational Readiness
Head of Branch: Nicole McArthur
Tel: 028 7744 2315
Email: nicole.mcarthur@daera-ni.gov.uk

Food Security Supply
Head of Branch: Brian Luke
Tel: 028 9056 9436
Email: brian.luke@daera-ni.gov.uk

Programme Management Office
Head of Branch: Patricia Walsh
Tel: 028 7129 0097
Email: patricia.walsh@daera-ni.gov.uk

Finance Division
Director of Finance: Roger Downey
Tel: 028 9052 4800
Email: roger.downey@daera-ni.gov.uk

Deputy Director of Finance: Declan McCarney
Tel: 028 9052 0915
Email: declan.mccarney@daera-ni.gov.uk

Financial Planning Branch
Head of Branch: Lynda Lowe
Tel: 028 9052 4585
Email: lynda.lowe@daera-ni.gov.uk

Strategic Planning Branch
Head of Branch: Briege Lafferty
Tel. 028 7744 2029
Email: briege.lafferty@daera-ni.gov.uk

Governance and EU Funding Branch
Head of Branch: Angela Millar
Tel: 028 9052 82466
Email: angela.millar@daera-ni.gov.uk

Department of Agriculture, Environment and Rural Affairs
www.daera-ni.gov.uk

Financial Reporting and Systems Branch
Head of Branch: Sharon O'Neill
Tel: 028 7744 2020
Email: sharonc.o'neill@daera-ni.gov.uk

Central Government Transformation Programme – Finance Workstream
Head of Branch: Tony Cooke
Tel: 028 9037 8390
Email: tony.cooke@daera-ni.gov.uk

Programme and Project Support Office (PPSO)
Head of Branch: Richard McAuley
Tel: 028 7744 2375
Email: richard.mcauley@daera-ni.gov.uk

European Services Branch (ESB)
Head of Branch: Leahann Donnelly
Tel: 028 9052 24186
Email: leahann.donnelly@daera-ni.gov.uk

Internal Audit Branch
Head of Branch: Alan McKee
Tel: 028 9052 0082
Email: alan.mckee@daera-ni.gov.uk

Rural Affairs, Forest Service, Estate Transformation, Brexit Operational Readiness and Food Supply Security
Deputy Secretary: Fiona McCandless
Tel: 028 7744 2306
Email: fiona.mccandless@daera-ni.gov.uk

DAERA Estate Transformation Division
Head of Division: Alison Caldwell
Tel: 028 7744 9336
Email: alison.caldwell@daera-ni.gov.uk

DAERA Estate Transformation Division
Head of Sub Division: Ambrose Tohill
Tel: 028 7744 2395
Email: ambrose.tohill@daera-ni.gov.uk

Project Delivery and Maintenance Branch
Head of Branch: Matthew Yeates
Tel: 028 7744 5139
Email: matthew.yeates@daera-ni.gov.uk

Estate Sustainability and Energy Efficiency Branch
Head of Branch: David O'Neill
Tel: 028 774 45126
Email: david.o'neill@daera-ni.gov.uk

Estate Transformation, Support and Development
Head of Branch: Claire McAllister
Tel: 028 7131 9748
Email: claire.mcallister@daera-ni.gov.uk

Office Estate and Resourcing
Head of Branch: Sheila Walker
Tel: 028 905 24162
Email: sheila.walker@daera-ni.gov.uk

Rural Affairs Division
Director of Rural Affairs: David Reid
Tel: 028 7744 2053
Email: davidp.reid@daera-ni.gov.uk

Sustainable Rural Communities
Head of Branch: Niall Heaney
Tel: 028 9076 5869
Email: niall.heaney@daera-ni.gov.uk

Rural Affairs West
Head of Branch: Gerard Treacy (acting)
Tel: 028 8225 3504
Email: gerard.treacy@daera-ni.gov.uk

Rural Affairs North
Head of Branch: Maria Bradley
Tel: 028 9052 4107
Email: maria.bradley@daera-ni.gov.uk

Rural Affairs South
Head of Branch: Jerome Burns
Tel: 028 3025 3259
Email: jerome.burns@daera-ni.gov.uk

Rural Affairs Division Corporate Services
Head of Branch: Joseph Kerr
Tel: 028 9076 5346
Email: joseph.kerr@daera-ni.gov.uk

Rural Affairs Division Customer Services Branch
Head of Branch: John White
Tel: 028 7131 9976
Email: john.white@daera-ni.gov.uk

Forest Service
Chief Executive: John Joe O'Boyle
Tel: 028 6634 3086
Email: johnjoe.o'boyle@daera-ni.gov.uk

Corporate Services
Head of Branch: Damian Larkin
Tel: 028 6634 3193
Email: damian.larkin@daera-ni.gov.uk

Forest Management and Inspection
Head of Branch: John Joe Cassidy
Tel: 028 4372 1279
Email: johnjoe.cassidy@daera-ni.gov.uk

Forest Policy, Regulation and Development
Head of Branch: Richard Schaible
Tel: 028 9052 4469
Email: richard.schaible@daera-ni.gov.uk

Department of Agriculture, Environment and Rural Affairs

www.daera-ni.gov.uk

Plant Health Inspection
Head of Branch: Jim Crummie
Tel: 028 9052 4426
Email: jim.crummie@daera-ni.gov.uk

Plant Health Policy and Legislation
Head of Branch: Diane Stevenson
Tel: 028 6634 3012
Email: diane.stevenson@daera-ni.gov.uk

Food and Farming Group
Deputy Secretary: Norman Fulton
Tel: 028 9052 4655
Email: norman.fulton@daera-ni.gov.uk

Brexit Division
Head of Division: Rosemary Agnew
Tel: 028 9052 4074
Email: rosemary.agnew@daera-ni.gov.uk

The Division is responsible for a programme of work linked to the end of the Transition Period and the strategic direction of the Department in terms of Future Agricultural Policy.

Brexit Secondary Legislation Team
Head of Branch: Kevin Murphy
Tel: 028 7744 2184
Email: kevin.murphy@daera-ni.gov.uk

Transition Programme / Ireland – Northern Ireland Protocol
Head of Branch: Catherine Coll (acting)
Tel: 028 9052 4369
Email: catherine.coll@deara-ni.gov.uk

Operational Preparedness / Ireland – Northern Ireland Protocol
Head of Branch: Diane Black (acting)
Tel: 028 9037 8387
Email: diane.blackl@deara-ni.gov.uk

DAERA Brussels Office
Head of Branch: Ciara Reynolds
Tel: 00 322 290 1337
Email: ciara.reynolds@daera-ni.gov.uk

Frameworks
Head of Branch: Julie-Ann Moorhead
Tel: 028 9076 5316
Email: julie-ann.moorhead@daera-ni.gov.uk

College of Agriculture, Food and Rural Enterprise (CAFRE)
The College is responsible for the delivery of education, training, knowledge transfer and innovation programmes to those entering or already working in the agri-food industry. Through these programmes CAFRE assists the competitive development of the industry and the sustainability of the rural economy.

CAFRE
Head of Division: Martin McKendry
Tel: 028 9442 6600
Email: martin.mckendry@daera-ni.gov.uk

College Services Branch
Head of Branch: Alan McCartney
Email: alan.mccartney@daera-ni.gov.uk

Education Service
Head of Service: James O'Boyle (acting)
Tel: 028 9442 6608
Email: james.o'boyle@daera-ni.gov.uk

Equine Branch
Head of Branch: Seamus McAlinney
Tel: 028 6634 4855
Email: seamus.mcalinney@daera-ni.gov.uk

Food Education Branch
Head of Branch: Shane McKinney
Tel: 028 8676 8242
Email: shane.mckinney@daera-ni.gov.uk

Agriculture Education Branch
Head of Branch: George Moffett
Tel: 028 9442 6633
Email: george.moffett@daera-ni.gov.uk

Horticulture Branch
Head of Branch: Paul Mooney
Tel: 028 9442 6675
Email: paul.mooney@daera-ni.gov.uk

Knowledge and Technology Transfer Operational Policy Branch
Head of Branch: Ian McCluggage
Tel: 028 9442 6760
Email: ian.mccluggage@daera-ni.gov.uk

Knowledge Advisory Service
Head of Service: Eric Long
Tel: 028 9442 6620
Email: eric.long@daera-ni.gov.uk

Food Technology Branch
Head of Branch: Peter Simpson
Tel: 028 8676 8130
Email: peter.simpson@daera-ni.gov.uk

Beef and Sheep Branch
Head of Branch: Paul McHenry
Tel: 028 9442 6922
Email: paul.mchenry@daera-ni.gov.uk

Dairy, Pigs, Poultry and Crops Branch
Head of Branch: Don Morrow
Tel: 028 9442 6845
Email: don.morrow@daera-ni.gov.uk

Department of Agriculture, Environment and Rural Affairs
www.daera-ni.gov.uk

Sustainable Land Management Branch
Head of Branch: Alan Galbraith
Tel: 028 9442 6853
Email: alan.galbraith@daera-ni.gov.uk

Agri-Business Branch
Head of Branch: Fiona Dickson
Tel: 028 9442 6941
Email: fiona.dickson@daera-ni.gov.uk

Policy, Economics and Statistics Division
The Division is responsible for the collation, analysis and publication of a broad range of statistics in relation to agriculture, environment, rural communities and the food sector. The Division provides economic analysis and advice as well as leading on the development, coordination and management of policy in relation to negotiations on free trade agreements and migration policy. The Division is policy lead for the Department's education and skills policy and also acts as Managing Authority for the NI Rural Development Programme (NIRDP) which includes monitoring and evaluation responsibilities as well as providing advice to the Department and its Arm's Length Bodies on State Aid requirements.

Policy, Economics and Statistics Division
Head of Division: Seamus McErlean
Tel: 028 9052 4675
Email: seamus.mcerlean@daera-ni.gov.uk

Policy Development Branch
Head of Branch: Zita Hale
Tel: 028 9037 8511
Email: zita.hale@daera-ni.gov.uk

CAP Reform, Brexit and Trade Policy Branch
Head of Branch: Mark McLean
Tel: 028 9052 4342
Email: mark.mclean@daera-ni.gov.uk

Future Partnerships Branch
Head of Branch: Carol O'Boyle
Tel: 028 9037 8520
Email: carol.oboyle@daera-ni.gov.uk

Strategic Economic Advice Branch
Head of Branch: Hazel Quinn
Tel: 028 9052 5010
Email: hazel.quinn@daera-ni.gov.uk

Resource Economics
Head of Branch: Jenny Hobson
Tel: 028 9052 24927
Email: jenny.hobson@daera-ni.gov.uk

Statistics and Analytical Services
Head of Branch: Maire Brolly
Tel: 028 9037 8346
Email: maire.brolly@daera-ni.gov.uk

Economics and Evaluation
Head of Branch: Paul Keatley
Tel: 028 9052 4063
Email: paul.keatley@daera-ni.gov.uk

Brexit Analysis and State Aid Policy Branch
Head of Branch: Brenda McGuigan
Tel: 028 9037 8591
Email: brenda.mcguigan@daera-ni.gov.uk

Rural Development
The Division exists to implement EU and Government rural development policies and programmes with the aim of achieving a thriving and sustainable rural community.

Rural Development Programme Management
Head of Branch: Alison Cranney
Tel: 028 9052 4355
Email: alison.cranney@daera-ni.gov.uk

Sustainable Agri-Food Development Division
The Division is responsible for the development of Departmental policies, legislation and programmes which support sustainable development of the agri-food Sector, including preparations for the end of the Transition Period and implementation of the Ireland/Northern Ireland Protocol. It also delivers a range of Rural Development Programme Schemes and other initiatives and provides policy support to a number of Arm's Length Bodies, including the Livestock and Meat Commission (LMC).

Director: Colette McMaster
Tel: 028 9052 4670
Email: colette.mcmaster@daera-ni.gov.uk

Deputy Director: Louise Millsopp
Tel: 028 7744 2057
Email: louise.millsopp@daera-ni.gov.uk

Agri-Food Brexit Policy I
Head of Branch: Elaine McCrory
Tel: 028 9052 4372
Email: elaine.mccrory@daera-ni.gov.uk

Agri-Food Brexit Policy II/Horse Racing (Amendment) Bill Team
Head of Branch: John Terrington
Tel: 028 9037 8510
Email: john.terrington@daera-ni.gov.uk

Agri-Food Brexit Policy III
Head of Branch: Samantha Swann
Tel: 028 9085 8039
Email: samantha.swann@daera-ni.gov.uk

Agri-Food Policy I
Head of Branch: Nichola Connery
Tel: 028 9052 4396
Email: nichola.connery@daera-ni.gov.uk

Department of Agriculture, Environment and Rural Affairs

www.daera-ni.gov.uk

Agri-Food Policy II
Head of Branch: Stephen Johnston
Tel: 028 9052 4804
Email: stephen.johnston@daera-ni.gov.uk

Future Capital Support Policy
Head of Branch: Brenda Cunning
Tel: 028 9052 4009
Email: brenda.cunning@daera-ni.gov.uk

Agri-food Support Branch
Head of Branch: Albert Johnston
Tel: 028 9442 6948
Email: albert.johnston@daera-ni.gov.uk

Pillar II Capital Investment
Head of Branch: Michael McLean
Tel: 028 9052 4578
Email: michael.mclean@daera-ni.gov.uk

Future Food Policy Branch
Head of Branch: Joy Alexander
Tel: 028 8676 8132
Email: joy.alexander@daera-ni.gov.uk

Science, Evidence and Innovation Policy
Head of Division: Alistair Carson
Tel: 028 9052 4391
Email: alistair.carson@daera-ni.gov.uk

Science Transformation Programme
Head of Branch: Pauline Rooney
Tel: 028 9052 4287
Email: pauline.rooney@daera-ni.gov.uk

Strategic Science Policy Project
Head of Branch: Katie Devlin
Tel: 028 9076 5370
Email: katie.devlin@daera-ni.gov.uk

Monitoring Science and Surveillance Evidence Project
Head of Branch: Thomas Gaston
Tel: 028 7744 9119
Email: thomas.gaston@daera-ni.gov.uk

Animal Health Sciences Building Project
Head of Branch: Janet Uhlemann
Tel: 028 9052 4231
Email: janet.uhlemann@daera-ni.gov.uk

Science and Innovation Strategy Project
Head of Branch: Michael Moorhead
Tel: 028 9052 5037
Email: michael.moorhead@daera-ni.gov.uk

Change Management Branch
Head of Branch: Caoimhe Treanor
Tel: 028 9052 0912
Email: caoimhe.treanor@daera-ni.gov.uk

Chief Scientific Advisers Office
Head of Branch: Paul Devine
Tel: 028 7744 2178
Email: paul.devine2@daera-ni.gov.uk

Research and Governance Programme
Head of Branch: Sharon O'Neill
Tel: 028 7744 2001
Email: sharon.o'neill@daera-ni.gov.uk

Area-based Schemes
The Division exists to deliver Direct Payments and other area-based schemes within the UK and EU integrated administration and control framework.

Area Based Schemes Division
Head of Division: Jason Foy
Tel: 028 7744 2363
Email: jason.foy@daera-ni.gov.uk

Area-based Schemes Delivery Unit
This unit exists to deliver financial support to farmers through Area-based schemes. It has responsibility for the development and delivery of processes and systems to support the application, administration and payments for all Area-based schemes.

Head of Area-based Schemes Delivery Unit:
Teresa O'Neill (acting)
Tel: 028 7131 9720
Email: teresa.o'neill@daera-ni.gov.uk

Area-based Schemes Delivery Support Branch
Head of Branch: Glenda Whiteside
Tel: 028 7131 9839
Email: glenda.whiteside@daera-ni.gov.uk

Area-based Schemes Operational Policy Branch
Head of Branch: Gregor Kerr
Tel: 028 7744 2163
Email: gregor.kerr@daera-ni.gov.uk

Area-based Schemes Systems Management Branch
Head of Branch: Noel McDonnell (acting)
Tel: 028 7131 9828
Email: noel.mcdonnell@daera-ni.gov.uk

Area-based Schemes Payments Branch
Head of Branch: John McGrath (acting)
Tel: 028 7131 9982
Email: john.mcgrath@daera-ni.gov.uk

Area-based Schemes Development Branch
Head of Branch: Anne-Marie McCosker
Tel: 028 7129 9001
Email: anne-marie.mccosker@daera-ni.gov.uk

Department of Agriculture, Environment and Rural Affairs
www.daera-ni.gov.uk

Countryside Management Unit

Countryside Management Unit ensures compliance with and control of DAERA's Area-based schemes to ensure that the correct payment is issued to eligible farm businesses. This includes carrying out inspections and the maintenance of a GIS Land Parcel Identification System (LPIS). The Unit also delivers DAERA's agri-environment schemes to mitigate climate change and enhance the environment. The Unit is currently reviewing cross compliance, land eligibility and the inspection processes and advancing the use of new technologies to assist in the Unit's work.

Head of Countryside Management Unit:
Lynne Martin (acting)
Tel: 028 2566 2813
Email: lynne.martin@daera-ni.gov.uk

Countryside Management Inspectorate Branch
Head of Branch: Manus McHenry
Tel: 028 2566 2829
Email: manus.mchenry@daera-ni.gov.uk

ASD Business Support Branch
Head of Branch: Roisin Quinn (acting)
Tel: 028 8675 7630
Email: roisin.quinn@daera-ni.gov.uk

Controls and Assurance Development Branch
Head of Branch: David Gillespie (acting)
Tel: 028 9052 4071
Email: david.gillespie@daera-ni.gov.uk

Countryside Management Delivery Branch
Head of Branch: Herbie Jones
Tel: 028 8675 7605
Email: herbie.jones@daera.ni.gov.uk

Integrated Controls Branch
Head of Branch: Jeanelle Cooke (acting)
Tel: 028 2566 2851
Email: jeanelle.cooke@daera-ni.gov.uk

Land Parcel Identification Systems Management Branch
Head of Branch: Wilma McMaster (acting)
Tel: 028 8765 7648
Email: wilma.mcmaster@daera-ni.gov.uk

Environment, Marine and Fisheries Group

The Environment, Marine and Fisheries Group is made up of the following:

- Environmental Policy Division;
- EU Transition Division;
- Regulatory and Natural Resources Policy Division;
- Marine and Fisheries Division; and
- Green Growth and Climate Action Division.

Deputy Secretary: Tracey Teague
Tel: 028 9056 9350
Email: tracey.teague@daera-ni.gov.uk

EMFG/NIEA Governance and Complaints Unit
Head of Branch: Brian Lamont
Tel: 028 9056 9726
Email: brian.lamont@daera-ni.gov.uk

Environmental Policy Division
Head of Division: Colin Breen
Tel: 028 7744 2343
Email: colin.breen@daera-ni.gov.uk

Head of Waste Policy: Michael McCallion (acting)
Tel: 028 9056 9509
Email: michael.mccallion@daera-ni.gov.uk

Single-Use Plastic, Waste Prevention and Recycling
Head of Branch: Rachael Hook (acting)
Tel: 028 7744 2087
Email: rachael.hook@daera-ni.gov.uk

Climate Change Bill Teams (2 teams)
Head of Branch: Arlene McGowan
Tel: 028 9056 9484
Email: arlene.mcgowan@daera-ni.gov.uk

Head of Branch: Anthony Courtney
Tel: 028 9056 9485
Email: anthony.courtney@daera-ni.gov.uk

Waste Framework, SUP Legislation and Environmental Liability
Head of Branch: Philip McMurray (acting)
Tel: 028 9056 9585
Email: philip.mcmurray@daera-ni.gov.uk

Climate Change Bill Team
Head of Branch: Arlene McGowan
Tel: 028 9056 9484
Email: arlene.mcgowan@daera-ni.gov.uk

Waste Framework and Environmental Liability
Head of Branch: Anthony Courtney
Tel: 028 9056 9485
Email: anthony.courtneyms@daera-ni.gov.uk

Radioactivity and Contaminated Land
Head of Branch: Alison Jeynes
Tel: 028 9056 9761
Email: alison.jeynes@daera-ni.gov.uk

Programme Support Team
Head of Branch: John Murray
Tel: 028 9052 4658
Email: john.murray@daera-ni.gov.uk

DAERA MyNI Digital Marketing Team
Head of Branch: Eileen Curry (acting)
Tel: 028 9056 9518
Email: eileen.curry@daera-ni.gov.uk

Department of Agriculture, Environment and Rural Affairs
www.daera-ni.gov.uk

EU Transition Division
Head of Division: John Mills
Tel: 028 9056 9554
Email: john.mills@daera-ni.gov.uk

Assistant Director: Janice Harris
Tel: 028 9056 9530
Email: janice.harris@daera-ni.gov.uk

Environmental Brexit and EU ETS
Head of Branch: Richard Coey
Tel: 028 9056 9787
Email: richard.coey@daera-ni.gov.uk

Waste Strategy
Head of Branch: Roderick Tate (acting)
Tel: 028 9037 8594
Email: roderick.tate@daera-ni.gov.uk

Environment Bill
Head of Branch: Karl Beattie
Tel: 028 9056 9496
Email: karl.beattie@daera-ni.gov.uk

Regulatory and Natural Resources Policy Division
Head of Division: Dave Foster
Tel: 028 9025 4706
Email: dave.foster@daera-ni.gov.uk

Air and Environmental Quality
Head of Branch: Amy Holmes
Tel: 028 9056 9543
Email: amy.holmes@daera-ni.gov.uk

Chemicals and Industrial Pollution Policy
Head of Branch: Caroline Barry (acting)
Tel: 028 9056 9584
Email: caroline.barry@daera-ni.gov.uk

Neighbourhood Environment Quality
Head of Branch: Simon Webb
Tel: 028 9056 9487
Email: simon.webb@daera-ni.gov.uk

Environmental Permitting
Head of Branch: Hazel Bleeks
Tel: 028 9056 9500
Email: hazel.bleeks@daera-ni.gov.uk

Natural Heritage
Head of Branch: Ken Bradley
Tel: 028 9056 9597
Email: ken.bradley@daera-ni.gov.uk

Water Policy, Finance and Co-ordination Team
Head of Branch: Terence Patton
Tel: 028 9056 9483
Email: terence.patton@daera-ni.gov.uk

Water Policy, Finance and Co-ordination Team
Head of Branch: Eamon Campbell
Tel: 028 9056 9483
Email: eamon.campbell@daera-ni.gov.uk

Carrier Bag Levy Team
Head of Branch: Rory O'Boyle
Tel: 028 7744 4225
Email: rory.o'boyle@daera-ni.gov.uk

Agri Emissions and Land Branch
Head of Branch: Peter Scott
Tel: 028 9037 8593
Email: peter.scott@daera-ni.gov.uk

Environmental Farming Branch
Head of Branch: Brian Ervine
Tel: 028 9052 5570
Email: brian.ervine@daera-ni.gov.uk

Ammonia Policy Branch
Head of Branch: Paddy Savage
Tel: 028 9076 5839
Email: patrick.savage@daera-ni.gov.uk

Marine and Fisheries Division
Head of Division: Owen Lyttle
Tel: 028 9056 9593
Email: owen.lyttle@daera-ni.gov.uk

Executive Support, Director's Office
Head of Branch: Mary Toland
Tel: 028 9056 9595
Email: mary.toland@daera-ni.gov.uk

Marine Conservation and Reporting
Head of Branch: Colin Armstrong
Tel: 028 9056 9235
Email: colin.armstrong@daera-ni.gov.uk

Aquaculture and Fish Health Policy Branch
Head of Branch: Donna Lyons (acting)
Tel: 028 4461 8039
Email: donna.lyons@daera-ni.gov.uk

Aquaculture and Fish Health Inspectorate
Head of Branch: David Mercer
Tel: 028 91825841
Email: david.mercer@daera-ni.gov.uk

Monitoring and Assessment
Head of Branch: Tim Mackie (acting)
Tel: 028 9262 3062
Email: tim.mackie@daera-ni.gov.uk

Marine Plan and Coordination
Head of Branch: Hugh Edwards (acting)
Tel: 028 9056 9556
Email: hugh.edwards@daera-ni.gov.uk

Department of Agriculture, Environment and Rural Affairs
www.daera-ni.gov.uk

Marine Licensing
Head of Branch: Diane Black
Tel: 028 9037 8387
Email: diane.black@daera-ni.gov.uk

Marine Strategy
Head of Branch: Claire Vincent
Tel: 028 9056 9250
Email: claire.vincent@daera-ni.gov.uk

Marine Plan
Head of Branch: Marcus McAuley
Tel: 028 9056 9765
Email: marcus.mcauley@daera-ni.gov.uk

Marine Strategy and Licensing
Head of Branch: Joe Breen (acting)
Tel: 028 9056 9828
Email: joe.breen@daera-ni.gov.uk

Sea Fisheries Policy and Grants
Head of Branch: Paddy Campbell
Tel: 028 4461 8007
Email: paddy.campbell@daera-ni.gov.uk

Sea Fisheries Inspectorate
Head of Branch: Mark McCaughan
Tel: 028 4461 8109
Email: mark.mccaughan@daera-ni.gov.uk

Inland Fisheries Inspectorate Delivery
Head of Branch: Seamus Connor
Tel: 028 9056 9465
Email: seamus.connor@daera-ni.gov.uk

Inland Fisheries Policy and Administration
Head of Branch: Damian McCann
Tel: 028 9056 9309
Email: damian.mccann@daera-ni.gov.uk

Fisheries EU Transition Team
Head of Branch: Ciaran Cunningham (acting)
Tel: 028 4461 8053
Email: ciaran.cunningham@daera-ni.gov.uk

Fisheries Bill Team
Head of Branch: David Steele
Tel: 028 9037 8386
Email: david.steele@daera-ni.gov.uk

Green Growth and Climate Action Division
Head of Division: Arron Wright (acting)
Tel: 028 9052 4510
Email: arron.wright@daera-ni.gov.uk

Green Growth Coordination
Head of Branch: Dera Watson
Tel: 029 9052 5030
Email: dera.watson@daera-ni.gov.uk

Green Growth Programme Branch
Head of Branch: Lisa-Jane McIlveen
Tel: 077 6425 4056
Email: lisa-jane.mcilveen@daera-ni.gov.uk

Green Growth Delivery Branch
Head of Branch: Judith Wilson
Tel: 079 7177 7488
Email: judith.wilson@daera-ni.gov.uk

Green Growth Climate Change Adaptation, International and Sustainability
Head of Branch: John Early
Tel: 028 9056 9561
Email: john.early@daera-ni.gov.uk

Green Growth Climate Change Mitigation Branch
Head of Branch: Rosemary McKee
Interim contact: Gordon Bell
Tel: 028 9056 831
Email: gordon.bell@daera-ni.gov.uk

The Northern Ireland Environment Agency (NIEA) Group

The NIEA Group is made up of the following:

- Resource Efficiency Division (NIEA) ;
- Natural Environment Division (NIEA); and
- Green Growth Division.

Deputy Secretary and Chief Executive NIEA
Head of Group: Tracey Teague (acting)
Tel: 028 9056 9210
Email: tracey.teague@daera-ni.gov.uk

EMFG/NIEA Business Support Team
Head of Branch: Peter Aiken
Tel: 028 9056 9275
Email: peter.aiken@daera-ni.gov.uk

Resource Efficiency Division (NIEA)
Head of Division: Keith Bradley (acting)
Tel: 028 9056 9285
Email: keith.bradley@daera-ni.gov.uk

Water Management Unit
Head of Unit: Kerry Anderson (acting)
Tel: 028 9262 3232
Email: kerry.anderson@daera-ni.gov.uk

South and East Catchment Management
Head of Branch: Gareth Greer
Tel: 028 8676 8191
Email: gareth.greer@daera-ni.gov.uk

Department of Agriculture, Environment and Rural Affairs
www.daera-ni.gov.uk

North and West Catchment Management
Head of Unit: Deirdre Quinn
Tel: 028 9262 3132
Email: deirdre.quinn@daera-ni.gov.uk

Water Assessment, Data and Evidence
Head of Branch: Wendy McKinley
Tel: 028 9262 3089
Email: wendy.mckinley@daera-ni.gov.uk

Water Chemistry
Head of Branch: Trudy McMurray
Tel: 028 9262 3025
Email: trudy.mcmurray@daera-ni.gov.uk

Business Group
Head of Branch: Nigel Donald (acting)
Tel: 028 9263 3475
Email: nigel.donald@daera-ni.gov.uk

Business Group
Head of Branch: Jenny Long
Tel: 028 9262 3118
Email: jenny.long@daera-ni.gov.uk

Integrated Catchment Management
Head of Branch: Silke Hartmann
Tel: 028 9262 3068
Email: silke.hartmann@daera-ni.gov.uk

Major Client Interface/Development Management
Head of Branch: Neil McAllister
Tel: 028 9262 3166
Email: neil.mcallister@daera-ni.gov.uk

Regulation Unit
Head of Unit: Theresa Kearney (acting)
Tel: 028 9056 9352
Email: theresa.kearney@daera-ni.gov.uk

Waste Management Licensing
Head of Branch: Brian McVeigh
Tel: 028 9056 9698
Email: brian.mcveigh@daera-ni.gov.uk

Control and Data Management
Head of Branch: Allison Townley
Tel: 028 9056 9313
Email: allison.townley@daera-ni.gov.uk

Water Regulation Team
Head of Branch: Stephanie Millar
Tel: 028 9262 3196
Email: stephanie.millar@daera-ni.gov.uk

Water Regulation Trade and Domestic Consents
Head of Branch: Liz Smyth
Tel: 028 9056 9570
Email: liz.smyth@daera-ni.gov.uk

Waste Permitting
Head of Branch: Colin Millar
Tel: 028 9262 3266
Email: colin.millar@daera-ni.gov.uk

Land, Groundwater and Regulatory Transformation
Head of Branch: Berni Corr (acting)
Tel: 028 9056 9479
Email: berni.corr@daera-ni.gov.uk

Drinking Water Inspectorate
Head of Branch: Catriona Davis
Tel: 028 9056 9294
Email: catriona.davis@daera-ni.gov.uk

Industrial Pollution and Radiochemical Inspectorate
Head of Unit: Gillian Wasson (acting)
Tel: 028 9056 9767
Email: gillian.wasson@daera-ni.gov.uk

COMAH Regulations/PPC/WID
Head of Branch: Phelim Sands
Tel: 028 9262 3263
Email: phelim.sands@daera-ni.gov.uk

Greenhouse Gas Regulation/PPC
Head of Branch: Hugh McGinn
Tel: 028 9056 9304
Email: hugh.mcginn@daera-ni.gov.uk

PPC Agriculture Team
Head of Branch: David Bruce
Tel: 028 9056 9283
Email: david.bruce@daera-ni.gov.uk

Radioactive Substances
Head of Branch: Stephen Wilson (acting)
Tel: 028 9262 3264
Email: stephen.wilson@daera-ni.gov.uk

PPC Regulation
Head of Branch: Philip Cummings
Tel: 028 2558 3063
Email: philip.cummings@daera-ni.gov.uk

Chemicals Regulation
Head of Branch: Helen Lewis
Tel: 028 9056 9400
Email: helen.lewis@daera-ni.gov.uk

Enforcement Branch
Head of Unit: Mark Cherry (acting)
Tel: 028 9056 5415
Email: mark.cherry@daera-ni.gov.uk

Department of Agriculture, Environment and Rural Affairs

www.daera-ni.gov.uk

Environmental Crime Section
Head of Section: Ian Walker (acting)
Tel: 028 9056 9462
Email: ian.walker@daera-ni.gov.uk

Financial Investigation Section
Head of Section: Niall Davey (acting)
Tel: 028 9056 9796
Email: niall.davey@daera-ni.gov.uk

Volume Crime/Incidents and Assessments
Head of Section: John Minnis (acting)
Tel: 028 9056 9343
Email: john.minnis@daera-ni.gov.uk

Natural Environment Division (NIEA)
Head of Division: Helen Anderson
Tel: 028 9056 9207
Email: helen.anderson@daera-ni.gov.uk

Natural Science
Head of Unit: Sara McGuckin
Tel: 028 9056 9375
Email: sara.mcguckin@daera-ni.gov.uk

Land Management
Head of Branch: James Warnock
Tel: 028 9056 9527
Email: james.warnock@daera-ni.gov.uk

Biodiversity
Head of Branch: Richard Gray
Tel: 028 9056 9685
Email: richard.gray@daera-ni.gov.uk

Conservation Science
Head of Branch: Mark Wright
Tel: 028 9056 9648
Email: mark.wright@daera-ni.gov.uk

Air Quality and Biodiversity
Head of Branch: Keith Finegan
Tel: 028 9056 9703
Email: keith.finegan@daera-ni.gov.uk

Conservation Designation and Protection
Head of Branch: Kieran McCavana
Tel: 028 9056 9647
Email: kieran.mccavana@daera-ni.gov.uk

Natural Environment Operations
Head of Unit: Mark Hammond
Tel: 028 9056 9579
Email: mark.hammond@daera-ni.gov.uk

Regional Operations
Head of Branch: Adam Reid
Tel: 028 9056 9446
Email: adam.reid@daera-ni.gov.uk

Future Funding and Partnership
Head of Branch: Pat Corker
Tel: 028 9052 4373
Email: pat.corker@daera-ni.gov.uk

Countryside, Coast and Landscapes
Head of Branch: Oonagh McCann
Tel: 028 9262 3149
Email: oonagh.mccann@daera-ni.gov.uk

Brexit and Operational Change
Head of Branch: Maia Taylor (acting)
Tel: 028 9056 9621
Email: maia.taylor@daera-ni.gov.uk

EMFG Planning Response Team
Head of Branch: Janice Riddell
Tel: 028 9056 9619
Email: janice.riddell@daera-ni.gov.uk

Green Growth Division
Head of Division: Arron Wright (acting)
Tel: 028 9052 4510
Email: arron.wright@daera-ni.gov.uk

Green Growth Coordination
Head of Branch: Dera Watson
Tel: 029 9052 5030
Email: dera.watson@daera-ni.gov.uk

Green Growth Programme Branch
Head of Branch: Lisa-Jane McIlveen
Tel: 077 6425 4056
Email: lisa-jane.mcilveen@daera-ni.gov.uk

Climate Change Adaptation, International and Sustainability
Head of Branch: John Early
Tel: 028 9056 9561
Email: john.early@daera-ni.gov.uk

Climate Change Mitigation Branch
Head of Branch: Vacant
Interim contact: Michael McCallion
Tel: 028 9056 9509
Email: michael.mccallion@daera-ni.gov.uk

Veterinary Service Animal Health Group (VSAHG)

VSAHG is responsible for the development of animal health and welfare policy for both farmed and non-farmed animals, and the implementation of that policy in respect of farmed animals, through the delivery of official controls and other official activities.

VSAHG also delivers official controls and activities in approved slaughterhouses, game handling establishments and co-located cutting plants; and in registered and approved establishments in relation to milk, egg and primary production hygiene on behalf of FSA NI.

Department of Agriculture, Environment and Rural Affairs
www.daera-ni.gov.uk

VSAHG is responsible for policy development and implementation in respect of food animal identification, imports of livestock and products of animal origin into Northern Ireland through ports of entry, and the export of animals and animal products internationally.

VSAHG contributes to DAERA's strategic goal to "Develop sustainable agricultural, fisheries and industrial sectors" by ensuring the health and welfare standards of farmed animals are such that producers have maximum access to all markets, locally and globally, and that production and environmental impacts are minimised.

VSAHG also leads for DAERA by supporting the Executive Office International Relations Strategy.

Veterinary Service Animal Health Group
Deputy Secretary: Robert Huey
Tel: 028 9052 4643
Email: robert.huey@daera-ni.gov.uk

Enzootic Disease and Animal Welfare Division
Head of Division: Michael Hatch
Tel: 028 7744 2319
Email: michael.hatch@daera-ni.gov.uk

PVP and RB Slaughter and Haulage Contract Management
Head of Branch: Emer McGowan
Tel: 028 7744 2388
Email: emer.mcgowan@daera-ni.gov.uk

TB Programme and Contracts, Welfare and Enforcement
Head of Section: Philip Johnston
Tel: 028 8775 4785
Email: philip.johnston@daera-ni.gov.uk

TB Strategy, Veterinary Epidemiology and Wildlife Unit
Head of Section: Raymond Kirke
Tel: 028 9052 0920
Email: raymond.kirke@daera-ni.gov.uk

Veterinary Epidemiology Unit
Head of Branch: Fraser Menzies
Tel: 028 9052 4376
Email: fraser.menzies@daera-ni.gov.uk

Management of Divisional Veterinary Offices and Delivery of Field Work Programmes
Contact: Gemma Daly
Tel: 028 774 42164
Email: gemma.daly@daera-ni.gov.uk

International Trade Facilitation
Head of Division: Dr Perpetua McNamee
Tel: 078 2514 6452
Email: perpetua.mcnamee@daera-ni.gov.uk

Trade Programme Manager (Exports):
Head of Programme: Dr Kirsten Dunbar
Tel: 028 9052 5058
Email: kirsten.dunbar@daera-ni.gov.uk

Trade Technical Support and Training Branch
Head of Branch: Peter Price
Tel: 028 9052 4114
Email: peter.price@daera-ni.gov.uk

Trade Certification and Standards Branch
Head of Branch: Heather Boyd
Tel: 028 9034 0949
Email: heather.boyd@daera-ni.gov.uk

Trade Governance Branch
Head of Branch: Vacant

International Programme
International and Divisional Governance Branch
Head of Branch: Lesley Fay
Tel: 028 9052 5042
Email: lesley.fay@daera-ni.gov.uk

Surveillance and Antimicrobial Resistance
Head of Programme: Owen Denny
Tel: 028 9052 4649
Email: owen.denny@daera-ni.gov.uk

Zoonoses / Medicines / Residues
Main Contact: Frances Kearney
Tel: 028 7744 2069
Email: frances.kearney@daera-ni.gov.uk

Surveillance
Main Contact: Anastasia Georgaki
Tel: 028 7131 9761
Email: anastasia.georgaki@daera-ni.gov.uk

Antimicrobial Resistance
Main Contact: Hilary Glasgow
Tel: 028 6634 3046
Email: hilary.glasgow@daera-ni.gov.uk

Epizootic Disease, Brucellosis, Animal By-Products, TSEs, Contingency Planning, Information & Communication, Animal Identification, Regulatory & Compliance
Head of Programme: Julian Henderson
Tel: 028 7744 2116
Email: julian.henderson@daera-ni.gov.uk

Identification Registration Movement
Main contact: Niall McAuley
Tel: 028 7744 2351
Email: niall.mcauley@daera-ni.gov.uk

TSE/ABP/BR/Epizootics
Head of Branch: Ignatius McKeown
Tel: 028 9052 4978
Email: ignatius.mckeown@daera-ni.gov.uk

Department of Agriculture, Environment and Rural Affairs
www.daera-ni.gov.uk

Contingency Planning for Epizootic Disease (CPED) and Information & Communication Branch (ICB)
Head of Branch: Vacant

Regulatory and Compliance and Cross Compliance
Head of Branch: Elvira McAleese
Tel: 028 7744 2373
Email: elvira.mcaleese@daera-ni.gov.uk

Director of Veterinary Public Health, Portal Controls and Imports Division:
Brian Dooher
Tel: 028 7744 2192
Email: brian.dooher@daera-ni.gov.uk

Veterinary Trade – Imports
Head of Programmes: Vacant

Portal Inspection/Change
Head of Branch: Jonathan Guy
Tel: 028 9037 8555
Email: jonathan.guy@daera-ni.gov.uk

Veterinary Public Health Programme
Manager: Jim McAlister
Tel: 028 2566 2828
Email: jim.mcalister@daera-ni.gov.uk

Manager – Region 1: Philip Kennedy
Tel: 028 7034 1035
Email: philip.kennedy@daera-ni.gov.uk

Manager – Region 2: Laura Wilson
Tel: 028 6634 3102
Email: laura.wilson@daera-ni.gov.uk

Manager – Region 3: Vanessa Whyte
Tel: 028 8775 4833
Email: vanessa.whyte@daera-ni.gov.uk

Manager – Audit and Training : Elaine Graham
(Carla Gongalves currently TP'd into post)
Tel: 028 9034 0934
Email: elaine.graham@daera-ni.gov.uk / carla.goncalves@daera-ni.gov.uk

Trade Manager: Elsie McGarvey
Tel: 028 9034 0931
Email: elsie.mcgarvey@daera-ni.gov.uk

DAERA representative on the UK Office for SPS Trade Assurance Project and Equines
Head of Division: David Cassells
Tel: 028 7744 2218
Email: david.cassell@daera-ni.gov.uk

Agri-Food Inspection
Head of Branch: John Finlay
Tel: 028 9052 4571
Email: john.finlay@daera-ni.gov.uk

Animal Health and Welfare Policy Division
Director: Neal Gartland
Tel: 028 7744 2190
Email: neal.gartland@daera-ni.gov.uk

Animal Health and Welfare, EU Legislation, Transition and Policy
Assistant Director: Naomi Callaghan
Tel: 028 7744 2159
Email: naomi.callaghan@daera-ni.gov.uk

Animal Disease Control and Trade
Assistant Director: Jim Blee
Tel: 028 7744 2074
Email: jim.blee@daera-ni.gov.uk

TB Strategy, BR and TBEP
Assistant Director: Seamus Murray
Tel: 028 9025 4056
Email: seamus.murray@daera-ni.gov.uk

TB/BR Policy and Research
Head of Branch: Lee Williamson
Tel: 028 7744 2137
Email: lee.williamson@daera-ni.gov.uk

TB Strategy Implementation
Head of Branch: Saoirse Kelly
Tel: 028 7744 2143
Email: saoirse.kelly@daera-ni.gov.uk

EU Transition and Legislation
Head of Branch: Darrin Fullerton (acting)
Tel: 028 7744 2310
Email: darrin.fullerton@daera-ni.gov.uk

AHS and TSE
Head of Branch: Colin Wilson
Tel: 028 9052 4476
Email: colin.wilson@daera-ni.gov.uk

Animal Identification and Welfare Branch
Head of Branch: Christopher Andrews
Tel: 028 7744 2067
Email: christopher.andrews@daera-ni.gov.uk

Sanitary and Phyto Sanitary (SPS) Policy and Logistics Division
Director: Catherine Fisher (acting)
Tel: 028 7744 2190
Email: catherine.fisher@daera-ni.gov.uk

SPS Policy Branch
Head of Branch: David Simpson
Tel: 028 7744 2177
Email: david.simpson@daera-ni.gov.uk

Department of Agriculture, Environment and Rural Affairs

www.daera-ni.gov.uk

VSAHG Organisation and Development
Director: David Torrens
Tel: 028 9052 4110
Email: david.torrens@daera-ni.gov.uk

Organisation and Development Programme
Head of Branch: Garry Corscadden (acting)
Tel: 028 3025 3244
Email: garry.corscadden@daera-ni.gov.uk

Business Change / ICT Development (incl APHIS):
Graeme Martin (acting)
Tel: 028 9037 8359
Email: graeme.martin@daera-ni.gov.uk

Business Management
Head of Branch: Anne Humphrys (acting)
Tel: 028 2566 5730
Email: anne.humphrys@daera-ni.gov.uk

Surveillance and Antimicrobial Resistance Division
Head of Division: Owen Denny
Tel: 028 9052 4649
Email: owen.denny@daera-ni.gov.uk

Agencies, public bodies and other organisations

Agri-Food and Biosciences Institute
Headquarters
18a Newforge Lane
Malone Upper, Belfast, BT9 5PX
Tel: 028 9025 5636
Web: www.afbini.gov.uk
Email: info@afbini.gov.uk
Chair: Colin Coffey
Chief Executive: Stanley McDowell

Finance and Corporate Affairs Division
AFBI Headquarters
18a Newforge Lane
Malone Upper, Belfast, BT9 5PX
Tel: 028 9025 5636

Sustainable Agri-Food Sciences Division
AFBI Headquarters
18a Newforge Lane
Malone Upper, Belfast, BT9 5PX
Tel: 028 9025 5293

Environment and Marine Sciences Division
AFBI Headquarters
18a Newforge Lane
Malone Upper, Belfast, BT9 5PX
Tel: 028 9025 5293

Veterinary Sciences Division
12 Stoney Road, Stormont
Ballymiscaw, Belfast, BT4 3SD
Tel: 028 9052 5690

The Livestock and Meat Commission for Northern Ireland
Lissue Industrial Estate (East)
1A Lissue Walk
Lisburn, BT28 2LU
Tel: 028 9263 3000
Web: www.lmcni.com
Email: info@lmcni.com
Chair: Gerard McGivern
Chief Executive: Ian Stevenson

Loughs Agency
22 Victoria Road
Derry, BT47 2AB
Tel: 028 7134 2100
Web: www.loughs-agency.org
Email: general@loughs-agency.org

Northern Ireland Fishery Harbour Authority
3 St Patrick's Avenue
Downpatrick, BT30 6DW
Tel: 028 4461 3844
Web: www.nifha.co.uk
Email: info@nifha.co.uk
Chair: Robert McConnell
Chief Executive: Kevin Quigley

Council for Nature Conservation and the Countryside (CNCC)
CNCC Secretariat, 2nd Floor
Klondyke Building
Cromac Street
Belfast, BT7 2JA
Tel: 028 9056 9290
Email: CNCC.Secretariat@daera-ni.gov.uk

Department for Communities (DfC)

Department for Communities
www.communities-ni.gov.uk

Causeway Exchange
1-7 Bedford Street
Belfast, BT2 7EG
Tel: 028 9082 9000

Minister:
Deirdre Hargey MLA

Permanent Secretary:
Tracy Meharg
Tel: 028 9082 3301
Email: tracy.meharg@communities-ni.gov.uk

Private Office
Tel: 028 9082 3320
Email: private.office@communities-ni.gov.uk

Permanent Secretary's Office
Tel: 028 9082 9034
Email: permsecsupport@communities-ni.gov.uk

In May 2016 the Department for Communities was established following the restructuring of Northern Ireland Departments. The Department's main functions include:

- the promotion of a healthy housing and the provision of decent, affordable, sustainable homes and housing support services;
- a social welfare system including focused support to the most disadvantaged areas;
- providing training and support to jobseekers and employers;
- bringing divided communities together by creating urban centres which are sustainable, welcoming and accessible to live, work and relax in peace;
- supporting local Government to deliver effective public services;
- maximising public benefits from the culture, arts and leisure sectors;
- tackling disadvantage and promoting equality of opportunity by reducing poverty, promoting and protecting the interests of children, older people, people with disabilities, and other socially excluded groups;
- addressing inequality and disadvantage.

Based on the final 2020/21 Budget the Department has over 8,000 staff and has an annual budget of almost £8.6 billion, including expenditure of £7.3 billion on social security and pension payments. The Department works with a total of 15 Arm's Length Bodies and six other Advisory Bodies to support delivery of its functions.

Strategic Policy and Professional Services Group
Deputy Secretary: Beverley Wall
Tel: 028 9051 5171
Email: beverley.wall@communities-ni.gov.uk

Financial Management Directorate
Director: Gavin Patrick
Tel: 028 9051 5168
Email: gavin.patrick@communities-ni.gov.uk

Financial Management Directorate
Director: Cherrie Arnold
Tel: 028 9051 5174
Email: cherrie.arnold@communities-ni.gov.uk

Governance and Commercial Services
Director: Linda Williams
Tel: 028 9082 9116
Email: linda.williams@communities-ni.gov.uk

Central Policy Division
Director: George Sampson
Tel: 028 9082 3558
Email: george.sampson@commuities-ni.gov.uk

Strategy, Communication and Engagement
Director: Anne Armstrong
Email: anne.armstrong@communities-ni.gov.uk

Organisational Development
Director: Eamon O'Kane
Tel: 028 9082 3374
Email: eamon.okane@communities-ni.gov.uk

Engaged Communities
Deputy Secretary: Moira Doherty
Tel: 028 9082 3556
Email: moira.doherty@communities-ni.gov.uk

Active Communities Directorate and Infrastructure Planning and Delivery Support Unit
Head of Division: Kathryn Hill
Tel: 028 9051 5180
Email: kathryn.hill@communities-ni.gov.uk

Government Departments

Northern Ireland Yearbook

Department for Communities
www.communities-ni.gov.uk

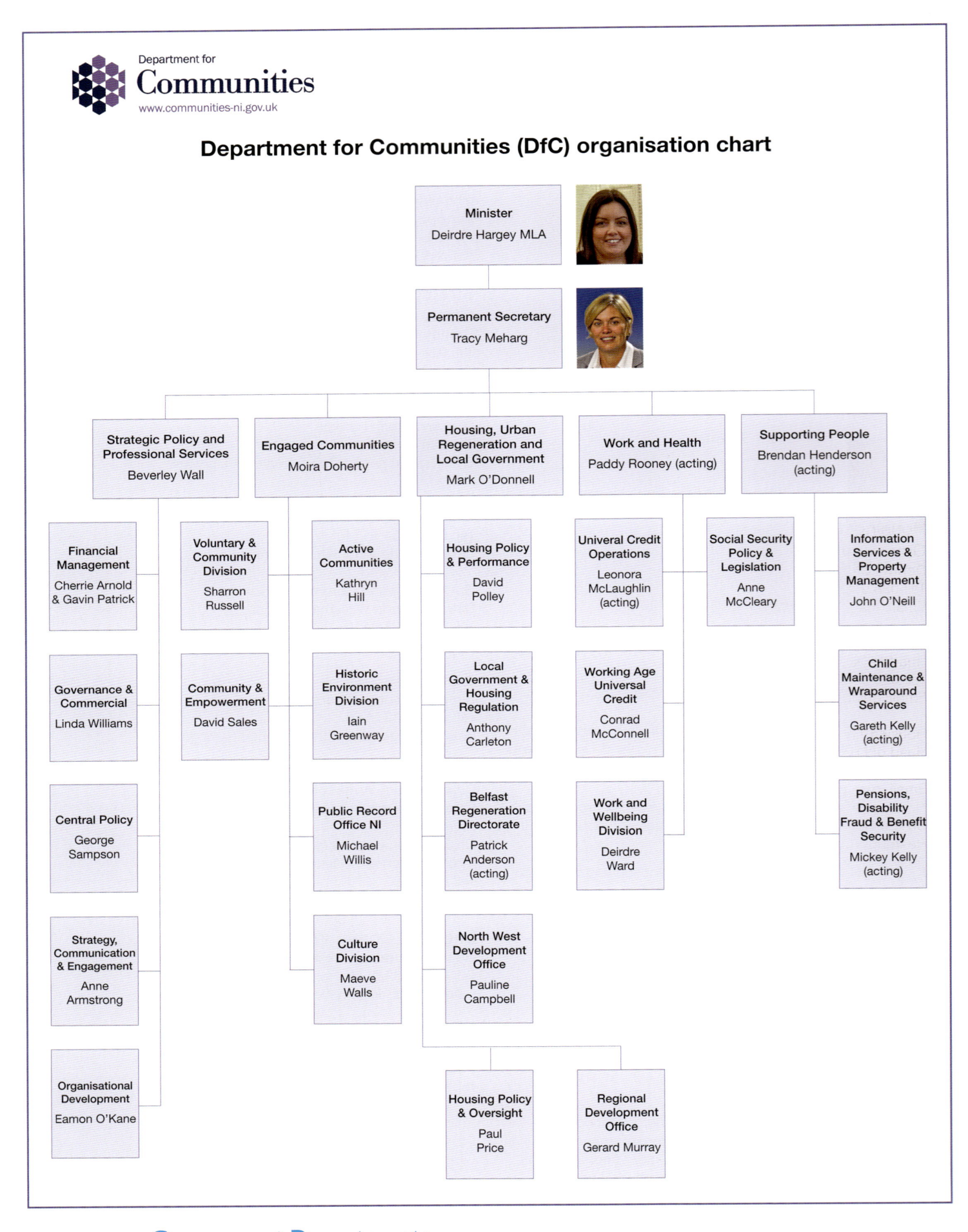

Department for Communities (DfC) organisation chart

- **Minister** — Deirdre Hargey MLA
  - **Permanent Secretary** — Tracy Meharg
    - **Strategic Policy and Professional Services** — Beverley Wall
      - Financial Management — Cherrie Arnold & Gavin Patrick
      - Governance & Commercial — Linda Williams
      - Central Policy — George Sampson
      - Strategy, Communication & Engagement — Anne Armstrong
      - Organisational Development — Eamon O'Kane
    - **Engaged Communities** — Moira Doherty
      - Voluntary & Community Division — Sharron Russell
      - Community & Empowerment — David Sales
    - **Housing, Urban Regeneration and Local Government** — Mark O'Donnell
      - Active Communities — Kathryn Hill
      - Historic Environment Division — Iain Greenway
      - Public Record Office NI — Michael Willis
      - Culture Division — Maeve Walls
      - Housing Policy & Performance — David Polley
      - Local Government & Housing Regulation — Anthony Carleton
      - Belfast Regeneration Directorate — Patrick Anderson (acting)
      - North West Development Office — Pauline Campbell
      - Housing Policy & Oversight — Paul Price
      - Regional Development Office — Gerard Murray
    - **Work and Health** — Paddy Rooney (acting)
      - Univeral Credit Operations — Leonora McLaughlin (acting)
      - Working Age Universal Credit — Conrad McConnell
      - Work and Wellbeing Division — Deirdre Ward
    - **Supporting People** — Brendan Henderson (acting)
      - Social Security Policy & Legislation — Anne McCleary
      - Information Services & Property Management — John O'Neill
      - Child Maintenance & Wraparound Services — Gareth Kelly (acting)
      - Pensions, Disability Fraud & Benefit Security — Mickey Kelly (acting)

Department for Communities
www.communities-ni.gov.uk

Historic Environment Division
Head of Division: Iain Greenway
Tel: 028 9081 9322
Email: iain.greenway@communities-ni.gov.uk

Public Record Office of Northern Ireland
Head of Division: Michael Willis
Tel: 028 9053 4902
Email: michael.willis@communities-ni.gov.uk

Culture Division
Head of Division: Maeve Walls
Tel: 028 9051 5340
Email: maeve.walls@communities-ni.gov.uk

Voluntary and Community Division
Head of Division: Sharron Russell
Tel: 028 9082 9357
Email: sharron.russell@communities-ni.gov.uk

Community and Empowerment Division
Head of Division: David Sales
Tel: 028 9082 9059
Email: david.sales@communities-ni.gov.uk

Housing, Urban Regeneration and Local Government Group (HURLG)
Deputy Secretary: Mark O'Donnell
Tel: 028 9082 9311
Email: mark.odonnell@communities-ni.gov.uk

Housing Policy and Performance
Head of Division: David Polley
Tel: 028 9051 5286
Email: david.polley@communities-ni.gov.uk

Housing Policy and Oversight
Head of Division: Paul Price
Tel: 028 9051 5225
Email: paul.price@communities-ni.gov.uk

Belfast Regeneration Directorate
Head of Division: Patrick Anderson (acting)
Tel: 028 9082 9274
Email: patrick.anderson@communities-ni.gov.uk

North West Development Office
Head of Division: Pauline Campbell
Tel: 028 7131 9782
Email: pauline.campbell@communities-ni.gov.uk

Regional Development Office
Head of Division: Gerard Murray
Tel: 028 9082 9307
Email: gerard.murray@communities-ni.gov.uk

Local Government and Housing Regulation
Head of Division: Anthony Carleton
Tel: 028 9082 3346
Email: anthony.carleton@communities-ni.gov.uk

Work and Health Group
Deputy Secretary: Paddy Rooney (acting)
Tel: 028 9051 5046
Email: paddy.rooney@communities-ni.gov.uk

Working Age Services and Universal Credit Programme
Director: Conrad McConnell
Tel: 028 9081 9132
Email: conrad.mcconnell@communities-ni.gov.uk

Universal Credit Operations
Director: Leonora McLaughlin (acting)
Tel: 028 9090 9343
Email: leonora.mclaughlin@communities-ni.gov.uk

Work and Wellbeing Division
Deputy Director: Deirdre Ward
Tel: 028 9082 3357
Email: deirdre.ward@communities-ni.gov.uk

Social Security Policy and Legislation and Decision-Making Services
Director: Anne McCleary
Tel: 028 9082 3332
Email: anne.mccleary@communities-ni.gov.uk

Supporting People Group
Deputy Secretary: Brenda Henderson (acting)
Tel: 028 9082 3455
Email: brenda.henderson1@dfcni.gov.uk

Information Services and Property Management
Director: John O'Neill
Tel: 028 9051 5342
Email: john.oneill@communities-ni.gov.uk

Child Maintenance and Wraparound Services
Head of Division: Gareth Kelly (acting)
Tel: 028 2132 6460
Email: gareth.kelly@dfcni.gov.uk

Pensions, Disability and Benefit Security and Debt
Head of Division: Mickey Kelly (acting)
Email: mickey.kelly@communities-ni.gov.uk

Government Departments

Department for Communities
www.communities-ni.gov.uk

Agencies, Non-Departmental Public Bodies and other organisations within DfC

Armagh Observatory and Planetarium
College Hill
Armagh, BT61 9DG
Tel: 028 3751 2966
Email: carol.corvan@armagh.ac.uk

Director: Professor Michael Burton
Email: michael.burton@armagh.ac.uk

Arts Council of Northern Ireland
Linen Hill House
23 Linenhall Street
Lisburn
BT28 1FJ
Tel: 028 9262 3555
Email: info@artscouncil-ni.org
Chief Executive: Roisin McDonough

Charity Commission for Northern Ireland
Marlborough House
Central Way
Craigavon, BT64 1AD
Tel: 028 3832 0220
Web: www.charitycommissionni.org.uk
Email: admin@charitycommissionni.org.uk
Chief Charity Commissioner: Nicole Lappin
Chief Executive: Frances McCandless

Commissioner for Older People for Northern Ireland
Equality House
7-9 Shaftesbury Square
Belfast, BT2 7DP
Tel: 028 9089 0892
Email: info@copni.org
Commissioner: Eddie Lynch
Chief Executive: Evelyn Hoy

Charities Advisory Committee
Email: NICIFIC@communities-ni.gov.uk

Fóras na Gaeilge
63-66 Amiens Street
Dublin 1
Tel: + 353 (0) 1 639 8400

2-4 Queen Street
Belfast
BT1 6ED
Tel: 028 (048) 9089 0970
Email: eolas@forasnagaeilge.ie
Chief Executive: Seán Ó Coinn

Historic Buildings Council
Statutory Advisory Councils Secretariat
c/o NINE Lanyon Place
Townparks
Belfast, BT1 3LP
Tel: 028 9081 9236 / 028 9081 9295
Email: hbc-hmcsecretariat@communities-ni.gov.uk
Chair: Peter Tracey

Historic Monuments Council
Statutory Advisory Councils Secretariat
c/o NINE Lanyon Place
Townparks
Belfast, BT1 3LP
Tel: 028 9081 9236 / 028 9081 9295
Email: hbc-hmcsecretariat@communities-ni.gov.uk
Chair: Audrey Gahan

Libraries NI
Lisburn City Library
23 Linenhall Street
Lisburn, BT28 1FJ
Tel: 0345 450 4580
Email: jim.o'hagan@librariesni.org.uk
Chief Executive: Jim O'Hagan
Chair: Prof Bernard Cullen

Local Government Boundaries Commissioner
c/o Local Government Division
Department for Communities
Causeway Exchange
1-7 Bedford Street
Belfast, BT2 7EG
Commissioner: Sarah Havlin

Ministerial Advisory Group for Architecture and the Built Environment
Causeway Exchange
1-7 Bedford Street
Belfast
BT2 7EG
Tel: 028 9051 5063
Email: magsecretariat@communities-ni.gov.uk

National Museums NI
Cultra
Holywood
BT18 0EU
Tel: 028 9039 5200
Email: kathryn.thomson@nmni.com
Director and Chief Executive: Kathryn Thomson

Northern Ireland Museums Council
153 Bangor Road
Holywood
BT18 0EU
Tel: 028 9055 0215
Email: siobhan.stevenson@nimc.co.uk
Director: Siobhan Stevenson

Northern Ireland Commissioner for Children and Young People (NICCY)
Equality House
7-9 Shaftesbury Square
Belfast, BT2 7DP
Tel: 028 9031 1616
Web: www.niccy.org
Email: info@niccy.org
Commissioner: Koulla Yiasouma
Chief Executive: Mairead McCafferty

Sport NI
House of Sport
2a Upper Malone Road
Belfast
BT9 5LA
Tel: 028 9038 1222
Email: info@sportni.net

Chief Executive: Antoinette McKeown
Tel: 028 9038 3802
Email: antoinettemckeown@sportni.net

Ulster Scots Agency
The Corn Exchange
31 Gordon Street
Belfast
BT1 2LG
Tel: 028 9023 1113
Email: info@ulsterscotsagency.org.uk
Chief Executive: Ian Crozier

Northern Ireland Housing Executive
The Housing Centre
2 Adelaide Street, Belfast, BT2 8PB
Tel: 03448 920 900
Web: www.nihe.gov.uk
Email: info@nihe.gov.uk
Chief Executive: Grainia Long

NI Local Government Officers' Superannuation Committee
Templeton House
411 Holywood Road
Belfast
BT4 2LP
Tel: 0345 3197320
Email: info@nilgosc.org.uk
Chief Executive and Secretary: David Murphy

Local Government Staff Commission for Northern Ireland
Commission House
18-22 Gordon Street
Belfast, BT1 2LG
Tel: 028 9031 3200
Email: info@lgsc.org.uk

Departmental Resource Accounts and Finance Systems
Causeway Exchange
1-7 Bedford Street
Belfast, BT2 7EG
Tel: 028 9051 2604
Email: colin.alderdice@communities-ni.gov.uk
Secretary: Colin Alderdice

Office of the Discretionary Support Commissioner
Level 2
James House
2-4 Cromac Avenue
Belfast
BT7 2JA
Tel: 0800 028 3074
Email: admin@odsc@nissa.gsi.gov.uk

Ulster Supported Employment Limited
182-188 Cambrai Street
Belfast
BT13 3JH
Tel: 028 9035 6600
Email: info@usel.co.uk
Chief Executive: Bill Atkinson

Department of Education (DE)

Rathgael House, Rathgill
Balloo Road
Bangor, BT19 7PR
Tel: 028 9127 9279
Web: www.education-ni.gov.uk

Minister:
Michelle McIlveen MLA

Permanent Secretary:
Mark Browne
Tel: 028 9127 9309

Private Office
Tel: 028 9127 9229

The Department of Education (DE) is responsible for the central administration of education and related services. Its primary statutory duties are to promote the education of the young people and to secure the effective execution of its policy in relation to the provision of the education service. The Department's main areas of responsibility are 0-4 provision, primary, post-primary and special education; the promotion of community relations within and between schools; youth and early years services and teacher education and salaries.

The Department's vision is: "Every young person achieving to his or her full potential at each stage of his or her development."

The Department of Education is headed by the Minister for Education and has 12 Directorates with three Deputy Secretaries overseeing them.

Deputy Secretary:
Linsey Farrell
Tel: 028 9127 9313
DD: 59330

Responsibility for the following Directorates: Inclusion and Wellbeing; Early Years, Children and Youth; Curriculum, Qualifications and Standards; Promoting Collaboration, Tackling Disadvantage; Children & Young People's Services and the Education Transformation programme.

Deputy Secretary:
Lianne Patterson
Tel: 028 9127 9524

Responsibility for the following Directorates: Education Workforce Development; Sustainable Schools, Policy & Planning; Finance; Corporate Services & Governance, Independent Review of Education.

Infrastructure, Transport, Food and Recovery Group
Division Deputy Secretary:
John Smith
Tel: 028 9127 9781

The main duties of each Directorate are as follows:

Investment and Infrastructure Directorate
Deputy Directors: Stephen Creagh/Seamus Gallagher
Tel: 028 9127 9573/028 9127 9861

This Directorate is responsible for management and delivery of the Department's key capital programmes – Major Works, Schools Enhancement Programme (SEP), minor works, youth capital projects and Fresh Start Agreement schemes. The Directorate also has responsibility for asset management and monitoring the Department's capital budget, including capital receipts.

Restart and Covid Management Directorate
Director: James Hutchinson
Tel: 028 9185 8031

Restart and Covid Management Directorate is responsible for the DE core response to the Covid-19 pandemic including co-ordinating the ongoing provision of guidance to schools and educational settings, reflecting the Executive's decisions. It has worked with practitioners, trade unions and other government bodies in both developing this guidance and providing ongoing policy support as the guidance evolves and in emerging issues such as the implementation of asymptomatic testing programmes. It has also led on ensuring appropriate information is available for educational settings, parents and carers, and children and young people.

Transport and Food in Schools Directorate
Director: Margaret Rose McNaughton
Tel: 028 9127 9830

This Directorate is responsible for policy on: school transport, food in schools, educational maintenance allowances, free school meals, school uniform guidance clothing allowances (school uniform grants), vaccination programmes in schools and elective home education. It also works with DfC on the Food Poverty Action plan.

Inclusion and Well-Being Directorate
Director: Ricky Irwin
Tel: 028 9127 9216

This Directorate is responsible for developing and maintaining policies that address a range of barriers to learning (including those experienced by children with special educational needs, newcomer pupils, Traveller children, looked after children, school-age mothers and young carers); safeguarding; behaviour; and promotion of emotional well-being.

The Directorate endeavours to bring a whole child/whole school approach to building resilience, supporting pupils to mitigate difficulties and addressing issues arising from learning and health or social impacts.

Promoting Collaboration, Tackling Disadvantage
Director: Alison Chambers
Tel: 028 9127 9332

This Directorate is responsible for teacher professional learning, tackling disadvantage, community relations, shared education, Irish Medium and Integrated Education.

Teacher professional learning includes policy for induction, early and continuing professional learning, school leadership development, intakes to initial teacher training and sponsorship of GTCNI.

Tackling disadvantage includes responsibility for delivery of "A Fair Start" report, Targeting Social Need, Extended Schools, Full Service Programmes and a range of geographical interventions in north, south east and west Belfast, Rathcoole and Greater Shantallow, Derry as well as Pupil Attendance policy, parental engagement and Community Use of Schools.

The Directorate also takes lead responsibility for oversight of Irish-medium and Integrated Education including the sponsor role for CnaG and NICIE. The Directorate leads on the role of Accountable Department in respect of the Peace IV Shared Education thematic area and the forthcoming Peace Plus Programme.

Early Years, Children and Youth Directorate
Director: Paul Brush
Tel: 028 9127 9826

This Directorate is responsible for policy on early childhood education and childcare; youth services and the Executive Children and Young People's Strategy. The Directorate's remit includes:
- Universal Pre-School Education Programme (PSEP);
- targeted early years support through the Sure Start Programme, Pathway Fund, and the Toybox project;
- Universal Getting Ready to Learn programme;
- universal youth services;
- development of an Executive Childcare Strategy; and
- coordination of the Executive Children and Young People's Strategy 2020-2030 and Executive input to the UN Convention on the Rights of the Child (UNCRC).

The Directorate undertakes the sponsor role for the Youth Council for Northern Ireland (currently non-operational).

Curriculum, Qualifications and Standards Directorate
Acting Director: Karen McCullough
Tel: 028 9127 9348

This Directorate's core responsibilities include policy on: promoting school improvement; improving pupil attainment, particularly in the areas of literacy and numeracy; and tackling educational disadvantage. It also leads on policy issues relating to: the statutory curriculum and the Entitlement Framework; the arrangements for assessing and recording pupil performance; and qualifications. It works closely with the Department for the Economy in respect of policy around 14–19 education, careers and pathways beyond school.

The Directorate is responsible for policy oversight of the Council for Curriculum, Examinations and Assessment (CCEA).

Children's and Young People's Services Directorate
Director: Margaret Rose McNaughton
Tel: 028 9127 9332

This Directorate is responsible for leading on the implementation of the Children's Services Co-operation Act (NI) 2015 including the development of the new Children's and Young People's Strategy, under the Act. It is responsible for policy on: school transport, food in schools, educational maintenance allowances, free school meals, uniforms, clothing allowances (school uniform grants) and elective home education. It also funds the school meals service in voluntary grammar and grant maintained integrated schools.

Corporate Services and Governance Directorate
Director: Andrew Scott
Tel: 028 9127 9321

This is the central corporate services Directorate for the Department. Its functions include:
- promotion of equality in education;
- North/South co-operation;
- communications: internal and external;
- business planning and risk management in DE and its Arm's Length Bodies;
- machinery of government and co-ordination services in support of the Minister and top management;
- civil contingencies/business continuity/emergency planning;
- information management/assurance/protective security;
- departmental ICT services.

The Directorate also has oversight responsibilities for governance, accountability and assurance issues between the Department and its Non-Departmental Public Bodies (NDPBs). It administers Ministerial public appointments and is responsible for policy on school governance, which includes the appointment of school governors and approval of school Schemes of Management and provides advice and support to interim Boards of Governors for school amalgamations. The Directorate currently provides funding by way of grant to three bodies: the Controlled Schools Support Council (CSSC); the

Department of Education organisation chart

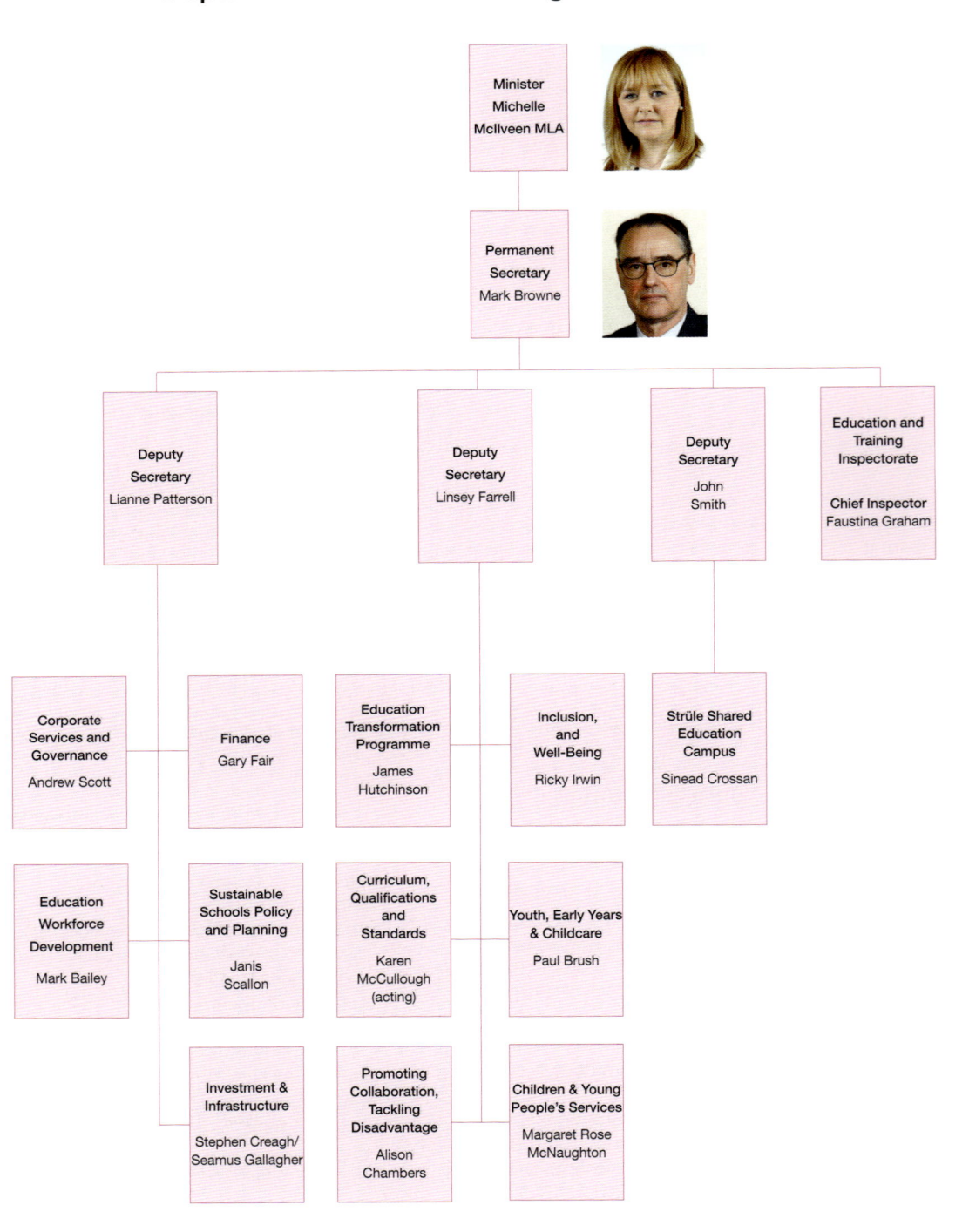

- **Minister** — Michelle McIlveen MLA
  - **Permanent Secretary** — Mark Browne
    - **Deputy Secretary** — Lianne Patterson
      - Corporate Services and Governance — Andrew Scott
      - Finance — Gary Fair
      - Education Workforce Development — Mark Bailey
      - Sustainable Schools Policy and Planning — Janis Scallon
      - Investment & Infrastructure — Stephen Creagh/Seamus Gallagher
    - **Deputy Secretary** — Linsey Farrell
      - Education Transformation Programme — James Hutchinson
      - Inclusion, and Well-Being — Ricky Irwin
      - Curriculum, Qualifications and Standards — Karen McCullough (acting)
      - Promoting Collaboration, Tackling Disadvantage — Alison Chambers
    - **Deputy Secretary** — John Smith
      - Strule Shared Education Campus — Sinead Crossan
      - Youth, Early Years & Childcare — Paul Brush
      - Children & Young People's Services — Margaret Rose McNaughton
    - **Education and Training Inspectorate** — Chief Inspector Faustina Graham

Catholic Schools' Trustee Service (CSTS); and the Governing Bodies Association (GBA).

Sustainable Schools Policy and Planning Directorate (SSPPD)
Director: Janis Scallon
Tel: 028 9127 9940

The SSPPD Directorate encompasses five teams. Three Area Planning Policy Teams (APPTs) (South West Region, North Region and Shared Education Campuses and East Region) and the Area Planning Development Team (APDT) who support the governance and development of the Area Planning process through the implementation of the Sustainable Schools Policy (SSP). APPTs support Area Planning governance structures at strategic and working group level through engagement with the EA, CSSC, CCMS, CSTS, GBA, NICIE, CnaG and TRC. Their primary focus is the provision of high-quality submissions to the Permanent Secretary and Minister on Development Proposals (DPs), responses to AQs and correspondence, input to cross-Departmental and policy development and Education Committee, responses to Judicial Reviews (JRs) and other briefing, as well as specific projects aimed at improving Area Planning to deliver in meeting the educational needs of children. The School Admissions Team (SAT) key responsibilities include processing Temporary Variations (TVs), review of approved admissions and enrolment numbers and overseeing the primary and post-primary transfer processes. The Directorate manages the delivery of DE commitments under the Together: Building a United Community strategy headline action on the development of Shared Education Campuses.

Strule Shared Education Campus Directorate
Business Change Manager: Sinead Crossan
Tel: 028 9185 8035

The Directorate is the Contracting Authority responsible for the direct delivery of the SSEC Programme which has a projected campus completion date of 2025. The Directorate is responsible for working with key educational, community and statutory stakeholders to deliver the programme. Projects include: the procurement, design and construction of the schools and shared areas; oversight of the development of an educational model; development of the ownership, governance and management arrangements for the campus, including funding arrangements; exploring opportunities for other services to be delivered from the campus; working with the Department for Infrastructure to ensure the delivery of required road improvements; and planning for effective migration prior to campus opening.

Finance Directorate
Director: Gary Fair
Tel: 028 9127 9240

The role of the Finance Directorate is to manage the Department's £2 billion Resource Budget in line with Ministerial priorities and to ensure financial probity, regularity and value for money. It prepares the Department's annual Budget, Estimates and Resource Accounts.

The Directorate is responsible for securing funding, allocating resources, monitoring expenditure and reporting financial results.

The Finance Directorate is also responsible for providing financial leadership, guidance and advice to the Department and its Arm's Length Bodies.

Education Workforce Development Directorate
Director: Mark Bailey
Tel: 028 9127 9257

This directorate has policy responsibility for all issues affecting the education workforce, including teachers and support staff. The purpose of the directorate is to provide the vision and set the framework to help deliver an education workforce which is able, qualified, rewarded and motivated to raise standards and close the educational achievement gap.

The directorate is responsible for: ensuring that pay and conditions of service are appropriate to maintain an able, committed and flexible workforce (both teaching and non-teaching) that will secure high and improving standards of school education for all children; ensuring pay remit business cases for all education sector staff are completed and approved according to Department of Finance guidance and the Executive's Public Sector Pay Policy.

The Directorate also co-ordinates the Departments' policy and role in relation to the implications of the EU referendum.

Education Transformation Programme
Director: James Hutchinson
Tel: 028 9185 8031

The focus of the Education Transformation Programme is to critically review aspects of the existing education system; identify where improvements can be made; and deliver a managed programme of transformation for the benefit of children and young people. The programme will involve work to develop policy and operational proposals to transform the education system to make it responsive to the needs of children and young people. Please note that work on the Education Transformation Programme has been temporarily suspended due to work pressures through Covid-19.

Department of Education
www.education-ni.gov.uk

Education Restart Programme
Director: James Hutchinson
Tel: 028 9185 8031

The Education Restart Programme, which, working alongside a wide range of stakeholders, will put in place the detailed measures and guidance which will enable a safe reopening of educational settings. Education Restart information is available for educational settings, parents and carers, and children and young people.

Education and Training Inspectorate
Chief Inspector: Faustina Graham
Tel: 028 9127 9738

The Education and Training Inspectorate (ETI) is a unitary inspectorate, which provides an independent inspection and policy advice service. Whilst ETI is formally a part of the Department of Education (DE), it also assists the Department for the Economy (DfE) and other commissioning Departments in the discharge of their responsibilities and gives policy advice to the Ministers and officials in these Departments. In addition, inspection services are also provided for the Criminal Justice Inspection (CJI) and the Home Office. ETI evaluates and reports on the quality of leadership and management, outcomes for learners and quality of provision in: early years, primary and post-primary schools, special education, further education, work-based learning, European Social Fund providers, youth, initial teacher education, education other than at school (EOTAS) as well as policy, planning and improvement work.

DE sponsored public bodies

Comhairle na Gaelscolaíochta
202 Falls Road
Belfast
BT12 6AF
Tel: 028 9032 1475
Web: www.comhairle.org
Email: eolas@comhairle.org
Chief Executive: Ciarán Mac Giolla Bhéin

Council for Catholic Maintained Schools
Linen Hill House
23 Linenhall Street
Lisburn
BT28 1FJ
Web: www.onlineccms.com
Email: info@ccmsschools.com
Chief Executive: Gerry Campbell

Education Authority
40 Academy Street
Belfast
BT1 2NQ
Tel: 028 9069 4964
Web: www.eani.org.uk
Email: info@eani.org.uk
Chief Executive: Sara Long

General Teaching Council for Northern Ireland
3rd Floor, Albany House
73-75 Great Victoria Street
Belfast, BT2 7AF
Tel: 028 9033 3390
Web: www.gtcni.org.uk
Email: info@gtcni.org.uk
Chief Executive Officer: Sam Gallaher

Middletown Centre for Autism Ltd
35 Church Street
Middletown
Armagh, BT60 4HZ
Tel: 028 3751 5750
Web: www.middletownautism.com
Email: admin@middletownautism.com
Chief Executive: Gary Cooper

Northern Ireland Council for Integrated Education
25 College Gardens
Belfast
BT9 6BS
Tel: 028 9097 2910
Web: www.nicie.org
Email: info@nicie.org
Chief Executive: Roisin Marshall

Northern Ireland Council for the Curriculum, Examinations and Assessment
29 Clarendon Road
Belfast
BT1 3BG
Tel: 028 9026 1200
Web: www.ccea.org.uk
Email: info@ccea.org.uk
Chief Executive: Margaret Farragher (interim)

Youth Council for Northern Ireland
c/o Rathgael House
43 Balloo Road
Rathgill
Bangor
BT19 7PR
Tel: 028 9127 9782

Department for the Economy (DfE)

Netherleigh House
Massey Avenue
Belfast, BT4 2JP
Tel: 028 9052 9900
Text Relay: 18001 028 9052 9900
Web: www.economy-ni.gov.uk
Email: dfemail@economy-ni.gov.uk

Minister: Gordon Lyons MLA

Permanent Secretary:
Mike Brennan
Tel: 028 9052 9441

Minister's Private Office
Private Secretary: Dan Cartland
Tel: 028 9052 9250
Email: dan.cartland@economy-ni.gov.uk

Press Office
Principal Information Officer: Ronan Henry
Tel: 028 9052 9611
Email: ronan.henry@economy-ni.gov.uk

Senior Information Officer: Leander Harding
Tel: 028 9052 9894
Email: leander.harding@economy-ni.gov.uk

Senior Information Officer: James Irwin
Tel: 028 9052 9433
Email: james.irwin@economy-ni.gov.uk

The Department for the Economy is responsible for economic development policy, energy, telecommunications, tourism, minerals and petroleum, health and safety at work, companies registry, insolvency service, consumer affairs, social economy, professional economic advice and research and labour market and economic statistics services, further and higher education, employment and skills programmes (including apprenticeships), employment rights, European fund management, credit union and societies. Financial and personnel management services are provided centrally within the department.

The Department has four agencies to assist in strategy implementation: Invest Northern Ireland; Tourism NI, the Health and Safety Executive for Northern Ireland and the Consumer Council for Northern Ireland.

The Department also works with the following bodies: Tourism Ireland Limited, Catalyst, Northern Ireland Authority for Utility Regulation, InterTradeIreland, The Certification Officer for Northern Ireland, The Labour Relations Agency, The Board of CITB Construction Skills, The Industrial Court, Office of the Industrial Tribunals and The Fair Employment Tribunals, Universities, FE Colleges.

Economic Strategy Group
Deputy Secretary: Paul Grocott
Tel: 028 9025 7567
Email: paul.grocott@economy-ni.gov.uk

Business Engagement
Head of Division: Trevor Connolly
Tel: 028 9052 6709
Email: trevor.connolly@economy-ni.gov.uk

Tourism and Telecoms / Project Stratum
Head of Division: Jeremy Gardner
Tel: 028 9037 8721
Email: jeremy.gardner@economy-ni.gov.uk

Strategic Policy
Head of Division: Keith Forster
Tel: 028 9052 9508
Email: keith.forster@economy-ni.gov.uk

Business Interventions
Head of Division: Michelle Scott
Tel: 028 9041 6803
Email: michelle.scott@economy-ni.gov.uk

City Deals Programme
Head of Division: Ciaran McGarrity
Tel: 028 9052 9448
Email: ciaran.mcgarrity@economy-ni.gov.uk

Energy Group
Deputy Secretary: Richard Rodgers
Tel: 075 8429 2495
Email: richard.rodgers@economy-ni.gov.uk

Heat, Minerals and Operations
Head of Division: Graham Miller
Tel: 028 9052 9527
Email: graham.miller@economy-ni.gov.uk

Energy Strategy
Head of Division: Thomas Byrne
Tel: 028 9052 9542
Email: thomas.byrne@economy-ni.gov.uk

Electricity Systems, Supply and Consumers
Head of Division: Joe Reynolds
Tel: 028 9052 9710
Email: joe.reynolds@economy-ni.gov.uk

Government Departments

Northern Ireland Yearbook

Department for the Economy
www.economy-ni.gov.uk

Department for the Economy organisation chart

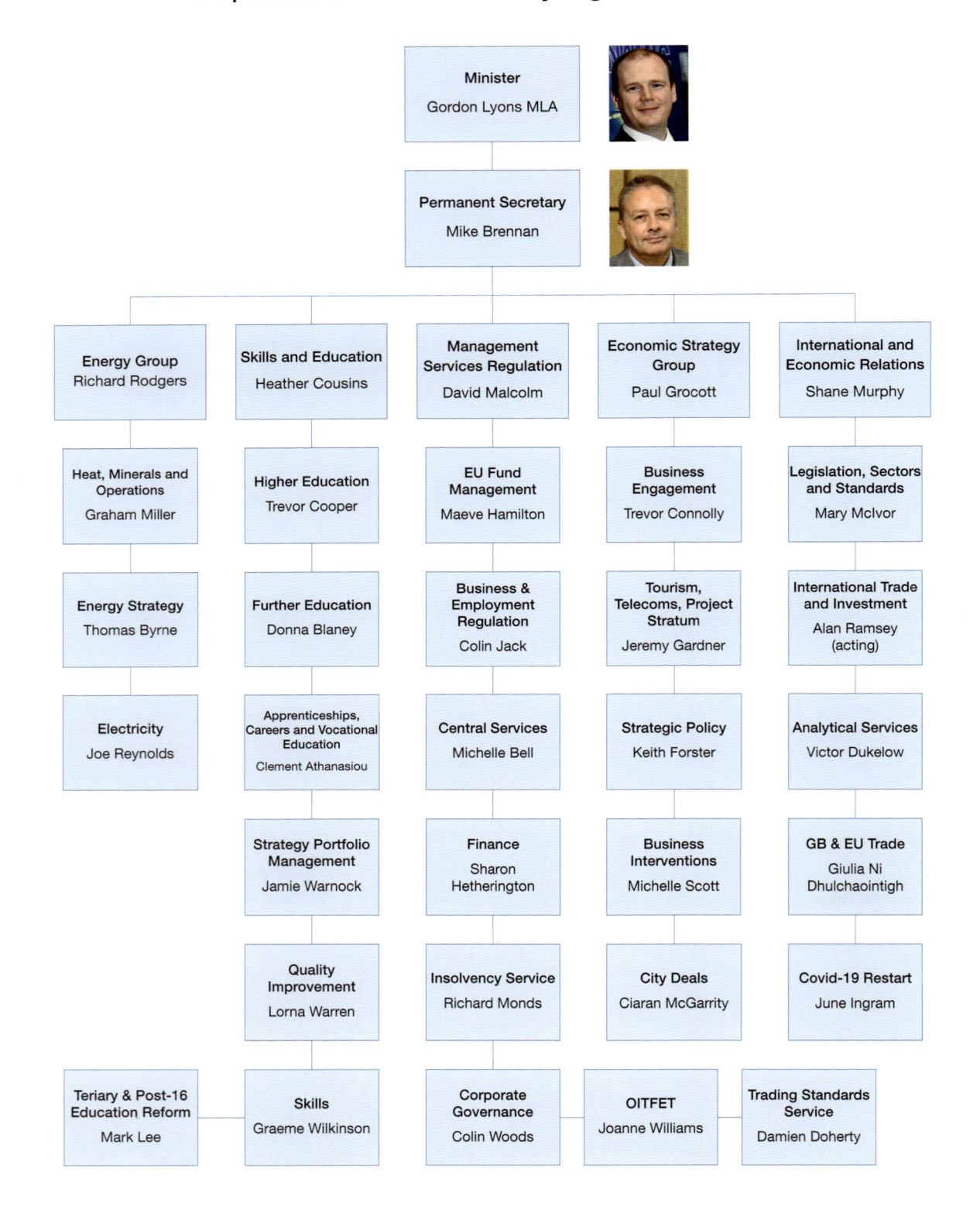

Minister — Gordon Lyons MLA

Permanent Secretary — Mike Brennan

- **Energy Group** — Richard Rodgers
  - Heat, Minerals and Operations — Graham Miller
  - Energy Strategy — Thomas Byrne
  - Electricity — Joe Reynolds
  - Teriary & Post-16 Education Reform — Mark Lee

- **Skills and Education** — Heather Cousins
  - Higher Education — Trevor Cooper
  - Further Education — Donna Blaney
  - Apprenticeships, Careers and Vocational Education — Clement Athanasiou
  - Strategy Portfolio Management — Jamie Warnock
  - Quality Improvement — Lorna Warren
  - Skills — Graeme Wilkinson

- **Management Services Regulation** — David Malcolm
  - EU Fund Management — Maeve Hamilton
  - Business & Employment Regulation — Colin Jack
  - Central Services — Michelle Bell
  - Finance — Sharon Hetherington
  - Insolvency Service — Richard Monds
  - Corporate Governance — Colin Woods

- **Economic Strategy Group** — Paul Grocott
  - Business Engagement — Trevor Connolly
  - Tourism, Telecoms, Project Stratum — Jeremy Gardner
  - Strategic Policy — Keith Forster
  - Business Interventions — Michelle Scott
  - City Deals — Ciaran McGarrity
  - OITFET — Joanne Williams

- **International and Economic Relations** — Shane Murphy
  - Legislation, Sectors and Standards — Mary McIvor
  - International Trade and Investment — Alan Ramsey (acting)
  - Analytical Services — Victor Dukelow
  - GB & EU Trade — Giulia Ni Dhulchaointigh
  - Covid-19 Restart — June Ingram
  - Trading Standards Service — Damien Doherty

Department for the Economy
www.economy-ni.gov.uk

International and Economic Relations Group
Deputy Secretary: Shane Murphy
Tel: 028 9041 6951
Email: shane.murphy@economy-ni.gov.uk

International Trade and Investment
Head of Division: Alan Ramsey (acting)
Email: alan.ramsey@economy-ni.gov.uk

GB and EU Trade
Head of Division: Giulia Ní Dhulchaointigh
Tel: 028 9041 6781
Email: giulia.nidhulchaointigh@economy-ni-gov.uk

Legislation, Sectors and Standards
Head of Division: Mary McIvor
Tel: 028 9025 7856
Email: mary.mcivor@economy-ni.gov.uk

Analytical Services
Head of Division: Victor Dukelow
Tel: 028 9025 7425
Email: victor.dukelow@economy-ni.gov.uk

Covid-19 Restart
Head of Division: June Ingram
Tel: 028 9025 7598
Email: june.ingram@economy-ni.gov.uk

Skills and Education Group
Deputy Secretary: Heather Cousins
Tel: 028 9025 7870
Email: heather.cousins@economy-ni.gov.uk

Higher Education
Head of Division: Trevor Cooper
Tel: 028 9025 7769
Email: trevor.cooper@economy-ni.gov.uk

Strategy Portfolio Management
Head of Division: Jamie Warnock
Email: strategyportfoliomanagement@economy-ni.gov.uk

Further Education
Head of Division: Donna Blaney
Tel: 028 9041 6822
Email: donna.blaney@economy-ni.gov.uk

Quality Improvement
Head of Division: Lorna Warren
Tel: 028 9041 6730
Email: lorna.warren@economy-ni.gov.uk

Skills
Head of Division: Graeme Wilkinson
Tel: 028 9025 7626
Email: graeme.wilkinson@economy-ni.gov.uk

Apprenticeships, Careers and Vocational Education
Head of Division: Clement Athanasiou
Tel: 028 9025 7412
Email: clement.athanasiou@economy-ni.gov.uk

Tertiary and Post-16 Education Reform
Head of Division: Mark Lee
Tel: 028 9025 7947
Email: mark.lee@economy-ni.gov.uk

Management Services and Regulation Group
Deputy Secretary: David Malcolm
Tel: 028 9052 9203
Email: david.malcolm@economy-ni.gov.uk

EU Fund Management
Head of Division: Maeve Hamilton
Tel: 028 9025 7872
Email: maeve.hamilton@economy-ni.gov.uk

Business and Employment Regulation
Head of Division: Colin Jack
Tel: 028 9025 7845
Email: colin.jack@economy-ni.gov.uk

Trading Standards Service
Chief Inspector: Damien Doherty
Tel: 028 9025 3969
Email: damien.doherty@economy-ni.gov.uk

Office of Industrial Tribunals and Fair Employment Tribunal (OITFET)
Secretary to the Tribunals: Joanne Williams
Tel: 028 9025 0065
Email: joanne.williams@economy-ni.gov.uk

Central Services
Head of Division: Michelle Bell
Tel: 028 9052 9920
Email: michelle.bell@economy-ni.gov.uk

Finance
Head of Division: Sharon Hetherington
Tel: 028 9025 7810
Email: sharon.hetherington@economy-ni.gov.uk

Insolvency Service
Head of Division: Richard Monds
Tel: 028 9054 8614
Email: richard.monds@economy-ni.gov.uk

Corporate Governance
Head of Division: Colin Woods
Tel: 028 9052 9390
Email: colin.woods@economy-ni.gov.uk

Department for the Economy
www.economy-ni.gov.uk

Agencies within the Department for the Economy

Invest NI

Invest Northern Ireland (Invest NI) supports business growth and inward investment, promotes innovation, research and development and in-company training, encourages exports and supports local economic development and company start up.

Chief Executive: Kevin Holland

Regional Business
Executive Director: Alan McKeown
Tel: 028 9069 8554
Email: alan.mckeown@investni.com

Entrepreneurship
Manager: Gren Armstrong
Tel: 028 9069 8072
Email: gren.armstrong@investni.com

Eastern Regional Office
Eastern Office Manager: Susan O'Kane
Tel: 028 9069 8422
Email: susan.okane@investni.com

North Western Regional Office / North Eastern Regional Office
North Western Office Manager: Des Gartland
Tel: 028 7127 8187
Email: des.gartland@investni.com

Southern Regional Office
Southern Office Manager: Mark Bleakney
Tel: 028 3025 8730
Email: mark.bleakney@investni.com

Western Regional Office
Western Office Manager: Ethna McNamee
Tel: 028 8224 8918
Email: ethna.mcnamee@investni.com

European and Partner Delivery
Manager: Mary Gormley
Tel: 028 8225 5622
Email: mary.gormley@investni.com

Communications
Executive Director: Peter Harbinson
Tel: 028 9069 8352
Email: peter.harbinson@investni.com

The Communications group comprises:

PR and Media Relations
Head of PR, Media Relations and Internal Comms: Jennifer Pleavin
Tel: 028 9069 8340
Email: jennifer.pleavin@investni.com

Sectors and International
Head: Una McCambridge
Tel: 028 9069 8492
Email: una.mccambridge@investni.com

Campaigns, Solutions and Digital Comms
Head: Rodney McMullan
Tel: 028 9069 8147
Email: rodney.mcmullan@investni.com

Business and Sector Development Group
Executive Director: Brian Dolaghan
Tel: 028 9069 8479
Email: brian.dolaghan@investni.com

The Business and Sector Development Group comprises:

Services (ICT, Financial, Professional, Business)
Director: George McKinney
Tel: 028 9069 8484
Email: george.mckinney@investni.com

Manufacturing and Advanced Engineering
Director: Gráinne McVeigh
Tel: 028 9069 8543
Email: grainne.mcveigh@investni.com

Food and Drink
Director: John Hood
Tel: 028 9069 8562
Email: john.hood@investni.com

International Business
Executive Director: Steve Harper
Tel: 028 9069 8048
Email: steve.harper@investni.com

The International Business Group comprises:

Americas
Head: Peta Conn
Tel: +1 617 207 2516
Email: peta.conn@investni.com

Asia Pacific
Head: Nick Caldwell
Tel: +65 6424 4200
Email: nick.caldwell@investni.com

Europe
Head: Derek Andrews
Tel: 028 9069 8486
Email: derek.andrews@investni.com

India, Middle East and Africa
Head: Swathi Sri
Tel: +971 4375 3859
Email: swathi.sri@investni.com

Trade and Investment
Director: Anne Beggs
Tel: 028 9069 8589
Email: anne.beggs@investni.com

Outcomes, Values and Impact
Executive Director: Donal Durkan
Tel: 028 9069 8527
Email: donal.durkan@investni.com

The Strategy group comprises:

Strategy Team
Head: Martin Robinson
Tel: 028 9069 8464
Email: martin.robinson@investni.com

Corporate Information Team
Head: David Greer
Tel: 028 9069 8289
Email: david.greer@investni.com

Economics Team
Head: Clare Mullan
Tel: 028 9069 8442
Email: clare.mullan@investni.com

Transform
Head: Paddy Robb
Tel: 028 9069 8334
Email: paddy.robb@investni.com

City and Growth Deals
Head: Gary Campbell
Tel: 028 9069 8789
Email: gary.campbell@investni.com

Business Solutions Group
Executive Director: Jeremy Fitch
Tel: 028 9069 8544
Email: jeremy.fitch@investni.com

The Business Solutions group comprises:

Innovation, Research and Development
Director: Vicky Kell
Tel: 028 9069 8382
Email: vicky.kell@investni.com

Skills and Competitiveness
Director: Niall Casey
Tel: 028 9069 8410
Email: niall.casey@investni.com

Technology Solutions, Compliance and New Programme Development
Director: Stephen Wightman
Tel: 028 9069 8458
Email: stephen.wightman@investni.com

Corporate Finance and Property Solutions
Director: William McCulla
Tel: 028 9069 8679
Email: william.mcculla@investni.com

Human Resources
Executive Director: Denise Black
Tel: 028 9069 8364
Email: denise.black@investni.com

Human Resources Group comprises:

Human Resources
Head: Carolyn McKenna
Tel: 028 9069 8332
Email: carolyn.mckenna@investni.com

Contracts Management
Head: Siobhan Haughey
Tel: 028 9069 8316
Email: siobhan.haughey@investni.com

Finance and Operations
Executive Director: Mel Chittock
Tel: 028 9069 8639
Email: mel.chittock@investni.com

The Finance and Operations Group comprises:

Finance, Risk and Assurance
Director: Katrina O'Dowd
Tel: 028 9069 8625
Email: katrina.odowd@investni.com

Internal Operations
Head: Steve Chambers
Tel: 028 9069 8345
Email: steve.chambers@investni.com

Business Performance, EU and Risk Management
Director: Ian Maxwell
Tel: 028 9069 8771
Email: ian.maxwell@investni.com

Legal Services
Head: Gillian Shaw
Tel: 028 9069 8268
Email: gillian.shaw@investni.com

Business Appraisal, Offers and Claims
Head: Nigel McKernan
Tel: 028 9069 8047
Email: nigel.mckernan@investni.com

Tourism NI
Floors 10-12
Linum Chambers
Bedford Square
Bedford Street
Belfast, BT2 7ES
Tel: 028 9023 1221
Web: www.tourismni.com
Email: info@tourismni.com

Chief Executive: John McGrillen
Director of Strategic Development: David Roberts
Chief Digital Officer: Dave Vincent
Director of Business Support and Events: Áine Kearney
Director of Marketing: Naomi Waite
Director of Finance: Lesley McKeown
Interim Director of Organisational Development and HR: Jill O'Reilly
Head of Strategy and Policy: Dorothy Erskine
Head of Programmes: Lesley Ann O'Donnell
Head of Regions: Ciaran Doherty

Department for the Economy
www.economy-ni.gov.uk

Tourism NI Dublin Office
2nd Floor, Riverview House
21-23 City Quay
Dublin Docklands
Dublin 2
Tel: +353 (0) 1 865 1880
Email: infodublin@tourismni.com

Tourism Northern Ireland (Tourism NI) is responsible for the development of tourism and the marketing of Northern Ireland as a tourist destination to domestic tourists, from within Northern Ireland, and to visitors from the Republic of Ireland.

The Department for the Economy also acts as co-sponsor to two organisations set up under the Belfast Agreement.

Tourism Ireland
Beresford House
2 Beresford Road
Coleraine, BT52 1GE
Tel: 028 7035 9200
Web: www.tourismireland.com
Email: corporate.coleraine@tourismireland.com

Chief Executive: Niall Gibbons
Director of Corporate Services, Policy and Northern Ireland: Shane Clarke
Director of Markets: Siobhan McManamy
Director of Central Marketing: Mark Henry

Dublin office
4th Floor, Bishop's Square
Redmond's Hill, Dublin 2, D02 TD99
Email: reception@tourismireland.com
Tel: +353 1 476 3400

Health and Safety Executive for Northern Ireland
83 Ladas Drive
Belfast, BT6 9FR
One-2-One Helpline: 0800 0320 121
Tel: 028 9024 3249
Web: www.hseni.gov.uk
Email: mail@hseni.gov.uk
Chief Executive: Robert Kidd

The Health and Safety Executive for Northern Ireland (HSENI) is the regional health and safety authority and is responsible for health, safety and welfare at work.

Deputy Chief Executive Services: Louis Burns
Deputy Chief Executive Market Surveillance and Operations: Kevin Neeson
Deputy Chief Executive Field Operations: Bryan Monson
Deputy Chief Executive Specialist Sectors: Nikki Monson

Heads of Group (G7 and Principal Inspectors)

Agriculture and Food: Camilla Mackey
Finance/Premises/Training/ Corporate Support: Michael Ditchfield
Information Management/Legislation: Pat Millen
Communications/ Notifications and Operational Support team: Danielle Mills
EU Exit: Nancy Henry / Malcolm Downey
Major Hazards, Gas and Transport: Kellie McNamara
Construction: Richard Meredith
Extractive Industries, Waste and Explosives: Brian Pryce
Major Investigation Team: Kyle Carrick
Manufacturing, Utilities and Docks: Anne Boylan
Trainee Inspector Co-ordination: Denise Donaghy
Occupational Health and Hygiene Group: Martin Rafferty
Public Sector: Cyril Anderson

The Consumer Council for Northern Ireland
Seatem House
Floor 3, 28-32 Alfred Street
Belfast, BT2 8EN
Tel: 028 9025 1600
Web: www.counsumercouncil.org.uk
Email: info@consumercouncil.org.uk
Chief Executive: Noyona Chundur

InterTradeIreland: The Cross-Border Trade and Business Development Body
The Old Gasworks Business Park
Kilmorey Street, Newry
Co Down, BT34 2DE
Tel: (048) 3083 4100
Web: www.intertradeireland.com
Email: info@intertradeireland.com
Chief Executive Officer: Margaret Hearty

InterTradeIreland is the economic agency responsible for promoting cross-border trade and innovation. The organisation is responsible for helping SMEs to access opportunities that cross-border trade presents, as well as building collaborative partnerships between businesses, academia and networks in both jurisdictions to drive innovation across the island.

It operates a wide range of services in particular to assist firms with growth, funding, capacity building, and research and innovation. Since 2017, InterTradeIreland has also been helping SMEs to manage the new trading relationship between Britain and the EU via its dedicated Brexit advisory service. To date it has assisted over 49,000 businesses, created/protected over 18,000 new jobs and has reported more than €1.3 billion in business development value, with cross-border trade currently sitting at €3.8 billion, its highest level in 20 years.

Department of Finance (DoF)

Clare House, 303 Airport Road West
Belfast, BT3 9ED
Tel: 028 9185 8111
Web: www.finance-ni.gov.uk

Minister:
Conor Murphy MLA
Tel: 028 9081 6216
Email: private.office@finance-ni.gov.uk

Interim Permanent Secretary:
Colum Boyle
Tel: 028 9081 6590
Email: colum.boyle@finance-ni.gov.uk

Director of Communications and Engagement:
Mark McLaughlin
Tel: 028 9081 6407
Email: mark.mclaughlin@finance-ni.gov.uk

Head of Media and External Communications: Ciarrai Conlan
Tel: 028 9081 6724
Email: dof.pressoffice@finance-ni.gov.uk

The Department of Finance, or DoF, has a wide range of functions, many of which are carried out centrally either by the department directly or through an agency on behalf of the Civil Service in Northern Ireland.

A key objective of the Department is to deliver high quality, cost effective and efficient public services and administration in the Department's areas of executive responsibility. DoF, through its Public Spending Directorate is responsible for the management of public expenditure in Northern Ireland, ensuring the optimal allocation of resources, including the formulation of the Executive's Budget, maximising value for money and promoting clear accountability alongside good governance.

NICS HR was established in 2017 to provide a centralised HR service for the NICS including resourcing, employee relations, learning and development.

The Department is also responsible for civil law reform and the provision of legal services to other Northern Ireland departments.

Construction and Procurement Delivery (CPD) provides procurement for supplies, services and construction works to the Northern Ireland Departments, agencies and associated public bodies. It is also responsible for the development of public procurement policy for the Civil Service in Northern Ireland, the dissemination of best practice and provides a single point of contact for advice on procurement matters. CPD also provides property management services to Northern Ireland Departments, agencies and associated public bodies.

Enterprise Shared Services within the Department provides shared services including HR, payroll, pensions, finance, IT, digital transformation and is responsible for nidirect – the official government website for Northern Ireland citizens.

The Integr8 Programme (formerly the Central Government Transformation Programme) has been established to take forward work on the development of an integrated operating model and to procure and implement replacement technology for Finance and HR systems and services.

The Department provides a valuation service to the public sector and, through Land & Property Services (LPS), collects rates in Northern Ireland and is also responsible for Land Registers Northern Ireland and Ordnance Survey Northern Ireland.

The Northern Ireland Statistics and Research Agency (NISRA) is an Agency within DoF, which supports decision makers in the formulation of evidence-based policy and informs public debate through the production and dissemination of high quality, trusted and meaningful analysis; facilitates research and delivers the decennial population census and every day civil registration services.

Strategic Policy and Reform (SPAR) shapes Executive Policy and interventions that contribute to a broad range of PfG outcomes through delivering strategic economic advice and reform of public services and ensuring that European income is maximised though overseeing the delivery of European Structural and Investment Funds.

A centralised Group Internal Audit and Fraud Investigation Service has been established within DoF. The Group Service provides fraud investigation services to NICS departments, executive agencies and arm's length bodies. The Group Service also comprises departmental internal audit teams who are outposted to the department to which they provide a service. While the Group Service is located in DoF, it is accountable to individual departmental accounting officers. Any fraud investigations or audit activity undertaken by the Group Service is undertaken on behalf of the relevant department and reported to the relevant department – there is no reporting line on these matters to DoF.

Public Spending Directorate
Budget Director: Joanne McBurney
Tel: 028 9081 6812
Email: joanne.mcburney@finance-ni.gov.uk

Central Expenditure Division
Head of Division: Jeff McGuinness
Tel: 028 9081 6828
Email: jeff.mcguinness@finance-ni.gov.uk

Department of Finance organisation chart

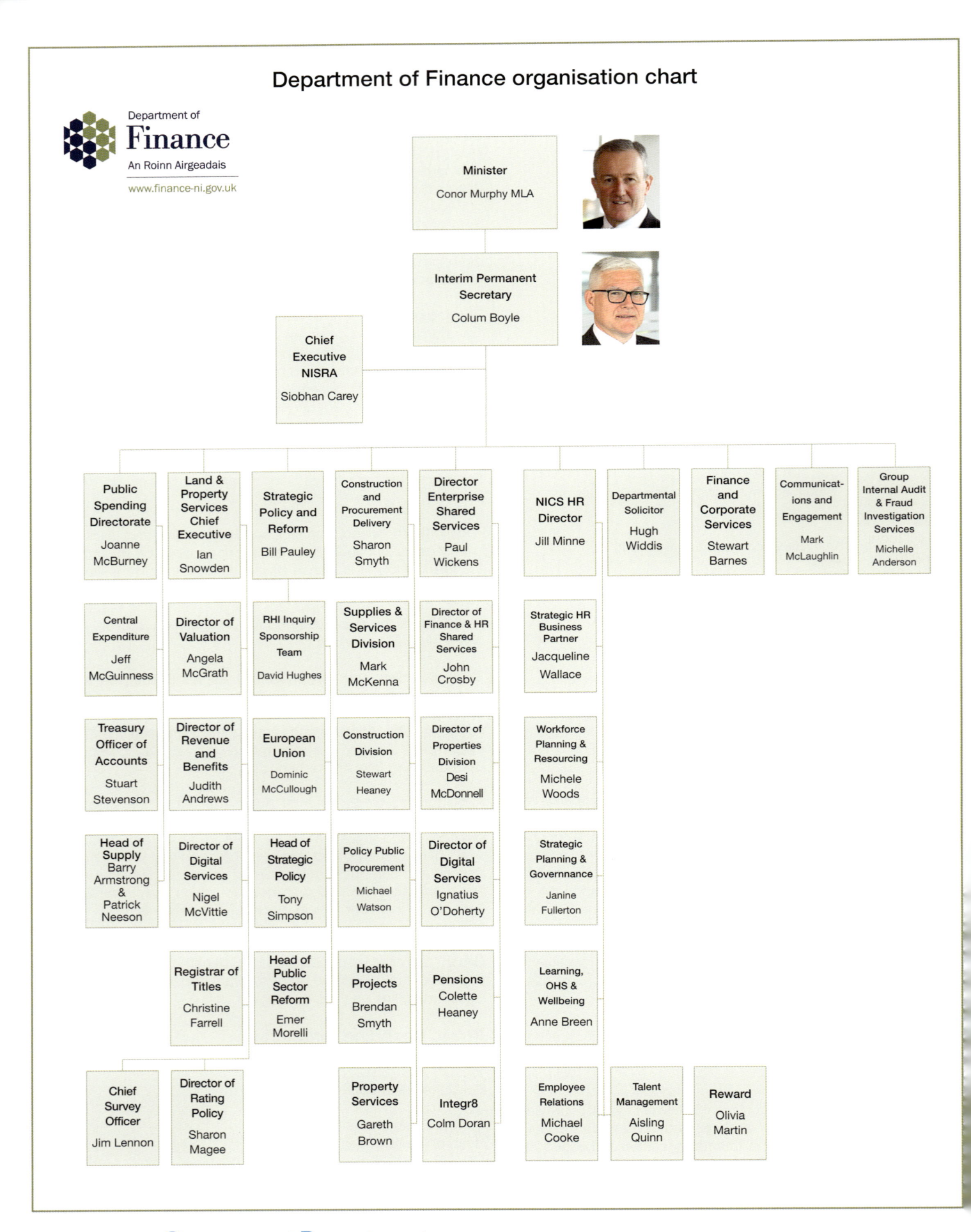

Department of Finance
An Roinn Airgeadais
www.finance-ni.gov.uk

- **Minister** — Conor Murphy MLA
  - **Interim Permanent Secretary** — Colum Boyle
    - **Chief Executive NISRA** — Siobhan Carey

Directorates

Public Spending Directorate — Joanne McBurney
- Central Expenditure — Jeff McGuinness
- Treasury Officer of Accounts — Stuart Stevenson
- Head of Supply — Barry Armstrong & Patrick Neeson

Land & Property Services Chief Executive — Ian Snowden
- Director of Valuation — Angela McGrath
- Director of Revenue and Benefits — Judith Andrews
- Director of Digital Services — Nigel McVittie
- Registrar of Titles — Christine Farrell
- Chief Survey Officer — Jim Lennon
- Director of Rating Policy — Sharon Magee

Strategic Policy and Reform — Bill Pauley
- RHI Inquiry Sponsorship Team — David Hughes
- European Union — Dominic McCullough
- Head of Strategic Policy — Tony Simpson
- Head of Public Sector Reform — Emer Morelli

Construction and Procurement Delivery — Sharon Smyth
- Supplies & Services Division — Mark McKenna
- Construction Division — Stewart Heaney
- Policy Public Procurement — Michael Watson
- Health Projects — Brendan Smyth
- Property Services — Gareth Brown

Director Enterprise Shared Services — Paul Wickens
- Director of Finance & HR Shared Services — John Crosby
- Director of Properties Division — Desi McDonnell
- Director of Digital Services — Ignatius O'Doherty
- Pensions — Colette Heaney
- Integr8 — Colm Doran

NICS HR Director — Jill Minne
- Strategic HR Business Partner — Jacqueline Wallace
- Workforce Planning & Resourcing — Michele Woods
- Strategic Planning & Governnance — Janine Fullerton
- Learning, OHS & Wellbeing — Anne Breen
- Employee Relations — Michael Cooke

Departmental Solicitor — Hugh Widdis

Finance and Corporate Services — Stewart Barnes
- Talent Management — Aisling Quinn

Communications and Engagement — Mark McLaughlin
- Reward — Olivia Martin

Group Internal Audit & Fraud Investigation Services — Michelle Anderson

122 Government Departments

Department of Finance
An Roinn Airgeadais
www.finance-ni.gov.uk

Supply Division
Joint Head of Division: Barry Armstrong
Tel: 028 9081 6817
Email: barry.armstrong@finance-ni.gov.uk

Supply Division
Joint Head of Division: Patrick Neeson
Tel: 028 9081 6837
Email: patrick.neeson@finance-ni.gov.uk

Treasury Officer of Accounts:
Stuart Stevenson
Tel: 028 9081 6795
Email: stuart.stevenson@finance-ni.gov.uk

Strategic Policy and Reform Directorate
Director: Bill Pauley
Tel: 028 9081 6824
Email: bill.pauley@finance-ni.gov.uk

European Union (EU) Division
Head of Division: Dominic McCullough
Tel: 028 9081 9633
Email: dominic.mccullough@finance-ni.gov.uk

RHI Inquiry Sponsorship Team
Head of Division: David Hughes
Tel: 028 9081 9631
Email: david.hughes@finance-ni.gov.uk

Strategic Policy Division
Head of Division: Tony Simpson
Tel: 028 9081 9654
Email: tony.simpson@finance-ni.gov.uk

Public Sector Reform Division
Head of PSRD: Emer Morelli
Tel: 028 9081 6842
Email: emer.morelli@finance-ni.gov.uk

NICS HR
NICS HR Director: Jill Minne
Tel: 028 9025 1735
Email: jill.minne@finance-ni.gov.uk

Strategic HR Business Partners
Head of Division: Jacqueline Wallace
Tel: 028 9025 1669
Email: jacqui.wallace@finance-ni.gov.uk

Workforce Planning and Resourcing
Head of Division: Michele Woods
Tel: 028 9025 1808
Email: michele.woods@finance-ni.gov.uk

Strategic Planning and Governance
Head of Division: Janine Fullerton
Tel: 028 9025 1765
Email: janine.fullerton@finance-ni.gov.uk

Learning, OHS and Wellbeing
Head of Division: Anne Breen
Tel: 028 9025 6715
Email: anne.breen@finance-ni.gov.uk

Employee Relations
Head of Division: Michael Cooke
Tel: 028 9047 5711
Email: michael.cooke2@finance-ni.gov.uk

Talent Management
Head of Division: Aisling Quinn
Tel: 028 90251195
Email: aisling.quinn2@finance-ni.gov.uk

Reward
Head of Division: Olivia Martin
Tel: 028 9025 1727
Email: olivia.martin@finance-ni.gov.uk

Construction and Procurement Delivery
Chief Executive: Sharon Smyth
Tel: 028 9081 6209
Email: sharon.smyth@finance-ni.gov.uk

Supplies and Services Division
Director: Mark McKenna
Tel: 028 9081 6225
Email: mark2.mckenna@finance-ni.gov.uk

Construction Division
Director: Stewart Heaney
Tel: 028 9081 6214
Email: stewart.heaney@finance-ni.gov.uk

Public Procurement Policy Division
Director: Michael Watson
Tel: 028 9081 6430
Email: michael.watson@finance-ni.gov.uk

Health Projects Division
Director: Brendan Smyth
Tel: 028 9081 6039
Email: brendan.smyth@finance-ni.gov.uk

Property Services Division
Director: Gareth Brown
Tel: 028 9081 6065
Email: gareth.brown2@finance-ni.gov.uk

Finance and Corporate Services
Director: Stewart Barnes
Tel: 028 9025 4723
Email: stewart.barnes@finance-ni.gov.uk

Department of Finance
An Roinn Airgeadais
www.finance-ni.gov.uk

Departmental Solicitor's Office
Departmental Solicitor: Hugh Widdis
Tel: 028 9025 1221
Email: hugh.widdis@finance-ni.gov.uk

Assistant Solicitor: Eugene O'Loan
Tel: 028 9025 1245
Email: eugene.o'loan@finance-ni.gov.uk

Assistant Solicitor: Patricia Haughan
Tel: 028 9025 1244
Email: patricia.haughan@finance-ni.gov.uk

Assistant Solicitor: Joanne Brundle
Tel: 028 9054 2403
Email: joanne.brundle@finance-ni.gov.uk

Assistant Solicitor: Mona McRoberts
Tel: 028 9025 1180
Email: mona.mcroberts@finance-ni.gov.uk

Assistant Solicitor: Louise Crilly
Tel: 028 9025 1292
Email: louise.crilly@finance-ni.gov.uk

Assistant Solicitor: Laura McPolin
Tel: 028 9025 1263
Email: laura.mcpolin@finance-ni.gov.uk

Enterprise Shared Services (ESS)
Goodwood House, 44-58 May Street
Belfast, BT1 4NN

Chief Executive: Paul Wickens
Tel: 028 9025 6880
Email: paul.wickens@finance-ni.gov.uk

Director of Strategic Programme: Paul Duffy
Tel: 028 9025 6814
Email: paul.duffy1@finance-ni.gov.uk

Director of Finance and HR Shared Services:
John Crosby
Tel: 028 9025 6813
Email: john.crosby@finance-ni.gov.uk

Director of Integr8 Programme:
Colm Doran
Tel: 028 9054 1703
Email: colm.doran@finance-ni.gov.uk

Director of Properties Division: Desi McDonnell
Tel: 028 9025 7001
Email: desi.mcdonnell@finance-ni.gov.uk

Director of Digital Shared Services: Ignatius O'Doherty
Tel: 028 9037 8337
Email: ignatius.o'doherty@finance-ni.gov.uk

Director of Pensions Division: Colette Heaney
Tel: 028 7132 1227
Email: colette.heaney@finance-ni.gov.uk

Land and Property Services
Lanyon Plaza
7 Lanyon Place, Town Parks
Belfast, BT1 3LP
Web: www.finance-ni.gov.uk/lps

Rates and Valuation Helpline: 0300 200 7801
Housing Benefit and Rate Rebate Helpline: 0300 200 7802
Land Registry Helpline: 0300 200 7803
Mapping Helpline: 0300 200 7804
Customer Complaints Helpline: 0300 200 7805

Chief Executive: Ian Snowden
Tel: 028 9033 6116
Email: ian.snowden@finance-ni.gov.uk

Director of Valuation and Commissioner of Valuation for Northern Ireland: Angela McGrath
Tel: 028 9033 6175
Email: angela.mcgrath@finance-ni.gov.uk

Director of Rating Policy: Sharon Magee
Tel: 028 9033 6126
Email: sharon.magee@finance-ni.gov.uk

Director of Digital Services: Nigel McVittie
Tel: 028 9033 6126
Email: nigel.mcvittie@finance-ni.gov.uk

Director of Registration and Registrar of Titles:
Christine Farrell
Tel: 028 9033 6314
Email: christine.farrell@finance-ni.gov.uk

Chief Survey Officer (Ordnance Survey NI): Jim Lennon
Tel: 028 9033 6502
Email: jim.lennon@finance-ni.gov.uk

Director of Revenues and Benefits: Judith Andrews
Tel: 028 9033 6780
Email: judith.andrews@finance-ni.gov.uk

Agencies within the Department of Finance

Northern Ireland Statistics and Research Agency (NISRA)
Colby House, Stranmillis Court
Belfast, BT9 5RR
Tel: 0300 200 7836
Web: www.nisra.gov.uk
Email: info.nisra@finance-ni.gov.uk

Chief Executive and Registrar General, NISRA:
Siobhan Carey
Tel: 028 9038 8430
Email: siobhan.carey@finance-ni.gov.uk

Director of Census, NISRA: David Marshall
Tel: 028 9038 8447
Email: david.marshall@nisra.gov.uk

Director of Analysis, NISRA: Tracy Power
Tel: 028 9038 8448
Email: tracy.power@nisra.gov.uk

Director of Sources, NISRA: Brian Green
Tel: 028 9038 8479
Email: brian.green@nisra.gov.uk

Northern Ireland Building Regulations Advisory Committee
Building Regulations Unit
Enterprise Shared Services
Floor 3, 3-5A Frederick Street
Belfast, BT1 2NR
Tel: 028 9025 7048
Email: karen.mckernon@finance-ni.gov.uk
Secretary: Karen McKernon

Internal Audit and Fraud Investigation Services
Room 14b, Hillview Buildings
Stormont, Belfast, BT4 3TA
Tel: 028 9052 0053 ext 20053
Group Head of Internal Audit and Fraud Investigation Services:
Michelle Anderson

Department of Health (DoH)

Department of Health
An Roinn Sláinte
Männystrie O Poustie
www.health-ni.gov.uk

**Castle Buildings, Stormont Estate
Upper Newtownards Road
Belfast, BT4 3SQ
Tel: 028 9052 0500
Web: www.health-ni.gov.uk**

Minister: Robin Swann MLA

Permanent Secretary:
Richard Pengelly
Tel: 028 9052 0559
Email: richard.pengelly@health-ni.gov.uk

The Permanent Secretary is also Chief Executive of the Health and Social Care system, as well as Principal Accounting Officer for all the Department's responsibilities. Within the Department, the key business groups are the Resources and Performance Management Group, the Healthcare Policy Group, the Social Care Policy Group, the Transformation, Planning and Performance Group and the Office of the Chief Medical Officer.

Private Office
Private Secretary: Kim Burns
Tel: 028 9037 8774
Email: private.office@health-ni.gov.uk

Director of Communications:
David Gordon
Tel: 028 9052 0543
Email: david.gordon@health-ni.gov.uk

Information Office
Principal Information Office: Karina Meredith (acting)
Tel: 028 9052 0575
Email: karina.meredith@health-ni.gov.uk

The Department of Health's mission is to improve the health and social well-being of the people of Northern Ireland. It endeavours to do so by:

- leading a major programme of cross-government action to improve the health and well-being of the population and reduce health inequalities. This includes interventions involving health promotion and education to encourage people to adopt activities, behaviours and attitudes which lead to better health and well-being. The aim is a population which is much more engaged in ensuring its own health and well-being; and

- ensuring the provision of appropriate health and social care services, both in clinical settings such as hospitals and GPs' surgeries, and in the community through nursing, social work and other professional services.

The Department has three main business responsibilities:

- Health and Social Care (HSC), which includes policy and legislation for hospitals, family practitioner services and community health and personal social services;

- public health, which covers policy, legislation and administrative action to promote and protect the health and well-being of the population; and

- public safety, which covers policy and legislation for fire and rescue services.

Resources and Performance Management Group

This group negotiates, and has management of financial resources for, the DoH departmental staffing policy and resources and internal audit arrangements for the Department. This group also manages the capital development programme and has responsibility for information analysis and information governance, as well as sponsorship of NIFRS.

Deputy Secretary: Deborah McNeilly
Tel: 028 9052 2667
Email: deborah.mcneilly@health-ni.gov.uk

Corporate Management Directorate
Director: La'Verne Montgomery
Tel: 028 9052 0501
Email: laverne.montgomery@health-ni.gov.uk

Finance Directorate
Director: Brigitte Worth
Tel: 028 9052 3814
Email: brigitte.worth@health-ni.gov.uk

Investment Directorate
Director: Preeta Miller
Tel: 028 9052 0504
Email: preeta.miller@health-ni.gov.uk

Internal Audit
Principal Auditor: Tracey Woods
Tel: 028 9054 7888
Email: tracey.woods@health-ni.gov.uk

Healthcare Policy Group

Healthcare Policy Group has lead responsibility for a wide range of policy and related issues across all aspects of Health and Social Care policy including Primary and Secondary Care, Connected Health and HSC workforce planning.

Deputy Secretary:
Jim Wilkinson
Tel: 028 9052 0156
Email: jim.wilkinson@health-ni.gov.uk

Primary Care Directorate
Director: Gearóid Cassidy
Tel: 028 9052 2123
Email: gearoid.cassidy@health-ni.gov.uk

Secondary Care Directorate
Director: Ryan Wilson
Tel: 028 9052 0265
Email: ryan.wilson@health-ni.gov.uk

Workforce Policy
Director: Philip Rodgers
Tel: 028 9052 0715
Email: philip.rodgers@health-ni.gov.uk

Hospital Services Reform
Director: Alastair Campbell
Tel: 028 9052 8374
Email: alastair.campbell@health-ni.gov.uk

Regional Health Services Transformation Directorate
Director: Peter Jakobsen
Tel: 028 9052 0022
Email: peter.jakobsen@health-ni.gov.uk

General Healthcare Policy Directorate
Director: Robbie Davis
Tel: 028 9052 0629
Email: robbie.davis@health-ni.gov.uk

Social Care Policy Group

The Social Care Policy Group, led by Sean Holland, Chief Social Services Officer/Deputy Secretary, comprises three sub-groups: the Office of Social Services Directorate; the Family and Children's Policy Directorate; and Mental Health, Disability & Older People Directorate.

Chief Social Services Officer/Deputy Secretary:
Sean Holland
Tel: 028 9052 0561
Email: sean.holland@health-ni.gov.uk

Office of Social Services Directorate (OSS)
Deputy Chief Social Services Officer: Jackie McIlroy
Tel: 028 9052 0704
Email: jackie.mcilroy@health-ni.gov.uk

The OSS provides professional advice and expertise to the Minister, the DoH, other government departments, including DoJ and DE, and social care and criminal justice agencies in the arena of social work and social care. The OSS has policy responsibility for the social work profession, professional training, qualification requirements, the education and training of the social care workforce and regulation of the social care workforce.

The OSS sponsors the Northern Ireland Social Care Council and has responsibility for the oversight of the professional governance arrangements in respect of the discharge of delegated statutory functions by the HSCB and HSC Trusts.

Family and Children's Policy Directorate (FCPD)
Director: Eilís McDaniel
Tel: 028 9052 3263
Email: eilis.mcdaniel@health-ni.gov.uk

The FCPD has responsibility for the development, maintenance and review of strategy, policy, legislation and guidance on family support, child protection, looked-after children and adoption in Northern Ireland. The FCPD also undertakes the role of Central Authority for inter-country adoption. The Directorate sponsors the Safeguarding Board for Northern Ireland and the Northern Ireland Guardian Ad Litem Agency. The Directorate has responsibility for the development of guidance on termination of pregnancy.

Mental Health, Disability and Older People Directorate
Director: Peter Toogood
Tel: 028 9052 8124
Email: mark.lee@health-ni.gov.uk

MH, D&OP has responsibility for the development, maintenance and review of strategy, policy, legislation and guidance for the full range of personal social services provided to adults in Northern Ireland as well as for mental health services.

Chief Medical Officer Group

The Chief Medical Officer Group is made up of all areas of responsibility overseen by the Chief Medical Officer, Dr Michael McBride. Areas of responsibility:

- professional medical and environmental health advice to Ministers and Departments, and to help inform policy decisions throughout the Department of Health;

- public health policy, including 'making life better' public health strategy, health promotion, disease prevention, emergency preparedness and response, civil contingencies policy, health protection and environmental health;

Government Departments — Northern Ireland Yearbook

Department of Health
An Roinn Sláinte
Männystrie O Poustie
www.health-ni.gov.uk

Department of Health organisation chart

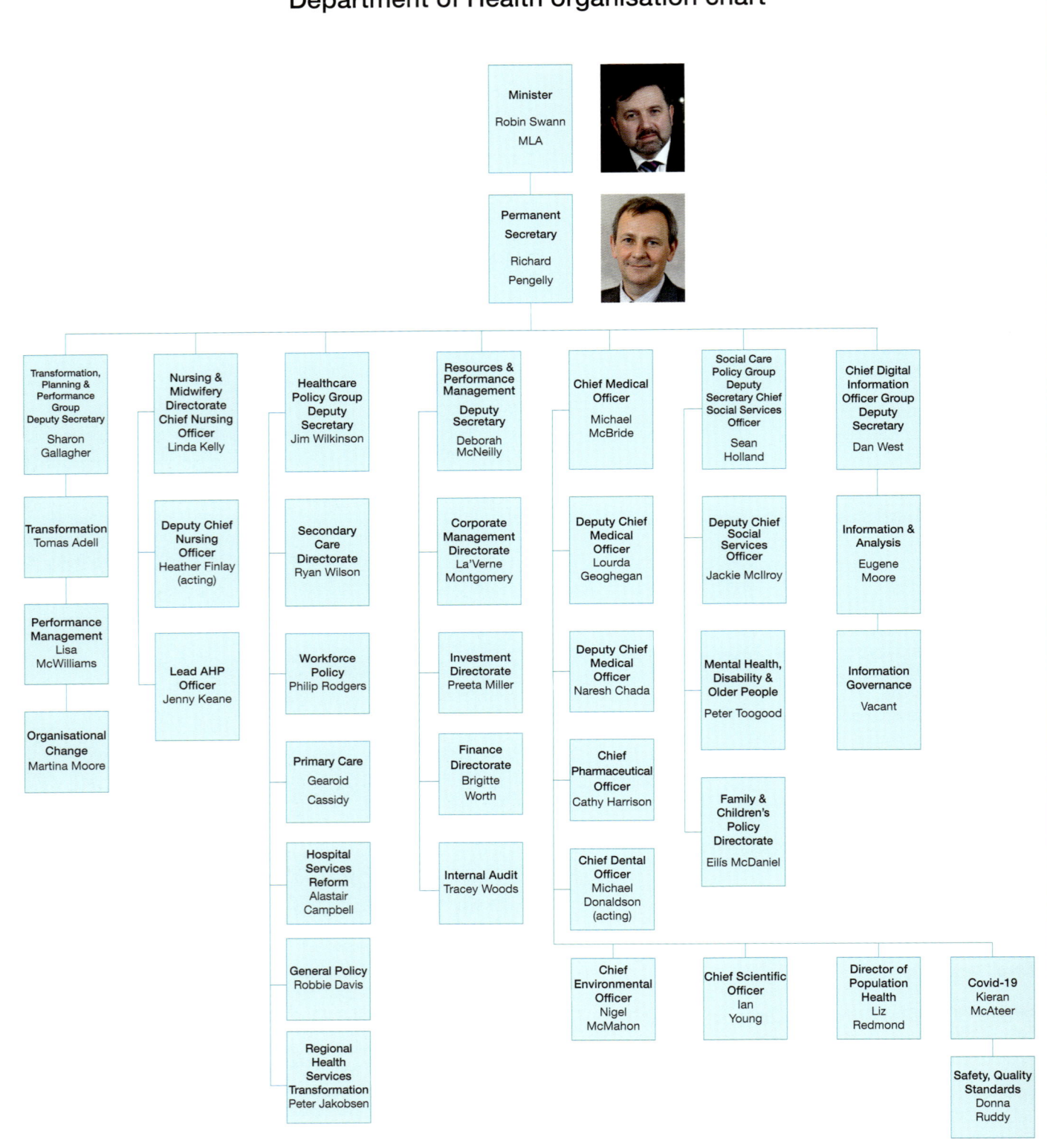

- **Minister** — Robin Swann MLA
  - **Permanent Secretary** — Richard Pengelly

Transformation, Planning & Performance Group
Deputy Secretary: Sharon Gallagher
- Transformation — Tomas Adell
- Performance Management — Lisa McWilliams
- Organisational Change — Martina Moore

Nursing & Midwifery Directorate
Chief Nursing Officer: Linda Kelly
- Deputy Chief Nursing Officer — Heather Finlay (acting)
- Lead AHP Officer — Jenny Keane

Healthcare Policy Group
Deputy Secretary: Jim Wilkinson
- Secondary Care Directorate — Ryan Wilson
- Workforce Policy — Philip Rodgers
- Primary Care — Gearoid Cassidy
- Hospital Services Reform — Alastair Campbell
- General Policy — Robbie Davis
- Regional Health Services Transformation — Peter Jakobsen

Resources & Performance Management
Deputy Secretary: Deborah McNeilly
- Corporate Management Directorate — La'Verne Montgomery
- Investment Directorate — Preeta Miller
- Finance Directorate — Brigitte Worth
- Internal Audit — Tracey Woods

Chief Medical Officer
Michael McBride
- Deputy Chief Medical Officer — Lourda Geoghegan
- Deputy Chief Medical Officer — Naresh Chada
- Chief Pharmaceutical Officer — Cathy Harrison
- Chief Dental Officer — Michael Donaldson (acting)
- Chief Environmental Officer — Nigel McMahon
- Chief Scientific Officer — Ian Young

Social Care Policy Group
Deputy Secretary / Chief Social Services Officer: Sean Holland
- Deputy Chief Social Services Officer — Jackie McIlroy
- Mental Health, Disability & Older People — Peter Toogood
- Family & Children's Policy Directorate — Eilís McDaniel
- Director of Population Health — Liz Redmond

Chief Digital Information Officer Group
Deputy Secretary: Dan West
- Information & Analysis — Eugene Moore
- Information Governance — Vacant

Covid-19
Kieran McAteer
- Safety, Quality Standards — Donna Ruddy

128

Department of Health

- safety and quality policy, including standards and guidelines, professional regulation and adverse incident reporting and learning, service frameworks, death certification and sustainable development;

- providing specialist advice on medicines and pharmaceutical issues to the Minister and development of policy relating to medicines optimisation;

- ensuring compliance with legislative requirements for medicines control in Northern Ireland including the monitoring of the production, import/export, possession, supply and administration of controlled drugs and other medicinal products; and

- dental services.

Chief Medical Officer: Michael McBride
Tel: 028 9052 0563
Email: michael.mcbride@health-ni.gov.uk

Deputy Chief Medical Officer: Lourda Geoghegan
Tel: 028 9052 8173
Email: lourda.geoghegan@health-ni.gov.uk

Safety, Quality and Standards Directorate
Director: Donna Ruddy
Tel: 028 9076 5615
Email: donna.ruddy@health-ni.gov.uk

Covid-19 Directorate
Director: Kieran McAteer
Tel: 028 9052 0112
Email: kieran.mcateer@health-ni.gov.uk

Deputy Chief Medical Officer: Naresh Chada
Tel: 028 9052 2049
Email: naresh.chada@health-ni.gov.uk

Director of Population Health: Liz Redmond
Tel: 028 9052 2045
Email: liz.redmond@health-ni.gov.uk

Senior Medical Officer: Carol Beattie
Tel: 028 9052 0717
Email: carol.beattie@health-ni.gov.uk

Chief Pharmaceutical Officer: Cathy Harrison
Tel: 028 9052 3219
Email: cathy.harrison@health-ni.gov.uk

Senior Principal Pharmaceutical Officer: Canice Ward
Tel: 028 9052 3703
Email: canice.ward@health-ni.gov.uk

Senior Principal Pharmaceutical Officer: Christopher Garland
Tel: 028 9052 0050
Email: christopher.garland@health-ni.gov.uk

Head of Medicines Policy and EU Exit: Eimear Smyth (acting)
Tel: 028 9052 0236
Email: eimear.smyth@health-ni.gov.uk

Chief Dental Officer: Michael Donaldson (acting)
Tel: 028 9052 2940
Email: michael.donaldson@hscni.net

Chief Environmental Officer: Nigel McMahon
Tel: 028 9052 0552
Email: nigel.mcmahon@health-ni.gov.uk

Chief Scientific Officer: Professor Ian Young
Tel: 028 9052 2029
Email: ian.young2@health-ni.gov.uk

Nursing, Midwifery and Allied Health Professionals Directorate
The Chief Nursing Officer (CNO) leads the nursing, midwifery and allied health professionals (AHP) contribution to the development and implementation of health and social care policy in Northern Ireland. The CNO's team of professional nurses provide advice on acute and children's services, mental health, elderly care, learning and physical disabilities, public health, community nursing, primary care, midwifery, and international issues in nursing. They also advise on the regulations of professions, education policy, workforce planning and development.

The Lead AHP Officer is also a member of the CNO's team, providing advice and support on a range of AHP issues including regulation, professional development/training and workforce planning.

Chief Nursing Officer: Linda Kelly (interim)
Tel: 028 9052 3136
Email: linda.kelly@health-ni.gov.uk

Deputy Chief Nursing Officer: Heather Finlay (interim)
Tel: 028 9052 0007
Email: heather.finlay@health-ni.gov.uk

Lead AHP Officer: Jenny Keane
Tel: 028 9052 0722
Email: jenny.keane@health-ni.gov.uk

Transformation, Planning and Performance Group
This group oversees the implementation and programme management of the transformation agenda across the HSC in line with Health and Wellbeing 2026: Delivering Together. The group also oversees the development of commissioning priorities, leads work on the closure of the Health and Social Care Board, and has responsibility for performance management across the HSC. It also has sponsorship responsibility for the HSC Trusts.

Government Departments

Department of Health
An Roinn Sláinte
Männystrie O Poustie
www.health-ni.gov.uk

Deputy Secretary: Sharon Gallagher
Tel: 028 9052 0781
Email: sharon.gallagher@health-ni.gov.uk

Transformation Directorate
Director: Tomas Adell
Tel: 028 9052 0042
Email: tomas.adell@health-ni.gov.uk

Organisational Change Directorate
Director: Martina Moore
Tel: 028 9052 0596
Email: martina.moore@health-ni.gov.uk

Performance Management Directorate
Director: Lisa McWilliams
Tel: 028 9536 3271
Email: lisa.mcwilliams@hscni.net

Chief Digital Information Officer Group
The role of this group is about using data and technology to improve health and care experiences and outcomes in the region, and to create an economically sustainable service for future generations.

Deputy Secretary: Dan West
Tel: 028 9052 0211
Email: dan.west@health-ni.gov.uk

Information Governance Directorate
Director: Vacant

Information and Analysis
Director: Eugene Mooney
Tel: 028 9052 0726
Email: eugene.mooney@health-ni.gov.uk

Trusts, Agencies, Non-Departmental Public Bodies and other organisations within DoH

Belfast Health and Social Care Trust
Trust Headquarters
A Floor, Belfast City Hospital
Lisburn Road, Belfast, BT9 7AB
Tel: 028 9504 0100
Web: www.belfasttrust.hscni.net
Email: info@belfasttrust.hscni.net
Chair: Peter McNaney
Chief Executive: Cathy Jack

Business Services Organisation
7th Floor, 2 Franklin Street
Belfast, BT2 8DQ
Tel: 0300 555 0113
Web: www.hscbusiness.hscni.net
Chair: Julie Erskine
Chief Executive: Karen Bailey (acting)

Food Standards Agency Northern Ireland
10A-C Clarendon Road
Belfast, BT1 3BG
Tel: 0330 3327149 option #4
Web: www.food.gov.uk/northern-ireland
Email: infosani@foodstandards.gsi.gov.uk
Director: Maria Jennings

Health and Social Care Board
Headquarters
12-22 Linenhall Street
Belfast, BT2 8BS
Tel: 0300 555 0115
Web: www.hscboard.hscni.net
Email: enquiry.hscb@hscni.net
Chair: Les Drew
Chief Executive: Sharon Gallagher

Northern Health and Social Care Trust
Trust Headquarters
Bretten Hall
Bush Road, Co Antrim
BT41 2RL
Tel: 028 9442 4000
Web: www.northerntrust.hscni.net
Chair: Bob McCann
Chief Executive: Jennifer Welsh

Patient and Client Council
5th Floor
14-16 Great Victoria Street
Belfast, BT2 7BA
Tel: 0800 917 0222
Web: www.patientclientcouncil.hscni.net
Email: info.pcc@pcc-ni.net
Chief Executive: Vivian McConvey

Public Health Agency
Linenhall Street Unit
12-22 Linenhall Street
Belfast, BT2 8BS
Tel: 0300 555 0114
Web: www.publichealth.hscni.net
Chair: Andrew Dougal
Chief Executive: Aidan Dawson

South Eastern Health and Social Care Trust
Ulster Hospital
Upper Newtownards Road
Dundonald
Belfast, BT16 1RH
Tel: 028 9048 4511
Web: www.setrust.hscni.net
Email: public.relations@setrust.hscni.net
Chair: Jonathan Patton (acting)
Chief Executive: Roisin Coulter

Southern Health and Social Care Trust
Southern College of Nursing
Craigavon Area Hospital
68 Lurgan Road
Portadown, BT63 5QQ
Tel: 028 3833 4444
Web: www.southerntrust.hscni.net
Email: corporate.hq@southerntrust.hscni.net
Chair: Eileen Mullan
Chief Executive: Shane Devlin

Western Health and Social Care Trust
MDEC Building
Altnagelvin Area Hospital site
Glenshane Road
Derry, BT47 6SB
Tel: 028 7134 5171
Web: www.westerntrust.hscni.net
Email: info.enquiry@westerntrust.hscni.net
Chair: Sam Pollock
Chief Executive: Neil Guckian

Northern Ireland Ambulance Service Trust
30 Knockbracken Healthcare Park
Saintfield Road
Belfast, BT8 8SG
Tel: 028 9040 0999
Web: www.niamb.co.uk
Chair: Nicole Lappin
Chief Executive: Michael Bloomfield

Northern Ireland Blood Transfusion Service
Belfast City Hospital Complex
51 Lisburn Road
Belfast, BT9 7TS
Tel: 028 9032 1414
Web: www.nibts.org
Email: inet@nibts.hscni.net
Chair: Bonnie Anley
Chief Executive: Karin Jackson

Northern Ireland Fire & Rescue Service
1 Seymour Street
Lisburn, BT27 4SX
Tel: 028 9266 4221
Web: www.nifrs.org
Chair: Carmel McKinney
Chief Fire & Rescue Officer: Peter O'Reilly

Northern Ireland Guardian Ad Litem Agency
Centre House
79 Chichester Street
Belfast, BT1 4JE
Tel: 0300 555 0102
Web: www.nigala.hscni.net
Email: admin@nigala.hscni.net
Chair: Gemma Loughran
Chief Executive: Dawn Shaw

Northern Ireland Medical and Dental Training Agency
Beechill House
42 Beechill Road
Belfast, BT8 7RL
Tel: 028 9040 0000
Web: www.nimdta.gov.uk
Email: nimdta@nimdta.gov.uk
Chair: Mark McCarey

Northern Ireland Practice and Education Council for Nursing and Midwifery (NIPEC)
79 Chichester Street
Belfast, BT1 4JE
Tel: 0300 300 0066
Web: www.nipec.hscni.net
Email: enquiries@nipec.hscni.net
Chief Executive: Angela McLernon

Northern Ireland Social Care Council
7th Floor, Millennium House
19-25 Great Victoria Street
Belfast, BT2 7AQ
Tel: 028 9536 2600
Web: www.niscc.info
Email: info@niscc.hscni.net
Chair: Paul Martin
Chief Executive: Patricia Higgins (interim)

Regulation and Quality Improvement Authority
7th Floor, Victoria House
15-27 Gloucester Street
Belfast
BT1 4LS
Tel: 028 9536 1111
Web: www.rqia.org.uk
Email: info@rqia.org.uk
Chair: Christine Collins (interim)
Chief Executive: Briege Donaghy

Department for Infrastructure (DfI)

Department for Infrastructure
An Roinn Bonneagair
www.infrastructure-ni.gov.uk

Clarence Court
10-18 Adelaide Street
Belfast, BT2 8GB
Tel: 028 9054 0540
Web: www.infrastructure-ni.gov.uk
Email: info@infrastructure-ni.gov.uk

Minister:
Nichola Mallon MLA

Permanent Secretary:
Katrina Godfrey
Tel: 028 9054 1175
Email: katrina.godfrey@infrastructure-ni.gov.uk

Special Advisor:
Tanya McCamphill
Email: private.office@infrastructure-ni.gov.uk

Private Office
Private Secretary:
Kathryn McFerran
Tel: 028 9054 0105
Email: private.office@infrastructure-ni.gov.uk

Communications Team
Principal Information Officer:
Áine Gaughran
Tel: 028 9054 0116
Email: aine.gaughran@infrastructure-ni.gov.uk

The Department's purpose statement is: 'Every day connecting people safely, supporting opportunities and creating sustainable living places'. Its responsibilities include: regional strategic planning, planning policy and legislation; transport strategy and sustainable transport policy; public transport policy and performance; management of public roads; road safety, vehicle and driver testing, driver licensing and enforcement; watercourse and coastal flooding; and policy on water, sewerage services and drainage.

Resources, Governance and EU Group
Deputy Secretary:
Declan McGeown
Tel: 028 9054 1180
Email: declan.mcgeown@infrastructure-ni.gov.uk

Roads and Rivers
Deputy Secretary:
Andrew Murray
Tel: 028 9054 0191
Email: andrew.murray@infrastructure-ni.gov.uk

Planning, Safety and Transport Policy Group
Deputy Secretary:
Julie Thompson
Tel: 028 9054 0175
Email: julie.thompson@infrastructure-ni.gov.uk

Resources, Governance and EU Group

Director, Gateways and EU Relations:
Bernie Rooney
Tel: 028 9054 2915
Email: bernie.rooney@infrastructure-ni.gov.uk

Public Transport Directorate:
Jackie Robinson
Tel: 028 9034 6247
Email: jackie.robinson@infrastructure-ni.gov.uk

Director of Finance:
Susan Anderson
Tel: 028 9054 0848
Email: susan.anderson@infrastructure-ni.gov.uk

Director of Corporate Support Services:
Linda MacHugh
Tel: 028 9054 1023
Email: linda.machugh@infrastructure-ni.gov.uk

Director of Corporate Policy and Planning:
Sian Kerr
Tel: 028 9034 6228
Email: sian.kerr@infrastructure-ni.gov.uk

Director of Water and Drainage Policy:
Alison Clydesdale
Tel: 028 9034 6200
Email: alison.clydesdale@infrastructure-ni.gov.uk

Director of Living with Water Programme:
Simon Richardson
Tel: 028 9054 0103
Email: simon.richardson@infrastructure-ni.gov.uk

Department for Infrastructure
An Roinn Bonneagair
www.infrastructure-ni.gov.uk

Planning, Safety and Transport Policy Group

Director of Transport Policy:
Liz Loughran
Tel: 028 9054 0843
Email: liz.loughran@infrastructure-ni.gov.uk

Director of Safe and Accessible Travel:
Chris Hughes
Tel: 028 9034 6242
Email: chris.hughes@infrastructure-ni.gov.uk

Director of Strategic Planning:
Alistair Beggs
Tel: 028 9054 0637
Email: alistair.beggs@infrastructure-ni.gov.uk

Chief Planner and Director of Regional Planning:
Angus Kerr
Tel: 028 9054 0636
Email: angus.kerr@infrastructure-ni.gov.uk

DVA Chief Executive:
Jeremy Logan
Tel: 028 9025 4125
Email: jeremy.logan@infrastructure-ni.gov.uk

Head of Internal Audit:
Lacey Walker
Tel: 028 9054 7888
Email: lacey.walker@infrastructure-ni.gov.uk

Roads and Rivers Group

Roads and Rivers HQ
Clarence Court
10-18 Adelaide Street
Belfast, BT2 8GB
Tel: 028 9054 0540
Web: www.infrastructure-ni.gov.uk

Director of Engineering:
David Porter (acting)
Tel: 028 9034 6273
Email: david.porter@infrastructure-ni.gov.uk

Director of Major Projects and Procurement:
John Irvine
Tel: 028 9054 0634
Email: john.irvine@infrastructure-ni.gov.uk

Director of Network Services:
Conor Loughrey
Tel: 028 9054 0462
Email: conor.loughrey@infrastructure-ni.gov.uk

Director of Rivers:
Jonathan McKee
Tel: 028 8675 7505
Email: jonathan.mckee@infrastructure-ni.gov.uk

Head of Roads Claims Unit:
Déaglán Coleman
Tel: 028 9054 0914
Email: deaglan.coleman@infrastructure-ni.gov.uk

Roads Regional Offices

Eastern Division
Tel: 0300 200 7899
Email: DfIRoads.eastern@infrastructure-ni.gov.uk
Divisional Manager: Kevin Monaghan

Northern Division
County Hall, Castlerock Road
Coleraine, BT51 3HS
Tel: 0300 200 7899
Email: DfIRoads.northern@infrastructure-ni.gov.uk
Divisional Manager: Colin Hutchinson

Southern Division
Marlborough House
Central Way
Craigavon, BT64 1AD
Tel: 0300 200 7899
Email: DfIRoads.southern@infrastructure-ni.gov.uk
Divisional Manager: Mark McPeak

Western Division
County Hall, Drumragh Avenue
Omagh, BT79 7AF
Tel: 0300 200 7899
Email: DfIRoads.western@infrastructure-ni.gov.uk
Divisional Manager: David McKinley

Consultancy Services
Rathkeltair House
Market Street
Downpatrick, BT30 6AJ
Tel: 028 4461 8220
Email: roads.consultancy@infrastructure-ni.gov.uk
Head of Consultancy Services: Ian McClung

Government Departments — Northern Ireland Yearbook

Department for Infrastructure organisation chart

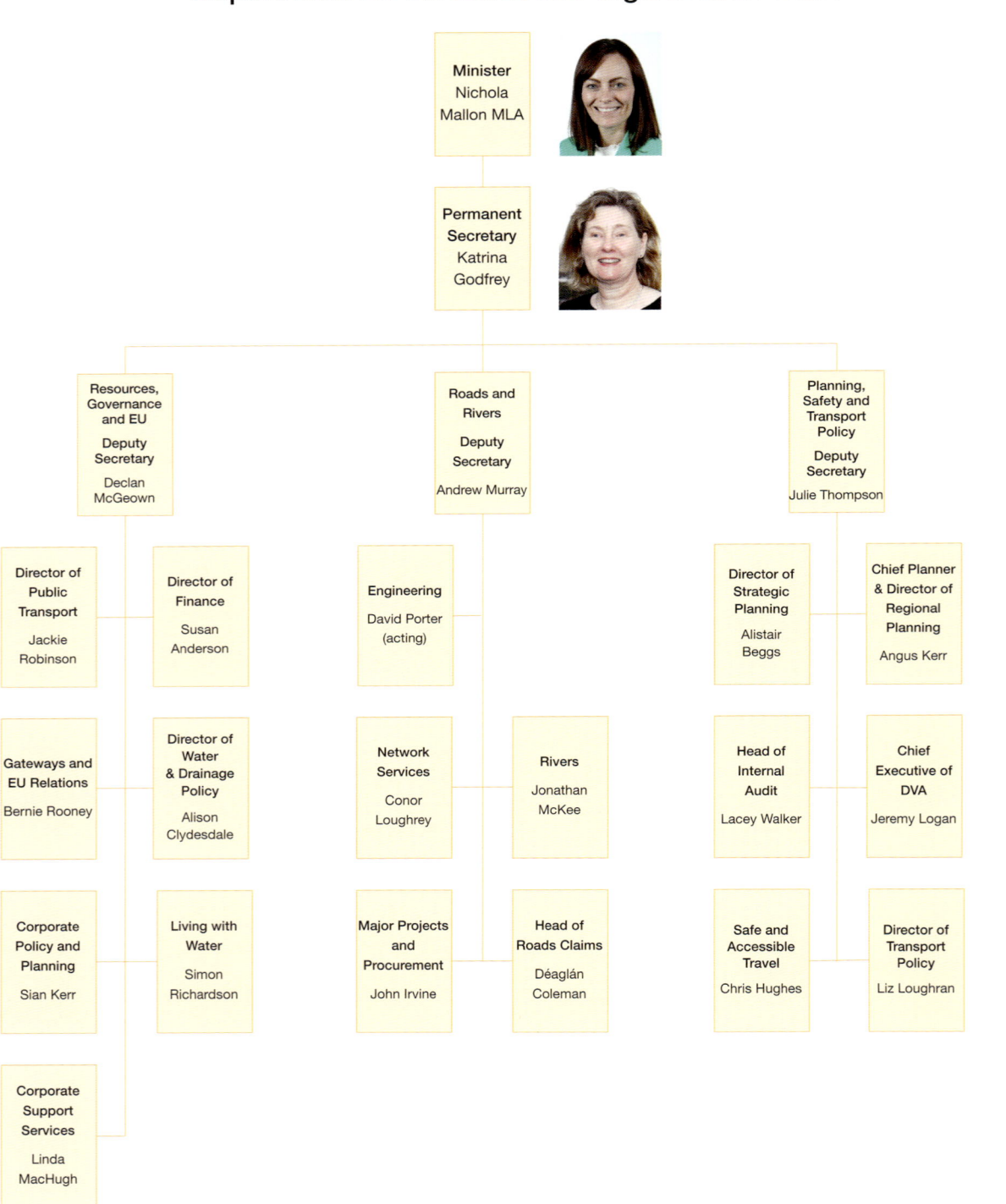

Minister — Nichola Mallon MLA

Permanent Secretary — Katrina Godfrey

Resources, Governance and EU
Deputy Secretary — Declan McGeown

- Director of Public Transport — Jackie Robinson
- Director of Finance — Susan Anderson
- Gateways and EU Relations — Bernie Rooney
- Director of Water & Drainage Policy — Alison Clydesdale
- Corporate Policy and Planning — Sian Kerr
- Living with Water — Simon Richardson
- Corporate Support Services — Linda MacHugh

Roads and Rivers
Deputy Secretary — Andrew Murray

- Engineering — David Porter (acting)
- Network Services — Conor Loughrey
- Rivers — Jonathan McKee
- Major Projects and Procurement — John Irvine
- Head of Roads Claims — Déaglán Coleman

Planning, Safety and Transport Policy
Deputy Secretary — Julie Thompson

- Director of Strategic Planning — Alistair Beggs
- Chief Planner & Director of Regional Planning — Angus Kerr
- Head of Internal Audit — Lacey Walker
- Chief Executive of DVA — Jeremy Logan
- Safe and Accessible Travel — Chris Hughes
- Director of Transport Policy — Liz Loughran

www.infrastructure-ni.gov.uk

Department for Infrastructure / An Roinn Bonneagair

www.infrastructure-ni.gov.uk

Operations and Maintenance
County Hall
182 Galgorm Road
Ballymena, BT42 1QG
Tel: 028 2565 3333
Email: operationsandmaintenance@infrastructure-ni.gov.uk
Head of Operations and Maintenance: Damien McQuillan

Agencies, Non-Departmental Public Bodies and other organisations within DfI

Arm's Length Bodies

Drainage Council for NI
Secretariat to the Drainage Council
c/o DfI Rivers
49 Tullywiggan Road
Loughry
Cookstown
Co Tyrone
BT80 8SG
Tel: 028 8676 8342
Email: rivers.registry@infrastructure-ni.gov.uk

Northern Ireland Water
Westland House
40 Old Westland Road
Belfast, BT14 6TE
Waterline: 0345 744 0088
Web: www.niwater.com
Email: waterline@niwater.com
Chief Executive: Sara Venning

Northern Ireland Transport Holding Company
Chamber of Commerce House
22 Great Victoria Street
Belfast, BT2 7LX
Tel: 028 9024 3456
Web: www.translink.co.uk/corporate
Chair: Michael Wardlow
Group Chief Executive: Chris Conway

North-South Body

Waterways Ireland
2 Sligo Road
Enniskillen
Co Fermanagh
BT74 7JY
Tel: 028 6632 3004
Email: info@waterwaysireland.org
Chief Executive: John McDonagh

Ports

Belfast Harbour Commissioners
Harbour Office
Corporation Square
Belfast, BT1 3AL
Tel: 028 9055 4422
Web: www.belfast-harbour.co.uk
Email: info@belfast-harbour.co.uk
Chair: Theresa Donaldson
Chief Executive: Joe O'Neill

Coleraine Harbour
Harbour Office
4 Riversdale Road
Coleraine, BT52 1XA
Tel: 028 7034 2012
Web: www.coleraineharbour.com
Email: info@coleraineharbour.com
Chair: James Millar
General Manager: Lisa McLaughlin

Foyle Port
Harbour Office
Port Road, Lisahally
Derry, BT47 6FL
Tel: 028 7186 0555
Web: www.foyleport.com
Chair: Bonnie Anley
Chief Executive: Brian McGrath

Warrenpoint Harbour Authority
The Docks
Warrenpoint, BT34 3JR
Tel: 028 4177 3381
Web: www.warrenpointport.com
Email: info@warrenpointharbour.co.uk
Chair: WG O'Hare
Chief Executive: David Holmes

Department of Justice (DoJ)

Department of Justice
www.justice-ni.gov.uk

Block B, Castle Buildings
Belfast, BT4 3SG
Tel: 028 9076 3000
Textphone: 028 9052 7668
Web: www.justice-ni.gov.uk

Minister:
Naomi Long MLA

Permanent Secretary:
Peter May
Tel: 028 9052 2992
Email: peter.may@justice-ni.gov.uk

Minister's Office
Private Secretary: Tim Logan
Tel: 028 9052 2704
Email: tim.logan@justice-ni.gov.uk

Press Office
Contact: Karen Fullerton
Tel: 028 9052 6250
Email: karen.fullerton@justice-ni.gov.uk

The Department of Justice (DOJ) has a range of devolved policing and justice functions set out in the Northern Ireland Act 1998 (Devolution of Policing and Justice Functions) Order 2010.

The DOJ's mission is: "We have a safe community where we respect the law and each other". The Departmental priorities can be described in terms of the following themes:

- **Support safe and resilient communities**
  We will work with our partners to help build safe and resilient communities and reduce the vulnerability of individuals to becoming a potential victim and/or offender. We will empower communities, businesses and individuals to protect themselves from becoming a victim of crime, and will provide support where people do become victims of crime. We will also work with within a multi-agency partnership model to provide for and link strategic and operational responses to cross-cutting community safety issues, and will address criminality and coercive control within our communities through proactive collaboration and local problem solving.

- **Address harm and vulnerability**
  We will work with partners to provide early stage diversionary approaches to address issues that contribute to offending behaviours. We will provide practical support to victims, and develop policies and legislation to protect those most vulnerable in our society.

- **Challenge offending behaviours and support rehabilitation**
  We will work with people who offend to challenge their behaviour and support them to become active and responsible citizens. Working with our partners we will promote rehabilitation; and when a custodial sentence is imposed our focus will be on resettlement leading to integration back into society.

- **Deliver an effective justice system**
  We will lead work to make our justice system faster and more effective, and more importantly, to serve the needs of those who engage with it. We will ensure appropriate access to justice for our citizens. We will also deliver a system which supports other court users in the early and proportionate resolution of civil and family proceedings. We will support and empower people working within the justice system to deliver effectively.

- **Secure confidence in the justice system**
  We will use new and innovative ways of engaging with communities, with our partners and stakeholders to explain the work that we do and build broad support for it; to ensure that we are responsive to the needs of citizens, and to enhance accountability around what we do.

The Department of Justice has an annual Department Expenditure Limit of approximately £1.2 billion. A number of major capital projects are currently in development.

The DOJ has four Directorates and five Agencies and also sponsors a number of Non-Departmental Public Bodies/bodies affiliated with policing and justice.

Directorates

Justice Delivery Directorate

Justice Delivery Directorate is responsible for helping the Department of Justice to meet its objectives through the provision of high-quality customer focused corporate services. The Directorate's role is pivotal in resource management and promoting 'Value For Money' in the Department. Its work includes specialist support within the key areas of Finance, Staff support services, Records management, Audit, Procurement and Information and Communication Technologies, Compensation Services for victims of crime, administrative support to the Victims' Payments Board and support to the DoJ Board. In addition it provides support to the Minister through the Private Office and Press Office functions.

Department of Justice
www.justice-ni.gov.uk

The Directorate also includes the Legal Services Agency and AccessNI.

Director: Deborah Brown
Tel: 028 9052 3732
Email: deborah.brown@justice-ni.gov.uk

The Director is supported by four Deputy Directors:

Financial Services Division
Deputy Director: Vacant
Tel: 028 9052 0140

Information Services Division
Deputy Director: John Napier
Tel: 028 9052 6373
Email: john.napier@justice-ni.gov.uk

Enabling Access to Justice
Deputy Director: Eamon O'Connor
Tel: 028 9016 9255
Email: eamon.oconnor@justice-ni.gov.uk

Corporate Engagement and Communications Division
Deputy Director: David Lennox
Tel: 028 9052 3787
Email: david.lennox@justice-ni.gov.uk

Access to Justice Directorate
Access to Justice Directorate is the Department's policy and legislation hub. It covers Criminal Justice, Civil Justice (although some aspects of civil law remain with other NI Departments) and Justice Performance. The Directorate also manages the greater part of the Department's legislation programme. The Directorate also includes one of the Department's largest Agencies, the Northern Ireland Courts and Tribunal Service (NICTS), and is the sponsor body for Criminal Justice Inspection NI (CJINI).

Director: Glyn Capper
Massey House
Tel: 028 9016 9574
Email: glyn.capper@justice-ni.gov.uk

The Director is supported by four Deputy Directors:

Criminal Justice Policy and Legislation Division (including Legacy of the Past)
Deputy Director: Brian Grzymek
Tel: 028 9016 9571
Email: brian.grzymek@justice-ni.gov.uk

Civil Justice Policy Division
Deputy Director: Laurene McAlpine
Tel: 028 9016 3570
Email: laurene.mcalpine@justice-ni.gov.uk

Justice Performance
Deputy Director: Vacant
Tel: 028 9016 9511

Gillen Review, Victims and Witness Branch and EU Exit Unit
Deputy Director: Julie Wilson
Tel: 028 9016 9630
Email: julie.wilson@justice-ni.gov.uk

Safer Communities Directorate
Safer Communities Directorate is the lead departmental interface with PSNI and has sponsorship responsibility for the majority of the Department's NDPBs, as well as shared governance responsibility for the Policing and Community Safety Partnerships with the Northern Ireland Policing Board. Forensic Science Northern Ireland also falls within SCD.

The Directorate is responsible for issues related to crime and community safety including serious and organised crime, violence against the person and public protection. SCD also leads on civil contingency planning and firearms and explosives.

Director: Julie Harrison
Tel: 028 9052 0442
Email: julie.harrison@justice-ni.gov.uk

The Director is supported by five Deputy Directors:

Policing Policy and Strategy Division
Deputy Director: Maura Campbell
Tel: 028 9052 2740
Email: maura.campbell@justice-ni.gov.uk

Protection and Organised Crime Division
Deputy Director: Cathy Galway
Tel: 028 9052 4219
Email: cathy.galway@justice-ni.gov.uk

Community Safety Division
Deputy Director: Katie Taylor
Tel: 028 9037 8649
Email: katie.taylor@justice-ni.gov.uk

Tackling Paramilitarism Programme Team
Programme Director: Adele Brown
Tel: 028 9052 2655
Email: adele.brown@justice-ni.gov.uk

Forensic Science Northern Ireland (FSNI)
Chief Executive: Gillian Morton
Tel: 028 9035 1800
Email: gillian.morton@justice-ni.gov.uk

Department of Justice
www.justice-ni.gov.uk

Reducing Offending Directorate

Reducing Offending Directorate (ROD) provides end to end support to individuals to reduce the risk of offending through diversion, intervention, rehabilitation and joined-up custodial services. ROD is responsible for setting reducing offending policy and for sponsorship of the Northern Ireland Prison Service (NIPS) and the Youth Justice Agency (YJA).

The Northern Ireland Prison Service (NIPS) is an agency within the Department of Justice. It is responsible for the operation and delivery of services within the Northern Ireland prison system and has overall responsibility for the Youth Justice Agency.

The overall aim of the Northern Ireland Prison Service is to improve public safety by reducing the risk of re-offending through the management and rehabilitation of offenders in custody.

Northern Ireland Prison Service
Headquarters
Dundonald House
Upper Newtownards Road
Belfast, BT4 3SU
Tel: 028 9052 2922
Web: www.justice-ni.gov.uk/topics/prisons

Director of Reducing Offending and Director General of the Northern Ireland Prison Service:
Ronnie Armour
Tel: 028 9052 5219
Email: ronnie.armour@justice-ni.gov.uk

The Director is supported by two Deputy Directors and three Governors.

Director of Prisons: David Kennedy
Tel: 028 9052 5319
Email: david.kennedy@justice-ni.gov.uk

Director of Rehabilitation: Paul Doran
Tel: 028 9052 5178
Email: paul.doran@justice-ni.gov.uk

Maghaberry Prison
Old Road, Ballinderry Upper
Lisburn, BT28 2PT
Tel: 028 9261 1888
Governing Governor: David Savage
Deputy Governor: Tom Ferguson

Magilligan Prison
Point Road
Limavady, BT49 0LR
Tel: 028 7776 3311
Governing Governor: Gary Milling
Acting Deputy Governor: Alan Platt

Hydebank Wood College and Women's Prison
Hospital Road
Belfast, BT8 8NA
Tel: 028 9025 3666
Governing Governor: Richard Taylor
Deputy Governor: Tracey Megrath

Prison Service College
Hydebank Wood College
Hospital Road
Belfast, BT8 8NA

Agencies

Northern Ireland Courts and Tribunals Service
Laganside House
23-27 Oxford Street
Belfast, BT1 3LA
Tel: 0300 200 7812

Director: Glyn Capper
Laganside House
Tel: 028 9016 9574
Email: glyn.capper@justice-ni.gov.uk

Chief Operating Officer: Mark Goodfellow
Laganside House
Tel: 028 9041 2329
Email: mark.goodfellow@courtsni.gov.uk

Chief Modernisation Officer: Karen Ward
Laganside House
Tel: 028 9041 2329
Email: karen.ward@courtsni.gov.uk

Head of Legacy Inquest Unit: Patrick Butler
Laganside House
Tel: 028 9044 6802
Email: patrick.butler@courtsni.gov.uk

Principal Private Secretary to the Lord Chief Justice:
Mandy Kilpatrick
Royal Courts of Justice
Tel: 028 9072 4614
Email: mandy.kilpatrick@courtsni.gov.uk

The Northern Ireland Courts and Tribunals Service (NICTS) provides administrative support for Northern Ireland's courts and tribunals, and to the Judiciary; enforces civil court judgments through the Enforcement of Judgments Office and manages funds held in court on behalf of minors and patients.

Legal Services Agency Northern Ireland
2nd Floor, Waterfront Plaza
8 Laganbank Road
Mays Meadow, Belfast
BT1 3BN
Tel: 028 9040 8888
Web: www.justice-ni.gov.uk/topics/legal-aid
Email: enquiries@lsani.gov.uk
Chief Executive: Paul Andrews

The Northern Ireland Legal Services Agency supports the justice system by administering publicly funded legal services impartially, effectively and efficiently within the legislative and policy framework set by the Department of Justice.

Forensic Science Northern Ireland (FSNI)
151 Belfast Road
Carrickfergus
BT38 8PL
Tel: 028 9036 1888
Web: www.justice-ni.gov.uk/topics/forensic-science
Email: FSNISM.ForensicScience@fsni.gov.uk

Chief Executive: Gillian Morton
Tel: 028 9036 1801
Email: gillian.morton@fsni.gov.uk

FSNI is an independent and impartial organisation providing objective scientific expertise to enhance the delivery of justice.

Youth Justice Agency of Northern Ireland
41 Waring Street
Belfast, BT1 2DY
Tel: 028 9031 6400
Web: www. justice-ni.gov.uk/topics/youth-justice
Email: info@yjani.gov.uk
Chief Executive: Stephen Martin

The Youth Justice Agency delivers a range of services, often in partnership with others, to help children address their offending behaviour, divert them from crime, assist their integration into the community, and to meet the needs of victims of crime.

Other organisations

Coroners Service for Northern Ireland
Laganside House
23-27 Oxford Street
Belfast, BT1 3LA
Tel: 0300 200 7811
Email: coronersoffice@courtsni.gov.uk

Criminal Justice Inspection Northern Ireland
Block 1
Knockview Buildings
Stormont Estate
Belfast, BT4 3SJ
Tel: 028 9076 5764
Web: www.cjini.org
Email: info@cjini.org
Chief Inspector of Criminal Justice: Jacqui Durkin

Lady Chief Justice for Northern Ireland
c/o Royal Courts of Justice
Chichester Street
Belfast, BT1 3JF
Tel: 0300 200 7812
Lady Chief Justice: Mrs Justice Siobhan Keegan

Northern Ireland Policing Board
Waterside Tower
31 Clarendon Road, Clarendon Dock
Belfast, BT1 3BG
Tel: 028 9040 8500
Web: www.nipolicingboard.org.uk
Email: information@nipolicingboard.org.uk
Chief Executive: Sinead Simpson

Parole Commissioners for Northern Ireland
Parole Commissioners Secretariat
Laganside Court
Mezzanine, 1st Floor
Oxford Street
Belfast, BT1 3LL
Tel: 028 9041 2969
Web: www.parolecomni.org.uk
Email: referrals@parolecomni.x.gsi.gov.uk
Chief Commissioner: Paul Mageean

Police Ombudsman for Northern Ireland
New Cathedral Buildings
Writer's Square
11 Church Street
Belfast, BT1 1PG
Tel: 028 9082 8600
Web: www.policeombudsman.org
Email: info@policeombudsman.org
Ombudsman: Marie Anderson

Department of Justice organisation chart

Minister — Naomi Long MLA

Permanent Secretary — Peter May

Agencies
- **Youth Justice Agency** — Stephen Martin
- **Forensic Science NI** — Gillian Morton
- **Probation Board NI** — Amanda Stewart
- **NI Courts & Tribunals Service** — Glyn Capper
- **Lady Chief Justice** — The Right Honourable Dame Siobhan Keegan
- **Legal services Agency NI** — Paul Andrews
- **NI Policing Board** — Sinead Simpson

Access to Justice — Glyn Capper
- **Criminal Justice Policy & Legislation Division** — Brian Grzymek
- **Civil Justice Policy** — Laurene McAlpine
- **Justice Performance** — Vacant
- **Gillen Review, Victims & Witness Branch & EU Exit** — Julie Wilson

Justice Delivery — Deborah Brown
- **Financial Services** — Vacant
- **Information Services** — John Napier
- **Corporate Engagement & Communications** — David Lennox
- **Enabling Access to Justice** — Eamon O'Connor

Safer Communities — Julie Harrison
- **Policing Policy and Strategy** — Maura Campbell
- **Protection & Organised Crime** — Cathy Galway
- **Community Safety** — Katie Taylor
- **Tackling Paramilitarism** — Adele Brown

NI Prison Service & Reducing Offending — Ronnie Armour
- **Prisons** — David Kennedy
- **Rehabilitation** — Paul Doran

Police Service of Northern Ireland
Headquarters
Brooklyn, 65 Knock Road
Belfast, BT5 6LE
Tel: 101
Crimestoppers: 0800 555 111
Web: www.psni.police.uk
Chief Constable: Simon Byrne
Deputy Chief Constable: Mark Hamilton

The Prisoner Ombudsman for Northern Ireland
Unit 2, Walled Garden
Department of Justice (DOJ)
Stormont Estate, Belfast
BT4 3SH
Tel: 028 9052 7771
Web: www.niprisonerombudsman.com
Email: pa@prisonerombudsman.x.gsi.gov.uk
Ombudsman: Lesley Carroll

Probation Board for Northern Ireland
80-90 North Street
Belfast, BT1 1LD
Tel: 028 9026 2400
Web: www.pbni.org.uk
Email: info@pbni.gsi.gov.uk
Chair: Dale Ashford
Chief Executive: Amanda Stewart

Public Prosecution Service
Central Management Unit
Belfast Chambers
93 Chichester Street
Belfast, BT1 3JR
Tel: 028 9089 7100
Web: www.ppsni.gov.uk
Email: info@ppsni.gov.uk
Director: Stephen Herron

State Pathologist's Department
Grosvenor Road
Belfast BT12 6BS
Tel: 028 9063 4648
State Pathologist: Dr J R Lyness

Advertise in the 2023 edition

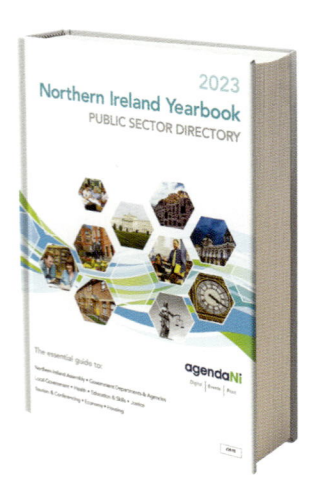

Advertise in the Northern Ireland Yearbook

With a shelf-life of at least a year, the Northern Ireland Yearbook presents an ideal platform for organisations to showcase their brand and services to a unique senior executive readership. Choice of marketing activity is key when communicating important messages to an already influential audience – our advertising team can help you to establish the most cost-effective return for your investment.

Creative marketing opportunities include advertisements, advertorials, sponsorship, gatefolds and many more. We work closely with all of our clients to guarantee maximum exposure and customer satisfaction and we are also happy to take care of any design requirements on behalf of the client (at no extra cost).

Benefits of sponsorship and advertising:

- An excellent platform for organisations to raise their profile
- Create awareness of the organisation's services
- Communicate key messages to important stakeholders
- Yearlong profiling opportunity
- Feature in a unique publication used as an essential reference guide across all sectors
- Prime positions available within particular chapters of key sectors
- Package options available across a series of bmf business services publications
- Be a thought leader in your area

Advertising opportunities:

- Display advertising
- Advertorials (branded-style articles)
- Front cover profile
- Sponsorship of the directory
- Sponsorship of individual chapters
- Roundtable discussion features

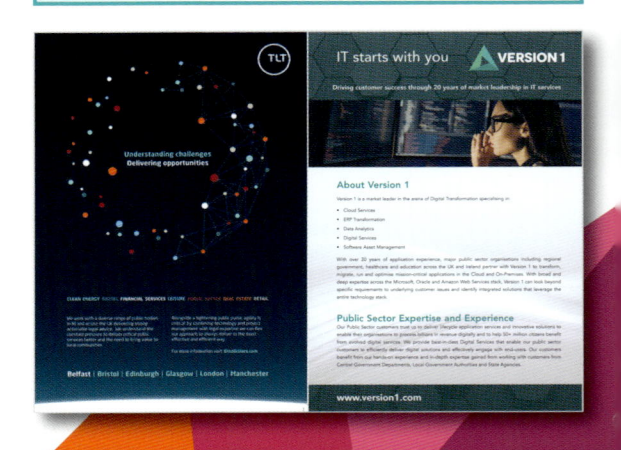

To discuss advertising opportunities in the Northern Ireland Yearbook 2022 contact us on 028 9261 9933 or email info@agendani.com.

Northern Ireland Yearbook | Government Departments

An A-Z Guide to government agencies and other public bodies

Agri-Food and Biosciences Institute
Headquarters, 18A Newforge Lane
Belfast, BT9 5PX
Tel: 028 9025 5636
Web: www.afbini.gov.uk
Email: info@afbini.gov.uk
Chair: Colin Coffey
Chief Executive:
Stanley McDowell

Armagh Observatory
College Hill, Armagh, BT61 9DG
Tel: 028 3752 2928
Web: www.armagh.ac.uk
Email: administrator@arm.ac.uk
Director: Michael Burton

Armagh Planetarium
College Hill, Armagh, BT61 9DB
Tel: 028 3752 4725
Web: www.armaghplanet.com
Email: info@armaghplanet.com
Chief Executive: Michael Burton

Arts Council of Northern Ireland
23 Linenhall Street
Lisburn, BT28 1FJ
Tel: 028 9262 3555
Web: www.artscouncil-ni.org
Email: info@artscouncil-ni.org
Chief Executive: Róisín McDonough

Attorney General for Northern Ireland
PO Box 1272
Belfast
BT1 9LU
Tel: 028 9072 5333
Web: www.attorneygeneralni.gov.uk
Email: contact@attorneygeneralni.gov.uk
Attorney General: Brenda King

The Bar of Northern Ireland
91 Chichester Street
Belfast, BT1 3JQ
Tel: 028 9024 1523
Web: www.barofni.com
Chair: Bernard Brady QC
Chief Executive: David Mulholland

Belfast Harbour Commissioners
Harbour Office, Corporation Square
Belfast, BT1 3AL
Tel: 028 9055 4422
Web: www.belfast-harbour.co.uk
Email: info@belfast-harbour.co.uk
Chair: Theresa Donaldson
Chief Executive: Joe O'Neill

Belfast Health and Social Care Trust
Trust Headquarters
A Floor, Belfast City Hospital
Lisburn Road, Belfast, BT9 7AB
Tel: 028 9504 0100
Web: www.belfasttrust.hscni.net
Email: info@belfasttrust.hscni.net
Chair: Peter McNaney
Chief Executive: Cathy Jack

Business Services Organisation
7th Floor, 2 Franklin Street
Belfast, BT2 8DQ
Tel: 0300 555 0113
Web: www.hscbusiness.hscni.net
Email: admin.office@hscni.net
Chair: Julie Erskine
Chief Executive: Karen Bailey (acting)

Charity Commission for Northern Ireland
Marlborough House
Central Way
Craigavon, BT64 1AD
Tel: 028 3832 0220
Textphone: 028 3834 7639
Web: www.charitycommissionni.org.uk
Email: admin@charitycommissionni.org.uk
Chief Commissioner: Nicole Lappin
Chief Executive: Frances McCandless

Coleraine Harbour Comissioners
Harbour Office
4 Riversdale Road
Coleraine, BT52 1XA
Tel: 028 7034 2012
Web: www.coleraineharbour.com
Email: info@coleraineharbour.com
Manager: Lisa McLaughlin

Comhairle na Gaelscolaíochta
Áras na bhFál
202 Falls Road
Belfast
BT12 6AF
Guthán: 028 9032 1475
Web: www.comhairle.org
R-Phost: eolas@comhairle.org
Príomhfheidhmeannach:
Ciarán Mac Giolla Bhéin

Commission for Victims and Survivors for Northern Ireland
Equality House
4th Floor, 7-9 Shaftesbury Square
Belfast, BT2 7DP
Tel: 028 9031 1000
Web: www.cvsni.org
Email: commission@cvsni.org
Twitter: @nivictimscom
Commissioner: Vacant
Chief Executive: Andrew Sloan

Commissioner for Older People Northern Ireland
Equality House, 6th Floor
7-9 Shaftesbury Square
Belfast, BT2 7DP
Tel: 028 9089 0892
Web: www.copni.org
Email: info@copni.org
Commissioner: Eddie Lynch
Chief Executive: Evelyn Hoy

Commissioner for Public Appointments for Northern Ireland
Dundonald House, Annexe B
Stormont Estate
Upper Newtownards Road
Belfast, BT4 3SB
Tel: 028 9052 4820
Web: www.publicappointmentsni.org
Email: info@publicappointmentsni.org
Commissioner: Vacant

Commissioner for Survivors of Institutional Childhood Abuse
5th Floor South
Queen's Court
55-66 Upper Queen Street
Belfast, BT1 6FD
Tel: 028 9054 4985
Email: info@cosica-ni.org
Commissioner: Fiona Ryan

Community Relations Council
Equality House, 2nd Floor
7-9 Shaftesbury Square
Belfast, BT2 7DP
Tel: 028 9022 7500
Web: www.community-relations.org.uk
Email: info@nicrc.org.uk
Chair: Martin McDonald
Chief Executive: Jacqueline Irwin

Consumer Council
Floor 3, Seatem House
28-32 Alfred Street
Belfast, BT2 8EN
Tel: 028 9025 1600
Complaints line: 0800 121 6022
Web: www.consumercouncil.org.uk
Email: info@consumercouncil.org.uk
Chief Executive: Noyona Chundur

Coroners Service Northern Ireland
Laganside House
23-27 Oxford Street
Belfast, BT1 3LA
Tel: 0300 200 7811
Email: coronersoffice@courtsni.gov.uk

Government Departments | Northern Ireland Yearbook

Council for Catholic Maintained Schools
Linen Hill House
23 Linenhall Street
Lisburn, BT28 1FJ
Tel: 028 9201 3014
Web: www.onlineccms.com
Email: info@ccmsschools.com
Chief Executive: Gerry Campbell

Council for Nature Conservation and the Countryside
The Secretariat
2nd Floor, Klondyke Building
Cormac Avenue, Malone Lower
Belfast, BT7 2JA
Tel: 028 9056 9290
Email: CNCC.secretariat@daera-ni.gov.uk

Criminal Justice Inspection Northern Ireland
Block 1, Knockview Buildings
Stormont Estate
Belfast, BT4 3SA
Tel: 028 9076 5764
Web: www.cjini.org
Email: info@cjini.org
Chief Inspector: Jacqui Durkin

Drainage Council
c/o DfI Rivers
49 Tullywiggan Road
Loughry, Cookstown
Co Tyrone, BT80 8SG
Tel: 028 8676 8342
Email: rivers.registry@infrastructure-ni.gov.uk
Chair: Alan Strong

Driver and Vehicle Agency Northern Ireland (DVA)
148-158 Corporation Street
Belfast, BT1 3TB
Tel: 0300 200 7861
Web: www.nidirect.gov.uk/motoring
Email: dva@infrastructure-ni.gov.uk

Chief Executive: Jeremy Logan
Email: chief.executivedva@infrastructure-ni.gov.uk

Licensing enquiries
County Hall, Castlerock Road
Coleraine, BT51 3HS
Tel: 0300 200 7861

Testing enquiries
County Hall
Castlerock Road
Coleraine, BT51 3TB
Tel: 0300 200 7861
Email: dva@infrastructure-ni.gov.uk

Passenger transport licensing enquiries
Tel: 028 9025 4100

Vehicle tax
Vehicles are taxed online by DVLA in Swansea using the following link: www.gov.uk/tax-disc

Vehicle registration
DVLA
Swansea, SA99 1BE
Tel: 0300 123 4321

Local Testing Offices

Armagh
47 Hamiltonsbawn Road
Armagh, BT60 1HW
Tel: 028 3752 2699

Ballymena
Pennybridge Industrial Estate
Larne Road, Ballymena, BT42 3ER
Tel: 028 2565 6801

Belfast
66 Balmoral Road, Belfast, BT12 6QL
Tel: 028 9068 1831

Dill Road, Castlereagh Road
Belfast, BT6 9HT
Tel: 028 9068 1831

Coleraine
2 Loughan Hill Industrial Estate
Gateside Road, Coleraine, BT52 2NJ
Tel: 028 7034 3819

Cookstown
Sandholes Road
Cookstown
BT80 9AR
Tel: 028 8676 4809

Craigavon
3 Diviny Drive, Carn Industrial Estate
Craigavon, BT63 5RY
Tel: 028 3833 6188

Derry
New Buildings Industrial Estate
Victoria Road, Derry, BT47 2SX
Tel: 028 7134 3674

Unit 4, Glenaden Complex
Altnaglevin Industrial Estate
Derry, BT47 2ED
Tel: 028 7134 3674

Downpatrick
Cloonagh Road, Flying Horse Road
Downpatrick, BT30 6DU
Tel: 028 4461 4565

Enniskillen
10 Coa Road, Enniskillen, BT74 4EG
Tel: 028 6632 2871

Larne
Ballyboley Road, Ballyloran
Larne, BT40 2SY
Tel: 028 2827 8808

Lisburn
1 Enterprise Cresent
Ballinderry Road, Lisburn, BT28 2BP
Tel: 028 9266 3151

Mallusk
Commercial Way
Hydepark Industrial Estate
Newtownabbey, BT36 4YY
Tel: 028 9084 2111

Newry
51 Rathfriland Road, Newry, BT34 1LD
Tel: 028 3026 2853

Newtownards
Jubilee Road, Newtownards, BT23 4XP
Tel: 028 9181 3064

Omagh
Gortrush Industrial Estate, Derry Road
Omagh, BT78 5EJ
Tel: 028 8224 2540

Education Authority
40 Academy Street
Belfast, BT1 2NQ
Tel: 028 9056 4000
Web: www.eani.org.uk
Email: info@eani.org.uk
Chief Executive: Sara Long

Equality Commission for Northern Ireland
Equality House
7-9 Shaftesbury Square
Belfast, BT2 7DP
Tel: 028 9050 0600
Web: www.equalityni.org
Email: information@equalityni.org
Chief Commissioner: Geraldine McGahey
Chief Executive: Evelyn Collins

Government Departments

Food Standards Agency
10C Clarendon Road
Belfast, BT1 3BG
Tel: 028 9041 7700
Web: www.food.gov.uk/northern-ireland
Email: infofsani@foodstandards.gsi.gov.uk
Director: Maria Jennings

Foras na Gaeilge
63-66 Amiens Street, Dublin 1
Tel: 00 353 1 639 8400

Westgate House
2-6 Queen Street, Belfast
BT1 6ED
Tel: 028 9089 0970
Web: www.forasnagaeilge.ie
Email: eolas@forasnagaeilge.ie
Chief Executive: Seán Ó Coinn

Forensic Science Northern Ireland
151 Belfast Road
Carrickfergus, BT38 8PL
Tel: 028 9036 1888
Web: www.justice-ni.gov.uk/fsni
Email: forensic.science@fsni.x.gsi.gov.uk
Chief Executive: Gillian Morton

Forest Service
Inishkeen House, Killyhevlin
Enniskillen, BT47 4EJ
Tel: 028 6634 3165
Web: www.daera-ni.gov.uk/forestry
Email: customer.forestservice@daera-ni.gov.uk
Chief Executive: John Joe O'Boyle

Foyle Port
Port Road, Lisahally
Derry, BT47 6FL
Tel: 028 7186 0555
Web: www.foyleport.com
Chief Executive: Brian McGrath

General Teaching Council for Northern Ireland
3rd Floor, Albany House
73-75 Great Victoria Street
Belfast, BT2 7AF
Tel: 028 9033 3390
Web: www.gtcni.org.uk
Chief Executive: Sam Gallaher

Health and Safety Executive for Northern Ireland
83 Ladas Drive, Belfast, BT6 9FR
Tel: 028 9024 3249
Helpline: 0800 0320 121
Web: www.hseni.gov.uk
Email: mail@hseni.gov.uk
Chief Executive: Robert Kidd

Health and Social Care Board
12-22 Linenhall Street
Belfast, BT2 8BS
Tel: 0300 555 0115
Web: www.hscboard.hscni.net
Email: enquiry.hscb@hscni.net
Chief Executive: Sharon Gallagher

Historic Buildings Council
HBC/HMC Secretariat
Department for Communities
Ground Floor
9 Lanyon Place
Town Parks, Belfast
BT1 3LP
Tel: 028 9081 9236
Web: www.communities-ni.gov.uk
Email: HBC-HMCSecretariat@communities-ni.gov.uk
Chair: Peter Tracey

Historic Monuments Council
HBC/HMC Secretariat
Department for Communities
Ground Floor
9 Lanyon Place
Town Parks, Belfast
BT1 3LP
Tel: 028 9081 9236
Web: www.communities-ni.gov.uk
Email: HBC-HMCSecretariat@communities-ni.gov.uk
Chair: Audrey Gahan

Integrated Education Fund
Forestview, Purdy's Lane
Belfast, BT8 7AR
Tel: 028 9069 4099
Web: www.ief.org.uk
Email: info@ief.org.uk
Chief Executive: Tina Merron

InterTradeIreland
Old Gasworks Business Park
Kilmorey Street, Newry, BT34 2DE
Tel: 028 3083 4100
Web: www.intertradeireland.com
Email: info@intertradeireland.com
Chief Executive: Margaret Hearty

Invest Northern Ireland
Bedford Square, Bedford Street
Belfast, BT2 7ES
Tel: 028 9069 8000
Web: www.investni.com
Email: eo@investni.com
Chief Executive: Kevin Holland

Land and Property Services
Lanyon Plaza, 7 Lanyon Place
Town Parks, Belfast
BT1 3LP
Tel: 028 9033 6116
Web: www.finance-ni.gov.uk
Chief Executive: Ian Snowden

Law Society of Northern Ireland
96 Victoria Street, Belfast, BT1 3GN
Tel: 028 9023 1614
Web: www.lawsoc-ni.org
Email: info@lawsoc-ni.org
President: Rowan White
Chief Executive: David Lavery

Legal Services Agency Northern Ireland
2nd Floor, Waterfront Plaza
8 Laganbank Road
Belfast, BT1 3BN
Tel: 028 9040 8888
Email: enquiries@lsani.gov.uk
Chief Executive: Paul Andrews

Libraries NI
2nd Floor
Portadown Library
24-26 Church Street
Portadown, BT62 3LQ
Tel: 0345 4504 580
Web: www.librariesni.org.uk
Email: enquiries@librariesni.org.uk
Chief Executive: Jim O'Hagan

Livestock and Meat Commission for Northern Ireland
Lissue Industrial Estate (East)
1A Lissue Walk
Lisburn, BT28 2LU
Tel: 028 9263 3000
Web: www.lmcni.com
Email: info@lmci.com
Chief Executive: Ian Stevenson

Local Government Boundaries Commissioner
c/o Local Government Division
Department for Communities
Causeway Exchange
1-7 Bedford Street
Belfast
BT2 7EG
Tel: 028 9051 5063
Email: magsecretariat@communities-ni.gov.uk

Local Government Staff Commission
Commission House
18-22 Gordon Street
Belfast, BT1 2LG
Tel: 028 9031 3200
Web: www.lgsc.org.uk
Email: info@lgsc.org.uk

Government Departments

Lady Chief Justice for Northern Ireland
Royal Courts of Justice
Chichester Street
Belfast, BT1 3JF
Tel: 028 9072 4616
Email: LCJOffice@judiciaryni.uk
Lady Chief Justice: The Rt Hon Dame Siobhan Keegan

The Loughs Agency
22 Victoria Road
Derry, BT47 2AB
Tel: 028 7134 2100
Web: www.loughs-agency.org
Email: general@loughs-agency.org
Designated Officer:
Sharon McMahon

Maze/Long Kesh Development Corporation
Halftown Road
Lisburn, BT27 5RF
Tel: 028 9250 1806
Web: www.mazelongkesh.com
Email: contact@mazelongkesh.com
Interim Chief Executive: Bryan Gregory

Middletown Centre for Autism
35 Church Street
Middletown
Armagh, BT60 4HZ
Tel: 028 3751 5750
Web: www.middletownautism.com
Email: admin@middletownautism.com
Chief Executive: Gary Cooper

National Museums Northern Ireland
Cultra, Hollywood, BT18 0EU
Tel: 028 9042 8428
Web: www.nmni.com
Email: info@nmni.com
Director: Kathryn Thomson

NI-CO
Landmark House
5 Cromac Quay, Belfast, BT7 2JD
Tel: 028 9034 7750
Web: www.nico.org.uk
Email: nicohq@nico.org.uk
Chief Executive: Graeme McCammon

Northern Health and Social Care Trust
Brettan Hall, Bush Road
Antrim, BT41 2RL
Tel: 028 9442 4000
Web: www.northerntrust.hscni.net
Email: info@northerntrust.hscni.net
Chief Executive: Jennifer Welsh

Northern Ireland Ambulance Service Trust
Site 30, Knockbracken Healthcare Park
Saintfield Road, Belfast, BT8 8SG
Tel: 028 9040 0999
Web: www.niamb.co.uk
Email: reception@nias.hscni.net
Chief Executive: Michael Bloomfield

Northern Ireland Audit Office
1 Bradford Court, Upper Galwally
Belfast, BT8 6RB
Tel: 028 9025 1000
Web: www.niauditoffice.gov.uk
Email: info@niauditoffice.gov.uk
Twitter: @NIAuditOffice
Comptroller and Auditor General:
Kieran Donnelly

Northern Ireland Fiscal Council
5th Floor
9 Lanyon Place
Belfast, BT1 3LP
Web: www.nifiscalcouncil.org
Email: info@nifiscalcouncil.org
Chair: Sir Robert Chote
Chief of Staff: Jonathan McAdams

Northern Ireland Blood Transfusion Service Agency
Belfast City Hospital Complex
51 Lisburn Road, Belfast, BT9 7TS
Tel: 028 9032 1414
Web: www.nibts.org
Email: inet@nibts.hscni.net
Chief Executive: Karin Jackson

Northern Ireland Building Regulations Advisory Committee
Floor 3
3-5A Federick Street
Belfast, BT1 2NR
Tel: 028 9185 8111
Chair: Mabel Higgins
Secretary: Karen McKernon

Northern Ireland Commissioner for Children and Young People
Equality House
7-9 Shaftesbury Square
Belfast, BT2 7DP
Tel: 028 9031 1616
Web: www.niccy.org
Email: info@niccy.org
Commissioner: Koulla Yiasouma

Northern Ireland Council for Integrated Education
25 College Gardens
Belfast, BT6 6BS
Tel: 028 9097 2910
Web: www.nicie.org
Email: info@nicie.org.uk
Twitter: @niciebelfast
Chief Executive: Roisin Marshall

Northern Ireland Council for the Curriculum, Examinations and Assessment (CCEA)
29 Clarendon Road
Belfast, BT1 3BG
Tel: 028 9026 1200
Web: www.ccea.org.uk
Email: info@ccea.org.uk
Chief Executive: Margaret Farragher (interim)

Northern Ireland Courts and Tribunal Service
Laganside House
23-27 Oxford Street, Belfast, BT1 3LA
Tel: 0300 200 7812
Web: www.courtsni.gov.uk
Email: communicationsgroup@courtsni.gov.uk

Northern Ireland Environment Agency
Headquarters, Klondyke Building
Cromac Avenue
Gasworks Business Park
Lower Ormeau Road, Belfast, BT7 2JA
Tel: 0300 200 7856
Email: nieainfo@daera-ni.gov.uk
Chief Executive: Paul Donnelly

Northern Ireland Fishery Harbour Authority
3 St Patrick's Avenue
Downpatrick, BT30 6DW
Tel: 028 4461 3844
Web: www.nifha.co.uk
Email: info@nifha.co.uk
Chief Executive: Kevin Quigley

Northern Ireland Fire and Rescue Service
1 Seymour Street, Lisburn, BT27 4SX
Tel: 028 9266 4221
Web: www.nifrs.org
Chief Fire Officer: Peter O'Reilly

Northern Ireland Yearbook | Government Departments

Northern Ireland Guardian Ad Litem Agency
Centre House, 79 Chichester Street
Belfast, BT1 4JE
Tel: 0300 555 0102
Web: www.nigala.hscni.net
Email: admin@nigala.hscni.net
Chief Executive: Dawn Shaw

Northern Ireland Housing Executive
The Housing Centre
2 Adelaide Street
Belfast, BT2 8PB
Tel: 03448 920 900
Web: www.nihe.gov.uk
Email: info@nihe.gov.uk
Twitter: @nihecommunity
Chief Executive: Grainia Long

Northern Ireland Judicial Appointments Commission
Headline Building
10-14 Victoria Street
Belfast, BT1 3GG
Tel: 028 9056 9100
Web: www.nijac.gov.uk
Email: judicialappointments@nijac.gov.uk
Chair: Lady Chief Justice of Northern Ireland, Dame Siobhan Keegan
Chief Executive: Tonya McCormac

Northern Ireland Local Government Officers' Superannuation Committee
Templeton House
411 Holywood Road
Belfast, BT4 2LP
Tel: 0345 3197 320
Web: www.nilgosc.org.uk
Email: info@nilgosc.org.uk
Chief Executive: David Murphy

Northern Ireland Medical and Dental Training Agency
Beechill House
42 Beechill Road
Belfast, BT8 7RL
Tel: 028 9040 0000
Web: www.nimdta.gov.uk
Email: nimdta@hscni.net
Chief Executive: Mark McCarey (acting)

Northern Ireland Museums Council
153 Bangor Road
Holywood, BT18 0EU
Tel: 028 9055 0215
Web: www.nimc.co.uk
Email: info@nimc.co.uk
Director: Siobhan Stevenson

Northern Ireland Policing Board
Waterside Tower
31 Clarendon Road
Clarendon Dock
Belfast, BT1 3BG
Tel: 028 9040 8500
Web: www.nipolicingboard.org.uk
Email: information@nipolicingboard.org.uk
Twitter: @nipolicingboard
Chair: Doug Garrett
Chief Executive: Sinead Simpson

Northern Ireland Practice and Education Council for Nursing and Midwifery (NIPEC)
2nd Floor, Centre House
79 Chichester Street
Belfast, BT1 4JE
Tel: 0300 300 0066
Web: www.nipec.hscni.net
Email: enquiries@nipec.hscni.net
Chief Executive: Angela McLernon

Northern Ireland Prison Service
Dundonald House
Upper Newtownards Road
Belfast, BT4 3SU
Tel: 028 9052 2922
Web: www.justice-ni.gov.uk
Email: info@niprisonservice.gov.uk
Director General: Ronnie Armour

Northern Ireland Social Care Council
7th Floor, Millennium House
19-25 Great Victoria Street
Belfast, BT2 7AQ
Tel: 028 9536 2600
Web: www.niscc.info
Email: info@niscc.hscni.net
Chief Executive: Patricia Higgins (interim)

Northern Ireland Statistics and Research Agency (NISRA)
Colby House
Stranmillis Court
Belfast, BT9 5RR
Tel: 0300 200 7836
Web: www.nisra.gov.uk
Email: info@nisra.gov.uk
Chief Executive: Siobhan Carey

Northern Ireland Transport Holding Company
Contact Centre
Falcon Road
Belfast, BT126PU
Tel: 028 9066 6630
Web: www.translink.co.uk/corporate
Chair: Michael Wardlow
Group Chief Executive: Chris Conway

Northern Ireland Water
Westland House
40 Old Westland Road
Belfast, BT14 6TE
Waterline: 0345 744 0088
Web: www.niwater.com
Email: waterline@niwater.com
Chief Executive: Sara Venning

Office of the Attorney General for Northern Ireland
PO Box 1272, Belfast, BT1 9LU
Tel: 028 9072 5333
Web: www.attorneygeneralni.gov.uk
Email: contact@attorneygeneralni.gov.uk
Attorney General: Brenda King

Office of the Northern Ireland Ombudsman
Progressive House
33 Wellington Place
Belfast, BT1 6HN
Tel: 028 9023 3821
Freephone: 0800 34 34 24
Web: www.nipso.org.uk
Email: nipso@nipso.org.uk

Parole Commissioners for Northern Ireland
Laganside Court, Mezzanine
1st Floor, Oxford Street
Belfast, BT1 3LL
Tel: 028 9041 2969
Web: www.parolecomni.org.uk
Email: referrals@parolecomni.x.gsi.gov.uk
Chief Commissioner: Paul Mageean

Patient and Client Council
5th Floor, 14-16 Great Victoria Street
Belfast, BT2 7BA
Freephone: 0800 917 0222
Web: www.patientclientcouncil.hscni.net
Email: info.pcc@hscni.net
Chief Executive: Vivian McConvey

Planning and Water Appeals Commission
Park House
87-91 Great Victoria Street
Belfast, BT2 7AG
Tel: 028 9024 4710
Web: www.pacni.gov.uk
Email: info@pacni.gov.uk
Chief Commissioner: Andrea Kells

Police Ombudsman for Northern Ireland
New Cathedral Buildings
Writer's Square
11 Church Street
Belfast, BT1 1PG
Tel: 028 9082 8600
Web: www.policeombudsman.org
Email: info@policeombudsman.org
Police Ombudsman: Marie Anderson

PSNI
65 Knock Road
Belfast, BT5 6LE
Non-Emergency Number: 101
Crimestoppers: 0800 555 111
Web: www.psni.police.uk
Chief Constable: Simon Byrne

Prisoner Ombudsman
Unit 2, Walled Garden
Stormont Estate
Belfast, BT4 3SH
Tel: 028 9052 7771
Freephone: 0800 783 6317
Web: www.niprisonerombudsman.gov.uk
Email: pa@prisonerombudsman.x.gsi.gov.uk
Ombudsman: Lesley Carroll

Probation Board for Northern Ireland
80-90 North Street
Belfast, BT1 1LD
Tel: 028 9026 2400
Web: www.pbni.org.uk
Email: info@pbni.gov.uk
Chief Executive: Amanda Stewart

Public Health Agency
Linenhall Street Unit
12-22 Linenhall Street
Belfast, BT2 8BS
Tel: 0300 555 0114
Web: www.publichealth.hscni.net
Twitter: @publichealthni
Chief Executive: Aidan Dawson

Public Prosecution Service
Central Management Unit
Belfast Chambers, 93 Chichester Street
Belfast, BT1 3JR
Tel: 028 9089 7100
Web: www.ppsni.gov.uk
Email: info@ppsni.gsi.gov.uk
Director: Stephen Herron

Public Record Office of Northern Ireland
2 Titanic Boulevard, Titanic Quarter
Belfast, BT3 9HQ
Tel: 028 9053 4800
Web: www.nidirect.gov.uk/proni
Email: proni@communities-ni.gov.uk

Regulation and Quality Improvement Authority
7th Floor, Victoria House
15-27 Gloucester Street
Belfast, BT1 4LS
Tel: 028 9536 1111
Web: www.rqia.org.uk
Email: info@rqia.org.uk
Chief Executive: Briege Donaghy

Rent Officer for Northern Ireland
Level 3
Causeway Exchange
1-7 Bedford Street
Belfast, BT2 7EG
Tel: 028 9051 5258
Email: info@rentofficer-ni.gov.uk

South Eastern Health and Social Care Trust
Trust Headquarters, Ulster Hospital
Upper Newtownards Road
Dundonald, BT16 1RH
Tel: 028 9055 3100
Web: www.setrust.hscni.net
Chief Executive: Roisin Coulter

Southern Health and Social Care Trust
Trust Headquarters
Craigavon Area Hospital
68 Lurgan Road
Portadown, BT63 5QQ
Tel: 028 3833 4444
Web: www.southerntrust.hscni.net
Email: corporate.hq@southerntrust.hscni.net
Chief Executive: Shane Devlin

Special EU Programmes Body (SEUPB)
The Clarence West Building
2 Clarence Street West
Belfast, BT2 7GP
Tel: 028 9026 6660
Web: www.seupb.eu
Email: info@seupb.eu
Twitter: @SEUPB
Chief Executive: Gina McIntyre

Sport NI
House of Sport
2A Upper Malone Road
Belfast, BT9 5LA
Tel: 028 9038 1222
Web: www.sportni.net
Email: info@sportni.net
Chief Executive: Antoinette McKeown

Strategic Investment Board Limited
9 Lanyon Place
Belfast, BT1 3LP
Tel: 028 9025 0900
Web: www.sibni.org
Email: contact@sibni.org
Twitter: @ContactSIBNI
Chief Executive: Brett Hannam

Tourism Ireland Limited
Beresford House
2 Beresford Road
Coleraine, BT52 1GE
Tel: 028 7035 9200
Web: www.tourismireland.com
Email: corporate.coleraine@tourismireland.com
Chief Executive: Niall Gibbons

Tourism NI
Floors 10-12, Linum Chambers
Bedford Square, Bedford Street
Belfast, BT2 7ES
Tel: 028 9023 1221
Web: www.tourismni.com
Email: info@tourismni.com
Chief Executive: John McGrillen

Utility Regulator
Queen's House, 14 Queen Street
Belfast, BT1 6ED
Tel: 028 9031 1575
Web: www.uregni.gov.uk
Email: info@uregni.gov.uk
Chief Executive: John French

Ulster Scots Agency
The Corn Exchange
31 Gordon Street
Belfast, BT1 2LG
Tel: 028 9023 1113
Web: www.ulsterscotsagency.com
Email: info@ulsterscotsagency.org.uk
Chief Executive: Ian Crozier

Regional Office
William Street
Raphoe, Co Donegal
Tel: + 353 749 173 876

Ulster Supported Employment Limited
182-188 Cambrai Street
Belfast, BT13 3JH
Tel: 028 9035 6600
Web: www.usel.co.uk
Email: info@usel.co.uk
Chief Executive: Bill Atkinson

Regional Offices
Gortfoyle House, 104 Spencer Road
Derry, BT47 6AG
Tel: 028 7116 1595

2 William Street, Millennium Court
Portadown, Craigavon, BT62 3NX
Tel: 028 3835 0202

Victims and Survivors Service
1st Floor, Seatem House
28-32 Alfred Street
Belfast, BT2 8EN
Tel: 028 9027 9100
Web: www.victimsservice.org
Email: enquiries@vssni.org
Chief Executive: Margaret Bateson

Warrenpoint Harbour Authority
The Docks
Warrenpoint, BT34 3JR
Tel: 028 4177 3381
Web: www.warrenpointport.com
Email: info@warrenpointharbour.co.uk
Chief Executive: David Holmes

Waterways Ireland
2 Sligo Road, Enniskillen, BT74 7JY
Tel: 028 6632 3004
Web: www.waterwaysireland.org
Email: info@waterwaysireland.org
Chief Executive: John McDonagh

Western Health and Social Care Trust
MDEC Building
Altnagelvin Area Hospital
Glenshane Road
Derry, BT47 6SB
Tel: 028 7134 5171
Web: www.westerntrust.hscni.net
Email: info.enquiry@westerntrust.hscni.net
Chief Executive: Neil Guckian

Youth Council
c/o Rathgael House
43 Balloo Road
Bangor, BT19 7PR
Tel: 028 9172 9782

Youth Justice Agency of Northern Ireland
41-43 Waring Street, Belfast, BT1 2DY
Tel: 028 9031 6400
Web: www.justice-ni.gov.uk
Email: info@yjani.gov.uk
Chief Executive: Stephen Martin

agendaNi Magazine

2022 features

February 2022
- Digital Govt
- Justice

April 2022
- Tourism
- Infrastructure

June 2022
- Housing
- Energy

September 2022
- Economy/ Social Economy
- Education/ Skills

December 2022
- Health
- Environment/ Waste

Key benefits

- Direct contact with over 7,000 key decision-makers in the public, private and voluntary sectors in Northern Ireland
- Deliver key messages to Northern Ireland's senior figures in government, local government and business
- Enhance your profile, showcase your work and highlight important issues to an influential audience
- Engage with stakeholders
- Increase the profile of senior people with the organisation
- Gain recognition as a thought leader

Opportunities available

- **Front cover profile interview:** very high profile opportunity, offers maximum exposure
- **Round table discussion,** hosted by organisation to include four/five leading professionals/stakeholders
- **Report sponsorship:** Combination of editorial, advertising and branding
- **Advertorials:** editorial style branded articles; used to promote the benefits, capabilities and services of an organisation
- **Advertisements:** build a high profile image within the market place; premium positions available including outside back cover

For further information contact us at leanne.brannigan@agendani.com or on 028 9261 9933

Northern Ireland Yearbook

Local Government

Northern Ireland Local government

Alongside Westminster and Stormont, Northern Ireland has a third tier of government administration in the form of its 11 local councils, which are involved in policy and decision-making and particularly the direct delivery of a range of services at a local level. In 2015, local government in Northern Ireland underwent its most significant shake-up in over 40 years, with the previous 26 local councils merging to form 11 new 'super-councils', with responsibility for a wider range of services, many of which have transferred from either government departments or other agencies or non-departmental public bodies.

Prior to 1 April 2015, local councils in Northern Ireland's primary responsibilities were:

- arts and entertainment;
- building control;
- burial grounds;
- community relations;
- dog control;
- environmental health;
- leisure and recreation;
- parks and green spaces;
- small harbours;
- street cleaning; and
- waste management.

See below for a summary of the powers which are available to the 11 councils, including where responsibility for these functions previously lay.

Department of Agriculture, Environment and Rural Affairs

- Local development planning;
- Development control;
- Enforcement;
- Nominating buildings for spot-listing;
- Listing buildings of architectural and/or historic interest;
- Delivery of rural development programme;
- Donaghadee Harbour (to North Down and Ards).

Department for Communities

- Community development programmes;

Northern Ireland Yearbook | Local Government

- Environmental improvement schemes;
- Area based regeneration;
- Water recreational facilities;
- Sports policy (more input for local government in decision-making);
- Armagh County Museum (to Armagh City, Banbridge and Craigavon Borough Council).

Northern Ireland Housing Executive
- Registration of houses in multiple occupation;
- Housing unfitness (including repair and demolition notices).

Northern Ireland Tourist Board/Tourism NI
- Business start-up advice;
- Small scale tourism accommodation development;
- Advice to developers on tourism policy.

Department for Infrastructure
- Off-street parking (excluding park-and-ride facilities).

Invest NI
- Local economic development;
- Enterprise shows;
- Youth and female entrepreneurship;
- Social entrepreneurship;
- Supporting women in business.

Local government districts are sub-divided into district election areas (DEAs) with Belfast having 10 DEAs and all of the other councils each having seven. Each council has either 40 or 41 councillors, with Belfast having 60 – a total of 462 councillors for Northern Ireland (previously 582).

Local government elections are generally held every four years, with a number of councillors elected to each DEA using proportional representation.

The first election for the 11 new councils took place on 22 May 2014, alongside the European Parliament election, with the councillors operating in 'shadow form', alongside the councillors from the 26 former councils, between May 2014 and 1 April 2015.

The most recent local government election took place in 2019. See the end of this chapter for an overview and full results from each council.

Status of districts

At present, there are five different statuses of council: city, borough, district, and city and district. All office-bearers are elected at the annual general meetings of each council.

City status is granted by royal charter. The three city councils (Belfast, Derry and Strabane, and Lisburn and Castlereagh) can designate up to one quarter of their members as aldermen and confer the freedom of the city or borough.

Derry and Lisburn are chaired by mayors whilst Belfast is led by a lord mayor. Newry is also a city but is part of Newry, Mourne and Down District Council rather than having its own local authority.

The five borough councils can also designate aldermen, grant freedoms and appoint mayors in the same manner as city councils. The following councils have borough status: Ards and North Down; Antrim and Newtownabbey; Armagh, Banbridge and Craigavon; Causeway Coast and Glens; Mid and East Antrim.

The three district councils are chaired by chairpersons. These are Fermanagh and Omagh; Mid Ulster and Newry, Mourne and Down. Armagh, uniquely, has a city and district council with a lord mayor but no aldermen.

Principal characteristics of local government in Northern Ireland
Area and population of local authorities June 2021

Council	Area (km²)	2020 Population	Annual Growth %	Population change % 2010-2020
Antrim and Newtownabbey	728	143,800	0.2	4.1
Ards and North Down	565	162,100	0.2	3.5
Armagh City, Banbridge and Craigavon	1,436	217,200	0.5	9.6
Belfast	138	342,600	-0.3	2.7
Causeway Coast and Glens	1,984	144,900	0.1	3.5
Derry City and Strabane	1,249	151,100	-0.1	2.0
Fermanagh and Omagh	3,006	117,300	-0.1	3.9
Lisburn and Castlereagh	510	146,500	0.3	9.4
Mid and East Antrim	1,061	139,400	0.1	3.2
Mid Ulster	1,955	149,000	0.3	8.5
Newry, Mourne and Down	1,682	181,700	0.2	6.2
Total	**14,314**	**1,895,500**	**0.1**	**5.0**

Sources: Land and Property Services, NISRA

Local Government

Councils' political breakdown

Council	DUP	SF	UUP	SDLP	Alliance	Other	Seats
Antrim & Newtownabbey	14	5	9	4	6	2	40
Ards & North Down	13	0	8	1	10	8	40
Armagh, Banbridge & Craigavon	11	10	10	6	3	2	41
Belfast	15	18	3	6	9	9	60
Causeway Coast & Glens	14	9	6	5	2	4	40
Derry & Strabane	6	11	3	10	2	8	40
Fermanagh & Omagh	5	15	9	5	1	5	40
Lisburn & Castlereagh	14	2	11	2	9	1	40
Mid & East Antrim	16	2	6	1	7	8	40
Mid Ulster	9	17	6	5	0	3	40
Newry, Mourne & Down	3	16	4	11	2	5	41
Total	**120**	**105**	**75**	**56**	**51**	**53**	**462**

*as of January 2022

Roles and functions of local government

The local government workforce numbers around 12,500 people. Councils essentially have three roles: the direct provision of services; representing the interests of their areas on external bodies; and a consultative role whereby councillors reflect the views of their communities regarding the operation of certain regional services.

Direct service provision

The services currently provided by councils include arts, leisure and entertainment, building control, community relations, environmental health, and street cleaning. The councils are members of three sub-regional waste management groups: arc21 (covering greater Belfast); the North West Region Waste Management Group; and the Southern Waste Management Partnership. Waste is collected by councils and disposed of by the waste management groups.

Representative role

Councils also appoint their elected members to certain statutory bodies. Appointees are not delegates but are free to exercise their own judgement. In practice, they tend to represent the interests of their council area.

The Education Authority includes eight political members, nominated by the main parties under the d'Hondt system, although these will not be required to be elected representatives. The majority of members on the board of Libraries NI are required to be councillors; the number varies between each term of office.

Roles and functions of local government

Direct service provision
- Arts and entertainment
- Building control
- Burial grounds
- Community relations
- Dog control
- Environmental health
- Leisure and recreation
- Parks and green spaces
- Small harbours
- Street cleaning
- Waste management

New services (since April 2015)
- Community development
- Development control
- Housing unfitness
- Local area planning
- Local economic development
- Off-street parking
- Planning enforcement
- Rural Development Programme
- Small scale tourism development
- Water recreational facilities

Representative role
- Education and library boards
- Education Authority
- Local commissioning groups (health and social care)
- Northern Ireland Housing Executive board
- Policing and community safety partnerships
- Public Health Agency Board

Consultative role
- Infrastructure and utilities
- Northern Ireland Housing Council
- Regional planning
- Roads

In health, each of the five local commissioning groups (LCGs) – which correspond with health and social care trust areas – include four councillors. Two local government seats are also allocated on the Public Health Agency (PHA) board.

Policing and community safety partnerships (PCSPs) replaced district policing partnerships and community safety partnerships in 2012. At present, these include eight to 10 councillors, who are nominated by councils and sit as political members, and seven to nine independent members nominated by the Northern Ireland Policing Board.

Representatives from seven external organisations also sit on each PCSP: the Education Authority; the PSNI; the Probation Board; the Fire and Rescue Service; the Youth Justice Agency; the Housing Executive; and the local health and social care trust.

There are currently 11 PCSPs, one for each council; Belfast has a further four district policing and community safety partnerships (DPCSPs) covering the north, south, east and west of the city.

Consultative role

Where services are provided by a government department or another public body (e.g. roads or water), the council provides a locally elected arena in which decisions are discussed. Local authorities may put forward the views of the community but have no rights of decision in these matters.

In most cases, the consultative role is carried out at council meetings where representatives of public bodies attend and discuss issues with councillors. In addition, the Northern Ireland Housing Council is a formal consultative body which advises the Northern Ireland Housing Executive. It comprises one councillor from each council area and four of its members fulfil a representative role by serving on the Housing Executive board.

The role of the Department for Communities

The Department for Communities (DfC) is the central government department responsible for local government policy. Its Local Government Policy Division is responsible for developing policy and legislation in this area, paying the general grant to councils, and developing methods to improve the administration, finance and audit of local government.

Local government policy was previously under the remit of the former Department of the Environment and transferred to the new Department for Communities in 2016.

Planning policy was originally a local government matter but was centralised in 1973 with the formation of the Town and Country Planning Service. This was reconstituted as an executive agency – the Planning Service – in 1996.

The Planning Service was then integrated into the DoE in 2011 in preparation for the transfer to local government. Strategic planning policy is the responsibility of the Department for Infrastructure.

The new councils have a statutory duty of community planning (to require all relevant organisations to work together) and a power of well-being (to take any reasonable action to improve the well-being of the community or area). A mandatory code of conduct has also taken effect.

Credit: Mid and East Antrim Borough Council

Paving the way for a prosperous future

Newry, Mourne and Down District Council is putting in place plans to ensure the momentum which has transformed the district in recent years remains.

Rarely before has Newry and district had such an exciting future ahead of it.

Having already transformed itself in recent years – as a place to live, work and play – it is now on the cusp of supercharging its fortunes with the help of the £1 billion Belfast Region City Deal (BRCD).

It will deliver a bespoke package of funding to six Northern Ireland councils including Newry, Mourne and Down and help develop key infrastructure projects, such as the Southern Relief Road and the regeneration of the city centre, including public realm, theatre, conference and innovation space.

Across the Belfast City Deal region, the deal will generate up to 20,000 jobs as it is delivered over the next 10 years – an exciting, once-in-a-generation opportunity to accelerate economic growth for the region in an inclusive and sustainable way.

For Newry, the deal is the key to unlocking the district's potential.

It is expected to be transformational and act as the catalyst for sustained economic growth, helping create thousands of new and better jobs and put pathways in place to make those jobs accessible to people from all communities.

The BRCD will deliver projects for Newry which are designed to attract business and visitor investment. New economic opportunity will emerge that can begin to address the challenges of high economic inactivity and low levels of productivity.

The ambition includes delivering modern, fit-for-purpose infrastructure such as the Southern Relief Road as well as developing new grade A offices in the city, an enhanced night-time economy with new conferencing and event space and a range of other projects.

From an economic point of view, the planned interventions will put in place the support Newry's entrepreneurs need to start to scale their businesses and will create an environment that investors, both from the locality and globally, want to invest.

When it comes to the environment, the interventions will integrate commitments to sustainability into project design and development while also holding projects to account for their inclusion and sustainability commitments.

"The importance of Belfast Region City Deal for Newry and the district's future cannot be underestimated," Councillor Cathy Mason, Chair of Newry, Mourne and Down District Council, says. "It will help fund a number of key projects which will improve our infrastructure, our public spaces, our arts sector, our workspace and a host of other schemes, which will unleash this great district's potential and allow it to flourish.

"We have come a long way in a short space of time and this city deal, along with the collective will of the Council and other leaders throughout the district, will provide the extra impetus we need to create a prosperous future for all. Working together with the private and third sectors, we can put Newry and district on the global map, attract investment, encourage entrepreneurship and build on our reputation as a great place to live."

Marie Ward, Chief Executive of Newry, Mourne and Down District Council, agrees: "We have a hugely exciting future ahead of us, one which will not just be enjoyed by this generation, but our children and our children's children. The Belfast Region City Deal will help us tackle some transformative investment projects which will be the fuel this district needs to grow its economy, to enhance its society and to become a powerhouse able to compete with Belfast and Dublin."

Of course, Newry and district has already been transformed in recent years, thanks to the foresight of a group of civic and business leaders who fought hard for its city status, which was bestowed in 2002.

It was a hugely important moment for a town, which was reawakening its civic and economic pride with the help of an incredible amount of grit and determination by its people.

Those leaders saw potential in a city which had just emerged from the epicentre of a 30-year conflict but had remained resilient and could now move forward with the glowing sparks of belief, optimism and partnership.

That belief was well placed, as the intervening years have shown.

Newry has transformed itself to become a city which is fuelled by entrepreneurialism and resilience and is now home to some of the best and most innovative companies in the world such as FD Technologies Norbrook, Statsports, MJM Marine and Glen Electrics. Of course, it has long been renowned for its excellent schools and colleges, whose students fuel the talent corridor between Belfast and Dublin.

Alongside the business, academic and skills success, it has developed a retail and hospitality offering which pulls shoppers from all corners of the island and sits cupped by some of the most stunning landscapes on this island, driving a visitor economy across the district with distinct and natural tourism assets which is able to compete with any global destination.

While the journey has been impressive, the next generation of civic and business leaders are determined to build on the work of their predecessors and continue to transform the district.

"Newry has become a city where people want to live, work, study, visit and invest," Councillor Cathy Mason, Chair of Newry, Mourne and Down District Council, says. "We have those forward-thinking leaders to thank for creating the conditions which have allowed the city to flourish and have primed it for an unprecedented period of growth.

"It is now incumbent on the city's current leadership – some of whom remain from 20 years ago – to grab the baton. We need to act with the same foresight and entrepreneurial spirit as those leaders of 20 years ago who saw the potential for Newry to emerge from the shadows of Belfast and Dublin.

"We need to implement as much of the vision which they had for the district by using the support which they helped us win so that we can leave a similar legacy for the next generation."

"In addition to the BRCD, evidence of progress and investment can already be seen through the announcement from the Executive for £16.2 million for the Albert Basin Park project, which will see a world-class city park created in Newry. This is central to our vision for the regeneration of Newry City Centre and will provide a welcome attraction for visitors and residents alike, offering an accessible and sustainable sanctuary in the centre of the city."

As a support lever, there are few to compare to the BRCD and, with the collective will of the current crop of leaders, Newry and district looks set for a bright future.

Newry, Mourne and Down District Council
T: 0330 137 4000
E: info@nmandd.org
W: newrymournedown.org

EMPOWERING NMD
A DECADE OF OPPORTUNITY

Belfast Region City Deal (BRCD) is made up of:

- **6** LOCAL COUNCILS
- PRIVATE SECTOR
- **6** UNIVERSITIES & REGIONAL COLLEGES
- NI EXECUTIVE & UK GOVERNMENT

SECURING UP TO £1 billion of co-investment shared across

20+ HIGHLY AMBITIOUS PROJECTS & PROGRAMMES

6 REGIONAL ECONOMIES

Where did the money come from?

| NI EXECUTIVE £350m | UK GOVERNMENT £350m | BRCD £150m | PRIVATE INVESTMENT |

Projects fall under 4 key pillars

| INNOVATION | DIGITAL | TOURISM & REGENERATION | INFRASTRUCTURE |
| £230 million | £120 million | £210 million | £140 million |

UNDERPINNED THROUGH INVESTMENT IN EMPLOYABILITY & SKILLS

Impact of BRCD projects will deliver up to

20,000 JOBS CREATED REGIONALLY

£400m OF GROSS VALUE ADDED (GVA)

#BRCityDeal

Antrim and Newtownabbey Borough Council

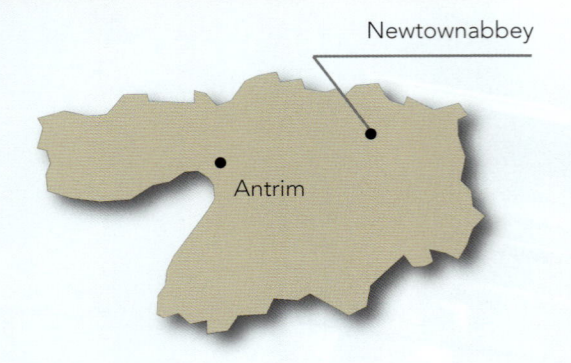

Population: 143,800
Councillors: 40
Residents per councillor: 3,595

Council contacts

Council offices
Antrim Civic Centre
50 Stiles Way
Antrim, BT41 2UB
Tel: 028 9446 3113

Mossley Mill
Carnmoney Road North
Newtownabbey, BT36 5QA

Tel: 028 9034 0000
Web: www.antrimandnewtownabbey.gov.uk
Email: info@antrimandnewtownabbey.gov.uk

Mayor: Councillor WJ Webb (APNI)
Deputy Mayor: Councillor Stephen Ross (DUP)

Senior Officers

Chief Executive: Jacqui Dixon

Deputy Chief Executive of Economic Growth: Majella McAlister
Deputy Chief Executive of Operations: Geraldine Girvan
Deputy Chief Executive of Finance and Governance: Sandra Cole
Director of Community Planning: Ursula Fay
Director of Organisation Development: Debbie Rogers

Committees

Community Planning Committee
Chair: Councillor Roisin Lynch (SDLP)

Operations Committee
Chair: Councillor Anne Marie Logue (SF)

Planning Committee
Chair: Councillor Sam Flanagan (DUP)

Policy and Governance Committee
Chair: Alderman Paul Michael (UUP)

Audit Committee
Chair: Councillor Andrew McAuley (APNI)

Councillor	Party	Councillor	Party
Fraser Agnew	UUP	Anne Marie Logue	SF
Jeannie Archibald-Brown	DUP	Roisin Lynch	SDLP
Alison Bennington	DUP	Matthew Magill	DUP
Matthew Brady	DUP	Ben Mallon	DUP
Phillip Brett	DUP	Andrew McAuley	APNI
Thomas Burns	SDLP	Noreen McClelland	SDLP
Tom Campbell	APNI	Julian McGrath	APNI
Linda Clarke	DUP	Taylor McGrann	SF
Mark Cooper	DUP	Vera McWilliam	UUP
Mark Cosgrove	UUP	Paul Michael	UUP
Henry Cushinan	SF	Jim Montgomery	UUP
Paul Dunlop	DUP	Norrie Ramsey	UUP
Glenn Finlay	IND	Victor Robinson	DUP
Robert Foster	UUP	Stephen Ross	DUP
Sam Flanagan	DUP	John Smyth	DUP
Julie Gilmour	APNI	Leah Smyth	UUP
Mandy Girvan	DUP	Michael Stewart	Ind
Michael Goodman	SF	Roderick Swann	UUP
Neil Kelly	APNI	Billy Webb	APNI
Rosie Kinnear	SF	Ryan Wilson	SDLP

Northern Ireland Yearbook | Local Government

Ards and North Down Borough Council

Council contacts

Civic Headquarters
Town Hall
The Castle
Bangor, BT20 4BT

Tel: 0300 013 3333
Web: www.ardsandnorthdown.gov.uk
Email: enquiries@ardsandnorthdown.gov.uk

Mayor: Councillor Mark Brooks (UUP)
Deputy Mayor: Councillor Robert Adair (DUP)

Senior Officers

Chief Executive:
Stephen Reid

Director of Community and Wellbeing: Graeme Bannister
Director of Environment: David Lindsay
Director of Finance and Performance: Simon Christie
Director of Organisational Development and Administration: Wendy Swanston
Director of Regeneration, Development and Planning: Susie McCullough

Committees

Planning Committee
Chair: Councillor Alistair Cathcart (DUP)

Environment Committee
Chair: Councillor Janice MacArthur (DUP)

Regeneration and Development Committee
Chair: Alderman McDowell (APNI)

Corporate Services Committee
Chair: Councillor Connie Egan (APNI)

Community and Wellbeing Committee
Chair: Councillor Eddie Thompson (DUP)

Audit Committee
Chair: Alderman Scott Wilson (APNI)

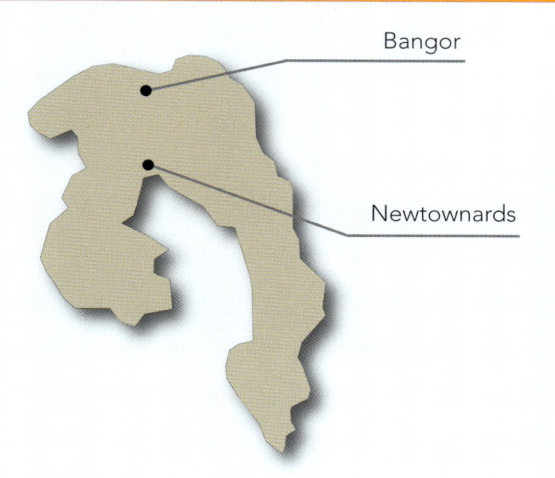

Population: 162,100
Councillors: 40
Residents per councillor: 4,053

Councillor	Party	Councillor	Party
Robert Adair	DUP	Bill Keery	Ind
Naomi Armstrong-Cotter	DUP	Lauren Kendall	Green
Craig Blaney	UUP	Colin Kennedy	DUP
Joe Boyle	SDLP	Janice MacArthur	DUP
Mark Brooks	UUP	Nick Mathison	APNI
Angus Carson	UUP	Lorna McAlpine	APNI
Alistair Cathcart	DUP	Carl McClean	UUP
David Chambers	UUP	Alan McDowell	APNI
Stephen Cooper	TUV	Stephen McIlveen	DUP
Trevor Cummings	DUP	Barry McKee	Green
Karen Douglas	APNI	Ray McKimm	Ind
Stephen Dunlop	Green	Martin McRandal	APNI
Nigel Edmund	DUP	Jimmy Menagh	Ind
Connie Egan	APNI	Richard Smart	UUP
Robert Gibson	DUP	Marion Smith	UUP
Jennifer Gilmour	DUP	Philip Smith	UUP
Deborah Girvan	APNI	Tom Smith	Ind
Gillian Greer	APNI	Eddie Thompson	DUP
Wesley Irvine	DUP	Gavin Walker	APNI
Peter Johnston	DUP	Scott Wilson	APNI

Local Government | Northern Ireland Yearbook

Armagh City, Banbridge and Craigavon Borough Council

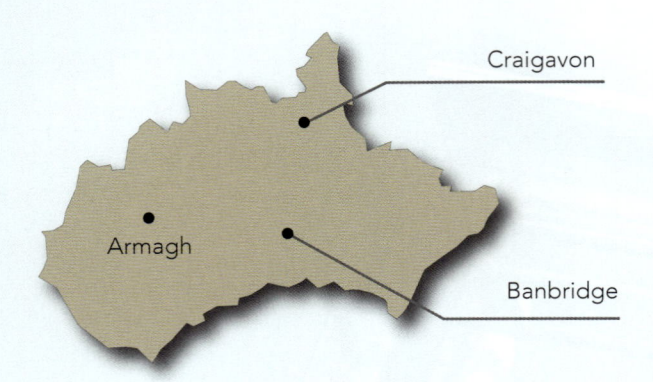

Population: 217,200
Councillors: 41
Residents per councillor: 5,298

Council contacts

The Palace Demesne
Armagh, BT60 4EL

Downshire Road
Banbridge, BT32 3JY

Craigavon Civic and
Conference Centre
Lakeview Road, Craigavon
BT64 1AL

Tel: 0300 0300 900
Web: www.armaghbanbridgecraigavon.gov.uk
Email: info@armaghbanbridgecraigavon.gov.uk

Lord Mayor: Alderman Glenn Barr (UUP)
Deputy Lord Mayor: Councillor Jackie Donnelly (SF)

Senior officers

Chief Executive: Roger Wilson

Deputy Chief Executive Officer: Mark Parkinson
Strategic Director Neighbourhood Services: Sharon O'Gorman
Strategic Director Community and Growth: Olga Murtagh
Strategic Director Strategy and Performance: Sharon McNicholl

Head of Community Planning: Elaine Gillespie
Head of Planning: Damian Mulligan
Head of Building Control: Tom Lavery
Head of Estates and Asset Management: Jonathan Hayes
Head of Economic Development: Nicola Wilson
Head of Tourism, Arts and Culture: Brian Johnston
Head of Environmental Health: Gillian Topping
Head of Environmental Services: Barry Patience
Head of Health and Recreation: Jonathan Hayes
Head of Community Development: Seamus McCrory

Councillor	Party	Councillor	Party
Sydney Anderson	DUP	Lavelle McIlwrath	DUP
Glenn Barr	UUP	Louise McKinstry	UUP
Mark Baxter	DUP	Darren McNally	SF
Paul Berry	Ind	Eamon McNeill	SDLP
Ian Burns	UUP	Stephen Moutray	DUP
Darryn Causby	DUP	Catherine Nelson	SF
Jackie Donnelly	SF	Sam Nicholson	UUP
Paul Duffy	SF	Thomas O'Hanlon	SDLP
Julie Flaherty	UUP	Gráinne O'Neill	SDLP
Paul Greenfield	DUP	Brian Pope	APNI
Bróna Haughey	SF	Paul Rankin	DUP
Keith Haughian	SF	Kevin Savage	SF
Garath Keating	SF	Kyle Savage	UUP
Gordon Kennedy	UUP	Jim Speers	UUP
Thomas Larkham	SDLP	Eóin Tennyson	APNI
Peter Lavery	APNI	Margaret Tinsley	DUP
Jill Macauley	UUP	Ciarán Toman	SDLP
Liam Mackle	SF	Kenneth Twyble	UUP
Declan McAlinden	SDLP	Gareth Wilson	DUP
Tim McClelland	DUP	Ian Wilson	DUP
Sorchá McGeown	SF		

Committees

Economic Development and Regeneration Committee
Chair: Councillor Declan McAlinden (SDLP)

Environmental Services Committee
Chair: Alderman Gordon Kennedy (UUP)

Governance, Resources and Strategy Committee
Chair: Councillor Tim McClelland (DUP)

Leisure and Community Services Committee
Chair: Councillor Keith Haughian (SF)

Performance and Audit Committee
Chair: Councillor Ciarán Toman (SDLP)

Planning and Regulatory Services Committee
Chair: Councillor Peter Lavery (APNI)

Northern Ireland Yearbook | Local Government

Belfast City Council

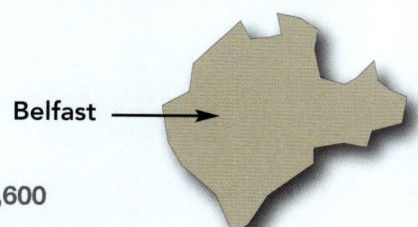

Council contacts

Council offices
City Hall
Belfast, BT1 5GS
Tel: 028 9032 0202
Textphone: 028 9027 0405
Web: www.belfastcity.gov.uk
Email: generalenquires@belfastcity.gov.uk
Twitter: @belfastcc

Mayor: Alderman Councillor Kate Nicholl (APNI)
Deputy Mayor: Alderman Tom Haire (DUP)

Senior Officers

Chief Executive:
Vacant

Deputy Chief Executive and Strategic Director of Finance and Resources: Ronan Cregan
Director of City and Organisational Strategy: John Tully
Legal and Civic Services, City Solicitor: John Walsh
Strategic Director of City and Neighbourhood Services: Vacant
Director of Place and Economy: Alistair Reid
Director of Physical Programmes: Sinead Grimes
Climate Commissioner: Debbie Caldwell
Head of Corporate Communications: Lisa Caldwell

Committees

Strategic Policy and Resources Committee
Chair: Councillor Áine Grogan (Green Party)

City Growth and Regeneration Committee
Chair: Councillor Ryan Murphy (SF)

People and Communities Committee
Chair: Councillor Fred Cobain (DUP)

Planning Committee
Chair: Councillor Arder Carson (SF)

Licensing Committee
Chair: Councillor Micheal Donnelly (SF)

Belfast Waterfront and Ulster Hall Ltd Shareholders' Committee
Chair: Councillor Áine McCabe (SF)

Brexit Committee
Chair: Councillor Daniel Baker (SF)

Population: 342,600
Councillors: 60
Residents per councillor: 5,710

Councillor	Party	Councillor	Party
Danny Baker	SF	John Kyle	Ind
Ciarán Beattie	SF	Michael Long	APNI
Christina Black	SF	Donal Lyons	SDLP
Nichola Bradley	SF	JJ Magee	SF
David Brooks	DUP	Stephen Magennis	SF
Sarah Bunting	DUP	Conor Maskey	SF
Claire Canavan	SF	Nuala McAllister	APNI
Arder Carson	SF	Geraldine McAteer	SF
Fred Cobain	DUP	Áine McCabe	SF
Matthew Collins	PBPA	Frank McCoubrey	DUP
Michael Collins	PBPA	Dean McCullough	DUP
Sonia Copeland	UUP	Paul McCusker	SDLP
Steven Corr	SF	Emmet McDonough-Brown	APNI
Séamas de Faoite	SDLP	Gary McKeown	SDLP
Michael Donnelly	SF	Ronan McLaughlin	SF
George Dorrian	DUP	Ross McMullan	APNI
Fiona Ferguson	PBPA	Peter McReynolds	APNI
Anthony Flynn	Green	Sian Mulholland	APNI
Matt Garrett	SF	Ryan Murphy	SF
John Gormley	SF	Adam Newton	DUP
Áine Groogan	Green	Kate Nicholl	APNI
Tom Haire	DUP	Mal O'Hara	Green
Eric Hanvey	APNI	Dale Pankhurst	DUP
Brian Heading	SDLP	Jim Rodgers	UUP
Carole Howard	UUP	Tommy Sandford	DUP
John Hussey	DUP	Brian Smyth	Green
Billy Hutchinson	PUP	Gareth Spratt	DUP
Michelle Kelly	APNI	Nicola Verner	DUP
Tracy Kelly	DUP	Séanna Walsh	SF
Brian Kingston	DUP	Carl Whyte	SDLP

Local Government 161

Causeway Coast and Glens Borough Council

Population: 144,900
Councillors: 40
Residents per councillor: 3,623

Council contacts

Cloonavin
66 Portstewart Road
Coleraine, BT52 1EY
Tel: 028 7034 7034

7 Connell Street
Limavady, BT49 0HA
Tel: 028 7772 2226

Council offices
Riada House
14 Charles Street
Ballymoney, BT53 6DZ
Tel: 028 2766 0200

Sheskburn House
7 Mary Street
Ballycastle, BT54 6QH
Tel: 028 2076 2225

Web: www.causewaycoastandglens.gov.uk
Email: info@causewaycoastandglens.gov.uk

Mayor: Councillor Richard Holmes (UUP)
Deputy Mayor: Councillor Ashleen Schenning (SDLP)

Senior Officers

Chief Executive: David Jackson

Director of Corporate Services (Deputy Chief Executive): Moira Quinn
Director of Leisure and Development: Richard Baker
Director of Environmental Services: Aidan McPeake
Chief Finance Officer: David Wright
Head of Planning: Denise Dickson
Head of Performance: Stephen McMaw

Committees

Environmental Services Committee
Chair: Councillor Darryl Wilson (UUP)

Leisure and Development Committee
Chair: Councillor John McAuley (DUP)

Corporate Policy and Resources Committee
Chair: Alderman Michelle Knight-McQuillan (DUP)

Planning Committee
Chair: Alderman Joan Baird (UUP)

Audit Committee
Chair: Councillor Dermot Nicholl (SF)

Finance Committee
Chair: Alderman Normal Hillis (UUP)

Councillor	Party	Councillor	Party
Philip Anderson	DUP	Kathleen McGurk	SF
Joan Baird	UUP	Tom McKeown	UUP
Seán Bateson	SF	Margaret Anne McKillop	SDLP
Orla Beattie	SDLP	Sharon McKillop	DUP
Yvonne Boyle	APNI	Cathal McLaughlin	SF
Aaron Callan	DUP	Alan McLean	DUP
Brenda Chivers	SF	Oliver McMullan	SF
Helena Dallat O'Driscoll	SDLP	Adrian McQuillan	DUP
George Duddy	DUP	Cara McShane	SF
Mark Fielding	DUP	Pádraig McShane	Ind
John Finlay	DUP	Angela Mulholland	Ind
Norman Hillis	UUP	Dermot Nicholl	SF
Richard Holmes	UUP	Leanne Peacock	SF
Sandra Hunter	UUP	Stephanie Quigley	Ind
Michelle Knight-McQuillan	DUP	Alan Robinson	DUP
John McAuley	DUP	Ashleen Schenning	SDLP
William McCandless	Ind	Edgar Scott	DUP
Chris McCaw	APNI	Ivor Wallace	DUP
James McCorkell	DUP	Russell Watton	PUP
Seán McGlinchey	SF	Darryl Wilson	UUP

Northern Ireland Yearbook | Local Government

Derry City and Strabane District Council

Council contacts

Council offices
98 Strand Road
Derry, BT48 7NN

47 Derry Road
Strabane, BT82 8DY

Tel: 028 7125 3253
Web: www.derrystrabane.com
Email: info@derrystrabane.com
Twitter: @dcsdcouncil

Mayor: Alderman Graham Warke (DUP)
Deputy Mayor: Councillor Christopher Jackson (SF)

Senior Officers

Chief Executive: John Kelpie

Director of Environment and Regeneration: Karen Philips
Director of Business and Culture: Stephen Gillespie
Director of Health and Community: Karen McFarland

Lead Finance Officer: Alfie Dallas
Lead Human Resources Officer: Paula Donnelly
Lead Democratic Services and Improvement Officer: Ellen Cavanagh
Lead Assurance Officer: Denise McDonnell
Lead Legal Services Officer: Philip Kingston

Committees

Audit, Assurance and Risk Committee
Chair: Councillor Paul Gallagher (Independent)

Business and Culture Committee
Chair: Councillor Conor Heaney (SF)

Environment and Regeneration Committee
Chair: Councillor Ruairi McHugh (SF)

Governance and Strategic Planning Committee
Chair: Councillor Martin Reilly (SDLP)

Health and Community Committee
Chair: Councillor Paul Fleming (SF)

Planning Committee
Chair: Councillor Philip McKinney (APNI)

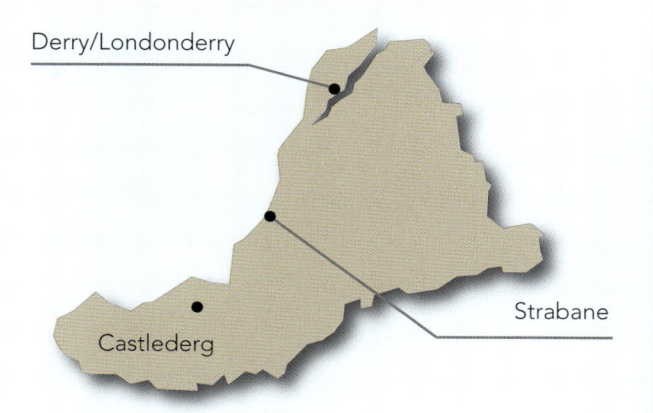

Population: 151,100
Councillors: 40
Residents per councillor: 3,778

Derry City & Strabane District Council
Comhairle Chathair Dhoire & Cheantar an tSratha Báin
Derry Cittie & Stràbane Destrick Cooncil

Councillor	Party	Councillor	Party
Jason Barr	SDLP	Derek Hussey	UUP
Raymond Barr	Ind	Christopher Jackson	SF
John Boyle	SDLP	Dan Kelly	SF
Michaela Boyle	SF	Keith Kerrigan	DUP
Allan Bresland	DUP	Patricia Logue	SF
Seán Carr	Ind	Hilary McClintock	DUP
Shauna Cusack	SDLP	Ryan McCready	UUP
Maurice Devenney	DUP	Emma McGinley	SF
Angela Dobbins	SDLP	John McGowan	SF
Gary Donnelly	Ind	Kieran McGuire	SF
Emmet Doyle	Aontú	Ruairí McHugh	SF
Sandra Duffy	SF	Jim McKeever	Ind
Steven Edwards	SDLP	Philip McKinney	APNI
Rory Farrell	SDLP	Seán Mooney	SDLP
Rachael Ferguson	APNI	Maeve O'Neill	PBPA
Paul Fleming	SF	David Ramsey	DUP
Paul Gallagher	Ind	Martin Reilly	SDLP
Darren Guy	UUP	Lilian Seenoi-Barr	SDLP
Shaun Harkin	PBPA	Brian Tierney	SDLP
Conor Heaney	SF	Graham Warke	DUP

Fermanagh and Omagh District Council

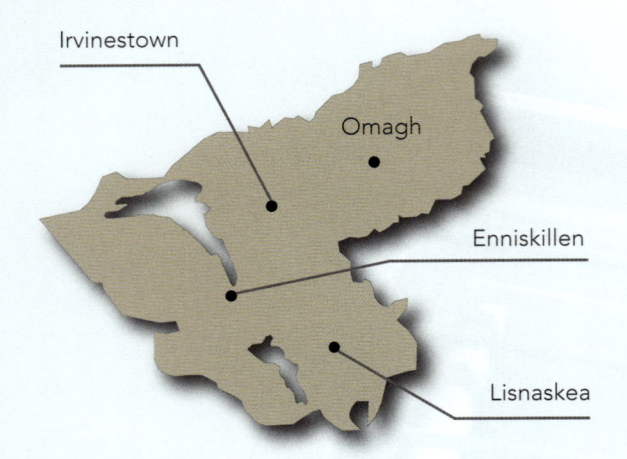

Population: 117,300
Councillors: 40
Residents per councillor: 2,933

Fermanagh & Omagh District Council
Comhairle Ceantair Fhear Manach agus na hÓmaí

Council contacts

Council offices

Townhall
2 Townhall Street
Enniskillen
Co Fermanagh
BT74 7BA

The Grange
Mountjoy Road
Lisnamallard
Omagh
Co Tyrone
BT79 7BL

Tel: 0300 303 1777
Textphone: 028 8225 6216
Web: www.fermanaghomagh.com
Email: info@fermanaghomagh.com
Twitter: @fermanaghomagh
Facebook: @fermanaghomagh
Instagram: @fermanaghomaghdc
LinkedIn: Fermanagh and Omagh District Council

Chair: Councillor Errol Thompson (DUP)
Vice-Chair: Councillor Chris McCaffrey (SF)

Senior Officers

Chief Executive: Alison McCullagh

Director of Corporate Services and Governance: Celine McCartan
Director of Regeneration and Planning: Kim McLaughlin
Director of Environment and Place: John News
Director of Community and Wellbeing: John Boyle

Committees

Regeneration and Community Committee
Chair: Councillor Victor Warrington (UUP)

Planning Committee
Chair: Councillor Glenn Campbell (SF)

Environmental Services Committee
Chair: Councillor Mark Buchanan (DUP)

Policy and Resources Committee
Chair: Councillor Howard Thornton (UUP)

Brexit Committee
Chair: Councillor Anthony Feely (SF)

Rural Affairs Sub Committee
Chair: Sheamus Greene (SF)

Health and Social Care Service Sub Committee
Chair: Vacant

Councillor	Party	Councillor	Party
Diana Armstrong	UUP	Catherine Kelly	SF
Alex Baird	UUP	Pádraigín Kelly	SF
Matthew Bell	UUP	Thomas Maguire	SF
Paul Blake	SDLP	Emmet McAleer	Ind
Mark Buchanan	DUP	Stephen McCann	SF
Glenn Campbell	SF	Chris McCaffrey	SF
Seán Clarke	SF	John McClaughry	UUP
John Coyle	SDLP	Barry McElduff	SF
Siobhán Currie	SF	Garbhan McPhillips	SDLP
Josephine Deehan	Ind	Dónal Ó Cofaigh	CCLA
Ann-Marie Donnelly	SF	Thomas O'Reilly	SF
Stephen Donnelly	APNI	Allan Rainey	UUP
Keith Elliott	DUP	Paul Robinson	DUP
Anthony Feely	SF	Paul Stevenson	DUP
Anne Marie Fitzgerald	SF	Bernice Swift	Ind
Adam Gannon	SDLP	Errol Thompson	DUP
Mary Garrity	SDLP	Howard Thornton	UUP
Sheamus Greene	SF	Victor Warrington	UUP
Robert Irvine	UUP	Bert Wilson	UUP
Eamon Keenan	Ind	Patrick Withers	SF

Northern Ireland Yearbook | Local Government

Lisburn and Castlereagh City Council

Council contacts

Civic Headquarters
Lagan Valley Island
Lisburn, Co Antrim
BT27 4RL

Tel: 028 9244 7300
Web: www.lisburncastlereagh.gov.uk
Email: enquiries@lisburncastlereagh.gov.uk
Twitter: @lisburnccc
Facebook: @LisburnCastlereagh

Mayor: Alderman Stephen Martin (APNI)
Deputy Mayor: Councillor Tim Mitchell (UUP)

Senior Officers

Chief Executive: David Burns

Director of Finance and Corporate Services: Cara McCrory
Director of Environmental Services: Heather Moore
Director of Leisure and Community Wellbeing: Louise Moore
Director of Service Transformation: Donal Rogan

Committees

Capital Projects Committee
Chair: Councillor Sharon Lowry (APNI)

Corporate Services Committee
Chair: Councillor John Laverty (DUP)

Development Committee
Chair: Alderman Amanda Grehan (APNI)

Environmental Services Committee
Chair: Councillor Andrew Ewing (DUP)

Governance and Audit Committee
Chair: Councillor John Palmer (UUP)

Leisure and Community Development Committee
Chair: Councillor Sharon Skillen (DUP)

Planning Committee
Chair: Councillor Alex Swan (UUP)

Population: 146,500
Councillors: 40
Residents per councillor: 3,663

Councillor	Party	Councillor	Party
Nathan Anderson	Ind	Stuart Hughes	UUP
James Baird	UUP	John Laverty	DUP
Thomas Beckett	DUP	Simon Lee	Green
Ryan Carlin	SF	Hazel Legge	UUP
Scott Carson	DUP	Sharon Lowry	APNI
Jonathan Craig	DUP	Uel Mackin	DUP
Jim Dillon	UUP	Stephen Martin	APNI
David Drysdale	DUP	Johnny McCarthy	SDLP
Sorcha Eastwood	APNI	Gary McCleave	SF
Allan Ewart	DUP	Caleb McCready	DUP
Andrew Ewing	DUP	Aaron McIntyre	APNI
John Gallen	SDLP	Ross McLernon	UUP
Owen Gawith	APNI	Tim Mitchell	UUP
Alan Givan	DUP	John Palmer	UUP
Andrew Gowan	DUP	Jenny Palmer	UUP
Martin Gregg	APNI	Paul Porter	DUP
Amanda Grehan	APNI	Sharon Skillen	DUP
Michelle Guy	APNI	Alex Swan	UUP
Michael Henderson	UUP	James Tinsley	DUP
David Honeyford	APNI	Nicholas Trimble	UUP

Local Government | Northern Ireland Yearbook

Mid and East Antrim Borough Council

Population: 139,400
Councillors: 40
Residents per councillor: 3,485

Council contacts

Council HQ
The Braid, 1-29 Bridge Street
Ballymena, BT43 5EJ

Ardeevin, 80 Galgorm Road
Ballymena, BT42 1AB

Museum and Civic Centre
11 Antrim Street
Carrickfergus, BT38 7DG

Smiley Buildings
Victoria Road, Larne, BT40 1RU

Tel: 0300 1245 000
Email: enquiries@midandeastantrim.gov.uk
Web: www.midandeastantrim.gov.uk
Twitter: @mea_bc

Mayor: Councillor William McCaughey (DUP)
Deputy Mayor: Councillor Matthew Armstrong (TUV)

Senior Officers

Chief Executive: Anne Donaghy

Director of Corporate Services: Louise Kennedy
Director of Community: Katrina Morgan
Director of Operations: Philip Thompson
Director of Development: Nicola Rowles

Committees

Planning Committee
Chair: Alderman Audrey Wales (DUP)

Policy and Resources Committee
Chair: Alderman Billy Ashe (DUP)

Direct Services Committee
Chair: Alderman Noel Williams (APNI)

Borough Growth Committee
Chair: Councillor Gregg McKeen (DUP)

Audit and Scrutiny Committee
Chair: Councillor Keith Turner (UUP)

Councillor	Party	Councillor	Party
Beth Adger	DUP	William McCaughey	DUP
Matthew Armstrong	TUV	John McDermott	DUP
Billy Ashe	DUP	Stewart McDonald	TUV
Cheryl Brownlee	DUP	Gregg McKeen	DUP
John Carson	DUP	James McKeown	SF
Robin Cherry	UUP	William McNeilly	UUP
Andrew Clarke	DUP	Maureen Morrow	UUP
Brian Collins	TUV	Geraldine Mulvenna	APNI
Marc Collins	DUP	Tommy Nicholl	DUP
Danny Donnelly	APNI	Patricia O'Lynn	APNI
Julie Frew	DUP	Rodney Quigley	Ind
Ian Friary	SF	David Reid	APNI
Timothy Gaston	TUV	Eugene Reid	SDLP
Thomas Gordon	DUP	Paul Reid	DUP
Lauren Gray	APNI	Angela Smyth	DUP
Bobby Hadden	Ind	Robin Stewart	UUP
James Henry	Ind	Keith Turner	UUP
Christopher Jamieson	TUV	Audrey Wales	DUP
Peter Johnston	DUP	Noel Williams	APNI
Robert Logan	APNI	Andrew Wilson	UUP

Mid Ulster District Council

Council contacts

Council offices
70 Burn Road
Cookstown, BT80 8DT

Circular Road
Dungannon
BT71 6DT

50 Ballyronan Road
Magherafelt, BT45 6EN

Tel: 03000 132 132
Web: www.midulstercouncil.org
Email: info@midulstercouncil.org

Chair: Councillor Paul McLean (DUP)
Deputy Chair: Councillor Christine McFlynn (SDLP)

Senior Officers

Chief Executive:
Adrian McCreesh

Director of Communities and Place: Vacant
Director of Environment: Anne-Marie Campbell
Director of Corporate Service: JJ Tohill
Director of Organisational Development, Strategy and Performance: Marissa Canavan
Director of Planning: Chris Boomer

Committees

Policy and Resources Committee
Chair: Councillor Derek McKinney (UUP)

Planning Committee
Chair: Councillor Kyle Black (DUP)

Development Committee
Chair: Councillor Dominic Molloy (SF)

Environment Committee
Chair: Councillor Wesley Browne (DUP)

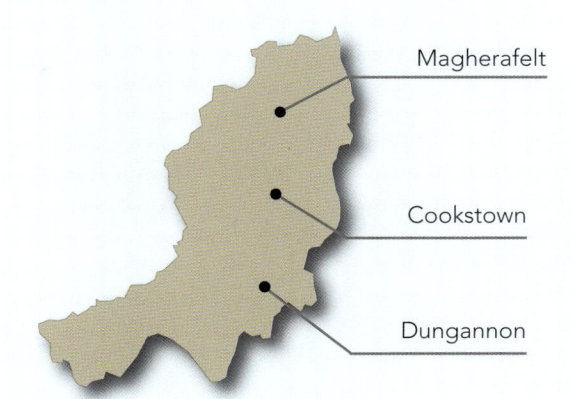

Population: 149,000
Councillors: 40
Residents per councillor: 3,725

Councillor	Party	Councillor	Party
Kim Ashton	DUP	Cathal Mallaghan	SF
Gavin Bell	SF	Niall McAleer	SF
Kyle Black	DUP	Sharon McAleer	SDLP
Wesley Brown	DUP	Christine McFlynn	SDLP
Wilbert Buchanan	DUP	Brian McGuigan	SF
Frances Burton	DUP	Seán McGuigan	SF
Sean Clarke	SF	Derek McKinney	UUP
Robert Colvin	UUP	Paul McLean	DUP
Cora Corry	SF	John McNamee	SF
Walter Cuddy	UUP	Donal McPeake	SF
Clement Cuthbertson	DUP	Seán McPeake	SF
Niamh Doris	SF	Ian Milne	SF
Catherine Elattar	SF	Dominic Molloy	SF
Anne Forde	DUP	Barry Monteith	Ind
Phelim Gildernew	SF	Denise Mullen	Aontú
Mark Glasgow	UUP	Joe O'Neill	SF
Meta Graham	UUP	Malachy Quinn	SDLP
Kerri Hughes	SDLP	Wills Robinson	DUP
Martin Kearney	SDLP	Darren Totten	SF
Dan Kerr	Ind	Trevor Wilson	UUP

Newry, Mourne and Down District Council

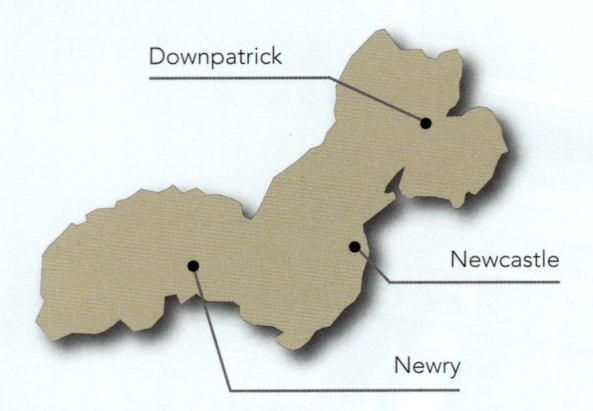

Population: 181,700
Councillors: 43
Residents per councillor: 4,226

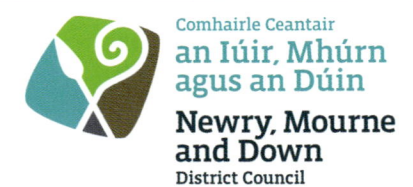

Councillor	Party	Councillor	Party
Terry Andrews	SDLP	Cathy Mason	SF
Patrick Brown	APNI	Declan McAteer	SDLP
Robert Burgess	UUP	Leeanne McEvoy	SF
Pete Byrne	SDLP	Harold McKee	UUP
Charlie Casey	SF	Karen McKevitt	SDLP
Willie Clarke	SF	Andrew McMurray	APNI
Dermot Curran	SDLP	Róisín Mulgrew	SF
Laura Devlin	SDLP	Declan Murphy	SF
Seán Doran	SF	Gerry O'Hare	SF
Cadogan Enright	Ind	Barra Ó Muirí	SF
Aoife Finnegan	SF	Kathryn Owen	DUP
Hugh Gallagher	SDLP	Henry Reilly	Ind
Mark Gibbons	Ind	Mickey Ruane	SF
Oonagh Hanlon	SF	Michael Savage	SDLP
Glyn Hanna	DUP	Gareth Sharvin	SDLP
Valerie Harte	SF	Gary Stokes	SDLP
Róisín Howell	SF	David Taylor	UUP
Mickey Larkin	SF	Jarlath Tinnelly	Ind
Alan Lewis	UUP	John Trainor	SDLP
Gavin Malone	Ind	Billy Walker	DUP
Oonagh Magennis	SF		

Council contacts

Oifig an Iúir
Newry Office
O'Hagan House
Monaghan Row
Newry, BT35 8DJ

Oifig Dhún Pádraig
Downpatrick Office
Downshire Civic Centre
Downshire Estate, Ardglass Road
Downpatrick, BT30 6GQ

Council: 0300 013 2233
Planning: 0300 200 7830
Email: info@nmandd.org

Chairperson: Councillor Cathy Mason (SF)
Deputy Chairperson: Councillor Oonagh Magennis (SF)

Senior Officers

Chief Executive:
Marie Ward

Director of Enterprise, Regeneration and Tourism:
Conor Mallon
Director of Active and Healthy Communities: Michael Lipsett
Director of Neighbourhood Services: Johnny McBride (acting)
Director of Corporate Services: Dorinnia Carville

Committees:

Active and Healthy Communities Committee
Chair: Councillor Karen McKevitt (SDLP)

Enterprise, Regeneration and Tourism Committee
Chair: Councillor Roisin Howell (SF)

Neighbourhood Services
Chair: Councillor Kathryn Owen (DUP)

Planning Committee
Chair: Councillor Declan McAteer (SDLP)

Strategy, Policy and Resources Committee
Chair: Councillor Oonagh Hanlon (SF)

agendaNi digital

The magazine's content is delivered over a number of digital platforms including all articles posted on the agendaNi.com website, a full digital version of the magazine online, a newsletter with selected articles from the current issue emailed to readers and focused newsletters with individual industry specific reports emailed to selected readers. **Sign up today to ensure you can access agendaNi anywhere.**

www.agendaNi.com/subscribe-now

Get the latest content delivered to your inbox with every issue!

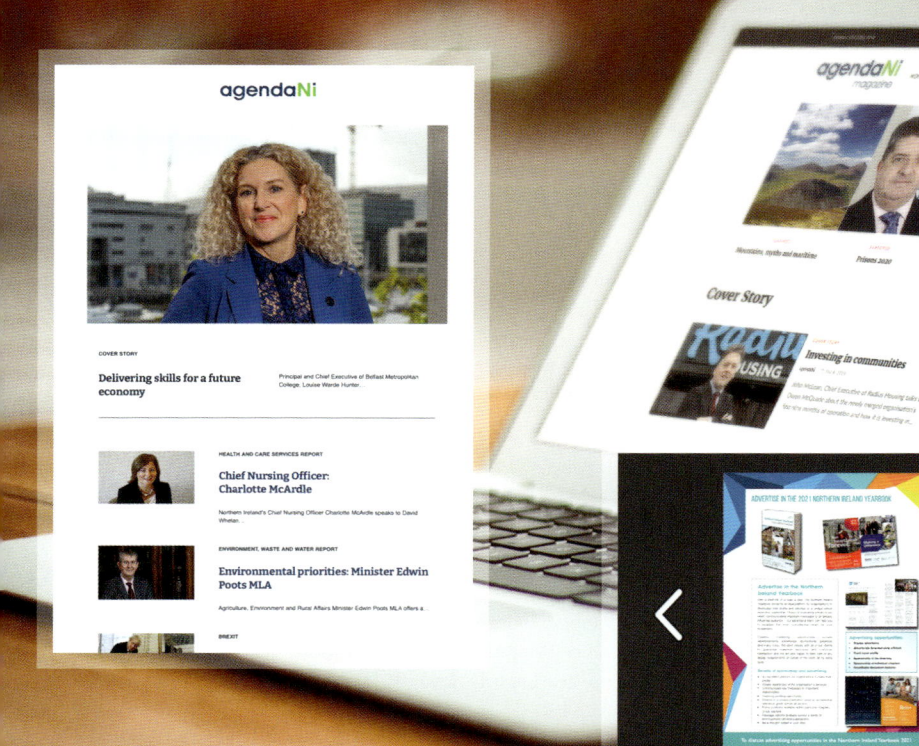

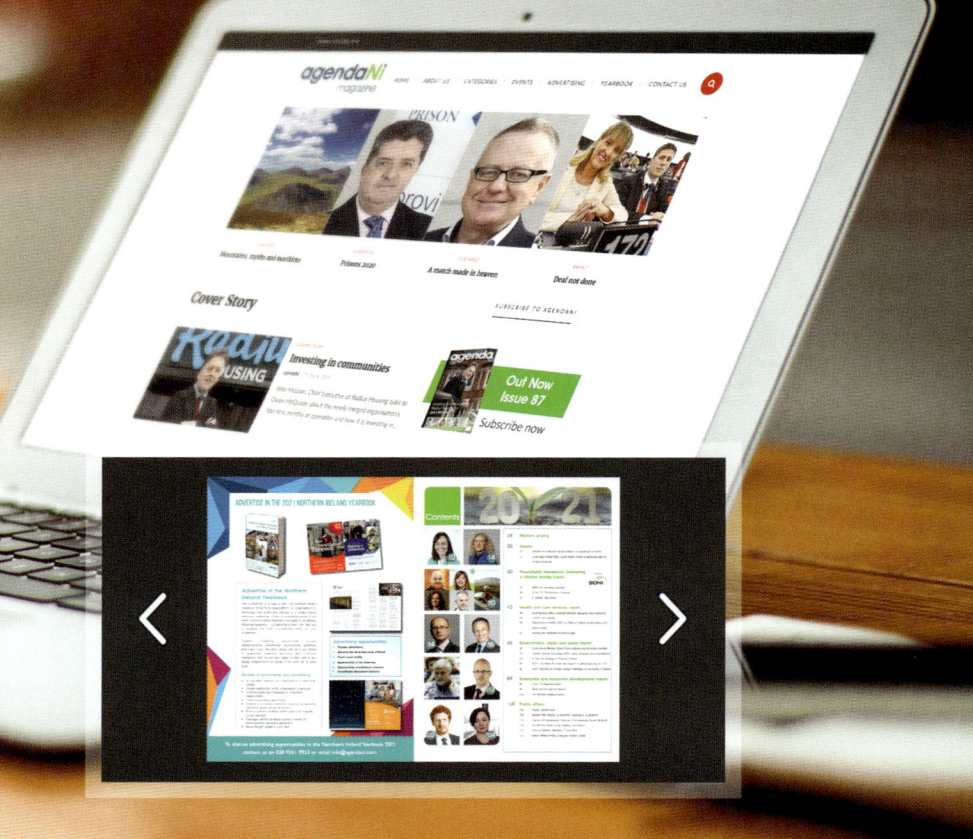

Subscribe to our mailing list today!

agendaNi

Digital | Events | Print

Follow agendaNi on twitter
agendaNi
Join the debate with #agendaNi

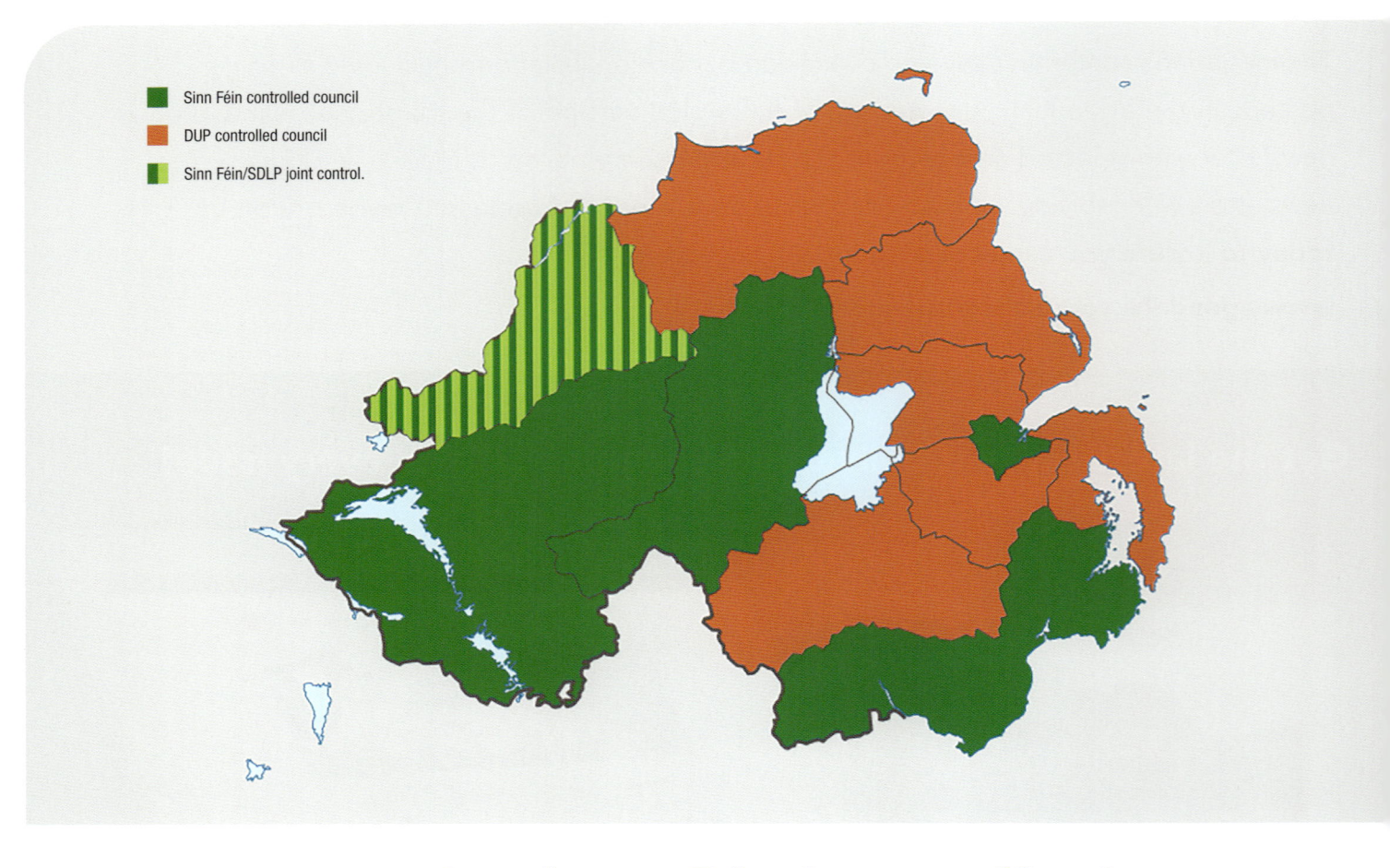

2019 local elections: Big four suffer losses

The DUP remained the largest party in terms of seats in Northern Ireland's local government makeup. However, such a stat does not tell the full story of an election where Sinn Féin was the only of the traditional big four parties not to lose seats from their 2014 tallies and all unionist parties suffered losses.

Despite the loss of eight seats, the DUP remained the largest party with 122 seats spread across Northern Ireland's 11 local councils. Again, this stat does not tell the full story, with the DUP being the only one of the big four parties to increase its share of first preference votes. The party's 1 per cent rise — from 23.1 per cent in 2014 to 24.13 per cent in 2019 — suggests a consolidation of its core vote, but its loss of seats suggests a lack of transfers and a falling out of favour in non-unionist areas.

While they maintained control of the six councils that they had controlled before the election, the DUP suffered a loss of seats in all but one of these areas. Only Causeway Coast and Glens Borough Council saw the DUP increase its number of seats in a previously held area, from 11 seats to 14. Significant losses include the loss of five seats – from 20 to 15 – in Lisburn and Castlereagh, where Sinn Féin won two seats for the first time and the Alliance gained two seats.

The party may take some encouragement from the gaining of one seat on Belfast City Council, rising from 14 to 15, where Sinn Féin lost one seat, but still retained control with 18 seats.

The election was one of loss for unionism as a whole, with 29 seats lost overall by unionist parties (DUP, UUP, Traditional Unionist Voice and Progressive Unionist Party). First preference votes for unionism also saw a decline: the previously mentioned four parties and UKIP and the NI Conservatives saw their total share of first preference votes fall from 47.5 per cent in 2014 to 39.87 per cent this time around.

The UUP tallied 75 seats, 95,320 first

Northern Ireland Yearbook

Local Government

Seats by party 2014 and 2019

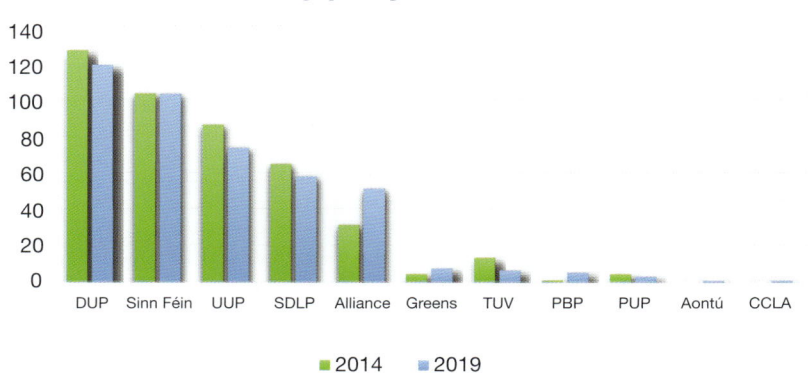

(Bar chart showing 2014 and 2019 seat counts for DUP, Sinn Féin, UUP, SDLP, Alliance, Greens, TUV, PBP, PUP, Aontú, CCLA)

First preference votes by party 2014 and 2019

(Bar chart showing 2014 and 2019 first preference vote shares for DUP, Sinn Féin, UUP, SDLP, Alliance, TUV, Greens, PBP, PUP, UKIP, Aontú, NI Conservatives)

preference votes and a 14.1 per cent share of the first preference votes when all counting had finished; their lowest postings in all three categories since local government in Northern Ireland was reorganised by the Local Government (Boundaries) Act (Northern Ireland) 1971 and the Local Government Act (Northern Ireland) 1972. Their loss of 13 seats from 2014, and the Alliance Party's gain of 21 seats would seem to suggest that the moderate unionist vote has migrated not to the DUP, as some may have predicted, but to the centrist cross-community party, whose roots lie in the moderate unionist New Ulster Movement, who gained a previously UUP seat in the Lisnasharrgh electoral district of Belfast.

For Sinn Féin, the election was a static affair. Having entered with 105 seats as the second biggest party in that regard, they exited with 105 seats, still the second biggest party. Having won outright control of four councils in 2014, while sharing Newry, Mourne and Down with the SDLP, Sinn Féin now outright control four councils and share control of Derry and Strabane District Council with the SDLP. Its first preference vote fell from 24.1 per cent in 2014 to 23.22 per cent, allowing the DUP to overtake it as the biggest party in Northern Ireland in that regard.

While Sinn Féin had hoped to make gains within Belfast City Council, it ended the election with one less seat in City Hall, but still as the largest party. The gain of an SDLP seat in Black Mountain was chalked off after the party was outflanked to the left by People Before Profit in Colin DEA and to the centre by Alliance in the Titanic DEA.

Explicitly republican/nationalist parties also saw a drop in their number of seats. In 2014, Sinn Féin and the SDLP won a combined 171 seats; in 2019, Sinn Féin, the SDLP and Aontú, the anti-abortion republican party led by ex-Sinn Féin TD Peadar Tóibín, won a combined total of 165. First preference shares across republicanism and nationalism also fell, from 37.7 per cent of the vote in 2014 to 35.49 per cent in 2019.

It was another disappointing electoral campaign for the SDLP, whose loss of six seats was paired with a 1.59 percentage point drop in their share of first preference votes. What little consolation they may be able to draw will come from the party's performance in Derry and Strabane, where three seats were gained, meaning the party is now the joint-biggest on the council along with Sinn Féin.

The truest and easiest to identify gains were made outside of Northern Ireland's traditional political dichotomy of unionism versus republicanism. The Alliance Party was the clearest winner of the day, with a gain of 21 seats and the largest rise in first preference votes of any party. The rise from 6.7 per cent in 2014 to a vote share of 11.5 per cent almost approaches the party's 1977 high of 14.4 per cent. The Green Party doubled its seat tally, from four to eight, and more than doubled its first preference vote share, jumping from 0.8 per cent to 2.11 per cent.

Leftist parties that remain non-aligned on the national question also experienced a boon, with the Cross Community Labour Alternative party winning its first seat ever, on the Fermanagh and Omagh District Council. The highest profile among the leftist parties, People Before Profit, also enjoyed its best ever local election results, again more than doubling its first preference vote share from 0.3 per cent to 1.4 per cent and jumping from one seat to five. Notable performances include that of Matt Collins, the only non-Sinn Féin councillor elected in Black Mountain, who topped the poll with 2,268 first preference votes.

With three of the big four declining in their number of seats and a different group of three declining in terms of first preference votes, the latest round of local elections in Northern Ireland suggest that the term "big four" may just be on its way to becoming irrelevant.

2019 council elections

Antrim and Newtownabbey

Summary of Council

Electorate 98,899 Valid vote 47,989 Turnout 53%

Party	Seats	Change since 2014
DUP	14	-1
SF	5	+2
UUP	9	-3
SDLP	4	
APNI	7	+3
Others	1	-1

Airport (5 seats)

Electorate	14,042	Total valid votes	7,052
Votes polled	7,121	Turnout %	50.71
Quota	1,176		

Candidate	Party	1st Pref	Elected
Thomas Burns	SDLP	1,125	5th count
Anne-Marie Logue	SF	1,095	5th count
Matthew Magill	DUP	1,164	3rd count
Ben Mallon	DUP	481	
Vikki McAuley	APNI	1,221	1st count
Paul Michael	UUP	893	4th count
Mervyn Rea	UUP	568	
Cathy Rooney	SF	505	

Antrim (6 seats)

Electorate	15,051	Total valid votes	6,432
Votes polled	6,512	Turnout %	43.27
Quota	919		

Candidate	Party	1st Pref	Elected
Richard Cairns	TUV	347	
Adrian Cochrane-Watson	Ind	359	
Paul Dunlop	DUP	603	6th count
Neil Kelly	APNI	1,689	1st count
Roisin Lynch	SDLP	723	2nd count
Gerard Magee	SF	583	
Karl McMeekin	DUP	363	
Jim Montgomery	UUP	416	7th count
John Smyth	DUP	734	5th count
Leah Smyth	UUP	615	7th count

Ballyclare (5 seats)

Electorate	13,190	Total valid votes	6,758
Votes polled	6,821	Turnout %	51.71
Quota	1,127		

Candidate	Party	1st Pref	Elected
Jeannie Archibald	DUP	739	6th count
David Arthurs	Ind	457	
Gary English	APNI	775	
Mary Girvan	DUP	861	6th count
Danny Kinahan	UUP	1,253	1st count
Vera McWilliam	UUP	707	6th count
Austin Orr	DUP	443	
Norrie Ramsey	UUP	341	
Michael Stewart	Ind	1,182	1st count

Dunsilly (5 seats)

Electorate	12,519	Total valid votes	6,514
Votes polled	6,590	Turnout %	52.64
Quota	1,086		

Candidate	Party	1st Pref	Elected
Linda Clarke	DUP	965	5th count
Henry Cushinan	SF	1,064	3rd count
Glenn Finlay	APNI	989	4th count
Jordan Greer	DUP	907	
Andrew Maguire	SF	552	
Roderick Swann	UUP	711	5th count
Gareth Thompson	UUP	424	
Ryan Wilson	SDLP	902	4th count

Glengormley Urban (7 seats)

Electorate	15,810	Total valid votes	7,939
Votes polled	8,046	Turnout %	50.89
Quota	993		

Candidate	Party	1st Pref	Elected
Alison Bennington	DUP	856	6th count
Phillip Brett	DUP	1,099	1st count
Samantha Burns	DUP	373	
Mark Cosgrove	UUP	891	5th count
Michael Goodman	SF	904	7th count
Rosie Kinnear	SF	801	7th count
Michael Maguire	UUP	337	
Noreen McClelland	SDLP	992	2nd count
Julian McGrath	APNI	1,345	1st count
Paul Veronica	Green	341	

Macedon (6 seats)

Electorate	13,593	Total valid votes	6,258
Votes polled	6,331	Turnout %	46.58
Quota	895		

Candidate	Party	1st Pref	Elected
Robert Foster	UUP	956	1st count
Paul Hamill	DUP	1,043	1st count
Robert Hill	UKIP	154	
Thomas Hogg	DUP	999	1st count
David Hollis	TUV	223	
Dean McCullough	DUP	321	7th count
Taylor McGrann	SF	765	7th count
Victor Robinson	DUP	327	
Stafford Ward	Ind	343	
Billy Webb	APNI	1,127	1st count

Three Mile Water (6 seats)

Electorate	14,694	Total valid votes	7,036
Votes polled	7,105	Turnout %	48.35
Quota	1,006		

Candidate	Party	1st Pref	Elected
Fraser Agnew	UUP	1,100	1st count
Norman Boyd	TUV	234	
Tom Campbell	APNI	1,075	1st count
Mark Cooper	DUP	1,230	1st count
Sam Flanagan	DUP	489	7th count
Julie Gilmour	APNI	749	7th count
Gary Grattan	Ind	223	
Stephen McCarthy	UUP	514	
Stephen Ross	DUP	1,103	1st count
Raymond Stewart	UKIP	319	

Northern Ireland Yearbook | Local Government

2019 council elections

Ards and North Down

Summary of Council

Electorate 116,536 Valid vote 50,206 Turnout 45%

Party	Seats	Change since 2014
DUP	14	-3
SF	0	+3
UUP	8	-1
SDLP	1	
APNI	10	+3
Others	7	+1

Ards Peninsula (6 seats)

Electorate 17,582 Total valid votes 7,837
Votes polled 7,956 Turnout % 45.30
Quota 1,120

Candidate	Party	1st Pref	Elected
Robert Adair	DUP	2,189	1st count
Joe Boyle	SDLP	1,621	2nd count
Angus Carson	UUP	832	5th count
Matt Davey	UKIP	234	
Nigel Edmund	DUP	735	3rd count
Lorna McAlpine	APNI	832	6th count
Murdoch McKibben	SF	196	
Tim Mullen	Conservative	58	
Michele Strong	Green	319	
Eddie Thompson	DUP	821	4th count

Bangor Central (6 seats)

Electorate 18,166 Total valid votes 7,357
Votes polled 7,450 Turnout % 41.90
Quota 1,052

Candidate	Party	1st Pref	Elected
Craig Blaney	UUP	757	4th count
Alistair Cathcart	DUP	787	3rd count
James Cochrane	DUP	255	
Karen Douglas	APNI	1,346	1st count
Stephen Dunlop	Green	1,046	2nd count
Ian Henry	UUP	542	
Wesley Irvine	DUP	878	5th count
Maria Lourenco	Ind	362	
Ray McKimm	Ind	503	6th count
John Montgomery	UKIP	215	
Gavan Reynolds	Ind	33	
Noelle Robinson	Ind	423	
Frank Shivers	Conservative	210	

Bangor East & Donaghadee (6 seats)

Electorate 17,416 Total valid votes 7,598
Votes polled 7,696 Turnout % 44.19
Quota 1,086

Candidate	Party	1st Pref	Elected
Mark Brooks	UUP	1,327	1st count
David Chambers	UUP	963	3rd count
Bill Keery	DUP	764	5th count
Paul Leman	Conservative	137	
Janice MacArthur	DUP	702	
Peter James Martin	DUP	902	4th count
Hannah Irwin McNamara	Green	735	
Tom Smith	Ind	765	6th count
Gavin Walker	APNI	1303	2nd count

Bangor West (5 seats)

Electorate 13,585 Total valid votes 5,709
Votes polled 5,794 Turnout % 42.65
Quota 952

Candidate	Party	1st Pref	Elected
Connie Egan	APNI	1,151	1st count
Ben English	Conservative	114	
Jennifer Gilmour	DUP	990	2nd count
Alan Graham	DUP	749	
Kieran Maxwell	SF	71	
Barry McKee	Green	949	4th count
Marion Smith	UUP	982	3rd count
Scott Wilson	APNI	703	5th count

Comber (5 seats)

Electorate 14,244 Total valid votes 6,527
Votes polled 6,587 Turnout % 46.24
Quota 1,088

Candidate	Party	1st Pref	Elected
Ricky Bamford	Green	372	
Stephen Cooper	TUV	695	5th count
Trevor Cummings	DUP	843	3rd count
Robert Gibson	DUP	985	4th count
Deborah Girvan	APNI	1,516	1st count
John Montgomery	DUP	643	
Michael Palmer	UUP	318	
John Sloan	Ind	73	
Philip Smith	UUP	1,082	

Holywood & Clandeboye (5 seats)

Electorate 15,052 Total valid votes 6,837
Votes polled 6,904 Turnout % 45.87
Quota 1,140

Candidate	Party	1st Pref	Elected
Roberta Dunlop	DUP	677	
Stephen Dunne	DUP	1,139	4th count
Gillian Greer	APNI	1,249	3rd count
Tim Lemon	UUP	416	
Carl McClean	UUP	507	5th count
Andrew Muir	APNI	1,397	1st count
Andrew Turner	Conservative	141	
Rachel Woods	Green	1,311	2nd count

Newtownards (7 seats)

Electorate 20,491 Total valid votes 8,341
Votes polled 8,479 Turnout % 41.38
Quota 1,043

Candidate	Party	1st Pref	Elected
Naomi Armstrong	DUP	1,232	2nd count
Paul Corry	UKIP	223	
Ian Dickson	UUP	481	
Colin Kennedy	DUP	570	5th count
Ben King		24	
Maurice McCartney	Green	374	
Nick Mathison	APNI	1,091	3rd count
Alan McDowell	APNI	574	7th count
Stephen McIlveen	DUP	898	4th count
Jimmy Menagh	Ind	2,138	1st count
Richard Smart	UUP	736	6th count

2019 council elections

Armagh, Banbridge and Craigavon

Summary of Council

Electorate 137,075　Valid vote 78,144　Turnout 54%

Party	Seats	Change since 2014
DUP	11	-2
SF	10	+2
UUP	10	-2
SDLP	6	
APNI	3	+3
Others	1	

Armagh (6 seats)

Electorate 21,982　Total valid votes 12,723
Votes polled 12,914　Turnout % 58.75
Quota 1,818

Candidate	Party	1st Pref	Elected
Mealla Campbell	SDLP	1,246	5th count
Jackie Coade	APNI	674	
Freda Donnelly	DUP	1,638	
Jackie Donnelly	SF	1,677	4th count
Garath Keating	SF	2,037	1st count
Martin Kelly	Aontu	822	
Darren McNally	SF	1,413	5th count
Sam Nicholson	UUP	1,697	5th count
Pól Ó-hÓgáin	Ind	28	
Thomas O'Hanlon	SDLP	1,491	5th count

Banbridge (7 seats)

Electorate 24,418　Total valid votes 12,138
Votes polled 12,274　Turnout % 50.27
Quota 1,518

Candidate	Party	1st Pref	Elected
Glenn Barr	UUP	1,764	1st count
Ian Burns	UUP	1,273	3rd count
Seamus Doyle	SDLP	1,309	
Paul Greenfield	DUP	1,563	1st count
Jill MacAuley	UUP	1,350	6th count
William Martin	TUV	508	
Vincent McAleenan	SF	676	
Junior McCrum	DUP	1,232	6th count
Brian Pope	APNI	1,425	8th count
Kevin Savage	SF	1,038	4th count

Craigavon (5 seats)

Electorate 18,796　Total valid votes 9,675
Votes polled 9,851　Turnout % 52.4
Quota 1,613

Candidate	Party	1st Pref	Elected
Kate Evans	UUP	871	
Sean Hagan	APNI	899	
Thomas Larkin	SDLP	1,244	5th count
Fergal Lennon	Aontu	230	
Declan McAlinden	SDLP	1,041	7th count
Catherine Nelson	SF	1,332	4th count
Robert Smith	DUP	1,105	
Michael Tallon	SF	727	
Margaret Tinsley	DUP	1,416	7th count
Kenneth Twyble	UUP	1,037	7th count

Cusher (5 seats)

Electorate 18,496　Total valid votes 11,457
Votes polled 11,569　Turnout % 62.55
Quota 1,910

Candidate	Party	1st Pref	Elected
Paul Berry		2,009	1st count
Paul Bowbanks	Ind	241	
Quincey Dougan	DUP	1,215	
Bróna Haughey	SF	1,519	4th count
Gareth Hay	APNI	462	
Gordon Kennedy	UUP	1,229	6th count
Seamus Livingstone	SDLP	901	
Jim Speers	UUP	1,633	5th count
Gareth Wilson	DUP	2,248	1st count

Lagan River (5 seats)

Electorate 17,249　Total valid votes 8,884
Votes polled 8,959　Turnout % 51.94
Quota 1,481

Candidate	Party	1st Pref	Elected
Mark Baxter	DUP	1,876	1st count
Tony Gorrell	SF	227	
Tim McClelland	DUP	678	9th count
Olive Mercer	UUP	871	
Samuel Morrison	TUV	499	
Sammy Ogle	Ind	217	
John O'Hare	SDLP	369	
Paul Rankin	DUP	1,444	2nd count
Kyle Savage	UUP	1,614	1st count
Jordan Stewart	UKIP	129	
Eoin Tennyson	APNI	96	8th count

Lurgan (7 seats)

Electorate 25,336　Total valid votes 12,044
Votes polled 12,295　Turnout % 48.53
Quota 1,506

Candidate	Party	1st Pref	Elected
Keith Haughan	SF	1,974	1st count
Peter Lavery	APNI	1,321	5th count
Liam Mackle	SF	1,190	3rd count
Noel McGeown	SF	454	
Sorcha McGeown	SF	823	6th count
Louise McKinstry	UUP	1,524	1st count
Terry McWilliams	DUP	1,282	
Stephen Moutray	DUP	1,504	6th count
Joe Nelson	SDLP	1,046	4th count
Ciaran Toman	SDLP	926	

Portadown (6 seats)

Electorate 21,698　Total valid votes 11,223
Votes polled 11,447　Turnout % 52.76
Quota 1,604

Candidate	Party	1st Pref	Elected
Sydney Anderson	DUP	1,696	1st count
Darryn Causby	DUP	2,077	1st count
Paul Duffy	SF	1,675	1st count
Julie Flaherty	UUP	1,512	3rd count
Darrin Foster	TUV	547	
Arnold Hatch	UUP	506	
Emma Hutchinson	APNI	570	
David Jameson	UKIP	149	
David Jones	Ind	266	
Lavelle McIlwrath	DUP	866	8th count
Eamon McNeill	SDLP	967	8th count
Callum Ó Dufaigh	SF	392	

Northern Ireland Yearbook | Local Government

2019 council elections

Belfast

Summary of Council

Electorate 247,245   Valid vote 112,859   Turnout 51%

Party	Seats	Change since 2014
DUP	15	+2
SF	18	-1
UUP	2	-5
SDLP	6	-1
APNI	10	+2
Others	9	+3

Balmoral (5 seats)

Electorate 17,864   Total valid votes 9,210
Votes polled 9,326   Turnout % 52.21
Quota 1,536

Candidate	Party	1st Pref	Elected
Sarah Louise Bunting	DUP	1,025	8th count
Jeffrey Dudgeon	UUP	660	
David Graham	DUP	1,442	4th count
Donal Lyons	SDLP	1,306	6th count
Geraldine McAteer	SF	1,283	7th count
Pádraigín Mervyn	PBPA	202	
Michael Mulhern	SDLP	813	
Kate Nicholl	APNI	1,842	1st count
Caoimhe O'Connell	Green	504	
William Traynor	UKIP	133	

Black Mountain (7 seats)

Electorate 26,022   Total valid votes 14,053
Votes polled 14,398   Turnout % 55.33
Quota 1,757

Candidate	Party	1st Pref	Elected
Ciaran Beattie	SF	1,893	1st count
Conor Campbell	The Workers Party	162	
Arder Carson	SF	1,634	6th count
Matt Collins	PBPA	2,268	1st count
Steven Corr	SF	1,864	1st count
Paul Doherty	SDLP	783	
Michael Donnelly	SF	1,535	6th count
Eoin Geraghty	Aontú	750	
Emma Groves	SF	1,431	6th count
Stevie Maginn	Green	204	
Ronan McLaughlin	SF	1,316	6th count
Liam Norris	APNI	213	

Botanic (5 seats)

Electorate 21,987   Total valid votes 9,738
Votes polled 9,842   Turnout % 44.76
Quota 1,624

Candidate	Party	1st Pref	Elected
Declan Boyle	Ind	609	
Graham Craig	DUP	615	
Billy Dickson	South Belfast Unionists	233	
Áine Groogan	Green	1,401	6th count
Deirdre Hargey	SF	1,325	9th count
John Hiddleston	TUV	82	
Tracy Kelly	DUP	1,365	7th count
Ian Shanks	PUP	170	
Richard Kennedy	UUP	333	
Paul Loughran	PBPA	383	
Paddy Lynn	The Workers Party	87	
Caitríona Mallaghan	SF	229	
Emmet McDonough-Brown	APNI	1,143	11th count
Gary McKeown	SDLP	1,009	12th count
Micky Murray	APNI	754	

Castle (6 seats)

Electorate 22,262   Total valid votes 11,300
Votes polled 11,436   Turnout % 51.37
Quota 1,615

Candidate	Party	1st Pref	Elected
David Browne	UUP	1,014	
Mary Ellen Campbell	SF	1103	
Fred Cobain	DUP	1,439	8th count
Patrick Convery	Ind	377	
John Finucane	SF	1,650	1st count
Riley Johnston	PBPA	204	
Nuala McAllister	APNI	1,787	1st count
Cathal Mullaghan	Ind	76	
Mal O'Hara	Green	882	
Guy Spence	DUP	1,407	8th count
Gemma Weir	The Workers Party	159	
Carl Whyte	SDLP	951	9th count
Heather Wilson	SDLP	551	

Colin (6 seats)

Electorate 23,300   Total valid votes 12,102
Votes polled 12,323   Turnout % 52.89
Quota 1,729

Candidate	Party	1st Pref	Elected
Danny Baker	SF	2,196	1st count
Michael Collins	PBPA	1,565	3rd count
Paddy Crossan	The Workers Party	109	
Matt Garrett	SF	1,264	8th count
Brian Heading	SDLP	970	8th count
Donnamarie Higgins	APNI	443	
Stephen Magennis	SF	1,616	8th count
Nichola McClean	Aontú	670	
David McKee	DUP	309	
Ellen Murray	Green	241	
Charlene O'Hara	SF	1,187	
Fred Rodgers	UUP	130	
Séanna Walsh	SF	1,402	7th count

Court (6 seats)

Electorate 22,116   Total valid votes 11,310
Votes polled 11,528   Turnout % 52.12
Quota 1,616

Candidate	Party	1st Pref	Elected
Dave Anderson	UUP	385	
Tina Black	SF	1,396	11th count
Jolene Bunting	Ind	351	
Ciara Campbell	APNI	253	
Claire Canavan	SF	1,447	11th count
Tiernan Fitzlarkin	SDLP	298	
Billy Hutchinson	PUP	929	10th count
Brian Kingston	DUP	1,648	1st count
Joanne Lowry	The Workers Party	166	
Sinead Magner	Green	147	
Cailin McCaffrey	PBPA	686	
Frank McCoubrey	DUP	2,227	1st count
Eric Smyth	TUV	259	
Nicola Verner	DUP	1,119	6th count

Lisnasharragh (6 seats)

Electorate 20,783   Total valid votes 11,066
Votes polled 11,182   Turnout % 53.8
Quota 1,581

Candidate	Party	1st Pref	Elected
Ivanka Antova	PBPA	133	
David Brooks	DUP	1,479	12th count
Séamas De Faoite	SDLP	988	14th count
Amy Ferguson	Cross-Community Labour Alternative	160	
Gwen Ferguson	PUP	363	
Aileen Graham	DUP	660	
Eric Hanvey	APNI	1,429	3rd count
Stevie Jenkins	SF	619	
Michael Long	APNI	1,755	1st count
Ben Manton	UUP	415	
Catherine McComb	UKIP	169	
Chris McGimpsey	UUP	508	
Kate Mullan	Ind	204	
Tommy Sandford	DUP	951	13th count
Brian Smyth	Green	1,233	10th count

Local Government   175

2019 council elections

Belfast (continued)

Oldpark (6 seats)

Electorate	22,024	Total valid votes	11,327
Votes polled	11,545	Turnout %	52.42
Quota	1,619		

Candidate	Party	1st Pref	Elected
Jack Armstrong	APNI	390	
Chris Bailie	The Workers Party	93	
Shauneen Baker	SF	1,107	10th count
Mary Clarke	SF	796	
Julie-Anne Corr-Johnston	PUP	575	
Jason Docherty	UUP	239	
Fiona Ferguson	PBPA	447	11th count
JJ Magee	SF	1,134	11th count
Paul McCusker	SDLP	2,856	1st count
Ryan Murphy	SF	1,185	9th count
Dale Pankurst	DUP	1,701	1st count
Gillian Simpson	DUP	573	
Lesley Veronica	Green	231	

Ormiston (7 seats)

Electorate	25,617	Total valid votes	13,285
Votes polled	13,432	Turnout %	52.4
Quota	1,661		

Candidate	Party	1st Pref	Elected
William Ennis	PUP	394	
Anthony Flynn	Green	1,301	4th count
Tom Haire	DUP	1,462	7th count
John Hussey	DUP	1,269	8th count
Peter Johnston	UUP	757	
Keith Lonsdale	UKIP	221	
Ross McMullan	APNI	2,622	1st count
Peter McReynolds	APNI	1,764	1st count
Laura Misteil	SF	57	
Sian O'Neill	APNI	1,165	2nd count
Jim Rodgers	UUP	1,416	7th count
Gareth Spratt	DUP	857	

Titanic (6 seats)

Electorate	22,653	Total valid votes	9,468
Votes polled	9,652	Turnout %	42.6
Quota	1,353		

Candidate	Party	1st Pref	Elected
Karl Bennett	Ind	448	
John Kyle	PUP	1,027	7th count
Sonia Copeland	UUP	852	8th count
Adam Newton	DUP	913	
George Dorrian	DUP	1,270	4th count
Mairéad O'Donnell	SF	1,102	
Paul Girvan	UKIP	228	
Lee Reynolds	DUP	586	
Colin Hall-Thompson	UUP	278	
Ben Smylie	Green	641	
Carole Howard	APNI	1,055	6th count
Michelle Kelly	APNI	1,068	7th count

2019 council elections

Causeway Coast and Glens

Summary of Council

| Electorate | 98,930 | Valid vote | 50,638 | Turnout | 52% |

Party	Seats	Change since 2014
DUP	14	+3
SF	9	+2
UUP	7	-3
SDLP	6	
APNI	2	+1
Others	2	-3

Ballymoney (7 seats)

Electorate	17,213	Total valid votes	8,751
Votes polled	8,885	Turnout %	51.62
Quota	1,094		

Candidate	Party	1st Pref	Elected
William Blair	TUV	479	
John Finlay	DUP	1,322	1st count
David Hanna	UKIP	117	
Peter McCully	APNI	734	
Tom McKeown	UUP	512	7th count
Cathal McLaughlin	SF	906	7th count
Alan McLean	DUP	827	7th count
Leanne Peacock	SF	1,153	1st count
Ian Stevenson	Ind	220	
Ivor Wallace	DUP	826	7th count
Darryl Wilson	UUP	1,420	1st count
John Wilson	TUV	217	

Bann (5 seats)

Electorate	12,656	Total valid votes	7,275
Votes polled	7,350	Turnout %	58.08
Quota	1,213		

Candidate	Party	1st Pref	Elected
Seán Bateson	SF	1,403	1st count
Sam Cole	DUP	639	
Elizabeth Collins	TUV	214	
Helena Dallat O'Driscoll	SDLP	686	5th count
Richard Holmes	UUP	964	5th count
William King	UUP	799	
Michelle Knight-McQuillan	DUP	781	5th count
Charlie McConaghy	APNI	491	
Adrian McQuillan	DUP	1,047	5th count
Timmy Reid	PUP	251	

Benbradagh (5 seats)

Electorate	12,560	Total valid votes	7,049
Votes polled	7,121	Turnout %	56.7
Quota	1,175		

Candidate	Party	1st Pref	Elected
Orla Beattie	SDLP	922	3rd count
Proinsias Brolly	Aontú	655	
Robert Carmichael	UUP	410	
Boyd Douglas	TUV	581	
Seán McGlinchey	SF	1,574	1st count
Kathleen McGurk	SF	677	5th count
Dermot Nicholl	SF	1,002	5th count
Edgar Scott	DUP	896	5th count
Christine Turner	APNI	332	

Causeway (7 seats)

Electorate	16,918	Total valid votes	8,131
Votes polled	8,220	Turnout %	48.59
Quota	1,017		

Candidate	Party	1st Pref	Elected
David Alexander	Ind	552	
Mark Coulson	Green	331	
Mark Fielding	DUP	1,276	1st count
Rebecca Hanna	UKIP	132	
Norman Hillis	UUP	758	8th count
Sandra Hunter	UUP	774	8th count
John McAuley	DUP	831	4th count
Chris McCaw	APNI	1,212	1st count
Sharon McKillop	DUP	1,010	2nd count
Stewart Moore	TUV	167	
Angela Mulholland	SDLP	496	8th count
Cyril Quigg	TUV	325	
Emma Thompson	SF	267	

Coleraine (6 seats)

Electorate	15,879	Total valid votes	7,131
Votes polled	7,208	Turnout %	45.39
Quota	1,019		

Candidate	Party	1st Pref	Elected
Philip Anderson	DUP	901	4th count
Ciaran Archibald	SF	417	
Yvonne Boyle	APNI	732	5th count
Trevor Clarke	DUP	769	
George Duddy	DUP	866	5th count
David Harding	Conservative	112	
William McCandless	UUP	633	5th count
Stephanie Quigley	SDLP	983	4th count
Amanda Ranaghan	UKIP	101	
Russell Watton	PUP	1,325	1st count
John Wisener	UUP	292	

Limavady (5 seats)

Electorate	11,197	Total valid votes	5,565
Votes polled	5,616	Turnout %	50.16
Quota	928		

Candidate	Party	1st Pref	Elected
Francie Brolly	Aontú	337	
Aaron Callan	DUP	385	6th count
Colin Cartwright	TUV	176	
Brenda Chivers	SF	1,034	1st count
Kevin Hayward	APNI	557	
Raymond Kennedy	UUP	405	
James McCorkell	DUP	654	2nd count
Alan Robinson	DUP	1,498	1st count
Ashleen Schenning	SDLP	519	6th count

The Glens (5 seats)

Electorate	12,507	Total valid votes	6,736
Votes polled	6,812	Turnout %	54.47
Quota	1,123		

Candidate	Party	1st Pref	Elected
Joan Baird	UUP	758	6th count
Bill Kennedy	DUP	843	
Ambrose Laverty	Ind	1,267	1st count
Margaret Anne McKillop	SDLP	1,080	3rd count
Oliver McMullan	SF	1,097	2nd count
Cara McShane	SF	1,102	2nd count
Kieran Mulholland	SF	589	

2019 council elections

Derry and Strabane

Summary of Council

Electorate 107,975 Valid vote 60,695 Turnout 57%

Party	Seats	Change since 2014
DUP	7	-1
SF	11	-5
UUP	2	
SDLP	11	+1
APNI	2	+2
Others	7	+3

Ballyarnett (6 seats)

Electorate 17,425 Total valid votes 9,575
Votes polled 9,774 Turnout % 56.09
Quota 1,368

Candidate	Party	1st Pref	Elected
Nuala Crilly	PBPA	826	
Angela Dobbins	SDLP	1,392	1st count
Sandra Duffy	SF	899	6th count
Rory Farrell	SDLP	1,170	6th count
Anne McCloskey	Aontú	1,032	6th count
Danny McCloskey	APNI	340	
Caoimhe McKnight	SF	656	
Neil McLaughlin	SF	538	
Aileen Mellon	SF	848	6th count
Warren Robinson	Ind	639	
Brian Tierney	SDLP	1,235	4th count

Derg (5 seats)

Electorate 12,996 Total valid votes 8,004
Votes polled 8,120 Turnout % 62.48
Quota 1,335

Candidate	Party	1st Pref	Elected
Cara Hunter	SDLP	1,032	5th count
Derek Hussey	UUP	1,267	3rd count
Keith Kerrigan	DUP	1,090	3rd count
Thomas Kerrigan	DUP	771	
Kieran McGuire	SF	1,075	5th count
Maoliosa McHugh	SF	798	
Ruairí McHugh	SF	1,086	5th count
Anne Murray	APNI	150	
Andy Patton	Ind	735	

Faughan (5 seats)

Electorate 13,601 Total valid votes 7,143
Votes polled 7,246 Turnout % 53.28
Quota 1,191

Candidate	Party	1st Pref	Elected
Rachael Ferguson	APNI	738	7th count
Paul Fleming	SF	854	7th count
Gus Hastings	SDLP	491	
Conor Heaney	SF	324	
Paul Hughes	Ind	733	
William Jamieson	UUP	710	
Ryan McCready	DUP	940	4th count
Jim McKeever	SDLP	565	7th count
Brenda Stevenson	SDLP	693	
Graham Warke	DUP	1,050	4th count

Foyleside (5 seats)

Electorate 13,233 Total valid votes 7,358
Votes polled 7,520 Turnout % 56.83
Quota 1,227

Candidate	Party	1st Pref	Elected
Sean Carr	Ind	822	6th count
Michael Cooper	SF	888	6th count
Shauna Cusack	SDLP	1,129	3rd count
John Doherty	APNI	305	
Mary Durkan	SDLP	1,231	1st count
Hayleigh Fleming	SF	632	
Shaun Harkin	PBPA	977	4th count
Eric McGinley	SF	653	
Lilian Seenoi-Barr	SDLP	721	

Sperrin (7 seats)

Electorate 18,048 Total valid votes 10,911
Votes polled 11,087 Turnout % 61.43
Quota 1,364

Candidate	Party	1st Pref	Elected
Jason Barr	SDLP	832	9th count
Raymond Barr	Ind	920	
Michaela Boyle	SF	1,153	8th count
Allan Bresland	DUP	1,156	4th count
Maurice Devenney	DUP	899	9th count
Steven Edwards	SDLP	794	
French Corey	Ind	104	
Paul Gallagher	Ind	1,106	9th count
Dan Kelly	SF	756	8th count
Patsy Kelly	Ind	595	
Pauline McHenry	Ind	128	
Andy McKane	UUP	560	
Brian McMahon	SF	731	
Scott Moore	APNI	437	
Cathal Ó hOisín	SF	740	

The Moor (5 seats)

Electorate 13,114 Total valid votes 7,748
Votes polled 7,917 Turnout % 60.37
Quota 1,292

Candidate	Party	1st Pref	Elected
John Boyle	SDLP	1,082	6th count
Cathy Breslin	SDLP	669	
Tina Burke	SF	738	6th count
Kevin Campbell	SF	712	
Colm Cavanagh	APNI	122	
Gary Donnelly	Ind	1,374	1st count
Emmett Doyle	Ind	496	
Sharon Duddy	SF	594	
Patricia Logue	SF	778	6th count
Eamonn McCann	PBPA	1,035	5th count
Niree McMorris	DUP	148	

Waterside (7 seats)

Electorate 19,558 Total valid votes 9,956
Votes polled 10,134 Turnout % 51.82
Quota 1,245

Candidate	Party	1st Pref	Elected
Darren Guy	UUP	1,589	1st count
Christopher Jackson	SF	825	7th count
Hilary McClintock	DUP	1,250	1st count
Phillip McKinney	APNI	715	8th count
Sharon McLaughlin	SF	784	
Sinéad McLaughlin	SDLP	1,483	1st count
Maeve O'Neill	PBPA	752	
David Ramsey	DUP	839	8th count
Martin Reilly	SDLP	939	5th count
Drew Thompson	DUP	780	

2019 council elections

Fermanagh and Omagh

Summary of Council

Electorate	84,313	Valid vote	51,913	Turnout	62%

Party	Seats	Change since 2014
DUP	5	
SF	15	-2
UUP	9	
SDLP	5	-3
APNI	1	+1
Others	5	+4

Enniskillen (6 seats)

Electorate	13,048	Total valid votes	7,225
Votes polled	7,312	Turnout %	56.04
Quota	1,033		

Candidate	Party	1st Pref	Elected
Matthew Beaumont		310	
Paul Blake	SDLP	955	4th count
Debbie Coleman	Green	136	
Debbie Coyle	SF	761	
Donald Crawford	TUV	492	
Keith Elliott	DUP	1,161	1st count
Robert Irvine	UUP	753	6th count
Tommy Maguire	SF	946	7th count
Donal O'Cofaigh	Cross Community Labour Alternative	720	7th count
Howard Thorton	UUP	651	6th count
Simon Wiggins	DUP	340	

Erne East (6 seats)

Electorate	11,963	Total valid votes	8,456
Votes polled	8,568	Turnout %	71.62
Quota	1,209		

Candidate	Party	1st Pref	Elected
Sheamus Greene	SF	1,032	6th count
Noeleen Hayes	SF	738	
Brian McCaffrey	SF	620	
John McCluskey	Ind	1,286	1st count
Gerry McHugh	Aontú	174	
Garbhan McPhillips	SDLP	839	6th count
Thomas O'Reilly	SF	829	6th count
Paul Robinson	DUP	1,382	1st count
Victor Warrington	UUP	1,352	1st count
Caroline Wheeler	Ind	204	

Erne North (5 seats)

Electorate	10,983	Total valid votes	6,849
Votes polled	6,941	Turnout %	63.2
Quota	1,142		

Candidate	Party	1st Pref	Elected
Deborah Armstrong	DUP	668	7th count
Diana Armstrong	UUP	1,186	1st count
John Coyle	SDLP	911	2nd count
Siobhán Currie	SF	1,055	3rd count
Alex Elliott	TUV	465	
John Feely	SF	769	
Lewis Jennings	Democrats and Veterans	20	
Diane Little	APNI	413	
David Mahon	DUP	732	
John McClaughry	UUP	630	7th count

Erne West (5 seats)

Electorate	10,825	Total valid votes	7,385
Votes polled	7,473	Turnout %	69.03
Quota	1,231		

Candidate	Party	1st Pref	Elected
Trevor Armstrong	Ind	512	
Alex Baird	UUP	1,333	1st count
Anthony Feely	SF	1,208	3rd count
Adam Gannon	SDLP	611	4th count
Carol Johnston	DUP	547	
Fionnuala Leonard	SF	879	
Chris McCaffrey	SF	1,136	4th count
Bernice Swift	Ind	1,159	3rd count

Mid Tyrone (6 seats)

Electorate	12,556	Total valid votes	8,088
Votes polled	8,202	Turnout %	65.32
Quota	1,156		

Candidate	Party	1st Pref	Elected
Richard Bullick	APNI	306	
Seán Clarke	SF	889	6th count
Seán Donnelly	SF	778	6th count
Catherine Kelly	SF	964	6th count
Pádraigín Kelly	SF	995	6th count
James Managh	DUP	931	
Emmet McAleer	Ind	897	5th count
Kevin McColgan	SF	287	
Bernard McGrath	SDLP	598	
Rosemarie Shields	Aontú	464	
Bert Wilson	UUP	979	6th count

Omagh (6 seats)

Electorate	12,737	Total valid votes	6,363
Votes polled	6,461	Turnout %	50.73
Quota	910		

Candidate	Party	1st Pref	Elected
Barry Brown	Citizens Ind Social Thought Alliance	101	
Charles Chittick	TUV	115	
Will Convey	Ind	43	
Josephine Deehan	Ind	728	8th count
Joanne Donnelly	Ind	128	
Stephen Donnelly	APNI	616	11th count
Anne Marie Fitzgerald	SF	589	11th count
Susan Glass	Green	141	
Lee Hawkes	SDLP	256	
Sorcha McAnespy	Ind	194	
Marty McColgan	SF	509	
Barry McElduff	SF	900	4th count
Jacinta McKeown	SDLP	258	
Christopher Smyth	UUP	633	11th count
Margaret Swift	Aontú	182	
Errol Thompson	DUP	970	1st count

West Tyrone (6 seats)

Electorate	12,201	Total valid votes	7,547
Votes polled	7,663	Turnout %	62.81
Quota	1,079		

Candidate	Party	1st Pref	Elected
Mark Buchanan	DUP	1,546	1st count
Glenn Campbell	SF	983	5th count
Fia Cowan	APNI	390	
Ann-Marie Donnelly	SF	752	2nd count
Frankie Donnelly	SF	653	
Mary Garrity	SDLP	1,047	2nd count
Stephen McCann	SF	839	6th count
Cathal McCrory	Aontú	242	
Allan Rainey	UUP	1,095	1st count

2019 council elections

Lisburn and Castlereagh

Summary of Council

Electorate 102,151　Valid vote 50,268　Turnout 50%

Party	Seats	Change since 2014
DUP	15	-5
SF	2	+2
UUP	11	+3
SDLP	2	-1
APNI	9	+2
Others	1	-2

Castlereagh East (6 seats)

Electorate 14,963　Total valid votes 6,982
Votes polled 7,047　Turnout % 47.1
Quota 998

Candidate	Party	1st Pref	Elected
David Drysdale	DUP	849	5th count
Andrew Girvan	TUV	637	
Martin Gregg	APNI	1,212	1st count
Tommy Jeffers	DUP	638	
John Laverty	DUP	813	5th count
Hazel Legge	UUP	723	5th count
Tim Morrow	APNI	936	2nd count
Sharon Skillen	DUP	1,174	1st count

Castlereagh South (7 seats)

Electorate 17,351　Total valid votes 9,077
Votes polled 9,130　Turnout % 52.62
Quota 1,135

Candidate	Party	1st Pref	Elected
Nathan Anderson	DUP	1,503	1st count
Ryan Carlin	SF	1,069	8th count
Sorcha Eastwood	APNI	1,629	1st count
Jason Elliott	DUP	335	
John Gallen	SDLP	975	7th count
Nicola Girvin	TUV	146	
Michelle Guy	APNI	1,236	1st count
Michael Henderson	UUP	628	10th count
Vasundhara Kamble	DUP	208	
Simon Lee	Green	648	8th count
Rachael McCarthy	SDLP	463	
Geraldine Rice	Ind	237	

Downshire East (5 seats)

Electorate 12,214　Total valid votes 6,175
Votes polled 6,222　Turnout % 50.94
Quota 1,030

Candidate	Party	1st Pref	Elected
James Baird	UUP	950	3rd count
Owen Beckett	SDLP	422	
Andrew Gowan	DUP	1,133	1st count
Janet Gray	DUP	721	
Uel Mackin	DUP	905	4th count
Aaron McIntyre	APNI	1,318	1st count
Alex Swan	UUP	726	4th count

Downshire West (5 seats)

Electorate 12,385　Total valid votes 6,234
Votes polled 6,301　Turnout % 50.88
Quota 1,040

Candidate	Party	1st Pref	Elected
Morgan Crone	SDLP	308	
Vince Curry	DUP	647	
Jim Dillon	UUP	667	7th count
Allan Ewart	DUP	670	7th count
Owen Gawith	APNI	1,616	1st count
Neil Johnston	Conservative	169	
Caleb McCready	DUP	1,012	3rd count
John Palmer	UUP	915	5th count
Luke Robinson	Green	230	

Killultagh (5 seats)

Electorate 14,361　Total valid votes 7,515
Votes polled 7,591　Turnout % 52.86
Quota 1,253

Candidate	Party	1st Pref	Elected
Thomas Beckett	DUP	1,006	7th count
Stuart Brown	Ind	107	
Ally Haydock	SDLP	695	
David Honeyford	APNI	1,524	1st count
William Leathem	DUP	871	
Gary McCleave	SF	994	6th count
Ross McLernon	UUP	707	4th count
Alexander Redpath	UUP	632	
James Tinsley	DUP	979	7th count

Lisburn North (6 seats)

Electorate 15,356　Total valid votes 7,323
Votes polled 7,412　Turnout % 48.27
Quota 1,457

Candidate	Party	1st Pref	Elected
Scott Carson	DUP	846	6th count
Jonathan Craig	DUP	1,187	1st count
Joe Duffy	SF	654	
Stuart Hughes	UUP	578	7th count
Gary Hynds	Cons	423	
Alan Love	UKIP	156	
Stephen Martin	APNI	1,483	1st count
Johnny McCarthy	SDLP	852	2nd count
Lindsay Reynolds	DUP	425	
Nicholas Trimble	UUP	719	7th count

Lisburn South (6 seats)

Electorate 15,521　Total valid votes 6,962
Votes polled 7,044　Turnout % 45.38
Quota 995

Candidate	Party	1st Pref	Elected
Alison Chittick	TUV	384	
Brendan Corr	SDLP	649	
Andrew Ewing	DUP	738	4th count
Alan Givan	DUP	735	6th count
Amanda Grehan	APNI	929	5th count
Helen Love	UKIP	99	
Tim Mitchell	UUP	715	6th count
Jonny Orr	Ind	534	
Jenny Palmer	UUP	877	4th count
Paul Porter	DUP	706	6th count
Ricky Taylor	Democrats & Veterans	242	
Rhoda Walker	DUP	354	

Northern Ireland Yearbook | Local Government

2019 council elections

Mid and East Antrim

Summary of Council

Electorate	98,410	Valid vote	46,827	Turnout	48%

Party	Seats	Change since 2014
DUP	15	-1
SF	2	-1
UUP	7	-2
SDLP	1	
APNI	7	+4
Others	8	

Ballymena (7 seats)

Electorate	15,896	Total valid votes	6,956
Votes polled	7,023	Turnout %	44.18
Quota	870		

Candidate	Party	1st Pref	Elected
Matthew Armstrong	TUV	765	3rd count
John Carson	DUP	527	5th count
Reuben Glover	DUP	498	
Philip Gordon	TUV	286	
Patrice Hardy	SF	521	
James Henry	Ind	872	1st count
William Logan	DUP	402	
Stephen Nicholl	UUP	485	
Patricia O'Lynn	APNI	578	6th count
Rab Picken	UKIP	143	
Rodney Quigley	Ind	433	8th count
Eugene Reid	SDLP	848	2nd count
Conal Stewart	Ind	107	
Audrey Wales	DUP	491	8th count

Bannside (6 seats)

Electorate	14,393	Total valid votes	8,073
Votes polled	8,169	Turnout %	56.76
Quota	1,154		

Candidate	Party	1st Pref	Elected
Philip Burnside	APNI	750	
Ian Friary	SF	971	6th count
Timothy Gaston	TUV	1,433	1st count
Thomas Gordon	DUP	744	4th count
Stewart McDonald	TUV	1,504	1st count
William McNeilly	UUP	783	3rd count
Jackson Minford	UUP	449	
Tommy Nicholl	DUP	690	4th count
Andrew Wright	DUP	749	

Braid (7 seats)

Electorate	16,951	Total valid votes	8,840
Votes polled	8,936	Turnout %	52.72
Quota	1,106		

Candidate	Party	1st Pref	Elected
Beth Adger	DUP	975	2nd count
Roni Browne	Ind	146	
Muriel Burnside	APNI	703	3rd count
Robin Cherry	UUP	1,084	1st count
Brian Collins	TUV	872	5th count
Julie Frew	DUP	926	3rd count
Sam Hanna	DUP	605	
Christopher Jamieson	TUV	902	5th count
Marian Maguire	Ind	371	
Collette McAllister	SF	631	
William McCaughey	DUP	825	5th count
Keith Turner	UUP	800	

Carrick Castle (5 seats)

Electorate	13,323	Total valid votes	5,653
Votes polled	5,721	Turnout %	42.94
Quota	943		

Candidate	Party	1st Pref	Elected
Billy Ashe	DUP	1,069	1st count
Lauren Gray	APNI	1,210	1st count
Si Harvey	Democrats and Veterans	265	
Cheryl Johnston	DUP	953	1st count
Noel Jordan	Ind	431	
John Kennedy	UKIP	104	
Jim McCaw	PUP	119	
John McDermott	UUP	445	5th count
Robin Stewart	UUP	813	4th count
Nicholas Wady	Ind	244	

Coast Road (5 seats)

Electorate	12,429	Total valid votes	5,616
Votes polled	5,686	Turnout %	45.75
Quota	937		

Candidate	Party	1st Pref	Elected
Andrew Clarke	DUP	973	1st count
James McKeown	SF	873	4th count
Maureen Morrow	UUP	728	4th count
Gerardine Mulvenna	APNI	1,217	1st count
Angela Smyth	DUP	764	5th count
Martin Wilson	Ind	460	
Ruth Wilson	TUV	601	

Knockagh (5 seats)

Electorate	12,289	Total valid votes	5,703
Votes polled	5,762	Turnout %	46.89
Quota	951		

Candidate	Party	1st Pref	Elected
David Barnett	PUP	185	
May Beattie	TUV	328	
Marc Collins	DUP	846	3rd count
Bobby Hadden	Ind	798	3rd count
Peter Johnston	DUP	967	1st count
Lindsay Millar	UUP	624	
Noel Williams	APNI	1,173	1st count
Andrew Wilson	UUP	782	5th count

Larne Lough (5 seats)

Electorate	13,129	Total valid votes	5,986
Votes polled	6,086	Turnout %	46.36
Quota	998		

Candidate	Party	1st Pref	Elected
Danny Donnelly	APNI	1,057	1st count
Robert Logan	APNI	719	5th count
Gregg McKeen	DUP	1,166	1st count
Mark McKinty	UUP	983	3rd count
Paul Reid	DUP	806	4th count
Robert Robinson	Green	256	
James Strange	TUV	435	
Andy Wilson	UUP	564	

2019 council elections

Mid Ulster

Summary of Council

Electorate	99,728	Valid vote	59,108	Turnout	60%

Party	Seats	Change since 2014
DUP	9	+1
SF	17	-1
UUP	6	-1
SDLP	0	
APNI	6	
Others	2	+1

Carntogher (5 seats)

Electorate	12,332	Total valid votes	7,947
Votes polled	8,029	Turnout %	65.16
Quota	1,325		

Candidate	Party	1st Pref	Elected
James Armour	Ind	138	
Kyle Black	DUP	1,228	4th count
Cora Groogan	SF	990	6th count
Paul Henry	SF	763	
Martin Kearney	SDLP	1,071	5th count
Brian McGuigan	SF	1,406	1st count
Seán McPeake	SF	1,164	6th count
Christopher Reid	UUP	555	
Pádraigín Uí Raifeartaigh	Aontú	632	

Clogher Valley (6 seats)

Electorate	14,030	Total Valid Poll	8,528
Total Votes Polled	8,665	Quota	1,219
Turnout	61.76%		

Candidate	Party	1st Pref	Elected
Frances Burton	DUP	1,891	1st count
Phelim Gildernew	SF	1,352	1st count
Meta Graham	UUP	990	4th count
Sharon McAleer	SDLP	1,635	1st count
Seán McGuigan	SF	1,494	1st count
Robert Mulligan	UUP	650	
Wills Robinson	DUP	1,083	3rd count

Cookstown (7 seats)

Electorate	16,472	Total valid votes	9,241
Votes polled	9,394	Turnout %	57.8
Quota	1,156		

Candidate	Party	1st Pref	Elected
Gavin Bell	SF	840	7th count
Wilbert Buchanan	DUP	1,225	1st count
Alan Day	TUV	230	
Mark Glasgow	UUP	793	6th count
Kerri Hughes	SDLP	1,339	1st count
Cáthal Mallaghan	SF	1,710	1st count
John McNamee	SF	1,369	1st count
Grace Neville	DUP	694	
Trevor Wilson	UUP	1,041	5th count

Dungannon (6 seats)

Electorate	15,014	Total valid votes	8,294
Votes polled	8,629	Turnout %	57.47
Quota	1,185		

Candidate	Party	1st Pref	Elected
Kim Ashton	DUP	807	8th count
Niall Bowen	Ind	345	
Mel Boyle	APNI	431	
Walter Cuddy	UUP	607	7th count
Clement Cuthbertson	DUP	1,833	1st count
Kim McNeill	UUP	434	
Dominic Molloy	SF	995	6th count
Barry Monteith	Ind	1,414	1st count
Denise Mullen	SDLP	710	8th count
Deirdre Varsani	SF	718	

Magherafelt (5 seats)

Electorate	12,944	Total valid votes	7,560
Votes polled	7,646	Turnout %	59
Quota	1,261		

Candidate	Party	1st Pref	Elected
Wesley Brown	DUP	1,218	5th count
Seán Clarke	SF	1,058	3rd count
Kevin Donnelly	Aontú	214	
Christine McFlynn	SDLP	1,206	2nd count
Paul McLean	DUP	1,203	5th count
George Shiels	UUP	996	
Darren Totten	SF	1,665	1st count

Moyola (5 seats)

Electorate	12,727	Total valid votes	7,873
Votes polled	7,984	Turnout %	62.73
Quota	1,313		

Candidate	Party	1st Pref	Elected
Aidan Bradley	APNI	298	
Catherine Elattar	SF	1,388	1st count
Anne Forde	DUP	1,619	1st count
Denise Johnston	SDLP	920	
Derek McKinney	UUP	937	4th count
Donal McPeake	SF	906	3rd count
Ian Milne	SF	1,710	1st count
Hugh Scullion	Workers	95	

Torrent (6 seats)

Electorate	15,458	Total valid votes	9,098
Votes polled	9,236	Turnout %	61
Quota	1,300		

Candidate	Party	1st Pref	Elected
Robert Colvin	UUP	1,018	4th count
Niamh Doris	SF	1,002	5th count
Mickey Gillespie	SF	856	
Dan Kerr	Ind	1,525	1st count
Ian McCrea	DUP	899	
Ronan McGinley	SF	1,173	5th count
Joe O'Neill	SF	994	5th count
Malachy Quinn	SDLP	1,631	1st count

2019 council elections

Newry, Mourne and Down

Summary of Council

	Electorate	125,496	Valid vote	69,339	Turnout	56%

Party	Seats	Change since 2014
DUP	3	-1
SF	16	+2
UUP	4	+1
SDLP	11	-3
APNI	2	
Others	5	+1

Crotlieve (6 seats)

Electorate	19,863	Total valid votes	11,480
Votes polled	11,649	Turnout %	58.65
Quota	1,641		

Candidate	Party	1st Pref	Elected
Jim Boylan	Ind	788	
Michael Carr	SDLP	808	
Mark Gibbons	**Ind**	**1,189**	**9th count**
Joshua Lowry	UUP	712	
Declan McAteer	**SDLP**	**1,175**	**9th count**
Wilma McCullough	DUP	371	
Lorcan McGreevy	APNI	483	
Karen McKevitt	**SDLP**	**1,116**	**9th count**
Oksana McMahon	SF	809	
Gerry O'Hare	**SF**	**1,286**	**6th count**
Mickey Ruane	**SF**	**812**	**9th count**
Jarlath Tinnelly	**Ind**	**1,412**	**5th count**
Mary Tinnelly	SF	519	

Downpatrick (5 seats)

Electorate	14,620	Total valid votes	7,388
Votes polled	7,474	Turnout %	51.12
Quota	1,232		

Candidate	Party	1st Pref	Elected
Alex Burgess	UUP	345	
Dermot Curran	**SDLP**	**940**	**6th count**
Macartan Digney	Aontú	475	
Cadogan Enright	**Ind**	**1,052**	**5th count**
Oonagh Hanlon	**SF**	**1,032**	**7th count**
Jamie Kennedy	Green	128	
Tiernan Laird	APNI	375	
Jordan Madden	SF	833	
James Savage	DUP	149	
Gareth Sharvin	**SDLP**	**1,395**	**1st count**
John Trainor	**SDLP**	**664**	**7th count**

Newry (6 seats)

Electorate	19,400	Total valid votes	9,900
Votes polled	10,098	Turnout %	52.05
Quota	1,415		

Candidate	Party	1st Pref	Elected
Charlie Casey	**SF**	**1,230**	**2nd count**
Valerie Harte	**SF**	**1,045**	**5th count**
Liz Kimmins	**SF**	**1,374**	**2nd count**
Gavin Malone	**Ind**	**2,296**	**1st count**
Sarah McAllister	SF	784	
Ricky McGaffin	UUP	341	
Michael Savage	**SDLP**	**1,231**	**2nd count**
Gary Stokes	**SDLP**	**878**	**6th count**
Helena Young	APNI	721	

Rowallane (5 seats)

Electorate	14,896	Total valid votes	7,766
Votes polled	7,839	Turnout %	52.62
Quota	1,295		

Candidate	Party	1st Pref	Elected
Terry Andrews	**SDLP**	**1,211**	**2nd count**
Patrick Brown	**APNI**	**1,416**	**1st count**
Robert Burgess	**UUP**	**842**	**6th count**
Emma Cairns	Green	182	
Marianne Cleary	SF	622	
Harry Harvey	**DUP**	**1,265**	**4th count**
Walter Lyons	UUP	667	
Liam Mulhern	Aontú	99	
Martyn Todd	Ind	477	
William Walker	**DUP**	**985**	**6th count**

Slieve Croob (5 seats)

Electorate	14,846	Total valid votes	8,179
Votes polled	8,290	Turnout %	55.84
Quota	1,364		

Candidate	Party	1st Pref	Elected
Gregory Bain	**APNI**	**863**	**6th count**
Hugh Gallagher	**SDLP**	**880**	**6th count**
Maynard Hanna	DUP	868	
Tracy Harkin	Aontú	481	
Róisín Howell	**SF**	**1,035**	**5th count**
Alan Lewis	**UUP**	**1,303**	**3rd count**
Cathy Mason	**SF**	**1,069**	**5th count**
Mark Murnin	SDLP	796	
John Rice	SF	884	

Slieve Gullion (7 seats)

Electorate	20,858	Total valid votes	12,522
Votes polled	12,817	Turnout %	61.45
Quota	1,566		

Candidate	Party	1st Pref	Elected
Pete Byrne	**SDLP**	**1,643**	**1st count**
Balazs Gazdag	APNI	361	
Terry Hearty	**SF**	**1,876**	**1st count**
Linda Henry	DUP	315	
Mickey Larkin	**SF**	**1,646**	**1st count**
Kate Loughran	SDLP	1,059	
Oonagh Magennis	**SF**	**1,622**	**1st count**
Róisín Mulgrew	**SF**	**1,362**	**4th count**
Barra Ó Muirí	**SF**	**1,351**	**2nd count**
David Taylor	**UUP**	**1,287**	**3rd count**

The Mournes (7 seats)

Electorate	21,013	Total valid votes	12,104
Votes polled	12,262	Turnout %	58.35
Quota	1,514		

Candidate	Party	1st Pref	Elected
Willie Clarke	**SF**	**1,154**	**7th count**
Laura Devlin	**SDLP**	**1,572**	**1st count**
Seán Doran	**SF**	**1,885**	**1st count**
Glyn Hanna	**DUP**	**1,944**	**1st count**
Leeanne McEvoy	**SF**	**1,097**	**7th count**
Harold McKee	**UUP**	**1,455**	**2nd count**
Andrew McMurray	APNI	943	
Brian Quinn	SDLP	607	
Henry Reilly	**Ind**	**1,447**	**2nd count**

Local Government | **Northern Ireland Yearbook**

Speakers: Gareth Hetherington, Ulster University Economic Policy Centre (UUEPC); John Campbell, BBC Northern Ireland; Sinéad McLaughlin MLA, Northern Ireland Assembly; Chris Giles, Financial Times and Sir Robert Chote, Northern Ireland Fiscal Council.

Northern Ireland Economic Conference 2021

The 26th annual Northern Ireland Economic Conference took place in the Galgorm Resort & Spa in December 2021. Hosted by Mid & East Antrim Borough Council, Northern Ireland's premier economic analysis hybrid event brought together key players in the economy, across all sectors including policy makers, business leaders and economic stakeholders to discuss economic priorities for Northern Ireland, Covid-19 recovery, addressing the competitiveness challenge and cross border trade and business development.

Delegates in attendance heard from a number of local and visiting expert speakers including Minister for the Economy, Gordon Lyons MLA; Sir Robert Chote, Chair, Northern Ireland Fiscal Council and Former Chairman, Office for Budget Responsibility; Chris Giles, Economics Editor, Financial Times; Sinéad McLaughlin MLA, Chair, Committee for the Executive Office, Northern Ireland Assembly and Dr Frances Ruane, Chairperson, National Competitiveness and Productivity Council.

We would like to take this opportunity to thank our conference host, Mid & East Antrim Borough Council, all speakers and delegates who joined us, both in the Galgorm Resort & Spa and virtually, and made the conference a huge success.

Jackie Logan, NakedPR with Cllr Peter Johnston, Mid & East Antrim Borough Council.

Cllr William McCaughey, Mayor of Mid & East Antrim Borough Council, David Whelan, agendaNi and Minister for the Economy, Gordon Lyons MLA.

Ellen McCaffrey and Scott Hilland, Department for the Economy.

Wendy Lecky and Ashlee McVeigh, Department of Finance.

Speaker: Philip Thompson, Mid & East Antrim Borough Council.

Mark Hannify, North South Ministerial Council with Mary Coughlin, Calor Gas.

Northern Ireland Yearbook
Health

Health in Northern Ireland

The Health Service

The National Health Service, established in July 1948, provides publicly-funded health care free at the point of delivery to UK residents. Responsibility for most areas of health policy is devolved and decided by the Department of Health (DoH). In June 2021, 72,053 people were employed in the Northern Ireland health and social care workforce.

A small number of sensitive ethical matters – such as genetics, surrogacy and embryology – are reserved to the Department of Health at Westminster to ensure a common national approach.

Health administration

The Review of Public Administration restructured the Health Service in April 2009. Prior to the suspension of the Northern Ireland Assembly in January 2017, a further reform programme entitled Transforming Your Care was being taken forward focusing on several aspects of care from hospitals to community settings. In August 2017, the health trusts unveiled cost-saving proposals of £70 million. Power lies with the Department to introduce temporary measures.

In May 2018, the Department released details of a series of important initiatives being funded under the £100 million Health and Social Care transformation fund. It included an initial £5 million for the roll-out of Multi Disciplinary Teams (MDTs) at GP practices. Originally launched in GP Federations in Down and Derry, the scheme has been expanded to Federations covering west Belfast and Causeway and Newry & District.

Further projected investments included workforce development in the Health and Social Care sector, reforming community and hospital services, including mental health and pharmacy, targeted actions aimed at strengthening the voice of those who use and those who deliver HSC services and investment in children's social services to fund a new approach to working with parents and families and to provide a different offer to children in care to better meet their needs.

The need for transformation is widely accepted. However, the health service has been put under further pressure from tackling the Covid-19 pandemic, placing resources and waiting lists under further strain.

Details of the main organisations and their responsibilities are outlined below.

Department of Health (DoH)

The Department of Health's mission is to improve the health and social well-being of the people of Northern Ireland, by ensuring the provision of appropriate health and social care services, and health promotion and education. The Department has three main areas of responsibility:

- Health and social care which covers policy and legislation for hospitals, family practitioner services and community health and personal social services;
- Public health which covers policy, legislation and administrative action to promote and protect the health and well-being of the population; and
- Public safety which covers policy and legislation for fire and rescue services.

Health and Social Care Board

The Health and Social Care Board (HSCB) focuses on commissioning, resource management, performance management and service improvement for the whole of Northern Ireland. The board also comprises five local commissioning groups, covering the same geographical areas as the health and social care trusts.

Health and Social Care Trusts

There are a total of six health and social care (HSC) trusts in Northern Ireland. Five HSC trusts provide integrated health and social care services across Northern Ireland:

- Belfast: Belfast, Castlereagh;
- Northern: Antrim, Ballymena, Ballymoney, Carrickfergus, Coleraine, Cookstown, Larne, Magherafelt, Moyle, Newtownabbey;
- South Eastern: Ards, Down, Lisburn, North Down;
- Southern: Armagh, Banbridge, Craigavon, Dungannon, Newry and Mourne;
- Western: Derry, Fermanagh, Limavady, Omagh, Strabane.

HSC trusts manage and administer hospitals, health centres, residential homes, day centres and other health and social care facilities whilst also providing a wide range of health and social care services to the community.

The sixth trust is the Northern Ireland Ambulance Service, which operates a single Northern Ireland wide service to people in need and aims to improve the health and well-being of the community through the delivery of high quality ambulance services.

Patient and Client Council
The Patient and Client Council was established under legislation on the 1 April 2009 as part of the reform of Health and Social Care in Northern Ireland, replacing the health and social service councils. The role of the Patient and Client Council is to provide an independent voice for patients, clients, carers and communities on health and social care issues.

Business Services Organisation
A single Business Services Organisation (BSO) provides a range of regional business support functions and specialist professional services to the health and social care sector across Northern Ireland. Services provided include legal, procurement and logistics, finance, human resources, payments to family practitioners, counter fraud and probity as well as internal audit and information and technology services.

Employment Medical Advisory Service
Statutory advisory body within the Health and Safety Executive for Northern Ireland. Provides occupational medical advice to the work force and the wider business community.

Safefood
Works on a north/south basis promoting food safety and provides nutritional and scientific advice. Supports scientific research and co-operation.

Public Health Agency
The Public Health Agency was established to focus on improving health and well-being and with a wider responsibility for health protection, health improvement and development to address existing health inequalities and public health issues in Northern Ireland.

Institute of Public Health in Ireland
Promotes co-operation for public health between Northern Ireland and the Republic of Ireland by strengthening public health intelligence, building public health capacity, policy and programme development and evaluation.

Local Commissioning Groups
There are five local commissioning groups which cover the same five areas as the trusts. Within its area, each local commissioning group is responsible for:
- Assessing health and social care needs;
- Planning health and social care to meet current and emerging needs; and
- Securing the delivery of health and social care to meet assessed needs.

The five local commissioning groups cover the following areas:

1. **Belfast Local Commissioning Group**
   Belfast and Castlereagh

2. **Northern Local Commissioning Group**
   Antrim, Ballymena, Ballymoney, Carrickfergus, Coleraine, Cookstown, Larne, Magherafelt, Moyle and Newtownabbey

3. **South Eastern Local Commissioning Group**
   Ards, Down, Lisburn and North Down

4. **Southern Local Commissioning Group**
   Armagh, Banbridge, Craigavon, Dungannon and Newry and Mourne

5. **Western Local Commissioning Group**
   Derry, Fermanagh, Limavady, Omagh and Strabane

Northern Ireland Blood Transfusion Service
The NIBTS exists to fully supply the needs of all hospitals and clinical units in the province with safe and effective blood and blood products and other related services.

Northern Ireland Fire and Rescue Service
Provision of regional fire and rescue services.

Northern Ireland Guardian Ad Litem Agency
Establishes and maintains a panel of guardians appointed by the courts to safeguard the interests of children in legal proceedings.

Health

Northern Ireland Medical and Dental Training Agency
Oversees the postgraduate medical and dental education of doctors and dentists. It also develops and delivers vocational training and continuing medical education for general practitioners and general dental practitioners.

Northern Ireland Practice and Education Council for Nursing and Midwifery
Supports the professional development of nurses and midwives in best practice, education and performance.

Northern Ireland Social Care Council
Regulation of the social care work force as well as approving, monitoring and promoting social work education and training.

Regulation and Quality Improvement Authority (RQIA)
Independent body responsible for monitoring and inspecting the availability and quality of health and social care services in Northern Ireland, and encouraging improvements in the quality of those services. The RQIA has taken over the duties of the Mental Health Commission, including a range of responsibilities for people with a mental illness and those with a learning disability.

Department of Health (DoH)

Castle Buildings, Stormont
Belfast, BT4 3SQ
Tel: 028 9052 0500
Web: www.health-ni.gov.uk

Minister: Robin Swann MLA
Permanent Secretary: Richard Pengelly
Chief Medical Officer: Dr Michael McBride
Chief Social Services Officer: Sean Holland
Chief Nursing Officer: Linda Kelly (interim)
Chief Dental Officer: Simon Reid
Chief Pharmaceutical Officer: Cathy Harrison
Chief Allied Health Professions Officer: Jenny Keane

Health and Social Care Board
12-22 Linenhall Street
Belfast, BT2 8BS
Tel: 0300 555 0115
Web: www.hscboard.hscni.net
Email: enquiry.hscb@hscni.net
Chair: Les Drew
Chief Executive: Sharon Gallagher
Director of Planning and Commissioning: Paul Cavanagh (interim)
Director of Performance Management and Service Improvement: Lisa McWilliams (interim)
Director of Finance: Tracey McCaig (interim)
Director of Social Care and Children: Brendan Whittle

Local Commissioning Groups

Belfast Commissioning Group
12-22 Linenhall Street, Belfast, BT2 8BS
Tel: 0300 555 0115
Email: belfast.lcg@hscni.net
Commissioning Lead: Iain Deboys

Northern Commissioning Group
County Hall, 182 Galgorm Road
Ballymena, BT42 1QB
Tel: 0300 555 0115
Email: northern.lcg@hscni.net
Commissioning Lead: Bride Harkin

South Eastern Commissioning Group
12-22 Linenhall Street, Belfast, BT2 8BS
Tel: 0300 555 0115
Email: southeastern.lcg@hscni.net
Commissioning Lead: Paul Turley

Southern Commissioning Group
Tower Hill, Armagh, BT61 9DR
Tel: 0300 555 0115
Email: southern.lcg@hscni.net
Commissioning Lead: Sophie Lusby

Western Commissioning Group
Gransha Park House, 15 Gransha Park
Clooney Road
Derry, BT47 6FN
Tel: 0300 555 0115
Email: western.lcg@hscni.net
Commissioning Lead: Brian McAleer

Health and Social Care Trusts

Belfast Health and Social Care Trust
Trust Headquarters
A Floor, Belfast City Hospital
Lisburn Road
Belfast, BT9 7AB
Tel: 028 9504 0100
Web: www.belfasttrust.hscni.net
Email: info@belfasttrust.hscni.net
Chair: Peter McNaney
Chief Executive: Cathy Jack

Board Members
Prof Martin Bradley; Miriam Karp; Patrick Loughran; Nuala McKeagney; Anne O'Reilly; Gordon Smyth; David Jones

Executive Directors
Deputy Chief Executive and Director Covid Oversight, Imaging and Neurosciences Services:
Bernie Owens
Director of Medicine: Chris Hagan
Director of Finance, Estates and Capital Planning:
Maureen Edwards
Director of Adult Community and Older People's Services:
Gillian Traub
Executive Director of Social Work / Director of Children's Community Services: Carol Diffin

[The circuit]
The National Defibrillator Network

British Heart Foundation Northern Ireland

Put your defibrillator on the map

thecircuit.uk

To save more lives, we're mapping all defibrillators in the UK.

It is estimated that over 70,000 defibrillators are unknown to ambulance services in the UK, making them less likely to be used in the event of an emergency.

The Circuit's purpose is to locate and register the UK's estimated 100,000 defibrillators – connecting them directly and automatically to each 999 service so that bystanders can be pointed to them in an emergency.

Register yours on The Circuit – The National Defibrillator Network, and give your defibrillator its best chance at saving a life.

Register on The Circuit today.

Scan the QR code to find out more.

In partnership with: **British Heart Foundation Northern Ireland** | **ASSOCIATION OF AMBULANCE CHIEF EXECUTIVES** | **Resuscitation Council UK**

Director of Nursing and User Experience: Brenda Creaney
Director of Performance, Planning and Informatics:
Charlene Stoops
Director of Unscheduled and Older People's Services:
Brian Armstrong
Director of HR and Organisational Development:
Jacqui Kennedy (interim)
Interim Director of Child Health & NISTAR services:
Paula Cahalan
Interim Director Acute Services: Janet Johnston
Interim Director for Mental Health and Intellectual Disability
Services: Moira Kearney
Interim Director for Trauma, Orthopaedics, Rehab Services &
Maternity, Dental, ENT & Sexual Health: Heather Jackson

Northern Health and Social Care Trust

Brettan Hall, Bush Road
Antrim, BT41 2RL
Tel: 028 9442 4000
Web: www.northerntrust.hscni.net
Email: info@northerntrust.hscni.net
Chair: Bob McCann
Chief Executive: Jennifer Welsh

Board Members
Paul Corrigan; Billy Graham; Glenn Houston;
Jim McCall; Gerard McGivern

Executive Directors
Deputy Chief Executive / Executive Director of Finance:
Owen Harkin
Director of Operations: Wendy Magowan (interim)
Medial Director: Seamus O'Reilly
Executive Director of Social Work and Divisional Director of
Women, Children and Families Division: Maura Dargan
Executive Director of Nursing and User Experience:
Suzanne Pullins
Director of Human Resources, OD and Corporate
Communications: Jacqui Reid (interim)
Divisional Director of Community Care: Roy Hamill (interim)
Divisional Director of Surgical and Clinical Services:
Kevin McMahon (interim)
Divisional Director of Mental Health, Learning Disability and
Community Wellbeing: Petra Corr (interim)
Divisional Director of Medicine and Emergency Medicine:
Audrey Harris (interim)
Divisional Director of Strategic Development and Business
Services: Neil Martin (interim)
Divisional Director of Integrated Care: Paddy Graffin (interim)

Northern Ireland Ambulance Service HSC Trust

Site 30, Knockbracken Healthcare Park
Saintfield Road, Belfast, BT8 8SG
Tel: 028 9040 0999
Web: www.niamb.co.uk
Email: reception@nias.hscni.net
Chair: Nicole Lappin
Chief Executive: Michael Bloomfield

Board Members
William Abraham; Dale Ashford;
Jim Dennison; Trevor Haslett

Executive Directors
Director of Finance: Paul Nicholson (interim)
Director of Operations: Rosie Byrne
Director of Human Resources:
Michelle Lemon
Medical Director: Dr Nigel Ruddell (acting)

Belfast Area Headquarters
Broadway, Belfast, BT12 6BA
Tel: 028 9040 5272
Email: belfastarea.hq@nias.hscni.net
Belfast Area Manager: Gary Richardson

South Eastern Area Headquarters
Bangor Ambulance Station
92 Newtownards Road
Bangor, BT19 1SZ
Tel: 028 9040 5265
Email: east.clerical@nias.hscni.net
South Eastern Area Manager: Ruth McNamara

Western Divisional Headquarters
Altnagelvin Hospital, Glenshane Road
Derry, BT47 6GT
Tel: 028 9081 0653
Email: west.secretary@nias.hscni.net
Western Area Manager: Laura Coulter

Northern Divisional Headquarters
Ballymena Ambulance Station
121-125 Antrim Road
Ballymena, BT42 2HD
Tel: 028 2563 6760
Email: northdiv.secretary@nias.hscni.net
Northern Area Manager: Gareth Tumelty

Southern Divisional Headquarters
Craigavon Area Hospital, 68 Lurgan Road
Portadown, BT63 5QQ
Tel: 028 3861 2537
Email: lynn.lindsay@nias.hscni.net
Southern Area Manager: Mark Cochrane

Southern Health and Social Care Trust

Southern College of Nursing
Craigavon Area Hospital, 68 Lurgan Road
Portadown, BT63 5QQ
Tel: 028 3833 4444
Web: www.southerntrust.hscni.net
Email: corporate.hq@southerntrust.hscni.net
Chair: Eileen Mullan
Chief Executive: Shane Devlin

Board Members
Geraldine Donaghy; Pauline Leeson;
Hilary McCartan; Martin McDonald; John Wilkinson

Executive Directors
Director of Children and Young People's Services:
Paul Morgan
Director of Finance, Procurement and Estates:
Catherine Teggart
Director of HR and Organisational Development:
Vivienne Toal
Director of Performance and Reform: Aldrina Magwood

Director of Performance and Reform:
Aldrina Magwood
Medical Director: Maria O'Kane
Director of Acute Services: Melanie McClements
Director of Mental Health and Disability Services:
Maria O'Kane (interim)
Director of Nursing, Midwifery and Allied Health Professionals:
Heather Trouton
Director of Older People and Primary Care:
Brian Beattie (interim)

South Eastern Health and Social Care Trust

Trust Headquarters, Ulster Hospital
Upper Newtownards Road, Dundonald
Belfast, BT16 1RH
Tel: 028 9055 3100
Web: www.setrust.hscni.net
Email: public.relations@setrust.hscni.net
Chair: Jonathan Patton (acting)
Chief Executive: Roisin Coulter

Board Members
Noel Brady; Maura Briscoe; Maynard Mawhinney; Helen Minford; Joan O'Hagan

Executive Directors
Director of Primary Care, Elderly and Executive Director of Nursing:
Nicki Patterson
Medical Director: Charles Martyn
Director of Children's Services / Executive Director of Social Work:
Barbara Campbell
Director of Human Resources and Corporate Affairs: Claire Smyth (interim)
Director of Finance: Wendy Thompson
Director of Hospital Services:
David Robinson
Director of Adult Services and Prison Healthcare: Margaret O'Kane

Western Health and Social Care Trust

MDEC Building
Altnagelvin Area Hospital Site
Glenshane Road, Derry
BT47 6SB
Tel: 028 7134 5171
Web: www.westerntrust.hscni.net
Chair: Sam Pollock
Chief Executive: Neil Guckian

Board Members
Joe Campbell; Sean Hegarty; Ruth Laird; Judith McGaffin; Hugh McKenna; John McPeake; Catherine O'Mullan

Executive Directors
Director of Finance and Contracting:
Eimear McCauley (interim)
Director of Human Resources:
Karen Hargan
Director of Nursing / Director of Primary Care & Older People's Services:
Bob Brown
Director of Performance and Service Improvement: Teresa Molloy
Executive Director of Social Work / Director of Women and Children's Services: Deirdre Mahon
Director of Acute Hospital Services:
Geraldine McKay
Medical Director: Catherine McDonnell
Director of Adult Mental Health and Disability Services: Karen O'Brien
Head of Communications: Oliver Kelly

Other organisations

Business Services Organisation
2 Franklin Street, Belfast, BT2 8DQ
Tel: 0300 555 0113
Web: www.hscbusiness.hscni.net
Email: admin.office@hscni.net
Chair: Julie Erskine
Chief Executive: Karen Bailey (acting)

Non-Executive Directors
Robert Bannon; Mark Campbell; Patricia Gordon; Sean McKeever; Dorothy Whittington

Executive Directors
Interim Director of Operations:
Peter Wilson
Director of Finance: Karen Bryson
Director of HR and Corporate Services:
Paula Smyth
Director, Corporate, Governance, Planning and IT: Mark Bradley
Chief Legal Adviser: Alphy Maginness

Regional offices

Procurement and Logistics HQ
77 Boucher Cresent
Belfast, BT12 6HU

Procurement and Logistics Services
Gransha Hospital
Clooney Road
Derry
BT47 6FN
Tel: 028 7186 5140

Finance HQ
12-22 Linenhall Street, Belfast
BT2 8BS

BSO Payments Centre
Greenmount House
Woodside Road Industrial Estate
Ballymena, BT42 4TP
Tel: 028 9536 2996

Centre for Public Health
Institute of Clinical Science
Block B
Royal Victoria Hospital
Grosvenor Road, Belfast
BT12 6BJ
Tel: +44 (0) 28 9097 6350
Web: www.qub.ac.uk/research-centres/CentreforPublicHealth
Email: cph@qub.ac.uk
Director: Prof Frank Kee

Employment Medical Advisory Service
c/o Health and Safety Executive NI
83 Ladas Drive, Belfast, BT6 9FR
Tel: 028 9024 3249
Web: www.hseni.gov.uk
Email: emasmail@hseni.gov.uk

Food Standards Agency
10A-C Clarendon Road
Belfast, BT1 3BG
Tel: 028 9041 7700
Web: www.food.gov.uk/northern-ireland
Email: infosani@foodstandards.gsi.gov.uk
Director: Maria Jennings

Institute of Public Health in Ireland
6th Floor, City Exchange
Gloucester Street
Belfast, BT1 4LS
Tel: 028 9064 8494
Web: www.publichealth.ie
Email: info@publichealth.ie
Chief Executive: Suzanne Costello

Northern Ireland Blood Transfusion Service
Belfast City Hospital Complex
51 Lisburn Road, Belfast, BT9 7TS
Tel: 028 9032 1414
Web: www.nibts.org
Email: inet@nibts.hscni.net
Chair: Bonnie Anley
Chief Executive: Karin Jackson
Medical Director: Dr Joanne Murdock

Northern Ireland Clinical Trials Unit (NICTU)
7 Lennoxvale
Belfast, BT9 5BY
Tel: +44 (0)28 9615 1447
Web: www.nictu.hscni.net
Email: info@nictu.hscni.net
Director: Prof Mike Clarke

Health — Northern Ireland Yearbook

Northern Ireland Fire and Rescue Service
Headquarters, 1 Seymour Street
Lisburn, BT27 4SX
Tel: 028 9266 4221
Web: www.nifrs.org
Chief Fire Officer: Peter O'Reilly

Northern Ireland Guardian Ad Litem Agency (NIGALA)
Centre House, 79 Chichester Street
Belfast, BT1 4JE
Tel: 0300 555 0102
Web: www.nigala.hscni.net
Email: admin@nigala.hscni.net
Chair: Gemma Loughran
Chief Executive: Dawn Shaw

Northern Ireland Medical and Dental Training Agency
Beechill House, 42 Beechill Road
Belfast, BT8 7RL
Tel: 028 9040 0000
Web: www.nimdta.gov.uk
Email: nimdta@nimdta.gov.uk
Chair: Derek Wilson
Chief Executive: Mark McCarey

Northern Ireland Practice and Education Council for Nursing and Midwifery (NIPEC)
2nd Floor, Centre House
79 Chichester Street
Belfast, BT1 4JE
Tel: 0300 300 0066
Web: www.nipec.hscni.net
Email: enquiries@nipec.hscni.net
Chair: Carol Curran
Chief Executive: Angela McLernon

Northern Ireland Social Care Council
7th Floor, Millennium House
19-25 Great Victoria Street
Belfast, BT2 7AQ
Tel: 028 9536 2600
Web: www.niscc.info
Email: info@niscc.hscni.net
Chair: Paul Martin
Chief Executive: Patricia Higgins (interim)
Director of Registration and Corporate Services: Declan McAllister
Director of Regulation and Standards: Marian O'Rourke

Patient and Client Council
5th Floor, 14-16 Great Victoria Street
Belfast, BT2 7BA
Tel: 0800 917 0222
Web: www.patientclientcouncil.hscni.net
Email: info.pcc@hscni.net
Chair: Christine Collins
Chief Executive: Vivian McConvey
Head of Business Support: Jackie McNeill

Public Health Agency
12-22 Linenhall Street
Belfast, BT2 8BS
Tel: 0300 555 0114
Web: www.publichealth.hscni.net
Chair: Andrew Dougal
Chief Executive: Aidan Dawson

Non-Executive Directors
Phillip Brett; John-Patrick Clayton; Anne Henderson; Robert Irvine; Deepa Mann-Kler; Nichola Rooney; Joseph Stewart

Executive Directors
Director of Public Health: Dr Stephen Bergin (interim)
Director of Nursing and Allied Health Professionals: Rodney Morton
Director of Operations: Stephen Wilson (interim)

Regulation and Quality Improvement Authority
7th Floor, Victoria House
15-27 Gloucester Street
Belfast, BT1 4LS
Tel: 028 9536 1111
Web: www.rqia.org.uk
Email: info@rqia.org.uk
Chair: Christine Collins (acting)
Chief Executive: Briege Donaghy

Safefood
7 Eastgate Avenue, Eastgate
Little Island, Cork, T45 RX01
Tel: +353 (0) 21 230 4100
Helpline: 0800 085 1683
Web: www.safefood.eu
Email: info@safefood.eu
Chair: Helen O'Donnell
Chief Executive: Ray Dolan

Safeguarding Board for Northern Ireland
The Beeches
12 Hampton Manor Drive
Belfast, BT7 3EN
Tel: 028 9536 1810
Web: www.safeguardingni.org
Email: sbnisupport@hscni.net
Chair: Bernie McNally
Director: Helen McKenzie

Private healthcare providers

3Fivetwo Healthcare
21 Old Channel Road
Titanic Quarter
Belfast, BT3 9DE
Tel: 028 9066 7878
Web: www.3fivetwo.com
Email: admin@3fivetwo.com

Blackwell Associates
Strand House
102 Holywood Road
Belfast, BT4 1NU
Tel: 028 9065 6131
Web: www.blackwellassociates.co.uk
Email: enquiries@blackwellassociates.co.uk

Hillsborough Private Clinic
2 Main Street
Hillsborough, BT26 6AE
Tel: 028 9268 8899
Web: www.hillsboroughprivateclinic.com
Email: info@hillsboroughprivateclinic.com

Kingsbridge Private Hospital
811-815 Lisburn Road
Belfast, BT9 7GX
Tel: 028 9066 7878
Web: www.3fivetwo.com/kingsbridge
Email: info@kingsbridgeprivatehospital.com

Northern MRI
93 Malone Road, Belfast, BT9 6SP
Tel: 028 9066 0050
Web: www.northernmri.com
Email: info@northernmri.com

Northwest Independent Hospital
Church Hill House, Ballykelly
Limavady, BT49 9HS
Tel: 028 7776 3090
Web: www.nwih.co.uk
Email: info@nwih.co.uk

Ulster Independent Clinic
245 Stranmillis Road
Belfast, BT9 5JH
Tel: 028 9066 1212
Web: www.ulsterindependentclinic.com
Email: info@ulsterindependentclinic.com

Northern Ireland Yearbook
Housing

Credit: NIHE
Credit: NIHE
Credit: NIHE

Housing in Northern Ireland

The Department for Communities (DfC) is responsible for housing policy and tackling homelessness in Northern Ireland. Its Housing Division regulates the Northern Ireland Housing Executive (NIHE) and registered housing associations and oversees the private rented sector. The division works with the Housing Executive and housing associations to provide social housing and also has lead responsibility for tackling fuel poverty.

The current draft Programme for Government (PfG) published in 2016 has an outcome to improve the supply of social housing. The Department for Communities is committed to delivering approximately 200 shared social housing units per year as part of the Social Housing Development Programme. The Programme for Government shared housing commitment is badged 'Housing for All'. The Executive Office is currently developing a new PfG. Early indications are that housing will not be one of nine main outcomes and will instead feature within various indicators.

The Housing Executive was established in 1971 and 2021 marked 50 years since its creation. The Housing Executive has 86,000 homes across Northern Ireland and works to deliver new-build accommodation. A review of the organisation by PwC was commissioned by then Social Development Minister Alex Attwood in October 2010 and reported in June 2011. The review recommended a new three-fold structure: a housing regulator, a strategic housing authority and a social enterprise landlord.

In January 2013, Attwood's successor, Nelson McCausland, announced his intention to move landlord functions out of the public sector and establish a regional housing body for non-landlord functions. This would be accompanied by an independent social housing rent panel.

In November 2020 plans to "revitalise" the Housing Executive were published by interim Housing Minister Carál Ní Chuilín. Among these proposals was the empowerment of the Housing Executive to borrow, allowing for stock investment and to begin building homes again. Additionally, the Minister proposed a review of the Housing Executive's House Sales Scheme, ring-fenced funding of the Social Housing Development Programme for areas of highest need and reformed the social housing allocations system.

In April 2021, Minister Deirdre Hargey announced that 2,403 new social homes were started in 2020/21, 30 per cent above the target for the year (1,850). The budget for new social housing for 2021/22 was announced as £162 million, around £26 million above 2020/21 levels. In Q3 2021 the house price index recorded a standardised price for Northern Ireland as a whole at £159,109, ranging from £140,983 in Armagh City, Banbridge and Craigavon to £183,392 in Lisburn and Castlereagh. The House Price Index increased by 10.7 per cent from Q3 2020. 7,529 residential properties were sold during Q3 2021. The House Price Index is now 43.4 per cent higher than Q1 2015.

Table 6.1 Total occupied housing stock by tenure 2012–13 to 2019–20

Tenure (%)	12-13	13-14	14-15	15-16	16-17	17-18	18-19	19-20
Owned outright	36	38	37	37	39	40	42	43
Owned with mortgage	30	29	31	28	27	29	28	27
Rented (NIHE)	12	12	11	13	13	12	12	10
Rented (housing associations)	4	3	4	4	4	4	4	5
Rented (privately)	16	16	16	17	16	14	13	14
Rent free	1	21	1	1	1	1	1	1

Source: DfC

Table 6.2 The Northern Ireland housing sector

%	13-14	14-15	15-16	16-17	17-18	18-19	19-20	20-21
Population (000s)	1,830	1,841	1,852	1,862	1,871	1,882	1,894	1,896
Average household size	2.5	2.5	2.5	2.5	2.5	2.5	2.5	2.5
Total housing stock (000s)	762.3	767.4	771.1	776.5	783.3	790.3	799.0	807.8
Total stock per 1,000 population	417	417	416	417	419	420	422	426
New dwellings started	5,315	5,501	5,808	6,461	7,096	7,808	7,314	6,459

Source: DfC

Revitalising the Housing Executive

Grainia Long, Chief Executive of the Housing Executive visited Linda Roy, who has been a Housing Executive tenant since 1971, as part of the organisation's 50th anniversary celebrations.

As the Housing Executive begins its 51st year, it is fitting that the discussion of the organisation's revitalisation will be a key topic on the Northern Ireland agenda in 2022, writes Chief Executive of the Housing Executive Grainia Long.

Our breadth and scope remain after our first 50 years: a landlord at scale, we manage more than 84,000 homes, keeping 170,000 people safe, warm and dry – that is almost 10 per cent of the population living in our properties. Alongside this, we remain the strategic housing authority for Northern Ireland, continuing to meet our fundamental purpose of ensuring housing is administered in a fair and impartial manner.

However, the organisation goes far beyond that, with responsibility for homelessness, assessing housing need, providing private sector grants, administering Housing Benefit, enabling thousands of new homes through the Social Housing Development Programme, and acting as the Home Energy Conservation Authority for Northern Ireland.

The need for transforming the organisation, however, has never been more pressing nor more urgent. The level of required investment in our own homes is double what the organisation can afford. At the same time, there are real pressures on the affordable housing market, a continued rise in demand for social housing and increased numbers of individuals and families who are homeless.

The Minister for Communities' statement in November 2020 proposed the revitalisation of the Housing Executive. This offers the key to a future that will deliver additional, better, energy efficient and more appropriate homes to those in need and it also provides the prospect of creating new jobs and skills training that will boost the economy.

Revitalising the Housing Executive is critical to our ambitions to reinvest in our stock, add to new social housing supply and help reinvigorate neighbourhoods. We are hopeful that 2022 will be the beginning of a new era for housing in Northern Ireland.

T: 03448 920 900
E: information@nihe.gov.uk
W: www.nihe.gov.uk
Twitter: @nihecommunity
Facebook: www.facebook.com/housingexecutive/

Housing Executive

Arbour HOUSING

Building a new future for Arbour Housing

(L-R) Kieran Matthews, Chief Executive Arbour Housing; Angela Clarke, Chair Arbour Housing; Grainia Long, Chief Executive of the Northern Ireland Housing Executive; Ben Collins, Chief Executive of the Northern Ireland Federation of Housing Associations (NIFHA).

Angela Clarke, Chair of Arbour Housing explains the new brand identity, future plans and why tenant engagement is at the heart of the Association.

Arbour Housing is one of Northern Ireland's larger providers of social housing. Previously under the name of South Ulster Housing Association, it was established more than 40 years ago, and since its inception in 1978 is well-known for developing social housing in areas of high housing need.

Arbour Housing's growth over the last three years prompted the Association, under the guidance of Chief Executive Kieran Matthews, to re-think its brand and name to reflect more accurately who it is rather than where it operates. The new name suggests shelter; family and community, a welcoming and safe space; perhaps even refuge. And at heart, that's what housing is all about.

Chief Executive of Arbour Housing, Kieran Matthews said: "When we started the rebranding process we wanted something that expressed our vision of being more than a landlord. We also put our tenants' voice at the heart of what we do. This fed into discussions, workshops and research and in the end, we all agreed on Arbour. We liked the natural element of shelter and protection it suggests. It feels like a very good fit for us.

While external signage will change, very little will change for tenants. There will be no impact on their rents or tenancy agreements, and Arbour is confident it will continue to provide exceptional service and support for everyone involved with the Association."

Arbour currently has social housing developments in Newcastle, Newry, Newtownabbey, Lurgan and Lisburn and future developments coming in Omagh, Derry, Portadown – all going some way to addressing the social housing challenge that currently exists in Northern Ireland.

Northern Ireland Yearbook | Housing

Housing associations like Arbour exist to provide quality homes to people who otherwise might not be able to secure these via the private housing ladder. But housing associations also have an important role to play in shaping communities, ensuring they are safe, welcoming and provide attractive places that people want to live in, where they can nurture their families and feel secure and part of a community.

And an important thing that makes a crucial contribution to delivering these is tenant engagement. Throughout its work, Arbour has strived to ensure the voice of tenants is not just captured but is heard and increasingly we want to ensure this plays a greater part in influencing and shaping the local physical, social and economic environment.

All of us have been living through the most extraordinary times due to the pandemic and this has made the need for safe, good quality and affordable housing even more essential than ever.

In addition to the continuing effects of the pandemic, there are numerous other challenges ahead for the broader social housing sector. Not only concerns around funding and affordability, increasing health and safety pressures and growing housing need but also issues around sustainability, the climate emergency and the green economy are also becoming more central considerations, for government, business and tenants alike.

Looking forward, Arbour will be putting sustainability at the heart of both its new-build programme, and its upgrade and maintenance of existing housing stock, through the use of low-impact materials and techniques, and energy-saving approaches and techniques. Value for money will remain crucial, for tenants, for Arbour as well as for its suppliers and partners.

Grainia Long, Chief Executive of The Northern Ireland Housing Executive, who spoke at the launch of the new brand, said: "Social housing providers are a key partner for us in addressing housing need across Northern Ireland. Arbour Housing have a strong track record of delivery and they have ambitious plans. I look forward to working with them in the future."

Arbour Housing
T: 028 3833 9795
E: www.arbourhousing.org

(L-R) Ben Collins, Chief Executive of the Northern Ireland Federation of Housing Associations (NIFHA); Miss Stephanie Walsh, Arbour Housing Tenant; Angela Clarke, Chair Arbour Housing.

During the last 18 months Arbour has therefore worked even harder than ever to ensure continuity of service to tenants in these most difficult of circumstances responding promptly to needs, finding new and inventive ways to provide services and address issues. In the midst of so much fear, anxiety and uncertainty, that's been invaluable to the wellbeing of our tenants and its important I think to recognise and thank staff and management for their continuing commitment and hard work.

Who is Arbour Housing?

Arbour Housing is the new name for the South Ulster Housing Association. Although the label has changed, our values remain the same.

We have a clear vision:

"To be more than just a landlord, to put our tenants' voice at the heart of what we do and to deliver great homes and services, supporting communities and improving lives."

That vision is the inspiration behind Arbour, which is reinforced by our strapline:

Live. Share. Grow.

Housing | Northern Ireland Yearbook

Table 6.3 House Price Index and standardised price in each council area Q3 2021

Local government district	Index (quarter 3 2021)	Percentage change on previous quarter	Percentage change over 12 months	Standardised price (quarter 3 2021)
Antrim and Newtownabbey	141.8	2.8%	10.0%	£163,057
Ards and North Down	133.8	2.6%	9.4%	£179,557
Armagh City, Banbridge and Craigavon	143.0	4.0%	11.2%	£140,983
Belfast	142.2	2.5%	9.6%	£150,267
Causeway Coast and Glens	161.8	1.7%	12.7%	£174,664
Derry City and Strabane	151.8	6.8%	13.9%	£143,674
Fermanagh and Omagh	149.0	1.7%	10.1%	£142,846
Lisburn and Castlereagh	136.6	1.1%	7.1%	£183,392
Mid and East Antrim	139.8	0.7%	10.6%	£144,737
Mid Ulster	137.3	5.7%	14.1%	£153,549
Newry, Mourne and Down	153.0	5.6%	13.1%	£172,085
Northern Ireland	143.4	3.0%	10.7%	£159,109

Source: NISRA

Table 6.4 Northern Ireland House Price Index by property type

Property type	Index (quarter 3 2021)	Percentage change on previous quarter	Percentage change change over 12 months	Standardised price (quarter 3 2021)
Detached	142.7	2.10%	11.60%	£239,839
Semi-Detached	140.3	3.50%	9.70%	£153,285
Terrace	150.6	4.80%	13.30%	£113,617
Apartment	134.8	-1.50%	3.40%	£117,784
All	143.4	3.00%	10.70%	£159,109

Source: NISRA

Although most residential properties in Northern Ireland are owner-occupied, a substantial proportion is rented either by a private landlord or a social housing provider. A breakdown of the housing market by type of ownership is shown in table 6.1.

In 2020-2021, 15,991 households presented as homeless. Single males (36 per cent) and families (29 per cent) were the biggest presenters of homelessness. Within the single males category, those aged between 26 and 59 were the highest presenters of homelessness with 4,312 cases.

In 2020-2021 the number of new dwelling completions in Northern Ireland was 6,446, a decrease of 12 per cent on the previous year. Of these, 653 completions were social sector and 5,793 were private. There were 6,459 new dwelling starts – 693 were social sector and 5,766 were private.

The total housing stock in April 2021 was 814,210. Average household size in 2020-21 was 2.5 people.

The Housing Executive holds data on all housing applications and allocations made through the social housing selection scheme in the Housing Management System. The total number of applicants on the waiting list (with no existing NIHE/housing association tenancy) at 31 March 2021 was 43,971. Of these applicants, 30,288 were in 'housing stress'. This means they have 30 or more points under the social housing selection scheme. The local government districts with the highest number of applicants were Belfast (11,858) and Derry City and Strabane (5,557).

In 2020-21, dwellings that were owned outright and dwellings that were owned with a mortgage accounted for 70 per cent of households (43 per cent and 27 per cent respectively). In the same period, 14 per cent of properties were privately rented and 5 per cent were rented from housing associations. NIHE rented properties made up 10 per cent of households.

Figure 6.1 Household tenure 2019-2020

- Owned outright: 43%
- Owned with mortgage: 27%
- Rented from Northern Ireland Housing Executive: 10%
- Rented from housing associations: 5%
- Privately rented: 14%
- Rent free: 1%

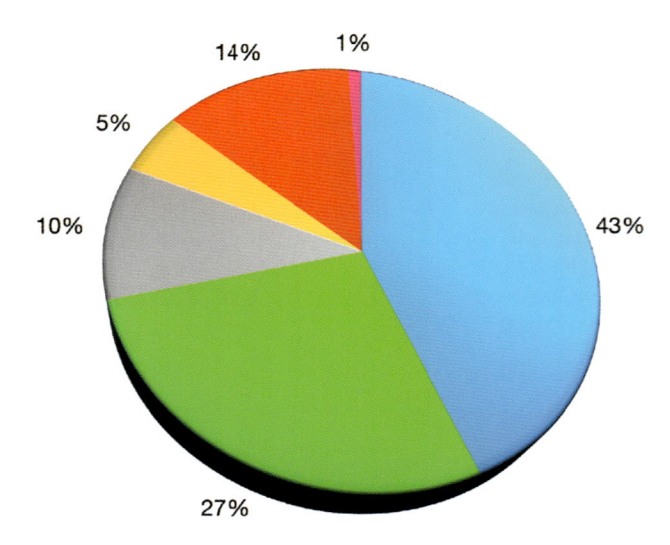

Social Housing Development Programme

The Social Housing Development Programme (SHDP) is a three-year rolling programme used by the Department to inform social housing funding investment decisions. Both the Northern Ireland Housing Executive (NIHE) and Registered Housing Association movement are involved in the programme.

Since 2010/11, 16,313 social houses have been completed through this scheme. Of these houses, 97 per cent were self-contained and 3 per cent were shared. In 2020-21, there were 2,403 SHDP starts, a 216 per cent increase on the previous year (761). In the same period, there were 1,304 SHDP completions, a 20 per cent decrease on the previous year (1,626).

Department for Communities

Causeway Exchange
1-7 Bedford Street
Belfast, BT2 7EG
Tel: 028 9082 9000
Web: www.communities-ni.gov.uk
Minister: Deirdre Hargey MLA
Permanent Secretary: Tracy Meharg
Deputy Secretary, Housing, Urban Regeneration and Local Government: Mark O'Donnell (acting)

Northern Ireland Housing Executive

The Housing Centre
2 Adelaide Street
Belfast, BT2 8PB
Tel: 03448 920 900
Web: www.nihe.gov.uk
Email: info@nihe.gov.uk
Chief Executive: Grainia Long

Directors
Director of Corporate Services:
David Moore
Director of Housing Services:
Colm McQuillan
Director of Asset Management:
Paul Isherwood
Director of Regional Services:
Siobhan McCauley
Head of Corporate Communications:
Jonny Blease

Housing Executive Board
Chairman: Professor Peter Roberts
Vice-Chairman: John McMullan
Members: Allan Bresland, Catherine Elattar, Amanda Grehan, Pauline Leeson, Jim McCall, Derek Wilson, Chris Welch

Regional offices
Tel: 03448 920 900

Belfast Region
1-11 May Street
Belfast, BT1 4NA
Email: belfastarea@nihe.gov.uk
Manager: Jennifer Hawthorne

Covers: North Belfast, South Belfast, East Belfast, West Belfast and Shankill districts.

North Region (Ballymena)
Twickenham House, Mount Street
Ballymena, BT43 6BP
Email: northeastarea@nihe.gov.uk
Manager: Frank O'Connor

Covers: Antrim, Ballycastle, Ballymena, Ballymoney, Carrickfergus, Coleraine, Larne and Newtownabbey 1 and 2 districts.

North Region (Derry)
Richmond Chambers
The Diamond
Derry, BT48 6QP
Email: westarea@nihe.gov.uk
Manager: Frank O'Connor

Covers: Waterloo Place, Waterside, Collon Terrace, Limavady, Magherafelt, Strabane, Cookstown and Omagh districts.

South Region (Craigavon)
Marlborough House, Central Way
Craigavon, BT64 1AJ
Email: southarea@nihe.gov.uk
Manager: John McCartan

Covers: Armagh, Banbridge, Craigavon, Dungannon, Fermanagh, Lurgan, Newry, Portadown and Cookstown, Magherafelt and Omagh areas.

South Region (Newtownards)
Strangford House, 28 Court Street
Newtownards, BT23 3NX
Email: southeastarea@nihe.gov.uk
Manager: John McCartan

Covers: Bangor, Downpatrick, Newtownards office districts.

Homelessness Services

Belfast Homelessness Services Unit
1-11 May Street
Belfast, BT1 4NA
Manager: Des Marley

Housing Benefit Units

Belfast Housing Benefit Unit (Private)
4th Floor, The Housing Centre
2 Adelaide Street, BT2 8PB
Email: belfasthb@nihe.gov.uk
Manager: Colette McCorry

Belfast Housing Benefit Unit (Public)
4th Floor, The Housing Centre
2 Adelaide Street, BT2 8PB
Email: belfast.housingbenefit@nihe.gov.uk
Manager: Colette McCorry

Lisburn Housing Benefit Recovery Unit
29 Antrim Street
Lisburn, BT28 1AU
Tel: 028 9598 1580
Email: hb.recoveryoffice@nihe.gov.uk
Manager: Norman Dougan

North East Housing Benefit Unit
Twickenham House
Mount Street
Ballymena, BT43 6BP
Tel: 03448 920 902
Email: northeast.housingbenefit@nihe.gov.uk
Manager: Kieron Murphy

Omagh Housing Benefit Unit
MacAllister House
Woodside Avenue
Omagh, BT79 7BP
Tel: 03448 920 902
Email: omagh.housingbenefit@nihe.gov.uk
Manager: Sean Cullen

South East Housing Benefit Unit
Strangford House
28 Court Street
Newtownards, BT23 7NX
Tel: 03448 920 902
Email: southeast.housingbenefit@nihe.gov.uk

West Housing Benefit Unit
Richmond Chambers
The Diamond
Derry, BT48 6QP
Tel: 03448 920 902
Email: westarea.housingbenefit@nihe.gov.uk

Local offices (A-Z)
Tel: 03448 920 900

Antrim
45 High Street, Antrim, BT41 4AN
Email: antrim@nihe.gov.uk
Area Manager: Breige Mullaghan

Covers: Antrim Town, Ballycraigy, Crumlin, Dublin Road, Firfields, Glenburn, Greystone, Menin Road, Moylena Grove, Muckamore, Newpark, Parkgate, Parkhall, Randalstown, Rathenraw, Rathglynn, Rathkyle, Springfarm, Steeple, Stiles, Templepatrick, Toome and Townparks North and South.

Armagh
48 Dobbin Street, Armagh, BT61 7QQ
Email: armagh@nihe.gov.uk
Area Manager: John McCartan

Covers: Ahorey, Annaghmore, Annahugh, Armagh Estates, Ballyards, Ballymacnab, Benburb, Blackwatertown, Carrickaness, Charlemont, Clady, Darkley, Derrynoose, Drumhillery, Drumnahuncheon, Edenveys, Eglish, Glenanne, Hamiltonsbawn, Keady, Killylea, Loughgall, Loughgilly, Madden, Markethill, Middletown, Milford, Mountnorris, Poyntzpass, Richhill, Tandragee, and Tynan.

Ballymena
Twickenham House, Mount Street
Ballymena, BT43 6BP
Email: ballymenadistrict@nihe.gov.uk
Area Manager: Mairead Myles-Davey

Covers: Adair, Ahoghill, Aughafatten, Ballee, Ballykeel, Ballymarlow, Ballymena Town, Broughshane, Cargan, Carninney, Clough, Craigwarren, Cullybackey, Doury Road, Dunclug, Dunvale, Fisherwick Crescent, Galgorm, Glarryford, Glenwherry, Gracehill, Harryville, Herbison Park, Kells, Loughlougan, Martinstown, Millfield, Moorfields, Moorlands, Newtowncrommelin, Portglenone, Procklis, Rectory, Slatt, Straid, Taylorstown, and Tullygarley.

Ballymoney
54 Main Street, Ballymoney, BT53 6AL
Email: ballymoney@nihe.gov.uk
Area Manager: Mark Alexander

Covers: Ballybogey, Balnamore, Bendooragh, Carnany, Clintyfinnan, Cloughmills, Corkey, Dervock, Druckendult, Dunaghy, Dunloy, Eastermeade, Glebeside, Killyrammer, Loughgiel, Macfin, Margaret Avenue, Rasharkin, Seacon, Stranocum, Townparks, Trinity Drive, and Westgate.

Banbridge
56 Bridge Street, Banbridge, BT32 3JU
Email: banbridge@nihe.gov.uk
Area Manager: Mark Ingham

Covers: Annaclone, Ashfield, Ballyvarley, Ballyward, Banbridge Estates, Closkelt, Corbet, Dromore Town, Gilford, Katesbridge, Kinallen, Laurencetown, Lenaderg, Lisnagade, Loughbrickland, Rathfriland, Scarva, Seapatrick, Tullyheenan and Tullylish.

Bangor
2 Alfred Street, Bangor, BT20 5DH
Email: bangor@nihe.gov.uk
Area Manager: Owen Brady

Covers: Bangor Estates, Conlig, Crawfordsburn, Groomsport, Helen's Bay and Holywood.

Causeway Area (Ballycastle office)
Fleming House
1B Coleraine Road
Ballycastle
Co Antrim, BT54 6EY
Tel: 03448 920 900
Email: ballycastle@nihe.gov.uk
Area Manager: Mark Alexander

Covers: Armoy, Ballintoy, Ballycastle Town, Cushendun, Ballyvoy, Bushmills, Cushendall, Liscolman, Mosside, Rathlin and Waterfoot.

Causeway Area (Limavady office)
2A Fleming Way, 57-59 Main Street
Limavady, BT49 0FB
Email: limavady@nihe.gov.uk

Homes, Lives and Communities

Habinteg Housing Association is a registered housing association in Northern Ireland. The Association plans, develops and manages integrated housing schemes in both urban and rural areas throughout the region and works with a number of partner organisations in providing supported housing projects.

Habinteg currently has over 2,215 properties at more than 100 locations and 18 partnership schemes.

Habinteg's vision: Homes, Lives and Communities, encapsulates the Association's central aim of providing homes which combines a range of dwelling types: family houses, apartments and bungalows, in order to appropriately meet the needs of the widest range of users, including older persons and persons with a disability.

Quality, sustainable developments include a wide range of housing. This includes family sized suburban housing developments, apartments, and specialised housing schemes. Partnership projects include sensitively designed housing with care schemes, temporary accommodation and housing initiatives for people with additional support needs.

The standard and quality of these developments has been recognised at local and national level with an impressive list of high-profile awards, including the UK Housing Award for Outstanding Achievement in Social Housing in Northern Ireland, the RICS Award for the Northern Ireland region and a succession of NIHE Housing Council Awards for Best Scheme in Northern Ireland. Habinteg is a Customer Service Excellence organisation and has Investor in People Silver status.

Habinteg embraces its vision of 'Homes, Lives and Communities' by working closely with the people who live in its properties. The Habinteg team understands that people need homes they can feel safe and comfortable in and conducts focus groups and site days where they can listen to people's needs as well as their ideas which help design the Association's services.

Habinteg has an active tenant and community engagement team who ensure people feel involved in the Habinteg family. Activities are provided for all tenants regardless of age, from Ukulele classes and Understanding Governance and training to opportunities to join Habinteg's committees or board, Habinteg has countless opportunities for people to engage with the Association, shaping how services are delivered in a unique and vibrant environment.

Habinteg has an expert and caring staff team covering all aspects of a dynamic Housing Association.

The Association will move to its new home on Newforge Lane toward the later part of 2022.

More information about Habinteg and the work it does can be found online at www.habinteg-ulster.co.uk

T: 028 9042 7211
E: info@habinteg-ulster.co.uk
W: www.habinteg-ulster.co.uk

Housing | Northern Ireland Yearbook

Covers: Aghanloo, Alexander Road, Ardgarvan, Aughill, Ballycrum, Ballykelly, Ballymacallion, Ballymonie, Ballyquin, Bellarena, Bonnanboigh, Caman Park, Carnabane, Carrowclare, Carrydoo, Church Street, Connell Street, Crawford Square, Crebarkey, Dernaflaw, Dromore, Drumachose Park, Drumavalley, Drumneechy, Drumsurn, Dungiven, Dungiven Road, Feeny, Glack, Gortgar, Gortnaghey, Greysteel, Greystone, Josephine Avenue, Killylane, King's Lane, Largy, Magherabuoy, Massey Avenue, Muldonagh, Myroe, Owenbeg, Protestant Street, Rathbeg Crescent, Rathbrady Road, Roemill Gardens, Roeview Park, Sistrokeel, William Street and Windsor Avenue.

Carrickfergus
19 High Street, Carrickfergus, BT38 7AN
Email: carrick@nihe.gov.uk
Area Manager: Mairead Myles-Davey

Covers: Agnes Street/McKeen's Avenue, Carrickfergus Town, Castlemara, Davys Street, Drumhoy/Salia/Ederny, Eden, Glenfield, Greenisland, Sunnylands, Taylors Avenue, Victoria, Whitehead, Windmill, Upper/Lower Woodburn.

Castlereagh
30 Church Road, Dundonald, BT16 2LN
Email: lisburndistrict@nihe.gov.uk
Area Manager: Des Marley

Covers: Ballybeen, Brooklands, Carryduff, Coronation Park, Mawhinney Park, Moatview Park, Moneyreagh, Newtownbreda, Ryan Park.

Coleraine
19 Abbey Street, Coleraine, BT52 1DU
Email: colerainedistrict@nihe.gov.uk
Area Manager: Mark Alexander

Covers: Aghadowey, Articlave, Ballyrashane, Ballysally, Ballywoodock, Boveedy, Brook Green, Burnside Park, Castlerock, Castleroe, Cherry Place, Coleraine Town, Craigmore, Curraghmore Park, Drumadraw, Dunluce, Farrenlester, Garvagh, Glenkeen, Glenleary, Glenmanus, Grove, Harpurs Hill, The Heights, Killowen, Kilrea, Macosquin, Maybuoy, Millburn, Newmills, Portballintrae, Portrush, Portstewart, Society Street, The Crescent and Windyhall.

Collon Terrace
14 Collon Terrace
Derry, BT48 7QP
Tel: 03448 920 900
Email: collonterrace@nihe.gov.uk
Area Manager: Eddie Doherty

Covers: Ballymagroarty, Ballynagard, Belmont, Bloomfield, Bradley Park, Bracken Park, Brookdale, Capal Court, Cashelhill Park, Carnhill, Culmore Road, Coshquin, Earhart Park, Ederowen Park, Elaghmore Park, Fergleen Park, Fern Park, Galliagh Park, Glencaw, Knockalla Park, Hazelbank, Slievemore Park, Leafair, Moss Park, Shantallow and Woodlands.

Cookstown
15 Morgan's Hill Road, Cookstown, BT80 8HA
Email: cookstown@nihe.gov.uk
Area Manager: Sharon Crooks

Covers: Ardboe, Ballylifford, Ballyronan, Blackhill, Coagh, Clare, Cluntoerichardson, Coagh Street, Cooke Crescent, Cookstown Estates, Coolreaghs, Derrychrin, Donaghy, Drum, Drumallan, Dunamore, Dunman, Gortacladdy, Keenaghan, Kildress, Killymoon, Killygonland, Lisnahull, Lissan, Loup, Maloon, Moneymore, Monrush, Moortown, Mourneview, Orritor, Pomeroy, Rock, Sandholes, Sherrygroom, Sperrinview, Stewartstown, Tullyhogue, Tullyreavey and Tullywiggan.

Downpatrick
2nd Floor, Downshire Civic Centre, Downshire Estate
Ardglass Road, Downpatrick, BT30 6RA
Email: downpatrick@nihe.gov.uk
Area Manager: Liam Gunn

Covers: Annacloy, Annsborough, Annadorn, Ardglass, Ballyhornan, Ballykinlar, Ballymacarn, Ballynahinch, Burrenreagh, Castlewellan, Clonvaraghan, Clough, Crossgar, Derryboye, Downpatrick Estates, Drumaness, Drumee, Drummaroad, Dundrum, Dunmore, Dunsford, Kilclief, Kilcoo, Killough, Kilmore, Killyleagh, Loughlinisland, Newcastle, Raffrey, Saintfield, Seaforde, Shrigley, Spa, Strangford, Teconnaught and Tyrella.

Dungannon
4 Ballygawley Road, Dungannon, BT70 1EL
Email: dungannon@nihe.gov.uk
Area Manager: Sharon Crooks

Covers: Ackinduff, Augher, Aughnacloy, Ballygawley, Benburb, Brantry, Bush, Caledon, Cappagh, Castlecaulfield, Clogher, Coalisland, Derrylee, Donaghmore, Drumkee, Dungannon Estates, Fivemiletown, Galbally, Granville, Killyman, Laghey, Mountjoy, Moy, Moygashel, Mullenakill, Newmills and Tamnamore.

Larne
Sir Thomas Dixon Buildings
47 Victoria Road, Larne, BT40 1RT
Email: larne@nihe.gov.uk
Area Manager: Mairead Myles-Davey

Covers: Antiville, Ballycarry, Carnlough, Craigyhill, Ferris Park, Glenarm, Gleno, Glynn, Islandmagee, Larne Town, Magheramorne, Millbrook, Mount Hill, Old Glenarm Road and Riverdale.

Lisburn – Antrim Street
29 Antrim Street, Lisburn, BT28 1AU
Email: lisburndistrict@nihe.gov.uk
Area Manager: Des Marley

Covers: Aghalee, Ballinderry, Ballycrune, Ballynadolly, Ballymacash, Ballymacoss, Beattie Park, Conway, Culcavey, Derriaghy, Dromara, Drumbo, Dunmurry Rural Cottages, Feumore, Glenavy, Hilden, Hillhall, Greenwood, Hillsborough, Islandkelly, Manor, Tonagh, Knockmore, Lambeg, Lisburn Estates, Long Kesh, Maghaberry, Magheragall, Maze, Milltown, Moira, Purdysburn, Ravarnette, Rockview, Seymour Hill, Warren/Old Warren.

Northern Ireland Yearbook | Housing

Lurgan
122 Hill Street, Lurgan, BT66 6BH
Email: lurganbrownlow@nihe.gov.uk
Area Manager: Mark Ingham

Covers: Aghagallon, Avenue Road/Queen Street, Bleary, Carrick Drive, Dollingstown, Donacloney, Edward Street, Gilpinstown, Gratton Street, Grey, Hill Street/Sloan Street, Hospital, Kilwilkie, Lurgan Tarry, Lurgan Town Centre, Maheralin, Manor Park/Drive, Mourneview, Shankill, Taghnevan, Wakehurst, Waringstown, Aldervale, Altmore, Ardowen, Burnside, Carn, Clonmeen, Derrymacash, Derrytrasna, Drumbeg North/South, Drumellan, Drumgor Heights, Drumnacanvey, Edenbeg, Enniskeen, Kinnego, Legahory Green, Meadowbrook, Moyravery Centre, Parkmore, Rosmoyle, Westacres.

Magherafelt
3 Ballyronan Road
Magherafelt, BT45 6BP
Email: magherafelt@nihe.gov.uk
Area Manager: Sharon Crooks

Covers: Ballinahone, Ballymaguigan, Ballynease, Beagh, Bellaghy, Beagh, Carmean, Castledawson, Clady, Creagh, Culnady, Curran, Desertmartin, Draperstown, Drumderg, Fallahogey, Gulladuff, Innisrush, Kilross, Knockloughrim, Lislea, Lisnamorrow, Lisnamuck, Longfield, Luney, Maghera, Magherafelt, Mayogall, Moneyneaney, Moneysallin, Portglenone, Ritchies Villas, Rocktown, St Treas, Swatragh, Tamlaght, Tobermore, Tullyherron, and Upperlands.

Newry
35-45 Boat Street, Newry, BT34 2DB
Email: newrydistrict@nihe.gov.uk
Area Manager: Liam Gunn

Covers: Barmeen, Belleek, Bessbrook, Burren, Camlough, Creggan, Crossmaglen, Cullyhanna, Cullaville, Derramore, Drumintee, Forkhill, Hilltown, Jonesboro, Killen, Lurganare, Mayobridge, Meigh, Mullaghbawn, Mullaghglass, Newry (Rural), Newry Town, Newtowncloughoge, Newtownhamilton, Shinn, Silverbridge, The Commons, Warrenpoint, Whitecross, Annalong, Attical, Ballymaderphy, Ballymartin, Dunnaman, Glassdrumman, Longstone, Rostrevor and Kilkeel.

Newtownabbey 1
Rantalard House, Rathcoole Drive
Newtownabbey, BT37 9BL
Email: newtownabbey1@nihe.gov.uk
Area Manager: Breige Mullaghan

Covers: Abbeyville, Bawnmore, Bleachgreen, Glenville, Hightown, Longlands, Rathcoole, Rathfern, Rushpark and Whiteabbey.

Newtownabbey 2
2 Ballyearl Drive, New Mossley
Newtownabbey, BT36 5XJ
Email: newtownabbey2@nihe.gov.uk
Area Manager: Breige Mullaghan

Covers: Ballyclare, Ballyduff, Ballynure, Doagh, Glengormley, Glenvarna, Hyde Park, Jennings Estate, Kelburn Park, Monkstown, New Mossley, Oakview, Old Mossley, Parkmount, Queen's Avenue, Queen's Park and Roughfort.

Newtownards
28 Court Street
Newtownards, BT23 7NX
Email: newtownardsdistrict@nihe.gov.uk
Area Manager: Owen Brady

Covers: Ballydrain, Ballygowan, Ballyhalbert, Ballywalter, Bowtown, Carrowdore, Cloughey, Comber, Cottown, Donaghadee, Glen, Greyabbey, Killinchy, Kircubbin, Lisbarnett, Loughries, Millisle, Movilla, Portaferry, Portavogie, Scrabo and West Winds.

North Belfast
1-11 May Street
Belfast, BT1 4NA
Email: belfastnorth@nihe.gov.uk
Area Manager: Gerard Flynn

Covers: Ardavon Park, Ashfield, Carlisle, Carrick Hill, Duncairn Gardens, Dunmore, Fairhill, Fairknowne, Fortwilliam, Gainsborough Area, Glandore, Graymount, Gray's Lane, Mount Vernon, New Lodge Area, Parkmount Flats, Ross House Flats, Shore Crescent, Shore Road, Skegoneill, Whitewell, Antrim Road, Ardoyne, Ballysillan, Benview, Cavehill, Cliftondene, Cliftonville, Glenbank, Glenbryn, Hesketh, Ligoniel, Oldpark, Silverstream, Sunningdale, Torrens, Tyndale, Westland, Wheatfield.

Portadown
41 Thomas Street, Portadown, BT62 3AF
Email: portadown@nihe.gov.uk
Area Manager: Mark Ingham

Covers: Anville Crescent, Loughview Crescent, Maghery, Marion Avenue, Magown House, Obra Avenue, Portadown Estates, Portadown Rural, Robinstown and Tartaraghen.

South and East Belfast Area (Dundonald office)
30 Church Road
Dundonald, BT16 2LN
Email: sandebelfast@nihe.gov.uk
Area Manager: Carole Johnston

Covers: Annadale, Ardcarn, Ashfield, Belvoir, Braniel , Upper Castlereagh Road, Cherryvalley, Clarawood, Clonduff, Cregagh, Downshire, Dundela, Edenvale, Garnerville, Geary Road, Inverary, Knocknagoney, Milltown, Ravenhill, Rosebery, Rosewood Park, Summerhill, Sunderland Road, Sydenham, Tullycarnet, Vionville, Wandsworth, Willowfield, and Woodstock.

South & East Belfast Area (The Housing Centre)
The Housing Centre
1-11 May Street
Belfast, BT1 4NA
Tel: 03448 920 900
Email: fermanaghdistrict@nihe.gov.uk
Area Manager: Oonagh McAvinney

Covers: Arney, Ballinamallard, Belcoo, Bellanaleck, Belleek, Brookeborough, Clabby, Derrygonnelly, Derrylin, Donagh, Ederney, Enniskillen Estates, Florececourt, Garrison, Irvinestown, Kesh, Killadeas, Kinawley, Lack, Letterbreen, Lisbellaw, Lisnarick, Lisnaskea, Magheraveely, Maguiresbridge, Monea, Newtownbutler, Rosslea, Spingfield, Tamlaght, Tempo, and Trory.

South West Area (Omagh office)
MacAllister House, Woodside Avenue
Omagh, BT79 7BP
Email: omaghdistrict@nihe.gov.uk
Area Manager: Oonagh McAvinney

Covers: Beragh, Brookmount Road, Cannondale, Carrickmore, Castleview, Culmore/O'Kane Park, Derry Road, Dromore, Drumquin, Fintona, Fox Park, Gallows Hill, Glenhull, Gortin, Greencastle, Kevlin Road, Killyclogher, Kilskeery, Knockmoyle, Lammy, Lisanelly, Loughmacrory, Mountfield, Mountjoy, Mullaghmore, O'Brien Park, Rouskey, Shandon Park, Sixmilecross, Strathroy, Strule Park/Centenary Park and Trillick.

Strabane
40-46 Railway Street, Strabane, BT82 8EH
Email: strabane@nihe.gov.uk
Area Manager: Eddie Doherty

Covers: Alexander Place Lower, Ardmore, Ardstraw, Artigarvan, Ballycolman (old and new), Ballymagorry, Burdennett, Carlton Drive, Castlederg, Castletown, Churchtown, Clady, Cullion, Donemana, Douglas Bridge, Dublin Road, Erganagh, Fountain, Glebe, Killen, Killeter, Lisnafin Park, Magheramason, Main Street, Melmount Road, Millbrook Gardens, Newtown Place, Newtownkennedy, Newtownstewart, Plumbridge, Sion Mills, Spamount, Springhill Park and Urney Road.

Waterloo Place
Ulster Bank Buildings
Waterloo Place
Derry, BT48 6BS
Tel: 03448 920 900
Email: waterlooplace@nihe.gov.uk
Area Manager: Eddie Doherty

Covers: Academy Road, Bishop Street, Brandywell, Cloughglass, Creggan, Elmwood, Fountain, Foyle Road, Ivy Terrace, Lower Creggan, Maureen Avenue, Meenan Park, Nixon's Corner, Northland Road, Orchard Row, Rosemount and Rossville.

Waterside
2 Glendermott Road
Waterside
Derry, BT47 1AU
Tel: 03448 920 900
Email: waterside@nihe.gov.uk
Area Manager: Eddie Doherty

Covers: Altnagelvin, Ard Na Brocky, Ardmore, Caw, Claudy, Clooney, Currynierin, Fountain Hill, Drumahoe, Eglinton, Gobnascale, Hollymount Park, Irish Street (Lisnagelvin), Kilfennan, Knockdara, Lettershandoney, Maydown, Melvin Court, New Buildings Park, Rossdowney, Strathfoyle, Tullyalley and the Waterside Triangle.

West Belfast Area (Dairy Farm office)
Stewartstown Road, Belfast, BT17 0SB
Email: dairyfarm@nihe.gov.uk
Area Manager: Paddy Kelly

Covers: Andersonstown, Glen Road, Glencolin, Hannahstown, Lenadoon, Poleglass, Turf Lodge, Gortnamona, Twinbrook, Lagmore.

West Belfast Area (The Housing Centre)
The Housing Centre
1-11 May Street
Belfast
Co Antrim, BT1 4NA
Tel: 03448 920 900
Email: belfastwest@nihe.gov.uk
Area Manager: Paddy Kelly

Covers: Ardmoulin, Ballymurphy, Beechmount, Cavendish Street, Cluain Mor, Dermotthill, Divis, Falls Court, Clonard, Lower Falls, Gransha, John Street, Moyard, New Barnsley, Rockmount, Roden Street, Springfield Park, Lower Springfield, Lower Suffolk, Springhill, St. James, Westrock, Whiterock.

West Belfast Area (Shankill Office)
The Shankill Wellbeing Centre
83 Shankill Road
Belfast, BT13 1PD
Tel: 03448 920 900
Email: belfastshankill@nihe.gov.uk
Area Manager: Paddy Kelly

Covers: Ainsworth, Ballygomartin, Brown Square, Woodvale, Dover, Glencairn, Highfield, Glenbank, Lawnbrook, Lower Shankill, Springmartin, Tudor, Upper Woodvale.

Home Improvement Grant Offices
Tel: 03448 920 900

Belfast & South East Area Grants
4th Floor, The Housing Centre
2 Adelaide Street, Belfast
BT2 8PB
Email: belfast.grants@nihe.gov.uk
Manager: Tom Hall

Covers: Belfast City Council, Ards and North Down Borough Council, Lisburn and Castlereagh City Council areas.

Derry Grants
Richmond Chambers, The Diamond
Londonderry, BT48 6QP
Email: derry-londonderrygrants@nihe.gov.uk
Manager: PJ Mulrine

Covers: Derry and Strabane Council areas.

North East Grants
Twickenham House, Mount Street
Ballymena, BT43 6BP
Email: northeast.grants@nihe.gov.uk
Manager: Conor Bell

Covers: Antrim and Newtownabbey, Causeway Coast and Glens, Mid and East Antrim Council areas.

South Grants
35-45 Boat Street, Newry, BT34 2DB
Email: south.grants@nihe.gov.uk
Manager: Malcolm McKeown

Covers: Armagh, Banbridge and Craigavon & Newry, Mourne and Down Council areas.

West Grants
MacAllister House, Woodside Avenue
Omagh, BT79 7BP
Email: west.grants@nihe.gov.uk
Manager: PJ Mulrine

Covers: Cookstown, Dungannon, Omagh, Magherafelt Council areas.

West Grants – Sub Office
Riverview House, Head Street
Enniskillen, BT74 7DB
Email: west.grants@nihe.gov.uk
Manager: PJ Mulrine

Covers: Fermanagh Council area.

Accounts and Customer Service Units

Belfast Accounts Unit
1-11 May Street
Belfast, BT1 4NA
Email: belfast.publicsectoraccounts@nihe.gov.uk
Manager: Ciaran Stitt

Covers: West Belfast, East Belfast, South Belfast, North Belfast, Shankill and Lisburn areas.

North East Accounts Unit
Twickenham House
Mount Street
Ballymena
Co Antrim, BT43 6BP
Tel: 03448 920 900
Email: northeastarea.accounts@nihe.gov.uk
Manager: Brendan Doherty

Covers: Antrim, Ballycastle, Ballymoney, Ballymena, Carrickfergus, Coleraine, Larne and Newtownabbey 1 & 2 Districts.

Omagh Accounts Unit
MacAllister House
Woodside Avenue
Omagh
Co Tyrone, BT79 7BP
Tel: 03448 920 900
Email: omagh.servicecentre@nihe.gov.uk
Accounts Manager: Christine Marks

Covers: Cookstown, Omagh, Fermanagh and Dungannon Districts.

South Accounts Unit
6th Floor
Marlborough House
Central Way, Craigavon
BT64 1AJ
Tel: 03448 920 900
Email: southaccounts@nihe.gov.uk
Rent Accounting Manager: Christine Marks

Covers: Banbridge, Armagh, Lurgan, Newry and Portadown Districts.

South Customer Services Unit
Strangford House
28 Court Street
Newtownards, BT23 7NX
Tel: 03448 920 900
Email: southeastarea.accounts@nihe.gov.uk
Manager: Danny Simpson

Covers: Ards, Castlereagh, Down and North Down Districts.

South East Accounts Unit
Strangford House
28 Court Street
Newtownards, BT23 7NX
Tel: 03448 920 900
Email: southeastarea.accounts@nihe.gov.uk
Manager: Christine Marks

West CSU & Accounts Unit
Richmond Chambers
The Diamond
Derry, BT48 6QP
Tel: 03448 920 900
Email: westareaaccounts@nihe.gov.uk
Manager: Kevin McDowell

Covers: Derry, Magherafelt, Limavady and Strabane Districts.

Housing in Multiple Occupation (HMO) Office
The Housing Centre, 2 Adelaide Street
Belfast, BT2 8PB
Tel: 03448 920 900
Email: hmo.belfast@nihe.gov.uk
Manager: Kevin Bloomfield

Regional HMO Office
19 Abbey Street, Coleraine, BT52 1DU
Tel: 03448 920 900
Email: hmo.coleraine@nihe.gov.uk
Manager: Kevin Bloomfield

Emergency Repairs
Tel: 03448 920 901

Homelessness
Tel: 03448 920 900

Out of hours service
Tel: 03448 920 908

Rent Officer for Northern Ireland
Level 3
Causeway Exchange
1-7 Bedford Street
Belfast
BT2 7EG
Tel: 028 9051 5258
Email: info@rentofficer-ni.gov.uk

The Rent Officer is an independent public appointment responsible for determining the status of a tenancy. If a tenancy is subject to rent control, he or she determines the appropriate rent and also maintains the public register of controlled rents.

Northern Ireland Housing Council
The Housing Centre, 2 Adelaide Street
Belfast, BT2 6PB
Tel: 028 9024 0588
Web: www.nihousingcouncil.org
Email: info@nihousingcouncil.org

The Housing Council currently has one councillor from each local authority in Northern Ireland. The Housing Executive consults the council on all issues relating to housing policy. In addition, four members of the Housing Council are appointed to sit on the board of the Housing Executive.

Members
Chair: Alderman Tommy Nicholl, Mid and East Antrim Borough Council
Alderman Allan Bresland, Derry City and Strabane District Council
Councillor Mark Cooper, Antrim and Newtownabbey Borough Council
Councillor Catherine Elattar, Mid Ulster Council
Councillor Anne Marie Fitzgerald, Fermanagh and Omagh District Council
Alderman John Finlay, Causeway Coast and Glens Borough Council
Alderman Amanda Grehan, Lisburn and Castlereagh City Council
Councillor Michelle Kelly, Belfast City Council
Councillor Nick Mathison, Ards and North Down Borough Council
Alderman Jim Speers, Armagh, Banbridge and Craigavon Borough Council
Councillor Michael Ruane, Newry, Mourne and Down District Council

Housing associations

Northern Ireland Federation of Housing Associations (NIFHA)
6C Citylink Business Park
Albert Street
Belfast, BT12 4HQ
Tel: 028 9023 0446
Web: www.nifha.org
Email: info@nifha.org
Chief Executive: Ben Collins

NIFHA is the umbrella organisation promoting, representing and supporting the activities of registered and non-registered housing associations in Northern Ireland.

Non-registered associations are members who provide housing but are not registered housing associations with DfC and therefore do not receive DfC funding.

Housing

Housing associations A-Z

Abbeyfield and Wesley Housing Association
2 Wesley Court
Carrickfergus, BT38 8HS
Tel: 028 9336 3558
Web: www.abbeyfieldandwesley.org.uk
Email: info@abbeyfieldandwesley.org.uk
Chief Executive: Geraldine Gilpin

Abbeyfield Belfast Housing Society*
Agapé Centre
238-266 Lisburn Road
Belfast, BT9 6GF
Tel: 028 9038 1332
Web: www.abbeyfieldbelfast.org.uk
Email: admin@abbeyfieldbelfast.co.uk

Alpha Housing (NI) Ltd
6 Edgewater Road, Belfast, BT3 9JQ
Tel: 028 9078 7750
Web: www.alphahousingni.org
Email: info@alphahousingni.org

Apex Housing Group
10 Butcher Street
Derry, BT48 6HL
Tel: 028 7130 4800
Web: www.apex.org.uk
Email: info@apexhousing.org.uk
Chief Executive: Sheena McCallion

Arbour Housing
18-22 Carleton Street
Portadown, BT62 3NE
Tel: 028 3833 9795
Web: www.arbourhousing.org
Email: housing@arbourhousing.org
Chief Executive: Kieran Matthews

Ark Housing Association
Unit 1, Hawthorn Office Park
43 Stockmans Way
Belfast, BT9 7ET
Tel: 028 9075 2310
Web: www.arkhousing.co.uk
Email: info@arkhousing.co.uk
Chief Executive: Jim McShane

Choice Housing Ireland
Leslie Morrell House
37-41 May Street, Belfast, BT1 4DN
Tel: 0300 111 2211
Web: www.choice-housing.org
Email: enquiries@choice-housing.org
Chief Executive: Michael McDonnell

Clanmil Housing Association
Northern Whig House
3 Waring Street
Belfast, BT1 2DX
Tel: 028 9087 6000
Web: www.clanmil.org
Email: housing@clanmil.org.uk
Chief Executive: Clare McCarty

Connswater Homes
Unit 5, Citylink Business Park
Albert Street, Belfast, BT12 4HQ
Tel: 028 9065 6155
Web: www.connswater.org.uk
Email: housing@connswater.org.uk
Chief Executive: Jacqueline Locke

Co-Ownership Housing
Moneda House
25-27 Wellington Place
Belfast, BT1 6GD
Tel: 028 9032 7276
Web: www.co-ownership.org
Email: hello@co-ownership.org
Chief Executive: Mark Graham

Grove Housing Association Ltd
171 York Road, Belfast, BT15 3HB
Tel: 028 9077 3330
Web: www.groveha.org.uk
Email: info@groveha.org.uk
General Manager: Agnes Crawford

Habinteg Housing Association (Ulster) Ltd
Alex Moira House, 22 Hibernia Street
Holywood, BT18 9JE
Tel: 028 9042 7211
Web: www.habinteg-ulster.co.uk
Email: info@habinteg-ulster.co.uk
Chief Executive: Darren McKinney

Habitat for Humanity Northern Ireland*
The Riverside Centre
Lisburn, BT27 5EA
Tel: 028 9263 5635
Web: www.habitatni.co.uk
Email: info@habitatni.co.uk
Chief Executive: Jenny Williams

Newington Housing Association Ltd
63-75 Duncairn Gardens
Belfast, BT15 2GB
Tel: 028 9074 4055
Web: www.newingtonha.co.uk
Email: admin@newingtonha.co.uk
Chief Executive: Anthony Kerr

NB Housing Association
Gatelodge, 8 Flax Street
Belfast, BT14 7EQ
Tel: 028 9059 2110
Web: www.nb-housing.org
Email: info@nb-housing.org

Radius Housing
38-52 Lisburn Road
Belfast, BT9 6AA
Tel: 0300 123 0888
Web: www.radiushousing.org
Email: info@radiushousing.org
Chief Executive: John McLean

Rural Housing Association Ltd
2 Killyclogher Road
Omagh, BT79 0AX
Tel: 028 8224 6118
Web: www.ruralhousing.co.uk
Email: info@ruralhousing.co.uk
Chief Executive: Stephen Fisher

St Matthew's Housing Association Ltd
58 Harper Street, Belfast
BT5 4EN
Tel: 028 9045 1070
Web: www.smha.co.uk
Email: office@smha.co.uk
Chief Executive: Jim Black

Threshold*
432 Antrim Road, Belfast
BT15 5GB
Tel: 028 9087 1313
Web: www.threshold-services.co.uk
Email: bernie.ross@threshold-services.co.uk
Chief Executive: Raman Kapur

Triangle Housing Association Ltd
60 Eastermeade Gardens
Ballymoney, BT53 6BD
Tel: 028 2766 6880
Web: www.trianglehousing.org.uk
Email: info@trianglehousing.org.uk
Chief Executive: Chris Alexander

*non-registered association

Northern Ireland Yearbook

Education and Skills

Credit: Queen's University Belfast

Education in Northern Ireland

Stages

Children in Northern Ireland are legally obliged to attend school between the ages of four and 16. They may continue their schooling for a further two years, but this is not compulsory. The maximum upper school leaving age is 19.

Pre-school education is non-compulsory and caters for children in the year immediately before they enter the first school year (Primary 1). It is provided through nursery schools, nursery and reception classes in primary schools, and places in voluntary and private pre-school education centres.

The Northern Ireland Curriculum is taught at primary and secondary level and requires schools to:

- promote the spiritual, emotional, moral, cultural, intellectual and physical development of pupils at the school and thereby of society; and
- prepare such pupils for the opportunities, responsibilities and experiences of life by equipping them with appropriate knowledge, understanding and skills.

A revised curriculum that applies to all 12 years of compulsory education, provided by the Education (Northern Ireland) Order 2006, was introduced in schools on a phased basis from September 2007 and was fully implemented in the 2009-2010 academic year. It provides a more flexible framework for teaching and learning and has a greater focus on developing skills for life after school.

The revised curriculum includes a Foundation Stage to cover Primary 1 and 2. Key Stage 1 now covers Primary 3 and 4 and Key Stage 2 remains as Primary 5, 6 and 7. At post-primary, Key Stage 3 remains as Years 8, 9 and 10 and Key Stage 4 Years 11 and 12.

Primary education in Northern Ireland is geared towards the completion of the first three stages of the curriculum: Foundation Stage (years 1 to 2); Key Stage 1 (years 3 to 4); and Key Stage 2 (years 5 to 7).

At Foundation Stage, the curriculum is as follows:

- language and literacy – talking and listening, reading, writing;
- mathematics and numeracy – number, measures, shape and space, sorting, patterns and relationships;
- the arts – art and design, music, drama;
- the world around us;
- communication;
- ICT;
- thinking skills and personal capabilities;
- personal development and mutual understanding – personal understanding and health, mutual understanding in the local and wider community;
- physical development and movement; and
- religious education.

Education continues at Key Stages 1 and 2, within the following areas of learning:

- language and literacy – talking and listening, reading, writing;
- mathematics and numeracy – processes in mathematics, number, measures, shape and space, handling data;
- communications;
- ICT;
- thinking skills and personal capabilities;
- the arts – art and design, music, drama;
- the world around us – history, geography, science and technology;
- personal development and mutual understanding – to become independent and responsible citizens, mutual understanding in the local and wider community;
- physical education; and
- religious education.

Queen's University awarded Silver Diversity Mark accreditation

(L-R): Professor Karen McCloskey, Director of Queen's Gender Initiative; Conor Curran, Head of Diversity and Inclusion, Queen's University Belfast; Joanne Clague, Registrar and Chief Operating Officer of Queen's University Belfast; Nuala Murphy, Interim Head of Business, Diversity Mark NI; Alistair Finlay, Interim Director of Human Resources, Queen's University Belfast; and Professor Margaret Topping, Pro-Vice-Chancellor for Internationalisation, Queen's University Belfast.

Recognising diversity in the workplace is a key element of all forward thinking, inclusive organisations.

Queen's University Belfast is one of only 10 organisations in Northern Ireland to be awarded a Silver Diversity Mark recognising its progress in advancing gender, race and disability equality and its ambitious plans in this space.

The Diversity Mark accreditation is awarded to organisations following an independent assessment process which ensures they have reached the required standard of commitment to advancing diversity and inclusion. It is also a visible acknowledgement of an organisation's commitment to building and supporting a more diverse and inclusive workplace for all employees.

Queen's Vice-Chancellor, Professor Ian Greer, says the university is committed to ensuring it is a welcoming and inclusive place for staff, students and visitors: "We are extremely proud of the diversity of our staff, students and community and of the work that continues to be done by them to embed equality, diversity and inclusivity at our university.

"Our 2030 strategy places significant emphasis on the importance of equality, diversity and inclusion. It resonates with our students, our staff and our focus on internationalisation, positive culture change and sustainability.

"This award will also ensure that we continue to hold ourselves to a high standard of achievement in this important area and continue to attract the students and staff from around the world to study, research, work and live in Belfast."

Professor Karen McCloskey, Director of Queen's Gender Initiative, adds: "The silver accreditation reflects significant progress since the University was awarded bronze almost three years ago. This award not only reflects the progress made at Queen's on gender, race, and disability equality, but also recognises our ambitious plans to do more in these spaces.

"To maintain the Silver Diversity Mark, Queen's will report annually on the initiatives we are delivering to drive forward further progress and meet agreed targets."

Conor Curran, Head of Diversity and Inclusion, explains: "We are delighted to be one of only 10 employers in Northern Ireland to have achieved Silver Award status now.

"It reflects the significant progress which has been made since we were awarded bronze almost three years ago, and the important work by carried out by many colleagues on campus, in various faculties, schools and directorates.

"It also gives us added determination to push on and address many other equality and diversity issues over the next few years."

Interim Head of Business, Diversity Mark, Nuala Murphy, says: "We are delighted that Queen's University Belfast have been awarded the Silver Diversity Mark in recognition of their progress and ongoing commitment to diversity and inclusion and we congratulate all the team on this very significant achievement.

"The independent assessment panel noted their submission included many considerable strengths and evidenced an ambition in the organisation to strive for further excellence in diversity and inclusion.

"We look forward to them continuing their progressive and innovative initiatives moving forward."

Further information at www.qub.ac.uk

QUEEN'S UNIVERSITY BELFAST

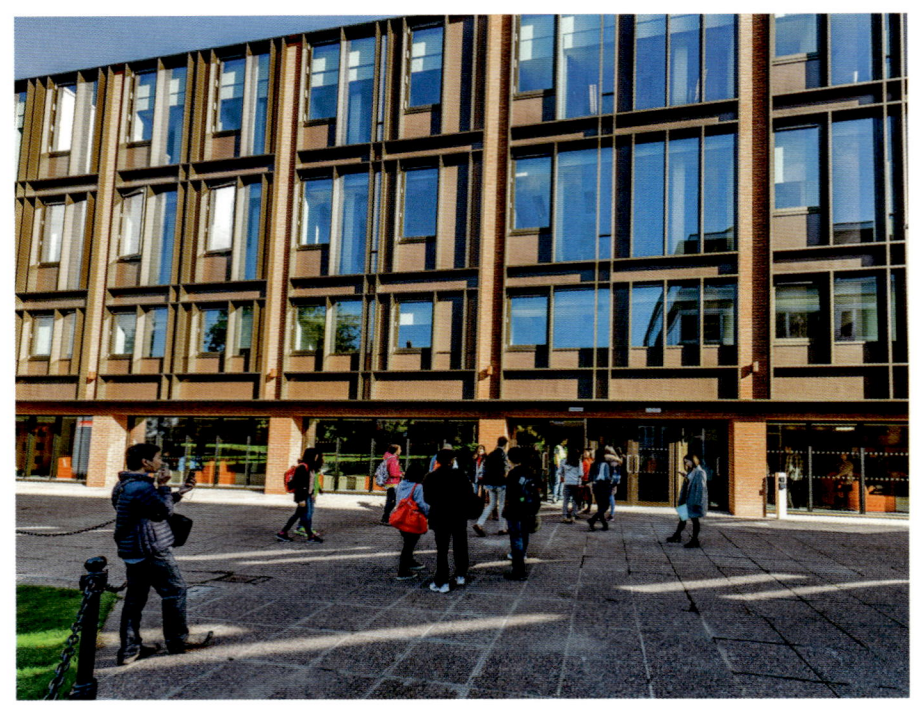

Education and Skills | Northern Ireland Yearbook

Credit: Queen's University Belfast.

Transfer to secondary school

The official transfer test exam, commonly known as the 11-plus, a component of academic selection, was last sat in November 2008, for transfer in September 2009. The Department of Education then recommended that academic criteria should not be used when transferring Primary 7 children to post-primary schools. Instead, it listed non-academic criteria which can be used to admit children. The first criterion is entitlement to free school meals, with the number of admissions matching the number of applications from children in that category.

Other recommended criteria, in no order, are whether:

- the child's sibling attends the post-primary school;
- the child is the eldest child in their family;
- the child is from a named feeder primary school;
- the child lives within a defined catchment area or parish; and
- the school is nearest to the child's place of residence.

Random selection is recommended as a tie-breaker. The post-primary transfer system is unregulated as schools are not obliged to follow the departmental guidance. Grammar schools have instead used independent entrance tests. These tests are commissioned by the Association for Quality Education (AQE) and the Post-Primary Transfer Consortium (PPTC); the latter group mostly consists of Catholic grammar schools. While both tests are based on Key Stage 2 maths and English, they are not regulated and the tests differ in structure, style and format.

In September 2016, then Minister for Education, Peter Weir MLA, released revised guidance on transfer, reversing the previous policy on preventing primary schools from facilitating unregulated tests.

Secondary education

Secondary education covers Key Stage 3 (years 8 to 10) and Key Stage 4 (years 11 to 12) of the curriculum. The revised post-primary curriculum includes a dedicated area for learning which includes the following contributory subject strands: Learning for Life and Work, made up of employability, personal development, local and global citizenship and home economics (at Key Stage 3). In addition, it incorporates the following areas of learning:

- language and literacy – English, Irish (in Irish-speaking schools), media education;
- mathematics and numeracy – problem solving, financial capability;
- modern languages – any official language of the European Union (other than English and, in Irish-speaking schools, Irish);
- the arts – art and design, music, drama;
- environment and society – history, geography;
- learning for life and work;
- physical education;
- communications;
- ICT;
- thinking skills and personal capabilities;
- planning for skills;
- science and technology – science, technology and design; and
- religious education.

At Key Stage 4, the statutory requirements have been reduced to provide greater choice and flexibility for pupils and will enable them to access the wider range of opportunities schools will have to provide through the Curriculum Entitlement Framework. The broad areas of learning are:

- language and literacy;
- mathematics and numeracy;
- modern languages;
- the arts;
- communications;
- ICT;
- other skills;
- environment and society;
- science and technology;
- learning for life and work – employability, local and global citizenship, personal development;
- physical education; and
- religious education.

Across each area of learning, children develop the skills and capabilities – cross-curricular skills, thinking skills and personal capabilities – for life-long learning and for effective contributions to society:

Cross-curricular skills

- communication;
- using mathematics; and
- using ICT.

CITB NI: Improving training and skills within the local construction industry

CITB NI Chief Executive Barry Neilson.

The construction industry is a resilient one, despite the restrictions in place, the pressures of the pandemic and impact of Brexit, the industry kept moving forward over the past year and continued to train and support their workforce, writes Barry Neilson, Chief Executive CITB NI.

With recent research published by the Construction Skills Network predicting a steady recovery within Northern Ireland (3.9 per cent over the next five years) and an increase in recruitment by 1,000 new workers each year over the period to meet the increase in activity within Northern Ireland, CITB NI continued to help, support and guide construction employers to train and invest in skills.

CITB NI finished the 2020-2021 year having delivered £1.3 million in direct grant support to industry. The CITB NI Grant scheme and training programmes are widely recognised within the industry, and are not limited to only construction trades. Registered employers are encouraged to make use of the grant scheme to help improve skills within their workforce.

Throughout 2021, CITB NI delivered a series of initiatives to help further support the industry. With a focus on apprenticeship recruitment and funded by the Department for the Economy, CITB NI launched a new scheme called Apprenticeship Connect (NI) which helped match construction employers and prospective craft apprentices. A media campaign supported the scheme with 25 employers providing 45 opportunities across nine occupations.

It has been recognised amongst industry bodies that mental health is a significant and ongoing issue within the industry. As part of our Training in Partnership programme a series of mental health and wellbeing training courses were launched aimed at helping employers to minimise stress and support employees.

CITB NI will continue to promote construction to the younger generation, help them consider the varied pathways within the industry as well as being a serious career option for the future. Following the launch of the Annual CITB NI Built Environment Student Bursary Award last year 12 students, who commenced and completed their first year of a full-time 3rd level Built Environment related construction qualification with a local training provider, were awarded a £1,000 bursary.

Skills competitions remain a focus for CITB NI and it hosts the annual Skillbuild NI Finals each year. SkillBuild NI is a great opportunity to showcase and celebrate the high level of skills within our college and training network. The competition has been heavily disrupted by Covid-19 but plans are in place to host the 2022 finals in May.

Looking towards the future, CITB NI will continue to follow the strategic road map published in recent years, under our themes to benefit the Industry Training Hub, Quality Standards, Partnership Work, Commercial Opportunities and Embracing Innovation, as well as continuing to focus on supporting training to rebuild and recover.

For further information on what we can do to help you and your construction training log on to www.citbni.org.uk, like us on Facebook http://www.facebook.com/CITBNorthernIreland or follow the discussion on Twitter @CITBNI, Instagram @citbni1 and LinkedIn http://linkd.in/1GBeyLf

CITB NI
Nutts Corner Training Centre
17 Dundrod Road
Crumlin, Co Antrim, BT29 4SR
T: 028 90825 466
E: info@citbni.org.uk

Education and Skills | Northern Ireland Yearbook

Other skills

- being creative;
- working with others;
- self-management;
- managing information; and
- thinking, problem-solving and decision-making.

Following Key Stage 4, pupils can undertake advanced subsidiary (AS) and advanced (A) levels after completing GCSEs. Study takes place in years 13 and 14 at schools which offer those qualifications. The AS-level is a standalone qualification and is worth half a full A-level.

The Curriculum is designed to provide a flexible framework for teaching and learning. The core syllabus for religious education at all levels is drafted by the four main churches – Catholic, Presbyterian, Church of Ireland and Methodist – and specified by the Department of Education.

Assessment for learning takes place up to Key Stage 3 inclusive. This concept places an emphasis on improvement, raising achievement in pupils' learning and celebrating success. Teachers are required to assess levels of progression in communication, mathematics and ICT skills in Key Stages 1-3.

Primary school teachers for Years 4 to 7 assess pupils' literacy and numeracy skills through computer-based assessments. These take place in the autumn term (September to December).

English, mathematics and science tests at the end of Key Stage 3 are available from the Council for the Curriculum, Examinations and Assessment, to corroborate the results of teacher assessment, but these have not been compulsory since 2006-2007.

From September 2017, post-primary schools must offer pupils a minimum of 21 courses at Key Stage 4 and 27 at the post-16 level. At least one third of these courses should be general and at least one third applied. General courses develop knowledge, understanding and skills within a subject. Applied courses develop knowledge, understanding and skills in relation to employment.

Schools are required to report to parents on a child's progress, using clear and meaningful information.

The Department of Education

Most education matters are devolved and fall within the remit of the Northern Ireland Assembly, although the province also follows UK-wide frameworks on issues such as qualifications and child protection.

The Department of Education (DE) is responsible for the central administration of nursery, primary, secondary and special education, and related services. Its remit also covers youth policy (up to the age of 19), the promotion of community relations within and between schools, and teachers' pay and pensions.

Further and higher education is covered by the Department for the Economy, while the Department for Communities is responsible for library policy. The Department of Education also includes the Education and Training Inspectorate (ETINI), which inspects all education services in Northern Ireland and is independent of all service users and providers.

Sectors

The education system in Northern Ireland is complex and divided between a number of sectors which differ according to their school management. All grant-aided schools are funded under the common funding formula.

Controlled schools are under the management of the Education Authority.

Some controlled schools were originally Church schools and were transferred to state control. The main Protestant churches – Presbyterian, Church of Ireland and Methodist – are known as 'transferors' and are represented on the boards of governors of controlled schools.

Number of pupils by school type

	2015/16	2016/17	2017/18	2018/19	2019/20	2020/21	2021/22
Nursery schools							
Full-time	4,011	3,955	3,944	3,930	3,934	3,935	3,930
Part-time	1,893	1,909	1,894	1,902	1,890	1,900	1,866
Nursery classes (primary school)							
Full-time	5,195	5,174	5,146	5,194	5,163	5,121	5,188
Part-time	4,117	4,292	4,377	4,360	4,508	4,152	4,479
Primary schools							
Reception	241	224	186	168	184	180	151
Years 1–7	166,912	169,908	172,035	172,863	172,255	171,7076	170,793
Preparatory	1,757	1,704	1,710	1,660	1,601	1,560	1,530
Post-primary schools							
Secondary (non-grammar)	77,753	77,432	77,727	79,377	81,662	84,520	85,594
Grammar	63,359	62,981	62,818	62,862	63,423	64,398	65,314
Other							
Special	5,173	5,407	5,735	5,959	6,174	6,403	6,653
Independent	658	514	604	611	608	625	716
Total (all schools) and pre-school education centres	339,785	341,771	344,178	364,979	349,536	352,364	354,528

Source: Department of Education

Northern Ireland Yearbook | Education and Skills

Integrated schools bring children and staff from Catholic and Protestant traditions, as well as those of other faiths, or none, together in one school. There are currently 65 grant-aided integrated schools in Northern Ireland, made up of 38 grant-maintained integrated schools and 27 controlled integrated schools. There are nearly 24,200 pupils enrolled in integrated schools – 10,640 in primary schools and nearly 13,500 in post-primary schools. The number enrolled has increased by 600 pupils compared to the previous year, and over 2,800 pupils compared to five years ago.

Controlled integrated schools are controlled schools which have been granted integrated status as they have a significant enrolment from the minority community in their area.

Grant-maintained integrated schools are managed by boards of governors which include parents who have sought to establish the school i.e. 'foundation parents'. They are funded by the Department and their boards employ all staff in each school. These schools have more autonomy than controlled integrated schools.

Other maintained schools fall outside the controlled, integrated and Catholic maintained school categories. They are mostly Irish medium schools. A small number of schools which are linked to the Protestant churches and have opted not to be transferred are also maintained.

Voluntary grammar schools are managed by boards of governors which include their trustees or representatives of their original founders and have more autonomy than controlled grammar schools. Voluntary schools are funded by the department and their boards of governors employ all staff in each school.

Most voluntary grammar schools are owned by the Catholic Church and their trustees are therefore the Catholic bishops. A number of other schools in this sector were founded by other interests and include their representatives on their boards of governors.

Maintained schools are linked to the Catholic Church and include representatives of the Catholic bishops (trustees) on their boards of governors.

Independent schools include the independent Christian schools, which do not seek public funds so they can maintain their own curriculum.

Others include schools, especially in the Irish medium and integrated sectors, which are seeking but which have not yet received public funds. There is also one independent school in the public school tradition: Rockport School in Holywood, County Down. The Belfast Hospital School caters for children aged 4-18 in hospitals, an education centre for post-primary pupils, and through home tuition. Northern Ireland also has 39 special schools which serve children with special educational needs.

Schools

The overall percentage of children entitled to free school meals has remained steady at 28.4 per cent in 2020/21. This 28.4 per cent equates to over 97,500 free school meal entitled pupils in nursery, primary, post-primary and special schools.

In terms of ethnical diversity in schools, there are approximately 18,500 pupils in Northern Ireland in 2020/21 recorded as "non-white", and this represents 5.2 per cent of the school population. This is an increase of almost 6,000 pupils and 1.5 percentage points compared to five years prior.

There is also a rise year-on-year in the number of pupils whose first language is not English (an increase of over 1,000 from last year). In 2020/21, there are approximately 89 first languages spoken by pupils, with Polish and Lithuanian being the most common behind English.

Covid-19 and education

The Covid-19 pandemic has impacted schools since the first lockdown in March 2020 saw remote learning introduced. Since then, there have been spells of classroom learning and remote learning depending on the current Government guidance. In January 2021 post-primary transfer tests in Northern Ireland were cancelled just four days before thousands of pupils were due to sit the first of a series of exams. Summer exams for GCSEs, AS and A-Levels did not take place in spring 2021.

Education administration

The Education Authority (EA) was established on 1 April 2015 and replaced the previous five Education and Library Boards and the Staff Commission for Education and Library Boards. The EA has responsibility for education, youth and library services throughout Northern Ireland with a headquarters and five regional offices. It is a non-departmental body sponsored by the Department of Education.

The EA employs over 39,000 people across Northern Ireland in a wide variety of roles. This includes teachers in controlled schools, school-based support staff and staff in administrative headquarters.

Currently there is no change to how services are provided. The five regional offices are located at the sites of the former education and library boards and continue to deliver the same services as the former boards within their geographic areas. A significant change programme to harmonise policies and the delivery of services in the new organisation is under way and will continue for a number of years.

Responsibility for public libraries was transferred to Libraries NI in April 2009, although the Education Authority remains responsible for school libraries. Libraries NI is accountable to the Department for Communities.

The education and library boards were to be replaced by the Education and Skills Authority (ESA) in January 2010 and a Bill to establish the ESA was brought before the Assembly in October 2012 but, in the absence of political agreement, the then Education Minister John O'Dowd decided in May 2014 not to proceed further.

The Executive then agreed in September 2014 to merge the existing transitional education and library boards (and the Staff Commission for the boards) into the Education Authority.

Sectoral bodies will represent the interests of the controlled, maintained, integrated and Irish medium sectors. The existing sectoral bodies are the Council for Catholic Maintained Schools (CCMS), Northern Ireland Council for Integrated Education

Continues on page 218

Educational overview 2021

Amid two years of disrupted learning, agendaNi provides a broad overview of the state of play in education.

Appointed June 2021, Michelle McIlveen MLA was chosen by short-lived DUP leader Edwin Poots MLA to replace Peter Weir MLA as Minister for Education. A former teacher of history and politics, McIlveen has previously served as a Junior Minister, Minister for Regional Development, and Minister of Agriculture, Environment and Rural Affairs.

Budget

Totalling £2,323 million, the Department of Education's opening resource budget for 2021/2022 is broken down as:

- £2,083 million in funding for schools and students;
- £97.6 million for Education Authority earmarked budgets;
- £27.6 million for other non-departmental public bodies;
- £10.9 million for other education services (including funding for third-party organisations);
- £32.8 million for Early Years Provision;
- £33.5 million for youth (mainly comprising mainly budgets for the Education Authority's Youth Services Programme);
- £32.7 million on Department of Education costs;
- £4.8 million for NDNA commitments; and
- £103.3 million in Covid-19 funding commitments.

Programme for Government 2021 (draft)

A public consultation on the Programme for Government (PfG) draft Outcomes Framework 2021 ran from late January to late March 2021. The first of nine strategic framework outcomes contained within the draft is 'Our children and young people have the best start in life'.

Acknowledging the correlation between early life experiences and future health and wellbeing, this outcome focuses on "ensuring all out children and young people grow up in a society which provides the support they need to achieve their potential".

For children and young people, the PfG states, this is about providing access to high quality education and instilling skills to facilitate better life choices, while also ensuring "good health, quality physical environments with space to play, opportunities for cultural and artistic expression and to make a positive contribution to society, and protection from violence and harm".

Key priority areas across this outcome, therefore, include:

- access to education;
- capability and resilience;
- care;
- early years; and
- skills and attainment.

216   ◂········ **Education and skills**

Northern Ireland Yearbook | Education and Skills

Within access to education, objectives include mitigating resourcing pressures, adopting a strategic approach to planning, and "supporting our education sector, including integrated and shared education".

Similarly, within the skills and attainment priority, aims include delivering a high-quality curriculum, enhancing careers advice delivery, improving educational attainment and opportunities, tackling persistent underachievement, and facilitating access to the curricula for children with additional needs, such as those with special educational needs and newcomer children whose first language is not English.

Free School Meals

As identified in *A Fair Start*, statistics indicate that in each school, further education, and higher education, "boys, especially those entitled to Free School Meals (FSME) from both sides of the community divide, are underachieving".

A total of 28.4 per cent of all pupils, or 97,631 students were entitled to free school meals, with almost three-quarters availing of them on school meal census day 2020/2021.

According to School Leavers Data for 2019/2020, only 50.5 per cent of male school leavers entitled to free school meals achieved >5 GCSEs at A* to C, including maths and English, while 60.9 per cent of their female counterparts did likewise. Overall, significantly fewer school leavers entitled to free school meals (55.7 per cent) achieved >5 GCSEs at A* to C, including maths and English when compared with the average for all school leavers (76.2 per cent).

Destinations of school leavers

In 2019/2020, a majority of school leavers entered into higher (47.9 per cent) or further education (29.2 per cent). A further 8.7 per cent entered employment and 9.5 per cent went into training. However, 2.8 per cent entered unemployment and the destinations of an additional 2.0 per cent is unknown.

Teacher workforce

Teacher workforce statistics published by the Department of Education and NISRA for 2020/2021 indicate that there are 20,410 teachers in Northern Ireland, 16,374 are full-time and 4,036 are part-time. This represents an increase of 506 teachers when compared with 2019/2020. Overall, 77.2 per cent of teachers are female.

A Fair Start

Following the *New Decade, New Approach* agreement, in July 2020, then Education Minister Peter Weir appointed an Expert Panel on Educational Underachievement to explore examine the correlation between socioeconomic disadvantage and educational underachievement. The independent panel was tasked with proposing recommendations as well as a costed action plan.

In May 2021, *A Fair Start*, the final report and action plan of the Expert Panel was submitted to the Education Minister and subsequently endorsed by the Executive. The panel's objectives were to:

- explore correlation between persistent educational underachievement and socio-economic background;
- examine the "long-standing issues facing working-class, Protestant boys", and produce specific actions to alleviate these;
- publish an interim report;
- create an action plan for change to "ensure all children and young people, regardless of background are given the best start in life"; and
- estimate the cost of action plan implementation.

Having conducted its work between September 2020 and May 2021, the final report is unambiguous in determining: "There has been almost unanimous agreement that addressing educational underachievement brought about as a consequence of social-economic disadvantage is wider than education alone and if we are serious about wanting to see fundamental change for the benefit of our most disadvantaged, everyone in Northern Ireland must prioritise education and learning as the route out of poverty."

Reflecting on the written and oral evidence it received, the panel allocated actions across eight key areas.

£2,323 million

The Department's opening resource budget for 2021/2022

These are:

1. Redirecting the focus to Early Years.
2. Championing emotional health and wellbeing.
3. Ensuring the relevance and appropriateness of curriculum and assessment.
4. Promoting a whole community approach to education.
5. Maximising boys' potential.
6. Driving forward Teachers' Professional Learning (TPL).
7. Supporting the professional learning and wellbeing of school leadership.
8. Ensuring Interdepartmental collaboration and delivery.

Replete with 47 cross-departmental actions across each of these eight areas, *A Fair Start* asserts: "We believe the actions set out in this Action Plan are capable of making a significant, long-lasting impact on children's learning now and for the foreseeable future however, this can only be achieved if we invest appropriately and significantly in education for the long-term."

Welcoming the final report, Weir thanked the panel chair and members, outlining: "Educational underachievement is an area of policy which many have endeavoured over recent years to change, but despite numerous policy interventions and significant financial investment, it has remained stubbornly entrenched… No child should suffer the burden of circumstance in determining his or her outcomes. The Northern Ireland Executive has considered and endorsed *A Fair Start Final Report* and *Action Plan* with the expectation that budget will be considered at the appropriate time. This will not be an easy task and there will be many competing priorities."

Education and Skills | Northern Ireland Yearbook

Credit: Queen's University Belfast.

(NICIE) and Comhairle na Gaelscolaíochta (CnaG). In September 2016, a new Controlled Schools' Support Council (CSSC) was established.

The integrated and Irish medium sectors are supported by two trust funds i.e. the Integrated Education Fund (IEF) and Iontaobhas na Gaelscolaíochta (InaG).

Ownership of maintained and voluntary schools remains with their trustees while the ownership of controlled schools transferred to the Education Authority. The employing authorities for staff is now the Education Authority (for controlled and controlled integrated schools), the CCMS and the boards of governors of grant maintained integrated schools.

The Education and Training Inspectorate and the General Teaching Council for Northern Ireland, which registers teachers and advises government on the profession, will remain independent.

In December 2015, it was announced that the Education Authority was to take over all youth services funded by the department as the Youth Council of Northern Ireland was abolished. The Department of Education remains responsible for overall strategy and policy.

Further and higher education

There are six further education (FE) colleges, and three universities: Queen's University Belfast, The Open University and Ulster University, split between campuses at Jordanstown, Coleraine, Derry and Belfast. Teacher training is delivered via two university colleges: Stranmillis University College and St Mary's University College. The College of Agriculture, Food and Rural Enterprise provides further and higher courses for the agri-food industry.

Agencies and organisations in education

Department of Education

Rathgael House
Balloo Road, Bangor, BT19 7PR
Tel: 028 9127 9279
Web: www.education-ni.gov.uk
Email: de.dewebmail@education-ni.gov.uk

Minister: Michelle McIlveen MLA
Permanent Secretary: Mark Browne
Deputy Secretaries: Fiona Hepper; John Smith; Lianne Patterson
Chief Inspector of Education and Training Inspectorate: Faustina Graham

Education Authority

40 Academy Street
Belfast, BT1 2NQ
Tel: 028 9056 4000
Web: www.eani.org.uk
Email: info@eani.org.uk

Board: Amanda Adams; Frances Boyd; David Cargo; Patricia Carville; Jonathan Craig; Giovanni Doran; Ronnie Hassard; Robert Herron; Maurice Johnston; Paul Kavanagh; Sarah Kelly; Gerry Lundy; Frank Maskey; Nelson McCausland; Gillian McGrath; Andy McMorran; Barry Mulholland (Chair); Angela Mervyn; Kieran Mulvenna; Liam Ó Flannagáin; Rosemary Rainey

Chief Executive: Sara Long

Interim Director of Children and Young People's Services: Una Turbitt
Director of Education: Michele Corkey
Director of Finance and ICT: Seamus Wade
Director of Operations and Estates: Dale Hanna
Director of Human Resources and Corporate Services: Clare Duffield

Belfast office
40 Academy Street
Belfast, BT1 2NQ
Tel: 028 9056 4000

Armagh office
3 Charlemont Place
The Mall, Armagh, BT61 9AX
Tel: 028 3751 2200

Antrim office
182 Galgorm Road
Ballymena, BT42 1HN
Tel: 028 2566 1111

Dundonald office
Grahamsbridge Road
Dundonald, Belfast, BT16 2HS
Tel: 028 9056 6200

Omagh office
1 Hospital Road
Omagh, BT79 0AW
Tel: 028 8241 1411

Ballee Centre
2-6 Ballee Road West
Ballymena
BT42 2HS
Tel: 028 2566 1111

Universities

Queen's University Belfast

University Road
Belfast, BT7 1NN
Tel: 028 9024 5133
Web: www.qub.ac.uk
Email: comms.office@qub.ac.uk

Senior officers

President and Vice-Chancellor: Professor Ian Greer
Registrar and Chief Operating Officer: Joanne Claque

Pro Vice-Chancellors

Education and Students: Professor David Jones
Internationalisation: Professor Margaret Topping
Engineering and Physical Sciences:

Northern Ireland Yearbook | Education and Skills

Professor Chris Johnson
Research and Enterprise:
Professor Emma Flynn
Arts, Humanities and Social Services:
Professor Nola Hewitt-Dundas
Medicine, Health and Life Sciences:
Professor Stuart Elborn

Ulster University
Tel: 028 7012 3456
Web: www.ulster.ac.uk
Email: corporatecomms@ulster.ac.uk

Belfast campus
York Street
Belfast, BT15 1ED

Coleraine campus
Cromore Road
Coleraine, BT52 1SA

Jordanstown campus
Shore Road
Newtownabbey, BT37 0QB

Magee campus
Northland Road
Derry, BT48 7JL

Senior officers
Vice-Chancellor and President:
Professor Paul Bartholomew
Chancellor: Dr Colin Davidson
Deputy Vice-Chancellor:
Professor Paul Seawright

The Open University
110 Victoria Street
Belfast, BT1 3GN
Tel: 028 9024 5025
Web: www.open.ac.uk
Email: northernireland@open.ac.uk
National Director: John D'Arcy

University colleges

St Mary's University College
191 Falls Road
Belfast, BT12 6FE
Tel: 028 9032 7678
Web: www.smucb.ac.uk
Principal: Professor Peter Finn

Stranmillis University College
Stranmillis Road
Belfast, BT9 5DY
Tel: 028 9038 1271
Web: www.stran.ac.uk
Email: info@stran.ac.uk
Principal: Dr Jonathan Heggarty

Further education

Belfast Metropolitan College
7 Queens Road
Belfast, BT3 9DT
Tel: 028 9026 5000
Web: www.belfastmet.ac.uk
Chair: Frank Bryan
Principal and Chief Executive:
Louise Warde Hunter

Main campuses: Castlereagh, Millfield, Titanic, Springvale.

Northern Regional College
Ballymena Campus
Farm Lodge Building
Ballymena, BT43 7DF
Tel: 028 2565 2871
Web: www.nrc.ac.uk
Principal and Chief Executive:
Mel Higgins

Main campuses: Ballymena, Ballymoney, Coleraine, Larne, Magherafelt, Newtownabbey.

CCMS – Council for Catholic Maintained Schools

World-class teachers wanted
028 9201 3014 • www.onlineccms.com

CCMS Chief Executive Gerry Campbell

At CCMS we see leading and teaching in our Catholic schools as a vocation that requires much more than an ability to raise academic standards and provide high quality learning and teaching. The pupils in our schools deserve teachers who will be committed to the mission, values, and ethos of Catholic education and who will set the benchmark for those in their care, in terms of their own values, interpersonal relationships and commitment to Catholic education.

- We want the most talented, dedicated and vocationally called people to teach in our schools.
- We want teachers who are committed to the ideal that no child should be left behind.
- We want teachers who will educate and inspire every child and young person to develop themselves so that they will contribute to building the society and economy of our shared future.
- We want teachers that are wholly committed to the pursuit of genuine excellence whilst remaining faithful to the distinctive culture, vision, and approach of a Catholic faith-based education.

The Council for Catholic Maintained Schools (CCMS) is the managing authority for 447 schools in Northern Ireland, employing approximately 6,500 teachers. Our schools, pupils and staff are part of a global network of Catholic education where 60 million pupils of all faiths and none are welcomed, cherished, and supported to realise their potential and to contribute positively to the Common Good. Catholic Schools are very much valued across society and continue to increase their capacity for diversity, academic excellence, and achievement for all.

If you feel that you are the teacher we are looking for, then look us up online at: www.onlineccmsschools.com / www.getgotjobs.co.uk

Education and Skills | Northern Ireland Yearbook

North West Regional College
Strand Road
Derry, BT48 7AL
Tel: 028 7127 600
Web: www.nwrc.ac.uk
Email: info@nwrc.ac.uk
Principal and Chief Executive:
Leo Murphy

Main campuses: Derry, Limavady, Strabane.

South Eastern Regional College
Lisburn Campus
Castle Street
Lisburn, BT27 4SU
Tel: 0345 600 7555
Web: www.serc.ac.uk
Email: info@serc.ac.uk
Principal and Chief Executive:
Ken Webb

Campuses: Ballynahinch, Bangor, Downpatrick, Holywood, Lisburn, Newtownards, Newcastle.

Southern Regional College
Newry Campus
East/West Buildings
Patrick Street, Newry, BT35 8DN
Tel: 0300 123 1223
Web: www.src.ac.uk
Email: info@src.ac.uk
Chief Executive: Brian Doran

Campuses: Armagh, Banbridge, Lurgan, Kilkeel, Newry, Portadown.

South West College
Omagh Campus
2 Mountjoy Road, Omagh
BT79 7AH
Tel: 0845 603 1881
Web: www.swc.ac.uk
Email: enquiries@swc.ac.uk
Director and Chief Executive:
Colin Lewis (interim)

Campuses: Cookstown, Dungannon, Erne, Omagh.

College of Agriculture, Food and Rural Enterprise (CAFRE)
Tel: 0800 028 4291
Web: www.cafre.ac.uk
Email: enquiries@cafre.ac.uk
Director: Martin McKendry

Main campuses: Enniskillen, Greenmount, Loughry.

Sectoral organisations

Comhairle na Gaelscolaíochta
200-202 Falls Road
Belfast, BT12 6AH
Tel: 028 9032 1475
Web: www.comhairle.org
Email: eolas@comhairle.org
Chief Executive:
Ciarán Mac Giolla Bhéin

Controlled Schools' Support Council
Second Floor, Main Building
Stranmillis University College 
Stranmillis Road
Belfast, BT9 5DY
Tel: 028 9531 3030
Email: info@csscni.org.uk
Chief Executive: Mark Baker

Council for Catholic Maintained Schools (CCMS)
Linen Hall House, 23 Linenhall Street
Lisburn, BT28 1FJ
Tel: 028 9201 3014
Web: www.onlineccms.com
Chief Executive: Gerry Campbell

Integrated Education Fund
Forestview, Purdy's Lane
Belfast, BT8 7AR
Tel: 028 9069 4099
Web: www.ief.org.uk
Email: info@ief.org.uk
Chief Executive: Tina Merron

Iontaobhas na Gaelscolaíochta (InaG)
199 Falls Road
Belfast, BT12 6FB
Tel: 028 9024 1510
Web: www.iontaobhasnag.com
Email: eolas@iontaobhasnag.com
Chief Executive: Pilib Ó Ruanaí

Northern Ireland Council for Integrated Education (NICIE)
25 College Gardens
Belfast, BT9 6BS
Tel: 028 9097 2910
Web: www.nicie.org.uk
Email: info@nicie.org.uk
CEO: Roisin Marshall

Other public bodies

Council for the Curriculum, Examinations and Assessment (CCEA)
29 Clarendon Road
Clarendon Dock
Belfast, BT1 3BG
Tel: 028 9026 1200
Web: www.ccea.org.uk
Email: info@ccea.org.uk
Interim Chief Executive:
Margaret Farragher

Northern Ireland Yearbook | Education and Skills

Education and Training Inspectorate

Inspection Services Branch
Department of Education
Room F29
Rathgael House, 43 Balloo Road
Bangor, BT19 7PR
Tel: 028 9127 9726
Web: www.etini.gov.uk
Email: eti@education-ni.gov.uk
Chief Inspector: Faustina Graham

General Teaching Council for Northern Ireland

3rd Floor, Albany House
73-75 Great Victoria Street
Belfast, BT2 7AF
Tel: 028 9033 3390
Web: www.gtcni.org.uk
Email: info@gtcni.org.uk
Chief Executive: Sam Gallaher

Libraries NI

Lisburn City Library
23 Linenhall Street
Lisburn, BT28 1FJ
Tel: 028 9263 5322
Web: www.librariesni.org.uk
Email: chiefexecutive@librariesni.org.uk
Chief Executive: Jim O'Hagan

Other organisations

Open College Network Northern Ireland

Sirius House, 10 Heron Road
Sydenham Business Park
Belfast, BT3 9LE
Tel: 028 9046 3990
Web: www.ocnni.org.uk
Email: info@ocnni.org.uk
Chief Executive: Martin Flynn

Pearson

80 Strand
London, WC2R 0RL
Tel: 020 7010 2000
Territory Manager, Ireland:
Fiona Callaghan

Skills

The most recent UK Commission for Employment and Skills' Employer Skills Survey published in 2019 found that 13 per cent of employers in Northern Ireland reported a skills gap with shortages of team working, technical and practical skills being the most common. While historically employers in Northern Ireland have found vacancies much less hard to fill than the rest of the UK, in 2019 the density of skill-shortage vacancies in Northern Ireland were broadly in line with the UK average (22 per cent compared with 24 per cent).

The former Department for Employment and Learning published a skills strategy, entitled 'Success through Skills', in February 2006. Its successor strategy, 'Success through Skills – Transforming the Future', was published in May 2011.

It aims to enable people to improve their skills, in order to:

- raise the skills level of the whole workforce;
- raise productivity;
- increase levels of social inclusion by enhancing the employability of those currently excluded from the labour market; and
- secure Northern Ireland's future in a global marketplace.

Four strategic goals that were set for 2020:

- increase the proportion of those people in employment with Level 2 skills and above to 84-90 per cent, from a baseline of 71.2 per cent in 2008;
- increase the proportion of those people in employment with Level 3 skills and above to 68-76 per cent, from a baseline of 55.6 per cent in 2008;
- increase the proportion of those people in employment with Level 4-8 skills and above to 44-52 per cent, from a baseline of 33.2 per cent in 2008;
- increase the proportion of those qualifying from Northern Ireland higher education institutions with graduate and postgraduate level courses in STEM subjects (with an emphasis on physical and biological sciences, mathematical and computer science, engineering and technology) to 25-30 per cent, from a baseline of 18 per cent in 2008.

This was supplemented by the 'Pathways to Success' strategy for young people who are not in education, employment or training (NEET), published in June 2012, and the 'Securing our Success' apprenticeships strategy, announced in June 2014. Together with the then Department of Enterprise, Trade and Investment, former Employment and Learning Minister Stephen Farry published a strategy to tackle economic inactivity in April 2015.

The Success through Skills Strategy ended in 2020, with the Department currently developing a new Skills Strategy to take Northern Ireland through the next decade.

The draft Skills Strategy for Northern Ireland: Skills for a 10X Economy was published in May 2021 as part of the 10X Economy strategy, which envisions the growth of Northern Ireland's economy by 10 times from its current standing. Having opened the consultation process for the skills strategy upon its publication, the consultation period ended on 19 August 2021.

Delivering an economy that performs at 10 times the rate that it currently does will require a transformation of the skills capacity in Northern Ireland, which will "mean investing in the skills that will drive our key strategic clusters, boosting the research and innovation potential of our workforce and developing Northern Ireland as a global hub of knowledge through strong collaboration between government, business and our world class research institutions", the strategy says.

The consultation document lays out the three major policy objectives within the strategy: addressing skills imbalances; creating a lifelong culture of learning; and enhancing digital skills in order to create a "digital spine". The three policy enablers that will underpin these objectives are: enhancing policy cohesion; building strong relationships; and investment in the skills system. These objectives and enablers have been formulated in part through the use of the Skills Barometer for Northern Ireland, which has shown that three key issues to address social and economic development are: the prevalence of individuals with low, or no qualifications; limited opportunities for high paying jobs and pathways for career progression; and a 'skills deficit' and comparatively poor productivity performance.

The actions included in the plan to achieve the goal of addressing skills imbalances include increasing the proportion of people graduating from higher education institutions with degrees and post-graduate qualifications in STEM subjects such as physical, environmental and computer

Education and Skills | Northern Ireland Yearbook

sciences, engineering and mathematics, "significantly" increasing the proportion of individuals achieving level 3, 4 and 5 qualifications, and increasing the proportion of the working age population with qualifications at level 2 and above. In order to achieve the second goal of the creation of a lifelong culture of learning, initiatives such as investment in apprenticeships, a Flexible Skills Fund to support upskilling and reskilling, and proposals for investment in leadership and management training are mentioned.

Key to the development of digital skills and the digital spine, the plan proposes is the publication of a separate plan. "It is proposed that a 'Digital Skills Action Plan' is developed to support the objectives of our economic vision: driving our decade of innovation and providing everyone with the opportunity to participate in our 10X Economy," the report says. This digital action plan would utilise the same co-design principles used for the skills strategy, appoint an expert panel to consider the changing digital skills needs of the economy and identify the changes needed in education to meet the needs of the labour market and society.

The report concludes on a familiar note, by emphasising the need for multi-year budgets in Northern Ireland: "Not only do we need to reprioritise our investment in education and skills, but we need a commitment to introduce the multi-year budgets which will underpin strategic planning and the transformational change in our skills system that will be required to deliver our 10X Economy."

Skills organisations

Department for the Economy
Netherleigh
Massey Avenue
Belfast
BT4 2JP
Tel: 028 9052 9900
Web: www.economy-ni.gov.uk
Email: dfemail@economy-ni.gov.uk
Minister: Gordon Lyons MLA
Permanent Secretary: Mike Brennan

Federation for Industry Sector Skills and Standards
64A Cumberland Street
Edinburgh, EH3 6RE
Tel: 0300 303 4444
Web: www.fisss.org
Email: info@fisss.org

Cogent
Sector: Chemical, pharmaceutical, nuclear, petroleum, polymers and life sciences business
Tel: 01925 515 200
Web: www.cogentskills.com

Construction Industry Training Board Northern Ireland (CITBNI)
Sector: Construction
Tel: 028 9082 5466
Web: www.citbni.org.uk

Creative and Cultural Skills
Sector: Craft, cultural heritage, design, literature, music, performing, and visual arts
Tel: 078 8023 0594
Web: www.ccskills.org.uk
Email: belfast@ccskills.org.uk

Creative Skillset
Sector: TV, film, radio, interactive media, animation, computer games, facilities, photo imaging, publishing, advertising and fashion and textiles
Tel: 020 7713 9800
Web: www.creativeskillset.org
Email: info@creativeskillset.org

Energy and Utility Skills
Sector: Electricity, gas, waste management and water industries
Tel: 0121 713 8255
Web: www.euskills.co.uk
Email: enquiries@euskills.co.uk

Institute of the Motor Industry (IMI)
Sector: Retail motor industry
Tel: 01992 511 521
Web: www.theimi.org.uk

InvestNI
Sector: Skills development support and advice
Tel: 0800 181 4422
Web: www.investni.com

Lantra
Sector: Land management and production, animal health and welfare and environmental industries
Tel: 028 7963 9290
Web: www.lantra.co.uk
Email: ni@lantra.co.uk

People 1st
Sector: Hospitality, leisure, passenger transport, travel and tourism
Tel: 028 9066 9669
Web: www.people-1st.co.uk
Email: people@people-1st.co.uk

SEMTA
Sector: Science, engineering and manufacturing technologies
Tel: 0845 643 9001
Web: www.semta.org.uk
Email: customerservices@semta.org.uk

SkillsActive
Sector: Active leisure, learning and well-being
Tel: 0330 004 0005
Web: www.skillsactive.com

Skills for Care and Development
Sector: Social care, social work, children, young people and families
Tel: 0113 241 1240
Web: www.skillsforcareanddevelopment.org.uk
Email: info@niscc.hscni.net

Skills for Health
Sector: Health sector
Tel: 0117 922 1155
Web: www.skillsforhealth.org.uk
Email: office@skillsforhealth.org.uk

Skills for Justice
Sector: Justice, community safety and legal services
Tel: 0117 922 1155
Web: www.sfjuk.com
Email: contactus@sfjuk.com

National Skills Academy
Sector: Food and drink
Tel: 0845 644 0558
Web: www.nsafd.co.uk
Email: info@nsafd.co.uk

Northern Ireland Yearbook
Justice

Justice in Northern Ireland

The Government of Ireland Act 1920 tasked the new devolved administration with maintaining the "peace, order and good government" of Northern Ireland. Criminal justice powers were devolved in 1921 but returned to Westminster in 1972 when direct rule was introduced.

Due to its sensitive nature, policing and justice policy was not initially devolved to the Northern Ireland Assembly. The Hillsborough Castle Agreement, in February 2010, allowed for the devolution of most aspects of policing and justice on 12 April of that year. The main devolved areas are as follows:

- creation of offences and penalties;
- prevention and detection of crime;
- powers of arrest and detention;
- prosecution policy, prison and probation;
- public order;
- the establishment, organisation and control of the Police Service of Northern Ireland; and
- courts and coroners policy.

The Minister of Justice, accountable to the Northern Ireland Assembly, is responsible for policy and legislation in all of the above areas.

The Police Service of Northern Ireland is responsible for policing the region as a whole. It was constituted in 2001, to succeed the Royal Ulster Constabulary which had been formed in 1922. The PSNI is overseen by the Northern Ireland Policing Board and also held to account by the independent Police Ombudsman for Northern Ireland.

Crime is investigated by the PSNI and prosecuted by the Public Prosecution Service (PPS), which is also independent of government. Forensic Science Northern Ireland – an executive agency of the Department of Justice – provides assistance to PSNI investigations.

Magistrates' courts hear minor criminal cases and those involving young people. The Crown Court hears all serious criminal cases. Appeals can be made to the Court of Appeal in Belfast.

In the civil justice system, county courts hear a wide range of civil actions. The High Court in Belfast hears complex or important civil cases and appeals from the county court. Coroners' courts investigate unexplained deaths. The Enforcement of Judgments Office enforces civil judgments.

The judiciary is led by the Lord Chief Justice of Northern Ireland, who oversees the standards and conduct of judges. Administrative support is provided by the Northern Ireland Courts and Tribunals Service. Final appeals, in both civil and criminal cases, can be made to the Supreme Court of the United Kingdom, on points of law in cases of major public importance.

The Northern Ireland Judicial Appointments Commission selects nominees for judicial office up to and including the level of High Court judge.

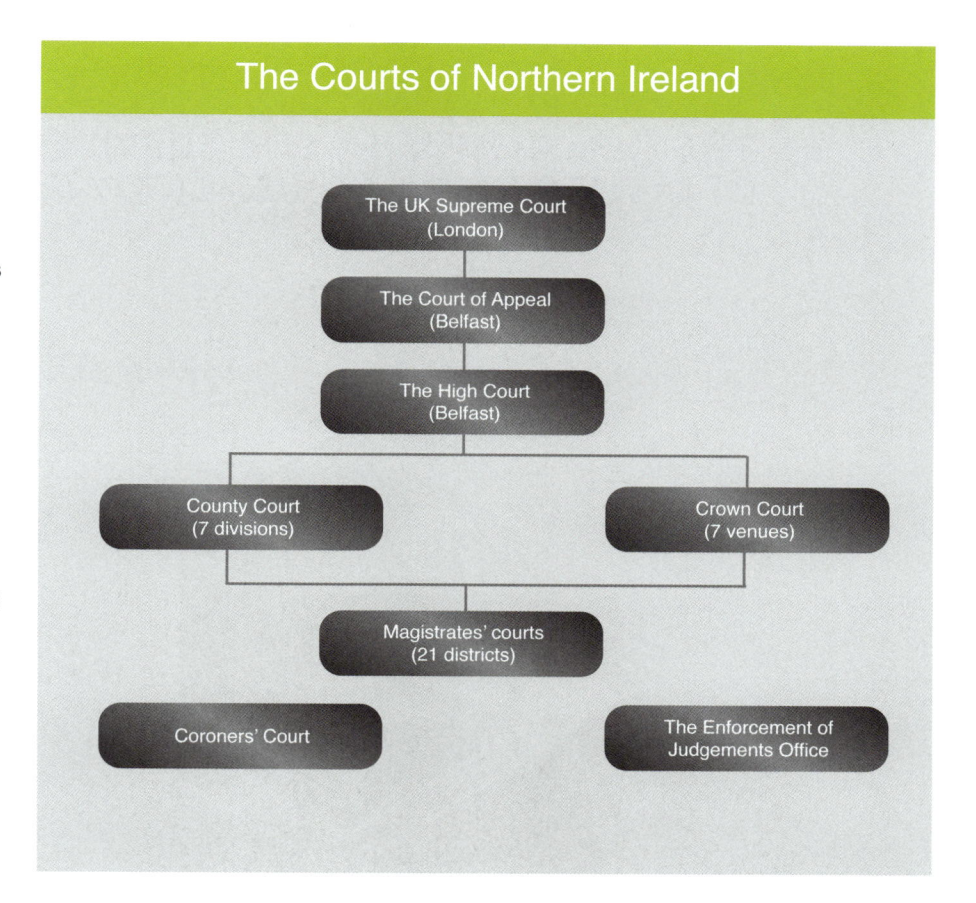

The Courts of Northern Ireland

- The UK Supreme Court (London)
- The Court of Appeal (Belfast)
- The High Court (Belfast)
- County Court (7 divisions)
- Crown Court (7 venues)
- Magistrates' courts (21 districts)
- Coroners' Court
- The Enforcement of Judgements Office

DELIVERING EFFECTIVE INDEPENDENT OVERSIGHT OF POLICING

Northern Ireland Policing Board

Our Work...

The Policing Board is responsible for ensuring that the Police Service of Northern Ireland is effective, efficient, impartial, representative and accountable to the community it seeks to serve. This means holding the Chief Constable to account for all his actions and those of his staff.

Through our work, we aim to ensure a continually improving police service, which contributes to a safe society and which has the support, trust and confidence of the community it serves.

Find out more about what we do and how we do it at:

- www.nipolicingboard.org.uk
- policingboard
- @nipolicingboard
- 028 9040 8500
- information@nipolicingboard.org.uk
- Northernirelandpolicingboard
- nipolicingboard

INVESTORS IN PEOPLE

Justice | Northern Ireland Yearbook

THE COMMISSIONER FOR SURVIVORS OF INSTITUTIONAL CHILDHOOD ABUSE

Representing and promoting the interests of victims and survivors of historical institutional childhood abuse

Fiona Ryan, Commissioner.

The principal aim of the Commissioner is to represent and promote the interests of any person who suffered abuse while a child and while resident in an institution within Northern Ireland at some time between 1922 and 1995.

Commissioner Fiona Ryan took up post in December 2020 saying: "Victims and survivors of institutional childhood abuse endured pain, suffering and trauma at the most vulnerable time of their lives: the time when they most needed love, care and protection. A time when they were children.

"It has been a long hard road for victims and survivors. Many have seen fellow survivors, friends, and family, pass on this journey for justice and acknowledgement. Many others continue to live with the trauma of their childhood experiences."

One year in office

Throughout 2021, the Commissioner has prioritised engaging with victims and survivors and their representative groups to better understand their needs and concerns. The Commissioner has advocated for the remaining recommendations of the Historical Institutional Abuse Inquiry to be implemented. This includes a public apology by the Executive and relevant institutions.

The Commissioner's office has also engaged with individual survivors, answering over 519 queries on a range of issues. Half of these queries related to the redress process, reflecting the Commissioner's statutory responsibility to provide general information and advice on making an application for redress.

In response to these queries and to let victims and survivors know about redress, available services, and the role of the Commissioner and how she can be

Northern Ireland Yearbook | Justice

contacted; the office established the new website www.cosica-ni.org. Specifically in relation to redress, there is a comprehensive FAQ section based on queries received, designed to help when completing an application.

Over the course of the year, the Commissioner has commented and provided information on issues affecting victims and survivors including that of the redress process and public apology, a recommendation of the Historical Institutional Abuse Inquiry report 2017. The Commissioner is independent and part of her role is to provide briefings to the Executive Office and the Committee for the Executive Office, before whom she appeared four times in 2021.

Her priorities have been to underline the need for improved communications and a comprehensive understanding of the needs of victims and survivors. This also includes identifying gaps in order to meet these needs. She has engaged with service providers supporting victims and survivors as well as with those providing more general services. In addition, the Commissioner has met with the Mental Health Policy Group (NI) consisting of leading organisations working in the field of mental health and made a submission to the Northern Ireland Mental Health Strategy 2021-2031.

The future

Moving forward, the Commissioner will continue working to ensure the implementation of the remaining recommendations published, as part of the Historical Institutional Abuse Inquiry. In response to victims and survivors' voiced concerns around government's insufficient public awareness on the services available, the Commissioner has recommended that the Executive leads on an integrated communications and engagement campaign. Recommendations include providing information on support services, the redress process and on her own office advocating for the campaign to get underway early in 2022.

In addition, the Commissioner has called for a programme of research to commence. Outcomes of this research will support the design of a plan for increased future engagement with victims and survivors, improving representation of their interests. This will also ensure that any lessons learned along the way will go towards supporting agencies on providing vital care now and possibly into the future. Research topics to consist of 'identifying where victims and survivors are currently living', with the aim of reaching out to provide information to those within Northern Ireland and beyond.

"The reality is that while most victims and survivors continue to reside in Northern Ireland, a significant number now live in Great Britain, the Republic of Ireland or further afield. It is my intention in the coming months to extend engagement and knowing where survivors are based would certainly help with that."

Commissioner Ryan concludes: "My vision is one where we work to represent and promote the interests of victims and survivors, not just through those measures set out in law to address the wrongs of the past, but also those that address the needs of victims and survivors now and in the future."

> "My vision is one where we work to represent and promote the interests of victims and survivors, not just through those measures set out in law to address the wrongs of the past, but also those that address the needs of victims and survivors now and in the future."
>
> **Fiona Ryan,** Commissioner for Survivors of Institutional Childhood Abuse

---

To contact The Commissioner for Survivors of Institutional Childhood Abuse:
5th Floor, South Queens Court, 56-66 Upper Queen Street, Belfast, BT1 6FD

T: 028 9054 4985
E: info@cosica-ni.org
W: www.cosica-ni.org

Justice | Northern Ireland Yearbook

A separate Judicial Appointments Ombudsman investigates complaints from applicants for judicial appointment. The more senior positions of Lord Justice of Appeal and Lady or Lord Chief Justice are nominated by the Prime Minister. All judges at High Court level and above are formally appointed by Elizabeth II.

The Northern Ireland Legal Services Commission funds legal aid payments to legal professionals and other advice providers.

The Northern Ireland Prison Service operates three prisons at Maghaberry (near Lisburn), Magilligan (near Limavady) and Hydebank Wood College and Women's Prison (in south Belfast). In less serious cases, offenders are supervised by the staff of the Probation Board for Northern Ireland or the Youth Justice Agency, if the offender is aged under 18.

The Prisoner Ombudsman investigates complaints from prisoners. The Parole Commissioners make decisions on the release and recall of all life sentence and public protection sentence prisoners, and the recall and further release of other prisoners sentenced to custody.

All aspects of the criminal justice system, aside from the judiciary, are inspected by Criminal Justice Inspection Northern Ireland. The Attorney General for Northern Ireland is the chief legal adviser to the Northern Ireland Executive and protects the public interest in matters of law. The Northern Ireland Law Commission is responsible for keeping the civil and criminal law under review.

The UK Government controls a number of significant policing, security and justice policy areas.

The Northern Ireland Office (NIO) oversees national security in Northern Ireland and intelligence support is provided by the Security Service (MI5). The NIO also appoints the Parades Commission, which decides conditions and restrictions on sensitive parades. The Home Office is responsible for overall national security, immigration law (implemented by the Border Force), the classification of illicit drugs and the regulation of the security industry (implemented by the Security Industry Authority). Her Majesty's Inspectorate of Constabulary and Fire and Rescue services monitors the performance of police and fire and rescue services in England, Wales and Northern Ireland.

The Advocate General for Northern Ireland advises the UK Government on Northern Ireland law. The position is held by the Attorney General for England and Wales, who also oversees the Serious Fraud Office.

The National Crime Agency (NCA) became operational in October 2013 and tackles serious and organised crime in non-devolved policy areas e.g. customs and immigration. The NCA is accountable to the Home Secretary.

Department of Justice

Block B, Castle Buildings
Stormont Estate, Belfast, BT4 3SG
Tel: 028 9076 3000
Textphone: 028 9052 7668
Web: www.justice-ni.gov.uk
Minister: Naomi Long MLA
Permanent Secretary: Peter May

Policing

Police Service of Northern Ireland
Command Secretariat
Brooklyn, 65 Knock Road
Belfast, BT5 6LE
Non-Emergency Number: 101
Crimestoppers: 0800 555 111
Web: www.psni.police.uk

Chief Constable: Simon Byrne
Deputy Chief Constable (Performance and Change Management): Mark Hamilton
Assistant Chief Constable (Crime Operations): Mark McEwan
Assistant Chief Constable (District Policing): Alan Todd
Temporary Assistant Chief Constable (Operational Support): Jonathan Roberts
Temporary Assistant Chief Constable (Community Safety): Bobby Singleton
Chief Operating Officer: Pamela McCreedy
Temporary Assistant Chief Constable (HR, Health and Wellbeing, Health and Safety): Jonathan Roberts
Temporary Assistant Chief Officer Corporate Services Director of Finance and Support Services and Human Resources: Mark McNaughten

Northern Ireland Policing Board
Waterside Tower, 31 Clarendon Road
Clarendon Dock, Belfast, BT1 3BG
Tel: 028 9040 8500
Web: www.nipolicingboard.org.uk
Email: information@nipolicingboard.org.uk

Chair: Doug Garrett
Chief Executive: Sinead Simpson

Police Ombudsman for Northern Ireland
New Cathedral Buildings
Writers' Square
11 Church Street, Belfast, BT1 1PG
Tel: 028 9082 8600
Web: www.policeombudsman.org
Email: info@policeombudsman.org

Police Ombudsman: Marie Anderson
Chief Executive: Olwen Laird
Senior Director of Investigations: Paul Holmes
Director of Current Investigations: Susie Harper

Courts, judiciary and prosecutions

Northern Ireland Courts and Tribunals Service
Laganside House, 23-27 Oxford Street
Belfast, BT1 3LA
Tel: 0300 200 7812
Web: www.courtsni.gov.uk
Email: communicationsgroup@courtsni.gov.uk
Acting Chief Executive: Peter Luney

Office of the Lady Chief Justice
c/o Royal Courts of Justice
Chichester Street, Belfast, BT1 3JF
Tel: 028 9072 4616
Email: LCJOffice@judiciaryni.uk

Lady Chief Justice:
The Right Hon Dame Siobhan Keegan

Coroners Service
Laganside House
23-27 Oxford Street
Belfast, BT1 3LA
Tel: 0300 200 7811
Email: coronersoffice@courtsni.gov.uk
Coroners: M Dougan, L Fee, J McCrisken, A-L Toal

Northern Ireland Yearbook | Justice

Public Prosecution Service Northern Ireland
Central Management Unit
93 Chichester Street
Belfast, BT1 3JR
Tel: 028 9089 7100
Web: www.ppsni.gov.uk
Email: info@ppsni.gsi.gov.uk
Director of Public Prosecutions:
Stephen Herron

Northern Ireland Legal Services Agency
2nd Floor, Waterfront Plaza
8 Laganbank Road, Mays Meadow
Belfast, BT1 3BN
Tel: 028 9040 8888
Web: www.justice-ni.gov.uk
Email: enquiries@lsani.gov.uk
Chief Executive: Paul Andrews

Northern Ireland Judicial Appointments Commission
Headline Building, 10-14 Victoria Street
Belfast, BT1 3GG
Tel: 028 9056 9100
Web: www.nijac.gov.uk
Email: judicialappointments@nijac.gov.uk

Chair: The Right Hon Dame Siobhan Keegan
(ex officio as Lady Chief Justice)
Chief Executive: Tonya McCormac

Northern Ireland Judicial Appointments Ombudsman
Progressive House
33 Wellington Place
Belfast, BT1 6HN
Tel: 028 9023 3821
Freephone: 0800 343 424
Web: www.nipso.org.uk
Email: nipso@nipso.org.uk
Ombudsman: Marie Anderson

Judiciary NI
Royal Courts of Justice
Chichester Street
Belfast, BT1 3JF
Tel: 028 9072 4616
Web: www.judiciaryni.uk
Email: LCJOffice@judiciaryni.uk

Prisons and probation

Northern Ireland Prison Service
Dundonald House
Upper Newtownards Road
Belfast, BT4 3SU
Tel: 028 9052 2922
Web: www.justice-ni.gov.uk
Email: info@niprisonservice.gov.uk
Director General: Ronnie Armour

Probation Board for Northern Ireland
80-90 North Street
Belfast, BT1 1LD
Tel: 028 9026 2400
Textphone: 028 9026 2400
Web: www.pbni.org.uk
Email: info@pbni.gsi.gov.uk

Chair: Dale Ashford
Chief Executive: Amanda Stewart

Prisoner Ombudsman for Northern Ireland
Unit 2, Walled Garden
Stormont Estate
Belfast, BT4 3SH
Tel: 028 9052 7771
Web: www.niprisonerombudsman.gov.uk
Email: pa@prisonerombudsman.x.gsi.gov.uk
Ombudsman: Lesley Carroll

Parole Commissioners for Northern Ireland
Laganside Court
Mezzaine 1st Floor
Oxford Street, Belfast, BT1 3LL
Tel: 028 9041 2969
Web: www.parolecomni.org.uk
Email: info@parolecomni.x.gsi.gov.uk
Chief Commissioner: Paul Mageean

Youth Justice Agency of Northern Ireland
41-43 Waring Street, Belfast, BT1 2DY
Tel: 028 9031 6400
Web: www.justice-ni.gov.uk
Email: info@yjani.gov.uk
Chief Executive: Stephen Martin

Other organisations

Attorney General for Northern Ireland
PO Box 1272
Belfast, BT1 9LU
Tel: 028 9072 5333
Web: www.attorneygeneralni.gov.uk
Email: contact@attorneygeneralni.gov.uk
Attorney General: Brenda King

Criminal Justice Inspection Northern Ireland
Block 1, Knockview Buildings
Stormont Estate, Belfast, BT4 3SJ
Tel: 028 9076 5764
Web: www.cjini.org
Email: info@cjini.org
Chief Inspector of Criminal Justice:
Jacqui Durkin

Parades Commission
2nd Floor, Andras House
60 Great Victoria Street
Belfast, BT2 7BB
Tel: 028 9089 5900
Web: www.paradescommission.org
Email: info@paradescommissionni.org
Chair: Graham Forbes

National policing, security and justice

Advocate General for Northern Ireland
20 Victoria Street
London, SW1H 0NF
Tel: 020 7271 2492
Web: www.gov.uk/ago
Email: correspondence@attorneygeneral.gsi.gov.uk
Advocate General for Northern Ireland:
The Rt Hon Suella Braverman QC MP

Border Force
Lunar House
40 Wellesley Road
Croydon, CR9 2BY
Web: www.gov.uk/government/organisations/border-force
Director General:
Paul Lincoln

HM Inspectorate of Constabulary and Fire & Rescue Service
6th Floor, Globe House
89 Eccleston Square
London, SW1V 1PN
Tel: 020 3513 0500
Web: www.hmic.gov.uk
Email: contact@hmic.gsi.gov.uk
HM Chief Inspector: Thomas Winsor

National Crime Agency
1-6 Citadel Place
Tinworth Street
London, SE11 5EF
Tel: 0370 496 7622
Web: www.nationalcrimeagency.gov.uk
Email: communications@nca.x.gsi.gov.uk
Director General: Graeme Biggar

Security Industry Authority
PO Box 49768
London, WC1V 6WY
Tel: 0844 892 1025
Chief Executive: Michelle Russell

Security Service
The Enquiries Desk
PO Box 3255
London, SW1P 1AE
Web: www.mi5.gov.uk
Director General: Ken McCallum

Serious Fraud Office
2-4 Cockspur Street
London, SW1Y 5BS
Tel: 020 7239 7272
Web: www.sfo.gov.uk
Email: public.enquiries@sfo.gsi.gov.uk
Director: Lisa Osofsky

Representative organisations

The Bar of Northern Ireland
The Bar Library, 91 Chichester Street
Belfast, BT1 3JQ
Tel: 028 9024 1523
Web: www.barofni.com
Chair: Bernard Brady QC
Chief Executive: David Mulholland

Law Society of Northern Ireland
96 Victoria Street
Belfast, BT1 3GN
Tel: 028 9023 1614
Web: www.lawsoc-ni.org
Email: enquiry@lawsoc-ni.org
President: Rowan White
Chief Executive: David Lavery

National Association of Probation Officers
Boat Race House
65 Mortlake High Street
London, SW14 8HL
Tel: 020 7223 4887
Web: www.napo.org.uk
Email: info@napo.org.uk
General Secretary: Ian Lawrence

Police Federation for Northern Ireland
77-79 Garnerville Road
Belfast, BT4 2NX
Tel: 028 9076 4200
Web: www.policefed-ni.org.uk
Email: contactus@policefedni.com
Chair: Mark Lindsay

Prison Officers Association
c/o Cronin House
245 Church Street
London, N9 9HW
Tel: 020 8803 0255
Web: www.poauk.org.uk
Email: general@poauk.org.uk

Superintendents' Association of Northern Ireland
The Gate Lodge, PSNI College
Garnerville Road
Belfast, BT4 2NX
Tel: 028 9092 2201
Email: suptassociation@psni.pnn.police.uk

Legal services

Arthur Cox
Victoria House
Gloucester Street
Belfast, BT1 4LS
Tel: 028 9023 0007
Email: belfast@arthurcox.com
Managing Partner: Catriona Gibson

A&L Goodbody
42/46 Fountain Street
Belfast, BT1 5EF
Tel: 028 9031 4466
Web: www.algoodbody.com

Carson McDowell
Murray House, Murray Street
Belfast, BT1 6DN
Tel: +44 (0)28 9024 4951
Web: www.carson-mcdowell.com
Email: law@carson-mcdowell.com
Senior Partner: Neasa Quigley

Millar McCall & Wylie
Imperial House
Donegall Square East
Belfast, BT1 5HD
Tel: 028 9020 0050
Web: www.mmwlegal.com

Mills Selig
21 Arthur Street
Belfast, BT1 4GA
Tel: 028 9024 3878
Web: www.millsselig.com
Managing Partner: Chris Guy

Pinsent Masons
The Soloist Building, 1 Lanyon Place
Belfast, BT1 3LP
Tel: 028 9089 4800
Web: www.pinsentmasons.com
Head of Office: Andrea McIlroy-Rose

TLT NI LLP
River House
48-60 High Street
Belfast
BT1 2BE
Tel: 0333 006 0600
Web: www.tltsolicitors.com
Head of Office: Katharine Kimber

Tughans
Marlborough House
30 Victoria Street
Belfast, BT1 3GG
Tel: 028 9055 3300
Web: www.tughans.com

Northern Ireland Yearbook

Tourism and Conferencing

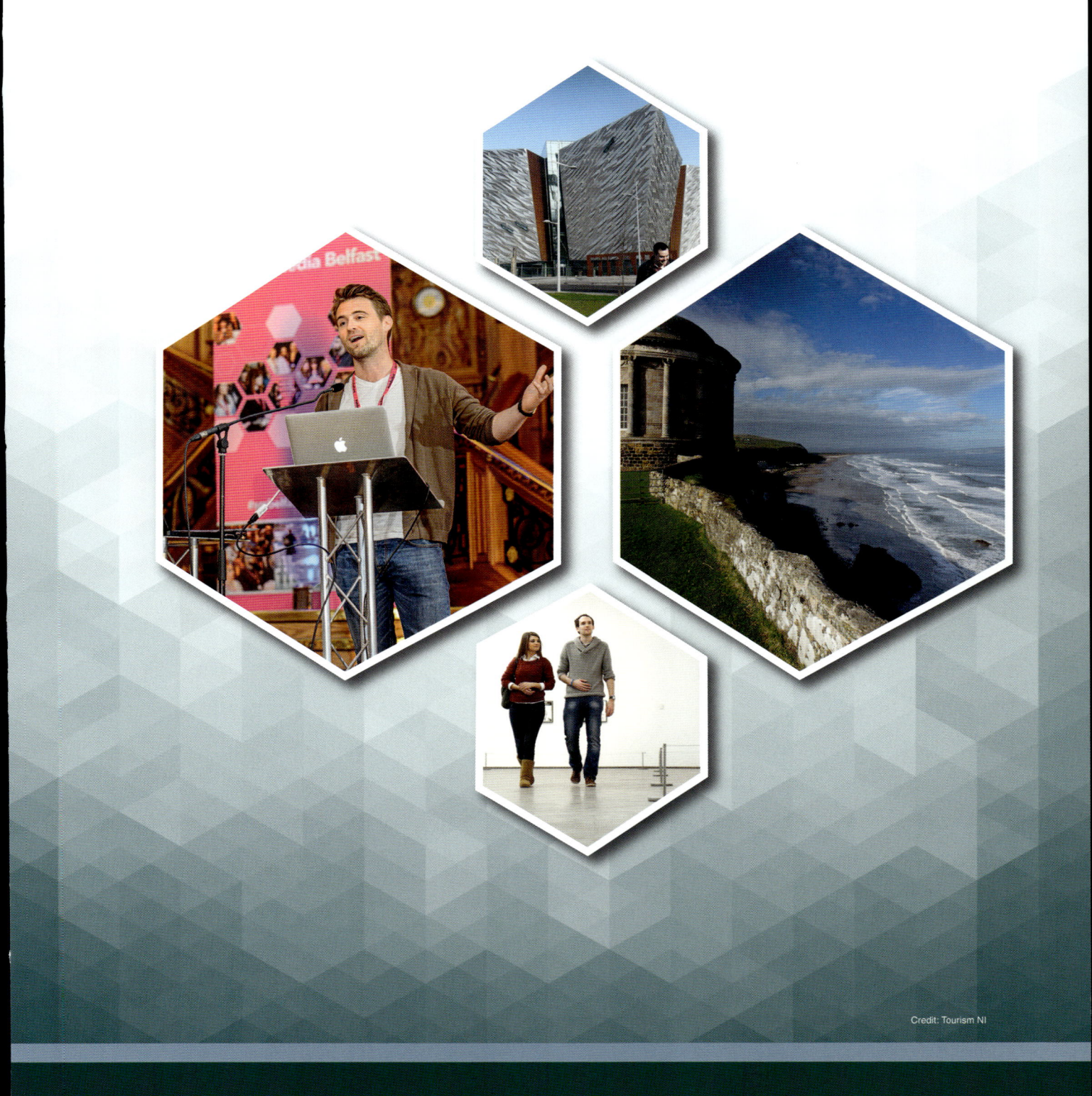

Credit: Tourism NI

Tourism and Conferencing | **Northern Ireland Yearbook**

tourism northernireland

Tourism in Action

Beyond the Bridge — Embrace a Giant Spirit. Credit Line: Courtesy of Tourism Northern Ireland

At Tourism NI's June 2021 conference we outlined how we intended to support the industry on its recovery journey. Since June, Tourism NI has continued to focus on the key themes of 'Survive, Revive and Thrive', rolling out initiatives in support of the tourism industry across Northern Ireland as well as activity that tourism organisations and businesses can get involved in, writes John McGrillen, Chief Executive, Tourism NI.

Tourism Enterprise Development

The Tourism Enterprise Development (TED) Programme 2021/22 supports tourism businesses to adapt their products and services to market opportunities and the new operating environment. It is all about businesses getting the professional advice and support needed at this critical time.

The TED programme has something for everyone in the industry including webinars, toolkits, instructional videos, top tips, tools, tactics and action plans. Expert mentors are also on hand to guide and advise. The programme spans all of the key topics and questions facing the industry including digital skills and innovation, people, and sustainable tourism.

A calendar of events is in place to March 2022 and key upcoming highlights include

Northern Ireland Yearbook | Tourism and Conferencing

market reviews of Great Britain and the Republic of Ireland, a customer service training programme, a sustainability masterclass and a recruitment and talent development masterclass. Those who sign up to the sessions at tourismni.com also receive newsletter updates on what is coming up in the future. Recordings of all previous webinars are also available at tourismni.com

City and Growth Deals

As well as investing in projects which can drive recovery in the short to medium term, a key element of Tourism NI's current work is progressing the delivery of key tourism projects across Northern Ireland under the City and Growth Deals. To return to accelerated growth and gain greater market share in the longer term, it is critical that Northern Ireland is in a position to compete with the Republic of Ireland and other tourism destinations. To do that, Northern Ireland must be able to offer a range of world class visitor attractions which appeal to our core market segments thus encouraging more people to visit, stay longer and spend more.

The delivery of this major capital investment programme will support the development of world class experiences across Northern Ireland promoting regional dispersal and sustainable tourism. Tourism NI acts as project sponsor to ensure that individual projects demonstrate they can meet market demand, are commercially viable in the longer term and deliver the highest possible economic return. This is an area the tourism sector will hear a lot more about next year as the key investments start to get delivered.

Skills

We recognise that attracting and retaining staff is a big challenge for many parts of the industry at the moment. There is a need to improve awareness too of the opportunities to develop a career in the sector.

With that in mind, we are working closely with the Hospitality and Tourism Skills Network to deliver a major recruitment and skills campaign early in 2022. The campaign will highlight the range of attractive roles and career choices in the industry. Running alongside the campaign, Tourism NI

John McGrillen, CEO Tourism NI

continues to champion the 'Hospitality and Tourism Commitment' as a way to spread good employment practice across the industry and boost the message that the sector is a positive career choice.

Events

Alongside financial assistance programmes, Tourism NI has delivered a suite of support for events that demonstrate compelling content with the potential to attract both local and out of state visitors.

We recently launched the National Tourism Events Sponsorship Scheme for events taking place between April 2022 and March 2023 and will be delivering an event specific series of webinars, workshops and masterclasses on key topics such as environmental sustainability, inclusivity and accessibility.

With the Covid-19 pandemic still very much with us, support will be available for both live and hybrid events.

Earlier this year, alongside the R&A, I was delighted to announce the return of The Open Championship in 2025 and, along with my colleagues, I look forward to working with multi agency partners to make it an even bigger success than the event delivered in 2019.

TNI.com/Insights and Market Intelligence

The website TourismNI.com plays a crucial role in delivery of information and guidance. It is an excellent resource for the industry who can receive targeted updates and information on a wide range of areas, including consumer sentiment, industry research and insight reports. The site also hosts other events and programme registration information and associated toolkits. By registering on the hub businesses can also manage their listing on discovernorthernireland.com. Updates on all activity can be viewed on tourismni.com, including participation in the TED programme and continued engagement with all of teams at Tourism NI for tailored support.

For more information on how Tourism NI can support businesses visit: www.tourismni.com/contact-us/covid-19-business-support-helpline/

*Twitter: @NITouristBoard
LinkedIn:
www.linkedin.com/company/northern-ireland-tourist-board*

Tourism and Conferencing

Tourism organisations

Department for the Economy
Netherleigh, Massey Avenue
Belfast, BT4 2JP
Tel: 028 9052 9900
Text Relay: 18001 028 9052 9900
Email: tourismpolicy@economy-ni.gov.uk
Head of Tourism: Geraldine Fee

Tourism NI
Floors 10-12
Linum Chambers
Bedford Square
Bedford Street
Belfast, BT2 7ES
Tel: 028 9023 1221
Web: www.tourismni.com
Email: info@tourismni.com

Dublin Office
The Cresent Building
Northwood Business Park
Santry, Dublin 9
Tel: +353 (0) 1 865 1880
Email: infodublin@tourismni.com

Chair: Terence Brannigan
Chief Executive: John McGrillen
Director of Business Support and Events: Áine Kearney
Interim Director of Organisational Development and HR: Jill O'Reilly
Director of Marketing: Naomi Waite
Director of Finance: Lesley McKeown
Chief Digital Officer: Dave Vincent
Director of Strategic Development: David Roberts
Head of Regions: Ciaran Doherty

Tourism NI is responsible for the development, promotion and marketing of Northern Ireland as a tourist destination.

Tourism Ireland Limited
Beresford House
2 Beresford Road
Coleraine, BT52 1GE
Tel: 028 7035 9200
Web: www.tourismireland.com
Email: corporate.coleraine@tourismireland.com

Dublin Office
5th Floor, Bishop's Square
Redmond's Hill, Dublin 2, D02 TD99
Tel: +353 (0)1 476 3400
Email: corporate.dublin@tourismireland.com

Chair: Joan O'Shaughnessy
Chief Executive: Niall Gibbons
Director of Markets: Siobhan McManamy
Marketing Director: Mark Henry
Director of Corporate Services, Policy and Northern Ireland: Shane Clarke

Tourism Ireland is responsible for marketing the island of Ireland overseas as a holiday and business tourism destination.

Northern Ireland Tourism Alliance
c/o 50 Bedford Street
Belfast
BT2 7FW
Tel: 077 4245 0283
Web: www.nitourismalliance.com
Email: info@nitourismalliance.com
Chief Executive: Joanne Stuart

Visitor information centres

Belfast
Visit Belfast (Belfast and Northern Ireland)
8-9 Donegall Square North, BT1 5GJ
Tel: 028 9024 6609
Email: info@visitbelfast.com

Airports
George Best Belfast City Airport
Sydenham Bypass, BT3 9JH
Tel: 028 9093 5372
Email: info@visitbelfast.com

Belfast International Airport
Arrivals Hall, BT29 4AB
Tel: 028 9448 4677
Email: info@visitbelfast.com

City of Derry Airport
Airport Road, Derry, BT47 3PY

County Antrim

Antrim
The Old Courthouse
Market Square, BT41 4AW
Tel: 028 9442 8331
Email: info@antrimandnewtownabbey.gov.uk

Ballymena
The Braid
1-29 Bridge Street, BT43 5EJ
Tel: 028 2563 5010
Email: reception@midandeastantrim.gov.uk

Cushendall
Old School House, 25 Mill Street
Cushendall, Co Antrim, BT44 0RR
Tel: +44 (0)28 2177 1180

Giant's Causeway
44 Causeway Road
Bushmills, BT57 8SU
Tel: 028 2073 1855
Email: giantscausewaytic@nationaltrust.org.uk

Newtownabbey
Carnmoney Road North
Newtownabbey, BT36 5QA
Tel: +44 (0) 28 9034 0000

Rathlin Island Boathouse Visitor's Centre
The Boathouse Demesne
Rathlin Island, BT54 6RT
Tel: +44 (0) 28 2076 2024

Credit: Tourism NI

The Voice for Tourism

The NI Tourism Alliance (NITA) was established in August 2018 to provide a united and independent voice for the tourism economy in Northern Ireland. Our members cover the diversity of sectors making up the tourism and travel economy – accommodation, attractions, airlines, airports, tour guides, destination marketing organisations, coach sector, taxi sector, travel agents, education providers and councils. In addition, we have strategic partnerships with Tourism NI and Tourism Ireland.

NITA's role is to represent our members and ensure the voice of industry is listened to in shaping the future growth of tourism and lobbying at all levels of government and beyond to raise awareness of and contributing to the solution of major strategic issues affecting the industry, which include everything from the UK's exit from the European Union, the impact of APD, VAT, access to talent and skills development and the ongoing uncertainty of the economic climate to the industry's overall competitiveness.

Over the last decade, tourism has been one of the most resilient and successful parts of the local economy, surpassing returns on investment made in other industrial sectors and outpacing the average in job creation.

In 2019, leisure and business visitors spent in excess of £1 billion, over 70 per cent of which was external sales, i.e., spend by visitors from outside of Northern Ireland. This spend supported over 72,000 jobs with the benefits spread across the region in rural, coastal and urban communities.

Tourism and travel suffered more than any other sectors throughout the pandemic, and it is down to the innovation and resilience of our businesses and strong destination proposition that we are in a position to look forward and build back stronger.

Tourism is an exciting and dynamic industry with a shared vision and ambition to double its economic impact by 2030. This will contribute to the wider regional economy bringing investment and jobs across the region.

NITA has supported our members and stakeholders throughout and will continue to work together to address the challenges the industry is facing. With revenues decimated, and international travel halted there is work to do to ensure the financial sustainability of a sector and to attract more people into the sector to support our ambition for growth.

The continued development of Northern Ireland as an exciting destination sends a positive message internationally. The significant investment in tourism and regeneration with the City and Growth deals, the return of The Open, the opening of the HBO Game of Thrones Studio Tour and hosting One Young World in 2023 are examples of the many developments that will enable us to maximise the transformational benefits that tourism presents in Northern Ireland.

Find out more about Northern Ireland Tourism Alliance at www.nitourismalliance.com and contribute to the professional debate on Facebook, Twitter and LinkedIn.

nita northern ireland tourism alliance

The Voice for Tourism

- Events and Conferencing
- Attractions, Guides, Agents and Operators
- Accommodation
- Destination Marketing Organisations
- Road/Air/Sea/Rail Transport
- Education and Skills

Tourism and Conferencing | Northern Ireland Yearbook

County Down

Banbridge
The Market House
1 Scarva Street, BT32 3DA
Tel: 028 4062 0232
Email: tic@armaghbanbridgecraigavon.gov.uk

Bangor
34 Quay Street, BT20 5ED
Tel: 028 9127 0069
Email: bangorvic@ardsandnorthdown.gov.uk

Downpatrick
The St Patrick Centre
53A Market Street, BT30 6LZ
Tel: 028 4461 2233
Email: downpatrick.vic@nmandd.org

Hillsborough
The Courthouse
The Square, BT26 6AG
Tel: 028 9268 9717
Email: vic.hillsborough@lisburncastlereagh.gov.uk

Kilkeel
The Nautilus Centre
Rooney Road, BT34 4AG
Tel: 028 4176 2525
Email: info@visitkilkeel.com

Newcastle
10-14 Central Promenade, BT33 0AA
Tel: 028 4372 2222
Email: newcastle.vic@nmandd.org

Newtownards
31 Regent Street, BT23 4AD
Tel: 028 9182 6846
Email: ardsvic@ardsandnorthdown.gov.uk

County Derry

Coleraine
Town Hall, 35 The Diamond, BT51 1DP
Tel: 028 7034 4723
Email: colerainevic@causewaycoastandglens.gov.uk

Limavady
Roe Valley Arts Cultural Centre
24 Main Street, BT49 0FJ
Tel: 028 7776 0650
Email: information@rvacc.co.uk

Derry
1-3 Waterloo Place, Derry, BT48 6BT
Tel: 028 7126 7284
Email: info@derryvisitor.com

Magherafelt
The Bridewell
6 Church Street, BT45 6AN
Tel: 028 7963 1510
Email: tourism@midulstercouncil.org

County Tyrone

Cookstown
The Burnavon
Burn Road, BT80 8DN
Tel: 028 8676 9949
Email: tourism@midulstercouncil.org

Dungannon
Hill of The O'Neill and
Ranfurly House Arts and Visitor Centre
26 Market Square, BT70 1AB
Tel: 028 8772 8600
Email: tourism@midulstercouncil.org

Omagh
Strule Arts Centre
Townhall Square, BT78 1BL
Tel: 028 8224 7831
Email: info@struleartscentre.co.uk

Strabane
The Alley Arts and Conference Centre
1a Railway Street, BT82 8EF
Tel: 028 7138 4444
Email: alleytheatre@derrystrabane.com

Travel / Transport links

Belfast Harbour
Harbour Office, Corporation Square
Belfast, BT1 3AL
Tel: 028 9055 4422
Web: www.belfast-harbour.co.uk
Email: info@belfast-harbour.co.uk
Chief Executive: Joe O'Neill

Belfast International Airport
Airport Road, Belfast, BT29 4AB
Tel: 028 9448 4848
Web: www.belfastairport.com
Managing Director: Graham Keddie

City of Derry Airport
Airport Road, Eglinton
Co Derry, BT47 3GY
Tel: 028 7181 0784
Web: www.cityofderryairport.com
Email: info@cityofderryairport.com
Managing Director: Steve Frazer

George Best Belfast City Airport
Airport Road, Belfast, BT3 9JH
Tel: 028 9093 9093
Web: www.belfastcityairport.com
Managing Director: Matthew Hall

Port of Larne
9 Olderfleet Road
Larne, BT40 1AS
Tel: 028 2887 2100
Web: www.portoflarne.co.uk
Email: info@portoflarne.co.uk
Harbour Master: Stuart Wilson

Tourist attractions

A small selection of Northern Ireland's tourist attractions are listed below.

Belfast Cathedral
Donegall Street, Belfast, BT1 2HB
Tel: 028 9032 8332
Email: admin@belfastcathedral.org

Belfast Zoo
Antrim Road, Belfast, BT36 7PN
Tel: 028 9077 6277
Web: www.belfastzoo.co.uk
Email: info@belfastzoo.co.uk

Carrick-a-Rede Rope Bridge
119a White Park Road, Ballintoy
Ballycastle, BT54 6LS
Tel: 028 2073 3335
Web: www.nationaltrust.org.uk/carrick-a-rede
Email: carrick-a-rede@nationaltrust.org.uk

Carrickfergus Castle
Marine Highway
Carrickfergus, BT38 7BG
Tel: 028 9335 1273
Email: scmenquiries@communities-ni.gov.uk

Crumlin Road Gaol
53-55 Crumlin Road, Belfast
BT14 6ST
Tel: 028 9074 1500
Web: www.crumlinroadgaol.com
Email: info@crumlinroadgaol.com

The Dark Hedges
Bregagh Road
(near Gracehill Golf Club)
Stranocum, Ballymoney, BT53 8TP
Tel: 028 2766 0230
Email: ballymoneyvic@causewaycoastandglens.gov.uk

Northern Ireland Yearbook | Tourism and Conferencing

Enniskillen Castle Museum
Enniskillen
Co Fermanagh, BT74 7HL
Tel: 028 6632 5000
Web: www.enniskillencastle.co.uk
Email: castle@fermanaghomagh.gov.uk

Giant's Causeway
44 Causeway Road
Bushmills, BT57 8SU
Tel: 028 2073 1855
Web: www.nationaltrust.org.uk/giants-causeway
Email: giantscauseway@nationaltrust.org.uk

Hillsborough Castle and Gardens
Main Street, Hillsborough
Co Down, BT26 6AG
Tel: +44 (0) 333 320 6000

HMS Caroline
Alexandra Dock
Queen's Road, Belfast
Co Antrim, BT3 9DT
Tel: 028 9045 4484

Irish Linen Centre and Lisburn Museum
Market Square, Lisburn
Co Antrim, BT28 1AG
Tel: 028 9266 3377
Web: www.lisburnmuseum.com
Email: reception@lisburncastlereagh.gov.uk

Marble Arch Caves UNESCO Global Geopark
43 Marlbank Road, Florencecourt
Enniskillen, BT92 1EW
Tel: 028 6634 8855
Web: www.marblearchcavesgeopark.com
Email: mac@fermanaghomagh.com

Mount Stewart
Portaferry Road, Newtownards
Co Down, BT22 2AD
Tel: 028 4278 8387
Web: www.nationaltrust.org.uk/mount-stewart
Email: mountstewart@nationaltrust.org.uk

Old Bushmills Distillery
2 Distillery Road, Bushmills, BT57 8XH
Tel: 028 2073 3218
Web: www.bushmills.com
Email: visitors.bushmills@bushmills.com

Seamus Heaney HomePlace
45 Main Street
Bellaghy, BT45 8HT
Tel: 028 7938 7444
Web: www.seamusheaneyhome.com
Email: seamusheaneyhome@midulstercouncil.org

Somme Museum
233 Bangor Road, Newtownards
Co Down, BT23 7PH
Tel: 028 9182 3202
Web: www.sommeassociation.com
Email: enquiry.shc@hotmail.co.uk

The Saint Patrick Centre
53A Market Street
Downpatrick, BT30 6LZ
Tel: 028 4461 9000
Web: www.saintpatrickcentre.com
Email: info@saintpatrickcentre.com

Titanic Belfast
1 Olympic Way, Queen's Road
Titanic Quarter
Belfast, BT3 9EP
Tel: 028 9076 6386
Web: www.titanicbelfast.com
Email: welcome@titanicbelfast.com

Tower Museum
Union Hall Place, Derry
BT48 6LU
Tel: 028 7137 2411
Web: www.derrystrabane.com/towermuseum
Email: tower.reception@derrystrabane.com

Ulster American Folk Park
2 Mellon Road, Castletown
Omagh, Co Tyrone, BT78 5QU
Tel: 028 8224 3292
Web: www.nmni.com/uafp
Email: info@nmni.com

Ulster Folk and Transport Museum
153 Bangor Road, Cultra
Holywood, Co Down, BT18 0EU
Tel: 028 9042 8428
Web: www.nmni.com/uftm
Email: uftm.info@nmni.com

Ulster Museum
Botanic Gardens, Belfast, BT9 5AP
Tel: 028 9044 0000
Web: www.nmni.com
Email: info@nmni.com

W5
SSE Arena, 2 Queen's Quay
Belfast, BT3 9QQ
Tel: 028 9046 7700
Web: www.w5online.co.uk
Email: info@w5online.co.uk

Beaches

Ballycastle Marina
14 Bayview Road
Ballycastle, BT54 6BT
Tel: 028 2076 8525
Web: www.causewaycoastandglens.gov.uk

Benone Strand
53 Benone Avenue, Limavady, Derry
Tel: 028 7776 0304
Web: www.causewaycoastandglens.gov.uk

Castlerock Beach
Contact: 35 The Diamond
Coleraine, BT52 1DE
Tel: 028 7034 4723
Web: www.visitcausewaycoastandglens.com
Email: colerainevic@causewaycoastandglens.gov.uk

Cranfield West Beach
Contact: Kilkeel Visitor Information Centre
28 Bridge Street, Kilkeel
Co Down, BT34 4AG
Tel: +44 (0) 330 137 4046
Email: info@newryandmourne.gov.uk

Credit: Tourism NI

Tourism and Conferencing

Crawfordsburn Country Park
Bridge Road South
Helen's Bay, BT19 1JT
Tel: 028 9185 3621
Web: www.daera-ni.gov.uk
Email: nieainfo@daera-ni.gov.uk

Downhill Beach
Contact: Cloonavon
66 Portstewart Road
Coleraine, BT52 1EY
Tel: 028 7034 7034
Web: www.visitcausewaycoastandglens.com

East Strand Beach, Portrush
Contact: Cloonavin
66 Portstewart Road
Coleraine, BT52 1EY
Tel: 028 7034 7234
Web: www.causewaycoastandglens.gov.uk

Newcastle and Murlough Beach
10-14 Central Promenade
Newcastle
Co Down, BT33 0AA
Tel: 028 4372 2222

Portstewart Strand and Barmouth
118 Strand Road, Portstewart
Co Derry, BT55 7PG
Tel: 028 7083 6396
Web: www.nationaltrust.org.uk/portstewart-strand
Email: portstewart@nationaltrust.org.uk

Tyrella Beach
Contact: Clanmaghery Road
Downpatrick, BT30 8SU
Tel: 028 4482 8333

West Strand Beach
Portstewart Road, Portrush
BT56 8EY
Tel: 028 7034 7234

Whiterocks Beach, Portrush
Contact: Coleraine Town Hall
35 The Diamond, Coleraine, BT52 1DE
Tel: 028 7034 4723
Web: www.visitcausewaycoastandglens.com
Email: colerainevic@causewaycoastandglens.gov.uk

Forest Parks

Castle Archdale Country Park
Rossmore, Lisnarick
Enniskillen, BT94 1PP
Tel: 0300 200 7856
Web: www.daera-ni.gov.uk
Email: nieainfo@daera-ni.gov.uk

Castlewellan Forest Park
East District Forest Office
The Grange, Castlewellan, BT31 9BU
Tel: 028 4377 8664
Email: customer.forestservice@daera-ni.gov.uk

Colin Glen Forest Park
163 Stewartstown Road
Belfast, BT17 0HW
Tel: 028 9061 4115
Web: www.colinglen.org
Email: reception@colinglen.org

Crawfordsburn Country Park
Bridge Road South, Helen's Bay
BT19 1JT
Tel: 028 9185 3621
Website: www.daera-ni.gov.uk
Email: nieainfo@daera-ni.gov.uk

Drum Manor Forest Park
Cookstown, Tyrone
Tel: 028 6634 3165
Web: www.forestserviceni.gov.uk
Email: tourism@midulstercouncil.org

Glenariff Forest Park
98 Glenariff Road
Glenariff
Co Antrim, BT44 0QX
Tel: 028 7034 0870
Email: customer.forestservice@daera-ni.gov.uk

Gosford Forest Park
7 Gosford Demesne, Markethill
Armagh, BT60 1GD
Tel: 028 3755 1277
Web: www.gosford.org.uk
Email: customer.forestservice@daera-ni.gov.uk

Gortnamoyagh Forest
6 Forest Road
Garvagh
Derry, BT51 5EF
Tel: 028 2955 6003
Web: www.nidirect.gov.uk/forests
Email: customer.forestservice@daera-ni.gov.uk

Hillsborough Forest Park
Hillsborough, Co Down
BT26 6DP
Tel: 028 4377 2240
Web: www.nidirect.gov.uk/forests
Email: customer.forestservice@daera-ni.gov.uk

Tollymore Forest Park
Bryansford Road
Tollymore Park, Newcastle
Co Down, BT33 0PR
Tel: 028 4372 2428
Email: customer.forestservice@daera-ni.gov.uk

Slieve Gullion Forest Park
89 Drumintee Road
Killeavy, Newry, BT35 8SW
Tel: 028 3031 3170
Web: www.ringofgullion.org
Email: newryvic@newryandmourne.gov.uk

Theatres

The Ardhowen
97 Dublin Road, Derrychara
Enniskillen, BT74 6FZ
Tel: 028 6632 5440
Web: www.ardhowen.com
Email: ardhowen@fermanaghomagh.com

Credit: Tourism NI

Northern Ireland Yearbook | Tourism and Conferencing

Burnavon Arts and Cultural Centre
Burn Road, Cookstown, BT80 8DN
Tel: 028 8676 9949
Web: www.burnavon.com
Email: burnavon@midulstercouncil.org

The Crescent Arts Centre
2-4 University Road
Belfast, BT7 1NH
Tel: 028 9024 2338
Web: www.crescentarts.org
Email: info@crescentarts.org

Grand Opera House
Great Victoria Street
Belfast, BT2 7HR
Tel: 028 9024 0411
Web: www.goh.co.uk
Email: info@goh.co.uk

Lyric Theatre
55 Ridgeway Street
Belfast, BT9 5FB
Tel: 028 9038 1081
Web: www.lyrictheatre.co.uk
Email: info@lyrictheatre.co.uk

The MAC
10 Exchange Street West
Belfast, BT1 2NJ
Tel: 028 9023 5053
Web: www.themaclive.com
Email: tickets@themaclive.com

The Market Place Theatre and Arts Centre
Market Street, Armagh, BT61 7BW
Tel: 028 3752 1820
Web: www.marketplacearmagh.com
Email: admin@marketplacearmagh.com

Millennium Forum
Newmarket Street
Derry, BT48 6EB
Tel: 028 7126 4455
Web: www.millenniumforum.co.uk

Theatre at the Mill
Mossley Mill, Carnmoney Road North
Newtownabbey, BT36 5QA
Tel: 028 9034 0202
Web: www.theatreatthemill.com

Riverside Theatre
Ulster University
Coleraine, BT52 1SA
Tel: 028 7012 3123
Web: www.ulster.ac.uk/riverside

Sightseeing Tours

City Sightseeing Belfast
10 Great Victoria Street
Belfast, BT2 7BA
Tel: 028 9032 1321
Web: www.belfastcitysightseeing.com
Email: info@citysightseeingbelfast.com

City Sightseeing Derry
8 Ballougry Road
Derry, BT48 9XJ
Tel: 028 7137 0067
Web: www.citysightseeingderry.com
Email: info@citysightseeingderry.com

Game of Thrones Tour
22 Donegall Road
Belfast, BT12 5JN
Tel: 028 9031 5333
Web: www.mccombscoaches.com/tours/game-of-thrones-tours
Email: info@mccombscoaches.com

Credit: Tourism NI

Planning for event success

In today's cost-conscious business environment, it is more important than ever for organisations wishing to put together an event, whatever its purpose, to ensure that everything goes smoothly and the event is a success. It is important to implement an effective planning process, to ensure everything runs efficiently, both in the run up to, and on the day itself. Below is a step by step guide to successful event planning.

Establish the purpose of the event and what format it's going to take

Before starting to organise any event it's important to establish what the event is going to be and why it's taking place. The objectives behind a company's annual drinks reception might simply be to get key stakeholders together for a sociable glass of wine whereas a gala awards dinner would aim to attract sponsorship and guests for dinner and obtain media coverage. The organisation would therefore have to be approached differently in terms of venues, invitations, catering etc.

Some of the various types of events organisations might wish to organise, for different purposes might include:

- conferences;
- webinars;
- dinners;
- awards ceremonies;
- report or product launches;
- drinks receptions;
- press conferences;
- 'openings' of new or refurbished premises;
- exhibitions;
- Q&A sessions with an expert;
- lecture series; and
- information sessions.

It is vital to think carefully about exactly what type of event is most appropriate to the organisation's business and objectives. Event objectives, in terms of what the planned event will achieve, should always be SMART: Specific, Measurable, Agreed, Realistic and Timed.

Covid-19: Online and hybrid events

The Covid-19 pandemic has meant that many events had to become virtual or hybrid depending on the Government restrictions at the time. It must first be considered if virtual suits the event – i.e. a large exhibition does not transfer to online as it is centred around a physical presence. If an event is suited to online, then a good video conferencing platform needs to be sourced with additional IT needs to be considered. The basic principles of event management remain the same whether the event is in person, online or a combination of both.

Agree a budget

It is important to set a budget at the outset and ensure this is adhered to throughout. To assist with budgeting, obtain two or three written quotations for any services required (e.g. photography, AV services, printing) to ensure prices are competitive. Keep records of any rates agreed for services to be provided and exactly what these include.

Consider whether it is possible for the event to generate any income to offset costs, e.g. it might be an option to sell exhibition space at a conference or obtain sponsorship for aspects of an event. If there are high-profile media personalities or other expert or celebrity speakers attending they will often have high fees and perhaps also require travel and accommodation expenses. Establish exactly what their fee is and what is included in it so it can be budgeted for at an early stage.

Date and venue

Obviously the 'where' and 'when' are two key elements of event planning. In deciding upon where and when an in-person event should take place, there are a number of important questions to consider:

Date issues

- availability of key people such as the company chairman/chief executive or a high-profile guest speaker or media personality;
- potential clashes with other events within the sector; and
- holiday times (christmas/easter/bank or public holidays) are best avoided if possible.

Venue issues

- where are people attending the event coming from?;
- does the venue need to be close to an airport if there are international guests attending?;
- is a city centre or out of town venue more appropriate? If people are invited for a glass of wine after work, city centre is likely to be better whereas for an all-day conference it won't be such an issue;
- is the venue accessible by public transport or is there sufficient car parking available?;
- is space required for exhibition/break-out rooms/media facilities etc.?;
- how will guests be seated? Consider classroom style/theatre style/cabaret style for conferences or informal seating arrangements for receptions and dinners;
- is there an interesting or quirky venue that would tie in with the objectives of the event or create interest?;
- will there be any social events running alongside the main event?;
- does the venue have accommodation on site or nearby?

A very basic consideration in any venue is the size of the facilities on offer – for conferences consider catering arrangements as well as the conference itself. Many venues can offer a large conference room but nowhere to actually give delegates a seated lunch if that's what is required!

An important factor in booking venues is cost and how the cost is arrived at. For conferences some venues will have a 'delegate rate' available which includes room hire, AV facilities and catering – it is worth checking that what is included is in line with what is required at the individual event e.g. if it is a two or three course lunch or how many coffee breaks are included. Depending on numbers and what's included it may be better value to pay for room hire and catering and AV services separately.

Marketing

Obviously depending on what type of event is being organised, the marketing will be approached in different ways. If it's for a major commercial conference or exhibition, it is most likely that brochures will be required for mailing out to potential delegates or attendees alongside email marketing and social

Tourism and Conferencing

media. However, for an annual dinner or drinks reception, a printed or perhaps emailed invitation may be sufficient.

Before embarking on any marketing activity it's important to establish who the target attendance is and what the best means of communicating with them might be. If it's a press conference or launch targeting a high level of media attendance, they can be invited by email but will require a follow-up call closer to the time of the event to confirm if they can attend. Depending on the type of event, it is worth considering if advertising it is appropriate and what might be the best outlet for this, not forgetting the value of local newspapers if it's an event targeting local attendance within a specific area.

In line with marketing, there will need to be a system for registering attendees or recording RSVPs – for something like an annual dinner it might be appropriate to follow up via telephone for those guests who have not replied by a set date. Give some consideration to any information attendees might need such as directions to the venue or dress code and record any information they provide such as dietary or access requirements.

Media

Alongside the event itself, there are often useful opportunities to be gained from media coverage surrounding the event. If the event is to attract media attention it's important that the media are engaged early and constructively. Find out the names of the appropriate correspondents from the various media outlets and send them notice of the event, including an invitation to attend, with as much information as possible. Follow up with a press release and appropriate photo (perhaps of the event launch or of someone who is participating in it) and check if they plan to attend.

It is important to have media facilities available on-the-day e.g. a quiet room for interviews, access to internet/power points for laptops, copies of any press releases etc. Following up with a good captioned photo and some additional information on the event can be a good way of obtaining post-event media coverage. Ensure a nominated person is allocated responsibility for media liaison so the media have a single point of contact for the event.

Audio-visual requirements

Establish what is required in terms of audio-visual services for the event – sound system, microphones, lighting, projection, screens, TVs, DVD players etc. AV can often be considered just another additional service but is actually highly central to the success or failure of any event. There is no point in paying huge amounts of money to secure a celebrity speaker if no one can see or hear them! If the AV doesn't run smoothly it will impact upon the entire event.

Don't assume that the AV that is included with venue hire will meet your requirements – establish exactly what is included and double-check it's actually working if you plan to use it. Also ensure you are briefed as to how it works as it's likely the one person in the venue that knows all about it will disappear at the key moment!

As with any service, obtain a number of written quotations for AV services and try and obtain recommendations from others that have used the company. Make sure the AV operator is fully aware of what is expected from him/her on the day and have a rehearsal if possible.

Catering

In many cases the venue will be responsible for catering but in some non-hotel venues outside caterers will be required. If this is the case, obtain two or three quotations and try to use a catering company that is familiar with the venue – usually the contact within the venue can recommend or suggest some good outside catering companies.

In all cases, establish exactly what is required in terms of numbers and menus (it is often worth estimating numbers on the lower side of what is expected to attend as there is usually some who find they can't make it at the last minute). Consider the option of a buffet (hot or cold) instead of a sit-down meal, if it's appropriate to the event, as this can often be less expensive and allow for better networking opportunities. Remember to allow for vegetarians and other special dietary requirements and try to choose menus that will appeal to a broad range of people.

The event itself

Alongside all the other considerations outlined above, there is one fundamental area that is central to the success of the planned event and that is the event itself! If it's a conference the success of the event will be centred around the programme so this is vitally important to get right so that people actually want to attend. There should be a mix of local and visiting speakers and the topics should address the key theme of the conference. Build in plenty of opportunities for networking and discussion so delegates feel they've had an opportunity to express their own views and meet and discuss with other attendees.

If the event is a dinner or a drinks reception or launch give some thought to who is going to speak, when and for how long, if any entertainment is required and how long the whole event is expected to last.

On-the-day

If all the planning and preparation has been put in place beforehand, the event should run smoothly on-the-day but it's important to always be prepared and in a position to respond to any last minute crises! Some important guidelines for on-the-day, regardless of the type of event being organised, include:

- arive early to ensure everything is set up properly;
- have a list of phone numbers for key people handy – speakers, AV provider, outside caterers etc;
- have a pre-event briefing, in the venue, for all those with a key role in the event so everyone knows what's happening when and who has responsibility for individual actions;
- ensure timings are adhered to as far as possible – at a conference one speaker running over his/her time can have a knock-on effect for the rest of the day;
- finalise your timetable with the venue and keep them informed of any changes;
- make sure the AV operator is fully briefed as to all AV requirements and has an up to date copy of the programme or running order to hand;
- have a box of essentials on hand containing anything you are likely to need such as sticky tape, drawing pins, a stapler etc.

Post-event

No matter what the event is, there is always some form of post-event activity required.

Typically this can include:

- sending thank you letters to anyone that has helped with the event;
- agreeing and paying any outstanding bills;
- returning any hired equipment;
- following up on any other promised actions from the event e.g. sending more information on something or setting up a meeting with a new contact;
- post-event evaluation – what worked well and what could be improved upon next time.

Success

No events guide can ever cover all of the considerations for every single event. As each event has its own needs and requirements, there will always be additional aspects to organise, the detail of which hasn't been included here. However, by sticking to the main guidelines outlined above, hopefully it will provide the recipe for a successful and stress-free event, whatever the occasion.

Tourism and Conferencing

Conference venues

Assembly Buildings Conference Centre
2-10 Fisherwick Place
Belfast, BT1 6DW
Tel: 028 9041 7200
Web: www.assemblybuildings.co.uk
Email: info@assemblybuildings.co.uk

Armagh City Hotel
2 Friary Road, Armagh, BT60 4FR
Tel: 028 3751 8888
Web: www.armaghcityhotel.com
Email: conference@armaghcityhotel.com

Belfast Cathedral
Donegall Street, Belfast, BT1 2HB
Tel: 028 9032 8332
Email: admin@belfastcathedral.org

Belfast Castle
Antrim Road, Belfast, BT15 5GR
Tel: 028 9077 6925
Email: bcr@belfastcastle.co.uk

The Braid
1-29 Bridge Street
Ballymena, BT43 5EJ
Tel: 028 2563 5077
Web: www.thebraid.com
Email: braid.enquiries@midandeastantrim.gov.uk

Canal Court Hotel
Merchants Quay, Newry
Co Down, BT35 8HF
Tel: 028 3025 1234
Web: www.canalcourthotel.com
Email: manager@canalcourthotel.com

City Hotel Derry
Queens Quay, Derry, BT48 7AS
Tel: 028 7136 5800
Web: www.cityhotelderry.com
Email: events@cityhotelderry.com

Clandeboye Lodge Hotel
10 Estate Road, Bangor
Co Down, BT19 1UR
Tel: 028 9185 2500
Web: www.clandeboyelodge.com
Email: events@clandeboyelodge.co.uk

Corick House
20 Corick Road, Clogher
Co Tyrone, BT76 0BZ
Tel: 028 8554 8216
Web: www.corickcountryhouse.com
Email: funtions@corickcountryhouse.com

The Crescent Arts Centre
2-4 University Road
Belfast, BT7 1NH
Tel: 028 9024 2338
Web: www.crescentarts.org
Email: info@crescentarts.org

Culloden Estate and Spa
Bangor Road, Holywood
Belfast, BT18 OEX
Tel: 028 9042 1066
Email: conf@cull.hastingshotels.com

Cultra Manor (Ulster Folk and Transport Museum)
153 Bangor Road, Hollywood
BT18 OEU
Tel: 028 9042 3578
Email: cultramanor@nmni.com

Craigavon Civic and Conference Centre
Armagh City, Banbridge and Craigavon Borough Council
Lakeview Road
Craigavon, BT64 1AL
Tel: 028 3831 2423
Web: www.craigavonciviccentre.com
Email: info@craigavonciviccentre.com
Contact: Denise Lavery

Northern Ireland Yearbook | Tourism and Conferencing

Dunadry Hotel
2 Islandreagh Drive, Dunadry
Antrim, BT41 2HA
Tel: 028 9443 4343
Web: www.dunadry.com
Email: banqueting@dunadry.com

Dunsilly Hotel
20 Dunsilly Road
Antrim, BT41 2JH
Tel: 028 9446 2929
Web: www.dunsillyhotel.com
Email: conference@dunsillyhotel.com

Edenmore Golf Club
70 Drumnabreeze Road
Magheralin, Craigavon, BT67 0RH
Tel: 028 9261 9241
Web: www.edenmore.com
Email: events@edenmore.com

Eikon Exhibition Centre
Balmoral Park, Sprucefield
Halftown Road
Lisburn, BT27 5RF
Tel: 028 9066 5225
Web: www.eikonexhibitioncentre.co.uk
Email: events@eikon.uk.com

Everglades Hotel
Prehen Road, Derry
BT47 2NH
Tel: 028 7132 1066
Email: conf@egh.hastingshotels.com

Galgorm Resort and Spa
136 Fenaghy Road
Galgorm, BT42 1EA
Tel: 028 2588 2568
Web: www.galgorm.com
Email: events@galgorm.com

Glenavon House Hotel
52 Drum Road, Cookstown
BT80 8JQ
Tel: 028 8676 4949
Web: www.glenavonhotel.com
Email: info@glenavonhotel.co.uk

Grand Central Hotel
9-15 Bedford Street
Belfast, BT2 7FF
Tel: 028 9023 1066
Email: res@gch.hastingshotel.com

Grand Opera House
Great Victoria Street
Belfast, BT2 7HR
Tel: 028 9027 7738
Web: www.goh.co.uk
Email: events@goh.co.uk

Hilton Belfast
4 Lanyon Place
Belfast, BT1 3LP
Tel: 028 9027 7221
Web: www.hilton.com
Email: belfast.events@hilton.com

Hilton Templepatrick
Castle Upton Estate
Templepatrick, BT39 0DD
Tel: 028 9043 5500
Web: www.hilton.com
Email: events.templepatrick@hilton.com

ICC Belfast
2 Lanyon Place, Belfast, BT1 3WH
Tel: 028 9033 4400
Web: www.iccbelfast.com
Email: iccinfo@iccbelfast.com

Killyhevlin Hotel
Killyhevlin, Enniskillen
BT74 6RW
Tel: 028 6632 3481
Web: www.killyhevlin.com
Email: events@killyhevlin.com

La Mon Hotel and Country Club
41 Gransha Road
Castlereagh, Belfast
BT23 5RF
Tel: 028 9044 8631
Web: www.lamon.co.uk
Email: events@lamon.co.uk

Tourism and Conferencing

Lagan Valley Island
Lisburn and Castlereagh City Council
Lisburn, Co Antrim, BT27 4RL
Tel: 028 9250 9292
Email: www.laganvalleyisland.co.uk
Email: lvi@lisburncastlereagh.gov.uk

The Lodge Hotel
Coleraine, BT52 1NF
Tel: 028 7034 4848
Web: www.thelodgehotel.com
Email: info@thelodgehotel.com

Lough Erne Resort
Belleek Road, Enniskillen
Fermanagh, BT93 7ED
Tel: 028 6634 5721
Web: www.lougherneresort.com
Email: events@lougherneresort.com

Lough Neagh Discovery Centre
Oxford Island National Nature Reserve
Craigavon, BT66 6NJ
Tel: 028 3832 2205
Web: www.oxfordisland.com
Email: oxford.island@armaghbanbridgecraigavon.gov.uk

Loughshore Hotel
75 Belfast Road
Carrickfergus, BT38 8PH
Tel: 028 9336 4556
Web: www.loughshorehotel.com
Email: reception@loughshorehotel.com

Malone Lodge Hotel
60 Eglantine Avenue, Malone Road
Belfast, BT9 6DY
Tel: 028 9038 8000
Web: www.malonelodgehotelbelfast.com
Email: info@malonelodgehotel.com

Manor House Country Hotel
Killadeas, Enniskillen, BT94 1NY
Tel: 028 6862 2200
Web: www.manorhousecountryhotel.com
Email: info@manorhousecountryhotel.com

The Merchant Hotel
16 Skipper Street
Belfast, BT1 2DZ
Tel: 028 9023 4888
Web: www.themerchanthotel.com
Email: events@themerchanthotel.com

The Mount Conference and Business Centre
Woodstock Link, Belfast, BT6 8DD
Tel: 028 9073 0188
Web: www.the-mount.co.uk
Email: enquiries@the-mount.co.uk

Nerve Centre
5-6 Magazine Street
Derry, BT48 6HJ
Tel: 028 7126 0562
Web: nervecentre.org
Email: info@nervecentre.org

Roe Park Resort
Limavady, BT49 9LB
Tel: 028 7772 2222
Web: www.roeparkresort.com
Email: reservations@roeparkresort.com

Slieve Donard Resort and Spa
Downs Road
Newcastle, BT33 0AH
Tel: 028 4372 1010
Email: conf@sdh.hastingshotels.com

Stormont Hotel
Upper Newtownards Road
Belfast, BT4 3LP
Tel: 028 9067 6007
Email: conf@stor.hastingshotels.com

Titanic Belfast
1 Olympic Way, Queen's Road
Belfast, BT3 9EP
Tel: 028 9076 6386
Web: www.titanicbelfast.com
Email: enquiries@titanicbelfast.com

W5
SSE Arena, 2 Queen's Quay
Belfast, BT3 9QQ
Tel: 028 9046 7700
Web: www.w5online.co.uk
Email: info@w5online.co.uk

Northern Ireland Yearbook

Economy

Economy | **Northern Ireland Yearbook**

10X Economy: Minister Gordon Lyons MLA

Economy Minister Gordon Lyons MLA speaks to David Whelan about recovery from the pandemic, plans to boost consumer confidence, Brexit frictions and a vision for a decade of growth.

East Antrim MLA Gordon Lyons brushes off suggestions that he has an unenviable task in the context of an ongoing pandemic, Brexit tensions, and energy transition, all with less than a year to go to the end of the current mandate.

"It is an exciting time," he states. "We have gone through a difficult time, and I hope the worst is behind us. It is now about not just getting back to where we were pre-pandemic but about setting the building blocks for future and long-lasting recovery and growth."

Asked about his immediate priorities, in August 2021, the Minister says: "First and foremost we need to see a reopening of the economy. Getting rid of those restrictions that are still holding us back but then preparing for what comes next post-Covid and post-Brexit."

To this end, the Minister points to two pieces of policy announced by one of his recent predecessors, Diane Dodds MLA, in the form of February's Economic Recovery Action Plan, including the £290 million High Street Stimulus scheme, and the longer-term looking *10X Economy* document, which the Minister describes as "a bold and ambitious vision for Northern Ireland's economy", focusing on "our strengths", as well as identified key industries and sectors.

Northern Ireland Yearbook | Economy

The 10X vision points to the likes of agri-tech, fintech, advanced manufacturing and engineering, and life and health sciences as areas of opportunity for Northern Ireland's economy over the next decade.

Pointing to his belief that the onus is on the Executive to rebuild confidence and in particular, consumer confidence, the Minister says that the High Street Stimulus scheme is an enabler.

"It is not just about a one-off payment to go on a one-off purchase. It hopefully builds consumer confidence over time, getting people on to the high street," the Minister states, highlighting the benefits to this approach over "giving money directly to businesses to close".

"I believe there is a demand there. We have to get back to normal and we have to help create those conditions," he adds.

Balance

Asked whether he felt the right balance had been struck between mitigating the economic impacts of the pandemic and managing the public health crisis, he says: "It is difficult to say with a great deal of certainty that we definitely got the right approach. I certainly feel that businesses have taken the brunt over the last number of months, and it has been exceptionally difficult for them.

"I understand the frustrations people express to me when they ask, 'what was the impact on health and did we really make a difference?' because a lot of businesses have found that very difficult," Lyons says.

"However, in terms of support, I think we did step in in many cases and we went further than the rest of the UK and Ireland with regards to the support that we offered.

"The Executive has always said that we would look at the health, societal and economic impacts. I think it is important that as we continue to relax restrictions, we continue to give consideration to the economic impacts."

Turning to the longer-term ambitions, Lyons identifies the 10X vision as the overall economic vision that requires buy-in from a wide range of stakeholders. Going "hand-in-hand" with that vision is the soon to be produced Skills Strategy.

Skills

Discussing the necessity for a focus on skills, Lyons explains: "There is no point having a 10X vision if we are not prepared to do the work to ensure we have people with the right skills. In focusing on those key areas and sectors, we need to ensure the people that we want to work in those industries have the skills to succeed.

"We want to stand out. We want Northern Ireland's economy to be among the elite of the small economies in the world and that is going to require work. We have the people and the talent. Our job now is to ensure that they are properly skilled."

Lyons admits that the pandemic has had an impact on the landscape of the labour market, particularly for certain industries. Using the example of a perceived exodus from the hospitality sector by some experienced and skilled workers into other sectors, he acknowledges that as well as looking to emerging sectors, some traditional sectors will require assistance in recruiting and retaining skills.

However, the Minister is also quick to point out opportunities presented by the pandemic. For example, a rise in flexible and remote working patterns lends itself to addressing regional imbalance, an ambition under the *New Decade, New Approach* agreement.

Budget

Asked whether he was confident the Department will have access to the necessary resources to deliver on its ambitions, in the context of other departments competing for a portion of the block grant, not least the Department of Health, Lyons says consideration must be given to the wider implications of investment in the economy.

"People who are in employment are generally healthier," he states. "We have heard the Chief Medical Officer stating that they do worry about the economic consequences of Covid because it reflects on people's health.

"Looking at the work we are doing in and around research and development, there is huge potential there to transform how we deliver healthcare and to support cutting-edge technologies to provide better health outcomes."

The Economy Minister is adamant that future ambitions should not be viewed in the context of a departmental competition. "We need to be putting resources in the places where we get the best outcomes for investment," he states. "This is not about health versus economy. It is about putting resources in the right place to deliver the right outcomes for the people we represent."

The Minister reaffirmed the value of a multi-year budget, highlighting the unsustainable nature of recent one-year budgets.

On what a multi-year allocation would offer, he says: "It will provide more certainty to the Department going forward. Our 10X vision is not a one-year document, it is a 10-year plan.

Economy 249

Economy | Northern Ireland Yearbook

Making sure we have a multiannual budget is crucial to delivering on our longer-term ambitions. We need longer-term thinking, longer-term planning and the requires longer-term budgeting as well."

Brexit

Having served in the Executive as a Junior Minister and as interim Agriculture Minister for a short period, since the resumption of the Northern Ireland Assembly, Lyons is well versed on the challenges presented by Brexit. In February 2021, the then Agriculture Minister sparked controversy when he ordered officials to halt construction of permanent inspection facilities for post-Brexit checks and further recruitment of inspection staff for the port facilities. He has consistently advocated for the Protocol to be removed.

Asked whether his opinion had changed upon taking up the Economy post, he says: "Do I still believe we can do better that what we have now? Yes, absolutely. The Protocol is causing huge frictions in the UK internal market and that is important not just from a political point of view but because it is our biggest market and we have integrated supply chains that have been disturbed."

Lyons says that having listened to complaints from businesses since January 2021, he believes a better arrangement can be agreed. In this sense, he says he is glad "there is the beginnings of an understanding" from the UK Government and "even an acknowledgement of the EU, in part".

The UK Government, through its command paper, has asked for a renegotiation of the Protocol. However, while former Brexit Minister David Frost has outlined his belief that the requirements to trigger Article 16 have been met, there is a clear reluctance to do so on the Government's part.

The Minister explains that while he would like to see a quick renegotiation, he doesn't believe the UK Government's command paper places the "impetus" on the European Union to return to the negotiating table.

"If they [the EU] are not prepared to recognise the problems and they are not prepared to offer anything more than piecemeal solutions, then they need to come back to the table. If Article 16 is the way to force that, then it needs to be done," he states.

Highlighting that the UK Government have set out the reasons why the triggering of Article 16 is now appropriate, he adds: "Article 16 is part of the Protocol. It is in there for a reason. I do not believe the EU or the UK Government thought there were going to be the problems we are currently experiencing."

The triggering of Article 16 risks ensuing a lengthy legal battle between the UK and the EU and another period of uncertainty for businesses in Northern Ireland who have endured years of uncertainty since the Brexit referendum. It also risks a further breakdown of relations and, potentially, a collapse of the current agreement which protects Northern Ireland's place in the single market and an open border on the island of Ireland.

Asked if he believed this was a risk worth taking, the Minister states: "There is a risk of those things happening versus the reality of what is actually happening now. People talk about the potential risks to the single market or to the border on the island of Ireland but what we are facing right now is the reality of trade between Great Britain and Northern Ireland, Northern Ireland's biggest trade partner, being disrupted.

"There is a risk to businesses and that is before we have any diversion and the end of grace periods. Once we move beyond that, we are in an even more difficult situation.

"There is a whole set of issues, some we are facing now and some we will face in the future, compared to the possibility of what might happen. The EU and the Republic of Ireland have made it very clear for a long time that there is not going to be a border on the island of Ireland and if that is the case then why don't we do something to sort out the disruption in trade between Northern Ireland and its biggest partner."

Asked to outline what tangible success might look like for his department with less than one year left of the mandate, the Minister points to the delivery of an Energy Strategy, the roll out of the High Street Stimulus scheme, progress under city deals and a continuation of work under the 10X vision and its associated documents, as key areas.

"Ideally, by April or May [2022] it would be great to say the worst effects of the pandemic are over and we are now on a pathway to growth. That is where I would like to leave the Department at the end of the mandate," he concludes.

"Article 16 is part of the Protocol. It is in there for a reason. I do not believe the EU or the UK Government thought there were going to be the problems we are currently experiencing."

10X skills for a 10X economy

Released as a key component of the *10X Economy* plan, the new draft skills strategy for Northern Ireland envisions economic growth driven by the rebalancing of skills imbalances, the creation of a culture of lifelong learning and the development of a "digital spine".

The draft *Skills Strategy for Northern Ireland: Skills for a 10X Economy* was published in May as part of the 10X Economy strategy, which envisions the growth of Northern Ireland's economy by 10 times from its current standing. Having opened the consultation process for the skills strategy upon its publication, the consultation period ended on 19 August 2021.

Delivering an economy that performs at 10 times the rate that it currently does will require a transformation of the skills capacity in Northern Ireland, which will "mean investing in the skills that will drive our key strategic clusters, boosting the research and innovation potential of our workforce and developing Northern Ireland as a global hub of knowledge through strong collaboration between government, business and our world class research institutions," the strategy says.

The consultation document lays out the three major policy objectives within the strategy: addressing skills imbalances; creating a lifelong culture of learning; and enhancing digital skills in order to create a "digital spine". The three policy enablers that will underpin these objectives are: enhancing policy cohesion; building strong relationships; and investment in the skills system. These objectives and enablers have been formulated in part through the use of the Skills Barometer for Northern Ireland, which has shown that three key issues to address social and economic development are: the prevalence of individuals with low, or no qualifications; limited opportunities for high paying jobs and pathways for career progression; and a 'skills deficit' and comparatively poor productivity performance.

The actions included in the plan to achieve the goal of addressing skills imbalances include increasing the proportion of people graduating from higher education institutions with degrees and post-graduate qualifications in STEM subjects such as physical, environmental and computer sciences, engineering and mathematics, "significantly" increasing the proportion of individuals achieving level 3, 4 and 5 qualifications, and increasing the proportion of the working age population with qualifications at level 2 and above. In order to achieve the second goal of the creation of a lifelong culture of learning, initiatives such as investment in apprenticeships, a Flexible Skills Fund to support upskilling and reskilling, and proposals for investment in leadership and management training are mentioned.

Key to the development of digital skills and the digital spine, the plan proposes is the publication of a separate plan. "It is proposed that a *'Digital Skills Action Plan'* is developed to support the objectives of our economic vision: driving our decade of innovation and providing everyone with the opportunity to participate in our 10X Economy," the report says. This digital action plan would utilise the same co-design principles used for the skills strategy, appoint an expert panel to consider the changing digital skills needs of the economy and identify the changes needed in education to meet the needs of the labour market and society.

The report concludes on a familiar note, by emphasising the need for multi-year budgets in Northern Ireland: "Not only do we need to reprioritise our investment in education and skills, but we need a commitment to introduce the multi-year budgets which will underpin strategic planning and the transformational change in our skills system that will be required to deliver our 10X Economy."

Economy | **Northern Ireland Yearbook**

Budget 2022-25: The inflation factor

Northern Ireland's first multiannual budget in almost a decade is expected to be published in March 2022 but Finance Minister Conor Murphy MLA has criticised the allocation for "a flat budget over the period".

In his Autumn Budget and Spending Review, UK Chancellor Rishi Sunak outlined an allocation which he described as the largest annual funding settlement for devolved governments since 1998.

However, an extra £1.6 billion per year for public services in Northern Ireland outlined by Sunak was quickly challenged by Murphy, who said that the reality was an additional £1.9 billion over three years, something he described as "nowhere near enough".

The Department of Finance's estimation is for a day-to-day increase of £450 million in year one, £670 million in year two and £866 million in year three, when compared to the Executive's 2021/22 budget.

While the Finance Minister welcomed the increase in cash, he said that it represented a "flat budget" by 2024/25 when factoring in inflation.

"This Spending Review was the opportunity to deliver a budget which would have enabled the Executive to rebuild public services and spur economic recovery. However, it provides a marginal real terms increase in funding next year which will be far outweighed by increased demands on public services, particularly in light of the ongoing pandemic," said Murphy.

In contrast, the Treasury says that the 2.1 per cent real term increase in day-to-day spending and 2.5 per cent a year increase in infrastructure spending out to

252   Economy

Northern Ireland Yearbook | Economy

	Non-ring-fenced DEL	Capital	FTC
2021-22	£12.485 billion	£1.611 billion	£74 million
2022/23	£12.936 billion	£1.686 billion	£163 million
2023/24	£13.155 billion	£1.784 billion	£66 million
2024/25	£13.351 billion	£1.759 billion	£62 million

Source: Department of Finance

"It provides a marginal real terms increase in funding next year which will be far outweighed by increased demands on public services, particularly in light of the ongoing pandemic."

Finance Minister Conor Murphy MLA

Northern Ireland Fiscal Council
Bringing transparency to NI's public finances

The Northern Ireland Fiscal Council, created in March 2021, is one of more than 40 independent fiscal institutions around the world.

The Council's mission is to bring greater transparency and scrutiny to the current and future condition of Northern Ireland's public finances, and to inform public debate and policy decisions.

The core functions of the Council reflect the New Decade, New Approach (NDNA) commitment to:

- prepare an annual assessment of the Executive's revenue streams and spending proposals and how these allow the Executive to balance their budget; and
- prepare a further annual report on the sustainability of the Executive's public finances, including the implications of spending policy and the effectiveness of long-term efficiency measures.

www.nifiscalcouncil.org   @NIFiscalCouncil   info@nifiscalcouncil.org

Economy | Northern Ireland Yearbook

The 11 successful Levelling Up Fund projects announced for Northern Ireland were:

1. upgrading the **electric vehicle charging network** across Northern Ireland;
2. the redevelopment of the **derelict Ministry of Defence site in Derry** into an urban community farm;
3. creating a new **bioscience research** centre at Ulster University;
4. redeveloping **Portrush Recreation Grounds**;
5. redeveloping the **Dundonald International Ice Bowl**;
6. replacing a former police station in **Glengormley with a new business hub**;
7. extending **Antrim's boardwalk** into the town centre;
8. regenerating **Daisyfield Community Sports Hub**;
9. regenerating **Omagh Health Centre**;
10. extending **cycle routes across the Belfast City** Region; and
11. providing new and upgraded **sports facilities in Castlederg**.

2025 gives the Executive "sufficient funding certainty" to plan in-year spending and to provide additional future investments in areas such as health, social care, and education.

Multiyear budget

The *New Decade, New Approach* agreement committed the Executive and the UK Treasury to multiyear budgets for Northern Ireland. Signed in January 2020, the emergence of the pandemic has been blamed on a delay to date.

Since 2008, two multiyear budgets (2008-11 and 2011/15) and two single-year budgets (2015/16 and 2016/17) have been set. Following the collapse of the Assembly, the Secretary of State set three single-year budgets, followed by a further 2020/21 budget set by the restored Executive.

The absence of multiyear budgets to enable long-term planning for transformative change across Northern Ireland's has pressurised sectors and workforce planning.

In June 2021, a report by Northern Ireland's Audit Office (NIAO) examining Northern Ireland's budget process identified the challenges, stating: "The short-term nature of annual budgets creates difficulties for future planning and innovation across the public sector. The absence of a medium-term dimension to financial planning and prioritisation has been the subject of significant criticism…"

The Northern Ireland Executive has agreed that health is its priority. The portfolio currently receives around half (£6.5 billion) of the annual day-to-day spending budget for Northern Ireland. During the pandemic, significant additional funding has had to be allocated to health to help meet the needs of Covid-19 and there are concerns that much of the extra £1.6 billion a year for public services announced in the UK's Autumn Budget will be needed just for services to stand still.

In June 2021, Health Minister Robin Swann MLA launched a roadmap for tackling Northern Ireland's waiting list crisis. The plan, which has yet to have funding agreed, would itself require £700 million over five years. Such a figure does not factor in investment in wider necessary health transformation and looks set to squeeze allocations for other departmental commitments included in *New Decade, New Approach* such as investment in education, delivering an energy strategy and Northern Ireland's environmental priorities.

Outlining the Executive's priorities, Murphy said: "The Executive has agreed to prioritise health. There is also consensus that additional resources should be diverted to support economic development including skills, the transition to net zero and tackling inequality. Departments have been asked to submit proposals against these priorities. It will be challenging to deliver on all of these given the limited funding available to us. The task for the Executive now is to make the best possible use of the resources available."

Air Passenger Duty

A move also partially welcomed by the Finance Minister during Autumn's Budget was the decision to cut Air Passenger Duty (APD) by half on internal UK flights. The call for APD to be removed in Northern Ireland by businesses and politicians in Northern Ireland has been long-standing for over a decade.

Those in favour believe that a reduction in the cost of air travel would boost connectivity for the region, increasing trade, tourism and making it more attractive for inward investment. Previously, EU law has meant that a Northern Ireland specific change to APD would come at a cost to Northern Ireland's block grant, a risk which raised some objection. However, Sunak's decision to set a new domestic band of APD at £6.50 to all flights between airports in England, Scotland, Wales, and Northern Ireland from April 2023, negates a specific approach for the region.

"Airports are a crucial part of our economic infrastructure and are key to regional connectivity. The fact that APD does not apply in the South creates an uneven playing field across the island. While it is disappointing that the Chancellor has not abolished APD it is welcome that it has been lowered. However, I would have preferred to have seen this reduction applied sooner than April 2023," said Finance Minister Murphy.

Levelling Up Fund

Outside of the Budget, Northern Ireland also received £50 million from the UK Government's Levelling Up Fund, billed as a programme to invest in infrastructure that improves everyday life across the UK.

The scheme has been criticised as lacking depth in long-term planning for those areas of the UK that are economically struggling, instead appearing to be project specific.

The Chancellor announced which projects had been successful in the first round of bids for the scheme, which is set to total £4.8 billion over four years. Of a total of 105 successful funding bids announced (£1.7 billion), 76 successful projects were announced for England, 11 for Northern Ireland, 10 for Wales and eight for Scotland.

Financial allocation of the scheme is not subject to the Barnett Formula.

In total, for the devolved regions, £170 million was allocated to Scotland, £120 million for Wales and £50 million for Northern Ireland.

The Finance Minister published the Executive's Draft Budget on 10 December 2021, beginning a 12 week consultation period.

The cost of the shift

Co-director of the Nevin Economic Research Institute, Paul Mac Flynn, outlines the ongoing shifts in the economy, some of which were masked by pandemic support.

The story of the labour market over the year to July 2021 was undoubtedly still centred on the extraordinary government support supplied to firms over the pandemic. With so much effort being expended to try and maintain and preserve the pre-pandemic economy, it was easy to miss the changes and shifts that are already taking place.

The Coronavirus Job Retention Scheme (CJRS) was a novel development in UK economic policy making, not just because of the scale of support it provided but because of the way it provided it. A furlough scheme keeps people in employment, even if they have no work. In terms of labour market statistics, the furloughed employee is considered to be 'in a job' but not 'at work'. Such a distinction is more than just pedantry.

In Dublin, the approach to supporting workers was quite different. There was a wage subsidy scheme for people working reduced hours, but for those with no work, they were offered the Pandemic Unemployment Payment (PUP). For most workers, the CJRS would be more generous than the equivalent PUP payment, but one of the main benefits of the CJRS is that it maintains the connection between employee and employer.

The objective of the CJRS is therefore not only to provide income protection for affected workers, but also to ensure that when restrictions ease, these same workers can move seamlessly back into work. Of course, the reality is far more complex. While many workers will hopefully move back into their pre-pandemic working patterns, for many the pandemic has fundamentally altered their jobs. Either their employer is no longer operating or their employer is operating in a way which significantly alters the nature or future of their job.

It is too early to know how successful the CJRS has been in preserving the pre-pandemic labour market. Data over the coming weeks and months will give an indication of the medium-term outlook. But looking to the data that we have already shows that substantial change may already be underway.

We now have data available for the first quarter of 2021 which can be compared with the first quarter of 2020 as the pre-pandemic benchmark. During that 1-year period there was a net loss of just over 7,000 jobs or 1 per cent of all jobs in the economy. Within that net figure there were over 15,000 jobs lost and just under 8,000 created. To put those figures into context, in the year between the first quarter of 2019 and the first quarter of 2020, there was a net gain of just under 4,000 jobs. Just under 10,000 jobs were created and 5,000 jobs lost.

Compared with the previous year, the scale of job losses experienced between 2020 and 2021 could be seen as a failure of the Government's labour market policy. However, when you take into account the scale of the disruption that the economy experienced, government policy actually did well to stem the loss of jobs to the extent that it did.

Northern Ireland Yearbook | Economy

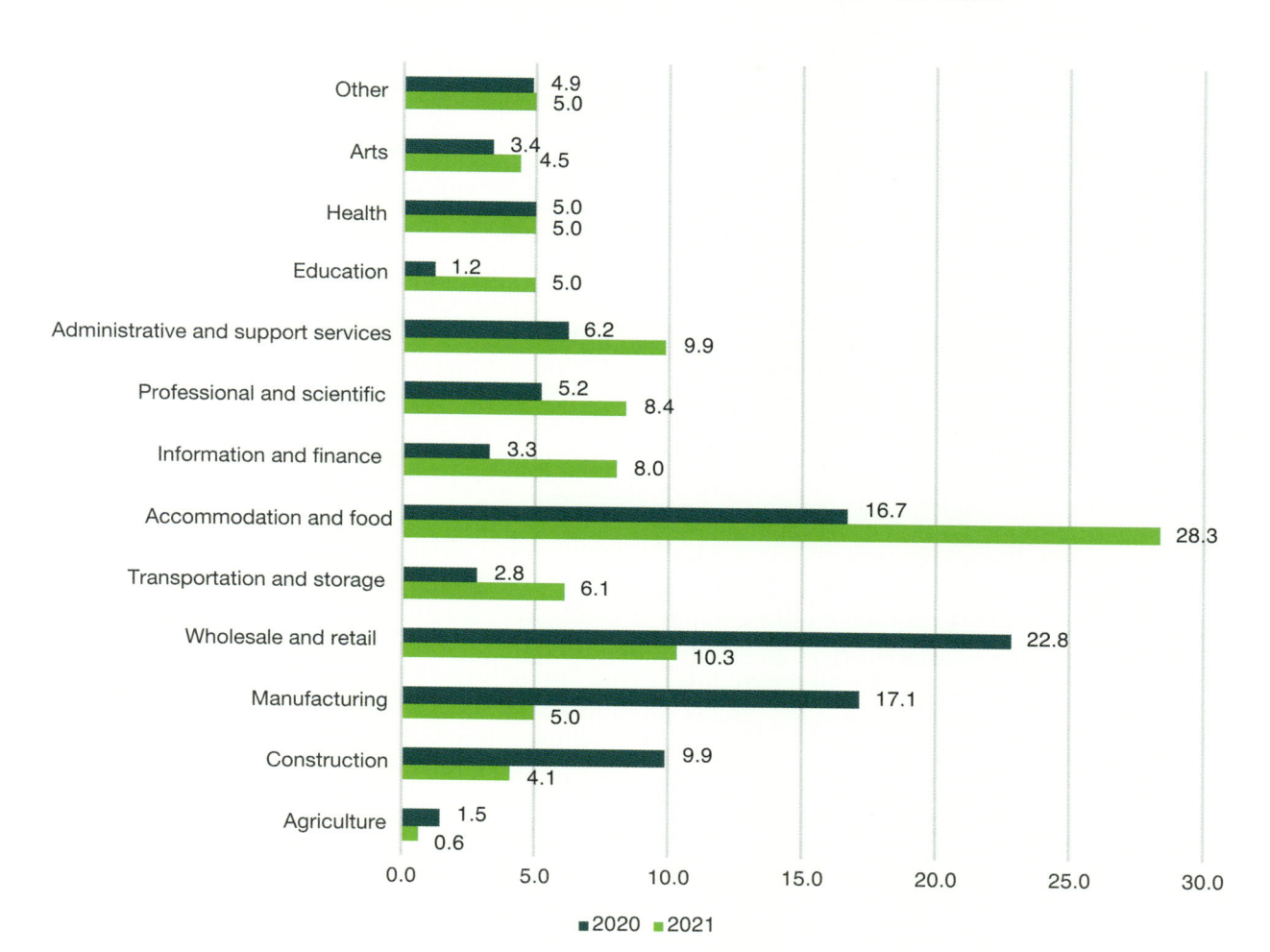

Figure 1: Percentage change in total employee jobs by sector in Northern Ireland between Q1 2020 and Q1 2021

Sector	2020	2021
Other	4.9	5.0
Arts	3.4	4.5
Health	5.0	5.0
Education	1.2	5.0
Administrative and support services	6.2	9.9
Professional and scientific	5.2	8.4
Information and finance	3.3	8.0
Accommodation and food	16.7	28.3
Transportation and storage	2.8	6.1
Wholesale and retail	22.8	10.3
Manufacturing	17.1	5.0
Construction	9.9	4.1
Agriculture	1.5	0.6

What the job loss figures for the last year can do is give us some idea of the prospects for jobs over the coming months. The sectors where we have seen job loss over the last year do not come as a surprise. As Figure 1 shows, accommodation and food has lost 10 per cent of jobs since last year. These are jobs lost in spite of government support, where the loss of trade could not be stemmed by grants or loans. The arts sector has lost over 8 per cent while wholesale and retail just under 5 per cent.

These three sectors also have the greatest take-up of the CJRS and so it is not surprising that they account for 85 per cent of jobs lost in the last year. There is hope that as public health restrictions continue to be unwound, some of these losses can be made back up as firms begin to expand again or as new firms step in to replace those that have ceased trading. However, such optimism may not hold across the rest of the labour market.

To investigate this, it is worthwhile to look at another sector of employment,

"We hear much talk of the benefits of flexible working for home life and the environment, but we have to accept that such an enormous change in the way we work is likely to have a significant negative effect on a section of our workforce."

administration and support services. We haven't heard as much about this sector, but it could be an important bellwether in the coming months. This sector not only includes people who work in offices but also people who work in the service of offices. It includes security services,

Economy | Northern Ireland Yearbook

Figure 2: Share of total furloughed employments by sector in Northern Ireland July 2020 and July 2021

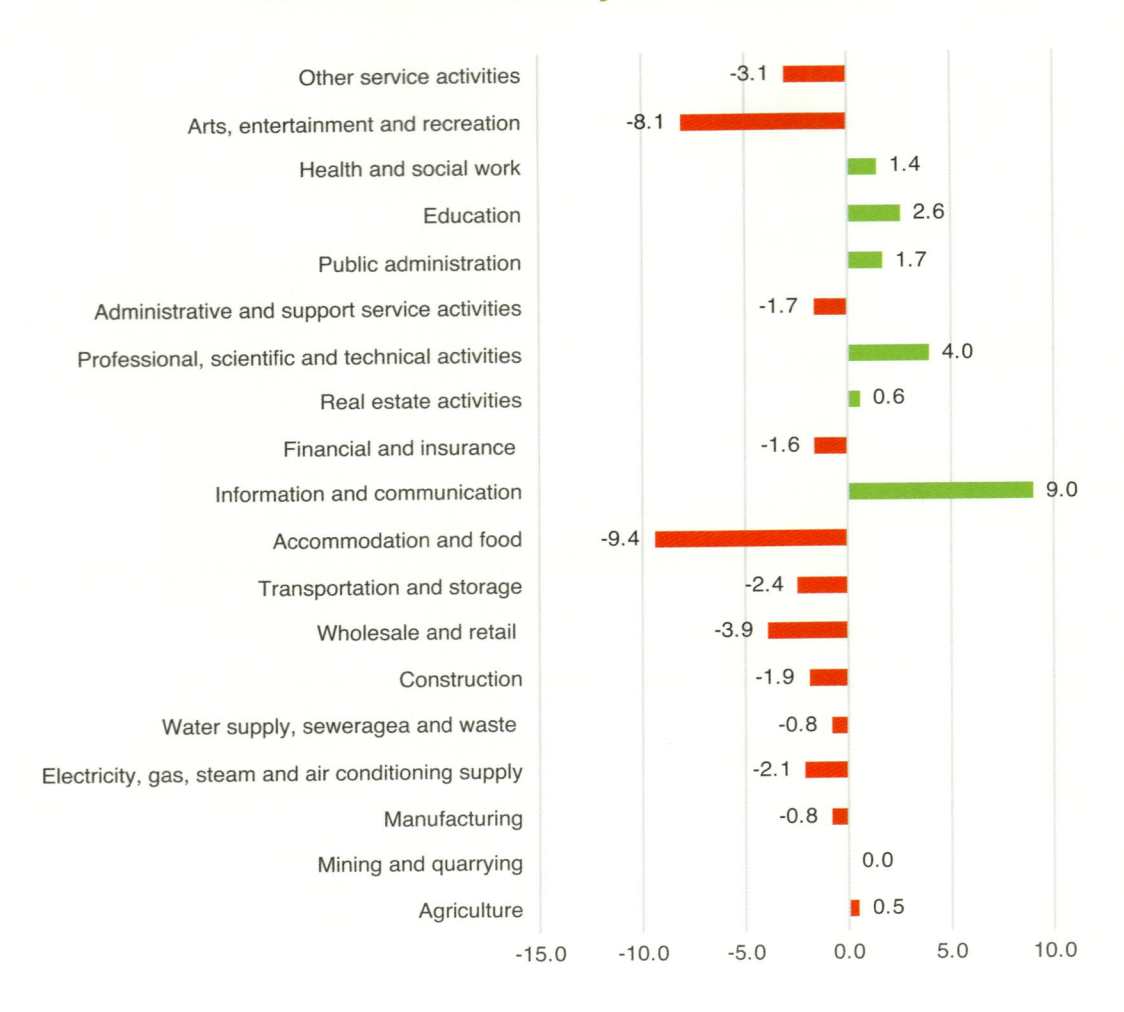

Sector	Value
Other service activities	-3.1
Arts, entertainment and recreation	-8.1
Health and social work	1.4
Education	2.6
Public administration	1.7
Administrative and support service activities	-1.7
Professional, scientific and technical activities	4.0
Real estate activities	0.6
Financial and insurance	-1.6
Information and communication	9.0
Accommodation and food	-9.4
Transportation and storage	-2.4
Wholesale and retail	-3.9
Construction	-1.9
Water supply, seweragea and waste	-0.8
Electricity, gas, steam and air conditioning supply	-2.1
Manufacturing	-0.8
Mining and quarrying	0.0
Agriculture	0.5

cleaning services and facilities management. It also includes conference and event organisers along with travel agents and office temping agencies.

Administration and support services has lost just under 1,000 jobs in the last year. This can seem small compared to the loss of over 5,000 jobs in accommodation and food. However, administration is a big sector of employment in Northern Ireland accounting for 7 per cent of all jobs compared to accommodation and food which accounts for 6 per cent. It was also a significant job creator in the years following the financial crash accounting for 12 per cent of all new jobs created between 2013 and 2019 compared to 11 per cent for accommodation and food. As a sector it is as important as accommodation and food in terms of both its size and its ability to generate swift employment growth.

There are reasons to be worried about the prospects for the administration sector. Looking at the progress of the CJRS over the past year Figure 2 shows the sectoral make up of all furloughed employments in July 2020 and July 2021. Accommodation and food stands out as being the largest share of total furlough in both years and has increased its share substantially over the year. However, the administration sector has also increased its share of total furloughed employments and it now sits only just behind the retail sector.

While the road back for hospitality and other sectors looks simple enough, the path of the administration sector is an awful lot less clear. As public health restrictions are lifted, many hospitality businesses can reopen and take staff back on. For the administration sector, the lifting of restrictions may not be enough.

Many, if not most, office workers have been working from home since last March under government advice. Even when this restriction is lifted, it is not clear how many people will return to the office some, or even all of the time. We hear much talk of the benefits of flexible working for home life and the environment, but we have to accept that such an enormous change in the way we work is likely to have a significant negative effect on a section of our workforce.

The CJRS may help hospitality businesses return to pre-pandemic employment, but the same cannot be said for the administration sector. The move toward flexible working may be a positive one but there needs to be acceptance of the cost of this shift in terms of jobs. The CJRS may help many return to employment but we will also need a new financial commitment to those who cannot return to employment.

Social Enterprise NI

Representative Body for Social Enterprises in NI

With a seat on the Department of Finance Procurement Board and High Street Task Force

Learn more about:
- What is Social Value
- Measuring Social Impact
- Access to the Business Directory for Social Enterprises
- How to include Social Enterprises in your supply chain
- Access to training on intelligent commissioning

If you would like to find out more or become a corporate partner please contact either:

Colin Jess - Director
colin@socialenterpriseni.org
078 7247 0327

Amanda Johnston - Operations & Membership Manager
amanda@socialenterpriseni.org
07734 820180

socialenterpriseni.org
@socentni

028 9046 1810

Economy | Northern Ireland Yearbook

Pre-pandemic return restricted

While the reopening of further sectors of the economy was expected to generate a significant uplift in economic output for the second half of 2021, Northern Ireland's economy appears to be still some years away from a return to pre-pandemic levels.

Northern Ireland lost an estimated £6.1 billion in GVA terms between March 2020 and March 2021, the equivalent to £100 million per week of lost economic output.

While many advanced countries across the world are now experiencing strong economic recovery and have closed the gap with pre-pandemic levels in the first half of 2021, the recovery of Northern Ireland's economy is expected to be much slower, with major risks still identified.

Despite evident exceptional economic consequences of the pandemic for the economy, the easing of restrictions and subsequent growth in output of customer-facing services have led to optimism for steady growth the second quarters of 2021 and into 2022, however there is a recognition that it could take years for Northern Ireland's economy to even attain pre-pandemic levels of output and employment.

It is estimated that over 10,000 businesses in Northern Ireland were either closed or impacted by restrictions from 26 December 2020 to May 2021. At the start of 2021, the UK was adjudged to have the sixth strictest lockdown in the world and the second harshest in Europe.

Northern Ireland's GDP is projected to have decreased by roughly 25 per cent below pre-pandemic levels of £48.9 billion per annum at the height of lockdown in spring 2020, however estimates over the whole of 2020 are for a 10 per cent decrease over the year.

During Q1 of 2021, real term economic output was down 1.6 per cent over the quarter. Northern Ireland's services sector is the largest sector of the economy and output of services was significantly lower than pre-Covid-19 levels in the first quarter. Output in the production sector was only slightly below pre-pandemic levels for the first three months of 2021 but construction output for Q1 was 5.3 per cent below the last quarter of 2020, when recovery looked to have been back on track before the reintroduction of more stringent restrictions.

Northern Ireland's economy can expect to experience greater levels of recovery in forthcoming data as renewed levels of activity in retail and recreation, alongside the reopening of all non-essential retail start to factor into statistics. While other global economies have experienced a significant uptick in consumer spending as a result of pent-up demand, on 6 August 2021

Northern Ireland Yearbook | Economy

Economic activity in Northern Ireland by quarterly NI Composite Economic Index (NICEI) Quarter 1 (January – March) 2021

Quarterly growth
-1.6%
Q1 2021 compared with Q4 2020

Annual growth
-0.6%
Q1 2021 compared with Q1 2020

Annualised growth
-5.8%
Q2 2020 to Q1 2021 compared with Q2 2019 to Q1 2020

Private Sector
Quarterly **-2.2%**
Annual -1.1%
Annualised -7.7%

Public Sector
Quarterly **0.3%**
Annual 0.9%
Annualised 0.8%

Source: NISRA

movement within retail and recreation in Northern Ireland was still 3 per cent below normal levels. It is expected that the narrative is similar for footfall in towns and cities.

Labour market

Northern Ireland's labour market has, to some degree, been shielded from the worst impacts of the pandemic due to UK Government and Northern Ireland Executive supports. However, these supports have not been able to prevent dramatic shifts in the shape of the labour market. Over 2020, Northern Ireland's claimant count doubled to almost 60,000 people. This number has been gradually reducing in 2021.

HMRC data shows that some 44,000 workers in Northern Ireland were furloughed at the end of June 2021. The reopening of the economy generated a reduction in the number of people on furlough support. Some 50,000 people were taken off furlough between 30 April 2021 and 30 June 2021 (down from 92,900 to 44,000), many of whom are in the retail and hospitality sectors. Around 53,000 self-employed people claimed the fourth SEISS grant up to 6 June 2021, down from 78,000 for the first grant up to 31 July 2020.

With CJRS and SEISS having ended on 30 September 2021, a serious risk of a

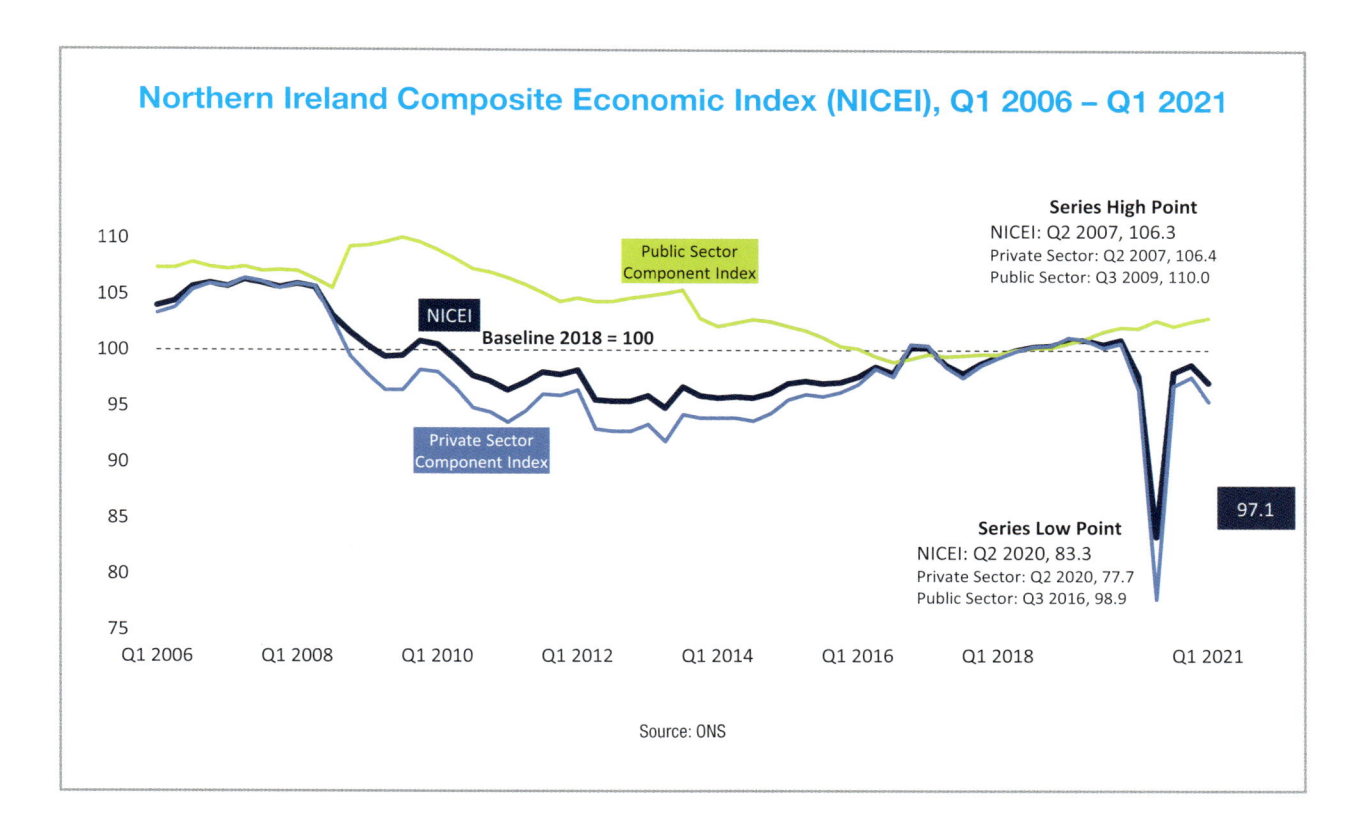

Northern Ireland Composite Economic Index (NICEI), Q1 2006 – Q1 2021

Series High Point
NICEI: Q2 2007, 106.3
Private Sector: Q2 2007, 106.4
Public Sector: Q3 2009, 110.0

Baseline 2018 = 100

Series Low Point
NICEI: Q2 2020, 83.3
Private Sector: Q2 2020, 77.7
Public Sector: Q3 2016, 98.9

97.1

Source: ONS

Economy 261

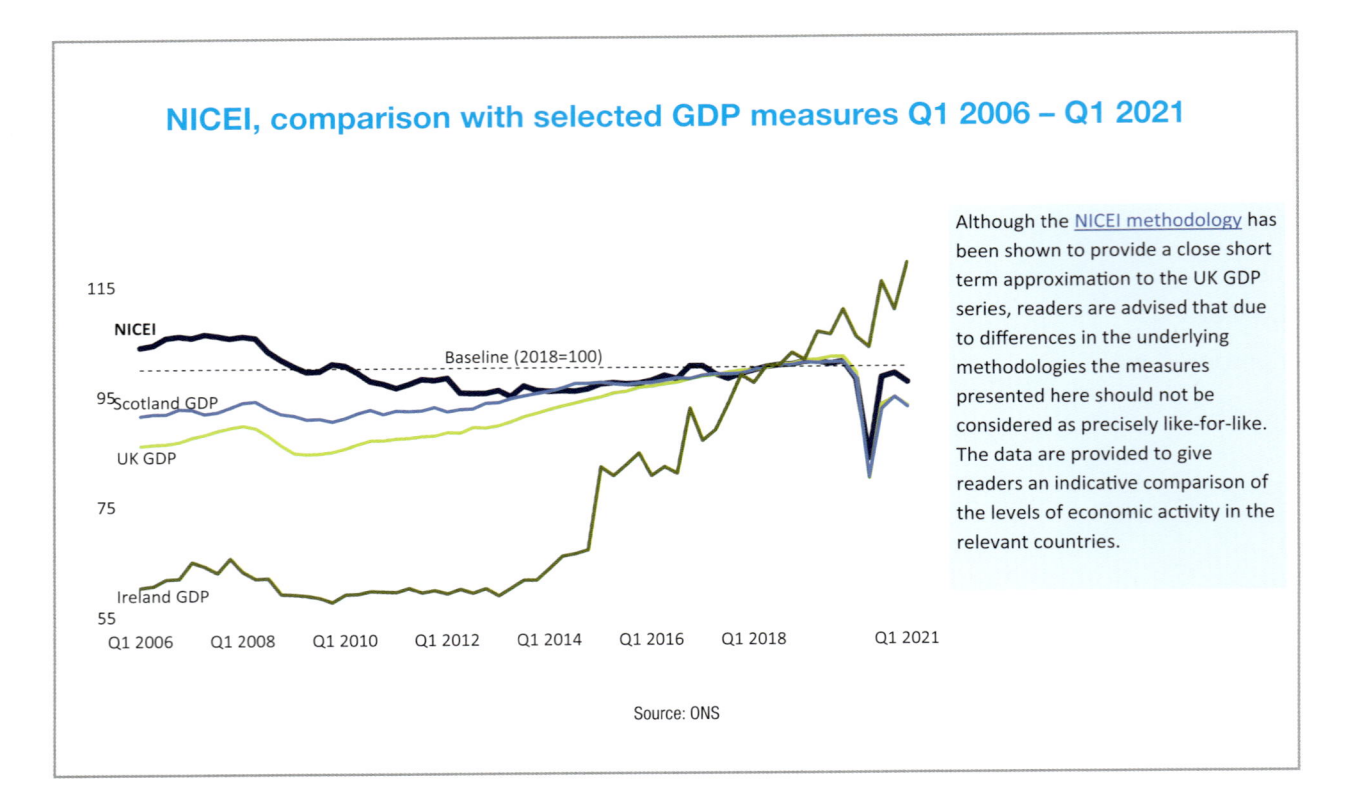

NICEI, comparison with selected GDP measures Q1 2006 – Q1 2021

Although the NICEI methodology has been shown to provide a close short term approximation to the UK GDP series, readers are advised that due to differences in the underlying methodologies the measures presented here should not be considered as precisely like-for-like. The data are provided to give readers an indicative comparison of the levels of economic activity in the relevant countries.

Source: ONS

further rise in unemployment remains. Despite the easing of restrictions, thousands of customer-facing industries still have workers furloughed. Additionally, sectors such as manufacturing continue to recognise disruption from lockdown and are experiencing a slower unfurloughing process.

Despite the risk to jobs, the Department for the Economy has published analysis showing online job postings in July 2021 were 12 per cent higher than the three-year average and 68 per cent higher than July 2020. However, July 2021's figures are a 13 per cent decrease on postings in June 2021.

Lasting impacts

While many sectors of the economy have been boosted by the reopening, there are lasting impacts on industry from the pandemic. Prior to the pandemic, the volume of online retail sales in Northern Ireland had risen to 19 per cent but by 2020, following the outbreak of Covid-19, that figure had risen to 28 per cent.

Additionally, research by Queen's University Belfast (QUB) highlights that significant progress had been made in the adoption and implementation of digital technologies among Northern Ireland's small- and medium-sized enterprises (SMEs), as a result of restrictions on face-to-face business operations.

Risks

While SMEs have sought to adapt to the pandemic, significant risks still exist even with the lifting of restrictions. QUB research found that the effect of Covid-19 was more severe for small- and medium-sized enterprises than larger businesses. According to the research, higher proportions of SMEs were reporting very limited cash reserves as well as low confidence in survival in the near future.

According to the Centre for Economics and Business Research (CEBR), Northern Ireland firms have borrowed over £2 billion in government loan schemes since Covid-19 struck and some sectors face more of a burden of debt repayments than others.

Research from the Ulster University Economic Policy Centre (UUEPC) published in March 2021 highlights the disparity of the impact of the pandemic across the labour market. Among the findings was that the self-employed, young people and females have been disproportionately affected.

Recovery

Northern Ireland's last economic strategy was published in 2012. In May 2021, the Department for the Economy published an economic vision for the next decade in Northern Ireland. The *A 10X Economy* strategy was not the costed action plan that many had hoped for, instead it offered a high-level vision of the sectors of the Northern Ireland economy that could lead the way in economic recover post-pandemic. Prior to this, the then Minister for the Economy had launched the *Economic Recovery Action Plan*, described as the "blueprint to rebuild a stronger economy in Northern Ireland". £275.8 million for resource funding and £11 million in capital funding was agreed by the Executive for the recovery plan. The Department had previously stated that £290 million (including the cost of delivery of the High Street Stimulus Scheme) would be required in 2021/22 to deliver the action plan.

Alongside the Economic Recovery Action Plan and the 10X Economy, the Department has also published a *Tourism Recovery Action Plan* and is currently consulting on a new Skills Strategy and Energy Strategy, both of which are to be published later this year.

Discernibly, central to the Department's ambitions for economic recovery is a desire to boost consumer confidence and spending. Northern Ireland's median household income sits 3.25 per cent behind the UK average, meaning that any increase in consumer spending is unlikely to underpin recovery to the

Northern Ireland Yearbook | Economy

same extent it has in the UK.

In response, the Northern Ireland Executive has unveiled a high street voucher scheme, giving every adult in Northern Ireland a £100 pre-paid card, hoping to encourage spending at retailers that have been badly affected by Covid-19 lockdowns. The hope is that the eligible public will use the money to make out-of-the-ordinary purchases, thereby producing a stimulus. However, as some economists have pointed out, with limited restrictions on how the money can be spent, use of the scheme's funds to simply replace regular expenditure will dramatically reduce the stimulus effect of the scheme.

While much must play out before a full assessment of the state of recovery of the Northern Ireland economy can be completed, not least the ending of labour market supports, impact of economic investment and the UK's upcoming Spending Review, the fulfilment of a full recovery remains some way off. The UUEPC forecasts that the pre-Covid GVA levels will not be reached until mid-2023, while employment will take until 2024. EY also identifies 2023 as a date for recovery to 2019 output levels and 2024 to 2019 employment levels. More optimistically, however, Danske Bank expects economic activity to return to its pre-pandemic levels in the first half of 2022.

"According to the Centre for Economics and Business Research (CEBR), Northern Ireland firms have borrowed over £2 billion in government loan schemes since Covid-19 struck and some sectors face more of a burden of debt repayments than others."

UK economy

The UK economy's substantial growth (close to 5 per cent) in the second quarter of 2021 masks the lag in economic performance in the UK when compared to other advanced economies.

August's figures are representative of an easing of restrictions and a correlated uptick in consumer spending but largely fail to reflect an expected slowdown in July due to the spread of the delta variant.

Consumer spending rose by 7.3 per cent in the second quarter, underpinning the growth, however, business investment also increased by 2.4 per cent.

The 4.8 per cent growth for the second quarter is the latest quarter-on-quarter growth, meaning the UK economy has recovered much of the ground lost to the pandemic over the past two years.

The growth rate for the second quarter of 2021 was the fastest among G7 countries but the UK's overall economic performance means that it still trails behind, with output continuing to perform below pre-pandemic levels. For instance, GDP was still 4.4 per cent below the pre-pandemic peak of the Q4 2019.

UK Chancellor Rishi Sunak said that August's figures were evidence the UK economy was "bouncing back" but many economists believe that a rise of Covid-19 cases and the associated necessity for more people to isolate may see recovery stall.

While the full impact of any obstruction to recovery has yet to be assessed, economists estimate that the UK economy will see a return to its pre-pandemic scale by the end of the year.

Record payroll employees figure masks unemployment rise

A rise of payrolled employees in Northern Ireland above pre-pandemic levels may be masking a potential wave of redundancies and an absence of recovery for the self-employed, writes David Whelan.

At face value, a 2.6 per cent annual rise in the number of workers in Northern Ireland to 757,200 in June 2021 is welcome news. The figure puts the number of employees receiving HMRC PAYE above pre-pandemic levels recorded in March 2020 and the 1.4 per cent monthly rise from May to June in 2020 suggests an increasingly improving picture.

However, caution is urged in using these figures as a measurement of the strength of the recovery of Northern Ireland's labour market.

The Northern Ireland Statistics and Research Agency's (NISRA) latest report uses HMRC payroll data and is seen as the most-timely and best single, overall indicator of the labour market but remains, by its nature, retrospective in its outlook.

A number of reasons lie behind the need for caution. Firstly, payroll figures include furloughed employees, estimated at around 60,000 at the end of October.

Additionally, while payrolled employee numbers may have increased over the year, in the same time period, Northern Ireland witnessed its annual record total of confirmed redundancies since 2001.

A trend of increasing numbers of redundancies is set to continue. A rise from 150 proposed redundancies in May 2021 to 490 in June and to 850 in just the first two weeks of July is evidence of an evolving labour market and these figures are likely to be compounded by the proposed ending of furlough.

Employers have had to pay 10 per cent of their furloughed workers' pay since 1 July but that is set to rise to 20 per cent in August and September before the scheme is removed entirely. Concerns have been raised that thousands of jobs currently retained under the furlough scheme could disappear then, either because they are no longer viable or because staff have moved to another job.

Official redundancy figures only include cases of companies making at least 20 people redundant and so do not capture the whole picture, particularly in a time when small-to medium-sized businesses appear to be hardest hit by restrictions.

Further indication that the labour market's recovery to pre-pandemic status may take some years is a 3.6 per cent increase in the unemployment rate over the year from March to May 2021. Additionally, Northern Ireland's employment rate (the proportion of people aged 16 to 64 in work) decreased over the year to 70.3 per cent.

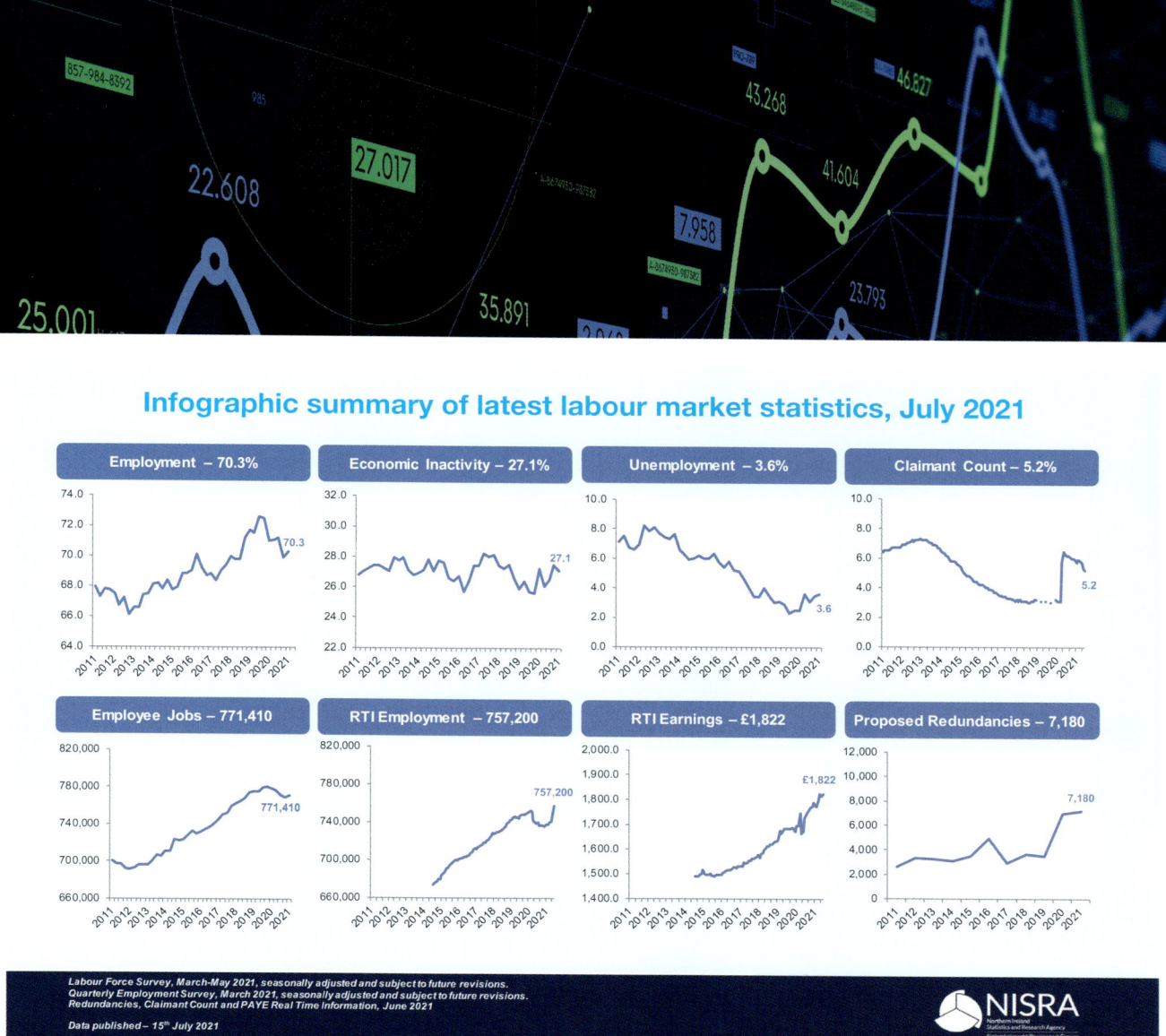

Northern Ireland Yearbook | Economy

Infographic summary of latest labour market statistics, July 2021

Employment – 70.3%
Economic Inactivity – 27.1%
Unemployment – 3.6%
Claimant Count – 5.2%

Employee Jobs – 771,410
RTI Employment – 757,200
RTI Earnings – £1,822
Proposed Redundancies – 7,180

Labour Force Survey, March-May 2021, seasonally adjusted and subject to future revisions.
Quarterly Employment Survey, March 2021, seasonally adjusted and subject to future revisions.
Redundancies, Claimant Count and PAYE Real Time Information, June 2021

Data published – 15th July 2021

Economic Overview Dashboard - https://datavis.nisra.gov.uk/economy-and-labour-market/economic-overview.html

NISRA Northern Ireland Statistics and Research Agency

The Northern Ireland employment rate continues to be below the UK rate of 74.8 per cent, as does the economic inactivity rate, which is 27.1 per cent in Northern Ireland compared to the UK rate of 21.3 per cent.

A 13 per cent rise over the year of the total number of weekly hours worked in Northern Ireland is also a positive indicator but should be read in the context that this figure remains 7 per cent below pre-pandemic value.

While some recovery in the labour market is evident from the height of the pandemic, self-employment appears to be showing no signs of recovery. The estimated 96,000 people self-employed in the quarter March-May is a significant decrease from the 131,000 recorded in the same quarter in 2020.

"A rise from 150 proposed redundancies in May 2021 to 490 in June and to 850 in just the first two weeks of July is evidence of an evolving labour market."

Northern Ireland employee jobs seasonally adjusted March 2021

	Total	Change on quarter (%)	Change on year (%)
Manufacturing	86,120	0.3	-0.8
Construction	34,910	-0.9	-2
Services	625,970	0.4	-0.9
Other	24,410	-0.7	-0.1
Total	**771,410**	**0.3**	**-0.9**

Economy

Cross-border trade up almost 60 per cent

The value of trade across the island of Ireland has risen by over 57 per cent since the UK left the European Union at the end of 2020.

The value of combined imports and exports between north and south were almost six times greater in the first five months of 2021, compared to the same period last year.

Brexit and checks on goods travelling from Great Britain to Ireland, north and south, since the introduction of the Northern Ireland Protocol in January 2021, have been attributed to the drastic rise in the levels of exports and imports this year.

The value of goods travelling from Northern Ireland to the Republic of Ireland rose 77 per cent between January to May 2021 compared to the same period in 2020, while the value of goods travelling from the Republic of Ireland to Northern Ireland rose by 38 per cent.

The surge in cross-border trade was described by the then Brexit Minister David Frost as representing the "problem" of the Northern Ireland Protocol.

Frost claimed the rise as evidence that Northern Irish businesses could not use their "first choice" suppliers and told a House of Lords committee that it did not make sense for the UK Government to "encourage more of that development".

In May 2021, the value of goods travelling from Northern Ireland to the Republic of Ireland was €356 million, compared to €138 million in May 2020, a 158 per cent rise. The value of goods travelling in the opposite direction was €256 million in May 2021, compared to €159 million in 2020, a 61 per cent increase.

The trend of rising cross-border trade looks set to continue given the steady month on month increase in both imports and exports between north and south in 2021. Figures from the CSO show that the value of goods travelling from Northern Ireland to the Republic of Ireland has increased every month of

Northern Ireland Yearbook | Economy

2021 up until May, rising from €144 million in December 2020, the month before the Northern Ireland Protocol came into effect, to €356 million in May 2021.

The value of goods travelling from the Republic of Ireland to Northern Ireland has also increased from December 2020's figure of €168 million to €256 million in May 2021, however, a €30 million drop in the value of exports from the Republic of Ireland to Northern Ireland was recorded between April and May.

For the first quarter of 2021, Northern Ireland's exports to the Republic of Ireland were up for 44 per cent, while exports from the Republic of Ireland to Northern Ireland were up 22 per cent.

Great Britain

The rise in the value of cross-border trade is happening in the context of a probable decrease in levels of trade between Ireland, north and south, and Great Britain. Statistics on trade between Great Britain and Northern Ireland are only produced once a year and the current release is not reflective of the trade period post-Protocol, however, figures for trade between Republic of Ireland and Great Britain are available from the CSO.

The Republic of Ireland increased the value of its exports to Great Britain by over €260 million in May 2021 compared to May 2020. The 28 per cent rise to €1.2 billion means that Great Britain now accounts for 9 per cent of the Republic of Ireland's total exports.

The value of goods exports to Great Britain from the Republic of Ireland in the first five months of 2021 was €5.3 billion, an increase of 12 per cent on the first five months of 2020. However, imports from Great Britain decreased by 24 per cent (€301 million) to €927 million compared with May 2020. Imports from Great Britain were 11 per cent of the value of total imports in May 2021.

The value of goods imports from Great Britain for January to May 2021 was €4.2 billion, a 35 per cent decrease compared with January to May 2020.

Speaking to the Northern Ireland Assembly's Economy Committee in May,

RoI and NI: Goods exports and imports Dec 2020-May 2021

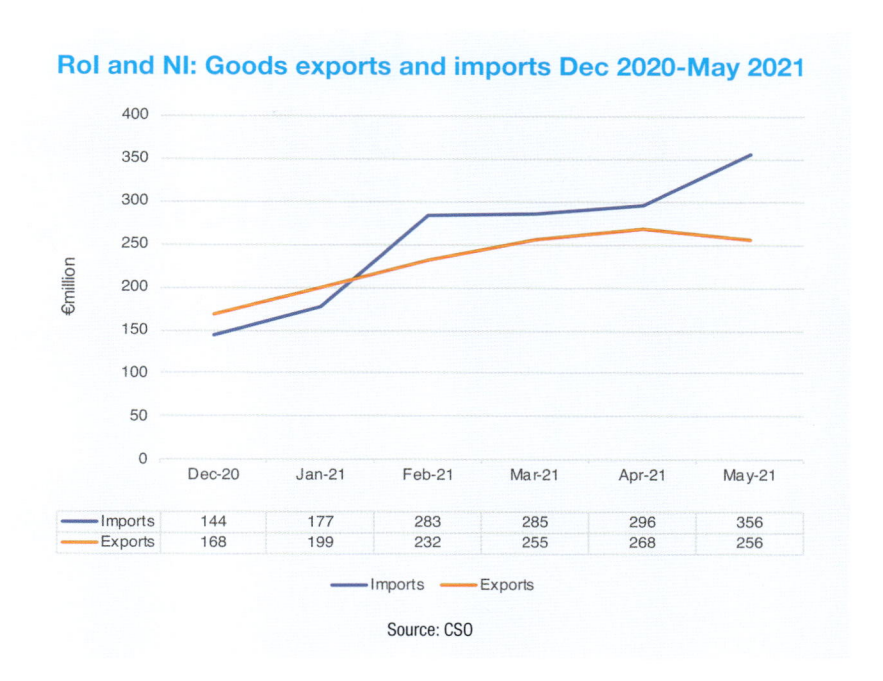

	Dec-20	Jan-21	Feb-21	Mar-21	Apr-21	May-21
Imports	144	177	283	285	296	356
Exports	168	199	232	255	268	256

Source: CSO

RoI to GB: Goods exports and imports Dec 2020-March 2021

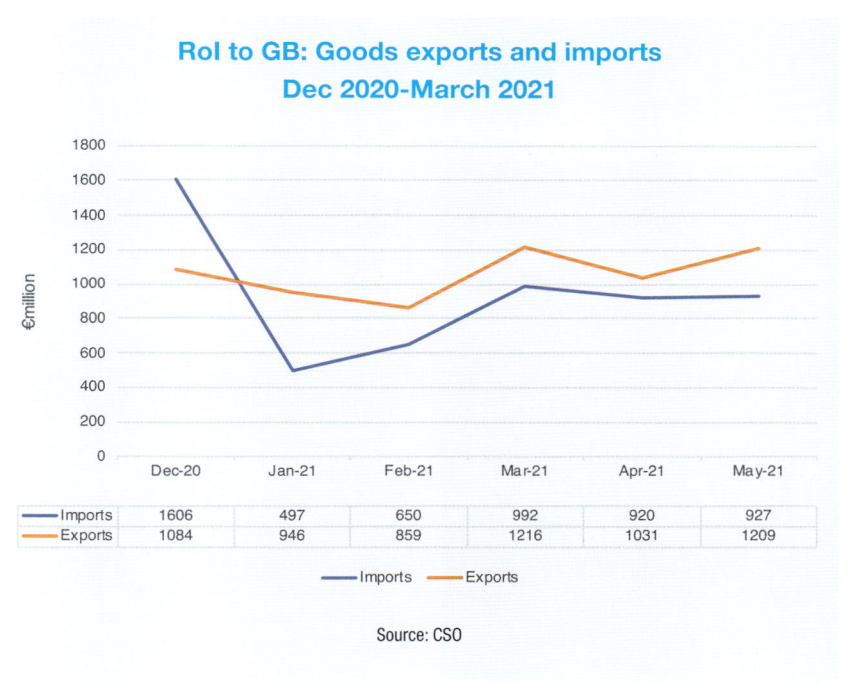

	Dec-20	Jan-21	Feb-21	Mar-21	Apr-21	May-21
Imports	1606	497	650	992	920	927
Exports	1084	946	859	1216	1031	1209

Source: CSO

a senior department official suggested that Great Britain traders exporting to Northern Ireland needed further education around the new processes and systems for sending goods to Northern Ireland.

Giulia Ní Dhulchaointigh said: "We know from the HMRC survey of businesses that nearly every business here [in Northern Ireland] has heard about the Trader Support Service (TSS) and are registered for it if they need it. In Great Britain, those figures are much lower. There simply is not the awareness that we would like to see there.

"There are a lot of different things in the mix, such as pressures that Great Britain businesses face with trade with the EU, but we definitely feel that there is a need for greater communication to those businesses."

Economy

Deepening cooperation on the Dublin-Belfast Economic Corridor

Ulster University economist Eoin Magennis overviews the findings of a joint report from Dublin City University and Ulster University on the challenges facing and potential opportunities of the Dublin-Belfast Economic Corridor.

Since 2018, a new local government and higher education network has been emerging in the region between the two cities of Dublin and Belfast. In March 2021, eight local authorities from either side of the border came together to launch the Dublin Belfast Economic Corridor.

The network came together with a shared recognition of the potential benefits that could arise from such an initiative and the challenges that might face it in the coming years, not least the outcome of a UK exit from the EU. Since then, the Covid-19 pandemic has struck and the economic trajectory has shifted significantly.

The region has historically been a centre for economic and population concentration on the island. Our research has shown how the strengths, in particular the road and rail infrastructure, and levels of entrepreneurship and innovation, have emerged over a long time. Since the 1990s and the calls by George Quigley, there has been great interest in the idea of an economic corridor.

A key strength of the corridor region is its two million population and the spatial concentration, educational attainment and diversity of this. The population is younger than elsewhere on the island, a third are educated to university level and more than 15 per cent were not born in Ireland. By 2040, a third of the island's population could live on the corridor. This presents its own challenges, not least sustainable housing and transport solutions.

Inward investment

The other key strength is the recurrent inward investment in the corridor. Businesses, particularly multinationals, have found the region to be an attractive proposition and returned for repeat business. Dublin and Belfast are key to this success, but the other council areas have seen spillovers from this too.

Employment growth to more than a million jobs has created a demand for high levels of skills. The report notes how there are promotional opportunities for the network to build further on this three decades of success. Tourism, agrifood and emerging industries such as FinTech, cybersecurity and high-tech creative could all feature.

However, we believe that the region has not reached its full potential. Knowledge flows between multinational and domestic firms, between both and universities and between different skills levels have been limited.

The creation of new 'soft' infrastructure, such as shared research centres, 'smart city' initiatives and investment in environmental management can create new and inclusive development paths.

Dublin-Belfast Economic Corridor fact file

- Two million people living in the eight local government areas
- 12 per cent population increase since 2006
- 1.4 million of population aged 16-64 (working age), younger that elsewhere on the island
- 34 per cent educated to university level
- 15 per cent not born in Ireland
- 38 per cent of island's businesses located in the corridor
- 35 per cent of the island's jobs could be located on the corridor by 2040.

Northern Ireland Yearbook | Economy

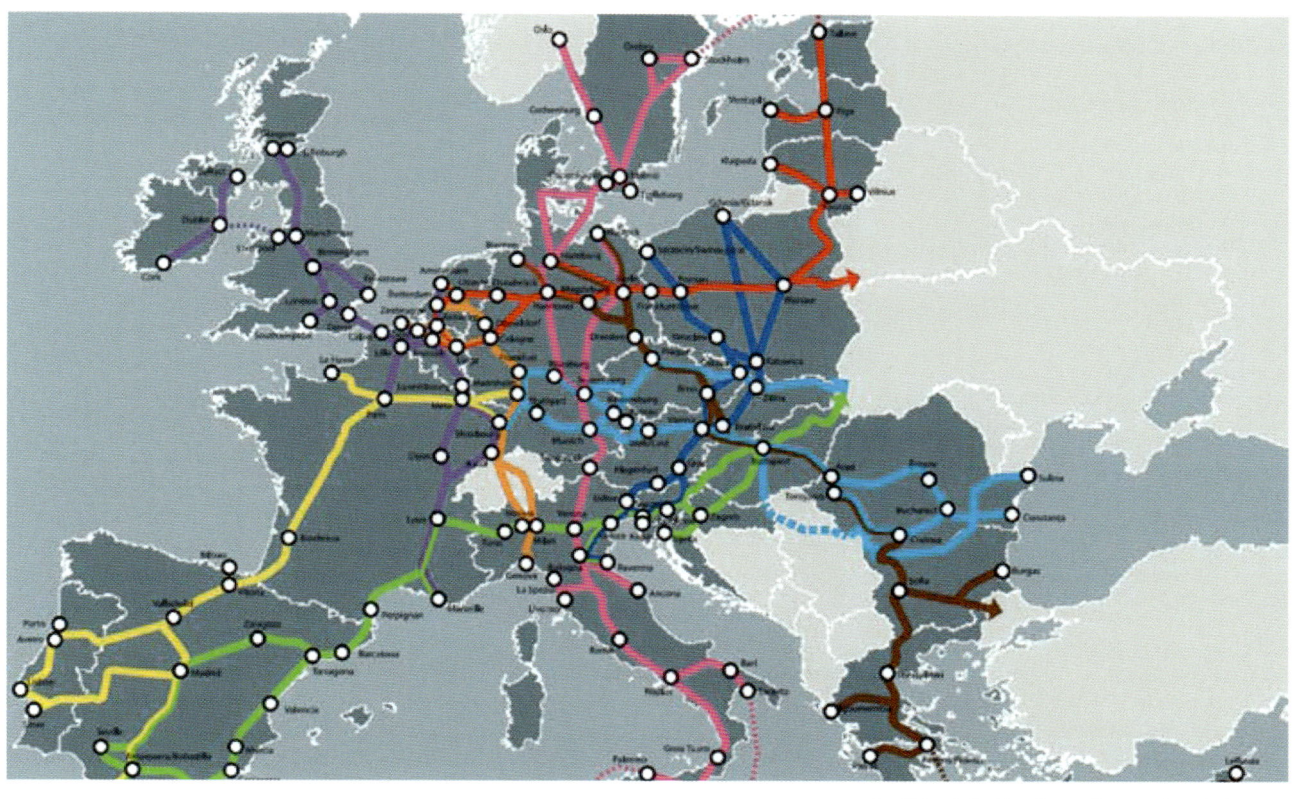

Core Network Corridors Source: European Commission, 2019

"…The island's potential will not be realised until there develops between Belfast and Dublin the normal economic and business interaction which one would expect to see between cities only 100 miles apart… and it needs to be genuinely an economic corridor and not simply a tunnel, with nothing happening in the space between the two cities."

George Quigley, 'Developing the North/South Economic Corridor' (1995)

The corridor initiative was launched online in March 2021 by ministers from the Irish and UK Governments and the Northern Ireland Executive. Several hundred attended to hear about the opportunities within the corridor and there has been strong demand since for definite next steps by the network. The first steps will be political and public engagement by the network this year to refine priorities for a plan of work to grasp the opportunities identified in the report.

Part of our research looks at other places and their cross-border economic corridors. The Øresund region has become best known for the bridge opened 20 years ago to link Denmark and southern Sweden. But growth there is about much more than a transport link. Networks of researchers, cultural links and education exchanges have all developed. Øresund shows how the key to success is effective partnership with all partners getting to know each other and building trust. This is once more developing in the Dublin-Belfast Economic Corridor.

The Dublin-Belfast Economic Corridor: Current Profile, Potential in Recovery and Opportunities for Cooperation report was compiled by Neale Blair (UU), Jordana Corrigan (TU Dublin), Eoin Magennis (UU) and Deiric Ó Broin (DCU).

The local authority members are currently Armagh City, Banbridge and Craigavon Borough Council, Belfast City Council, Dublin City Council, Fingal County Council, Lisburn & Castlereagh City Council, Louth County Council, Meath County Council and Newry, Mourne & Down District Council.

Economy

Economy | Northern Ireland Yearbook

Local enterprise agencies

Belfast

Argyle Business Centre Ltd
39 North Howard Street
Belfast, BT13 2AP
Tel: 028 9023 3777
Email: donna@abcni.biz
Manager: Donna Smyth

East Belfast Enterprise
City East Business Centre
68-72 Newtownards Road
Belfast, BT4 1GW
Tel: 028 9094 2010
Web: www.eastbelfast.org
Email: info@eastbelfast.org
Chief Executive: Jonathan McAlpin

Glenwood Business Centre
57-60 Springbank Place
Dunmurry
Belfast, BT17 0YU
Tel: 028 9061 0311
Web: www.glenwoodbc.com
Email: info@glenwoodbc.com

Inspire Business Centre Ltd
Inspire Business Park
Carrowreagh Road
Dundonald, Belfast, BT16 1QT
Tel: 028 9055 7557
Web: www.inspirebusinesscentre.co.uk
Email: enquiries@inspirebusinesscentre.co.uk
Chief Executive: Andy Tough

North City Business Centre
2 Duncairn Gardens
Belfast, BT15 2GG
Tel: 028 9074 7470
Web: www.north-city.co.uk
Email: mailbox@north-city.co.uk
CEO: Dave Murphy

Ormeau Business Park
8 Cromac Avenue, Belfast, BT7 2JA
Tel: 028 9033 9906
Web: www.ormeaubusinesspark.com
Email: info@ormeaubusinesspark.com
Manager: Patricia McNeill

ORTUS – The Business Development Agency
Filor Building
Twin Spires Complex
155 Northumberland Street
Belfast, BT13 2JF
Tel: 028 9031 1002
Web: www.ortus.org
Email: hq@ortus.org
Chief Executive: Seamus O'Prey

Townsend Enterprise Park
28 Townsend Street
Belfast, BT13 2ES
Tel: 028 9043 5778
Web: www.townsend.co.uk
Email: info@townsend.co.uk
Chief Executive:
Margaret Patterson McMahon

Work West Enterprise Agency
301 Glen Road, Belfast, BT11 8BU
Tel: 028 9061 0826
Web: www.workwest.co.uk
Email: info@workwest.co.uk
Agency Manager: Claire Ferris

Co Antrim

Antrim Enterprise Agency
58 Greystone Road
Antrim, BT41 1JZ
Tel: 028 9446 7774
Web: www.antrimenterprise.com
Email: admin@antrimenterprise.com
Manager: Jennifer McWilliams

Ballymena Business Centre
Galgorm Industrial Estate
62 Fenaghy Road, Galgorm
Ballymena, BT42 1FL
Tel: 0330 133 2092
Web: www.ballymenabusiness.co.uk
Email: info@ballymenabusiness.co.uk
Chief Executive: Melanie Christie-Boyle

Carrickfergus Enterprise
8 Meadowbank Road
Carrickfergus, BT38 8YF
Tel: 028 9336 9528
Web: www.ceal.co.uk
Email: info@ceal.co.uk
Manager: Kelli Bagchus

Larne Enterprise Development Company (LEDCOM)
Willowbank Business Park
Willowbank Road
Larne
BT40 2SF
Tel: 028 2826 9973
Web: www.ledcom.org
Email: info@ledcom.org
Chief Executive: Ken Nelson

Lisburn Enterprise Organisation
6 Enterprise Crescent
Ballinderry Road
Lisburn, BT28 2BP
Tel: 028 9266 1160
Web: www.lisburn-enterprise.co.uk
Email: centre@lisburn-enterprise.co.uk
Chief Executive: Martina Crawford

Mallusk Enterprise Park
2 Mallusk Drive
Newtownabbey, BT36 4GN
Tel: 028 9083 8860
Web: www.mallusk.org
Email: business@mallusk.org
Chief Executive: Emma Garrett

Co Armagh

Armagh Business Centre
2 Loughgall Road
Armagh, BT61 7NH
Tel: 028 3752 5050
Web: www.abcarmagh.com
Email: info@abcarmagh.com
Manager: Eileen Stewart

Craigavon Industrial Development Organisation Ltd (CIDO)
73 Charlestown Road
Portadown
BT63 5PP
Tel: 028 3839 6520
Web: www.cido.co.uk
Email: info@cido.co.uk
Chief Executive: Cara Dallat

Co Derry
Causeway Enterprise Agency
17 Sandel Village
Knocklynn Road
Coleraine
BT52 1WW
Tel: 028 7035 6318
Web: www.enterprisecauseway.co.uk
Email: info@enterpriseccauseway.co.uk
Chief Executive: Jayne Taggart

Ballymoney office
2 Riada Avenue
Ballymoney
BT53 7LH
Tel: 028 2766 6133
Email: ballymoney@enterprisecauseway.co.uk

Ballycastle / Moyle office
61 Leyland Road
Ballycastle
BT54 6EZ
Tel: 028 2076 3737
Email: moyle@enterprisecauseway.co.uk

Creggan Enterprises Ltd
Unit 9 Ráth Mór, Bligh's Lane
Creggan, Derry, BT48 0LZ
Tel: 028 7137 3170
Web: www.rathmor.com
Email: info@rathmor.com
Development Executive: Conal McFeely

Glenshane Community Development Ltd
114 Main Street
Dungiven, BT47 4LG
Tel: 028 7774 2494
Email: glenshane@btconnect.com

Roe Valley Enterprise Centre
Aghanloo Industrial Estate
Aghanloo Road, Limavady, BT49 0HE
Tel: 028 7776 5655
Web: www.roevalleyenterprises.com
Email: info@roevalleyenterprises.co.uk

Enterprise North West
North West Business Complex
Skeoge Industrial Estate
Beraghmore Road
Derry, BT48 8SE
Tel: 028 7135 2693
Web: www.enterprisenw.com
Email: info@enterprisenw.com

Workspace Enterprises Ltd
The Business Centre
5-7 Tobermore Road
Draperstown, BT45 7AG
Tel: 028 7962 8113
Web: www.workspace.org.uk
Email: info@theworkspacegroup.org
Chief Executive: Georgina Grieve

Co Down
Ards Business Centre Ltd
Sketrick House
Jubilee Road
Newtownards, BT23 4YH
Tel: 028 9181 9787
Web: www.ardsbusiness.com
Email: info@ardsbusiness.com
Chief Executive: Nichola Lockhart

Banbridge District Enterprises Ltd
Scarva Road Industrial Estate
Banbridge, BT32 3QD
Tel: 028 4066 2260
Web: www.bdelonline.com
Email: info@bdelonline.com
Manager: Ciaran Cunningham

Down Business Centre
46 Belfast Road
Downpatrick, BT30 9UP
Tel: 028 4461 6416
Web: www.downbc.co.uk
Email: business@downbc.co.uk
Manager: Janice McDonald

Newry and Mourne Enterprise Agency
WIN Business Park
Canal Quay, Newry, BT35 6PH
Tel: 028 3026 7011
Web: www.nmea.net
Email: info@nmea.net
Chief Executive: Conor Patterson

North Down Development Organisation
Enterprise House
2-4 Balloo Avenue
Bangor, BT19 7QT
Tel: 028 9127 1525
Web: www.nddo.co.uk
Email: mail@nddo.co.uk
Chief Executive: Lynne Vance

SIGNAL Centre of Business Excellence
2 Innotec Drive, Balloo Road
Bangor, Co Down, BT19 7PD
Tel: 028 9147 3788
Web: www.signalni.com
Email: signal@ardsandnorthdown.gov.uk
Head of Economic Development:
Clare McGill

Co Fermanagh
Fermanagh Enterprise Limited
Enniskillen Business Centre
21 Lackaghboy Road
Tempo Road, Enniskillen
Fermanagh, BT74 4RL
Tel: 028 6632 7348
Web: www.fermanaghenterprise.com
Email: info@fermanaghenterprise.com
Manager: John Treacy

Irvinestown Community Development
116-122 Sallyswood
Irvinestown, BT94 1HQ
Tel: 028 6862 8741
Web: www.archlc.com
Email: info@archlc.com
Chief Executive: Jenny Irvine

Lisnaskea Community Enterprise Limited
158 Lisnagole Road
Drumbrughas North
Lisnaskea, BT92 0PE
Tel: 028 6772 1081
Web: www.lisnaskeabusinesscomplex.com
Email: lcel@btconnect.com

Co Tyrone
Cookstown Enterprise Centre Ltd
Derryloran Industrial Estate
Sandholes Road
Cookstown, BT80 9LU
Tel: 028 8676 3660
Web: www.cookstownenterprise.com
Email: info@cookstownenterprise.com
Manager: Jim Eastwood

Dungannon Enterprise Centre
2 Coalisland Road
Dungannon, BT71 6JT
Tel: 028 8772 3489
Web: www.dungannonenterprise.com
Email: info@dungannonenterprise.com
Chief Executive: Brian MacAuley

Omagh Enterprise Company Limited
Great Northern Road
Omagh, BT78 5LU
Tel: 028 8224 9494
Web: www.omaghenterprise.co.uk
Email: info@omaghenterprise.co.uk
Chief Executive: Nicholas O'Shiel

Strabane Enterprise Agency
Orchard Road Industrial Estate
Orchard Road, Strabane, BT82 9FR
Tel: 028 7138 2518
Web: www.seagency.co.uk
Email: info@seagency.co.uk
Chief Executive: Christina Mullen

Join the #agendaNi conversation

Keep up-to-date with what's happening and news on the latest events!

Action for Children NI
@Actn4ChildrenNI
After recent research revealed one-in-four children across NI are growing up in poverty, Sheena McMullen, @SCUKNI and @ncb_ni_tweets spoke to @agendani about why child poverty must be a key focus for all parties.

Tweets from our readers

RiverRidge
@RiverRidge_
Great to see @AgendaNI roundtable discussion on how we can develop a #CircularEconomy in Northern Ireland, in this month's magazine.

Danske Bank
@DanskeBank_UK
Our fraud and cybercrime manager @Chr1sWynne spoke to @agendani this month about the fight against fraudsters, and our top tips on spotting and stopping a scam

Ark Housing
@arkhousing
Our Chief Executive, Jim McShane, has published an article in the June edition of AgendaNi, setting out our plans for growth

@agendani   agendaNimagazine

Northern Ireland Yearbook

Representative groups and organisations

nicva
PROMOTING THE VOLUNTARY SECTOR

CBI
THE VOICE OF BUSINESS
NORTHERN IRELAND

Representative groups

Introduction

Northern Ireland has a vast number of representative groups and associations, large and small, commercial and not-for-profit, covering a wide spectrum of the economic and social life of its people. The main groups are listed A–Z below under appropriate categories.

These listings have been extensively researched but they are by no means exhaustive. The listings provide contact details for each organisation and for the larger ones some information on their structuring and activities.

Anglo North Irish Fish Producers Organisation Limited
The Harbour, Kilkeel, BT34 4AX
Tel: 028 4176 2855
Web: www.seasource.com
Email: info@seasource.com
Chief Executive: Alan McCulla

Armagh City Centre Management
Tel: 028 3752 8888
Email: art@cps-property.com
Chairperson: Art O'Hagan

Arts and Business Northern Ireland
Bridge House, Paulett Avenue
Belfast, BT5 4HD
Tel: 028 9073 5150
Web: www.artsandbusinessni.org.uk
Email: m.nagele@artsandbusinessni.org.uk
Chief Executive: Mary Nagele

ARC Northern Ireland
Wildflower Way
Belfast, BT12 6TA
Tel: 028 9038 0960
Web: www.arcuk.org.uk/northernireland
Email: arc.ni@arcuk.org.uk
Director: Leslie-Anne Newton

Belfast City Centre Management
2nd Floor, Sinclair House
95-101 Royal Avenue, Belfast, BT1 1FE
Tel: 07799 526 930
Web: www.belfastcentre.com
Email: info@belfastcentre.com
Belfast City Manager: Geraldine Duggan

The Bar of Northern Ireland
Bar Library
91 Chichester Street
Belfast, BT1 3JQ
Tel: 028 9024 1523
Web: www.barofni.com
Email: contact@barlibrary.com
Chief Executive: David Mulholland

British Council – Northern Ireland
The Boat, 7th Floor
49 Queen's Square
Belfast, BT1 3FG
Tel: 028 9019 2200
Web: nireland.britishcouncil.org
Email: general.enquiries@britishcouncil.org
Director: Jonathan Stewart

British Dental Association
The Mount, 2 Woodstock Link
Belfast, BT6 8DD
Tel: 020 7935 0875
Web: www.bda.org
Email: northernirelandoffice@bda.org
NI Director: Tristen Kelso

British Medical Association
16 Cromac Place, Cormac Wood
Ormeau Road
Belfast, BT7 2JB
Tel: 028 9026 9666
Web: www.bma.org.uk
Email: bmanorthernireland@bma.org.uk
Chair: Dr Tom Black

Bryson Charitable Group
2 Rivers Edge, 13-15 Ravenhill Road
Belfast, BT6 8DN
Tel: 028 9032 5835
Email: info@brysongroup.org
Chief Executive: Shane Logan

CBI Northern Ireland
2nd Floor, Hamilton House
3 Joy Street, Belfast, BT2 8LE
Tel: 028 9010 1100
Web: www.cbi.org.uk
Email: ni.mail@cbi.org.uk

Centre for Competitiveness
Innovation Centre
Queens Road
Belfast, BT3 9DT
Tel: 028 9073 7950
Web: www.cforc.org
Email: compete@cforc.org
Chief Executive: Bob Barbour

Chartered Institute of Marketing
Moor Hall, Cookham
Maidenhead, Berkshire, SL6 9QH
Tel: 01628 427 500
Web: www.cim.co.uk
Email: philip.preston@cim.co.uk
Volunteer Partnerships Manager:
Philip Preston

Construction Employers Federation
143 Malone Road
Belfast, BT9 6SX
Tel: 028 9087 7143
Web: www.cefni.co.uk
Email: mail@cefni.co.uk
Managing Director: Mark Spence

CITB Northern Ireland
Nutts Corner Training Centre
17 Dundrod Road, Crumlin, BT29 4SR
Tel: 028 9082 5466
Web: www.citbni.org.uk
Email: info@citbni.org.uk
Chief Executive: Barry Neilson

Dairy Council Northern Ireland
Shaftesbury House
Edgewater Office Park
Edgewater Road, Belfast, BT3 9JQ
Tel: 028 9077 0113
Web: www.dairycouncil.co.uk
Email: info@dairycouncil.co.uk
Chief Executive: Mike Johnston

Electrical Contractors Association
25 Prospect Road
Bangor, BT20 5DA
Tel: 028 9147 9527
Web: www.eca.co.uk
Email: alfie.watterson@eca.co.uk
Regional Manager: Alfie Watterson

Northern Ireland Yearbook | Representative groups

EEF Northern Ireland
7 Pilots View, Heron Road
Belfast, BT3 9LE
Tel: 028 9059 5050
Web: www.eefni.org
Email: info@eefni.org
Director: Peter Bloch

Federation of Master Builders
Unit 10, Kilbegs Business Centre
8 Plasketts Close, Antrim, BT41 4NN
Tel: 028 9446 0416
Web: www.fmb.org.uk
Email: fmbni@fmb.org.uk
Director: Gavin McGuire

Federation of Small Businesses (FSB)
Cathedral Chambers
143 Royal Avenue
Belfast, BT1 1FH
Tel: 028 9032 6035
Web: www.fsb.org.uk/ni
Email: fsbni@fsb.org.uk
Chair: Tina McKenzie

Logistics UK
109 Airport Road West
Belfast, BT3 9ED
Tel: 028 9046 6699
Web: www.logistics.org.uk

Hospitality Ulster
91 University Street
Belfast, BT7 1HP
Web: www.hospitalityulster.org
Email: enquiries@hospitalityulster.org
Chief Executive: Colin Neill

Institute of Directors Northern Ireland
Riddel Hall, 185 Stranmillis Road
Belfast, BT9 5EE
Tel: 028 9694 6209
Web: www.iod.com
Email: Chelsea.brennan@iod.com
National Director: Kirsty McManus

Livestock and Meat Commission for Northern Ireland
Lissue Industrial Estate (East)
1A Lissue Walk
Lisburn, BT28 2LU
Tel: 028 9263 3000
Web: www.lmcni.com
Email: istevenson@lmcni.com
Chief Executive: Ian Stevenson

Newry Business Improvement District
Unit 8, Monaghan Court Business Park
Newry, BT35 6BH
Tel: 028 3025 0303
Web: www.newry.com
Email: admin@newry.com
Managing Director: Eamonn Connelly

NICMA – the Childminding Association
Elizabeth House, Suite 3
116-118 Holywood Road
Belfast, BT4 1NU
Tel: 028 9181 1015
Web: www.nicma.org
Email: info@nicma.org

Northern Ireland Agricultural Producers' Association
15 Molesworth Street
Cookstown, BT80 8NX
Tel: 028 8676 5700

British Association of Social Workers Northern Ireland
Douglas House, 397 Ormeau Road
Belfast, BT7 3GP
Tel: 028 9064 8873
Web: www.basw.co.uk
Email: carolyn.ewart@basw.co.uk
NI Manager: Carolyn Ewart

Northern Ireland Council for Voluntary Action (NICVA)
61 Duncairn Gardens
Belfast, BT15 2GB
Tel: 028 9087 7777
Web: www.nicva.org
Email: info@nicva.org
Chief Executive: Seamus McAleavey

Northern Ireland Dyslexia Centre
17A Upper Newtownards Road
Belfast, BT4 3HT
Tel: 028 9065 4670
Web: www.nidyslexiacentre.co.uk
Email: info@nidyslexiacentre.co.uk

Northern Ireland Fish Producers' Organisation
1 Coastguard Cottages
Portavogie, BT22 1EA

The Harbour, Rooney Road
Kilkeel, BT34 4AG
Tel: 028 4277 1946
Web: www.nifpo.co.uk
Email: info@nifpo.co.uk
Chief Executive: Harry Wick

Northern Ireland Food and Drink Association
Belfast Mills, 71-75 Percy Street
Belfast, BT13 2HW
Tel: 028 9024 1010
Web: www.nifda.co.uk
Email: info@nifda.co.uk
Executive Director: Michael Bell

Northern Ireland Grain Trade Association (NIGTA)
86 Donnybrewer Road
Eglinton, BT47 3PD
Tel: 078 7088 5176
Web: www.nigta.co.uk
Email: info@nigta.co.uk
Chief Executive: Gill Gallagher

Northern Ireland Hotels Federation
The McCune Building, 1 Shore Road
Belfast, BT15 3PG
Tel: 028 9077 6635
Email: office@nihf.co.uk
Chief Executive: Janice Gault

Northern Ireland Local Government Association (NILGA)
Bradford Court, Upper Galwally
Castlereagh, BT8 6RB
Tel: 028 9079 8972
Web: www.nilga.org
Chief Executive: Derek McCallan

Northern Ireland Meat Exporters Association
Lissue House, 31 Ballinderry Road
Lisburn, BT28 2SL
Tel: 028 9262 2510
Web: www.nimea.co.uk
Email: info@nimea.co.uk
President: Campbell Tweedie

Northern Ireland Museums Council
153 Bangor Road, Holywood
BT18 0EU
Tel: 028 9055 0215
Web: www.nimc.co.uk
Director: Siobhan Stevenson

Northern Ireland Tourism Alliance
c/o 50 Bedford Street
Belfast, BT2 7FW
Tel: 0774 2450 283
Web: www.nitourismalliance.com
Email: info@nitourismalliance.com
Chief Executive: Joanne Stuart

Mineral Products Association Northern Ireland
Unit 10, Nutts Corner Business Park
Dundrod Road, Crumlin, BT29 4SR
Tel: 028 9082 4078
Web: www.mpani.org
Email: info@mpani.org
Regional Director: Gordon Best

Retail Trade NI
245 Upper Newtownards Road
Ballyhackamore, Belfast, BT4 3JF
Tel: 028 9022 0004
Web: www.retailni.com
Email: info@retailni.com
Chief Executive: Glyn Roberts

Representative groups | Northern Ireland Yearbook

Ulster Archaeological Society
16 Knockbreda Park
Belfast, BT6 0HB
Web: www.qub.ac.uk/sites/uas/
Email: ulsterarchaeolsoc@gmail.com

Ulster Chemists' Association
5 Annadale Avenue
Belfast, BT7 3JH
Tel: 028 9065 6576
Web: www.uca.org.uk
Email: office@uca.org.uk

YMCA Ireland
National Centre Greenhill YMCA
Donard Park, Newcastle, BT33 0GR
Tel: 028 4372 3172
Web: www.ymca-ireland.net
Email: admin@ymca-ireland.net

Chambers of Commerce

The Northern Ireland Chamber of Commerce and Industry
40 Linenhall Street
Belfast, BT2 8BA
Tel: 028 9024 4113
Web: www.northernirelandchamber.com
Email: mail@northernirelandchamber.com
Chief Executive: Ann McGregor

Newtownards Chamber of Trade
Web: www.ardschamber.com
Email: hello@ardschamber.com
President: Derek Wright

Ballycastle Chamber of Commerce
Tel: 028 2076 2294
Email: ballycastlechamber@yahoo.co.uk

Ballymena Borough Chamber of Commerce and Industry
4 Wellington Court
Ballymena, BT43 6EQ
Tel: 078 0173 8359
Web: www.ballymenachamber.co.uk
Email: office@ballymenachamber.co.uk

Bangor Chamber of Commerce
Studio 12, 1st Floor
80 Main Street
Bangor, BT20 3AH
Tel: 028 9187 7957
Web: www.bangorchamber.co.uk
Email: office@bangorchamber.co.uk

Belfast Chamber of Trade and Commerce
Arthur House, 41 Arthur Street
Belfast, BT1 4GB
Tel: 028 9033 1399
Web: www.belfastchamber.com
Email: info@belfastchamber.com

Belfast Junior Chamber of Commerce
Web: www.jcibelfast.org.uk
Email: president@jcibelfast.org.uk
Local President: Phil Hunter

Causeway Chamber of Commerce and Industry
2A Abbey Street
Coleraine, BT52 1DS
Tel: 028 7034 3111
Web: www.causewaychamber.com
Email: info@causewaychamber.com

Cookstown Chamber of Commerce
c/o CFC Interiors, 73 Church Street
Cookstown, BT80 8HT
Web: www.cookstownchamberofcommerce.co.uk
Email: paul@cfcinteriors.com
Contact: Paul Wilson

Kilkeel Chamber of Commerce
18 Mountain Road, Kilkeel, BT34 4AG
Tel: 028 4176 9494

Lisburn Chamber of Commerce
11-13 Market Square
Lisburn, BT28 1AD
Tel: 028 9266 2449
Web: www.lisburnchamber.co.uk
Email: office@lisburnchamber.co.uk

Londonderry Chamber of Commerce
16 Bishop Street
Derry, BT48 6PW
Tel: 028 7126 2379
Web: www.londonderrychamber.co.uk
Email: info@londonderrychamber.co.uk

Newry Chamber of Commerce and Trade
Granite Exchange
5-6 Kildare Street
Newry, BT34 1DQ
Tel: 028 3025 0303 ext 2
Web: www.newrychamber.com
Email: admin@newrychamber.com

Omagh Chamber of Commerce and Industry
Unit VSC1, Omagh Enterprise Centre
Omagh, BT78 5LU
Tel: 028 8224 9494 ext 259
Web: www.omaghchamber.com
Email: admin@omaghchamber.com

Portadown Chamber of Commerce
Chairperson: Adrian Farrell
Contact: Helen Donnelly
Tel: 07436 796 283
Email: info@portadownchamber.co.uk

Roe Valley Chamber of Commerce
c/o 26 Main Street, Limavady
Contact: Julie Brolly
Tel: 028 777 62845 (closed Monday)
Email: julie@cafepiazza.co.uk

Professional institutes and associations

Architects Registration Board
8 Weymouth Street
London, W1W 5BU
Tel: 020 7580 5861
Web: www.arb.org.uk
Email: info@arb.org.uk
Chief Executive: Hugh Simpson

Association of Chartered Certified Accountants (ACCA)
The Adelphi, 1-11 John Adam Street
London, WC2N 6AU
Tel: 020 7059 5701
Web: www.accaglobal.com
Email: info@accaglobal.com
Chief Executive: Helen Brand

The Bar of Northern Ireland
Bar Library
91 Chichester Street
Belfast, BT1 3JQ
Tel: 028 9024 1523
Web: www.barofni.com
Email: contact@barlibrary.com
Chief Executive: David Mulholland

British Dental Association
The Mount, 2 Woodstock Link
Belfast, BT6 8DD
Tel: 020 7935 0875
Web: www.bda.org
Email: northernirelandoffice@bda.org
NI Director: Tristen Kelso

British Medical Association
Tel: 028 9026 9666
Web: www.bma.org.uk
Email: bmanorthernireland@bma.org.uk
Chair: Dr Tom Black

Chartered Institution of Building Services Engineers
Web: www.cibse.org
Email: northernireland@cibse.org

Chartered Institute of Housing
Carnmoney House
Edgewater Office Park
Belfast, BT3 9JQ
Tel: 028 9077 8222
Web: www.cih.org
Email: ni@cih.org
Director: Justin Cartwright

Northern Ireland Yearbook | Representative groups

Chartered Institute of Management Accountants (CIMA)
The Helicon, One South Place
London EC2M 2RB
Tel: 020 8849 2251
Web: www.cimaglobal.com

Chartered Institute of Public Finance and Accountancy
Riddel Hall
185 Stranmillis Road
Belfast, BT9 5EE
Web: www.cipfa.org
Email: nitraining@cipfa.org
Chair: Catherine McFarland

Chartered Institute of Purchasing and Supply
Easton House, Church Street
Easton on the Hill, Stamford
Lincolnshire, PE9 3NZ
Tel: 0345 880 1188
Email: northernireland@cipsbranch.org
Web: www.cips.org
Chair: Mark Osmer

Chartered Institute of Public Relations
Tel: 020 7631 6900
Web: www.cipr.co.uk
Email: AlastairM@cipr.co.uk
Chief Executive: Alastair McCapra

Chartered Society of Physiotherapy (CSP)
Scottish Provident Building
Donegall Square West
Belfast, BT1 6JH
Tel: 028 9521 5533
Email: northernireland@csp.org.uk
Contact: Hilary McErlean

Chief Executives' Forum
Clare House, 303 Airport Road West
Belfast, BT3 9ED
Tel: 028 9081 6440
Web: www.ceforum.org
Email: mail@ceforum.org
Executive Director: Anne Dickson

The Institute of Chartered Accountants in Ireland
The Linenhall, 32-38 Linenhall Street
Belfast, BT2 8BG
Tel: 028 9043 5840
Web: www.charteredaccountants.ie
Email: UlsterSociety@charteredaccountants.ie
Head of Chartered Accountants Northern Ireland: Zara Duffy

Institution of Chemical Engineers
Davis Building
Railway Terrace
Rugby, CV21 3HQ
Tel: 01788 578 214
Web: www.icheme.org
Email: membersupport@icheme.org
Chief Executive: Jon Prichard

Institution of Civil Engineers (ICE)
143 Malone Road
Belfast, BT9 6SX
Web: www.ice.org.uk
Email: iceni@ice.org.uk
Regional Director: Jenny Green

Institution of Engineering and Technology (IET)
Michael Faraday House, Six Hills Way
Stevenage, Hertfordshire, SG1 2AY
Tel: 01438 313 311
Web: www.theiet.org
Email: postmaster@theiet.org
Chief Executive: Nigel Fine

Institute of Financial Accountants
CS111, Clerkenwell Workshops
27-31 Clerkenwell Close
Farringdon, London, EC1R 0AT
Tel: 020 3567 5999
Web: www.ifa.org.uk
Email: mail@ifa.org.uk
Chief Executive: John Edward

Institute of Management Services
Lichfield Business Village
Staffordshire University Centre
Friary Way, Lichfield
WS13 6QG
Tel: 01543 308 605
Web: www.ims-productivity.com
Email: admin@ims-productivity.com

Institution of Mechanical Engineers
One Birdcage Walk
London, SW1H 9JJ
Tel: 020 7304 6862
Web: www.imeche.org
Email: enquiries@imeche.org

The Law Society of Northern Ireland
96 Victoria Street, Belfast, BT1 3GN
Tel: 028 9023 1614
Web: www.lawsoc-ni.org
Chief Executive: David Lavery

Royal College of General Practitioners
4 Cromac Place
Ormeau Road
Belfast, BT7 2JB
Tel: 020 3188 7722
Web: www.rcgp.org.uk/ni
Email: nicouncil@rcgp.org.uk
Chair: Laurence Dorman

Royal College of Midwives
4 College House, Citylink Business Park
Belfast, BT12 4HQ
Tel: 0300 303 0444 opt 2
Web: www.rcm.org.uk

Royal College of Nursing
17 Windsor Avenue, Belfast, BT9 6EE
Tel: 028 9038 4600
Web: www.rcn.org.uk/northernireland
Email: ni.board@rcn.org.uk

Royal Institute of Chartered Surveyors
12 Great George Street
London, SW1P 3AD
Tel: 024 7686 8555
Web: www.rics.org
Email: ricsni@rics.org
Chair of Northern Ireland:
Sharon McClements

Royal Society of Ulster Architects
2 Mount Charles, Belfast, BT7 1NZ
Tel: 028 9032 3760
Web: www.rsua.org.uk
Email: info@rsua.org.uk
Director: Ciarán Fox

Royal Town Planning Institute (Northern Ireland Branch)
PO Box 69, Carrickfergus, BT38 8WX
Tel: 020 7929 8193
Web: www.rtpi.org.uk
Email: northernireland@rtpi.org.uk
Director: Roisin Willmott

Society of Radiographers (SOR)
207 Providence Square
Mill Street, London, SE1 2EW
Tel: 020 7740 7200
Web: www.sor.org
Chief Executive: Richard Evans

Trade unions

Irish Congress of Trade Unions Northern Ireland Committee (ICTUNI)
45-47 Donegall Street
Belfast, BT1 2FG
Tel: 028 9024 7940
Web: www.ictuni.org
Email: info@ictuni.org
Assistant General Secretary: Owen Reidy

Bakers, Food and Allied Workers Union (BFAWU)
Suite 105, City East Business Centre
68-72 Newtownards Road
Belfast, BT4 1GW
Tel: 028 9094 1693
Web: www.bfawu.org
Email: region7@bfawu.org
Regional Officer: Laura Graham

Representative groups

Broadcasting, Entertainment, Communications and Theatre Union (BECTU)
373-377 Clapham Road
London, SW9 9BT
Tel: 020 7346 0900
Web: www.bectu.org.uk
Email: info@bectu.org.uk
General Secretary: Mike Clancy

Communication Workers' Union (CWU)
CWU Office, 3rd Floor
26-34 Antrim Road
Belfast, BT15 2AA
Tel: 028 9032 1771
Web: www.cwu.org
Email: northernirelandregion@cwu.org
Regional Secretary: Erin Massey

Financial Services Union (FSU)
5th Floor, Quaygate House
15 Scrabo Street, Belfast, BT5 4BD
Tel: 028 9020 0130
Web: www.fsunion.org
Email: info@fsunion.org
General Secretary: John O'Connell

Fire Brigades' Union (FBU)
14 Bachelors Walk, Lisburn
BT28 1XJ
Tel: 028 9266 4622
Web: www.fbu.org.uk
Email: jim.quinn@fbu.org.uk
Contact: Jim Quinn

First Division Association
93-95 Borough High Street
London, SE1 1NL
Tel: 020 7401 5555
Web: www.fda.org.uk
Email: allan@fda.org.uk
Contact: Allan Sampson

GMB
Victoria House, 1A Victoria Road
Holywood, BT18 9BA
Tel: 028 9039 3340
Web: www.gmb.org.uk
Email: holywood@gmbnorthwest.com

Irish National Teachers Organisation (INTO)
23-24 College Gardens, Belfast, BT9 6BS
Tel: 028 9038 1455
Web: www.into.ie
Email: infoni@into.ie
Northern Secretary: Gerry Murphy

National Association of Head Teachers
Carnmoney House
Edgewater Office Park
Belfast, BT3 9JQ
Tel: 028 9077 6633
Web: www.naht.org.uk
Email: nahtni@naht.org.uk

National Association for Probation Officers (NAPO)
65 Mortlake High Street, London, SW14 8HL
Tel: 020 7223 4887
Web: www.napo.org.uk
Email: info@napo.org.uk
General Secretary: Ian Lawrence

National Association of Schoolmasters / Union of Women Teachers (NASUWT)
Ben Madigan House, Edgewater Road
Belfast, BT3 9JQ
Tel: 028 9078 4480
Web: www.nasuwt.org.uk
Email: rc-nireland@mail.nasuwt.org.uk

National Education Union
41-45 York Road
Belfast, BT15 3GU
Tel: 028 9078 2020
Web: www.neu.org.uk
Email: ni@neu.org.uk

National Union of Journalists (NUJ)
2nd Floor, Spencer House
Spencer Row
Dublin 1, D01 R9T8
Tel: +353 (0)1 817 0340
Web: www.nuj.org.uk
Email: info@nuj.ie
Irish Secretary: Séamus Dooley

National Union of Rail, Maritime and Transport Workers (RMT)
Unity House, 39 Chalton Street
London, NW1 1JD
Tel: 020 7387 4771
Web: www.rmt.org.uk
Email: info@rmt.org.uk

National Union of Students – Union of Students in Ireland (NUS-USI)
42 Dublin Road
Belfast, BT2 7HN
Tel: 028 9024 4641
Web: www.nus-usi.org
Email: info@nistudents.org

Northern Ireland Public Service Alliance (NIPSA)
54 Wellington Park
Belfast, BT9 6DP
Tel: 028 9066 1831
Web: www.nipsa.org.uk
Email: info@nipsa.org.uk
General Secretary: Alison Millar

Prospect
45-47 Donegal Street
Belfast, BT1 2FG
Tel: 028 9024 6331
Web: www.prospect.org.uk
Email: ni@prospect.org.uk
General Secretary: Mike Clancy

Public and Commercial Services Union (PCS)
40 Wellington Park, Belfast, BT9 6DP
Tel: 0141 225 5150
Web: www.pcs.org.uk
Email: belfast@pcs.org.uk
Regional Secretary: Gayle Matthews

Belfast Met Students' Union
Titanic Quarter, Level 1, Room 43
7 Queens Road, Belfast, BT3 9DT
Tel: 028 9026 5099
Email: studentsunion@belfastmet.ac.uk
Contact: Paul Docherty/Eugene McKenna

Queen's University of Belfast Students' Union
3 Elmwood Avenue
Belfast, BT9 6AZ
Tel: 028 9097 3726
Web: www.qubsu.org
Email: studentsunion@qub.ac.uk
Director: Ciaran Higgins

University and College Union (UCU)
Suite 1, Shaftesbury House
Belfast, BT3 9JQ
Tel: 028 9037 2870
Web: www.ucu.org.uk
Regional Official: Katharine Clarke

Ulster University Students' Union

Belfast Campus
York Street, Belfast, BT15 1ED
Tel: 028 9036 6050
Web: www.uusu.org
Email: vp.belfast@uusu.org
Contact: Robert Millar

Coleraine Campus
Cromore Road, Coleraine, BT52 1SA
Web: www.uusu.org
Email: vp.coleraine@uusu.org
Contact: Curtis Donnan

Jordanstown Campus
Shore Road, Jordanstown
Newtownabbey, BT37 0QB
Web: www.uusu.org
Email: vp.jordanstown@uusu.org
Contact: Rebecca Allen

Magee Campus
Northland Road
Derry/Londonderry, BT48 7JL
Tel: 028 7167 5290
Web: www.uusu.org
Email: vp.magee@uusu.org
Contact: Ryan Harling

Northern Ireland Yearbook | Representative groups

Services Industrial Professional and Technical Union (SIPTU)
3 Antrim Road, Belfast, BT15 2BE
Tel: 028 9031 4000
Web: www.siptu.ie
Email: martinorourke@siptu.ie
Lead Organiser: Martin O'Rourke

Ulster Farmers' Union
475 Antrim Road, Belfast, BT15 3DA
Tel: 028 9037 0222
Web: www.ufuni.org
Email: info@ufuhq.com
Chief Executive: Wesley Aston

Ulster Teachers' Union (UTU)
94 Malone Road, Belfast, BT9 5HP
Tel: 028 9066 2216
Web: www.utu.edu
Email: office@utu.edu
General Secretary: Jacquie White

Union of Shop, Distributive and Allied Workers (USDAW)
First Floor, Unit 2
41 Stockmans Way, Belfast, BT9 7ET
Tel: 028 9066 3773
Web: www.usdaw.org.uk
Email: belfast@usdaw.org.uk

UNISON
Galway House
165 York Street, Belfast, BT15 1AL
Tel: 028 9027 0190
Web: www.unison-ni.org.uk
Email: unisonnorthernireland@unison.co.uk
Regional Secretary: Patricia McKeown

Unite the Union
26-34 Antrim Road
Belfast, BT15 2AA
Tel: 028 9023 2381
Web: www.unitetheunionireland.org
Regional Secretary: Jackie Pollock

Charities

Action Cancer
Action Cancer House
20 Windsor Avenue
Belfast, BT9 6EE
Tel: 028 9080 3344
Web: www.actioncancer.org
Email: info@actioncancer.org
Chief Executive: Gareth Kirk

Action for Children
10 Heron Road
Belfast, BT3 9LE
Tel: 028 9046 0500
Web: www.actionforchildren.org.uk
Email: nioffice@actionforchildren.org.uk
Chief Executive: Melanie Armstrong

Age NI
3 Lower Crescent, Belfast, BT7 1NR
Tel: 028 9024 5729
Web: www.ageni.org
Email: info@ageni.org
Chief Executive: Linda Robinson

Alcoholics Anonymous
North City Business Centre
Unit 11, 2 Duncairn Gardens
Belfast, BT15 2GG
Tel: 028 9035 1222
Web: www.alcoholicsanonymous.ie
Email: gso@alcoholicsanonymous.ie

Alzheimer's Society
30 Skegoneill Street
Belfast, BT15 3JL
Tel: 028 9066 4100
Web: www.alzheimers.org.uk
Email: nir@alzheimers.org.uk

Amnesty International
397 Ormeau Road, Belfast, BT7 3GP
Tel: 028 9064 3000
Web: www.amnesty.org.uk
Email: grainne.teggart@amnesty.org.uk
Contact: Grainne Teggart

Arts and Disability Forum
University of Atypical
Ground Floor
Cathedral Quarter Workspaces
109-113 Royal Avenue
Belfast, BT1 1FF
Tel: 028 9023 9450
Web: www.universityofatypical.org
Email: info@universityofatypial.org

Advice NI
Forestview, Purdy's Lane
Newtownbreda, Belfast
BT8 7AR
Tel: 0800 915 4604
Web: www.adviceni.net
Email: advice@adviceni.net
Chief Executive: Bob Stronge

Autism NI
Donard, Knockbracken Healthcare Park
Saintfield Road, Belfast, BT8 8BH
Tel: 028 9040 1729
Web: www.autismni.org
Email: info@autismni.org
Chief Executive: Kerry Boyd

Barnardo's
542-544 Upper Newtownards Road
Belfast, BT4 3HE
Tel: 028 9067 2366
Web: www.barnardos.org.uk
Email: receptionNI@barnardos.org.uk
NI Director: Lynda Wilson

BBC Children in Need
Broadcasting House
Ormeau Avenue
Belfast, BT2 8HQ
Tel: 028 9033 8221
Web: bbcchildreninneed.co.uk
Email: pudsey@bbc.co.uk

Belfast Central Mission
Grosvenor House, 5 Glengall Street
Belfast, BT12 5AD
Tel: 028 9024 1917
Web: www.belfastcentralmission.org
Email: info@belfastcentralmission.org
CEO: Nicky Conway

Brainwaves NI
35 Loy Street, Cookstown
Co Tyrone, BT80 8PZ
Tel: 028 8676 6000
Web: www.brainwaves-ni.org
Email: info@brainwaves-ni.org
Chair: Colin McMillan

British Deaf Association
Unit 5c, Weavers Court
Linfield Road
Belfast, BT12 5GH
Tel: 028 9043 7480
Web: www.bda.org.uk
Email: busdeve.niscot@bda.org.uk
Contact: Majella McAteer

British Heart Foundation Northern Ireland
2nd Floor, 14 Cromac Place
The Gasworks
Belfast, BT7 2JB
Tel: 028 9053 8301
Web: www.bhf.org.uk
Email: mckinneyf@bhf.org.uk
Head of Northern Ireland:
Fearghal McKinney

British Red Cross
12 Heron Road
Belfast, BT3 9LE
Tel: 028 9073 5350
Web: www.redcross.org.uk
Email: contactus@redcross.org.uk

Bryson Charitable Group
2 Rivers Edge, 13-15 Ravenhill Road
Belfast, BT6 8DN
Tel: 028 9032 5835
Web: www.brysongroup.org
Email: info@brysongroup.org
Chief Executive: Shane Logan

Cancer Focus Northern Ireland
40-44 Eglantine Avenue
Belfast, BT9 6DX
Tel: 028 9066 3281
Web: www.cancerfocusni.org
Email: hello@cancerfocusni.org
Chief Executive: Richard Spratt

Representative groups

Carers Northern Ireland
58 Howard Street, Belfast, BT1 6PJ
Tel: 028 9043 9843
Web: www.carersuk.org/northernireland
Email: info@carersni.org
Contact: Lyn Campbell

Cancer Fund for Children
Curlew Pavilion, Portside Business Park
Airport Road West, Belfast, BT3 9ED
Tel: 028 9080 5599
Web: www.cancerfundforchildren.com
Email: info@cancerfundforchildren.com
Chief Executive: Phil Alexander

Cancer Research UK
PO Box 1561
Oxford, OX4 9GZ
Tel: 0300 123 1022
Web: www.cancerresearchuk.org
Email: margaret.carr@cancer.org.uk
Contact: Margaret Carr

Cara Friend
Belfast LGBTQI+ Centre
23-31 Waring Street
Belfast, BT1 2DX
Tel: 028 9089 0202
Web: www.cara-friend.org.uk
Email: admin@cara-friend.org.uk
Director: Steve Williamson

The Cedar Foundation
Malcolm Sinclair House
31 Ulsterville Avenue
Belfast, BT9 7AS
Tel: 028 9066 6188
Web: www.cedar-foundation.org
Email: communications@cedar-foundation.org
Chief Executive: Elaine Armstrong

Children in Northern Ireland (CiNI)
Unit 9, 40 Montgomery Road
Belfast, BT6 9HL
Tel: 028 9040 1290
Web: www.ci-ni.org.uk
Email: info@ci-ni.org.uk
Chief Executive: Pauline Leeson

Children in Crossfire
2 St Joseph's Avenue
Derry, BT48 6TH
Tel: 028 7126 9898
Web: www.childrenincrossfire.org
Email: info@childrenincrossfire.org
Chief Executive: Richard Moore

Children's Law Centre
Rights House
127-131 Ormeau Road
Belfast, BT7 1SH
Tel: 028 9024 5704
Web: www.childrenslawcentre.org.uk
Email: chalky@childrenslawcentre.org
Director: Paddy Kelly

Christian Aid Ireland
Linden House, Beechill Business Park
96 Beechill Road, Belfast, BT8 7QN
Tel: 028 9064 8133
Web: www.christianaid.ie
Email: belfast@christian-aid.org
Chief Executive: Rosamond Bennett

Cleft Lip and Palate Association
The Green House
244-254 Cambridge Heath Road
London, E2 9DA
Tel: 020 7833 4883
Web: www.clapa.com
Email: info@clapa.com

Committee on the Administration of Justice
1st Floor, Community House
City Link Business Park, 6A Albert Street
Belfast, BT12 4HQ
Tel: 028 9031 6000
Web: www.caj.org.uk
Email: info@caj.org.uk
Director: Brian Gormally

Community Arts Partnership
7 Donegall Street Place, Donegall Street
Belfast, BT1 2FN
Tel: 028 9092 3493
Web: www.capartscentre.com
Email: info@capartscentre.com
Chief Executive: Conor Shields

Community Relations Council
2nd Floor, Equality House
7-9 Shaftesbury Square
Belfast, BT2 7DB
Tel: 028 9022 7500
Web: www.community-relations.org.uk
Email: info@nicrc.org.uk
Chief Executive: Jacqueline Irwin

Concern Worldwide NI
47 Frederick Street, Belfast, BT1 2LW
Tel: 028 9033 1100
Web: www.concern.org.uk
Email: enquiries.info@concern.net

Conservation Volunteers NI
Beech House, 159 Ravenhill Road
Belfast, BT6 0BP
Tel: 028 9064 5169
Web: www.tcv.org.uk/northernireland
Email: tcvni@tcv.org.uk
Regional Director: Debbie Adams

Co-operation Ireland
5N Weavers Court Business Park
Linfield Road, Belfast, BT12 5GH
Tel: 028 9032 1462
Web: www.cooperationireland.org
Email: info@cooperationireland.org
Chief Executive: Peter Sheridan

Corrymeela Community
5 Drumaroan Road
Ballycastle, BT54 6QU
Tel: 028 2076 2626
Web: www.corrymeela.org
Email: welcome@corrymeela.org

Crossroads Care NI
432 Upper Newtownards Road
Belfast, BT4 3GY
Tel: 028 9181 4455
Web: www.crossroadscare.co.uk
Email: info@crossroadscare.co.uk

CRUSE Bereavement Care NI
Prince Regent Commercial Centre
8 Prince Regent Road
Belfast, BT5 6QR
Tel: 028 9079 2419
Web: www.cruse.org.uk
Email: northern.ireland@cruse.org.uk
Director: Kathleen Laverty

Cystic Fibrosis Trust
Forsyth House, Cromac Square
Belfast, BT2 8LA
Tel: 07990 064 984
Web: www.cysticfibrosis.org.uk
Email: Nicola.holland@cysticfibrosis.org.uk
Contact: Nicola Holland

Diabetes UK
First Floor, Suite 1
Lisburn Square House
10 Haslems Lane
Lisburn, BT28 1TW
Tel: 028 9066 6646
Web: www.diabetes.org.uk
Email: n.ireland@diabetes.org.uk
National Director: Tina McCrossan

Disability Action
Portside Business Park
189 Airport Road West
Belfast, BT3 9ED
Tel: 028 9029 7880
Web: www.disabilityaction.org
Email: hq@disabilityaction.org
Interim Chief Executive: Andrea Brown

Down's Syndrome Association NI
Unit 2, Marlborough House
348 Lisburn Road, Belfast, BT9 6GH
Tel: 028 9066 5260
Web: www.downs-syndrome.org.uk/northernireland
Email: enquiriesni@downs-syndrome.org.uk

Early Years
6C Wildflower Way
Apollo Road, Boucher Road
Belfast, BT12 6TA
Tel: 028 9066 2825
Web: www.early-years.org
Email: info@early-years.org
Chief Executive: Pauline Walmsley

Northern Ireland Yearbook | Representative groups

East Belfast Independent Advice Centre
55 Templemore Avenue
Belfast, BT5 4FP
Tel: 028 9073 5690
Web: www.ebiac.org
Email: advice@ebiac.org
Manager: Gerard Morgan

Employers for Childcare
Blaris Industrial Estate
11 Altona Road, Lisburn, BT27 5QB
Tel: 028 9267 8200
Web: www.employersforchildcare.org
Email: hello@employersforchildcare.org
Chief Executive: Marie Marin

Family Planning Association Belfast
3rd Floor, Ascot House
Belfast, BT2 7DB
Tel: 0845 122 8687
Web: www.fpa.org.uk
Email: fpadirect@fpa.org.uk
Director: Mark Breslin

Federation of Women's Institutes of Northern Ireland
209-211 Upper Lisburn Road
Belfast, BT10 0LL
Tel: 028 9030 1506
Web: www.wini.org.uk
Email: irene@wini.org.uk
Acting General Secretary: Kathleen Dicky

Fostering Network
Unit 22, 40 Montgomery Road
Belfast, BT6 9HL
Tel: 028 9070 5056
Web: www.thefosteringnetwork.org.uk
Email: ni@fostering.net
NI Director: Kathleen Toner

Friends of the Earth Northern Ireland
7 Donegall Street Place
Belfast, BT1 2FN
Tel: 028 9023 3488
Web: www.friendsoftheearth.uk/northern-ireland
Email: foe-ni@foe.co.uk
NI Director: James Orr

Guide Dogs for the Blind
Unit 17, 18 Heron Road
Belfast, BT3 9LE
Tel: 0345 143 0193
Web: www.guidedogs.org.uk
Email: belfast@guidedogs.org.uk

Habitat for Humanity Northern Ireland
Riverside Centre, Young Street
Lisburn, BT28 5EA
Tel: 028 9263 5635
Web: www.habitatni.co.uk
Email: info@habitatni.co.uk
Chief Executive: Jenny Williams

Home-Start UK
NICVA Building, 61 Duncairn Gardens
Belfast, BT15 2GB
Tel: 077 1891 2772
Web: www.home-start.org.uk
Email: jmurray@home-start.org.uk
Contact: Jayne Murray

Homeless Connect
3rd Floor, Andras House
60 Great Victoria Street
Belfast, BT2 7BB
Tel: 028 9024 6440
Web: www.homelessconnect.org
Email: info@chni.org.uk
CEO: Nicola McCrudden

International Fund for Ireland
Seatem House, 28-32 Alfred Street
Belfast, BT2 8EN
Tel: 028 9031 2884
Web: www.internationalfundforireland.com
Email: info.ifi@finance-ni.gov.uk
Joint Director General: Joe Mullan

Leukaemia and Lymphoma NI
Patrick G Johnston Centre for Cancer Research
97 Lisburn Road, Belfast, BT9 7AE
Tel: 028 9097 2928
Web: www.llni.co.uk
Email: info@llni.co.uk
Contact: Joanne Badger

Macmillan Cancer Support
Support and Information Centre
77-81 Lisburn Road
Belfast, BT9 7A13
Tel: 028 9615 0077
Web: www.macmillan.org.uk
Email: cancer.info@belfasttrusthscni.net

Marie Curie
Kensington Road, Belfast, BT5 6NF
Tel: 028 9088 2000
Web: www.mariecurie.org.uk
Email: Belfast.hospice@mariecurie.org.uk
Associate NI Director: Paula Heneghan

Mencap Centre
5 School Road, Newtownbreda
Belfast, BT8 6BT
Tel: 028 9069 1351
Web: www.northernireland.mencap.org.uk
Email: helpline.ni@mencap.org.uk
NI Director: Gráinne Close

Mindwise
Pinewood House
46 Newforge Lane
Belfast, BT9 5NW
Tel: 028 9040 2323
Web: www.mindwisenv.org
Email: info@mindwisenv.org
Chief Executive: Anne Doherty

MS Society Northern Ireland
The Resource Centre
34 Annadale Avenue
Belfast, BT7 3JJ
Tel: 028 9080 2802
Web: www.mssociety.org.uk
Email: nireception@mssociety.org.uk
NI Director: David Galloway

The National Trust
Northern Ireland Regional Office
Rowallane Stableyard
Saintfield, Ballynahinch, BT24 7LH
Tel: 028 9751 0721
Web: www.nationaltrust.org.uk
Email: ni.customerenquiries@nationaltrust.org.uk
Director: Heather McLachlan

NCB Northern Ireland
NICVA Building
61 Duncairn Gardens
Belfast, BT15 2GB
Tel: 028 9087 5006
Web: www.ncb.org.uk
Email: enquiriesni@ncb.org.uk
NI Assistant Director: Deirdre McAliskey

Nexus NI
59 Malone Road
Belfast, BT9 6SA
Tel: 028 9032 6803
Web: www.nexusni.org
Email: info@nexusni.org
CEO: Joanne Barnes

Inspire Wellbeing
Lombard House
10-20 Lombard Street
Belfast, BT1 1RD
Tel: 028 9032 8474
Web: www.inspirewellbeing.org
Email: hello@inspirewellbeing.org
Chief Executive: Kerry Anthony

Northern Ireland Chest Heart and Stroke
21 Dublin Road
Belfast, BT2 7HB
Tel: 028 9032 0184
Web: www.nichs.org.uk
Email: mail@nichs.org.uk
Chief Executive: Declan Cunnane

Northern Ireland Hospice
Head Office
18 O'Neill Road
Newtownabbey, BT36 6WB
Tel: 028 9078 1836
Web: www.nihospice.org
Chief Executive: Heather Weir

Northern Ireland Children's Hospice
Horizon House
18 O'Neill Road
Newtownabbey, BT36 6WB
Tel: 028 9077 7635
Web: www.nihospice.org/childrens-hospice
Chief Executive: Heather Weir

NSPCC NI
1st Floor, Lanyon Building
Jennymount Business Park
North Derby Street, Belfast, BT15 3HL
Tel: 028 9035 1135
Web: www.nspcc.org.uk
Email: northernirelandappeals@nspcc.org.uk

Oxfam Northern Ireland
Elizabeth House, Suite 1
116-118 Holywood Road
Belfast, BT4 1NY
Tel: 028 9023 0220
Web: www.oxfamireland.org
Email: irl-info@oxfam.org
CEO: Jim Clarken

Oxygen Therapy Centre
100 Shore Road
Magheramorne
Larne, BT40 3HT
Tel: 028 2827 4670
Web: www.oxygentherapycentre.co.uk
Email: info@oxygentherapycentre.co.uk

Parenting NI
First Floor, Unit 3
Hawthorn Office Park
39a Stockman's Way
Belfast, BT9 7ET
Tel: 028 9031 0891
Web: www.parentingni.org
Email: info@parentingni.com
CEO: Charlene Brooks

Parkinson's UK
Wellington Park Business Centre
3 Wellington Park, Malone Road
Belfast, BT9 6DJ
Tel: 028 9092 3370
Web: www.parkinsons.org.uk
Email: northernireland@parkinsons.org.uk
Country Director: Nicola Moore

PIPS
281 Antrim Road
Belfast, BT15 2HE
Tel: 0800 088 6042
Web: www.pipscharity.com
Email: info@pipscharity.com

Positive Life NI
20 Derryvolgie Avenue
Belfast, BT9 6FN
Tel: 0800 137 437
Web: www.positivelifeni.com
CEO: Jacquie Richardson

Praxis Care Group
25-31 Lisburn Road, Belfast, BT9 7AA
Tel: 028 9023 4555
Email: info@praxiscare.org.uk
Web: www.praxiscare.org.uk
NI Director: Deirdre Carr

The Prince's Trust
Unit 8, Weavers Court
Belfast, BT12 5GH
Tel: 028 9089 5000
Web: www.princes-trust.org.uk
Email: outreachni@princes-trust.org.uk
NI Director: Mark Dougan

The Rainbow Project
23-31 Waring Street
Belfast, BT1 2DX
Tel: 028 9031 9030
Web: www.rainbow-project.org
Email: info@rainbow-project.org
Director: John O'Doherty

Relate NI
3 Glengall Street
Belfast, BT12 5AB
Tel: 028 9032 3454
Web: www.relateni.org
Email: office@relateni.org
Chief Executive: Duane Farrell

RNID
Harvester House
4-8 Adelaide Street
Belfast, BT2 8GA
Tel: 028 9023 9619
Web: www.rnid.org.uk
Email: information.nireland@rnid.org.uk
Chief Executive: Mark Atkinson

Royal National Institute of Blind People (RNIB NI)
Victoria House
15-17 Gloucester Street
Belfast, BT1 4LS
Tel: 028 9032 9373
Web: www.rnib.org.uk
Email: rnibni@rnib.org.uk

Royal National Lifeboat Institution
West Quay Road
Poole, BH15 1HZ
Tel: 0300 300 9990
Web: www.rnli.org

Royal Society for the Protection of Birds (RSPB)
Northern Ireland Headquarters
Belvoir Park Forest
Belfast, BT8 7QT
Tel: 028 9049 1547
Web: www.rspb.org.uk
Email: rspb.nireland@rspb.org.uk
NI Director: Joanne Sherwood

Samaritans
5 Wellesley Avenue
Belfast, BT9 6DG
Tel: 0330 094 5717
Web: www.samaritans.org

Save the Children
Popper House
15 Richmond Park
Belfast, BT10 0HB
Tel: 028 9043 1123
Web: www.savethechilren.org.uk
Email: infoni@savethechildren.org.uk

Self Help Africa
NICVA Building
61 Duncairn Gardens
Belfast, BT15 2GB
Tel: 028 9087 7777
Web: www.selfhelpafrica.org
Email: info@selfhelpafrica.org

Shelter (Northern Ireland)
58 Howard Street, Belfast, BT1 6PJ
Tel: 028 9024 7752
Web: www.shelterni.org
Email: info@shelterni.org
Director: Tony McQuillan

Shine
PO Box 61
Cookstown, BT80 1AN
Tel: 01733 555 988
Web: www.shinecharity.org.uk
Email: firstcontact@shinecharity.org.uk
Contact: Marie McGonnell

Simon Community Northern Ireland
4th Floor, Arthur Place
24-26 Arthur Street
Belfast, BT1 4GF
Tel: 028 9023 2882
Web: www.simoncommunity.org
Email: info@simoncommunity.org
Chief Executive: Jim Dennison

Springboard Opportunities Ltd
112-114 Donegall Street
Belfast, BT1 2GX
Tel: 028 9031 5111
Web: www.springboard-opps.org
Email: james@springboard-opps.org
Contact: James Magee

St John's Ambulance
35 Knockbracken Healthcare Park
Saintfield Road, Belfast, BT8 8RA
Tel: 028 9079 9393
Web: www.sjani.org
Email: districthq@sjani.org
Chief Executive: Adrian Donaldson

Stroke Association
Tel: 028 9050 8020
Web: www.stroke.org.uk
Email: ni@stroke.org.uk
NI Director: Barry McAuley

Trócaire
50 King Street, Belfast, BT1 6AD
Tel: 028 9080 8030
Web: www.trocaire.org
Email: infoni@trocaire.org

Ulster Society for the Prevention of Cruelty to Animals (USPCA)
Unit 5-6, Carnbane East Industrial Estate
Newry, BT35 6QH
Tel: 028 3025 1000
Web: www.uspca.co.uk
Email: enquiries@uspca.co.uk
Chief Executive: Brendan Mullan

Ulster Wildlife Trust
McClelland House, 10 Heron Road
Belfast, BT3 9LE
Tel: 028 9045 4094
Web: www.ulsterwildlife.org
Email: info@ulsterwildlife.org
Chief Executive: Jennifer Fulton

Versus Arthritis
Unit 4, McCune Building
1 Shore Road, Belfast, BT15 3PG
Tel: 028 9078 2940
Web: www.versusarthritis.org
Email: northernireland@versusarthritis.org
Director: Sara Graham

Victim Support NI
Albany House
73-75 Great Victoria Street
Belfast, BT2 7AF
Tel: 028 9024 3133
Web: www.victimsupportni.com
Email: belfast@victimsupportni.org.uk
CEO: Geraldine Hanna

Volunteer Now
The Skainos Centre
239 Newtownards Road
Belfast, BT4 1AF
Tel: 028 9023 2020
Web: www.volunteernow.co.uk
Email: info@volunteernow.co.uk
Chief Executive: Denise Hayward

The Woodland Trust
The Courtyard, Clandeboye Estate
Bangor, BT19 1RN
Web: www.woodlandtrust.org.uk
Email: northernireland@woodlandtrust.org.uk
Director: Darren Moorcroft

Women's Aid Federation Northern Ireland
The Annex, 30 Adelaide Park
Belfast, BT9 6FY
Tel: 028 9024 9041
Web: www.womensaidni.org
Email: info@womensaidni.org
CEO: Sarah Mason

Women's Support Network
109-113 Royal Avenue
Belfast, BT1 1FF
Tel: 028 9023 6923
Web: www.wsn.org.uk
Email: info@wsn.org.uk
Director: Karen Sweeney

Youth and community organisations

Belfast Interface Project
2nd Floor
Cathedral Quarter Managed Workspace
109-113 Royal Avenue
Belfast, BT1 1FF
Tel: 028 9024 2828
Web: www.belfastinterfaceproject.org
Email: info@belfastinterfaceproject.org
Director: Joe O'Donnell

Belfast Unemployed Resource Centre
4-6 Donegall Street, Donegall Place
Belfast, BT1 2FN
Tel: 028 9096 1111
Web: www.burc.org
Email: info@burc.org

Business in the Community
Bridge House, Paulett Avenue
Belfast, BT5 4HD
Web: www.bitc.org.uk
Email: info@bitcni.org.uk
Managing Director: Kieran Harding

Catholic Guides of Ireland
St Francis De Sales
Beechmount Drive, Belfast, BT12 7LU
Tel: 028 9031 3639
Web: www.girlguidesireland.ie
Email: admin.nr@catholicguides.org.uk

Community Development and Health Network
30A Mill Street, Newry, BT34 1EY
Tel: 028 3026 4606
Web: www.cdhn.org
Email: info@cdhn.org
Director: Joanne Vance

Community Relations Council NI
2nd Floor, Equality House
7-9 Shaftesbury Square
Belfast, BT2 7DB
Tel: 028 9022 7500
Web: www.community-relations.org.uk
Email: info@nicrc.org.uk
Chief Executive: Jacqueline Irwin

Community Transport Association
Room 110 City East
68-72 Newtownards Road
Belfast, BT4 1GW
Tel: 028 9094 1661
Web: www.ctauk.org
Email: info@ctauk.org

East Belfast Community Development Agency
East Belfast Network Centre
55 Templemore Avenue
Belfast, BT5 4FP
Tel: 028 9045 1512
Web: www.ebcda.org
Email: info@ebcda.org
Executive Director: Michael Briggs

Falls Community Council
275-277 Falls Road, Belfast, BT12 6FD
Tel: 028 9020 2030
Web: www.fallscouncil.com
Email: info@fallscouncil.com
Director: Gerry McConville

Fermanagh Rural Community Initiative
Unit 3, 56A Tempo Road
Enniskillen, BT74 6HR
Tel: 028 6632 6478
Web: www.frci.org.uk
Email: info@frci.org.uk
Manager: Ciaran Rooney

Girls' Brigade Northern Ireland
C2 Kilbegs Business Park
Ferguson Way, Antrim, BT41 4LZ
Tel: 028 9454 8054
Web: www.gbni.co.uk
Email: info@gbni.co.uk
Secretary: Gail Clarke

Girlguiding Ulster
30 Station Road
Holywood, BT18 0BP
Tel: 028 9042 5212
Web: www.girlguidingulster.org.uk
Email: info@girlguidingulster.org.uk
Operations Manager: Tasha Crawford

Groundwork NI
63-75 Duncairn Gardens
Belfast, BT15 2GB
Tel: 028 9074 9494
Web: www.groundwork.org.uk
Email: info@groundworkni.co.uk
CEO: Cara Cash-Marley

Lifestart Foundation NI
Head Office
2 Springrowth House
Balliniska Road, Derry, BT48 0GG
Tel: 028 7136 5363
Web: www.lifestartfoundation.org
Email: headoffice@lifestartfoundation.org
Executive Director: Pauline McClenaghan

Representative groups | Northern Ireland Yearbook

Ligoniel Improvement Association
148 Ligoniel Road, Belfast, BT14 8DT
Tel: 028 9039 1225
Email: administration@ligonielvillage.com
CEO: Maria Morgan

Mediation Northern Ireland
83 University Street
Belfast, BT7 1HP
Tel: 028 9043 8614
Web: www.mediationnorthernireland.org
Email: info@mediationnorthernireland.org

NIACRO
Amelia House, 4 Amelia Street
Belfast, BT2 7GS
Tel: 028 9032 0157
Web: www.niacro.co.uk
Email: niacro@niacro.co.uk
Chief Executive: Olwen Lyner

Rural Community Network
38A Oldtown Street
Cookstown, BT80 8EF
Tel: 028 8676 6670
Web: www.ruralcommunitynetwork.org
Email: info@ruralcommunitynetwork.org
Policy and Public Affairs Officer:
Aidan Campbell

Sandy Row Community Forum
63-75 Sandy Row, Belfast, BT12 5ER
Tel: 028 9023 8446
Email: info@sandyrow.co.uk

The Boys' Brigade Northern Ireland
Newport, 117 Culcavey Road
Hillsborough, BT26 6HH
Tel: 028 9268 8444
Web: www.boys-brigade.org.uk
Email: nihq@boys-brigade.org.uk

The Duke of Edinburgh's Award
Stranmillis University College
Stranmillis Road
Belfast, BT9 5DY
Tel: 028 9069 9100
Web: www.dofe.org
Email: nireland@dofe.org
Director: Kate Thompson

The Scout Association
109 Old Milltown Road
Belfast, BT8 7SP
Tel: 028 9049 2829
Web: www.scoutsni.org
Email: enquiries@scoutsni.org
Chief Commissioner: Stephen Donaldson

Training for Women Network Ltd
Suite 2, Elizabeth House
116-118 Holywood Road
Belfast, BT4 1NY
Tel: 028 9031 9888
Web: www.twnonline.com
Email: info@twnonline.com
Chief Executive: Norma Shearer

Northern Ireland Yearbook

INDEX

2019 council election	172
Abbeyfield and Wesley Housing Association	207
Abbeyfield Belfast Housing Society	207
Ad hoc committees	29
Advocate-General	82, 229
Agriculture, Environment and Rural Affairs Committee	28, 30
Agri-Food and Biosciences Institute	104, 143
Aiken MLA, Steve	13
Allen MLA, Andy	13
Alliance Party	9, 12
Allister MLA, Jim	13
Alpha Housing	207
Antrim and Newtownabbey Borough Council	158
Apex Housing Group	207
Arbour Housing	196, 197, 207
Archibald MLA, Caoimhe	13
Ards and North Down Borough Council	159
Ark Housing Association	207
Armagh City, Banbridge and Craigavon Borough Council	160
Armagh Observatory and Planetarium	108, 143
Armstrong MLA, Kellie	13
Arts Council for Northern Ireland	108, 143
Assembly and Executive Review Committee	29, 32
Attorney General for Northern Ireland	82, 143, 229
Attorney-General's Office	73
Audit Committee	29, 32
Bailey MLA, Clare	13
Barton MLA, Rosemary	13
Beattie MLA, Doug	13
Beggs MLA, Roy	14
Begley MP, Órfhlaith	72
Belfast Agreement	6
Belfast City Council	161
Belfast Commissioning Group	188
Belfast Harbour Commissioners	135, 143
Belfast Health and Social Care Trust	130, 143, 188
Belfast Metropolitan College	219
Belfast North	36
Belfast South	38
Belfast West	40
Blair MLA, John	14
Border Force	229
Boylan MLA, Cathal	14
Boyle, Colum	121
Bradley MLA, Maurice	14
Bradley MLA, Paula	14
Bradley MLA, Sinead	14
Bradshaw MLA, Paula	14
Brady MP, Mickey	72
Brady, Jayne	83
Braverman QC MP, Suella	82
Brennan, Mike	115
British Heart Foundation	189
British-Irish Council	26
British-Irish Intergovernmental Conference	26
British-Irish Parliamentary Assembly (BIPA)	26
Brogan MLA, Nicola	14
Brown, Susie	27
Browne, Mark	110
Buchanan MLA, Keith	15
Buchanan MLA, Thomas	15
Buckley MLA, Jonathan	15
Budget 2022-2025	252
Bunting MLA, Joanne	15
Burns MP, Conor	82
Burns, David	165
Business Committee	29, 32
Business Services Organisation	130, 143, 187, 191
Butler MLA, Robbie	15
Cabinet Office	73
Cameron MLA, Pam	15
Campbell MP, Gregory	72
Carroll MLA, Gerry	15
Catney MLA, Pat	15
Causeway Coast and Glens Borough Council	162
Centre for Public Health	191
Chairpersons' Liaison Group	29, 33
Chambers MLA, Alan	16
Charities Advisory Committee	108
Charity Commission for Northern Ireland	108, 143
Choice Housing Ireland	207
Chundur, Noyona	10, 11
CITB NI	213, 222
Clanmill Housing Association	207
Clarke MLA, Trevor	16
Clarke, Angela	196, 197
Cogent	222
Coleraine Harbour	135, 143
Comhairle na Gaelscolaíochta	114, 143
Commission for Victims and Survivors for Northern Ireland	86, 88, 89, 143
Commissioner for Older People for Northern Ireland	108, 143
Commissioner for Public Appointments for Northern Ireland	86, 143
Commissioner for Survivors of Institutional Childhood Abuse	86, 143, 226, 227
Commissioners of Irish Lights	25
Committee for Communities	28, 30
Committee for Finance	29, 31
Committee for Health	29, 31
Committee for Infrastructure	29, 31
Committee for Justice	29, 32
Committee for the Economy	28, 30
Committee for the Executive Office	29, 31
Community Relations Council	143
Connswater Homes	207
Consumer Council	10, 11, 120, 143
Consumer Price Index	11
Controlled Schools' Support Council	
Co-Ownership Housing	207
COP26 President	73
Coroners Service Northern Ireland	143, 228
Council for Catholic Maintained Schools (CCMS)	114, 144, 219
Council for Nature Conservation and the Countryside (CNCC)	104, 144
Council for the Curriculum, Examinations and Assessment (CCEA)	220
Criminal Justice Inspection Northern Ireland	144, 229

Index → 285

INDEX — Northern Ireland Yearbook

Delargy MLA, Padraig	16
Democratic Unionist Party (DUP)	9, 12
Department for Business, Energy and Industrial Strategy	73
Department for Communities	199
Department for Digital, Culture, Media and Sport	74
Department for Education	74
Department for Environment, Food and Rural Affairs	74
Department for Infrastructure	132
Department for International Trade	74
Department for the Communities	105
Department for the Economy	115, 222, 234
Department for Transport	74
Department for Work and Pensions	74
Department of Agriculture, Environment and Rural Affairs	90
Department of Education	110, 218
Department of Finance	121
Department of Health	126, 186, 188
Department of Health and Social Care	74
Department of Justice	136, 228
Departmental Resource Accounts and Finance Systems	109
Derry City and Strabane District Council	163
Dickson MLA, Stewart	16
Dillon MLA, Linda	16
Dixon, Jacqui	158
Dodds MLA, Diane	16
Dolan MLA, Jemma	16
Donaghy, Anne	166
Donaldson MP, Jeffrey	72
Drainage Council for NI	135, 144
Driver and Vehicle Agency Northern Ireland	144
Dunne MLA, Stephen	16
Durkan MLA, Mark	17
East Antrim	42
East Londonderry	44
Easton MLA, Alex	17
Eastwood MP, Colum	72
Education and Training Inspectorate	221
Education Authority	114, 144, 218
Employment Medical Advisory Service	187, 191
Ennis MLA, Sinead	17
Equality Commission for Northern Ireland	86, 144
Erskine MLA, Deborah	17
Farry MP, Stephen	72
Federation for Industry Sector Skills and Standards	222
Ferguson MLA, Ciara	17
Fermanagh and Omagh District Council	164
Fermanagh and South Tyrone	46
Finucane MP, John	72
Flynn MLA, Orlaithi	17
Food Safety Promotion Board	24
Food Standards Agency Northern Ireland	130, 145, 191
Foras na Gaeilge	24, 108, 145
Foreign and Commonwealth Office	74
Forensic Science Northern Ireland	145
Forest Service	145
Foyle	48
Foyle Port	135, 145
Frew MLA, Paul	17
General Teaching Council for Northern Ireland	114, 145, 221
Gildernew MLA, Colm	17
Gildernew MP, Michelle	72
Girvan MP, Paul	72
Givan MLA, Paul	18, 83
Godfrey, Katrina	132
Good Friday Agreement	6
Government of Ireland Act 1920	224
Green Party	9, 12
Grove Housing Association	207
Habinteg Housing Association	201, 207
Habitat for Humanity Northern Ireland	207
Hanna MP, Claire	72
Harbinson, Anthony	90
Hargey MLA, Deirdre	105
Harvey MLA, Harry	18
Hazzard MP, Chris	72
Head of the Northern Ireland Civil Service	83
Health and Safety Executive for Northern Ireland	120, 145
Health and Social Care Board	130, 145, 186, 188
Health and Social Care Trusts	186, 188
Hilditch MLA, David	18
Hillsborough Castle Agreement	224
Historic Buildings Council	108, 145
Historic Monuments Council	108, 145
HM Treasury	74
Home Office	74
House of Commons	71
House of Lords	71
House Price Index	194
Humphrey MLA, William	18
Hunter MLA, Cara	18
Institute of Public Health in Ireland	187
Institute of the Motor Industry	222
Integrated Education Fund	145
Internal Audit and Fraud Investigation Services	125
InterTradeIreland	24, 120, 145
Invest NI	118, 145
Irwin MLA, William	18
Jackson, David	162
Jess, Colin	262
Johnson MP, Boris	73
Johnston, Amanda	262
Judiciary NI	229
Kearney MLA, Declan	18
Keep Northern Ireland Beautiful	7
Kelly MLA, Dolores	19
Kelly MLA, Gerry	19
Kelpie, John	163
Kimmins MLA, Liz	19
King, Brenda	82
Lady Chief Justice for Northern Ireland	146
Lagan Valley	50
Land and Property Services	145
Law Society of Northern Ireland	145, 230
Legal Services Agency Northern Ireland	145

Northern Ireland Yearbook | INDEX

Lewis MP, Brandon	82
Libraries NI	108, 145, 221
Lisburn and Castlereagh City Council	165
Livestock and Meat Commission for Northern Ireland	104, 145
Local Commissioning Groups	187, 188
Local Government Boundaries Commissioner	108, 145
Local Government Staff Commission for Northern Ireland	109, 145
Lockhart MP, Carla	72
Long MLA, Naomi	19, 136
Long, Grainia	195
Loughs Agency	24, 104, 146
Lunn MLA, Trevor	19
Lyons MLA, Gordon	19, 115, 222, 248
Lyttle MLA, Chris	19
Mallon MLA, Nichola	19, 132
Maskey MLA, Alex	20
Maskey MP, Paul	72
Matthews, Kieran	196, 197
May, Peter	136
Maze/Long Kesh Development Commission	87, 146
McAleer MLA, Declan	20
McCreesh, Adrian	167
McCrossan MLA, Daniel	20
McCullagh, Alison	164
McGlone MLA, Patsy	20
McGrath MLA, Colin	20
McGrillen, John	232, 233
McGuigan MLA, Philip	20
McHugh MLA, Maoliosa	20
McIlveen MLA, Michelle	21, 110, 218
McLaughlin MLA, Sinead	21
McMahon, Denis	83
McNulty MLA, Justin	21
Meharg, Tracy	105
Mid and East Antrim Borough Council	166
Mid Ulster	52
Mid Ulster District Council	167
Middleton MLA, Gary	21
Middletown Centre for Autism	114, 146
Minister of State for Northern Ireland	82
Ministerial Advisory Group for Architecture and the Built Environment	108
Ministry for Housing, Communities and Local Government	73
Ministry of Defence	74
Ministry of Justice	74
Molloy MP, Francie	72
Muir MLA, Andrew	21
Murphy MLA, Aine	21
Murphy MLA, Conor	21, 121
National Crime Agency	230
National Health Service	186
National Museums NI	108, 146
National Skills Academy	222
NB Housing Association	208
Neilson, Barry	213
Nesbitt MLA, Mike	21
New Decade New Approach	6
Newington Housing Association	207
Newry and Armagh	54
Newry, Mourne and Down District Council	156, 157, 168
Newton MLA, Robin	22
Ní Chuilín MLA, Carál	22
NI Community Relations Council	86
NI Local Government Officers' Superannuation Committee	109
NI-CO	146
North Antrim	56
North Down	58
North/South implementation bodies	24
North/South Inter-Parliamentary Association	25
North/South Ministerial Council	24
Northern Commissioning Group	188
Northern Health and Social Care Trust	130, 146, 190
Northern Ireland Affairs Committee	73
Northern Ireland Ambulance Service Trust	131, 146, 190
Northern Ireland Assembly	6, 8
Northern Ireland Assembly election 2017	35
Northern Ireland Audit Office	146
Northern Ireland Blood Transfusion Service	131, 146, 187, 191
Northern Ireland Building Regulations Advisory Committee	125, 146
Northern Ireland Clinical Trials Unit	191
Northern Ireland Commissioner for Children and Young People (NICCY)	109, 146
Northern Ireland Consumer Week	11
Northern Ireland Council for Integrated Education	146
Northern Ireland Council for the Curriculum, Examinations and Assessment (CCEA)	114, 146
Northern Ireland Courts and Tribunal Service	146, 228
Northern Ireland Environment Agency	146
Northern Ireland Federation of Housing Associations	206
Northern Ireland Fire and Rescue Service	131, 146, 187, 192
Northern Ireland Fiscal Council	146, 253
Northern Ireland Fishery Harbour Authority	104, 146
Northern Ireland Grand Committee	73
Northern Ireland Guardian Ad Litem Agency	131, 147, 187, 192
Northern Ireland Housing Council	206
Northern Ireland Housing Executive	109, 147, 195, 199
Northern Ireland Judical Appointments Commission	87, 147, 229
Northern Ireland Judical Appointments Ombudsman	229
Northern Ireland Legal Services Agency	229
Northern Ireland Local Government Officers' Superannuation Committee	147
Northern Ireland Medical and Dental Training Agency	131, 147, 188, 192
Northern Ireland Museums Council	109, 147
Northern Ireland Office	74, 82
Northern Ireland Policing Board	147, 225, 228
Northern Ireland Practice and Education Council for Nursing and Midwifery	131, 147, 188, 192
Northern Ireland Prison Service	147, 229
Northern Ireland Question Time	71
Northern Ireland Social Care Council	131, 147, 188, 192
Northern Ireland Statistics and Research Agency (NISRA)	125, 147
Northern Ireland Tourism Alliance	234, 235
Northern Ireland Transport Holding Company	135, 147
Northern Ireland Water	135, 147
Northern Regional College	219
O'Dowd MLA, John	22
Office of the Advocate-General for Scotland	73
Office of the Attorney General for Northern Ireland	87, 147
Office of the Discretionary Support Commissioner	109
Office of the Lady Chief Justice	228
Office of the Leader of the House of Commons	74
Office of the Leader of the House of Lords	74
Office of the Northern Ireland Ombudsman	147
O'Neill MLA, Michelle	22, 83
O'Toole MLA, Matthew	22

INDEX | Northern Ireland Yearbook

Paisley MP, Ian	72
Parades Commission	229
Parliamentary Under Secretary of State	82
Parole Commissioners for Northern Ireland	147, 229
Patient and Client Council	130, 147, 187, 192
Pengelly, Richard	126, 188
People Before Profit Alliance	9, 12
Planning and Water Appeals Commission	148
Police Ombudsman for Northern Ireland	148, 228
Police Service of Northern Ireland	228
Poots MLA, Edwin	22, 90
Prime Minister	73
Prisoner Ombudsman	148, 229
Probation Board for Northern Ireland	148, 229
Procedures Committee	29, 33
PSNI	148
Public Accounts Committee	29, 33
Public Health Agency	130, 148, 187, 192
Public Prosecution Service	148, 229
Public Record Office of Northern Ireland	148
Queen's University Belfast	211, 218
Radius Housing	208
Regulation and Quality Improvement Authority	131, 148, 188, 192
Reid, Stephen	159
Reilly MLA, Aisling	22
Rent Officer for Northern Ireland	148, 206
Review of Public Administration	186
Robinson MLA, George	22
Robinson MP, Gavin	72
Rogan MLA, Emma	23
Rural Housing Association	208
Ryan, Fiona	226, 227
Safefood	24, 187, 192
Safeguarding Board for Northern Ireland	192
Scotland Office	74
Secretary of State	82
Serious Fraud Office	230
Shannon MP, Jim	72
Sheehan MLA, Pat	23
Sheerin MLA, Emma	23
Sinn Fein	9, 12
Skills Strategy for Northern Ireland	251
Sloan, Andrew	86, 88, 89
Social Democratic and Labour Party (SDLP)	9, 12
Social Enterprise NI	262
Social Housing Development Programme	199
South Antrim	60
South Down	62
South Eastern Commissioning Group	188
South Eastern Health and Social Care Trust	131, 148, 191
Southern Health and Social Care Trust	131, 190
Special EU Programmes Body (SEUPB)	25, 148
Sport NI	109, 148
St Andrews Agreement	6
St Mary's University College	219
St Matthew's Housing Association	208
Stalford MLA, Christopher	23
Standards and Privileges Committee	29, 33
Standing committees	29, 32, 33
Standing Order	34
Statutory committees	28, 30, 31, 32
Stewart MLA, John	23
Storey MLA, Mervyn	23
Strangford	64
Stranmillis University College	219
Strategic Investment Board	87, 148
Stuart, Joanne	234, 235
Sugden MLA, Claire	23
Swann MLA, Robin	23, 126, 188
The Bar of Northern Ireland	143, 230
The Executive Office	83
The Open University	219
Threshold	208
Tourism Enterprise Development (TED) Programme 2021/2022	232, 233
Tourism Ireland	25, 120, 148, 234
Tourism NI	119, 148, 232, 233, 234
Traditional Unionist Voice	9, 12
Triangle Housing Association	208
UK Commission for Employment and Skills' Employer Skills Survey	221
UK Parliament	71
Ulster Scots Agency	25, 109, 149
Ulster Supported Employment	109, 149
Ulster Unionist Party (UUP)	9, 12
Ulster University	219
Upper Bann	66
Utility Regulator	148
Victims and Survivors Service	87, 149
Wales Office	74
Ward, Marie	168
Warrenpoint Harbour Authority	135, 149
Waterways Ireland	25, 135, 149
Weir MLA, Peter	24
Wells MLA, Jim	24
West Tyrone	68
Western Commissioning Group	188
Western Health and Social Care Trust	131, 149, 191
Westminster	71
Wilson MP, Sammy	72
Wilson, Roger	160
Woods MLA, Rachel	24
Youth Council for Northern Ireland	114, 149
Youth Justice Agency of Northern Ireland	149, 229